About the Author

Edwin G. Dolan, economist and educator, holds a PhD from Yale University. Early in his career, he was a member of the economics faculty at Dartmouth College, the University of Chicago, and George Mason University. From 1990 to 2001, he taught in Moscow, Russia, where he and his wife founded the American Institute of Business and Economics (AIBEc), an independent, not-for-profit MBA program. Since 2001, he has taught at several universities in Europe—including Central European University in Budapest, the University of Economics in Prague, and the Stockholm School of Economics in Riga, where he has an ongoing annual visiting appointment. During breaks in his teaching career, he worked in Washington, D.C., as an economist for the Antitrust Division of the Department of Justice and as a regulatory analyst for the Interstate Commerce Commission. He later served a stint in Almaty as an adviser to the National Bank of Kazakhstan. When not lecturing abroad, he makes his home in Washington state's San Juan Islands.

Brief Contents

Introduction to
MICROECONOMICS

Fifth Edition

Edwin G. **Dolan**

PhD Yale University

BVT
PUBLISHING

Project Development Manager: Terri Beaudette

Managing Editor: Joyce Bianchini

Production Manager: Della Brackett

Sales Manager: Robert Rappeport

Pre-Production: Tommi Morgenthal

Director of Business Development: Richard Schofield

Typesetting: Rhonda Minnema

Permissions Coordinator: Janai Bryand

Acquisitions Coordinator: Jenefier Winchell

Cover and Interior Design: Esther Scannell

Photo Researcher: Jacquelyn Wein

Text and Cover Printing: Quad/Graphics

For information address BVT Publishing, LLC, P.O. Box 492831, Redding, CA 96049-2831

Some ancillaries, including electronic and print components, may not be available to customers outside the United States.

Hardcover ISBN: 978-1-61882-292-5
Softcover ISBN: 978-1-61882-293-2
Looseleaf ISBN: 978-1-61882-296-3
eBook ISBN: 978-1-61882-301-4

Contents

Chapter 5

Understanding the Choices Consumers Make   134

Appendix to Chapter 8:

Cost and Output with Two Variable Inputs

Chapter 9

Supply under Perfect Competition

Chapter 10

The Theory of Monopoly   298

Chapter *14*

Insurance, Information and Uncertainty   412

Chapter *15*
Labor Markets, Discrimination, and Public Policy   436

Chapter 16

Income Distribution and Poverty

Preface

The spread of instant electronic communication has changed not only the economy itself but also the way students learn economics and the way instructors teach the subject. A textbook, perhaps supplemented by a few photocopied handouts, used to be almost the only source of information for students. A blackboard was often the instructor's only teaching tool. All this has changed, and so have the textbooks.

Today, both students and instructors rely on the Internet as their primary source of information about current economic events. They still need a good textbook to provide a framework for organizing all the information that is available, but that textbook needs to mesh with the material available from on-line news sources, blogs, and social media. This fifth edition of *Introduction to Microeconomics* from BVT Publishing includes several changes that integrate it more smoothly into the world of e-learning.

First, the book has a new look with more color and more pictures. The new design is not just decorative—it also makes the analytical graphics more readable.

Second, the book has a new style. A couple of years ago I started a blog, and the exercise of blogging regularly has affected the way I write. I have revised the entire text to make the language more active with shorter sentences, shorter paragraphs, and shorter chapters. Chapter titles are more descriptive and less technical. With all these changes, the book now reads less like a series of journal articles and more like something students might actually want to read.

In addition to a more inviting presentation, much of the content is new, including new case studies and examples throughout the book. Topics range from the price of chocolate to the latest clean air regulations to China's monopoly of rare earth elements to changes in the distribution of income and the way poverty is measured.

Furthermore, the range of new case studies and examples is not limited to those included in the book itself. Every week, Ed Dolan's Econ Blog provides new material to both students and instructors. The blog's Resource Center for Teaching Economics, found at dolanecon.blogspot.com, brings regular posts on micro- and macroeconomic topics. A Topic Index and Course Planning Guide helps instructors and students find relevant older posts by grouping them in a way that reflects the sequence of a typical economics course. In addition to original material, the blog regularly features links to news items, articles from the business press, government documents, and other material relevant to the course. Students and instructors can also follow @DolanEcon on Twitter to keep up with the latest economic news. I also invite instructors and students to suggest topics for blog posts or submit guest posts of their own on favorite subjects.

Finally, this edition recognizes the fact that instructors no longer rely solely on blackboards and photocopied handouts as teaching aids. Most instructors now regularly use slide shows, smartboards, and videos in class, and course web sites to help students with their studying between classes.

One important aid to e-teaching and e-learning is a complete set of PowerPoint™ slides, which include all of the graphs and tables from each chapter, plus other relevant material that is available as a supplement to *Introduction to Microeconomics* from BVT. Beyond the basic slides for each chapter, Ed Dolan's Econ Blog provides additional content in PowerPoint format that can be cut-and-pasted directly into classroom presentations or posted to a course web page.

Acknowledgements

As always, I thank the entire publishing and editorial staff of BVT Publishing for their highly professional support. They are a pleasure to work with, and I hope that all students and instructors who use this book benefit as much as I have from their unique and innovative approach to textbook publishing. Enjoy your teaching and learning!

Instructor Supplements

A complete teaching package is available to instructors who adopt this book. This package includes an **instructor's manual**, **test bank**, **course management software**, and **PowerPoint slides**.

Instructor's Manual

A comprehensive manual provides a wealth of teaching suggestions, objectives and resources, class activities, and discussion questions.

Test Bank

An extensive test bank is available to instructors in electronic form. Each chapter consists of multiple choice, true/false, and essay questions. Each question is referenced to the appropriate text section/topic to make test creation quick and easy.

Course Management Software

BVT's Course Management Software (Respondus) allows for the creation of randomly generated tests and quizzes that can be downloaded directly into a wide variety of course management environments such as Blackboard, Web CT, Desire 2 Learn, Angel, E Learning, and others.

PowerPoint Slides

A set of PowerPoint slides includes charts, tables, and graphs from the text, as well as overview slides and bullet-pointed lists designed to guide lectures and discussions.

Student Resources

Student resources are available for this textbook at www.BVTLab.com. These resources are geared towards students needing additional assistance as well as those seeking complete mastery of the content. The following resources are available:

Practice Questions

Students can work through hundreds of practice questions online. Questions are multiple choice or true/false format and are graded instantly for immediate feedback.

Flashcards

BVT*Lab* includes sets of flashcards for each chapter that reinforce the key terms and concepts from the textbook.

Chapter Summaries

A convenient and concise chapter summary is available as a study aid for each chapter.

Study Guide

A thorough and practical student study guide includes learning objectives, chapter outlines, questions, and ideas that help the student review the material presented in this text. The study guide is available in both physical and online formats.

Video Tutorials

Many of the graphing topics covered in this text are explained in a series of Easonomics® video tutorials. Links to these videos are available at BVTLab.com.

BVT*Lab*

BVT*Lab* is a simple, robust, online lab for college instructors and their students. Even if you do not use the lab as your online classroom, your students can still take advantage of the many student resources available in the lab.

BVT*Lab* for Instructors

Course Setup

BVT*Lab* has an easy-to-use, intuitive interface that allows instructors to quickly set up their courses and grade books, plus replicate them from section to section and semester to semester. Multiple choice and true/false questions can be delivered online as practice questions, homework assignments, quizzes, and tests—each of which draws from a separate bank of questions. Homework, quizzes, and tests have assigned start and end times; tests can be proctored in the computer lab or self-proctored for distance learners. Instructors can preview and manually select questions assigned to students, or they can use the "quick-pick" feature in BVT*Lab* to generate sets of questions.

Grade Book

Using an assigned passcode, students can register into the grade book. All homework, quizzes, and tests are automatically graded and recorded in the grade book. In addition, instructors can manually enter or modify scores, with provisions for extra credit, attendance, and participation grades. Grade books can be printed, or downloaded for transfer to various school course management systems.

Communications Tools

BVT*Lab*

Instructors can post discussion threads to a class forum and then monitor and moderate student replies. Important notifications can also be sent directly to each student via email.

BVT*Lab* for Students

BVT*Lab* is a comprehensive online learning environment designed to help students succeed. It provides a complete online classroom, as well as the practice questions, learning aids, and communication tools that students need for success. For classes taught within the lab, students can view their grades for all completed work and also review prior homework and quizzes to identify areas that require additional study.

An online discussion forum allows students to interact with each other and the instructor to explore challenging concepts and share other resources, while providing an online community for distance learning.

Even if a class is not taught in the lab, students with an access code are always welcome to login and explore the many student resources described above.

BVT Online Student Bookstore

For convenience, students have the added option of purchasing this textbook (and associated resources) in the various available formats at www.BVTLab.com.

Customization

BVT's Custom Publishing Division can help you modify this book's content to satisfy your specific instructional needs. The following are examples of customization:

- Rearrangement of chapters to follow the order of your syllabus

- Deletion of chapters not covered in your course

- Addition of paragraphs, sections, or chapters you or your colleagues have written for this course

- Editing of the existing content, down to the word level

- Addition of handouts, lecture notes, syllabus, etc.

- Incorporation of student worksheets into the textbook

All of these customizations will be professionally typeset to produce a seamless textbook of the highest quality, with an updated table of contents to reflect the customized content.

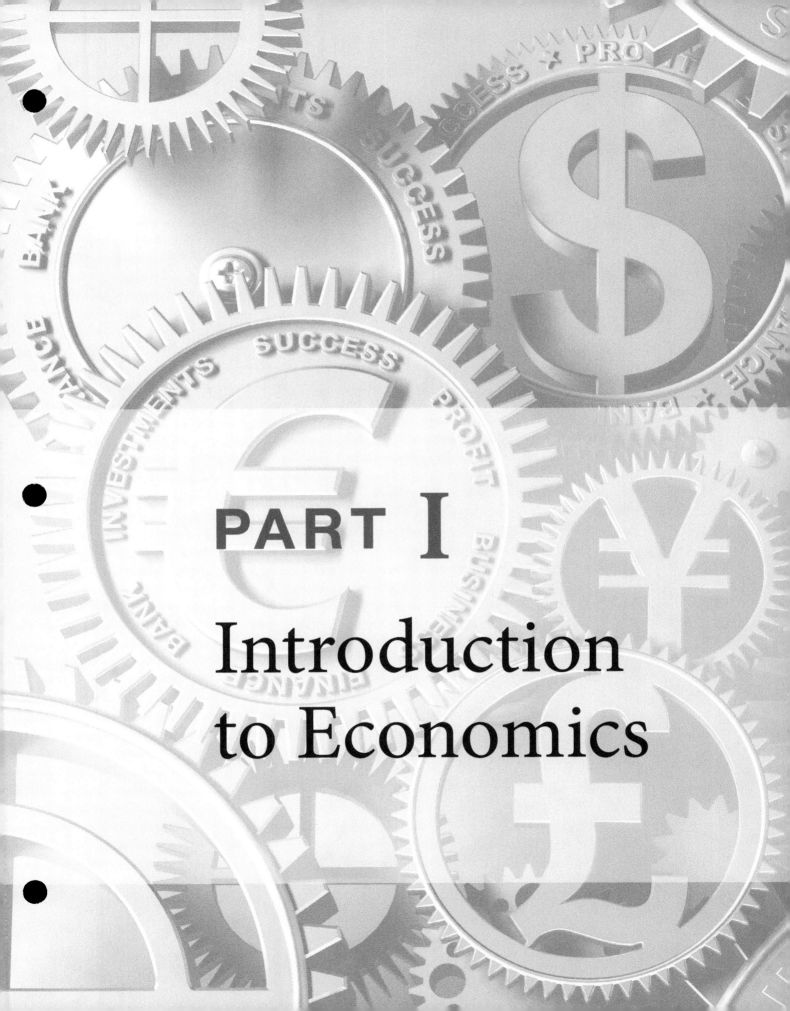

PART I

Introduction to Economics

Chapter 1

How Economists Think

After reading this chapter, you will understand the following:

1. What economics is really about

2. Four fundamental economic choices that all economies must make

3. How economic choices are coordinated

4. How economists use theory, graphs, and data in their work

2011 was a turbulent year for the world economy. In the first half of the year, global commodity prices soared. Gold and corn reached all-time highs while prices of oil, other foods, and rare earth metals approached records. At the same time other prices fell. Home prices in the United States continued a long decline. Natural gas prices fell as oil prices rose, producing a record gap between the two fuels. Financial markets were volatile, too. Interest rates on Greek, Irish, and Portuguese bonds rose alarmingly, leading to fears that those countries might not be able to pay their debts. The exchange rate of the Chinese yuan rose relative to the U.S. dollar, cheered by U.S. exporters but not welcomed so strongly by U.S. consumers of low-priced Chinese goods. Many factors lay behind these swings in prices—climate change, political deadlocks in Washington and the European Union, and rise of tens of millions of Brazilian, Indian, and Chinese families to middle class status. How can we understand these complex, yet interrelated, events?

There are many ways to understand what goes on in the world around us. Sociologists, poets and religious leaders each have a contribution to make. So do economists. Although reading this book will not make you an economist, it should give you a good overview of how economists think about things. By adding the economic perspective to others, you will better understand the world around you.

This chapter will take the first steps toward explaining the economic way of thinking by introducing a few big ideas that apply to all markets, in all countries, at all times. The most important of them is **scarcity**. Scarcity means any situation in which there is not enough of something to fill everyone's wants. For example, corn grown in the U.S. Midwest is scarce because there is not enough of it to meet all the competing needs of Chinese consumers, who want to eat more corn-fed pork as they become wealthier, and U.S. drivers, who are burning more corn-based ethanol in their cars. The scarcity of corn affects people's choices about how to use not only corn but also other goods. The effects on markets for wheat and gasoline are direct. The effects on exchange rates and stock markets are not quite so easy to trace, but they are no less important.

Scarcity and the way people deal with it are defining concepts of **economics**, the social science that seeks to understand the choices people make in using scarce resources to meet their wants. As this definition makes clear, economics is a study not of things, money, or wealth but of *people*. Economics is about people because scarcity itself is a human phenomenon. Wild strains of corn grew for millions of years and deposits of crude oil lay long undisturbed in the ground before they became the object of human wants. Only at that point did they become scarce in the sense that economists understand the term.

The focus on the human dimension of scarcity and choice is part of what makes economics a social science. Also, economics is a social science because people do not deal with scarcity in isolation. Instead, they can stretch scarce resources to meet their wants more effectively by trading with one another. As people trade, each person gives up something of value to others so that everyone gains from the

Scarcity

A situation in which there is not enough of a resource to meet all of everyone's wants

Economics

The social science that seeks to understand the choices people make in using scarce resources to meet their wants

exchange. Some economists think exchange is even more important than scarcity as a defining characteristic of economics.[1]

We can divide the wide range of topics covered by economics into two main branches. Understanding what determines corn prices belongs to the branch known as **microeconomics**. The prefix *micro*, meaning "small," indicates that this branch of economics deals with the choices of small economic units such as households, firms, and government agencies. Although microeconomics studies individual behavior, its scope can be worldwide, as when it focuses on global trade in goods such as food and energy.

Economics also has another branch, known as **macroeconomics**. The prefix *macro*, meaning "large," indicates that it deals with larger-scale phenomena. Typical problems in macroeconomics include how to combat unemployment, how to control inflation, and how to provide for a steady increase in living standards over time. Macroeconomics and microeconomics are not completely separate. Because macroeconomic phenomena like inflation represent the result of millions of individual choices about the prices of particular goods and services, macroeconomics ultimately rests on a microeconomic foundation.

1.1 What? How? Who? For Whom?

Among the most important economic choices people make are those concerning what goods will be produced, how people will produce them, who will do which jobs, and who will benefit from the goods and services that the economy produces. Scarcity makes each of these choices necessary. We can use each of them to introduce a key aspect of how economists think.

Deciding What to Produce: Opportunity Cost

The first choice is what goods to produce. In a real economy, there is an immense array of goods and services, but we can illustrate the basic concept with an economy that produces just two goods: cars and education. For many students, going without a car (or driving a used car instead of a new one) is a sacrifice they must make to get a college education. The economy as a whole faces the same trade-off that individual students face. It is not possible to give everyone all the cars and education they want, or just the kind and quality they would like. Somehow, someone must make choices.

The reason no economy can produce as much of everything as everyone wants is that the resources used to make all goods are, themselves, scarce. For example, making a car requires steel, glass, paint, welding machines, land for factories, and the labor of autoworkers. Traditionally, economists group all the various resources used in production into three basic categories called **factors of production**: labor, capital, and natural resources. **Labor** includes all of the productive

Microeconomics

The branch of economics that studies the choices of individual units—including households, business firms, and government agencies

Macroeconomics

The branch of economics that studies large-scale economic phenomena, particularly inflation, unemployment, and economic growth

Factors of production

The basic inputs of labor, capital, and natural resources used in producing all goods and services

Labor

The contributions to production made by people working with their minds and their hands

For many students, going without a car (or driving a used car instead of a new one) is a sacrifice they must make to get a college education.

Capital

All means of production that are created by people—including tools, industrial equipment, and structures

Natural resources

Anything that people can use as a productive input in its natural state, such as farmland, building sites, forests, and mineral deposits

Opportunity cost

The cost of a good or service measured in terms of the forgone opportunity to pursue the best possible alternative activity with the same time or resources

contributions made by people working with their minds and hands. **Capital** includes all the productive inputs created by people, including tools, machinery, buildings, and intangible items like computer software. **Natural resources** include anything that people can use as a productive input in its natural state—for example, farmland, building sites, forests, and mineral deposits.

We cannot use factors of production to satisfy two wants at the same time. We cannot use the same steel, concrete, and building sites both for automobile factories and for classrooms. People who work as teachers cannot spend the same time working on an automobile assembly line. Even students could spend their time working in an auto plant instead of studying. Whenever scarce inputs have more than one possible use, using them to produce one good means giving up the opportunity to produce something else instead. Economists express this basic truth by saying that everything has an **opportunity cost.** The opportunity cost of a good or service is its cost in terms of the forgone opportunity to pursue the best possible alternative activity with the same time or resources.

In our two-good economy, the opportunity cost of producing a college graduate can be expressed as the number of cars that could have been produced by using the same labor, capital, and natural resources. Suppose that the opportunity cost of educating a college graduate is four Toyota Camrys. That ratio (graduates per car or cars per graduate) is a useful way to express opportunity cost when only two goods are involved. More typically, though, we deal with situations in which there are many goods. Having more of one means giving up a little bit of many others.

In an economy with many goods, we can express opportunity costs in terms of a common unit of measurement, money. For example, rather than saying that a college education is worth four Camrys or that a Camry is worth one-fourth of a college education, we could say that the opportunity cost of a car is $30,000 and that of a college education is $120,000.

Useful as it is to have a common unit of measurement, we must take great care when expressing opportunity costs in terms of money because not all out-of-pocket money expenditures represent the sacrifice of opportunities to do something else. At the same time, not all forgone opportunities take the form of money spent. *Applying Economic Ideas 1.1*, which analyzes both the out-of-pocket expenditures and the opportunity costs of a college education, shows why.

We will stress the importance of opportunity cost repeatedly in this book. The habit of looking for opportunity costs is one of the distinguishing features of the economic way of thinking.

Applying Economic Ideas **1.1**

The Opportunity Cost of a College Education

How much does it cost you to go to college? If you are a resident student at a typical four-year private college in the United States, you can answer this question by making up a budget like the one shown in part A of the table. We can call this a budget of out-of-pocket costs because it includes all the items—and only those items—that you or your parents must actually pay for in a year.

Part A: Budget of Out-of-Pocket Costs		Part B: Budget of Opportunity Costs	
Item	**Amount**	**Item**	**Amount**
Tuition and fees	$14,000	Tuition and fees	$14,000
Books and supplies	1,200	Books and supplies	1,200
Transportation to and from home	1,100	Transportation to and from home	1,100
Room and board	7,000	Forgone income	16,000
Personal expenses	1,400		
Total out-of-pocket costs	**$24,700**	**Total opportunity costs**	**$32,300**

(Continues)

Your own out of pocket costs may be much higher or lower than those in the example. Chances are these are the main categories that first come to mind when you think about the costs of college. As you begin to think more like an economist, you may find it useful to restate your college budget in terms of opportunity costs. Which of the items in Part A represent opportunities that you have forgone in order to go to college? Are any forgone opportunities missing? To answer these questions, compare Part A with Part B, which shows a budget of opportunity costs.

Some items are both opportunity costs and out-of-pocket costs. The first three items in Part A show up again in Part B. To spend $14,000 on tuition and fees and $1,200 on books and supplies, you must give up the opportunity to buy other goods and services—maybe to buy a car or rent a ski condo. To spend $1,100 getting to and from school, you may have to pass up the opportunity to travel somewhere else or to spend the money on something other than travel. Not all out-of-pocket costs are also opportunity costs, however. Consider the last two items in the out-of-pocket budget. By spending $7,000 on room, board, and personal expenses during the year, you are not really giving up the opportunity to do something else. Whether or not you were going to college, you would have to eat, live somewhere, and buy clothes. Because you would have those expenses in any case, they do not count as opportunity costs of going to college.

Consider both the out-of-pocket expenses for your college education as well as the opportunity costs.

Finally, some items are opportunity costs without being out-of-pocket costs. Think about what you would be doing if you were not going to college. If you were not going to college, you probably would have taken a job and started earning money soon after leaving high school. As a high-school graduate, your earnings would be about $16,000 during the nine months of the school year. (You can work during the summer even if you are attending college.) Because this potential income is something that you must forgo for the sake of college, it is an opportunity cost even though it does not involve an outlay of money.

Which budget you use depends on the kind of decision you are making. If you have already decided to go to college and are doing your financial planning, the out-of-pocket budget will tell you how much you have to raise from savings, money earned, parents' contributions, loans, and scholarships to make ends meet. But if you are making the more basic choice between going to college and pursuing a career that does not require a college degree, the opportunity cost of college is what counts.

Deciding How to Produce: Efficiency and Entrepreneurship

A second basic economic choice is how to produce. There is more than one way to make almost anything. Auto firms can, for example, make cars in highly automated factories, using a lot of capital equipment and relatively little labor, or build them one by one in smaller shops, using a lot of labor and only a few general-purpose machines. Toyota builds its Camrys the first way; Lamborghini builds its Gallardo Spyder (priced at a thrifty $209,000) the second way. We could say the same about education. A professor can teach a course directly to twenty students in a small classroom using only a blackboard, or teach the same course online to hundreds of students.

Some cars are made in highly automated factories while others are built with lots of hand labor.

Efficiency Efficiency is one of the most important things to keep in mind when deciding how to produce something. In everyday language, efficiency means producing with a minimum of expense, effort, and waste. Economists use a more precise definition. **Economic efficiency,** they say, refers to a state of affairs in which it is impossible to make any change that satisfies one person's wants more fully without causing some other person's wants to be satisfied less fully.[2]

Although this formal definition of economic efficiency may be unfamiliar, it does not differ greatly from the everyday notion. If there is some way to make you better off without making me worse off, it is wasteful to pass up the opportunity. If I have a red pen that I am not using, and you need one just for a minute, it would be wasteful for you to buy a red pen of your own. It is more efficient for me to lend you my pen; it makes you better off and me no worse off.

In cases where there is a way to make us both better off, it would be all the more wasteful not to take advantage of the opportunity. You lend me your bicycle for the afternoon, and I will lend you my volleyball. If I do not ride a bicycle very often and you do not play volleyball very often, it would be inefficient for us both to own one of each.

The examples of the pen, the bicycle, and the volleyball did not involve production, but many applications of efficiency do. **Efficiency in production** refers to a situation in which it is not possible, given available productive resources and existing knowledge, to produce more of one good without forgoing the opportunity to produce some of another good. Like the broader concept of economic efficiency, efficiency in production has its roots in the everyday notion of avoiding waste. For example, a grower of apples finds that beyond some certain quantity, using more water per tree does not increase the yield of apples, so using more than that amount would be wasteful. Better to transfer the extra water to the production of, say, peaches. That way, the grower can get more peaches without reducing the apple crop.

The economist's definition also includes more subtle possibilities for improving the efficiency of production. For example, it is possible to grow apples in Georgia. It is also possible, by selecting the right tree varieties and using winter protection, to grow peaches in Vermont.

Economic efficiency

A state of affairs in which it is impossible to make any change that satisfies one person's wants more fully without causing some other person's wants to be satisfied less fully

Efficiency in production

A situation in which it is not possible, given available knowledge and productive resources, to produce more of one good without forgoing the opportunity to produce some of another good

Apples can be grown in Georgia, but it is more efficient to grow them commercially in Vermont.

Some hobbyists do grow both fruits in both states. However, growing them commercially would be inefficient even if growers in both states followed best practices and avoided any obvious waste.

An example will show why. Suppose that to start with, growers plant equal numbers of apple and peach trees in each state. Then compare a situation with five hundred fewer struggling peach trees growing in Vermont, with their place taken by five hundred thriving apple trees. At the same time, suppose growers plant five hundred fewer heat-stressed apple trees in Georgia, and peaches take their place. The second situation would increase the output of both fruits without increasing the total land, labor, and capital used in fruit production, showing that the original distribution of trees was inefficient.

How to Increase Production Potential   Once the economy is producing efficiently, we can get more of one good only by giving up the opportunity to produce something else—assuming we hold productive resources and knowledge constant. Over time, though, we can find new resources or new ways to use existing resources.

In the past, the discovery of new supplies of natural resources and population growth has been the most important way of increasing production potential. However, as we deplete the most easily tapped supplies of natural resources and as population growth slows in most parts of the world, capital will increasingly be the factor of production that contributes most to the expansion of production potential.

Economists use the term **investment** to refer to the act of increasing the economy's stock of capital, that is, its supply of productive inputs made by people. Investment involves a trade-off of present consumption for future consumption. To build more factories, roads, and computers, we have to divert resources from the production of bread, movies, haircuts, and other things that satisfy immediate wants. In return, we put ourselves in a better position to satisfy our future wants.

Increasing the quantities of labor, capital, and natural resources is not the only source of economic growth. Even more important are improvements in knowledge—the invention of new technology, new forms of organization, and new ways of satisfying wants. **Entrepreneurship** is the process of looking for new possibilities—making use of new ways of doing things, being alert to new opportunities, and overcoming old limits. It is a dynamic process that breaks

Investment

The act of increasing the economy's stock of capital, that is, its supply of means of production made by people

Entrepreneurship

The process of looking for new possibilities—making use of new ways of doing things, being alert to new opportunities, and overcoming old limits

down the constraints imposed by existing knowledge and limited supplies of factors of production.

Entrepreneurship does not have to mean inventing something or starting a new business, although it sometimes does. It may mean finding a new market for an existing product—for example, convincing people in Germany that Japanese sushi makes a quick and tasty lunch. It may mean taking advantage of price differences between one market and another—for example, buying hay at a low price in Pennsylvania, where growing conditions have been good in the past year, and re-selling it in Virginia, where the weather has been too dry.

We can be entrepreneurs in our roles as consumers and workers, too. We do not just repeat the same patterns of work and leisure every day. We seek variety—new jobs, new foods, and new places to visit. Each time we try something new, we are taking a step into the unknown. In that sense, we are all entrepreneurs.

Some people call entrepreneurship the fourth factor of production, but it differs from the three classical factors of production in important ways. Unlike labor, capital, and natural resources, we cannot measure entrepreneurship because it is intangible. Although entrepreneurs earn incomes reflecting the value that the market places on their accomplishments, we cannot speak of a price per unit of entrepreneurship; there are no such units. Also, unlike human resources (which grow old), machines (which wear out), and natural resources (which can be used up), the inventions and discoveries of entrepreneurs are not depleted as they are used. Once someone invents a new product or concept—lithium battery power for cars, taking pictures with cell phones, or hedge funds as a form of financial investment—the required knowledge does not have to be created again, although it may be supplanted by even better ideas. All in all, it is more helpful to think of entrepreneurship as a process of learning better ways of using the three basic factors of production than as a separate factor of production.

Deciding Who Will Do Which Work: The Division of Labor

Even a person living in complete isolation would have to choose what to produce and how to produce it. The fictional castaway Robinson Crusoe had to decide whether to fish or hunt birds. If he decided to fish, he had to decide whether to do so with a net or with a hook and line. Other important economic choices, including who will do which work and who will get the resulting output, exist only for people living in society. That is another reason economics is one of the social sciences.

Deciding who will do which work is a matter of organizing the social division of labor. Will everyone work independently—be a farmer in the morning, a tailor in the afternoon, and a poet in the evening? Or will people cooperate—specialize in one particular job, coordinate their work with other specialists, and trade the resulting goods and services? Economists have long argued that specialization and cooperation are the best strategies. Three things make cooperation pay off: teamwork, learning by doing, and comparative advantage.

First, consider *teamwork*. In a classic paper on this subject, Armen Alchian and Harold Demsetz used the example of workers unloading bulky crates from a truck.[3] The crates are so large that one worker alone cannot move them at all without unpacking them. Two people, each working independently, would take hours to unload the truck. However, if they work as a team, they can easily pick up the crates and stack them on the loading dock. This example shows that even when everyone is doing the same work, and even when little skill is involved, teamwork pays.

Working as a team, two people can get a job done more easily.

A second reason for cooperation applies when there are different jobs to do and different skills to learn. In a furniture plant, for instance, some workers operate production equipment, others use office equipment, and still others buy materials. Even if all the workers start out with equal abilities, each gets better at a particular job by doing it repeatedly. *Learning by doing* thus turns workers of average productivity into specialists, thereby creating a more productive team.

A third reason for cooperation comes into play when the differing skills of workers give them a *comparative advantage* in particular tasks. **Comparative advantage** is the ability to do a job or produce a good at a relatively lower opportunity cost than someone else. An example will show how two people can use comparative advantage to improve the efficiency of the division of labor.

Suppose two clerical workers, Bill and Jim, are working at the job of getting out a batch of invoices to clients. The invoices include both a personalized text and a table with data. Jim is very good at working

Comparative advantage

The ability to produce a good or service at a relatively lower opportunity cost than someone else

INVOICE

Fieldcom Inc.

Dear Mr. Gupta:

We were glad to learn that the P622.2 replacement modules for your Model A41 smartphone continue to perform well. If you would like any further technical assistance or advice, please contact Ms. Ivana Pleschko at ext. 517. As your firm grows, we hope that you will visit our web site frequently (www.fieldcom.biz) to learn of our latest product releases.

Below please find your account activity for the month. If you have any questions regarding your account, please feel free to contact me directly at ext. 032.

Yours truly,
Andrea Martin

Part No.	Quantity	Item	Price per unit	Total
P622.2	8	Replacement module	$56.27	$450.16
A41	2	Smartphone	$798.00	$1,596.00
Subtotal				$2,046.16
Preferred customer discount				–$204.62
Total due 30 days after receipt				$1,841.54

with both text and data. He can prepare the text section of an invoice in 5 minutes and do the data table in 1 minute. Working alone, he can finish ten invoices in an hour. Bill is not so good at either task. It takes him 10 minutes to do the text for an invoice and 5 minutes to prepare the data. Alone, he can do only four invoices an hour. In summary form:

Jim: Prepare 1 text, 5 min.
       Prepare 1 data table, 1 min.

Bill: Prepare 1 text, 10 min.
        Prepare 1 data table, 5 min.

Without cooperation, the two workers' limit is fourteen invoices per hour between them. Could they do better by cooperating? It depends on who does which job. One idea might be for Jim to prepare all the text while Bill does all the data because that way they can just keep up with each other. That turns out not to be such a good idea. At 5 minutes per invoice, that kind of cooperation cuts their combined output to twelve invoices per hour. It is worse than not cooperating at all.

Instead, they should divide the work according to the principle of *comparative advantage*. Even though Bill is slower at preparing the text, he has a comparative advantage in text preparation because the opportunity cost of that part of the work is lower for him: The ten minutes he takes to do the text for one invoice is equal to the time he needs to do two data tables. Jim could use the 5 minutes he takes to prepare text for one invoice to do the data for five invoices. For Bill, then, the opportunity cost of preparing one text is to forgo two data tables, whereas for Jim the opportunity cost of preparing one text is to forgo five data tables.

Because Bill gives up fewer data tables per text than Jim, the principle of comparative advantage says that Bill should spend all his time preparing text. If he does, he can produce the text for six invoices per hour. Meanwhile Jim can spend 45 minutes of each hour preparing the text for nine invoices, and the last 15 minutes of each hour doing the data for all fifteen invoices. By specializing according to comparative advantage, the two workers can increase their total output to fifteen invoices per hour, the best they can possibly do.

In this example, two people working side-by-side use comparative advantage to work out the efficient division of labor but the principle also has broader implications. It can apply to a division of labor between individuals or business firms working far apart—even in different countries. In fact, the earliest application of the principle was to international trade (see *Who Said It? Who Did It?* 1.1). Comparative advantage remains one of the primary principles of mutually beneficial cooperation, whether on the scale of the workplace or on that of the world as a whole.

Whatever the context, comparative advantage arises from opportunity cost. Suppose there are two tasks, A and B, and two parties, X and Y (individuals, firms, or countries), each capable of doing both tasks, but not equally well. First ask what the opportunity cost is for X of doing a unit of task A, measured in terms of how many units of task B could be done with the same time or resources. Then ask the same question for Y. The party with the lower opportunity cost for doing a unit of task A has the comparative advantage in doing that task. To check, ask what the opportunity cost is for each party of doing a unit of task B, measured in terms how many units of task A could be done with the same time or resources. The party with the lower opportunity cost for doing a unit of task B has the comparative advantage in doing that task. Both X and Y will be better off if each specializes according to comparative advantage.

Who Said It? Who Did It? 1.1

David Ricardo and the Theory of Comparative Advantage

David Ricardo was born in London in 1772, the son of an immigrant who was a member of the  London stock exchange. Ricardo's education was rather haphazard, and he entered his father's business at the age of fourteen. In 1793, he married and went into business on his own. These were years of war and financial turmoil. The young Ricardo developed a reputation for remarkable astuteness and quickly made a large fortune.

In 1799, Ricardo read Adam Smith's *The Wealth of Nations* and developed an interest in political economy (as people at that time called the field we now call economics). In 1809, he published his first writings on economics, a series of newspaper articles on "The High Price of Bullion." Several other short works added to his reputation in this area. In 1814, he retired from business to devote all his time to political economy.

Ricardo's major work was *Principles of Political Economy and Taxation*, first published in 1817. This work contains, among other things, a pioneering statement of comparative advantage as applied to international trade. Using a lucid numerical example, Ricardo showed why, even though Portugal could produce both wine and wool with fewer labor hours than England, it was to the advantage of both countries for England to export wool to Portugal and to import wine in return because the comparative cost was less in England.

International trade is only one topic in Ricardo's *Principles*. The book covers the whole field of economics, as it then existed, beginning with value theory and progressing to a theory of economic growth and evo-lution. Ricardo held that the economy was growing toward a future "steady state." At that point, economic growth would come to a halt and the wage rate would fall to the subsistence level. This gloomy view and the equally pessimistic views of Ricardo's contemporary, Thomas Malthus, gave political economy a reputation as "the dismal science."

Ricardo's comparative advantage describes exporting wool and importing wine between England and Portugal.

Ricardo's book was extremely influential. For more than half a century thereafter, much of the writing on economic theory published in England consisted of expansions and commentaries on Ricardo's work. Economists as different as Karl Marx, the revolutionary socialist, and John Stuart Mill, a defender of liberal capitalism, took Ricardo's theories as their starting point. Even today there are "neo-Ricardian" and "new classical" economists who look to Ricardo's works for inspiration.

Deciding for Whom Goods Will Be Produced

Together, the advantages of team production, learning by doing, and comparative advantage mean that people can produce more efficiently by cooperating than if each person worked in isolation. Cooperation raises a new issue, however: Who will benefit from the goods that the economy has produced? The question of the distribution of output among members of society matters for both efficiency and fairness.

Efficiency in Distribution   Suppose, first, that people have already produced the goods so that their supply is fixed. For example, imagine that thirty students get on a bus to go to a football game. The driver hands out bag lunches. Half the bags contain a ham sandwich and a root beer; the other half contain a tuna sandwich and a cola. What happens when the students open their bags? They do not just eat whatever they find—they start trading. Some swap sandwiches; others swap drinks. Maybe there is not enough of everything to give each person his or her first choice. Nevertheless, the trading makes at least some people better off than they were when they started. Moreover, no one ends up worse off. If some of the students do not want to trade, they can always eat what they got in the first place.

This example shows one sense in which the "for whom" question is partly about efficiency: Starting with any given quantity of goods, we can improve the distribution through trades that better satisfy preferences. Doing so permits some people to satisfy their wants more fully without making others worse off. That improves **efficiency in distribution** even while the total quantity of goods remains fixed.

So far, we have considered efficiency in distribution and efficiency in production in isolation. In practice, there is a close link between the two because rules for distribution affect patterns of production. For example, suppose wages of home healthcare workers increases relative to the wages of clothing workers. If so, two things will happen. One is that healthcare workers will receive a bigger share of total goods and services produced by the economy. Another is that the pattern of output will change, with more healthcare services produced, and less clothing. By the same token, the way output is distributed affects incentives for entrepreneurship. If there are great rewards for discovering new ways of doing things, people will make greater efforts to improve products, methods of production, and means of distribution.

Fairness in Distribution   Efficiency is not the whole story when it comes to distributing goods and services. We also need to ask whether a given distribution is fair. Questions of fairness often dominate discussions of distribution.

One widely held view judges fairness in distribution in terms of equality. That concept of fairness follows from the idea that all people, by virtue of their shared humanity, deserve a portion of the goods and services turned out by the economy. There are many versions of this concept. Some people think that people have a right to an

---

Efficiency in distribution

A situation in which it is not possible, by redistributing existing supplies of goods, to satisfy one person's wants more fully without causing some other person's wants to be satisfied less fully

equal share of all income and wealth. Others think that people have an equal right to a "safety net" level of income but that inequality in distributing any surplus beyond that level is not unfair. Still others think that the economy should distribute certain goods equally (for example, health care and education) but that it is fair to distribute other goods less equally.

An alternative view, which also has many adherents, judges fairness not in terms of how much each person receives but, instead, in terms of the process through which goods are distributed. In this view, fairness requires the observation of certain rules and procedures, such as respect for property or nondiscrimination on grounds of race and gender. As long as people follow those rules, any resulting distribution of income is acceptable. This view emphasizes equality of opportunity more than equality of outcome.

Efficiency versus Fairness   Most economists consider efficiency to be their primary area of expertise; but in practice, questions of fairness come into economic discussions in several ways. One is the selection of topics to investigate. An economist who sees unemployment as a glaring injustice may study that problem; one who sympathizes with victims of job discrimination may take up a different line of research. Considerations of fairness can also affect the ways economists collect data, which sources of data they treat as reliable, and so on. Some economists have argued that a purely objective economics could be developed, untouched by considerations of values and fairness. If so, they could resolve all disputes by reference to indisputable facts. Today that notion is less widely held, and it is more widely recognized that most major economic controversies, especially those that have to do with government policy, involve considerations of fairness as well as efficiency.

1.2 Coordinating Economic Choices

Every economy must have some way of coordinating the choices of millions of people about what to produce, how to produce it, who will do each job, and who will get the output. This section discusses how to accomplish the needed coordination.

A Non-Economic Example

You, like almost everyone, have probably had the experience of shopping at a supermarket where there are several long checkout lines. You and other shoppers want to get through checkout as fast as possible. The store, too, would like to avoid a situation in which customers in some lines have a long wait while the cashiers in other lines stand idle, but how to do it?

Grocery store checkout aisles are an example of coordinating people's choices by spontaneous order.

Hierarchy

A way of achieving coordination in which individual actions are guided by instructions from a central authority

Spontaneous order

A way of achieving coordination in which individuals adjust their actions in response to cues from their immediate environment

One way would be to have an employee on duty to direct people to the line with the shortest wait. Busy airports and government offices sometimes use that method, but supermarkets do not usually work that way. Instead, supermarkets leave you to decide for yourself which line to join, based on your own observations. As you approach the checkout area, you first look to see which lines are the shortest. You then make allowance for the possibility that some shoppers have heaped their carts full, while others have only a few items. Using your own judgment, you head for the line you think will be fastest.

The coordination system in which an airport employee directs customers to the shortest line is an example of **hierarchy**. Hierarchy is a way of achieving coordination in which a central authority issues instructions to guide individual actions. The approach used in supermarkets is an example of coordination by **spontaneous order**. Coordination comes about as people adjust their own actions as they see fit in response to cues received from their immediate environment. This method is *orderly* because it achieves an approximately equal waiting time in each checkout line. It is *spontaneous* in that coordination takes place without central direction. Even though no shopper has the specific goal of equalizing the lines, the result is approximate equalization.

Spontaneous Order in Markets

In economics, *markets* are the most important example of coordination through spontaneous order. A **market** is any arrangement people have for trading with one another. Some markets have formal rules and carry out trading all in one place, like an auction house that sells works of art. Other markets are more informal, such as the word-of-mouth networks through which domestic workers get in touch with people who need their services. Despite a variety of forms, all markets have one thing in common: They provide the information and incentives people need to coordinate their decisions.

Above all, people need information about the scarcity and opportunity costs of goods and factors of production. Markets use prices to transmit such information. If a good or factor of production becomes scarcer, people bid up its price. The rising price tells people it is worth more and signals producers to make greater efforts to increase supplies. For example, when automakers first began to use catalytic converters with platinum to reduce exhaust pollution, new buyers entered the market. As automakers began to compete with makers of jewelry and other traditional users, platinum became harder to acquire. Competition for available supplies bid up the price. That gave buyers a cue that the value of platinum had increased and an incentive to use it more carefully. At the same time, producers got a cue to look for ways to increase the quantity of platinum mined.

On another occasion, a new technology might reduce the cost of producing platinum. For example, it might become possible to extract platinum from wastes that miners had discarded in earlier periods when the metal was less valuable. Markets would transmit information about the new technology in the form of a lower price. People could then consider using more platinum.

At the same time markets provide information, they also provide incentives to act on it. Markets provide incentives to sell goods and services where they will bring the highest prices and to buy them where the price is lowest. Profits motivate business managers to improve production methods and to design goods that match consumer needs. Workers who stay alert to opportunities and work where they are most productive receive the highest wages. Consumers are motivated to use less expensive substitutes where feasible.

Adam Smith, often considered the father of economics, saw coordination through markets as the foundation of prosperity and progress. In a famous passage in *The Wealth of Nations*, he called markets an "invisible hand" that nudges people into the economic roles they can play best (see *Who Said It? Who Did It?* 1.2). To this day, an appreciation of markets as a means of coordinating choices remains a central feature of the economic way of thinking.

Market

Any arrangement people have for trading with one another

Who Said It? Who Did It? **1.2**

Adam Smith on the Invisible Hand

Economists consider Adam Smith to be the founder of their field of study, even though he wrote only one book on the subject: *The Wealth of Nations,* published in 1776. Smith was fifty-three years old at the time. His friend David Hume found the book such hard going that he doubted that many people would read it. Hume was wrong—people have been reading it for more than two hundred years.

   The wealth of a nation, in Smith's view, is not a result of the accumulation of gold or silver in its treasury, as many of his contemporaries believed. Rather, it is the outcome of the activities of ordinary people working and trading in free markets. To Smith, the remarkable thing about a market economy is that it produces wealth not a result of any organized plan, but rather as the unintended outcome of the actions of many people, each of whom is pursuing his or her own interests. As he put it:

It is not from the benevolence of the butcher, the brewer, or the baker that we expect our dinner, but from their regard to their own interest …. Every individual is continually exerting himself to find out the most advantageous employment for whatever capital he can command …. By directing that industry in such a manner as its produce may be of the greatest value, he intends only his own gain, and he is in this, as in many other cases, led by an invisible hand to promote an end which was no part of his intention. *

Much of the discipline of economics as it has developed over the past two centuries consists of elaborations on ideas found in Smith's work. The idea of the "invisible hand" of market incentives that channels people's efforts in directions that are beneficial to their neighbors remains the most durable of Smith's contributions to economics.

* Adam Smith, *The Wealth of Nations* (1776), Book 1, Chapter 2.

The Role of Hierarchy

Important as markets are, they are not the only way to coordinate economic activity. Hierarchy within formal organizations is a widely used alternative. Government agencies are one example. Government agencies do not make decisions through the spontaneous choices of individuals, but according to directives issued by a central authority. The directives tell people to submit tax forms by a certain date, to monitor pollution according to certain standards, to pay fines if they do not follow the rules, and so on. Business firms, especially large corporations, also use hierarchical forms of organization. For example, a company like Toyota uses directives from a central authority to make many important decisions—such as building a new hybrid version of its popular Camry in Kentucky rather than in Japan.

Although governments and corporations use hierarchies to make choices internally, they deal with one another and with consumers through markets. Markets and hierarchies play complementary roles. Some economies rely more on markets, others on government or corporate planning. At one extreme, the centrally planned economy of North Korea places heavy emphasis on government authority. Economies like that of the United States make greater use of markets. No economy uses one means of coordination to the exclusion of the other. Government regulatory agencies in the United States establish laws to control pollution or protect worker safety; on the other hand, North Korea permits small-scale street markets for some goods. Large corporations use commands from higher authority to make many decisions, but they also often subcontract with outside suppliers through markets. They also often encourage their own divisions to deal with one another on a market basis.

1.3 Economic Method

We have seen that when economists think about the world around them, they use concepts like scarcity, choice, and exchange. In doing so, they also have distinctive methods of approaching problems and expressing conclusions. We will conclude the chapter with a few comments about method.

Theories and Models

Economists try to understand the choices people make in terms of the context in which they make them. They call the relationships between choices and context **theories** or **models**. The terms mean almost the same thing although economists tend to use the term theory to refer to more general statements about economic relationships and the term model to refer to more particular statements, especially those that take the form of graphs or equations.

Economics needs theories and models because facts do not speak for themselves. Take, for example, the fact that in the spring of 2011 U.S. farmers planted more acres in corn than ever before. Economists have a theory as to why this happened. They relate the change in crop patterns to a record-high price for corn at the time of planting. The link between the price of corn and the choice of what crop to grow is as an example of a broader theory according to which an increase in the price of any good, other things being equal, leads producers to increase output of the good.

The theory, as stated, is a simple one. It relates crop choices to just one other fact, the price of corn. A more complete theory would bring in

Theory

A representation of the relationships among facts

Model

A synonym for theory; in economics, often applied to theories that take the form of graphs or equations

Farmers choose to plant corn based on the price of corn at the time of planting

other influences—such as the prices of gasoline, for which corn-based ethanol is a substitute; the price of soybeans, which can be grown on the same land as corn; tax advantages provided by Congress to producers of biofuels; and so on. Where does one draw the line? How much detail does it take to make a good theory?

There is no simple answer to this question. Adding detail to a theory involves a trade-off. On the one hand, if a theory leaves out essential details, it may fail altogether to fit the facts. On the other hand, adding too much detail defeats the purpose of understanding because key relationships may become lost in a cloud of complexity. The only real guideline is that a theory should have just enough detail to suit its purpose, and no more.

By analogy, consider the models that aircraft designers use. A scaled-down wind-tunnel model made to test the aerodynamics of a new design would need to represent the shapes of the wings, fuselage, and control surfaces accurately. It would not need to include tiny seats with tiny tables and magazine pockets. On the other hand, a full-scale model built to train flight crews would need seats and magazine pockets, but it would not need wings.

Extending the same analogy, the theories and models presented in this book are helpful in understanding economics in the same way that playing a flight simulation game on a laptop computer is helpful in understanding the basics of flying. Professional economists use more detailed models, just as professional pilots train with complex flight simulators rather than with simple computer games. Still, the basic principles of the simple models should not contradict those of the more complex ones. In the simple flight simulator games, just as in the complex professional version, adjusting the rudder makes the plane turn and adjusting the elevators makes it climb or dive.

Using Graphs

We have stated all the theories we have introduced so far in words. Words are a powerful tool for developing understanding, but they are even more powerful when we add pictures. An example will illustrate how economists use graphs together with words to represent theories.[4]

The Production Possibility Frontier   Earlier in the chapter, we discussed a trade-off between education and cars. Figure 1.1 shows that trade-off in graphical form for an economy that produces only those two goods. The horizontal axis measures the quantity of education in terms of the number of college graduates produced per year; the vertical axis measures the production of cars. Any combination of education and cars corresponds to a point in the space between the two axes. For example, point E represents production of 10 million graduates and 5 million cars.

FIGURE 1.1   PRODUCTION POSSIBILITY FRONTIER

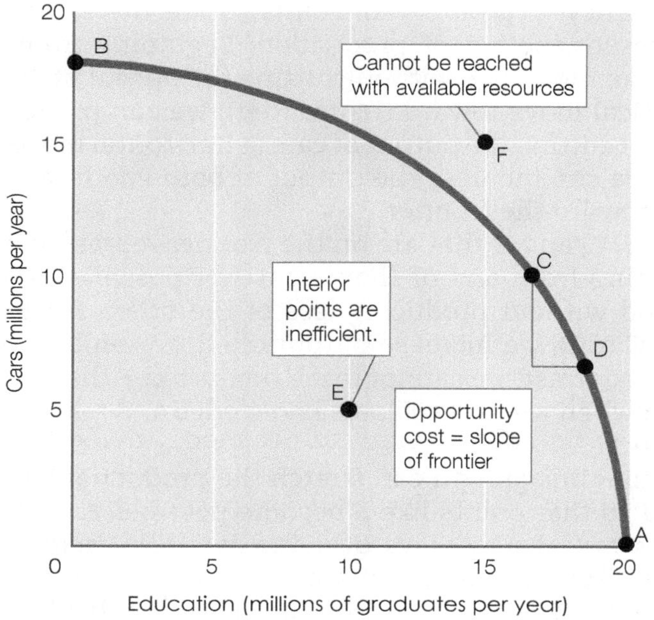

This figure shows combinations of cars and education that are possible for a simple economy in which they are the only two products. We assume that quantities of available factors of production and technologies are fixed. If we devote all factors to education, we can produce 20 million college graduates each year (point A). If we use all factors for making cars, we can produce 18 million cars each year (point B). Combinations of the two goods that we can produce when the available factors are used efficiently, for example, points C and D, lie along a curve called a production possibility frontier. The slope of the frontier indicates the opportunity cost of education in terms of cars. Interior points, such as E, represent inefficient use of resources. Beginning from such a point, we can produce more of one good without producing less of the other. However, we cannot reach points outside the frontier, such as F, using available factors of production and technology.

In drawing this graph, we assume that supplies of productive resources and technology remain constant. Even if all available resources go to education, the limit to the number of graduates that the economy can produce in a year is 20 million. The extreme possibility of producing 20 million graduates and no cars is shown by point A. Likewise, point B shows that the maximum number of cars the economy can produce is 18 million, if no resources go to education. Between those two extremes is a whole range of possible combinations of education and cars. Points such as C and D along the curve between A and B show points the economy can produce that include some cars and some graduates. We call that curve a **production possibility frontier**.

Production possibility frontier

A graph that shows possible combinations of goods that an economy can produce given available technology and factors of production

Efficiency and Economic Growth   A production possibility frontier based on given technology and productive resources serves nicely to illustrate efficiency in production. Points inside the frontier, such as point E, represent inefficient production. Beginning from such a point, we can make more cars without cutting the output of education (shown by a vertical move toward the frontier); we can produce more education without cutting the output of cars (a horizontal move toward the frontier); or we can increase the output of both goods (a move up and to the right toward the frontier).

Points like A, B, C, and D that are on the frontier represent efficient production. Starting from any of them, it is not possible to produce more of one good without producing less of the other. For example, in moving from C to D, we increase output of education but decrease output of cars. In contrast, we cannot reach points like F that lie outside the frontier even when we use available knowledge and resources with complete efficiency.

Over time, economic growth can stretch the production possibility frontier outward so that points like F become possible. As mentioned earlier, the discovery of new ways of using available factors of production is one source of growth. So are additions to the total stock of factors of production—for example, through growth of the labor force. Over time, the educational process itself improves the quality of the labor force, thus making a given number of people capable of producing more.

Opportunity Cost and Comparative Advantage   We can also use the production possibility frontier to illustrate opportunity cost. As we have seen, once the economy is producing efficiently at a point on the frontier, choosing to make more of one good means making less of the other. For example, suppose we start at point C, representing 16 million graduates and 10 million cars. If we want to increase the output of graduates to 18 million per year, we must give up some cars and use the labor, capital, and natural resources freed in this way to build and staff classrooms. In moving from point C to point D, we trade off production of 4 million cars for the extra 2 million graduates. Over that range of the frontier, the opportunity cost of each extra graduate is about two cars. The slope of the frontier shows the opportunity cost of graduates, measured in terms of cars.

As more students graduate and we move down and to the right along the frontier, the frontier becomes steeper and the opportunity cost of producing graduates increases. A major reason is that not all factors of production—especially not all workers—are alike. Suppose we start all the way up at point B, with no graduates, and then transfer enough resources to education to open one small college. The first people we would pull off the assembly line to staff the classrooms would be those who have a comparative advantage in teaching. By the time enough resources move to education from the auto industry to reach point D, we will begin to run out of the most suitable recruits for academic life. Increasingly, to produce still more education we have to take some of the best production workers with no assurance that they will be good teachers. The opportunity cost of increasing the output of education (shown by the slope of the frontier) is correspondingly greater.

Theory and Evidence

Theories are of no use in explaining relationships among facts unless they fit those facts. Theory building is a matter of constantly comparing proposed explanations with evidence gleaned from observations of the actual choices people make—that is, with *empirical* evidence. When **empirical** evidence is consistent with the relationships proposed in a theory, our confidence in the validity of the theory increases. When evidence is not consistent with the theory, we need to reexamine the theory. The relationships proposed in it may be invalid, or they may be valid only under different circumstances. We then need to modify the theory by changing the proposed relationships or adding detail.

Empirical

Based on experience or observation

Government agencies and private firms generate mountains of empirical data on economic activity. Economists constantly examine that data in an effort to confirm theories or find inconsistencies that point the way to better theories. Statistical analysis of empirical economic data is known as **econometrics**—the science of economic measurement.

Econometrics

The statistical analysis of empirical economic data

Theories and Forecasts

Economic theories can help us understand things that happened in the past—trends in crop patterns over the past decade, the effects of new communication technologies, and so on; but understanding the past is not always enough. People also want forecasts of future economic events.

Within limits, economic theory can be useful here, too. Any theory that purports to explain a relationship between past events can help predict what will happen under similar circumstances in the future. To put it more precisely, economic theory can be used to make **conditional forecasts** of the form "If A, then B, other things being equal." Thus, an economist might say, "If gasoline prices rise, and if at the same time consumer incomes and the prices of other goods do not change, purchases of SUVs will fall."

Conditional forecast

A prediction of future economic events in the form "If A, then B, other things being equal"

Thousands of economists make a living from forecasting. Decision-makers in business and government use economic forecasts extensively. Forecasts are not perfect, however; and forecasters sometimes make conspicuous mistakes. There are at least three reasons for these mistakes.

First, people sometimes pay insufficient attention to the conditional nature of forecasts. The news might report, for example, "Economists predict a drop in SUV sales." Yet people keep right on buying big vehicles. In such a case, the news report may have failed to note the forecasters' cautionary comments. The forecasters may have said that

A forecasted drop in SUV sales should include the forecaster's precautionary comments.

SUV sales would drop in response to a gas price increase if consumer incomes and technology remained the same; but consumers got richer and new technology made SUVs less gas-hungry, so SUV sales did not fall after all.

Second, a forecast may be invalid because the theory behind it is incorrect or incomplete. Economists do not always agree on what theory best fits the facts. Some theories give more weight to one fact, others to different facts. The competing theories may imply conflicting forecasts under some conditions. At least one of the forecasts will then turn out to be wrong. Finding out which theories yield better forecasts than others is an important part of the process through which economists distinguish valid theories from inadequate ones.

Third, economic forecasts can go wrong because some of the things that business managers and government officials most want to know are among the hardest to predict. For example, a competent economist could produce a fairly accurate forecast of car sales based on certain assumptions about incomes and the prices of gasoline and other goods. However, what the marketing people at General Motors would like to know is what will happen to the social image of SUVs: Will they continue to be a symbol of high status, or will they become an embarrassment in a more environmentally conscious society? Social attitudes are not among the variables that economists can forecast accurately.

Despite these limitations, most economists take the view that well-founded conditional forecasts, for all their limitations, are a better basis for business and public policy decisions than whims and guesswork. Still, they caution against relying too heavily on forecasts.

Theory and Policy

People often ask economists to use their theories to analyze the effects of public policies or forecast the effects of policy changes. The government may, for example, be considering new measures to aid unemployed workers, new responses to climate change, or new measures to regulate international trade. How will the effects of such policies spread through the economy? How will they affect people's lives?

Economists have their own characteristic way of thinking about public policy, just as they have their own way of thinking about other topics. In particular, economists want to understand not just the direct effects of policy, but also the indirect effects, some of which may be completely unintended. Here are some examples:

- Unemployment compensation has the intended effect of aiding unemployed workers, but it also has the unintended effect of increasing the number of workers who are unemployed. The reason is that workers who receive compensation can afford to take their time finding just the right new job. In some ways that is bad. In the short run, more people out of work means fewer goods and services produced. In other ways, it may be good. When people have more time to find jobs that match their skills, they can produce more goods and services in the long run.

- Regulations intended to improve the fuel efficiency of automobiles encourage production of cars that weigh less, but the lighter cars are somewhat less safe. Increased highway deaths may be an unintended consequence.

- After widespread banking failures in the 1980s, U.S. regulators made rule changes intended to stabilize the banking system by strengthening the balance sheets of commercial banks. Those regulations also raised the cost of bank loans relative to loans from sources outside the banking system. As an unintended consequence, much lending activity, including home mortgage lending, moved to an emerging "shadow banking system" consisting of mortgage brokers, securitized loans, and special purpose financial vehicles. When a new crisis came in 2008, the new financial system turned out, in some ways, to be not more but less stable than the old one.

It would be wrong to conclude that the government should never act simply because its policies may do some harm as well as some good. Sometimes the harm may outweigh the good, and sometimes not. What is important, economists say, is that policymakers look at the whole picture, not just part of it, before they make a decision. Henry Hazlitt seized on this idea to reduce the whole of economics to a single lesson:

The art of economics consists in looking not merely at the immediate but at the longer effects of any act or policy; it consists in tracing the consequences of that policy not merely for one group but for all groups.[5]

As you progress through your study of economics—both the macro and micro branches—you will repeatedly encounter examples of the way economic theory can help understand the choices people make and the complex effects of policies intended to regulate those choices.

Summary

1. **What is the subject matter of economics?** Economics is a social science that seeks to understand the choices people make in using scarce resources to meet their wants. Scarcity is a situation in which there is not enough of something to meet everyone's wants. *Microeconomics* is the branch of economics that studies choices that involve individual households, firms, and markets. *Macroeconomics* is the branch of economics that deals with large-scale economic phenomena, such as inflation, unemployment, and economic growth.

2. **What considerations underlie the choice of what an economy will produce?** Producing more of one good requires producing less of something else because productive resources that go into producing one good cannot produce another at the same time. Productive resources fall into three groups called *factors of production*. *Labor* means the productive contributions made by people working with their hands and minds. *Capital* means the productive inputs created by people. *Natural resources* include anything useful in its natural state as a productive input. The *opportunity cost* of a good or service is its cost in terms of the forgone opportunity to pursue the best possible alternative activity with the same time or resources.

3. **What considerations underlie the choice of how to produce?** The economy can produce goods and services in many different ways, some of which are more efficient than others. *Economic efficiency* means a state of affairs in which it is impossible to make any change that satisfies one person's wants more fully without causing some other person's wants to be satisfied less fully. *Efficiency in production* means a situation in which it is not possible, given the available productive resources and existing knowledge, to produce more of one good or service without forgoing the opportunity to produce some of another good or service. Once an economy achieves efficiency, it can expand production potential by increasing the availability of resources or by improving knowledge. The term *investment* refers to the process of increasing the economy's stock of capital. Entrepreneurship is the process of looking for new possibilities—making use of new ways of doing things, being alert to new opportunities, and overcoming old limits.

4. **What considerations underlie the choice of who will do which work?** Cooperation can greatly enhance economic efficiency. Three things make cooperation worthwhile: teamwork, learning by doing, and comparative advantage. Teamwork can enhance productivity even when there is no specialization. Learning by doing improves productivity even when all workers start with equal talents and abilities. Comparative advantage comes into play when people have different abilities or, after learning by doing, have developed specialized skills. Having a *comparative advantage* in producing a particular good or service means being able to produce it at a relatively lower opportunity cost than someone else.

5. **What considerations underlie the choice of who will benefit from goods and services that the economy produces?** In part, deciding who will benefit revolves around issues of efficiency. *Efficiency in distribution* refers to a state of affairs in which, with a given quantity of goods and services, it is impossible to satisfy one person's wants more fully without satisfying someone else's less fully. In addition, the choice of how we distribute goods depends on judgments about fairness.

6. **How are economic choices coordinated?** The two principle methods of coordinating choices are *hierarchy* and *spontaneous order*. Markets are the most important example of spontaneous order. The internal decisions made by large corporations and units of government are the most important examples of hierarchy.

7. **How do economists use theory, graphs, and evidence in their work?** A *theory* or *model* is a representation of the relationships among facts. Economists use graphs to display data and make visual representations of theories and models. For example, *a production possibility frontier* is a graph, using available factors of production and knowledge, which shows the boundary between combinations of goods that are possible to produce and those that are not. Economists refine theories in the light of *empirical* evidence, that is, evidence gleaned from observation of actual economic decisions. *Econometrics* means the economic analysis of empirical evidence. Economic models are a way to make *conditional forecasts* of the form "If A, then B, other things being equal.

Key Terms   Page

Problems and Topics for Discussion

1. **Opportunity cost**   Gasoline, insurance, depreciation, and repairs are all costs of owning a car. Which of these are opportunity costs in the context of each of the following decisions?

   a. You own a car and are deciding whether to drive one hundred miles for a weekend visit to a friend at another university.

   b. You do not own a car but are considering buying one so that you can get a part-time job located five miles from where you live.

   In general, why does the context in which you decide to do something affect the opportunity cost of doing it?

2. **Comparative advantage in international trade**   Suppose that companies in the United States can produce a car with 200 labor hours and a ton of rice with 20 labor hours. In China, it takes 250 labor hours to make a car and 50 labor hours to grow a ton of rice. What is the opportunity cost of producing rice in each country, stated in terms of cars? What is the opportunity cost of cars, stated in terms of rice? Which country has a comparative advantage in cars? Which in rice?

3. **Efficiency in distribution and the food stamp program**   The federal Supplemental Nutrition Assistance Program (SNAP), formerly known as food stamps, could have been designed so that every low-income family would receive a ration consisting of so much bread, so much milk, and so on. Instead, SNAP gives the family an allowance to spend on almost any kind of food the family prefers. For a given cost to the federal government, which plan do you think would better serve the goal of efficiency in distribution? Why?

   Now consider a program that would allow families to trade their SNAP credits for cash (some such trading does occur, but it is restricted by law) or one in which poor families are given cash, with which they can buy whatever they want. Compare these alternatives with the existing program in terms of both positive and normative economics.

   (Continues)

4. **Spontaneous order in the cafeteria**   Suppose that your college cafeteria does not have enough room for all the students to sit down to eat at once. It stays open for lunch from 11:30 a.m. to 1:30 p.m. Consider the following three methods of distributing diners over the two-hour lunch period in such a way that everyone can have a seat.

    a.   The administration sets a rule: First-year students must eat between 11:30 and 12:00, sophomores between 12:00 and 12:30, and so on for juniors and seniors.

    b.   The lunch period is broken up into half-hour segments with green tickets for the first shift, blue tickets for the second, and so on. There are an equal number of tickets of each color. At the beginning of each semester, the cafeteria holds an auction in which students bid for the ticket color of their choice.

    c.   Students can come to the cafeteria whenever they want. If there are no empty seats, they have to stand in line.

   Compare the three schemes in terms of the concepts of (1) spontaneous order and hierarchy, (2) information and incentives, and (3) efficiency.

5. **A production possibility frontier**   Bill Schwartz has four fields spread out over a hillside. He can grow either wheat or potatoes in any of the fields, but the low fields are better for potatoes and the high ones are better for wheat. Here are some combinations of wheat and potatoes that he could produce:

Number of Fields Used for Potatoes	Total Tons of Potatoes	Total Tons of Wheat
All 4	1,000	0
Lowest 3	900	400
Lowest 2	600	700
Lowest 1	300	900
None	0	1,000

Use these data to draw a production possibility frontier for wheat and potatoes. What is the opportunity cost of wheat, stated in terms of potatoes, when the farmer converts the highest field to wheat production? What happens to the opportunity cost of wheat as Schwartz switches more and more fields to wheat?

Case for Discussion

Cow Power

As natural resources go, it doesn't have much glamour; but unlike oil, the United States has plenty of it. We're talking about cow manure. The average cow puts out about thirty gallons a day. Multiply that by something like 8 million cows on the nation's sixty-five thousand dairy farms, and you have—well, what do you have—a big problem or a big opportunity?

In the past, manure was a problem. True, it makes good fertilizer, but with big drawbacks. Most dairy farms stored it in open lagoons before spreading it on fields. The smelly lagoons created a nuisance to neighbors. What is more, they were a big source of methane, a greenhouse gas that, pound for pound, contributes ten times more to global warming than carbon dioxide.

Methane burns, however; and that's where cow manure becomes an opportunity. If farmers pump it into an anaerobic digester instead of into an open lagoon, it produces a purified gas that the farm itself can burn to produce electricity or sell to a company that will transport it by pipeline to other customers.

Marie and Earl Audet's dairy farm in Bridport, Vermont, was one of the earliest farms to go on line with cow power. Already in 2006, they were expecting to sell $200,000 worth of cow power a year to Central Vermont Public Service, the local electric utility. In addition, they expected to benefit from a clear liquid byproduct that could serve as fertilizer and to save another $50,000 by using the dry, odorless, fluff that remains from the digester as bedding for the cows, in place of expensive sawdust.[6]

In addition to the Audet's early project, another larger digester has come on line on the Jordan Dairy Farm in Rutland, Vermont. That digester supplies enough electricity for three hundred homes. In addition to cow manure, the Jordan digester uses food scraps from four local food companies, making use of biomass that previously went to disposal. Working together with the Massachusetts energy company, National Grid, four neighboring dairy farms expect to add digesters soon.

Cow power, like other forms of alternate energy, is not a free lunch. It requires expensive capital investments. In many locations, electric companies encourage such investment by paying a premium rate for energy from biomass and other renewable resources.

Questions

1. Based on the information given in the case, do you think the out-of-pocket costs of producing electricity from cow manure are greater, less, or about the same as the cost of conventional power sources? On what information in the case do you base your answer?

2. Anaerobic digestion of cow manure reduces harm to neighbors (less smell) and harm to the environment (less greenhouse gas). How do these benefits enter into the calculation of the opportunity cost of producing cow power? Do these benefits tend to make the opportunity cost greater than, or less than, the out-of-pocket costs?

3. Based on information in the case, do you think the growth of the cow power industry illustrates the principle of spontaneous order or that of hierarchy? Or, is it a little bit of both? Explain your reasoning.

Endnotes

1. The Austrian economist Ludwig von Mises suggested that *catallactics,* meaning the science of exchange, would be a better term than *economics,* which has the original meaning of household management. For better or worse, the term catallactics has never come into wide use.

2. Economists sometimes call efficiency, defined this way, *Pareto efficiency* after the Italian economist Vilfredo Pareto.

3. Armen A. Alchian and Harold Demsetz, "Production, Information Cost, and Economic Organization," *American Economic Review* (December 1972): 777–795.

4. The appendix to this chapter provides a review of basic graphical concepts, including axes, points and number pairs, slopes, and tangencies.

5. Henry Hazlitt, *Economics in One Lesson* (New York: Arlington House, 1979), 17.

6. Martha T. Moore, "Cows Power Plan for Alternative Fuel," *USA Today,* Dec. 6, 2006, http://www.usatoday.com/news/nation/2006-12-03-cow-power_x.htm.

Appendix to Chapter 1:
Working with Graphs

Which is smarter—a computer or the human brain? The computer certainly does some things faster and more accurately, say, dividing one twenty-digit number by another. The human brain, however, has the ability to solve other kinds of problems with speed and accuracy beyond the ability of most computers. Working with pictures is one of the areas in which the human brain excels. Three key abilities give the brain a comparative advantage where pictures are involved.

1. An ability to store and retrieve a vast number of images quickly and accurately (Think of how many people's faces you can recognize.)

2. An ability to discard irrelevant detail while highlighting essentials (Think of how easily you can recognize a politician's face in a political cartoon that has just a few lines.)

3. An ability to see key similarities between patterns that are not exactly the same (That is why you can usually match two pictures of a person taken twenty years apart.)

Graphs are an aid to learning economics precisely because they make use of those three special abilities of the human brain. Economists do use graphs to make their theories easier to understand, not harder. All it takes to use graphs effectively as a learning tool is the inborn human skill in working with pictures plus knowledge of a few simple rules for extracting the information that graphs contain. This appendix outlines those rules in brief.

1A.1 Pairs of Numbers and Points

The first thing to master is how to use points on a graph to represent pairs of numbers. The table in Figure 1A.1 presents five pairs of numbers. The two columns are labeled "x" and "y." The first number in each pair is called the x value and the second the y value. Each pair of numbers is labeled with a capital letter. Pair A has an x value of 2 and a y value of 3, pair B has an x value of 4 and a y value of 4, and so on.

The diagram in Figure 1A.1 contains two lines that meet at the lower left-hand corner; we call them *coordinate axes*. The horizontal axis is marked off into units representing the x value and the vertical axis into unit representing the y value. Each pair of numbers from the table corresponds to a point in the space between the two axes. For example, we find point A by going two units to the right along the horizontal axis and then three units straight up, parallel to the vertical axis. That point represents the x value of 2 and the y value of 3. The other points are located in the same way.

FIGURE **1A.1** NUMBER PAIRS AND POINTS

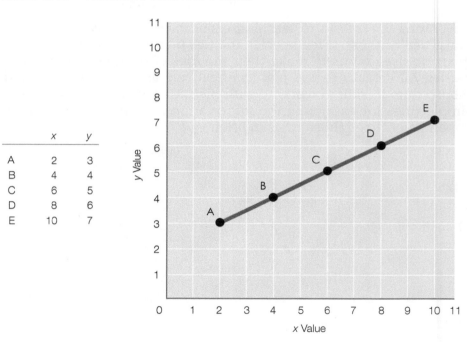

	x	y
A	2	3
B	4	4
C	6	5
D	8	6
E	10	7

Each lettered pair of numbers in the table corresponds to a lettered point on the graph. The x value of each point corresponds to the horizontal distance of the point from the vertical axis; the y value corresponds to its vertical distance from the horizontal axis.

We can often improve the visual effect of a graph by connecting the points with a line or a curve. That makes it possible to see the relationship between x values and y values at a glance: As the x value increases, the y value also increases.

1A.2 Slopes and Tangencies

Every line or curve in a graph has a slope. The **slope** of a straight line between two points is the ratio of the change in the y value to the change in the x value between the two points. In Figure 1A.2, for example, the slope of the line between points A and B is 2. The y value changes by six units between these two points, whereas the x value changes by only three units. The slope is the ratio 6/3 = 2.

We can express the slope of a line between the points (x_1, y_1) and (x_2, y_2) in terms of a simple formula that is derived from the definition just given:

$$\text{Slope} = \frac{(y_2 - y_1)}{(x_2 - x_1)}$$

Slope

For a straight line, the ratio of the change in the *y* value to the change in the *x* value between any two points on the line

---

FIGURE 1A.2   SLOPES OF LINES

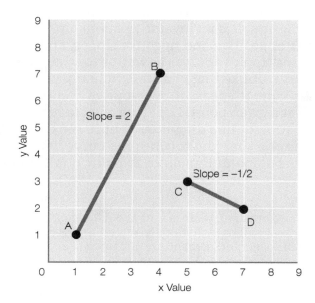

The slope of a straight line drawn between two points is defined as the ratio of the change in the y value to the change in the x value as one moves from one point to the other. For example, the line between points A and B in this Figure has a slope of +2, whereas the line between points C and D has a slope of −1/2.

Applied to the line between points A and B in Figure 1A.2, the formula gives the following result:

$$\text{Slope} = \frac{(7-1)}{(4-1)} = \frac{6}{3} = 2$$

A line such as that between A and B in Figure 1A.2, which slopes upward from left to right, is said to have a **positive slope** because the value of its slope is a positive number. A positively sloped line represents a **direct relationship** between the variable represented on the x axis and that represented on the y axis—that is, a relationship in which an increase in one variable is associated with an increase in the other. The relationship of the age of a tree to its height is an example of a direct relationship. An example from economics is the relationship between family income and expenditures on housing.

When a line slants downward from left to right, like the one between points C and D in Figure 1A.2, the x and y values change in opposite directions. Going from point C to point D, the y value changes by –1 (that is, decreases by one unit) and the x value changes by +2 (that is, increases by two units). The slope of this line is the ratio –1/2.

When the slope of a line has a negative value, we say has a **negative slope**. Such a line represents an **inverse relationship** between the x variable and the y variable—that is, a relationship in which an increase in the value of one variable is associated with a decrease in the value of the other variable. The relationship between the temperature in the room and the time it takes the ice in your lemonade to melt is an example of an inverse relationship. In economics, the relationship between the price of gasoline and the quantity that consumers purchase, other things being equal, is an inverse relationship.

The concepts of positive and negative slopes, and of direct and inverse relationships, apply to curves as well as to straight lines. However, the slope of a curve, unlike that of a straight line, varies from one point to the next.[1] We cannot speak of the slope of a curve in general, but only of its slope at a given point. The slope of a curve at any given point is the slope of a straight line drawn tangent to the curve at that point. (A **tangent** line is one that just touches the curve without crossing it.) In Figure 1A.3, the slope of the curve at point A is 1 and the slope at point B is –2.

---

[1] Economists try to be consistent; yet in talking about lines and curves, they fail. They have no qualms about calling something a "curve" that is a straight line. For example, later we will encounter "demand curves" that are as straight as a stretched string. Less frequently, they may call something a line that has a curved shape.

Positive slope

A slope having a value greater than zero

Direct relationship

A relationship between two variables in which an increase in the value of one variable is associated with an increase in the value of the other

Negative slope

A slope having a value less than zero

Inverse relationship

A relationship between two variables in which an increase in the value of one variable is associated with a decrease in the value of the other

Tangent

A straight line that touches a curve at a given point without intersecting it

FIGURE 1A.3   SLOPES OF CURVES

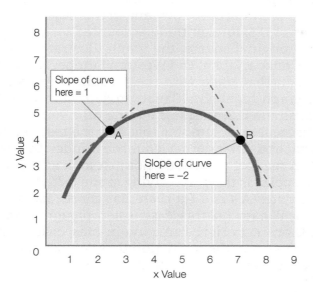

The slope of a curve at any point is the slope of a straight line drawn tangent to the curve at that point. A tangent line is one that just touches the curve without crossing it. In this figure, the slope of the curve at point A is 1, and the slope at point B is –2.

1A.3 Using Graphs to Display Data

Economists use graphs for two primary purposes: for display of data and for representation of economic relationships. Some graphs serve one purpose; some the other; and some a little of both. We begin with some common kinds of graphs whose purpose is to display data.

Figure 1A.4 shows three kinds of graphs that display data. Part (a) is a *pie chart*. We use pie charts to show the relative size of various quantities that add up to a total of 100 percent. In this case, the quantities are the percentages of U.S. foreign trade accounted for by various trading partners. In the original source, the graph illustrated a discussion of U.S. trade with Canada, Japan, and Western Europe. The author wanted to make the point that trade with these countries is very important. Note how the graph highlights Canadian, Japanese, and Western European trade with the U.S. and, at the same time, omits details not relevant to the discussion by lumping together the rest of Europe, Africa, the rest of Asia, and many other countries under the heading "rest of the world." In reading graphs, do not just look at the numbers; ask yourself, "What point is the graph trying to make?"

Part (b) of Figure 1A.4 is a *bar chart*. Bar charts, like pie charts, can display numerical data (in this case, unemployment rates) in relationship to a non-numerical category, in this case, education. Bar charts are not subject to the restriction that data displayed must total 100 percent. What point do you think the author of this graph was trying to make?

Part (c) of Figure 1A.4 is an example of a data display graph very common in economics—the *time-series graph*. A time-series graph shows the values of one or more economic quantities on the vertical axis and time (years, months, or whatever) on the horizontal axis. This graph shows the ups and downs of the U.S. unemployment rate by month from 2008 to early 2011.

Note one feature of this time-series graph: the scale on the vertical axis begins from 2 percent rather than from 0. By spreading out the data points in the range 2 to 12 percent, one can show the trend of unemployment in greater detail. The advantage of greater detail has an offsetting danger, however. Careless reading of the graph could cause one to exaggerate the amount by which unemployment rose during the 2007–2009 recession. For example, the unemployment line is almost three times higher above the horizontal axis in mid-2009 as at the beginning of 2008. However, careful reading of the graph shows that the unemployment rate was actually only twice as high (10 percent vs. 5 percent). The moral of the story: Always examine the vertical and horizontal axes of a graph carefully.

FIGURE 1A.4   USING GRAPHS TO DISPLAY DATA

(a)

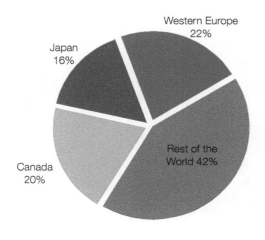

Western Europe
22%

Japan
16%

Rest of the
World 42%

Canada
20%

(b)

Unemployment Rate by Highest Level of Education Attainment

(Average Unemployment Rate 1992–2003)

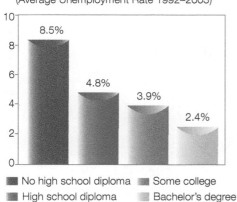

8.5%

4.8%

3.9%

2.4%

■ No high school diploma ■ Some college
■ High school diploma   ■ Bachelor's degree
                            or higher

(c)

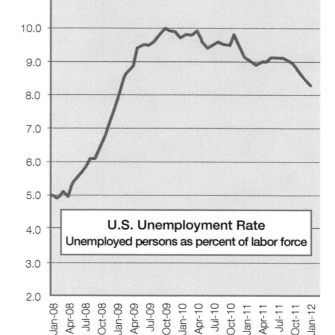

U.S. Unemployment Rate
Unemployed persons as percent of labor force

This figure shows three common kinds of data display graphs. The pie chart in part (a) is appropriate when the data items sum to 100 percent. The bar chart in part (b), like the pie chart, is good for reporting numerical data that are associated with non-numerical categories (in this case educational attainment). The bar chart does not require data items to sum to 100 percent. The time-series graph in part (c) shows the values of one or more economic quantities on the vertical axis and time on the horizontal axis

Source: Part (a), U.S. Council of Economic Advisers, *Economic Report of the President* (Washington, D.C.: Government Printing Office, 2002), Table B-105, 397; part (b), Bureau of Labor Statistics, *Current Population Survey*; and part (c), Bureau of Labor Statistics, The Employment Situation.

FIGURE 1A.5 USING GRAPHS TO SHOW RELATIONSHIPS

(a)

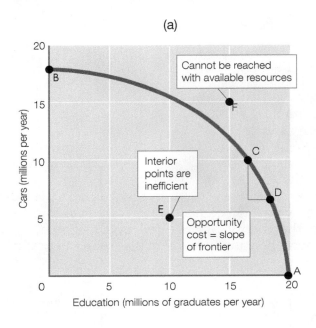

(b)

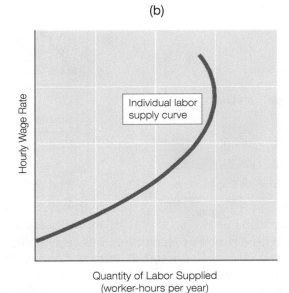

Quantity of Labor Supplied
(worker-hours per year)

Relational graphs are visual representations of theories, that is, of relationships among facts. This figure shows two typical relational graphs. Part (a) is the production possibility frontier discussed in Chapter 1. It relates quantities of cars to quantities of education the economy can produce with given factors of production and knowledge. Part (b) represents a theory of individual labor supply, according to which an increase in the hourly wage rate, after a point, will cause a person to reduce the quantity of labor supplied. Part (b) is an abstract graph in that it shows only the general nature of the relationship, with no numbers on either axis.

1A.4 Using Graphs to Display Relationships

Some graphs, rather than simply recording observed facts, represent theories and models. Instead of simply presenting facts, they highlight the relationships among facts. Figure 1A.5 shows two typical graphs whose primary purpose is to display relationships.

Part (a) of Figure 1A.5 is the production possibility frontier that we encountered in Chapter 1. The graph represents the inverse relationship between the quantities of cars and education that the economy can produce, given available knowledge and productive resources.

Part (b) of Figure 1A.5 represents a relationship between the number of hours per year a person is willing to work and the wage rate. The graph shows that raising the wage rate will, up to a point, induce a person to work more hours; beyond a certain point, however, a further increase in the wage will cause the person to work fewer hours. Why? According to the theory represented by the graph, once a person's income reaches a certain level, he or she tends to prefer the luxury of more leisure time to the alternative of more material goods.

Note one distinctive feature of this graph: There are no numbers on the axes. It is an abstract graph that represents only the qualitative relationships between the hours of labor per year and the wage rate. It makes no quantitative statements regarding how the change in hours worked associated with any given change in wage rate. In reality, the point where people prefer more leisure to additional income is different for different people, and many people never reach that point. We often use abstract graphs to represent theories that apply in a general way to many cases, regardless of differences in detail from one case to another.

1A.5 Packing Three Variables into Two Dimensions

Anything drawn on a flat piece of paper is limited to two dimensions. The relationships discussed so far fit a two-dimensional graph easily because they involve just two variables. In the case of the production possibility frontier, they are the quantity of education (horizontal axis) and the quantity of cars (vertical axis). In the case of labor supply, they are hours of work per year (horizontal axis) and wage rate (vertical axis). However, two-variable relationships often oversimplify the reality we are trying to understand. When that happens, we must find a way to represent three or more variables in two dimensions.

There are a number of ways to represent relationships among three or more variables on a flat piece of paper. For example, a map of the United States might use coordinates of latitude and longitude to indicate position, contour lines to indicate altitude, and colors to indicate vegetation. An architect might use a perspective drawing to give the illusion of three dimensions—height, width, and depth. This section deals with still another way of packing three variables into two dimensions. Although the method is a favorite of economists—we will use it in dozens of graphs in this book—we will show its generality by beginning with a non-economic example.

A Non-Economic Example

The example concerns heart disease, the leading cause of death in the United States. There is a close link between the risk of heart disease and the quantity of cholesterol in a person's blood. Studies have indicated, for example, that a 25 percent reduction in cholesterol can cut the risk of death from heart attack by nearly 50 percent. Knowing this, millions of people order tests of their cholesterol levels; and, if results are high, they use diet, exercise, or medications to reduce their risk of heart disease.

Important though cholesterol is, just knowing your cholesterol level is not enough to tell you your risk of dying of a heart attack in the coming year. Other variables also enter in, including age. For men aged twenty with average cholesterol levels, the mortality rate from heart disease is only about 3 per 100,000. For men aged sixty, the mortality rate rises to over 500 per 100,000, still assuming average cholesterol. We thus have three variables with which to deal—mortality, cholesterol, and age. How can we represent these three variables using a two-dimensional graph?

A possible approach would be to draw two separate graphs. One would show the relationship between age and heart disease for the male population as a whole, without regard to cholesterol levels. The other would show the relationship between cholesterol and heart disease for the male population as a whole, without regard to age. By looking from one diagram to the other, we could get an idea of the three-variable relationship.

However, such a side-by-side pair of graphs would be clumsy. A better way, shown in Figure 1A.6, is to use cholesterol and mortality as the x and y axes, and to take age into account by plotting separate lines for men of various ages. That chart is far easier to interpret than the side-by-side pair would be. If you are a man and know your age and cholesterol count, you just pick out the appropriate line and read off your risk. If you do not like what you see, you go on a diet.[2]

The multi-curve graph is a lovely invention. One of the great things about it is that it works for more than three variables. For example, we could add a fourth variable, gender, to the graph by drawing a new set of lines in a different color to show mortality rates for women of

---

[2] We could instead have started with the age-mortality chart and drawn separate lines for men with different cholesterol levels. Such a chart would show exactly the same information. We could even draw a chart with cholesterol and age on the axes, and separate contour lines to represent various levels of mortality. The choice often depends on what one wants to emphasize. Here, we emphasize the cholesterol-mortality relationship because cholesterol is something you can do something about. You cannot do anything about your age, so we give age slightly less emphasis by not placing it on one of the two axes.

various ages. Each line for women would have a positive slope similar to the men's lines, but it would lie below the corresponding line for men of the same age because women, other things being equal, experience lower mortality from heart disease.

Shifts in Curves and Movements along Curves

Now that it is clear how to read three-variable graphs, we can turn our attention to some special terminology. How can we best describe what happens to a man as he ages, given the relationship shown in Figure 1A.6?

FIGURE 1A.6   THREE VARIABLES IN TWO DIMENSIONS

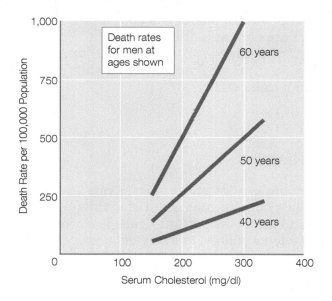

This graph shows a common way of representing a three-variable relationship on a two-dimensional graph. The three variables in this case are serum cholesterol (a measure of the amount of cholesterol in the blood), age, and death rate from heart disease for the U.S. male population. We can most easily interpret the relationship among the three variables if we represent all of them on one graph, by drawing separate cholesterol-death rate lines for each age group. As a man ages, his cholesterol-death rate line shifts upward.

One way to describe the effects of aging would be to say, "As a man ages, he moves from one curve to the next higher one on the chart." There is nothing at all wrong with saying that; but an economist would tend to phrase it a bit differently, saying, "As a man ages, his cholesterol-mortality curve shifts upward." The two ways of expressing the effects of aging have exactly the same meaning. Preferring one or the other is just a matter of habit.

If we express the effects of aging in terms of a shift of the cholesterol-mortality curve, how should we express the effects of a reduction in cholesterol for a man of a given age? An economist would say it this way: "Cutting a man's cholesterol count through diet or exercise will move him down along his cholesterol-mortality curve."

Before you finish this book, you will see the phrases "shift in a curve" and "movement along a curve" a great many times. How can you keep them straight? Nothing could be easier.

- If you are talking about the effect of a change in a variable that appears on one of the coordinate axes of the diagram, the effect will appear as a movement along one of the curves. For example, the effect of a change in cholesterol (horizontal axis) on mortality (vertical axis) appears as a movement along the line for a given age.

- If you are talking about the effect of a change in a variable that does not appear on one of the coordinate axes of the diagram, the effect appears as a shift in one of the curves. For example, the effect of a change in age (not the unit for either axis) on mortality (vertical axis) appears as a shift in the curve relating cholesterol to mortality.

1A.6 Study Hints

So much for the basic rules of graphics. Once you master them, how should you study a chapter that is full of graphs?

The first—and most important—rule is to *avoid trying to memorize graphs as patterns of lines*. In every economics course, at least one student comes to the instructor after failing an exam and exclaims, "But I learned every one of those graphs! What happened?" The reply is that the student should have learned economics instead of memorizing graphs. Following are some hints for working with graphs.

After reading through a chapter that contains several graphs, go back through the graphs one at a time. Cover the caption accompanying each graph, and try to express the graph's "picture" in words. If you cannot say as much about the graph as the caption does, reread the text. Once you can translate the graph into words, you have won half the battle.

Next, cover each graph and use the caption as a guide. Try to sketch the graph on a piece of scratch paper. What are the labels on the graph's axes? On the curves? What are the slopes of various curves? Are there important points of intersection or tangencies? If you can go back and forth between the caption and the graph, you will find that the two together are much easier to remember than either one separately.

Finally, try going beyond the graph that appears in the book. If the graph illustrates the effect of an increase in the price of butter, try sketching a similar diagram that shows the effect of a decrease in the price of butter. If the graph shows what happens to the economy during a period of rising unemployment, try drawing a similar graph that shows what happens during a period of falling unemployment. Doing practice exercises of this kind will give you an edge on your next exam.

Making Your Own Graphs

For some students, the hardest test questions to answer are ones that require original graphs as part of an essay. Suppose the question is, "How does a change in the number of students attending a university affect the cost per student of providing an education?" Here are some hints for making your own graph.

1. Write down the answer to the question in words. If you cannot, you might as well skip to the next question. Underline the most important quantities in your answer, such as "The larger the *number of students* who attend a college, the lower the *cost per student* of providing them with an education because it is not necessary to duplicate fixed facilities, such as libraries."

2. Decide how you want to label the axes. In our example, the vertical axis could be labeled "cost per student" and the horizontal axis "number of students."

3. Do you have specific numbers to work with? If so, the next step is to construct a table showing what you know, and use that table to sketch your graph. If you have no numbers, you must draw an abstract graph. In this case, all you know is that the cost per student goes down when the number of students goes up. Your graph would thus be a negatively sloped line.

4. If your graph involves more than one relationship between quantities, repeat steps 1 through 3 for each relationship you wish to show. When constructing a graph with more than one curve, pay special attention to points at which you think the curves should intersect. (Intersections occur whenever both the x and y values of the two relationships are equal.) Also, note the points at which you think two curves ought to be tangent (which requires that their slopes be equal), the points of maximum or minimum value, if any, and so on.

5. When your graph is finished, try to translate it back into words. Does it really say what you want it to?

A Reminder

As you read this book and encounter various kinds of graphs, turn back to this appendix now and then. Do not memorize graphs as patterns of lines; if you do, you will get lost. If you can alternate between graphs and words, the underlying point will be clearer than if you rely on either one alone. Keep in mind that the primary focus of economics is not graphs; it is people and the ways in which they deal with the challenge of scarcity.

Chapter 2

Supply *and* Demand:
The Basics

After reading this chapter, you will understand the following:

1. How the price of a good or service affects the quantity demanded by buyers

2. How other market conditions affect demand

3. How the price of a good affects the quantity supplied by sellers

4. How other market conditions affect supply

5. How supply and demand interact to determine the market price of a good or service

6. Why market prices and quantities change in response to changes in market conditions.

Before reading this chapter, make sure you know the meaning of the following concepts:

1. Spontaneous order

2. Markets

3. Opportunity cost

4. Law of unintended consequences

Frequent ups and downs in the prices of goods and services—corn, oil, gold, medical care—are among the most conspicuous features of economic life. Prices make headlines because they affect the way we live—our jobs, our incomes, the things we buy, and the things we sell. What determines the prices of goods at any time and the way they change from day to day? The short answer: supply and demand.

Economists use the term **supply** to refer to sellers' willingness and ability to provide goods for sale in a market. **Demand** refers to buyers' willingness and ability to purchase goods. This chapter will show how supply and demand work together to determine prices.

2.1 Demand

According to the **law of demand**, there is an inverse relationship between the quantity of a good that buyers demand and its price. The quantity demanded tends to rise as the price falls and to fall as the price rises. We expect that to happen for two reasons. First, if the price of one good falls while the prices of other goods stay the same, people are likely to substitute the cheaper good. Second, when the price of one good falls while incomes stay the same, people feel a little richer. They use their added buying power to buy a bit more of many things, including, in most cases, a little more of the good whose price went down.

Supply

The willingness and ability of sellers to provide goods for sale in a market

Demand

The willingness and ability of buyers to purchase goods

Law of demand

The principle that an inverse relationship exists between the price of a good and the quantity of that good that buyers demand, other things being equal

The terms *demand* and *quantity demanded*, as used in economics, are not the same as want or need. For example, I think a Porsche is a beautiful car. Sometimes when I see one on the street, I think, "Hey, I want one of those!" Alas, my income is limited. Although in the abstract I might want a Porsche, there are other things I want more. As a result, the quantity of Porsches I demand at the going price is zero.

On the other hand, I might *need* dental surgery to avoid losing my teeth. However, suppose I am poor. If I cannot pay for the surgery or find someone to pay for it on my behalf, I am out of luck. The quantity of dental surgery I demand, therefore, would be zero, however great my need.

Demand, then, combines both willingness and ability to buy. It is not desire in the abstract, but desire backed by the means and the intent to buy.

The Demand Curve

The law of demand defines a relationship between the quantity of a good that people are willing and able to buy, other things being equal, and the price of that good. Figure 2.1 represents this relationship for a familiar consumer good, chicken. It would be possible to discuss a single consumer's demand for chicken; but, more frequently, as in this figure, we focus on the total demand for the good by all buyers in the market.

FIGURE 2.1   A DEMAND CURVE FOR CHICKEN

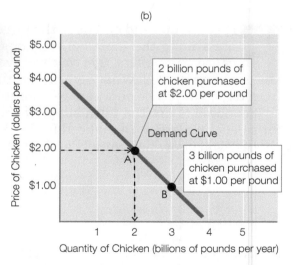

(a)

Price of Chicken (dollars per pound)	Quantity of Chicken Demanded (billions of pounds per year)		
	$3.50	0.5	
	$3.00	1	
	$2.50	1.5	
A	$2.00	2	
	$1.50	2.5	
B	$1.00	3	
	$0.50	3.5	

Both the table and the chart show the quantity of chicken demanded at various prices. For example, at a price of $2.00 per pound, buyers are willing and able to purchase 2 billion pounds of chicken per year. Row A in Part (a) and point A in Part (b) show this price-quantity combination.

The figure shows the demand relationship in two different ways. First look at Part (a). The first row of the table shows that when the price of chicken is $3.00 a pound, the quantity demanded per year is 1 billion pounds. Reading down the table, we see that as the price falls, the quantity demanded rises. At $2.50 per pound, buyers are willing and able to purchase 1.5 billion pounds per year; at $1.50, 2.5 billion pounds; and so on.

Part (b) of Figure 2.1 uses a graph to present the same information; we call it the **demand curve** for chicken. Suppose we want to use the demand curve to find out what quantity of chicken buyers will demand at a price of $2.00 per pound. Starting at $2.00 on the vertical axis, we move across, as shown by the arrow,

The demand curve is based upon quantity and price.

until we reach the demand curve at point A. Continuing to follow the arrow, we drop down to the horizontal axis. Reading from the scale on that axis, we see that the quantity demanded at a price of $2.00 per pound is 2 billion pounds per year. That is the quantity demanded in row A of the table in Part (a).

The effect of a change in the price of chicken, other things being equal, takes the form of a movement from one point to another along the demand curve. Suppose that the price drops from $2.00 to $1.00 per pound. In the process, the quantity that buyers plan to buy increases. The point corresponding to the quantity demanded at the new, lower price is point B (which corresponds to row B of the table). Because of the inverse relationship between price and quantity demanded, the demand curve has a negative slope.

Economists speak of a movement along a demand curve as a **change in quantity demanded**. Such a movement represents buyers' reactions to a change in the price of the good, other things being equal.

Demand curve

A graphical representation of the relationship between the price of a good and the quantity of that good that buyers demand

Change in quantity demanded

A change in the quantity of a good that buyers are willing and able to purchase that results from a change in the good's price, other things being equal, shown by a movement from one point to another along a demand curve

Shifts in the Demand Curve

The demand curve[1] in Figure 2.1 shows a relationship between two variables: the price of chicken and the quantity of chicken demanded. Changes in other variables can also affect people's buying decisions. For example, the prices of beef and pork would affect the demand for chicken. So would changes in consumer incomes. Changes in expectations about the future and changes in consumer tastes are still other factors that affect how much chicken people will buy. We could make a similar list for any good or service—the weather affects the demand for ice, the birthrate affects the demand for diapers, the won-lost record of the home team affects the demand for baseball tickets, and so on.

How do we handle all these other variables graphically? In brief, two rules apply.

1. When drawing a single demand curve for a good, such as the one in Figure 2.1, all other conditions other than the price of chicken are treated as constant, following the "other things being equal" clause of the law of demand. As long as that clause is in force, the

only two variables at work are quantity demanded (on the horizontal axis) and the price of chicken (on the vertical axis). The effect of a change in price on quantity demanded takes the form of a movement along the demand curve.

2. When we look beyond the "other things being equal" clause to discuss the effect of a change in any variable that does not appear on one of the axes, the situation changes. The effect of any other variable, such as a change in consumer income or the price of another good, takes the form of a shift in the demand curve. In its new position, the demand curve still represents a relationship between the price of chicken and the quantity demanded, but it is a slightly different relationship than before because one of the "other things" is no longer equal.

These two rules for demand curves are crucial to understanding the theory of supply and demand. It will be worthwhile to expand on them through a series of examples.

Changes in the Price of Another Good   We have already suggested that the demand for chicken depends on the price of beef, as well as the price of chicken. Figure 2.2, which shows demand curves for both goods, provides a closer look at how the two prices interact to determine demand.

Suppose that the price of beef starts at $3.00 per pound and then increases to $4.50. The effect of this change on the quantity of beef demanded appears in Part (a) of Figure 2.2 as a movement along the beef demand curve from point A to point B. Part (b) shows the effect on the demand for chicken. With the price of beef higher than before, people will tend to buy more chicken *even if the price of chicken does not change.* Suppose the price of chicken is steady at $2.00 per pound. When beef was selling at $3.00, consumers bought 2 billion pounds of chicken a year (point A´ on demand curve D_1). After the price of beef goes up to $4.50, they will buy 3.5 billion pounds (point B´ on demand curve D_2).

An increase in the price of beef would cause consumers to buy more chicken regardless of the price of chicken. If the price of chicken had started at $3.00 and remained there while the price of beef went up, people would have increased their chicken consumption from 1 billion pounds a year to 2.5 billion pounds a year. If the price of chicken were $1.00 a pound, the quantity bought would have increased from 3 billion pounds to 4.5 billion, and so on. An economist would say that a change in the price of beef causes the entire demand curve for chicken to shift. The chicken demand curve shifts because one of the "other things," this time the price of beef, is no longer equal. For the new demand curve, D_2, the price of beef is $4.50 a pound, rather than the $3.00 assumed in drawing demand curve D_1.

FIGURE 2.2
EFFECTS OF AN INCREASE IN THE PRICE OF BEEF ON THE DEMAND FOR CHICKEN

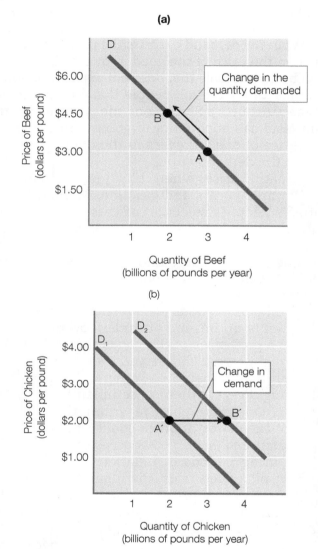

An increase in the price of beef from $3.00 to $4.50 per pound, other things being equal, causes a movement from point A to point B on the beef demand curve—a decrease in the quantity of beef demanded. With the price of chicken unchanged at $2.00 per pound, consumers will substitute chicken for beef. That will cause an increase in the demand for chicken, which takes the form of a shift in the chicken demand curve from D_1 to D_2.

Change in demand

A change in the quantity of a good that the buyers are willing and able to purchase that is caused by a change in some condition other than the price of that good; a shift in the demand curve

Substitute goods

A pair of goods for which an increase in the price of one causes an increase in demand for the other

Complementary goods

A pair of goods for which an increase in the price of one causes a decrease in demand for the other

If we call a movement along a demand curve a "change in quantity demanded," what do we call a shift in the curve? The correct term for a shift in a demand curve is a **change in demand**. A change in quantity demanded (a movement along the curve) is the result of a change in the price of the good in question. In our example, that means the price of chicken, which is the variable on the vertical axis. In contrast, a change in demand (a shift in the demand curve) is the result of a change in some variable other than the price of the good in question. In our example, it was the price of beef, a variable that does not appear on either axis.

In the example in Figure 2.2, people bought more chicken when the price of beef went up, replacing one meat with the other in their dinners. Economists call such pairs of goods **substitutes** because an increase in the price of one increases in the demand for the other—a rightward shift in the demand curve.

A different situation arises when consumers tend to use two goods together. One example is cars and gasoline. An increase in the price of gasoline affects people's selection of cars. For example, they buy fewer low-mileage, large SUVs—even if their price does not change. An increase in the price of gasoline thus causes a movement upward along the gasoline demand curve and a *leftward shift* in the demand curve for SUVs. We call pairs of goods that have this relationship to one another **complements**.

Whether a given pair of goods are substitutes or complements depends on buyers' attitudes toward those goods, not the properties of the goods themselves. Some people might regard cheese and beef as substitute sources of protein in their diets; others, who like cheeseburgers, might regard them as complements.

One more point regarding the effects of changes in the prices of other goods: It is the price of a good *relative to those of other goods* that counts for demand. During periods of inflation, when the average level of all prices rises, distinguishing between changes in *relative prices* and changes in *nominal prices* (the number of dollars actually paid per unit of a good) is of key importance. During a time of inflation, a good can become relatively less expensive even though its nominal price rises, if the prices of other goods rise even faster.

For example, between 1950 and 2005 the average retail price of broiler chicken rose by almost 40 percent, from $.59 per pound to $1.05 per pound. Over the same period, the average price of all goods and services purchased by consumers rose by about 600 percent. The relative price of chicken thus fell during the period even though its nominal price rose. The drop in the relative price of chicken had a lot to do with its growing popularity on the dinner table.

An increase in the price of gasoline will affect a consumer's choice of which vehicle to buy.

Changes in Consumer Incomes Changes in consumer incomes can also affect the demand for a good. People tend to buy larger quantities of many goods when their incomes rise, assuming that prices do not change.

Figure 2.3 shows the effect of an increase in consumer income on the demand for chicken. Demand curve D_1 is the same one as shown in Figure 2.1. Suppose now that consumer income rises. With higher incomes, people become choosier about what they eat. They do not just want calories; they want high-quality calories from foods that are tasty, fashionable, and healthful. Those considerations have made chicken increasingly popular as consumer incomes have risen.

FIGURE 2.3

EFFECTS OF AN INCREASE IN CONSUMER INCOME ON THE DEMAND FOR CHICKEN

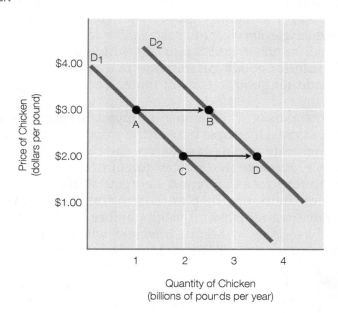

Demand curve D_1 assumes a given level of consumer income. If their incomes increase, consumers will want to buy more chicken at any given price, other things being equal. That will shift the demand curve rightward to, say, D_2. If the prevailing market price at the time of the demand shift is $3.00 per pound, the quantity demanded increases to 2.5 billion pounds (B) from 1 billion (A); if the prevailing price is $2.00 per pound, the quantity demanded will increase to 3.5 billion pounds (D) from 2 billion (C); and so on.

Suppose that after their incomes rise, people want to buy 2.5 billion pounds of chicken instead of 1 billion at $3.00 per pound. Figure 2.3 shows the change as an arrow drawn from point A to point B. If the price of chicken were instead $2.00, consumers would buy even more chicken at any level of income. When income was at its original low level, consumers would buy 2 billion pounds, as shown by point C. After their incomes went up, buyers would want 3.5 billion pounds, shown by point D.

The same reasoning applies to any given price of chicken. As a result, the effect of rising income is to shift the entire demand curve to the right, as shown. Later, if consumer incomes stay at the new, higher level but the price changes, the effects would appear as movements along the new demand curve. There is a chicken demand curve for every possible income level. Each represents a one-to-one relationship between price and quantity demanded for that income.

In our example just given, an increase in income causes an increase in demand. Because that is what happens for most goods, economists call goods like chicken **normal goods**.

Not all goods are normal, however. There are some goods that people buy less of when their incomes rise, other things being equal. For example, as the economy slipped into a deep recession in 2008, sales of new shoes fell, but demand for shoe repair services increased sharply. Hormel Foods Corp. reported a surge in sales of staple products like Spam and Dinty Moore beef stew, even while demand for its upscale single-serving microwaveable foods fell. We call goods like shoe repair services and Spam, for which demand increases as income falls, **inferior goods**. An increase in income shifts the demand curve for an inferior good to the left instead of to the right.

Changes in Expectations   Changes in buyers' expectations can also shift demand curves. If people expect the price of a good to rise, they will step up their rate of purchase before the change takes place.

For example, suppose that in May consumers rush to make airline reservations in response to a report saying that prices will go up after June 1. Some of them may be planning to travel late in the summer and would have waited several weeks before booking a flight. As a result, travelers will make more reservations in May than if they had not anticipated the June price increase. The surge in travel bookings sales in May takes the form of as a temporary rightward shift in the demand curve.

The same thing can happen if people expect something other than a price increase to raise the opportunity cost of the good. For example, not long ago people learned that starting in June 2009, they would need a passport to travel to Canada—an increased opportunity cost for people who did not already have a passport. Some of those people moved their planned Canadian vacations forward to avoid the extra hassle. The result was a temporary surge in demand for Canadian travel.

Normal goods

A good for which an increase in consumer income results in an increase in demand

Inferior goods

A good for which an increase in consumer incomes results in a decrease in demand

U.S. consumers have become more health conscious, leading to greater demand for such products as fish, organic vegetables, and gym memberships.

Changes in Tastes   Changes in tastes are still another source of changes in demand. Sometimes these changes occur rapidly, such as with popular music, clothing styles, and fast foods.

The demand curves for these goods and services shift often. In other cases, changes in tastes take longer but are more permanent. For example, over the years, U.S. consumers have been more health conscious. As that has happened, demand has fallen for cigarettes and fatty foods, while demand for fish, organic vegetables, and gym memberships has risen.

2.2 Supply

The Supply Curve

We now turn from the demand side of the market to the supply side. As before, we focus first on a one-to-one relationship between price and quantity, other things being equal. This time, though, the quantity is that which suppliers intend to offer for sale. Figure 2.4 shows such a relationship for chicken.

FIGURE 2.4   A SUPPLY CURVE FOR CHICKEN

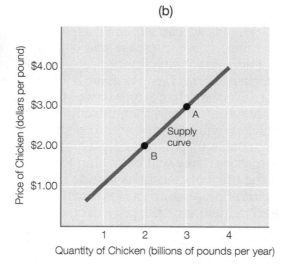

(a)	
Price of Chicken (dollars per pound)	**Quantity of Chicken Supplied** (billions of pounds per year)
$4.00	4
$3.50	3.5
A $3.00	3
$2.50	2.5
B $2.00	2
$1.50	1.5
$1.00	1

Parts (a) and (b) of this figure show the quantity of chicken supplied at various prices. As the price rises, the quantity supplied increases, other things being equal. The higher price gives farmers an incentive to raise more chickens, but the rising opportunity cost of doing so limits the supply produced in response to any given price increase.

Supply curve

A graphical representation of the relationship between the price of a good and the quantity of that good that sellers are willing to supply

We call the relationship shown in the figure a **supply curve** for chicken. The supply curve has a positive slope because the quantity supplied increases when the price goes up. Like demand curves, supply curves are based on an "other things being equal" condition. The supply curve shows how sellers respond to a change in the price of chicken, assuming no changes in conditions such as the prices of other goods, production techniques, input prices, expectations, or any other relevant condition.

Why do sellers, other things being equal, plan to supply more chicken when the prevailing market price is higher than when the price is lower? Without going too deeply into a discussion of microeconomic theory, we can consider some common-sense explanations.

One explanation is that the positive slope of the supply curve represents *producers' responses to market incentives*. When the price of chicken goes up, farmers have a reason to expand their capacity. Some who raise chickens as a sideline may decide to make chickens their main business. Other people may enter the chicken business for the first time. The same reasoning applies in every market. If parents are finding it hard to get babysitters, what do they do? They offer a bigger incentive in the form of a higher hourly rate. If a sawmill cannot buy enough timber, it raises the price it offers to loggers, and so on. Exceptions to the rule that a higher price causes a greater quantity supplied are rare.

Another way to explain the positive slope of the supply curve stems from the *rising cost of producing additional output in facilities of a fixed size*. A furniture factory with a fixed amount of machinery might be able to produce more chairs only by adding shifts or paying overtime. A farmer trying to grow more wheat on a fixed amount of land could increase the use of fertilizer; but beyond a point, each added ton of fertilizer would yield less additional output.

Finally, we can explain the positive slope of the supply curve in terms of *comparative advantage and opportunity cost*. Figure 2.5a shows a production possibility frontier for an economy the produces tomatoes and chicken. Some farmers have a comparative advantage in one product, some in the other. Suppose we start from a point where farmers produce only tomatoes and then introduce chicken. The first farmers to switch to chicken will be those with the strongest comparative advantage, that is, those able to produce chicken at the lowest opportunity cost relative to tomatoes. They will be willing to switch from tomatoes to chicken even if the price of chicken is low. As farmers add more and more chicken, the point of production moves down and to the right along the frontier. After each adjustment, the price of chicken must rise further to give the needed incentive for farmers with higher opportunity costs to make the switch.

The slope of the frontier at any point represents the price of chicken, relative to the price of tomatoes, that will cause one more farmer to switch. In Figure 2.5, the slopes at points A, B, and C in Part (a) are graphed on a new set of axes in Part (b). We can interpret the graph as a supply curve since it shows that the price of chicken must rise relative to the price of tomatoes to induce more farmers to switch to chicken.

Each of these common-sense explanations fits certain circumstances. Together, they provide an intuitive basis for the positive slope of the supply curve.

Figure 2.5
THE PRODUCTION POSSIBILITY CURVE AND THE SUPPLY CURVE

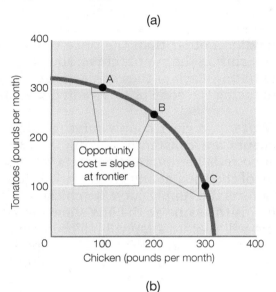

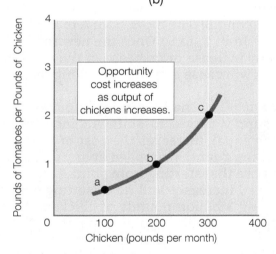

This figure offers an interpretation of the supply curve in terms of the production possibility frontier for an economy that produces two goods, tomatoes and chicken. Part (a) shows a production possibility frontier. The slope of the frontier, at any point, shows the opportunity cost of producing an additional pound of chicken measured in terms of the quantity of tomatoes that farmers could have produced using the same factors of production. The frontier curves because some farmers have a comparative advantage in producing tomatoes and others have a comparative advantage in producing chicken. As farmers raise more chicken, those with the greatest comparative advantage are the first to stop producing tomatoes. Because the frontier gets steeper as the quantity of chicken increases, the opportunity cost rises, as shown in Part (b). We can interpret the curve in Part (b) as a supply curve, in the sense that an incentive, in the form of a higher price, will cause producers to shift factors from tomatoes to chicken despite the rising opportunity cost of chicken.

Shifts in the Supply Curve

Change in quantity supplied

A change in the quantity of a good that suppliers are willing and able to sell that results from a change in some condition other than the good's price, shown by a shift in the supply curve

Change in supply

A change in the quantity of a good that suppliers are willing and able to sell that results from a change in the good's price, other things being equal, shown by a movement along a supply curve

As in the case of demand, we call the effects of a change in the price of chicken, other things being equal, a **change in quantity supplied**, shown as a movement along the supply curve. We call the effects of a change in a condition other than the price of chicken a **change in supply**, shown as a shift in the supply curve. Four sources of change in supply are worth noting. Each of them reflects a change in the opportunity cost of producing the good or service in question.

Changes in Technology   A given supply curve is based on a given technology. Entrepreneurs are constantly looking for new ways of doing things that lower costs. When production costs fall, it becomes worthwhile to sell more of the good at any given price. Figure 2.6 shows how new technology affects the supply curve for chicken.

Supply curve S_1 is the same as the one shown in Figure 2.4. It indicates that farmers will plan to supply 3 billion pounds of chicken per year at a price of $3.00 per pound (point A). Now suppose that the development of a faster-growing bird reduces feed requirements. With lower costs per unit, farmers will be willing to supply more chicken at any given price. They may, for example, be willing to supply 4 billion pounds of chicken at $3.00 (point B). The move from A to B is part of a shift in the entire supply curve from S_1 to S_2. Once the new methods of production are established, any increase or decrease in the price of chicken, other things being equal, will cause a movement along the new supply curve.

Changes in Input Prices   Changes in input prices are a second item that can cause supply curves to shift. An increase in input prices, other things being equal, increases the cost of producing the good in question and reduces quantity supplied at any given price. Refer again to Figure 2.6. Suppose that starting from point A on supply curve S_1, the price of chicken feed increases and no offsetting changes occur. Now, instead of supplying 3 billion pounds of chicken at $3.00 per pound, farmers will supply just 2 billion pounds (point C). The move from A to C is part of a leftward shift in the supply curve, from S_1 to S_3.

If the price of feed remains at the new level, changes in the price of chicken will cause movements along the new supply curve. For example, farmers could be induced to supply the original quantity of chicken—3 billion pounds—if the price of chicken was raised enough to cover the increased cost of feed. As you can see in Figure 2.6, that would require a price of $4.00 per pound for chicken (point D).

Changes in the Prices of Other Goods   Changes in the prices of other goods that producers could make using the same factors of production can also shift the supply curve. In our earlier example, farmers could use available resources for either chickens or tomatoes. Suppose that the price of tomatoes rises while the price of chicken stays at $3.00. The higher price of tomatoes gives some farmers who would otherwise have produced chickens an incentive to shift to tomatoes. The result would be a leftward shift in the chicken supply curve.

FIGURE 2.6   SHIFTS IN THE SUPPLY CURVE FOR CHICKEN

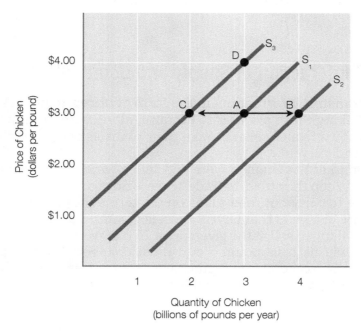

Quantity of Chicken
(billions of pounds per year)

Several kinds of changes can cause the supply of chicken to increase or decrease. For example, a new production method that lowers costs will shift the curve to the right, from S_1 to S_2. The shift is to the right because, taking into account the new, lower cost of production per unit, producers will be willing to supply more chicken at any given price. An increase in the price of inputs, other things being equal, will shift the curve to the left, from S_1 to S_3. The shift is to the left because, taking into account the new, higher price of inputs, producers will be willing to supply less chicken at any given price. Changes in sellers' expectations or in the prices of competing goods can also cause the supply curve to shift.

Changes in Expectations   Changes in expectations can cause supply curves to shift for much the same reason that they can cause demand curves to shift. For example, a farmer's selection of crops depends not so much on the prices that prevail at planting time as on those expected at harvest. Expectations over a time horizon longer than one growing season also affect supply. Each crop requires special equipment and know-how. We have just seen that an increase in the price of tomatoes gives farmers an incentive to shift from chicken to tomatoes. The incentive will be stronger if they expect the price of tomatoes to remain high. If it is, farmers are more likely to buy the special equipment needed for that crop and to learn the necessary production techniques.

2.3 The Interaction of Supply and Demand

Markets transmit information, in the form of prices, to people who buy and sell. Taking these prices into account, along with other knowledge they have, buyers and sellers make their plans as shown by the supply and demand curves[2].

Each market has many buyers and sellers who all make plans independently. When they meet to trade, there is no guarantee that all of them will be able to carry out their plans on the terms they expected. Perhaps the quantity of a good that buyers want is greater than the quantity suppliers are willing to sell at the given price. In that case, some of the would-be buyers will be disappointed and must change their plans. Perhaps planned sales exceed planned purchases at the given price. In that case, some would-be sellers will be unable to carry out their plans.

Market Equilibrium

Sometimes the total quantity of a good that buyers plan to purchase exactly matches the total quantity that producers plan to sell. When buyers' and sellers' plans exactly mesh when they meet in the marketplace, no one needs be disappointed or needs to change plans. In that case, the market is in **equilibrium**.

Equilibrium

A condition in which buyers' and sellers' plans exactly mesh in the marketplace, so that the quantity supplied exactly equals the quantity demanded at a given price

To give a graphical illustration of market equilibrium, we draw the supply and demand curves for a good on the same diagram, instead of separately, as in earlier figures. Figure 2.7 does this for the supply and demand curves for chicken. If we compare the quantity of planned sales at each price with the quantity of planned purchases, we can see that there is only one price where the two sets of plans mesh. (We can use either the table or the graph to make the comparison.) That price—$2.00 per pound—is the equilibrium price. If all buyers and sellers make their plans with the expectation of a price of $2.00, no one will be surprised and no one will have to change their plans.

FIGURE 2.7   EQUILIBRIUM IN THE CHICKEN MARKET

(a)

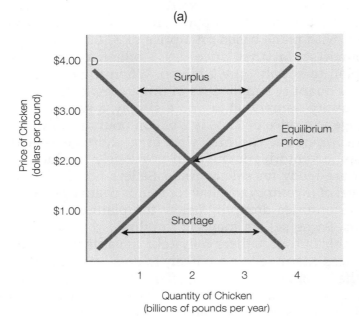

Quantity of Chicken
(billions of pounds per year)

(b)

Price (per pound)	Quantity Demanded (billions of pounds)	Quantity Supplied (billions of pounds)	Shortage (billions of pounds)	Surplus (billions of pounds)	Direction of Pressure on Price
$3.50	0.5	3.5	—	3	Downward
$3.00	1	3	—	2	Downward
$2.50	1.5	2.5	—	1	Downward
$2.00	2	2	—	—	Equilibrium
$1.50	2.5	1.5	1	—	Upward
$1.00	3	1	2	—	Upward
$.050	3.5	0.5	3	—	Upward

This figure shows the supply and demand curves for chicken presented earlier in graphical and numerical form. The demand curve shows how much buyers plan to purchase at a given price. The supply curve shows how much producers plan to sell at a given price. At only one price—$2.00 per pound—do buyers' and sellers' plans exactly match. That is the equilibrium price. A higher price causes a surplus of chicken and puts downward pressure on price. A lower price causes a shortage and puts upward pressure on price.

Shortages

What would happen if people were to base their plans on a price other than $2.00 a pound?[3] Suppose, for example, that they approach the market with plans based on a price of $1.00. As Figure 2.7 shows, planed purchases at that price are 3 billion pounds per year, but farmers plan to supply only 1 billion. When the quantity demanded exceeds the quantity supplied, as in this example, the difference is an **excess quantity demanded** or, more simply, a shortage. In Figure 2.7 the **shortage** at a price of $1.00 is 2 billion pounds per year.

Excess quantity demanded (shortage)

A condition in which the quantity of a good demanded at a given price exceeds the quantity supplied

Inventory

A stock of a good awaiting sale or use

In most markets, the first sign of a shortage is a decrease in **inventories**. Inventories include all previously produced stocks of a good that are ready for sale or issue. Sellers normally plan to hold a certain level of inventory to allow for minor changes in demand. When they see inventories dropping below the planned level, they change their plans. Some sellers may try to rebuild their inventories by increasing their output. Others may take advantage of strong demand to raise prices. Many sellers are likely to do a little of both. If sellers do not take the initiative, buyers will, offering to pay more if sellers supply more. Whatever the details, the result is an upward movement along the supply curve as both price and quantity increase.

As the shortage puts upward pressure on the market price, buyers change their plans, too. As the price rises, they cut back on their planned purchases, moving up and to the left along the demand curve. As both buyers and sellers change their plans, the market moves toward equilibrium. When the price reaches $2.00, both the shortage and the pressure to change buying and selling plans disappears.

In the markets for most goods, sellers hold inventories of goods that they are ready to sell. There are exceptions, though. Inventories are not possible in markets for services—knee surgery, tax preparation, lawn care, and the like. Also, it is not possible to hold some goods, such as custom-built houses and custom-designed machine tools, in inventory. Sellers in these markets do not begin production until they have a contract with a buyer.

In markets where there are no inventories, the sign of a shortage is a queue of buyers. The queue may take the form of a line of people waiting for service or a list of names in an order book. The queue is a sign that, at the prevailing price, people would like to buy more of the good than is being supplied. When that is the case, buyers cannot carry out all of their plans—at least not right away. They must wait for service on a first-come, first-served basis.

The formation of a queue of buyers has the same effect on the market as a decrease in inventories. Sellers react by increasing their rate of output, raising their prices, or both. Buyers react by reducing planned purchases or by offering higher prices. The market moves up and to the right along the supply curve and, at the same time, up and to the left along the demand curve until it reaches equilibrium.

One sign of a shortage is a line of people waiting to buy a particular product.

Surpluses

Let's turn now to the opposite case in which buyers and sellers start their planning from an expected price that is above equilibrium. For example, Figure 2.7 shows that if the expected price is $2.50 per pound, farmers will plan to supply 2.5 billion pounds of chicken—but their customers will plan to buy only 1.5 billion pounds. In that case, we say that there is an **excess quantity supplied,** or a **surplus.** In this case, the surplus at $2.50 per pound is 1 billion pounds per year.

When there is a surplus, suppliers will be unable to sell all that they had hoped at the expected price. Inventories will begin to grow. Suppliers will react to the inventory buildup by changing their plans. Some will cut back their output. Others will lower their prices in the hope of getting customers to buy more. Still others will do a little of both. These changes in plans will cause a movement down and to the left along the supply curve.

As unplanned inventory buildup puts downward pressure on the price, buyers change their plans, too. Finding that chicken costs less than they had expected, they buy more of it. The figure shows that reaction as a movement down and to the right along the demand curve. Taken together, buyers' and sellers' reactions to the surplus bring the market into equilibrium.

In markets in which there are no inventories, surpluses lead to the formation of queues of sellers looking for customers. Taxi queues at airports are a case in point. At some times of the day, the fare for taxi service from the airport to downtown is more than high enough to attract a number of taxis equal to the demand. A queue of cabs waiting for passengers then forms. In some cities drivers who are far back in the queue try to attract riders by offering cut-rate fares. Often, though, there are rules against fare cutting. The queue then grows until the next peak period when a surge in demand shortens it.

Excess quantity supplied (surplus)

A condition in which the quantity of a good supplied at a given price exceeds the quantity demanded

Taxi queues are a sign of a surplus of sellers looking for customers.

Changes in Market Conditions

In the examples we have given, finding the equilibrium price and quantity looks easy. In real life, though, it is a moving target. The market conditions that are covered by "other things being equal" change frequently. When they do, both buyers and sellers must revise their plans, and the point of equilibrium changes.

Response to a Shift in Demand   Let's start by looking at a market's response to a shift in demand. Suppose the news reports that an outbreak of food poisoning has been linked to eating chicken. As the news spreads, the demand for chicken decreases, which appears in Part (a) of Figure 2.8 as a leftward shift of the demand curve.

FIGURE 2.8
EFFECTS OF CHANGING CONDITIONS IN THE CHICKEN MARKET

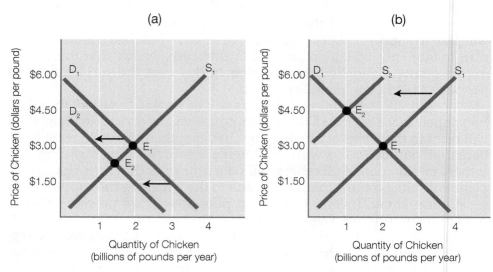

Part (a) of this figure shows the effects of a decrease in demand for chicken caused by news report linking food poisoning to eating chicken. Initially the market is in equilibrium at E_1. The report causes a shift in the demand curve. At the original equilibrium price of $3.00, there is a temporary surplus of chicken. That causes inventories to rise and puts downward pressure on the price. As the price falls, producers move down along the supply curve to a new equilibrium at E_2. There both the price and quantity of chicken are lower than before the shift in demand. Part (b) shows the effects of a decrease in supply caused by an increase in the price of chicken feed. The shift in the supply curve causes a shortage at the initial price of $3.00 per pound. The shortage puts upward pressure on price. As the price rises, buyers move up and to the left along the demand curve until they reach a new equilibrium at E_2. In each case, note that only one curve needs to shift to bring about the new equilibrium.

After the decrease in demand, there will be a surplus at the original price of $3.00. The price will not stay at that level for long, however. As soon as inventories start to rise, producers begin to revise their plans. They lower their prices and reduce quantities supplied. Their reactions appear as a movement along the supply curve, not a shift in the curve, because the producers are responding to a change in the price of chicken, the variable shown on the vertical axis. Nothing has happened to change the "other things being equal" conditions, such as technology or input prices, which could cause the supply curve to shift.

Eventually the adjustments reach a point where the plans of suppliers once again mesh with those of consumers. That happens at point E_2 in Part (a) of Figure 2.8, where the price has fallen to $2.25 and the quantity sold to 1.5 billion pounds. Later, if the conditions that caused the health warning are corrected, the demand curve will shift back to D_1, and the market will return to its original equilibrium.

Response to a Shift in Supply   Alternatively, the market equilibrium might be upset by a change in supply rather than a change in demand. For example, suppose that rising demand for corn used to make ethanol causes the price of chicken feed to increase. That would shift the supply curve to the left while the demand curve remained unchanged, as shown in Part (b) of Figure 2.8.

The shift in the supply curve will cause a shortage to develop if the price of chicken remains unchanged at $3 per pound. Inventories will fall in response to the shortage, putting upward pressure on the price. Producers will increase the amount they plan to sell, moving upward and to the right along the new supply curve. Buyers will move upward and to the left along the demand curve, which remains unchanged. A new equilibrium is established when the price reaches $4.50.

A Shift in One Curve or Both?   One of the most common mistakes people make in using supply and demand is to think that *both* curves always must shift in order to restore equilibrium. The examples given in Figure 2.8 show that this is not the case. In Part (a), after the demand curve shifts, a movement along the supply curve is enough to establish the new equilibrium. The supply curve does not need to shift. Similarly, in Part (b), after the supply curve shifts, the demand curve does not need to shift to reach the new equilibrium.

However, in the turmoil of real-world markets, it is easy to find cases where two separate changes occur at the same time, one acting on supply and the other on demand. *Economics in the News 2.1* provides an example of the way both demand and supply conditions affect prices for cocoa. In that market, a steady rightward shift in the demand curve has led to a long-term trend toward higher prices. Superimposed on the long-term, demand-driven trend are short-term changes in supply caused by political disturbances and changes in growing conditions.

Equilibrium as Spontaneous Order

The way that markets adjust to change is an example of economic coordination through spontaneous order. Consider the market for cocoa. The adjustment to changes in income, consumer tastes, political events and growing conditions involves decisions of thousands of farmers, wholesalers, retailers, as well as that of millions of consumers. Somehow their action must all be coordinated. But how?

A market economy needs no central planning agency or regulatory bureaucracy. The required changes in the use of scarce resources take place in response to information and incentives transmitted by changing market prices. As prices rise, farmers plant new cocoa trees, where possible. At the same time, researchers redouble their efforts to breed disease-resistant trees. Meanwhile candy makers in Europe and the United States employ new marketing strategies like introducing vintage estate-grown chocolates in an attempt to maintain the product's appeal as its price rises.

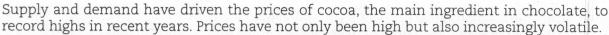

Economics in the News 2.1

Chocolate Lovers
Keep Nervous Eye on Cocoa Prices

Supply and demand have driven the prices of cocoa, the main ingredient in chocolate, to record highs in recent years. Prices have not only been high but also increasingly volatile.

The long upward trend in cocoa prices is mainly the result of changing demand conditions. Rising incomes are one factor affecting demand. Since chocolate is a normal good, people want more of it at any given price as their incomes rise. Changing tastes also play a role. For example, until recently chocolate was not especially popular in China. Per capita consumption hovered around 100 grams per person, some 100 times less than in Europe and the United States. That is a far bigger difference than income alone could explain. Now Chinese consumers are starting to see chocolate as trendy. Consumption has been growing by more than 10 percent per year.

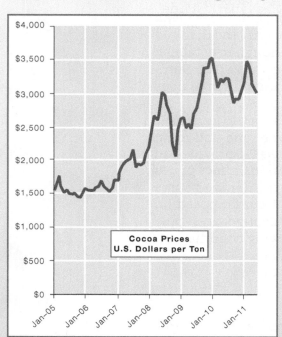

Both rising incomes and changing tastes shift the chocolate demand curve to the right. If supply conditions remained unchanged, the shift in demand by itself would be enough to push the price of cocoa steadily higher.

Supply conditions do not remain constant, however. Supply, more than demand, is subject to sharp short-term shifts. Politics are one source of these shifts. In 2010, a disputed election in Ivory Coast, the world's largest cocoa producer, threw the market into turmoil. As the country spiraled toward civil war, exports were disrupted, shifting the world supply curve to left and causing a spike in world prices. When the crisis was finally resolved in April 2011, normal supply conditions were restored and prices fell again.

Politics aside, cocoa supply, like that of any farm product, is subject to changes in growing conditions. For example, cocoa crops throughout West Africa, the largest producing region, suffer from periodic outbreaks of swollen shoot disease. The leaves of affected trees turn red, and the cocoa pods are ruined. In the summer of 2011, just as a return of political calm allowed the cocoa price to fall a bit, a new outbreak of swollen shoot disease threatened to shift the supply curve to the left once again, pushing the price back up.

The bottom line? You may have to get ready to pay more for your chocolate—or you may not. Any way you look at it, the complexities of supply and demand are likely to keep chocolate prices volatile. But look at the bright side. If high chocolate prices depress you, just remember that chocolate itself is a reliable cure for depression!

Source: Based on "Chocolate Lovers Keep Nervous Eye on Volatile Prices," Ed Dolan's Econ Blog, Oct. 11, 2010 (http://dolanecon.blogspot.com/2010/10/chocolate-lovers-keep-nervous-watch-on.html)

No central authority has to plan the process of adjustment. Equilibrium is not a compromise negotiated by a committee of consumers and producers. Just as shoppers manage to equalize the length of supermarket checkout lines without the guidance of a central authority, markets like that for cocoa move toward equilibrium spontaneously through the small, local adjustments that people make in their efforts to serve their own interests. As Adam Smith might have put it, we have not the benevolence of the International Cocoa Organization for our dessert; instead it is self-interest that puts that box of chocolates on the table.

2.4 Some Closing Thoughts

This chapter has covered the basics of the supply-and-demand model and described a few of its applications. There are many more applications in both macro- and microeconomics. In macroeconomics, supply and demand apply to financial markets, labor markets, and the problem of determining the rate of inflation and real output for the economy as a whole. In microeconomics, the model applies to product markets, markets for productive resources, and policy issues ranging from pollution to farm policy to international trade. As the great economist Alfred Marshall once put it, nearly all of the major problems of economics have a "kernel" that reflects the workings of supply and demand (see *Who Said It? Who Did It? 2.1*).

When we turn from the general outline presented in this chapter to some of the underlying details, the supply-and-demand model appears to fit some kinds of markets more closely than others. The fit is best for markets in which there are many producers and many customers, the goods sold by one producer are much like those sold by others, and all sellers and buyers have good information on market conditions. Markets for farm commodities, such as wheat and corn, and financial markets, such as the New York Stock Exchange, meet these standards reasonably well.

However, not all markets display all of these features. The market for chocolate is an example. Cocoa, the basic commodity, fits the supply-and-demand model closely. Markets for high-end chocolate confections do not. In those markets, the products of different producers are not alike, and just a few specialist firms dominate some segments of the market. Even in markets like those, however, the notions of supply and demand provide a useful framework to which we can add refinements and extensions.

Who Said It? Who Did It? **2.1**

Alfred Marshall on Supply and Demand

Alfred Marshall, who was probably the greatest economist of his day, was born in London in 1842. His father was a Bank of England cashier who hoped the boy would enter the ministry. Young Marshall had other ideas, however. He turned down a theological scholarship at Oxford to study mathematics, receiving his MA from Cambridge in 1865.

While at Cambridge, Marshall joined a philosophical discussion group. There he became interested in promoting the broad development of the human mind. He soon learned that harsh economic realities would prevent the realization of his ideas. Britain's economic potential as a country could, supposedly, never allow the masses sufficient leisure for education. This disillusioning episode appears to have triggered Marshall's fascination with economics.

At the time, the classical school founded by Adam Smith and David Ricardo dominated British economics. Marshall had great respect for the classical writers. At first, he saw his own work as simply applying his mathematical training to strengthen and systematize the classical system. Before long, however, he was breaking new ground and developing a system of his own. By 1890, when he brought out his famous *Principles of Economics*, he had laid the foundation of what we now call the neoclassical school.

In an attempt to explain the essence of his approach, Marshall included the following passage in the second edition of his *Principles*:

In spite of a great variety in detail, nearly all the chief problems of economics agree in that they have a kernel of the same kind. This kernel is an inquiry as to the balancing of two opposed classes of motives, the one consisting of desires to acquire certain new goods, and thus satisfy wants; while the other consists of desires to avoid certain efforts or retain certain immediate enjoyment ... in other words, it is an inquiry into the balancing of the forces of demand and supply.

Marshall's influence on economics—at least in the English-speaking world—was enormous. His *Principles* was the leading economics text for several decades, and modern students can still learn much from it. As a professor at Cambridge, Marshall taught a great many of the next generation's leading economists. Today his neoclassical school continues to dominate the profession. Many have challenged it, but so far it has held up.

Summary

1. **How does the price of a good or service affect the quantity of it that buyers demand?** The term demand means the willingness and ability of buyers to purchase goods and services. According to the *law of demand*, there is an inverse relationship between the price of a good and the quantity demanded. The *quantity demanded* is the quantity that buyers are willing and able to pay for. The law of demand can be represented by a negatively sloped *demand curve*. A movement along the demand curve shows a change in the quantity demanded.

2. **How do other market conditions affect demand?** A change in any of the variables covered by the "other things being equal" clause of the law of demand causes a shift in the demand curve, known as a *change in demand*. Examples include changes in the prices of goods that are *substitutes or complements* of the good in question as well as changes in consumer incomes, expectations, and tastes.

3. **How does the price of a good affect the quantity supplied by sellers?** The term *supply* means sellers' willingness and ability to offer products for sale in a market. In most markets an increase in the price of a good will increase the quantity of the good that sellers are willing to supply. This relationship takes the form a positively sloped *supply curve*. The higher price gives producers an incentive to supply more, but rising opportunity costs set a limit on the amount they will supply at any given price.

4. **How do changes in other market conditions affect supply?** A change in any of the items covered by the "other things being equal" clause of the supply curve will shift the curve. Examples include changes in technology, changes in the prices of inputs, changes in the prices of other goods that could be produced with the same resources, and changes in expectations.

5. **How do supply and demand interact to determine the market price of a good or service?** In a market with a positively-sloped supply curve and a negatively-sloped demand curve, there is only one price at which the quantity of a good that sellers plan to supply will exactly match the quantity that buyers plan to purchase. We call that the *equilibrium* price. At any higher price, there will be a surplus; and at any lower price there will be a shortage.

(Continues)

6. **Why do market prices and quantities change in response to changes in market conditions?** A change in any market condition that shifts the supply or demand curve will change the equilibrium price and quantity in a market. For example, the demand curve may shift to the right as a result of a change in consumer incomes. That causes a shortage at the old price, and the price begins to rise. As the price rises, suppliers move up along the supply curve to a new equilibrium. No shift in the supply curve is required. On the other hand, better technology may shift the supply curve to the right. In that case, there is a surplus at the old price, and the price will fall. As the price decreases, buyers will move down along their demand curve to a new equilibrium. No shift in the demand curve is required.

Key Terms   Page

Problems and Topics for Discussion

1. **A shifting demand curve**   A vending machine company has studied the demand for soft drinks sold in cans from machines. On a 70-degree day consumers in the firm's territory will buy about 2,000 cans at a price of $0.75. For each $.05 rise in price, the quantity sold falls by 200 cans per day; for each 5-degree rise in the temperature, the quantity sold rises by 150 cans per day. The same relationships hold for decreases in price or temperature. Using this information, draw a set of curves showing the demand for soft drinks on days when the temperature is 60, 70, and 85 degrees. Then draw a separate diagram with temperature on the vertical axis and quantity on the horizontal axis. Draw a line representing the relationship between temperature and quantity when the price is $0.75. Next, draw additional temperature-quantity lines for prices of $0.50 and $1.00. Do the two diagrams give the same information? Discuss. (Note: If you have any trouble with this exercise, review the appendix to Chapter 1, "Working with Graphs," especially the section entitled "Packing Three Variables into Two Dimensions.")

2. **Demand and the price of motor fuel**   From 2007 to 2008, the price of gasoline in the United States rose from $2.76 per gallon to $3.20 per gallon. The quantity used decreased from 3,389 million barrels to 3,290 million barrels. In 2009, the price fell again, to $2.30 per gallon, but the quantity used continued to decline, to $3,283 million barrels. Each year from 2007 to 2009, personal income of U.S. households increased.

   Which one or more of the following hypotheses do you think best explain(s) the behavior of motor fuel sales in 1981 and 1982? Illustrate your chosen hypothesis with an appropriate diagram.

   a. In 2008 the demand curve for gasoline had the usual negative slope. However, in 2009 the demand curve shifted to a positively sloped position.

   b. The demand curve had a negative slope throughout the period. However, it appears that gasoline changed from a normal good to an inferior good between 2008 and 2009.

   c. The demand curve has a negative slope at all times, but the shape depends partly on how much time consumers have to adjust to a change in prices. Over a short period, the demand curve is fairly steep because few adjustments can be made. Over the long term, it has a somewhat flatter slope because further adjustments, such as buying more fuel-efficient cars or moving closer to the job, can be made. As a result, falling gasoline sales in 2009 were a delayed reaction to the price increase the previous year.

(Continues)

3. **Shortages, price controls, and queues**   During the late 1980s and early 1990s, economic reforms initiated by Soviet President Mikhail Gorbachev began to raise consumer incomes; however, the Soviet government continued to impose price ceilings on basic goods like food, clothing, and household goods. As higher income led to increased demand, severe shortages of many goods and long lines at all kinds of stores became common. Finally, in January 1992, a new Russian government, under President Boris Yeltsin, removed retail price controls on most goods. Within a month, prices more than doubled on average and lines disappeared. Analyze these events using the supply and demand model. First draw a supply and demand diagram for some normal good such as butter. Show the market in equilibrium at a price of 1 ruble per kilo before the beginning of the Gorbachev reforms. Draw a horizontal line at that level to represent the price ceiling; no butter can be sold for more than 1 ruble per kilo. Next, show the effect of rising income. Does it shift the supply curve? Does it shift the demand curve? What is the shortage or surplus at the controlled price? After the price control ends, assuming no further shift in the supply and demand curve, what happens to the price? What happens to the shortage or surplus?

4. **Eliminating queues through flexible pricing**   You are a member of the Metropolitan Taxi Commission, which sets taxi fares for your city. You learn that long lines of taxis form at the airport during off-peak hours. At peak hours, in contrast, few taxis are available and there are long lines of passengers waiting for cabs. The Commission is considering a proposal to cut taxi fares from the airport to downtown by 10 percent during off-peak hours and raising them by 10 percent during peak hours. How do you think these changes would affect the queuing patterns of taxis and passengers? Do you think the proposal is a good one from the passengers' point of view? From the cabbies' point of view? From the standpoint of economic efficiency? What do you think would happen if the Taxi Commission stopped setting fares altogether, and allowed passengers and drivers to negotiate any price they wanted? Discuss.

Case for Discussion:

Will CNG Power Your Next Car?

There has been a lot of talk in the United States about the automotive fuel of the future. Most of it has centered on ethanol, electricity, and to some extent hydrogen. Yet the real fuel of the future may turn out to be compressed natural gas, or CNG.

CNG as an automotive fuel is not new technology. Thousands of busses and delivery vehicles use it every day in the United States. So do millions of passenger cars in other countries. Now market forces favor CNG as an automotive fuel in the United States. In 2011, while the price of crude oil soared to $100 per barrel, the price of the quantity of natural gas needed to supply the same energy fell under $25. It was a record gap between the two fuels. As recently as 2005, natural gas actually cost more than oil on an energy-equivalent basis.

What is behind the radical change in relative price? On the supply side, the main change is new technologies that allow greater production of nonconventional gas from shales, coal beds, and other sources. On the demand side, the change arises from greater environmental awareness on the part of consumers, regulations that encourage alternative fuels, and, yes, the rising price of oil.

So what is holding back widespread use of CNG for cars, an off-the-shelf technology already in wide use elsewhere? Two factors are causing the problem.

First, there is a chicken-and-egg issue. There are not enough filling stations that dispense natural gas. With the right kind of pump, filling you car's tank with CNG is just as quick and easy as using gasoline; however, it is not worth it for gas stations to install the pumps until there are lots of CNG-powered cars on the road. CNG cars, including a CNG-powered Honda, are already on the market, but demand will be limited until there are more filling stations.

Second, Federal regulations make it expensive to bring conversion kits to market that let people convert old cars and trucks to CNG. The technology is simple, but the regulations are not.

CNG will have its day, though, provided its price remains low. Over time, market forces will produce pressure to install more CNG pumps and simplify regulations. Then the fuel of the future—already quite ordinary in many parts of the world—will finally arrive in the United States.

Sources: Ed Dolan's Econ Blog (http://dolanecon.blogspot.com), "Technology, Environment, and the Future of Natural Gas," Feb. 27 2010, and "Move Over Ethanol: Market Forces Favor CNG," March 16, 2011. Used by permission of author

Questions

1. Beginning from a position of equilibrium, use supply and demand curves to show how the natural gas market is affected by new technologies that reduce the cost of producing gas from unconventional deposits. Does the supply curve shift? The demand curve? Both? Explain.

2. Now, starting from the end point of your answer to Question 1, show the effects of increased consumer preference for alternative fuels. Does the supply curve shift? The demand curve? Both? Explain.

3. Finally, draw a diagram that includes both long-term and short-term demand curves. How do the two differ, and why?

Endnotes

1. Before continuing, the reader may want to review the Chapter 1 appendix, "Working with Graphs," especially the section entitled "Packing Three Variables into Two Dimensions."

2. The "plans" referred to need not be formal, or thought out in detail, and are subject to change. A consumer might, for example, make out a shopping list for the supermarket based on the usual prices for various foods, but then revise it to take into account unexpected price increases or sales on certain items. On specific occasions, consumer decisions may even be completely impulsive, with little basis in rational calculation. The model of supply and demand does not require that every decision be based on precise analysis, only that consumer intentions, on the average, are influenced by prices and other economic considerations.

3. Why might buyers and sellers enter the market expecting a price other than the one that permits equilibrium? It may be, for example, that market conditions have caused the supply or demand curve to shift unexpectedly, so that a price that formerly permitted equilibrium no longer does so. It may be that buyers or sellers expect conditions to change, but they do not change after all; or it may be that government policy has established a legal maximum or minimum price that differs from the equilibrium price. Later sections of the chapter will explore some of these possibilities.

Chapter 3

Supply, Demand, *and* Elasticity

After reading this chapter, you will understand the following:

1. What economists mean by elasticity

2. The relationship of demand to revenue

3. How economists apply the concept of elasticity to changes in market conditions

4. How elasticity helps in understanding issues of public policy

Before reading this chapter, make sure you know the meaning of the following concepts:

1. Supply and demand

2. Demand, quantity demanded

3. Supply, quantity supplied

4. Substitutes and complements

5. Normal and inferior goods

How much did you pay for this textbook? Did it cost more or less than the books you buy for other courses? As a student, you probably have a strong desire to pay less for your books if you can. Have you ever wondered why your professors sometimes choose books that cost so much?

This chapter will help you understand the effect of price on choices that people make among goods like textbooks, foods, or medical services. It will focus *elasticity*, a concept economists use to describe how sensitive buyers are to prices. As a student, your choice of textbook is probably fairly sensitive to price—your demand is elastic, to use the economist's term. However, your professor, who does not personally pay for the books, may care less about how much they cost. Your professor's demand may be *inelastic*. In the following pages, you will learn how to define, measure, and apply the concept of elasticity.

3.1 Elasticity

We can express the responsiveness of quantity demanded to a change in price in many ways. Take demand for chicken, for example. A discussion of the choices made by a typical American household might find that an increase of ten cents per pound would decrease consumption by one pound per month. A study done in France might find that a price increase of one euro per kilogram would decrease consumption of all consumers in the city of Lille by twenty-five thousand kilos per month. Are the findings of these studies similar? It is hard to tell, not just because the currencies and units of weight are different, but also because we don't know the starting points for the prices or quantities. Ten cents a pound is not a very large increase if it refers to premium organic, boneless, chicken breasts that began at $5.49 a pound, but that increase would be much more significant for a commercial grade of chicken backs and necks intended for use in soup.

To avoid confusion arising from different units of measurement and different starting points for price changes, it is useful to standardize. One way to do so is to express all changes as percentages. Suppose that the studies of both American and French consumers found that a 20 percent increase in price was associated with a 10 percent decrease in quantity demanded. Stating changes in percentages would take the starting point of any change into account. The percentage changes would also be the same regardless of whether we record observations in dollars per pound, euros per kilo, or whatever.

Elasticity

A measure of the response of one variable to a change in another, stated as a ratio of the percentage change in one variable to the associated percentage change in another

Economists use the term **elasticity** to refer to relationships of changes in one variable to changes in another, expressed in percentages. Like equilibrium, elasticity is a metaphor borrowed from physics. Much as equilibrium calls to mind a pendulum that has come to rest hanging straight down, elasticity conjures up the image of a rubber band that stretches by a certain percentage of its length when the force applied to it is increased by a given percentage. This chapter introduces several applications of elasticity in economics.

Price Elasticity of Demand

Price elasticity of demand

The ratio of the percentage change in the quantity of a good demanded to a given percentage change in its price, other things being equal

The **price elasticity of demand** is the ratio of the percentage change in the quantity of a good demanded to a given percentage change in its price. Figure 3.1 presents five demand curves showing different degrees of price elasticity of demand. The different degrees of elasticity affect not only the shape of the curves but also the relationship between changes in price and changes in the revenue that sellers earn from the good in question. (Revenue means the price of the good times the quantity sold.)

Revenue

Price multiplied by quantity sold

In Part (a) of Figure 3.1, the percentage change in quantity demanded is greater than the percentage change in price. As a result, a decrease in price causes total **revenue** to increase. Revenue before and after the changes in price is shown as the area of a rectangle drawn under the demand curve, with a height equal to price and a width equal to quantity demanded. In this case, revenue before the price reduction ($5 per unit for 3 units = $15) is less than afterward ($3 per unit for 6 units = $18). When the quantity demanded changes by a greater percentage than price, so that a price decrease causes total revenue to increase, demand is **elastic**.

Elastic demand

A situation in which quantity demanded changes by a larger percentage than price, so that total revenue increases as price decreases

In contrast, Part (b) of Figure 3.1 shows a case where quantity demanded is only weakly responsive to a change in price. There, a $2 decrease in price, from $5 to $3 per unit, causes the quantity demanded to increase by just one unit—from three to four. Now the percentage

FIGURE 3.1   PRICE ELASTICITY OF DEMAND

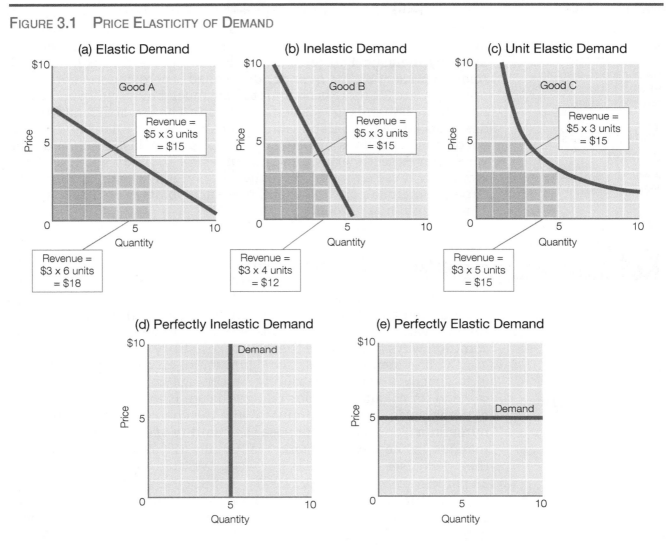

This figure shows five examples of demand curves with various degrees of elasticity over the indicated range of variation of price and quantity. The examples illustrate elastic, inelastic, unit elastic, perfectly inelastic, and perfectly elastic demand. The first three cases show the revenue change associated with a change in price. When demand is elastic, a price decrease causes revenue to increase. When demand is inelastic, a price decrease causes revenue to decrease. When demand is unit elastic, revenue does not change when price changes.

change in quantity demanded is less than the change in price, so a decrease in price causes total revenue to fall. In such a case, demand is **inelastic**.

    Part (c) shows still another possibility. There, a change in price causes an exactly proportional change in quantity demanded, so that total revenue does not change at all. When the percentage change in quantity demanded equals the percentage change in price, demand is **unit elastic**.

Inelastic demand

A situation in which quantity demanded changes by a smaller percentage than price, so that total revenue decreases as price decreases

Unit elastic demand

A situation in which price and quantity demanded change by the same percentage so that total revenue remains unchanged as price changes

Perfectly inelastic demand

A situation in which the demand curve is a vertical line

Perfectly elastic demand

A situation in which the demand curve is a horizontal line

The final two parts of Figure 3.1 show two extreme cases. Part (d) shows a vertical demand curve. Regardless of the price, the quantity demanded is five units—no more, no less. Such a demand curve is **perfectly inelastic**. Part (e) shows a demand curve that is horizontal. Above a price of $5, the quantity demanded is zero; but as soon as the price drops to $5, there is no limit to how much buyers will purchase. A horizontal demand curve is **perfectly elastic**. The law of demand, which describes an inverse relationship between price and quantity, does not encompass the cases of perfectly elastic and inelastic demand; and we do not expect market demand curves for ordinary goods and services to fit these extremes. Nonetheless, perfectly elastic and inelastic curves sometimes provide useful reference points even if they do not fit real-world market demand curves.

Calculating Elasticity of Demand

Sometimes it is enough to say that demand is elastic or inelastic, without being more precise. At other times, it is useful to give a numerical value for elasticity. This section outlines one of the most common ways to calculate the value of elasticity of demand.

The first step in turning the definition of elasticity into a formula is to specify a way of measuring percentage changes. The everyday method for calculating a percentage change is to use the initial value of the variable as the denominator and the change in the value as the numerator. For example, suppose the quantity of California lettuce demanded in the national market is initially 12,000 tons per week and then decreases by 4,000 tons per week. We then say there has been a 33 percent decrease (4,000/12,000 = .33) in quantity. The trouble with this convention is that the same change in the opposite direction gives a different percentage. Using the same everyday approach, an increase in the quantity of lettuce demanded from 8,000 tons per week to 12,000 tons per week is a 50 percent increase (4,000/8,000 = .5).

Decades ago, the economist R. G. D. Allen proposed avoiding the ambiguity of percentage increases and decreases by using the midpoint of the range over which change takes place as the denominator. To find the midpoint, take the sum of the value before the change and the value after, and then divide by 2. In our example, the midpoint of the quantity range is (8,000 + 12,000)/2 = 10,000). When we use that value as the denominator, a change of 4,000 units, whether an increase or a decrease, becomes a 40 percent change (4,000/10,000 = .4).

Using Q_1 to represent the quantity before the change and Q_2 to represent the quantity after the change, the midpoint formula for the percentage change in quantity is

$$\text{Percentage change in quantity} = \frac{Q_2 - Q_1}{(Q_1 + Q_2)/2}$$

We can use the same approach for price. Suppose that the price of lettuce increases from $700 per ton to $900 per ton. Using the midpoint of the range, or $800, as the denominator [(700+ + 900)/2 = 800], we see that the $200 increase in price is a 25 percent (200/800 = .25). The midpoint formula for the percentage change in price is

$$\text{Percentage change in price} = \frac{P_2 - P_1}{(P_1 + P_2)/2}$$

The Midpoint Formula for Elasticity   Expressing both changes in price and quantity in this way allows us to write a complete midpoint formula for price elasticity of demand. Simplifying by omitting the terms "/2", which cancel out, the midpoint formula is

$$\text{Price elasticity of demand} = \frac{(Q_2 - Q_1)/(Q_1 + Q_2)}{(P_2 - P_1)/(P_1 + P_2)}$$

$$= \frac{\text{Percentage change in quantity}}{\text{Percentage change in price}}$$

If an increase in price from $700 per ton to $900 per ton causes the quantity of lettuce demanded to fall from 12,000 tons to 8,000 tons, the complete calculations for the elasticity of demand are as follows:

P_1 = price before change = $700

P_2 = price after change = $900

Q_1 = quantity before change = 12,000

Q_2 = quantity after change = 8,000

$$\text{Elasticity} = \frac{(8{,}000 - 12{,}000)/(8{,}000 + 12{,}000)}{(\$900 - \$700)/(\$700 + \$900)}$$

$$= \frac{-4{,}000/20{,}000}{200/1{,}600}$$

$$= \frac{-.2}{.125}$$

$$= -1.6$$

Because demand curves have negative slopes, price and quantity change in opposite directions. As a result, the midpoint formula gives a negative value for elasticity. When the price decreases, the term $(P_2 - P_1)$, which appears in the denominator of the formula, is negative, whereas the term $(Q_2 - Q_1)$, which appears in the numerator, is positive. When the price increases, the numerator is negative and the denominator is positive. Sometimes economists use the minus sign when reporting price elasticity of demand, and sometimes they do not. In this book, we follow the second option and drop the minus sign when discussing price elasticity of demand. For example, we will refer to the elasticity of demand for lettuce in our example as approximately 1.6 over the range studied. A numerical elasticity value such as 1.6 means that the quantity demanded will increase by 1.6 percent for each 1 percent decrease in price[1].

Elasticity Numbers and Terminology   Earlier in the chapter, we defined *elastic, inelastic, unit elastic, perfectly elastic,* and *perfectly inelastic* demand. Each of those terms corresponds to a value or range of values of elasticity. A perfectly inelastic demand curve has a value of zero. There is no change in quantity demanded regardless of how great the change in price. *Inelastic demand* (but not perfectly inelastic) corresponds to values from 0 up to, but not including, 1. Unit elasticity means a numerical value of exactly 1; the percentage change in quantity equals the percentage change in price. *Elastic demand* means any value for elasticity that is greater than 1. *Perfectly elastic* demand, represented by a horizontal demand curve, is numerically undefined; as the demand curve approaches horizontal, the denominator of the elasticity formula approaches 0 and the measured value of elasticity increases without limit.

Varying- and Constant-elasticity Demand Curves

The midpoint formula shows elasticity of demand over a certain range of prices and quantities. Measured over some other range, the elasticity of demand for the same good may be the same or different, depending on the shape of the demand curve, as shown in Figure 3.2.

Part (a) of Figure 3.2 shows a demand curve that, like most of those in this book, is a straight line. The elasticity of demand is not constant for all points along the curve. For example, over the price range $8 to $9, elasticity is 5.66, but over the range $2 to $3, it is .33. (The figure shows the calculations.)

The calculations illustrate the general rule that elasticity decreases as one moves down and to the right along a straight-line demand curve. It is easy to see why. When the demand curve is a straight line, a $1 reduction in price always causes the same absolute increase in quantity demanded. At the upper end of the curve, a $1 change is a small percentage of the relatively high price, while the change in quantity is a large percentage of the relatively low quantity demanded. At the lower end, the situation is reversed: A $1 change is a large percentage of the relatively low price, while the increase in quantity is smaller in relation to the relatively larger quantity demanded.

If the demand curve is not a straight line, other results are possible. There is an important special case in which the demand curve has just the curvature needed to keep elasticity constant over its entire length. Part (b) of Figure 3.2 shows such a curve. As the figure shows, elasticity is 1.0 at every point on that curve. It is possible to construct demand curves with constant elasticities of any value. Econometric studies of demand elasticity often look for the constant-elasticity demand curve that most closely approximates buyers' average sensitivity to price changes as revealed by market data over time.

FIGURE 3.2   ELASTICITY AT VARIOUS POINTS ALONG A DEMAND CURVE

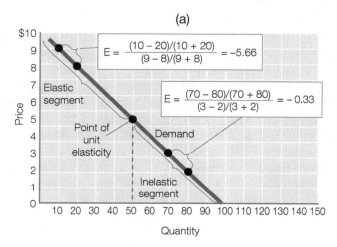

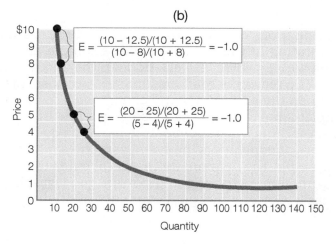

Elasticity varies along a straight-line demand curve, as Part (a) of this figure illustrates. At the upper end of the curve, where the price is relatively high, a $1 change in price is a relatively small percentage change. Because the quantity demanded is low, the corresponding percentage change in quantity is relatively large. That makes demand elastic near the top of the demand curve. At the lower end of the curve, the opposite is true: A $1 change in price is now a relatively large percentage change and the corresponding percentage change in quantity is smaller. Demand is inelastic. As Part (b) shows, we can also draw a demand curve with such a shape that elasticity is constant at all prices and quantities.

Determinants of Elasticity of Demand

The fact that elasticity often varies along the demand curve means that we must take care in making general statements about the elasticity of demand for a good. In practice, what such statements usually refer to is the elasticity, measured by the midpoint formula or some alternative method, over the range of price variation that usually occurs in the market. With that understanding, we can generalize about what makes the demand for some goods elastic and the demand for others inelastic.

Substitutes, Complements, and Elasticity　One important determinant of elasticity of demand is the availability of substitutes. When a good has close substitutes, the demand for it tends to be elastic because people willingly switch to the substitutes when the price of the good goes up. For example, the demand for corn oil is elastic because consumers can easily substitute other cooking oils. On the other hand, the demand for cigarettes is inelastic because for a habitual smoker there is no good substitute.

This principle has two corollaries. One is that the demand for a good tends to be more elastic the more narrow the definition of the good. For example, the demand for coffee as a whole is inelastic. However, the demand for medium-roast Colombian coffee is likely to be elastic because if the price of that particular type rises, people can switch to similar coffee from Nicaragua or Sumatra.

The other corollary is that demand for the product of a single firm tends to be more elastic than the demand for the output of all producers operating in the market. As one example, the demand for cigarettes as a whole will be less elastic than the demand for any particular brand. The reason is that consumers can substitute one brand for another when the price of a brand changes.

The complements of a good can also play a role in determining its elasticity. If something is a minor complement to a good that accounts for a large share of consumers' budgets, demand for it tends to be inelastic. For example, the demand for motor oil tends to be inelastic because it is a complement to a more important good, gasoline. The price of gasoline has a greater effect on the amount of driving a person does than the price of motor oil.

Price versus Opportunity Cost　Elasticity measures the responsiveness of quantity demanded to the price of a good. In most cases, the price, in money, is an accurate indicator of opportunity cost; but that is not always the case. We mentioned one example at the beginning of the chapter: The price of a textbook is an opportunity cost to the student who buys it, but it is not an opportunity cost to the professor who assigns it. The reason is that the students pay for the book, not the professor. As a result, publishers have traditionally assumed that professors will pay little attention to the price of the text, and demand will be highly inelastic. However, in recent years students have increasingly been making their influence felt, so that price-elasticity of demand for textbooks may be increasing.

The textbook market is a relatively small one, but there are other much more important markets where the responsibility for choice does not lie with the party who bears the opportunity cost. Medical care provides many examples. Doctors choose what drug to offer to patients, but either the patient or the patient's insurance company pays for the drug. As a result, demand for drugs is very inelastic, and doctors sometimes prescribe expensive brand-name drugs when cheaper generic drugs are available to do the same job.

Business travel is still another example of the separation of price and opportunity cost. Business travelers do not pay for their own airline tickets, hotels, and meals. As a result, their demand for these services tends to be inelastic. When vacationers purchase the same services, they bear the full opportunity cost. Not surprisingly, business travelers often choose more expensive options. Often airlines and hotels take advantage of the separation of price and opportunity cost by charging different rates to business and vacation travelers.

Textbook prices are opportunity costs for students.

Time Horizon and Elasticity   Still another determinant of elasticity of demand is the time horizon within which buyers make their decisions. For several reasons, demand is often less elastic in the short run than in the long run.

One reason is that full adjustment to a change in the price of a good may require changes in the kind or quantity of other goods that a consumer buys. For example, when the price of gasoline rises, people can cut out some nonessential driving; but the total quantity of gasoline demanded is only slightly affected. Econometricians have estimated short-run demand elasticity for gasoline at about .25. Over time, though, consumers can adjust to a higher price in several ways. They can buy fewer fuel-hungry SUVs and more higher-mileage, hybrid cars. They can change their jobs or move in order to shorten their daily commute. They can switch to public transportation, if it is available, or if it is not, demand that local governments expand public transportation options. The long-run demand for gasoline is about .6 to .8, considerably higher than the short-run elasticity.

Another reason elasticity tends to be greater in the long run is that an increase in the price of one good encourages entrepreneurs to develop substitutes. The availability of substitutes, in turn, makes demand more elastic. Consider the response to America's first energy crisis: a sharp increase early in the nineteenth century in the price of whale oil, then widely used as lamp fuel. At first candles were the only substitute for whale-oil lamps, and not a very good one. People therefore cut their use of whale oil only a little when the price began to rise. However, over time the high price of whale oil spurred entrepreneurs to develop a better substitute, kerosene. Once kerosene came onto the market, the quantity of whale oil demanded for lamp fuel dropped to zero. Today market forces are spurring the development of many alternative forms of energy, ranging from compressed natural gas as a motor fuel to wind, wave, and solar energy for generating electricity.

A final reason for greater long-run elasticity of demand is the slow adjustment of consumer tastes. The case of beef and chicken, featured in the preceding chapter, provides an example. Chicken, originally the more expensive meat, achieved a price advantage over beef many years ago, but eating lots of beef was a habit. Gradually, as chicken developed an image as a healthy, versatile food, it overtook beef as the number-one meat in the United States.

Income Elasticity of Demand

Determining the response of quantity demanded to a change in price is the most common application of the elasticity, but by no means the only one. We can also use elasticity to express the response of demand to changes in any of the conditions covered by the "other things being equal" assumption that underlies a demand curve. The response of demand to changes in consumer income is an important example.

Income elasticity of demand

The ratio of the percentage change in the quantity of a good demanded to a given percentage change in consumer incomes, other things being equal

The **income elasticity of demand** for a good is the ratio of the percentage change in the quantity demanded to a percentage change in income, assuming no change in price. Using Q_1 and Q_2 to represent quantities before and after the change in income, and y_1 and y_2 to represent income before and after the change, we can write the midpoint formula for income elasticity of demand as follows:

$$\text{Income elasticity of demand} = \frac{(Q_2 - Q_1)/(Q_1 + Q_2)}{(y_2 - y_1)/(y_1 + y_2)}$$

$$= \frac{\text{Percentage change in quantity}}{\text{Percentage change in income}}$$

For a normal good, an increase in income causes demand to increase. Because income and demand change in the same direction, the income elasticity of demand for a normal good is positive. For an inferior good, an increase in income causes demand to decrease. Because income and demand change in opposite directions, the income elasticity of demand for an inferior good is negative.

Some of the considerations that determine price elasticity also affect income elasticity. In particular, whether a good is normal or inferior depends on how narrowly we define it and on the availability of substitutes. For example, a study by Jonq-Ying Lee, Mark G. Brown, and Brooke Schwartz of the University of Florida looked at the demand for frozen orange juice[2]. Orange juice considered as a broad category is a normal good; people tend to consume more of it as their income rises. However, when the definition is narrowed so that house-brand and national-brand frozen orange juice are treated as separate products, the house-brand product turns out to be an inferior good. As their incomes rise, consumers substitute the higher-quality national brands, which have a positive income elasticity of demand.

Cross-elasticity of Demand

Another condition that can cause a change in the demand for a good is a change in the price of some other good. Changes in the price of beef affect the demand for chicken, changes in the price of gasoline affect the demand for SUVs, and so on. The **cross-elasticity of demand** for a good is the ratio of the percentage change in the quantity demanded of that good to a given percentage change in the price of another good. The midpoint formula for cross-elasticity of demand looks just like the one for price elasticity of demand, except that the numerator shows the percentage change in the quantity of one good while the denominator shows the percentage change in the price of some other good.

Cross-elasticity of demand provides a way of measuring the relationships of substitutes and complements. Because lettuce and cabbage are substitutes, an increase in the price of cabbage causes an increase in the quantity of lettuce demanded; the cross-elasticity of demand is positive. Because SUVs and gasoline are complements, an increase in the price of gasoline causes a decrease in the quantity of SUVs demanded; the cross-elasticity of demand is negative. The previously mentioned study of frozen orange juice found a positive cross-elasticity of demand between house-brand and national-brand juices, indicating that the two are substitutes.

Cross-elasticity of demand

The ratio of the percentage change in the quantity of a good demanded to a given percentage change in the price of some other good, other things being equal

Price Elasticity of Supply

Elasticity applies to supply as well as demand. The **price elasticity of supply** of a good is the percentage change in the quantity of the good supplied divided by the percentage change in its price. The midpoint formula for calculating price elasticity of supply looks like the one for determining price elasticity of demand, but the Qs in the numerator of the formula now refer to quantity *supplied* rather than quantity *demanded*. Because price and quantity change in the same direction along a positively sloped supply curve, the formula gives a positive value for the elasticity of supply. Figure 3.3 applies the elasticity formula to two supply curves, one with constant elasticity and the other with variable elasticity.

Price elasticity of supply

The ratio of the percentage change in the quantity of a good supplied to a given percentage change in its price, other things being equal

FIGURE 3.3 CALCULATING PRICE ELASTICITY OF SUPPLY

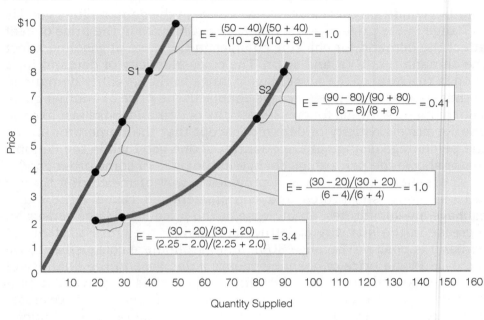

This figure gives four examples of the way price elasticity of supply is calculated. The figure gives price elasticity of supply for two ranges on each of the two supply curves. Supply curve S_1, which is a straight line passing through the origin, has a constant elasticity of 1.0. Supply curve S_2, which is not a straight line, is elastic for small quantities and inelastic for larger ones.

In later chapters, we will look in detail at the considerations that determine the elasticity of supply for various products. Two of those are important enough to be worth a preliminary discussion here.

One determinant of the elasticity of supply is the mobility of the factors of production used to produce a good. As used here, *mobility* means the ease with which a higher price can attract factors away from some other use, as well as the ease with which they can return to their original use. The trucking industry provides an example of mobile resources. When a crop such as lettuce or watermelons comes to harvest in a particular region of a country, the need for trucks to haul it to market increases. Shippers compete for available trucks, paying higher prices to truckers in the local market. Independent truckers throughout the country learn—from their own experience, from trucking brokers, and from Internet sites—where they can earn the best rates for hauling produce. It takes only a modest rise in the price for hauling a load of Georgia watermelons to attract enough truckers to Georgia to haul the crop to market. When the harvest is over, the truckers will move elsewhere to haul peaches, tomatoes, or whatever.

In contrast, other products require resources that are not so mobile. For example, when oil prices rise, producers have an incentive to drill more wells. However, there are only so many drilling rigs, and it is expensive to move them from place to place. For that reason, among others, even a substantial increase in the price of oil has only a small effect on output.

Time is a second determinant of elasticity of supply. As in the case of demand, price elasticity of supply tends to be greater in the long run than in the short run. Resource mobility is part of the explanation. In the short run, producers can increase output by using more of the most flexible inputs—for example, by adding workers at a plant or extending their hours of work.

When a crop is ready for harvest, the need for trucks to haul it to market increases.

Often such short-run measures mean higher costs per unit, however. If a firm expects market conditions to warrant an increase of supply in the long run, it will be worthwhile to invest in additional quantities of less mobile inputs such as specialized plants and equipment. Once a firm makes those investments, its costs per unit will decrease and quantity supplied will increase.

3.2 Applications of Elasticity

Elasticity has many applications in both macro- and microeconomics. In macroeconomics, it applies to financial markets, to the aggregate supply and demand for all goods and services, and to foreign-exchange markets, to name just a few. In microeconomics, elasticity plays a role in discussions of consumer behavior, business behavior, and government policy. We conclude this chapter with two examples.

Gas Tax or Mileage Standards?

In 2011, the U.S. government announced an increase in the Corporate Average Fuel Economy standard (CAFE standard) for passenger cars to 54 miles per gallon (mpg) by 2025. The new standard will be almost double the 27.5 mpg in force for the previous twenty years.

Many economists agree that some government policy to discourage excessive fuel consumption is a good idea. Using gasoline and diesel fuel on the highway has many undesirable spillover effects, which economists call negative externalities. Pollution, both in the form of local smog and global climate change, is one concern. National security problems stemming from dependence on oil from unstable and unfriendly countries are another. Highway congestion and wear and tear on roads and bridges are still others. Are CAFE standards the best way to reduce fuel consumption? Would an increase in the federal gasoline tax work better? It turns out that the answer depends on the price elasticity of demand for motor fuel.

The fundamental problem with CAFE standards is that they attack the spillover effects of fuel use only partially and indirectly. As a result, the cost of achieving a given reduction in fuel use via CAFE standards is higher than the cost of reaching the same goal through a tax increase.

To understand why, we need to consider the various ways consumers can cut back on fuel use. In the short run, they can buy an efficient hybrid instead of a gas-guzzling SUV, they can reduce discretionary driving, or they can shift some trips from their Ford F-250 to their Honda, if they happen to have one of each in the driveway. Given more time to adjust, they can make work and lifestyle changes, such as moving closer to public transportation, work, and shopping; changing jobs; or working at home.

In 2011, the U.S. government announced an increase in the Corporate Average Fuel Economy standard for passenger cars from the current 27.5 mpg to 54 mpg by 2025.

Higher fuel prices directly affect all of these choices. They encourage people to make whatever marginal adjustments best suit their circumstances. CAFE standards, in contrast, encourage fuel saving only with regard to the choice of what car to buy. Once a consumer buys a low-mileage vehicle, the cost of driving an extra mile goes down. That actually reduces the incentive for fuel-saving measures like moving closer to work, working at home, riding the bus to work, or consolidating errands.

Economists call the tendency of more fuel-efficient vehicles to induce additional driving the "rebound effect." The size of the rebound effect depends directly on elasticity of demand. For example, suppose that the elasticity of demand based on fuel-cost per mile is 0.3. If so, a 10 percent decrease in the price of gasoline would cause a 3 percent increase in miles driven, but so would a 10 percent increase in fuel efficiency, assuming no change in fuel prices. The increased miles driven would partly offset the increase in miles per gallon, so that total fuel consumption would decrease by only about 7 percent.

Even taking the rebound effect into account, higher CAFE standards are still somewhat helpful in reducing those negative externalities that are proportional to the quantities of fuel consumed, including pollution and national security concerns. However, the rebound effect causes an absolute increase in those externalities that are proportional to miles driven, including road congestion, traffic accidents, and road maintenance.

What is more, the very fuel-saving strategies that CAFE standards discourage, like moving closer to work or consolidating errands, are often the ones that have the lowest costs. That is why the total cost of reaching a given national fuel-saving target will be greater when achieved through CAFE standards than through fuel taxes. A 2004 study from the Congressional Budget Office concluded that an increase in the federal gasoline tax would achieve a given reduction in fuel economy at a cost 27 percent less than that of an equivalent tightening of CAFE standards. Furthermore, its effects would come more quickly because they would not have to wait for the gradual turnover of the national motor vehicle fleet. Over the fourteen-year time horizon of the CBO study, the gas tax increase would save 42 percent more total fuel.

We see, then, that the relative merits of CAFE standards vs. fuel taxes depend critically on the price-elasticity of demand for fuel. The less elastic is demand, the stronger is the case for CAFE standards; the more elastic, the larger the rebound effect and the stronger the case for raising fuel taxes. So what do we know about price elasticity?

Of all the many elasticity studies, the most widely cited is one by Molly Espey. She concluded that the best estimate for the price elasticity of gasoline demand was –0.26 in the short run and –0.58 in the long run. Those estimates strongly undermine the case for CAFE standards. However, recent estimates challenge Espey's results, which use data from 1936 through 1986. The new estimates show a decrease in elasticity in the early years of the twenty-first century. One such study found that the short-run price elasticity of gasoline for 2001–2006 had fallen to a range of –0.034 to –0.077. That finding would seem to strengthen the case for higher CAFE standards. The study suggested that elasticity may have fallen because suburban sprawl and longer commuting distances meant that a lower proportion of all driving was discretionary. Also, it is possible that after more than a decade in which CAFE standards had remained unchanged at 27.5 mpg, there were fewer opportunities for saving fuel by trading in an older car for a new one or shifting driving from one car to another within the family fleet.

Not so fast, however. Still more recent studies seem to show that the factors at work in 2001-2006 were temporary, and that after hitting a low, elasticity is on the rise again. A 2011 review of the latest literature on gasoline demand concluded that a short-run elasticity of demand around 0.3 is still realistic, and that long-run elasticity has returned to a range of –0.4 to –0.8. This latest study suggested that rising fuel prices and stagnating incomes have once more increased the share of fuel costs in consumer budgets. Also, as a larger share of the population reaches retirement, a higher percentage of driving becomes discretionary, and therefore more sensitive to fuel prices.

All this leaves one last question. If the economics of elasticity show that CAFE standards are a bad idea, why do they remain so popular? If you are an economist, choosing higher fuel taxes over CAFE standards looks like a no-brainer; but if you are a politician, fuel taxes have an obvious drawback. Fuel taxes make the cost of reducing consumption highly visible. You see the big dollars-per-gallon number right there in front of you every time you drive up to the pump. CAFE standards, in contrast, hide the cost. You pay the price of a higher-mileage car only when you buy a new one, and even then, the part of the price attributable to the mileage-enhancing features is not broken out as a separate item on the sticker. You may notice that your new car costs more than your old one did, but there are lots of other reasons for that besides fuel economy.

It is a classic case of the TANSTAAFL principle—There Ain't No Such Thing As A Free Lunch. If you try to make something look like it's free, it only ends up costing more in the long run. If you are a politician, you may well prefer a big hidden cost to a small visible cost. If you're a friend of the environment, you should know better.

Elasticity and Prohibition

The previous case showed how a tax or regulation could reduce the use of a product whose consumption has undesired spillover effects. Prohibition is a more extreme policy to accomplish the same end. The ultimate goal of prohibition is to reduce the quantity sold to zero. Alcoholic beverages were subject to prohibition in the United States during the 1920s; drugs like marijuana, heroin, and cocaine are subject to prohibition today. Environmental regulations sometimes also rely on prohibition. For example, regulations do not just tax the use of the pesticide DDT and lead additives for gasoline—they completely prohibit them.

On the surface, a policy of prohibition may seem very different from a tax. However, a closer economic analysis reveals similarities as well as differences between taxation and prohibition.

First, passage of a law prohibiting production and sale of a good does not make it impossible to supply the good—it simply makes it more expensive to do so. After the prohibition is in effect, the supplier must consider not only the direct costs of production but also the extra costs of covert transportation and distribution systems, the risk of fines or jail terms, the costs of hiring armed gangsters to protect illegal laboratories, and so on. From the law-breaking supplier's point of view, these costs are an implicit tax. If the price rises by enough to cover them, lawbreakers will still supply the good. Thus, the effect of prohibition of a good is to shift its supply curve to the left until each point on the new supply curve lies above the corresponding point on the old curve by a distance equal to the extra costs associated with evading the prohibition.

Second, the effects of the prohibition, like those of a tax, depend on the elasticities of demand and supply. Figure 3.4 illustrates this point

Drugs like heroin and cocaine are subject to prohibition in the United States.

FIGURE 3.4   ELASTICITY AND THE EFFECTS OF PROHIBITION

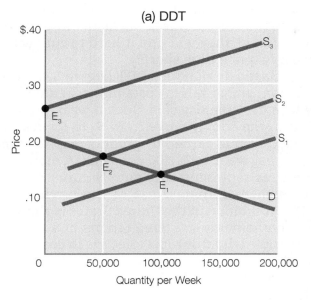

(a) DDT

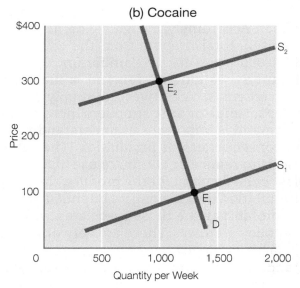

(b) Cocaine

A law prohibiting production and sale of a good, like a tax on the good, shifts its supply curve to the left. The new supply curve will lie above the old supply curve at any given quantity by a distance equal to the cost of evading the prohibition. The effects on price, quantity, and revenue depend on the elasticity of demand. Part (a) uses DDT to illustrate prohibition of a good with elastic demand. A weakly enforced prohibition (S_2) raises the price, reduces the quantity, and reduces total revenue earned by producers from sale of the product. A strongly enforced prohibition reduces quantity and revenue to zero (S_3). Part (b) uses cocaine to illustrate prohibition of a good with inelastic demand. In this case, even strong efforts to enforce prohibition do not reduce quantity sold to zero. Because quantity sold increases by a smaller percentage than price increases, there is an increased total revenue and expenditure on the good.

by comparing the effects of prohibition on the U.S. markets for DDT and cocaine. The demand for DDT is shown as elastic because effective substitutes are available at a price only a little higher than the banned pesticide. The demand for cocaine is inelastic, in part because once people become addicted, they will find it hard to cut back on their use of the drug even if its price rises sharply.

In the case of elastic demand for DDT (Figure 3.4a), even a weakly enforced prohibition, which raises costs of illegal supply only a little, will sharply reduce the quantity sold. Such a weak prohibition, represented by a shift in the supply curve from S_1 to S_2, is already enough to reduce the total revenue earned by producers (price times quantity sold) from \$14,000 per week to \$8,500 per week. A more vigorously enforced prohibition, as represented by supply curve S_3, raises the cost of supply by enough to eliminate use of the product altogether. In practice, the DDT prohibition in the United States is almost 100 percent effective, although one hears scattered reports of a tiny black market, fueled partly by people who think it is effective in combatting bedbugs.

In the case of cocaine, even a strongly enforced prohibition has a small effect on quantity sold. By the nature of the market, it is hard to get accurate price and quantity data for illegal drugs; however, the few studies that have been done suggest a short-run price elasticity of about .5 to .7. Accordingly, in Figure 3.4b, as prohibition shifts the supply curve to S_2, total revenue from the sale of cocaine rises sharply, from \$130,000 per week at equilibrium E_1 to \$300,000 per week at equilibrium E_2. As long as demand is inelastic, increasing strictness of enforcement, which drives the supply curve still higher, will make the sales revenue of drug suppliers increase still further.

Elasticity of demand is important in understanding the intended and unintended consequences of prohibition. The intended consequence, of course, is to reduce or eliminate use of the product. As we see, the more elastic the demand for the product, the more successful is the policy of prohibition in achieving its intended effects. The unintended effects of prohibition are those associated with the change in revenue that the policy produces. These are very different in the case of elastic and inelastic demand.

Where demand is elastic, there is a moderate loss of revenue to DDT producers and a small rise in the cost of growing crops as farmers switch to more expensive pesticides. Neither has major social consequences. Chemical companies offset the loss of revenue from producing DDT by increased revenue from production of substitutes. The benefits of a cleaner environment offset the increased cost of growing crops.

On the other hand, where demand is inelastic, the intended conse-quences are smaller and the unintended consequences greater. With in-elastic demand, prohibition increases total expenditure on the banned product. The social consequences may be severe. First, users of cocaine must spend more to sustain their habit. At best, this means impover-ishing themselves and their families; at worst it means an increase in muggings and armed robberies by users desperate for cash. Second, we must also consider the impact of the prohibition on suppliers. For sup-pliers, the increase in revenue does not just mean an increase in profit (although profits may increase) but also an increase in expenditures devoted to evading prohibition. In part, the result is simply wasteful, as when drug suppliers build special submersible boats that they discard after a single one-way smuggling voyage rather than shipping their product cheaply by normal transportation methods. Worse, some of suppliers' increased expenditures take the form of hiring armies of thugs to battle the police and other suppliers, further raising the level of violence on city streets, or bribing government officials, thereby cor-rupting the quality of government.

The issue of drug prohibition, of course, involves many normative issues that reach far beyond the concept of elasticity. One such issue is whether people have a right to harm themselves through consumption of substances like tobacco, alcohol, or cocaine; or whether, instead, the government has a duty to act paternalistically to prevent such harm. Another concerns the relative emphasis that should be placed on pro-hibition versus treatment in allocating resources to reduce drug use. The analysis given here cannot answer such questions. However, it does suggest that the law of unintended consequences applies in the area of drug policy, and that elasticity of demand is important in shaping those consequences.

BVT *Lab*

Visit www.BVTLab.com to explore the student resources available for this chapter.

Summary

1. **What do economists mean by elasticity?** *Elasticity* is the responsiveness of quantity demanded or supplied to changes in the price of a good (or changes in other factors), measured as a ratio of the percentage change in quantity to the percentage change in price (or other factor causing the change in quantity). The *price elasticity of demand* between two points on a demand curve is the percentage change in quantity demanded divided by the percentage change in the good's price.

2. **What is the relationship of demand to revenue?** If the demand for a good is elastic, a decrease in its price will increase total revenue. If it is inelastic, an increase in its price will increase total revenue. When the demand for a good is unit elastic, revenue will remain constant as the price varies.

3. **How do economists apply elasticity to changes in market conditions?** The concept of elasticity can be applied to many situations besides movements along demand curves. The *income elasticity of demand* for a good is the ratio of the percentage change in quantity demanded to a given percentage change in income. The *cross-elasticity of demand* between goods A and B is the ratio of the percentage change in the quantity of good A demanded to a given percentage change in the price of good B. The *price elasticity of supply* is the ratio of the percentage change in the quantity of a good supplied to a given change in its price.

4. **How does elasticity help in understanding changes in public policy?** Many issues of public policy depend on how responsive demand or supply is to changes in price. One example is the choice of mileage standards or higher fuel prices as a means of decreasing motor fuel use. Higher elasticity of demand would favor price mechanisms; lower elasticity would favor mileage standards. Prohibition is another example where elasticity is important. Prohibition is more likely to have harmful unexpected consequences when demand is inelastic.

Key Terms   Page

Key Term	Page #
Cross-elasticity of demand	89
Elastic demand	80
Elasticity	80
Income elasticity of demand	88
Inelastic demand	82
Perfectly elastic demand	82
Perfectly inelastic demand	82
Price elasticity of demand	80
Price elasticity of supply	89
Revenue	80
Unit elastic demand	82

Problems and Topics for Discussion

1. **Time horizon and elasticity**   Suppose a virus infects the California lettuce crop, cutting production by half. Consider three time horizons: (a) The "very short" run means a period that is too short to allow farmers to change the amount of lettuce that they plant. No matter what happens to the price, the quantity supplied will be the amount already planted, less the amount destroyed by the virus. (b) The "intermediate" run means a period that is long enough to allow farmers to plant more fields in lettuce, but not long enough to permit them to develop new varieties of lettuce, introduce new methods of cultivation, or acquire new specialized equipment. (c) The "long" run means a period that is long enough to allow farmers to develop new varieties of virus-resistant lettuce and improve cultivation techniques. Discuss these three time horizons in terms of the price elasticity of supply. Sketch a figure showing supply curves for each of the time horizons.

2. **Calculating elasticity**   Draw a set of coordinate axes on a piece of graph paper. Label the horizontal axis from 0 to 50 units and the vertical axis from $0 to $20 per unit. Draw a demand curve that intersects the vertical axis at $10 and the horizontal axis at 40 units. Draw a supply curve that intersects the vertical axis at $4 and has a slope of 1. Make the following calculations for these curves, using the midpoint formula:

    a. What is the price elasticity of demand over the price range $5 to $7?

    b. What is the price elasticity of demand over the price range $1 to $3?

    c. What is the price elasticity of supply over the price range $10 to $15?

    d. What is the price elasticity of supply over the price range $15 to $17?

3. **Elasticity and revenue**   Look at the demand curve given in Figure 2.1 of the preceding chapter. Make a third column in the table that gives revenue for each price-quantity combination shown. Draw a set of axes on a piece of graph paper. Label the horizontal axis as in Figure 2.1, and label the vertical axis from 0 to $5 billion of revenue in increments of $1 billion. Graph the relationship between quantity and revenue using the column you added to the table. Discuss the relationship of your revenue graph to the demand curve, keeping in mind what you know about elasticity and revenue and about variation in elasticity along the demand curve.

4. **Elasticity of demand and revenue**   Assume that you are an officer of your campus theater club. You are at a meeting called to discuss ticket prices. One member says, "What I hate to see most of all is empty seats in the theater. We sell out every weekend performance, but there are always empty seats on Wednesdays. If we cut our Wednesday night prices by enough to fill up the theater, we'd bring in more money." Would this tactic really bring in more revenue? What would you need to know in order to be sure? Draw diagrams to illustrate some of the possibilities.

5. **Cross-elasticity of demand**   During 2011, the price of natural gas in the United States fell to a record low relative to the prices of fossil fuels, including coal. In same year, the share of U.S. electricity output generated by gas increased and output generated by coal fell. What do these facts suggest to you about the cross-elasticity of demand between coal and gas? Illustrate your answer with a pair of diagrams showing the market for coal and that for natural gas. Which supply curves would have needed to shift to produce results consistent with the reported facts? Which demand curves? Why?

Case for Discussion

Does a Higher Price Promote Energy Efficiency? Results from a Natural Experiment in New York City

What does the demand curve for electricity look like? If we ask the question in the abstract, not everyone would agree.

Some people might say, "It's obvious. If the price goes up, people use more; if it goes down, they use less. Like this." Then they grab a pencil and draw a negatively sloped straight line that looks just like the demand curves they remember from their college econ textbook.

No, not so fast! Other people might say, "I agree that people are going to use more when the price is lower, but I'm not so sure about that straight line. It seems to me that if the price gets really low—for example, if electricity were completely free—there would be no real limit to how much they would use. The demand curve is more likely to look like this." Then they would take their own pencil and draw a curved line that flattens out as it approaches the horizontal axis—one that looks like what economists call a constant elasticity demand curve.

"Nonsense," still other people might say. "Electricity is a necessity in the modern world. Raising the price wouldn't do any good for promoting conservation. Rich people can afford to use as much as they want no matter what it costs, and poor people would still have to use the electricity they need to live. Raising the price would just make them even poorer." Someone from this third group would draw the demand curve as a vertical line.

Who is right? Fortunately, in this case, we don't have to guess. We have a natural experiment based on the experience of New York City apartments. About 1.75 million apartments in New York have electric meters. The average rate per kilowatt-hour is about 21 cents. Yet about 250,000 apartments have no electric meters. People who live in those apartments have unlimited electric power included in the rent. The price for them is effectively zero.

The people who live in unmetered apartments do use more electricity than those with meters. "My A.C. is pretty much running 24/7," says a twenty-eight-year-old TV producer with no meter, who likes to keep a cool apartment for his cat. In another unmetered apartment, a young couple recently left their A.C. on for four days in July when they left town for a funeral. They wanted to come home to a cool apartment.

Still, there is a limit to wasteful use. Total electric consumption in unmetered apartments is only about 30 percent greater than use in metered apartments.

Source: Based in part on "A Natural Experiment in Demand Elasticity: Metered vs. Un-metered Electricity," Ed Dolan's Econ Blog, Aug. 17 2010 (http://dolanecon.blogspot.com/2010/08/natural-experiment-in-demand-elasticity.html). Used by permission of author. Quotations and data from Sam Dolnick, "Air-Conditioners that Run When Nobody's Home," The New York Times, Aug. 16, 2010, p. A13.

Questions

1. What value of price elasticity of demand for electricity is assumed by people who draw the vertical demand curve? What evidence from the New York "experiment" is consistent with this hypothesis? What evidence is inconsistent?

2. What is assumed about price elasticity of demand by the people who draw the negatively-sloped straight-line demand curve? Does the elasticity of demand increase, decrease, or remain the same as the price approaches zero? What evidence from the New York "experiment" is consistent with this hypothesis? What evidence is inconsistent?

3. What is assumed about price elasticity of demand by the people who draw the curved demand curve that does not intersect the horizontal axis? What evidence from the New York "experiment" is consistent with this hypothesis? What evidence is inconsistent?

4. On balance, which of the three hypotheses about electricity demand does the New York "experiment" best support?

Endnotes

1. The midpoint formula (also sometimes called arc-elasticity) is not the only one for calculating elasticity. A drawback of that formula is that it can give misleading elasticity values if applied over too wide a range of price or quantity. Because of that limitation, the midpoint formula works best over small ranges of price or quantity. A more precise approach gives a value for elasticity for a single point on the demand curve. For a linear demand curve having the formula $q = a - bp$ (with q representing quantity demanded, p the price, and a and b being constants), the point formula for elasticity of demand (stated, as elsewhere, as a positive number) is

$$\text{Elasticity} = \frac{bp}{(a - bp)}.$$

2. Jonq-Ying Lee, Mark G. Brown, and Brooke Schwartz, "The Demand for National Brand and Private Label Frozen Concentrated Orange Juice: A Switching Regression Analysis," Western Journal of Agricultural Economics (July 1986): 1–7.

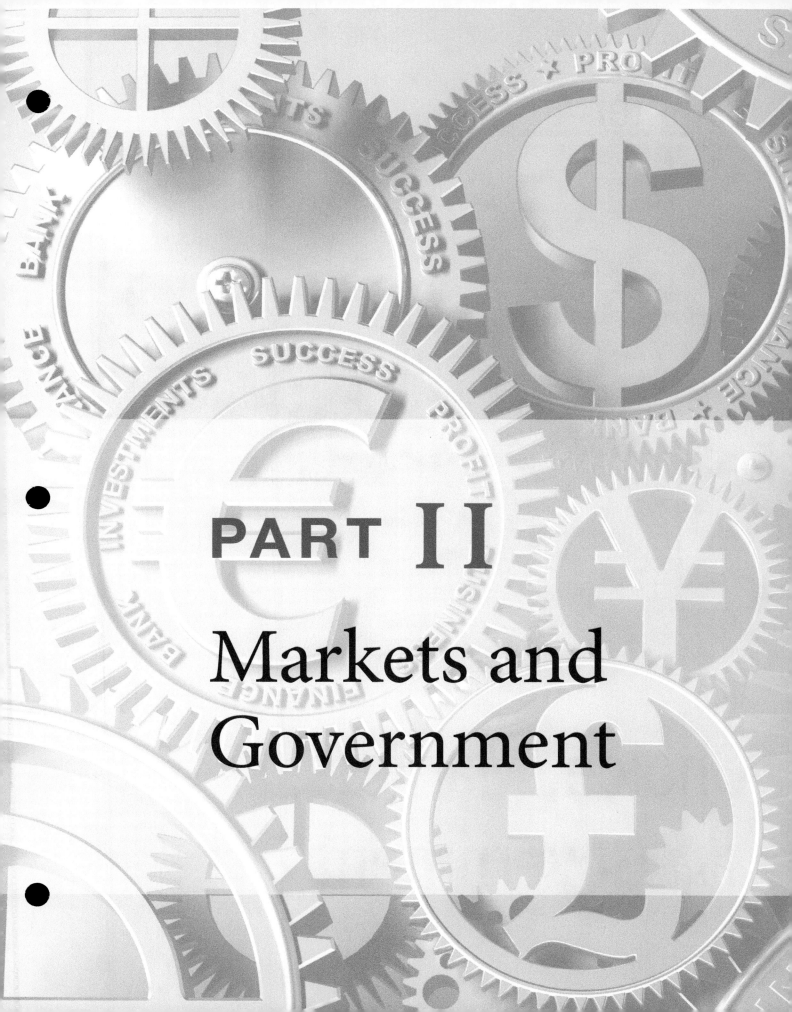

PART II

Markets and Government

Chapter 4

Choice, Markets, *and* Government

After reading this chapter, you will understand the following:

1. The basic structure of economic theory

2. Why rationality is central to economics

3. The meaning of market performance and market failure

4. Some theories of the economic role of government

Before reading this chapter, make sure you know the meaning of the following concepts:

1. Entrepreneurship

2. Law of unintended consequences

3. Supply and demand

Choices are central to economics. Chapter 1 introduced the basic choices of Who? What? How? and For Whom? Chapters 2 and 3 showed how the choices that lie behind supply and demand determine market prices and quantities. In this chapter and the next, we will take a still closer look at the economic choices people make. As we do so, we will ask some general questions about the structure of economic theory, the reliability with which markets work, and the nature of the individuals and organizations, including governments that populate the economist's world. Then, in Chapters 6 and 7, we will apply what we have learned to environmental policy and global trade.

4.1 The Structure of Economic Theory

To *analyze* something means to break it down into its component parts. A literary critic might analyze a novel in terms of plot, character, and dialog. A detective might analyze a murder in terms of motive, means, and opportunity. Similarly, economists analyze peoples' decisions in terms of the concepts of objectives, constraints, and choices.

Objectives, Constraints, and Choices

Statements About Objectives   An *objective* is anything people want to achieve. A business owner's objective may be to earn the greatest possible profit. A consumer may strive for maximum material satisfaction with a given income. People in any situation may blend their pursuit of material objectives with considerations like family values and social responsibilities. The terms *aims*, *goals*, and *preferences* are interchangeable with *objectives*.

Statements About Constraints on Opportunities   Statements about the constraints on the set of opportunities from which people may choose are a key part of every economic theory. Constraints are universal in a world of scarcity where alternatives are always limited.

Some constraints arise from what is physically possible. We can load only so many bales of hay onto a truck that can hold ten tons of cargo. A steel mill can get only so many tons of construction beams from a shipload of ore, given the available technology.

Other constraints take the form not of physical limits but of opportunity costs, often defined in terms of prices. For example, there is no physical limit to the number of pairs of shoes a person can own. However, there are economic limits. If shoes cost $60 a pair and sweaters cost $30 a piece, each pair of shoes purchased means forgoing the opportunity to buy two sweaters (or something else of equal value).

Still other constraints take the form of legal rules. One set of legal constraints defines property rights. **Property rights** establish what things people may use or control and the conditions under which they may exercise control. In short, they establish what a person owns.

Property rights

Legal rules that establish what things people may use or control, and the conditions under which they may exercise control

As an everyday example, consider the property rights that define ownership of a house. Those rights include the right to live in the house, to make improvements, and to arrange the furniture. In some communities, ownership may include the right to park a boat trailer in the driveway and to have a swing set on the front lawn. In others, those rights may be limited by zoning laws or the rules of a neighborhood association. As the example shows, the broad concept of "ownership" may be associated with different bundles of specific property rights depending on the circumstances.

Property rights extend to more complex situations, too. For example, owning a share of common stock in ConocoPhillips Corporation gives the shareholder a package of rights that includes voting on issues that affect the firm and sharing in the firm's profits.

Property rights in some neighborhoods allow a homeowner to park a boat trailer in the driveway, while zoning laws or rules of a neighborhood association may limit such rights in others.

Statements About Choices   The final component of an economic theory is a statement of the most likely choice, given the objectives and constraints on opportunities. For example, consumers have the objective of obtaining the greatest possible satisfaction, given the constraints placed on their opportunities by their budgets, the range of goods available, and the prices of those goods. Taking those objectives and constraints into account, the law of demand states that people will increase their purchases of a good when its price falls, other things being equal.

Economic Theory and Rationality

Although all economic theories contain the three types of statements just listed, a successful theory is more than just a list. Its elements need to form a coherent whole. One further key assumption holds the three elements of a theory together: the assumption that people choose the *best* way of accomplishing their objectives, given the constraints they face, that is, the assumption that people are *rational*.

Rationality, as economists use the term, means acting purposefully to achieve an objective, given the constraints on available opportunities. The concept of rationality is central to the definition of economics that we gave at the beginning of this book, which speaks of choosing the best way to use scarce resources to meet human wants. To say that some ways of using scarce resources are better than others, and that those are the ones people tend to choose, is to express the essence of rationality.

Some people misunderstand the assumption of rationality as a psychological or philosophical assertion about human nature—an assertion that people are always coolly calculating and not emotional or impulsive. A critic once ridiculed economists for seeing the human individual as a "lightning calculator of pleasures and pains, who oscillates like a homogeneous globule of desire under the impulse of stimuli ... [who] spins symmetrically about his own spiritual axis until the parallelogram of forces bears down upon him, whereupon he follows the line of the resultant."[1] Used properly, though, the rationality assumption does not imply that sort of caricature of "economic man."

The rationality assumption, as economists understand it, is simply a tool for giving structure to theories about the choices people make. Economists then fill in the specifics of the structure by observing what people do in various situations, that is, what choices they make when faced with certain opportunities.

Consider a very simple example. Suppose Bundy Hall, a dormitory, and Carpenter Hall, where economics classes meet, lie at opposite corners of a grassy quadrangle in the middle of a college campus. Across the diagonal of the quad between Bundy and Carpenter there is a well-worn path in the grass. Why is the path there, even though there are perfectly good sidewalks around all four sides of the quad?

If you ask an economist that question, the answer will probably be something like this: "The students' objective is to minimize the time it takes to get to class so that they can sleep as late as possible. Of the limited numbers of routes to class, the diagonal path is the shortest one; so that's the path they choose to take."

Most people would probably accept that theory as a reasonable explanation of the path across the quad. Why? First and most important, it is consistent with the observation that the path is there and students use it. Second, adding to its appeal, the theory corresponds with our intuition about what we would do in the same situation. Although economists are wary of relying too heavily on their own experience, in practice introspection plays a significant role. Finally, our theory about the path across the quad is appealing partly because it is simple.

Rationality

Acting purposefully to achieve an objective, given constraints on the opportunities that are available

Why is there a well-worn path in the grass between Bundy Hall and Carpenter Hall? Economists might say it's because it meets the students' objective to save time getting to class.

Ockham's razor

The principle that simpler theories are to be preferred to more complex ones when both are consistent with given observations

Economists, like their colleagues in other social and natural sciences, tend to prefer simple theories to complex ones when both are consistent with given observations. The preference for simple theories over complex ones is known as **Ockham's razor**, after a fourteenth-century philosopher who urged its use to "shave away" unnecessary theoretical complexities.

So far, so good. Suppose now that a transfer student arrives from another campus and says, "At Treelined University there is a big quad just like this one, and there is no diagonal path across it. Here's a picture to prove it. What do you say to that, O Wise Economist?"

This is not a far-fetched possibility. Observations that are inconsistent with previously accepted theories cross economists' desks frequently. When that happens, they look for a way to modify the theory so that it provides a rational basis for the new observation. Given the structure of economic theory, we can expect the search to take one of two directions.

First, closer investigation will often show that the original theory failed to allow for some *constraint* on available opportunities. For example, it might be that the campus police at Treelined University have a nasty practice of slapping a $20 fine on any student caught walking on the grass. A modified theory can take this constraint into account: "Even when the shortest distance to class is a diagonal across the quad, a fine that raises the opportunity cost of walking on the grass will induce some students to take the sidewalk. The number taking the sidewalk will increase as the fine increases, so that if the fine is large enough, not enough students will take the shortcut to wear a path in the grass." This more general theory is consistent with observations made on both campuses.

Second, if closer investigation fails to turn up some previously un-noticed constraint, it may turn out that the original theory included a mistaken understanding of the *objectives* of the people involved. In this case, we assumed that students on both campuses placed a high priority on getting to class on time. However, perhaps the students of Treelined University take great pride in the appearance of their campus. They would rather be late to class than trample on the grass. Thus, there is a path on one campus and not on the other because students at the two schools rank their objectives differently.

Clearly differing choices sometimes stem from differing objectives. For example, if Marcia buys pistachio ice cream while Mark buys chocolate ice cream, and the two flavors cost the same, we are comfortable concluding that their choices differ because their preferences do. However, as a rule, economists like first to see whether they can frame an explanation of different choices in terms of differing constraints on opportunities—prices, regulations, climate, and so on. If they don't check constraints first, explaining things in terms of differing preferences is simply too easy. Take, for example, the fact that people in the United States drive larger cars, on average, than people in Italy. Who would be satisfied just to say that Italians prefer little cars, without noting that drivers in Italy face different constraints, in particular, narrower streets and more expensive gasoline?

Italian drivers face different constraints than drivers in the U.S., particularly since Italy has narrower streets and more expensive gasoline.

We can say much the same about the rationality assumption. Just as economists are wary of relying too much on differences in preferences to explain choices, they are also wary of explaining choices in nonrational terms. Suppose, for example, that an economist sees a student, obviously late for class, who, instead of cutting across the quad or even hurrying around by the sidewalk, is walking slowly in circles in the middle of the grass. The economist questions the student: "Have you lost a contact lens? Are you exercising?" If the economist can't find an explanation in terms of constraints and the rational pursuit of objectives, then there is a dilemma. One alternative would be to give up on studying this particular aspect of human behavior and call in some other specialist, perhaps a psychotherapist. The other could be to rethink the concept of rationality itself. Increasingly, economists are choosing to rethink the concept of rationality.

Full and Bounded Rationality

One way to modify the rationality assumption is to distinguish between full and bounded rationality.

Theories based on **full rationality** assume that people make optimal use of all available information in planning how best to meet their objectives. Some versions of full rationality assume the cost of making decisions, the possibility of error, and often, the cost of acquiring

Full rationality

The assumption that people make full use of all available information in calculating how best to meet their objectives

information to be zero. Other versions assume that those aspects of decision-making are themselves handled with optimal efficiency.

On the other hand, theories based on **bounded rationality** assume that people intend to make choices that best serve their objectives, but that they have limited ability to acquire and process information. Rather than optimally weighing all available information, they rely on incomplete data and rules of thumb that do not always make full use of what they do know.

For example, consider the choice of which university to attend. If college applicants strictly followed the assumption of full rationality, they would make full use of all sources of information. They would carefully study the information on the website of every college, limiting their efforts only according to the opportunity cost of the time needed to make the search. On the basis of what they learned, they would outline preferred four-year programs of study at each school. Based on their web search, they would systematically interview people who had attended the schools that rated near the top of their list and would perhaps visit those schools. Only when all the information that they could gather in a cost-effective manner was in hand would they make a choice. In doing so, they might weigh such factors as the probable grades they would earn at each school, the influence of grades and choice of school on their lifetime incomes, and so on.

On the other hand, if applicants applied bounded rationality, they would conduct a more limited search. Perhaps they would look only at schools from a certain region. They might listen to what friends and relatives said and consult only the websites of schools where they had studied. They might base their final choice more on advice from trusted friends and less on systematic balancing of objective information.

In the chapters that follow, we will encounter examples of theories based both on full and on bounded rationality.

Self-regarding versus Other-regarding Preferences

Another way to modify the assumption of rationality is to expand the concept of objectives to include human feelings like fairness, compassion, trust, spite, and envy. We can capture these feelings by distinguishing between **self-regarding** and **other-regarding preferences.** People who are concerned only with their own material welfare have self-regarding preferences. People who balance considerations of their own material welfare with the welfare of others and take into account what others think about them have other-regarding preferences.

One simple example of other-regarding preferences comes to light in the "ultimatum game" described in *Applying Economic Ideas* 4.1. Results from repeated experiments around the world suggest that people often behave in ways that correspond more closely to other-regarding rather than strictly self-regarding preferences. Somewhat more controversial is the issue of whether to describe choices based on compassion, envy, and similar feelings as rational. The tendency in economics today seems to be toward expanding the concept of rationality in a way that allows for other-regarding preferences.

Bounded rationality

The assumption that people intend to make choices that best serve their objectives, but have limited ability to acquire and process information

Self-regarding preferences

A set of objectives that depend only on the material welfare of the decision maker

Other-regarding preferences

A set of objectives that includes not only the material welfare of the decision maker but also the material welfare of others and their attitudes

Applying Economic Ideas **4.1**

Ultimatums, Dictators, and Other Games

In recent years, games have become increasingly popular as a tool of economic research. One game that consistently produces results that contradict narrow definitions of economic rationality is the so-called ultimatum game.

The game works like this. One player, call her Ann, gets a sum of money, $10. She must then offer some share of the money to a second player, Bob. Bob can accept the offer or reject it. If he rejects Ann's offer, neither player gets to keep anything. If Bob accepts, they divide the money according to the terms that Ann proposed. The name of the game comes from the fact that there is only one offer and only one chance to refuse—there is no extended bargaining and no repeated play during which notions like developing a reputation or building trust might come into play.

Under the assumptions of full rationality and self-regarding preferences, the outcome of the game is easy to predict. First, we conclude that Bob will never rationally reject any nonzero offer. To do so would give up a certain (although perhaps small) reward in favor of getting nothing at all. Second, we conclude that Ann, knowing that Bob will never reject

In the ultimatum game, one player offers money to another.

any nonzero offer, no matter how small, will rationally make the smallest offer allowed. (Sometimes the rules set by the experimenter might say this is one cent, sometimes one dollar, or whatever.)

That is not what happens when people actually play the game. In reality, Player A—not always, but more often than not—offers a substantial amount, say 30 to 50 percent of the total. Furthermore, B typically rejects offers that seem too low, with the frequency of rejection rising sharply for offers below 20 percent or so of the total. Experimenters have repeated the game thousands of times, not only with American college students, but also with African hunter-gatherers, Wall Street brokers, Mongolian herders, and many other groups. The average amount offered and the threshold for rejection differ somewhat from one society to another, but it seems that the narrowly rational result is never observed.

What is going on? One hypothesis is that when placed in the Player A position, people behave altruistically. They take pleasure from pleasing Player B. Another hypothesis is that Player A is not altruistic but, rather, is strategically motivated by the fear that a too-low offer will be rejected. But if so, what motivates Player B? Why does that person reject low offers even though they can only lose, in material terms, by doing so? Does B have some innate aversion to inequality? Some spiteful wish to draw pleasure from punishing an insufficiently generous Player A?

(Continues)

One way to try to sort out the motives is to play the related dictator game with a similar group of subjects. In the dictator game, Player A gets to keep her share regardless of whether B accepts or rejects the offer. Since there is no fear of rejection, the motivation for any nonzero offer must be pure altruism. Interestingly, although the dictator game typically produces smaller offers than the ultimatum game, the offers are still substantially above zero. Seemingly, both altruism and fear of rejection play a role.

There are many, many variants of the games. Sometimes the players know each other; sometimes they are anonymous. Sometimes the game takes on a "double-blind" form where neither the players nor the experimenter knows the individual identities of the players or amount specific individuals offer or reject. (The double-blind variant is supposed to eliminate the possibility that Player A might be ashamed of appearing "too selfish" in the eyes of the experimenter.) No matter what, the offers never fall to zero. Human behavior is stubbornly more complex than narrowly rational, self-regarding preferences can account for!

In the nineteenth and early twentieth centuries, economists freely discussed emotional and psychological elements of economic behavior. As mathematical modeling came to dominate economics in the second half of the twentieth century, those elements largely disappeared. Today, the tide is turning once again with the rise of behavioral economics. Among other sources, behavioral economics draws on the work of Daniel Kahneman, a psychologist who won the 2002 Nobel Memorial Prize in Economic Science for his work with the late Amos Tversky. Richard H. Thaler of the University of Chicago, a leader of the new school, admits that it is harder to construct models that incorporate a full range of human behavior. However, doing so could once again make economics more of a social science, as in the past.[2]

4.2 Market Performance and Market Failure

People do not make economic choices in a vacuum. They make them in the context of institutions, of which markets and government are two of the most important. This section offers a preview of what coming chapters will have to say about markets, especially the key concepts of market performance and market failure. The next section will preview the role of government in the economy.

Market Performance

Market performance

The degree to which markets work efficiently in providing arrangements for mutually beneficial trade

Earlier, we defined a *market* as any arrangement that people have for trading with one another. When economists speak of **market performance**, then, they are referring to how efficiently markets do their job of providing arrangements for mutually beneficial trade.

Ideally, markets would make it possible to carry out every exchange that is to the mutual benefit of the parties involved. Suppose we are talking about the market for peaches. The parties to peach trading are farmers and consumers. An exchange will benefit consumers if the satisfaction they get from a peach is at least as great as the satisfaction they would get from spending the same amount on the next most attractive good (say, an apple). The exchange will benefit producers if the price paid for a peach is at least high enough to cover the opportunity cost of producing it. If there is a price that makes the trade beneficial both to consumers and to producers, then carrying out the trade will be *efficient* inasmuch as it will leave at least one party better off and neither worse off.

Farmers and consumers are the parties involved in the market for peaches.

Although the details will require several chapters to work out, a simple diagram can give an intuitive idea of efficient market performance. Figure 4.1 shows two curves that represent the market for peaches.

FIGURE 4.1 PERFORMANCE OF THE MARKET FOR PEACHES

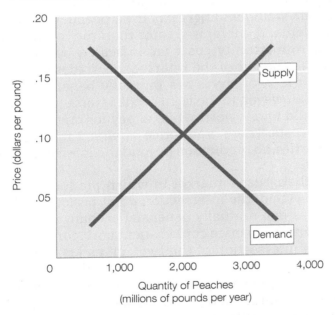

This exhibit shows hypothetical supply and demand curves for peaches. The demand curve reflects the willingness of consumers to buy peaches, given the price of peaches and the prices of alternative goods. The supply curve represents the willingness of farmers to sell peaches, given the price of peaches and the opportunity costs of production. At any point to the left of the intersection of the curves, the price that consumers would willingly pay for a peach (as indicated by the height of the demand curve) is greater than the minimum needed to cover farmers' costs (as indicated by the height of the supply curve). Thus, up to that point, exchanges carried out at a price between the two curves are mutually beneficial to consumers and producers. At any point to the right of the intersection, the maximum amount that consumers would be willing to pay for still more peaches is less than the amount needed to cover farmers' costs. Thus, production beyond the intersection point would not be efficient. It follows, then, that a market in which production continues just up to but not beyond the intersection performs efficiently.

The demand curve shows the benefit of peaches to consumers as reflected by their willingness to buy peaches, given the price of peaches, the prices of other goods, and so on. The supply curve shows the opportunity costs of producing an additional peach as reflected by the willingness of farmers to grow and sell it.

Transaction Costs and Market Performance

A supply curve like that in Figure 4.1 reflects the opportunity costs of producing the good in question. The demand curve in the figure, and others like it, show how much consumers are willing to buy, assuming that the price they pay is the only cost that they must bear in order to buy it. Neither the supply nor the demand curve allows for the possibility that buyers or sellers may incur other costs as part of carrying out an exchange.

At any point to the left of the intersection of the two curves, the price consumers would willingly pay for a peach (as indicated by the height of the demand curve) is greater than the minimum needed to cover farmers' opportunity costs (as indicated by the height of the supply curve). To the left of the intersection, trades carried out at any price between the two curves are mutually beneficial to consumers and producers. However, to the right of the intersection, the maximum consumers would find it worthwhile to pay for one more peach is less than farmers' costs. There is no price at which further trades would benefit both parties, so production beyond the intersection point would not be efficient.

It follows, then, that a market in which production proceeds just up to, but not beyond, the intersection point performs efficiently. At a lower quantity, some mutually beneficial exchanges would not occur. At a higher quantity, no price could benefit both parties. Not only is the quantity at the intersection of the two curves just right but so is the price. Any higher price would lead to a wasteful surplus of peaches, whereas any lower price would lead to a shortage in which some consumers' wants would remain unsatisfied.

It is hard to exaggerate the enthusiasm that economists have for markets that generate such efficient outcomes. From reformers in emerging market economies to ministers of finance in the world's richest countries, there is widespread agreement that within large areas of economic life, markets can efficiently solve basic economic problems. Yet even the most enthusiastic fans of markets admit that they do not always work perfectly. Several conditions must hold before markets reach a stable equilibrium exactly at the intersection of the supply and demand curves. Let's look briefly at some of the situations in which market performance falls short of the ideal, again leaving details to later chapters.

Among other things, the simple supply and demand model implicitly assumes that consumers are able, at no cost in terms of time, money, or mental effort, to obtain full information on the range of goods available, their quality, and their prices. It also implicitly assumes that neither buyers nor sellers need any time, money, or mental effort to negotiate the terms of a sale. Finally, the model implicitly assumes that all purchases and sales are clean and final. Once they reach an agreement, neither party runs a risk that the other will fail to do as promised; and there are no costs of renegotiating contracts if circumstances change.

In practice, costs of gathering information, finding potential partners, negotiating and enforcing agreements, and renegotiating when conditions change can be large. Economists use the term **transaction costs** to refer to all such costs. For a simple transaction, like buying a single peach, transaction costs are likely to be small. For a larger consumer purchase, like buying a house or condominium, transaction costs—in the form of brokers' commissions, bank closing costs, and fees paid to insurers and surveyors—can add greatly to the quoted price. In the case of complex business transactions, say the merger of two corporations, transaction costs can be enormous.

Transaction costs
The costs, other than production costs, of carrying out a transaction

When we account for transaction costs, it is harder to tell whether a market is efficient. It is no longer enough to say that efficiency means exactly hitting the point where the supply and demand curves intersect. Instead, before the market approaches the intersection, it may reach a point where the gap between the opportunity cost of production (as shown by the supply curve) and consumers' willingness to pay (as shown by the demand curve) is smaller than the transaction costs needed to carry out additional exchanges. To take a trivial example, you might be driving down the street when you feel a hunger for a luscious, ripe peach. You see a supermarket; but then you start thinking about the time it will take to park and stand in line for checkout, the chance that the store may not have any peaches for sale today, and the possibility that a peach that looks attractive on the shelf won't taste as good as you would like. The gap between your hunger for the peach and the price isn't great enough to make it worth the effort and uncertainty involved in stopping.

It would be going too far, however, to say that markets are necessarily operating efficiently when they reach the point where the gap between supply and demand curves is just equal to transaction costs. Sometimes transaction costs themselves may be inefficiently large. For example, the Japanese economy, which has a world-class reputation for efficiency in manufacturing, has an outdated retail trade system hampered by cumbersome regulations. As a result, transaction costs facing Japanese consumers are sometimes much greater than those for consumers in the United States, who are able to buy their peaches super-fresh from a farm stand, super-cheap in a big-box discounter, or super-fast in at 24-hour convenience store. In this sense, it would be reasonable to say that high Japanese transaction costs are a sign of inefficiency.

As we add detail to our discussion of markets in coming chapters, we will often return to the subject of transaction costs.

Market Failure

Market failure

A situation in which a market fails to coordinate choices in a way that achieves efficient use of resources

A **market failure** is a situation in which a market fails to coordinate choices in a way that achieves efficient use of resources. We should not consider every situation in which the market misses the exact intersection of supply and demand to be a market failure. We need to consider transaction costs, as well as production costs. Economists usually think of market failure as a situation where transaction costs are not the only conditions that keep buyers and sellers from carrying out all potentially beneficial exchanges. Of the many possible sources of market failure, three deserve special attention: externalities, public goods, and insufficient competition.

Externalities   One type of market failure arises when prices fail to transmit accurate information about scarcity. For markets to perform their job efficiently, prices should reflect the opportunity costs of producing the goods or services in question. Ordinarily, market prices do reflect at least a reasonable approximation of opportunity costs. However, situations arise in which producers' (and consumers') actions have effects on third parties, that is, people other than the buyer and seller who carry out a transaction. These third-party effects, which are not reflected in prices, are known as **externalities**. When externalities are present, the price system does not transmit accurate information about opportunity costs.

Externalities

The effects of producing or consuming a good whose impact on third parties other than buyers and sellers of the good is not reflected in the good's price

The classic example of an externality is pollution. Suppose a utility burns coal to generate electricity. The costs of fuel, capital, and labor come to $.10 per kilowatt-hour. We call those internal costs because they are borne by the utility itself. Internal costs are reflected in market transactions—payments to coal producers, workers, stockholders and bondholders, and so on. They represent the forgone opportunities of using the same natural resources, capital, and labor in some other industry. To stay in business, the utility must receive a price of at least $.10 per kilowatt-hour, that is, a price at least equal to the internal opportunity costs.

The internal costs of generating electricity are not the only ones, however. A coal-fired power plant spews out clouds of carbon dioxide, sulfur dioxide, soot, and other pollutants. The pollution damages health, kills trees, and corrodes buildings in areas downwind from the plant, and it contributes to climate change. We refer to those effects as external costs of generating electricity because they are borne by third parties—people who are neither buyers nor sellers of electricity or any of the inputs used in making it. From the viewpoint of the economy as a whole, external costs are also part of the opportunity cost of generating power. They represent the value of

The government can require a utility to install pollution control equipment or to pay the resulting imposed taxes.

the factors of production that are destroyed by the pollution (such as dead trees or workers in other firms taking extended sick leave) or required in order to repair its effects (repainting houses, treating pollution-related diseases).

Suppose that pollution damage of all kinds comes to $.02 per kilowatt-hour of power produced. Added to the $.10 in internal costs, the $.02 of external costs brings the overall opportunity cost of electricity to $.12 per kilowatt-hour. This figure reflects the value of the factors of production used directly by the utility plus those that the pollution destroys or diverts from other uses.

If supply and demand set the price of electric power, its equilibrium value will tend toward the level of $.10 per kilowatt-hour that just covers internal costs. That price, however, sends a false signal to users of electricity: It tells them that producing a kilowatt-hour puts a smaller drain on the world's scarce factors of production than is really the case. As a result, electricity users will use more power than they should. They will be less inclined to buy new, more efficient machinery, to design products to use less electricity, to shift to cleaner natural gas, and so on. In short, the market will fail to achieve efficient resource allocation because prices will have sent users the wrong information.

We will return to the economics of pollution in Chapter 6. There, we will examine several possible solutions to market failures resulting from externalities.

Public Goods   The goods and services discussed in all the examples used to this point—chicken, peaches, electricity, and so on—have two properties in common: (1) The supplier can decide to supply the good to some people and to exclude others, something that we call the property of *exclusion*. (For example, if I run a multiplex movie theater, I can exclude people who do not buy tickets.) (2) Use of a unit of the good by one person limits the possibility of use of that unit by other people, something we call the property of *rivalry*. (For example, if I sell you a peach, I cannot sell that same peach to someone else.) Some goods do not possess the properties of exclusion and rivalry, however. We call them **public goods**. Lacking the property of exclusion, it is not possible to provide them for one person without also providing them for others. Lacking the property of rivalry, once we provide them for one person, we can provide them for others at no extra cost. Public goods, like externalities, are a potential source of market failure.

Perhaps the closest thing to a pure public good is national defense. There is no way to protect one person against nuclear attack or invasion without extending the protection to everyone. Also, it costs no more to protect a single resident of an area than to safeguard an entire city or region.

Although pure public goods are rare, other goods may lack the properties of exclusion or rivalry to some extent. We can call them impure public goods. Police protection is an example. In their functions of promoting public safety in general and deterring street crime, the police are providing a public good; but in their function of solving

Public goods

Goods that (1) cannot be provided for one person without also being provided for others and (2) when provided for one person can be provided for others at zero additional cost

an individual crime, such as a burglary, they are providing a private good to the person who hopes to recover the stolen property. Maintenance of urban streets, the provision of parks, and even the space program are other examples of goods that are neither purely public nor purely private.

Private firms have difficulty making a profit selling products that, once provided to one customer, are available to others at no additional cost. To see why the market may fail in such cases, imagine that someone tries to set up a private missile defense system—call it Star Wars, Inc.—funded by selling subscriptions to people who want protection from a nuclear attack. Even if I think the system will work and that there is a real threat, there are two reasons I might choose not to subscribe. First, I know that if my neighbors subscribe and get their homes protected, my home will be protected too, even if I do not pay. I could take a *free ride* on a public good paid for by others. Second, I might be willing to contribute if I had *assurance* that at least, say, one thousand of my neighbors did so. That would raise enough money to buy at least one missile. However, I would not contribute without the assurance that others will also contribute at least the minimum amount. Contributing along with just five hundred neighbors would buy only half a missile, which would be useless—and my contribution would be pointless.

The free-rider problem and the assurance problem can make it difficult for private firms to make a profit on selling such products as a private missile defense system.

Some economists argue that the *free-rider problem* and the *assurance problem,* which make people reluctant to contribute voluntarily to the support of public goods, mean that government must provide those goods if they are to be provided at all. There are two problems with that view. First, as *Applying Economic Ideas* 4.2 illustrates, private firms provide some things that have the characteristics of public goods.

Second, many goods and services that the government provides at public expense are public goods only to a small extent, if at all. Take education, for example. The principal beneficiaries of public education are students. It is not impossible to exclude students from the schools. Only a few schools, public or private, operate on an "open admission" basis. Others select their students according to neighborhood, ability to pay, or scholastic achievement. Moreover, education clearly has the property of rivalry in consumption. A school cannot add students without some additional expense for teachers, classrooms, laboratories, and other facilities. Thus, education fits the definition of a public good, if at all, only to the extent that it has some benefit beyond that received by individual students, for example, promoting good citizenship in a way that makes life better for everyone in the community.

Applying Economic Ideas 4.2

Private Provision of Public Goods

Some economists argue that private firms cannot supply public goods because of the assurance and free rider problems that arise whenever goods have the properties of non-exclusion and nonrivalry. In practice, however, many private firms and voluntary organizations do find methods of providing goods that have these properties. Examples include broadcast radio and television, computer software, and amenities like streets and parks in residential neighborhoods.

A public road ceases to be a public good when a tollbooth is installed.

In some cases, private firms simply alter the product in a way that makes it possible to exclude free riders. Thus, satellite television providers typically scramble their signals so that only subscribers who rent a decoder can receive them; computer software can be copy-protected so that the original purchasers cannot easily make free copies for their friends; and roads can be equipped with tollbooths. In this case, the good ceases to be a public good, even though it continues to have the property of nonrivalry.

Exclusion has its disadvantages, however. The necessary technology may be expensive and less than fully reliable, and the attempt to exclude may be offensive to customers the firm would like to attract. To avoid these disadvantages, private firms and voluntary organizations often use other techniques to provide public goods.

- One approach is to link the public good to an ordinary good, offering the two as a package deal. Thus, some public radio stations send their contributors magazines with movie reviews and program guides, computer software companies provide advice via telephone or Internet chat to legitimate registered purchasers; and real estate developers find it worthwhile to build residential streets as part of a package included with the sale of private homes.

- Another approach is to tap the power of other-regarding preferences. Voluntary organizations build on the psychological satisfaction of contributing to a good cause or the psychological discomfort of recognition as a free rider. This works best in small communities where everyone knows everyone else; but organizations, like public radio stations, can achieve something of the same effect by publicly thanking contributors over the air.

(Continues)

- Still another device is the "assurance contract." Sometimes people hesitate to contribute to a good cause because they fear their contribution will be in vain unless others join them. In such a case, the provider can accept pledges of support that will become effective only if support reach as an agreed minimum level. Thus, families might contribute checks to a fund to build a neighborhood playground on the understanding that organizers will return the checks if a there is insufficient support.

As these examples show, the economic category of "public good" does not always mean a good that government must provide.

Monopoly

A situation in which there is only a single seller of a good or service

Electric utilities are examples of a monopoly.

Insufficient Competition A third source of market failure is insufficient competition. As we have seen, market prices should reflect opportunity costs if they are to guide resource allocation efficiently. In the case of harmful externalities, market failure occurs because prices fall below opportunity costs. Where competition is insufficient, however, market failure can occur because prices are too high.

As an extreme case, consider a market in which there is only a single seller of a good or service—such a market is termed a **monopoly**. Residential electric service is a frequently cited example. Suppose that Metropolitan Electric can generate power at an opportunity cost of $.10 per kilowatt-hour. Selling electric power at that price would guide customers in choosing between electricity and other energy sources, such as oil or gas, and in undertaking energy-saving investments, such as home insulation and high-efficiency lighting.

If homeowners could buy electricity from anyone they chose the way they buy eggs or gasoline, the forces of competition, acting through supply and demand, would push the market price toward the level of opportunity costs. In a competitive market, other firms would undercut any seller that tried to raise prices much above opportunity costs; and the utility would not sell power at a price below opportunity costs because doing so would put it out of business.

However, utilities do not compete in selling to residential customers. Every home normally has a connection to only one set of power lines. In this case, if government regulation did not restrain it, a utility could substantially increase its profits by charging a price higher than opportunity cost. Of course, raising the price would mean selling less power as customers moved up and to the left along their demand curves. Up to a point, however, the greater profit per kilowatt-hour sold would more than outweigh the effects of the reduction in quantity demanded.

If utilities charge too high a price, homeowners will get a false message regarding the opportunity cost of electricity. They may make substitutions that are not economically justified. For example, they may switch from electricity to oil for heat, even in regions where cheap hydroelectric power is available, or from electric air conditioning to gas air conditioning, even in areas where the opportunity cost of electricity is below that of gas.

Market failures due to insufficient competition are not necessarily limited to the extreme case of monopoly. Under some circumstances, competition among a small number of firms may also lead to prices that are above opportunity costs, especially if the firms engage in collusion. The circumstances under which competition is or is not sufficient to ensure the efficient operation of markets is the subject of a large body of economic research and of more than a few controversies, as we will see in coming chapters.

Other Market Failures   Some economists would list other sources of market failure in addition to the three just discussed. For example, some consider the macroeconomic phenomena of inflation and unemployment to be market failures. Certainly, an economy that is subject to excessive inflation and unemployment provides a poor environment in which to coordinate the actions of buyers and sellers. However, the effects of inflation and unemployment, together with policies intended to keep them under control, lie outside the scope of the microeconomics course.

As we have defined it, market failure means failure to achieve an *efficient* allocation of scarce resources. In addition, the market may or may not achieve a *fair* allocation of resources. Whether we should refer to unfairness, inequality, and economic injustice in a market economy as market failures is more a matter of terminology than of substance. In this book, we define *market failure* in a way that makes it an issue of efficiency alone; however, in doing so, we do not mean to deny the importance of issues of economic justice. We will discuss many such issues in the following chapters, although not under the heading of market failure.

4.3 The Economic Role of Government

Although markets play a big role in answering the key questions of who, what, how, and for whom, markets are not the only context in which people make economic decisions. People also make many decisions in hierarchies. Allocation of resources within a business firm is one example of hierarchical decision making; we will focus on that later. Here we are concerned with the role of government, the other major example of hierarchy in economics.

If we want to understand the microeconomic role of government, a good place to begin is by asking: Why does government play any role in the economy at all? Why can't people coordinate all of their activities using decisions made in markets? Economists offer two answers, one based on the notion of market failure, the other on that of *rent seeking*. The answers are partly contradictory and partly complementary. Each will figure prominently in coming chapters, and each deserves a brief preview here.

The Market Failure Theory of Government

According to the market failure theory of government, the principal economic role of government is to step in where markets fail to allocate resources efficiently and fairly. Each type of market failure calls for a particular type of governmental intervention.

Take the case of pollution. Earlier we gave the example of a utility whose contribution to air pollution caused $.02 worth of damage for every kilowatt-hour of electricity. Government can do a number of things to correct the resulting market failure. For example, it can require the utility to install pollution control equipment that will prevent poisonous gas from escaping into the atmosphere or impose a tax equal to the external costs of pollution.

To correct market failure, government may require installation of pollution control equipment to prevent poisonous gas from escaping into the atmosphere.

When markets fail to supply public goods, government also has a role to play. Often, as in the case of national defense, the government simply becomes the producer of the public good. In other cases, such as education, which some economists consider to be in part a public good, the government need not be the sole producer. Private schools and colleges are encouraged with subsidies and tax benefits to add to the supply of education produced by public institutions.

Governments attempt to remedy market failures arising from insufficient competition in a variety of ways. In some cases, they use *antitrust laws* to preserve competition by preventing mergers of competing firms, or even by breaking large firms up into a number of smaller ones. In other cases, such as the electric power industry, *regulation* controls prices charged by a monopoly firm. In a few cases, such as the Tennessee Valley Authority's electric power facilities, the government itself may become a monopoly producer of a good or service. We will discuss regulation in a later chapter.

The Public Choice Theory of Government

Some people criticize the market failure theory of government as being more about what the government ought to do than about what it actually does. In practice, many government programs, rather than correcting market failures, seem to promote inefficiency or inequality in markets that would function well without government intervention.

Public choice theory

The branch of economics that studies how people use the institutions of government in pursuit of their own interests

Critics of the market failure theory prefer to interpret government policies not in terms of broad social goals like efficiency and fairness but in terms of how people use the institutions of government to pursue their own self-interest. This approach to policy analysis goes by the name of **public choice theory**.

Rents and Rent Seeking   One of the key concepts of public choice theory is economic rent. In everyday language, a *rent* is simply a payment made for the use of something, say, an apartment or a car. Public choice theorists use the term in a more specialized sense, however. An **economic rent** is any payment to a factor of production in excess of its opportunity cost. An example is the huge income a popular author like James Patterson or Danielle Steel earns from a new novel—an income much higher than the author could earn spending the same amount of time in the next-best paying line of work.

When firms earn rents through innovation in competitive markets, we call them *economic profits*. Entrepreneurs are always on the lookout for ways to earn such profits—for example, by introducing a new product superior to that of rival firms or by being the first to implement a cost-saving production method. When they are successful, the income they earn may be substantially higher than what others are able to earn by employing similar factors of production in less imaginative ways.

Profit that entrepreneurs earn through private market activity is not the only category of economic rent, however. Firms, workers, and resource owners often turn to government in search of rents, rather than trying to outwit their rivals in the marketplace. A dollar earned because of a regulation that raises the price at which a firm sells its output or lowers the prices at which it buys its inputs is worth just as much as a dollar of profit earned through purely private efforts at innovation. In some cases, it may even be better. Profits earned from innovation in a competitive market may be short lived because rivals will soon come out with an even better product or introduce an even cheaper production method. However, government regulations can not only create opportunities to earn rents but also shield those opportunities from competitors. Economists call the process of obtaining and defending rents through government action **political rent seeking**, or often simply as **rent seeking**, with the political aspect implied.[3]

Consider the case of subsidies for corn-based ethanol used as a gasoline substitute. Politicians attempt to justify those subsidies as a way to offset externalities—in this case, the carbon dioxide produced from burning gasoline. However, many economists argue that the process of producing ethanol releases nearly as much carbon dioxide into the atmosphere as burning gasoline does, or even more. Public choice theorists see ethanol subsidies as a classic case of political *rent seeking*. The benefits of ethanol subsidies go not just to small family farms but also to large agribusinesses, owners of ethanol refineries, even growers of competing crops like wheat and soybeans whose prices rise when corn acreage expands. The result is a program that draws wide political support even though its environmental benefits are often overstated.

Economic rent

Any payment to a factor of production in excess of its opportunity cost

Political rent seeking (rent seeking)

The process of seeking and defending economic rents through the political process

Ethanol subsidies are a classic case of political rent seeking.

Government restrictions on competition are another way of generating rents. For example, tariffs and import quotas on clothing, cars, sugar, steel, and other products shield domestic firms and their employees from foreign competition. Thus, the firms are able to earn rents by raising prices above the competitive market level, and the employees are able to earn rents in the form of higher wages. We can find examples of government restrictions on competition in the domestic economy, too. For example, licensing fees and examinations restrict the number of competitors who can enter such professions as law and medicine, and often even such occupations as manicuring and hair styling.

From the Law of Unintended Consequences to Government Failure   The notion that government policies do not always promote efficiency and equity is not new. Economists have long been aware of the law of unintended consequences—the tendency of government policies to have effects other than those desired by their proponents. Public choice theory goes beyond the notion of unintended consequences, which can arise simply from incomplete analysis on the part of policy makers. Rather, the element of rent seeking in the formulation of government policy suggests that the inefficient results of many government programs are not unintended at all. In this view, there is a systematic tendency for government programs to cause rather than to cure economic inefficiencies—a tendency, that is, toward **government failure**.

Government failure

A situation in which a government policy causes inefficient use of resources

In introducing the notion of government failure, public choice theorists do not intend to imply that government always makes a mess of things or that the market always functions perfectly. Rather, they want to level the playing field by showing that both markets and government are imperfect institutions. In deciding whether government or the market better performs a given function, we must weigh the possibilities of government failure against those of market failure.

Neoclassical and Other Approaches to Microeconomics

This chapter began by introducing the idea of economics as the study of rational choice when objectives and constraints are given. Rational choice lies at the core of neoclassical economics, a school of thought that began with the work of Alfred Marshall at the end of the nineteenth century (see *Who Said It? Who Did It?* 2.1), and has long been the dominant school of economics in the United States. Much of the material in the following chapters, including the theory of consumer choice, the theory of profit maximization by firms, and the theory of factor markets, comes from the neoclassical tradition. In addition to the general principles of rational choice that we have already discussed, neoclassical economics often incorporates additional simplifying assumptions:

1. An assumption of full rationality where decision makers have well-defined objectives (for example, profit maximization) and are competent to make use of all available information in choosing how best to pursue those objectives

2. An assumption of self-regarding preferences, models in which decision makers are motivated by material gain for themselves

3. An emphasis on the price system as the economy's key mechanism for transmitting information, where the prices of all goods and services are public information available free to all households and firms and there are few or any costs of acquiring information or other transaction costs

4. An emphasis on formal models of economic behavior stated in graphical or mathematical terms, and a focus on conditions of equilibrium

5. Treatment of households, firms, and government agencies as "black boxes" with the main focus on the interactions of these units in the marketplace and relatively little attention to the workings of their internal hierarchies

The very restrictiveness of these assumptions is the source of much of the success of neoclassical theory. Neoclassical economics is like a spotlight that is able to illuminate objects brightly precisely because its focus is narrow. In the following chapters, we will encounter one situation after another, ranging from highway safety to negotiations among OPEC oil ministers, where neoclassical economics provides insights of striking clarity and predictions that stand up remarkably well to the test of experience.

Despite the successes of neoclassical microeconomics, economists have long been aware that there are some problems that its narrowly focused spotlight cannot adequately illuminate. We have already mentioned difficulties posed by bounded rationality, other-regarding preferences, and transactions costs—all of which require modifications or extensions of neoclassical models. Also, neoclassical economics tends to take market and government institutions as given, without asking why they exist and how they evolve. Finally, the focus on equilibrium in neoclassical economics has limited its ability to address issues of innovation, change, and entrepreneurship. In coming chapters, we will discuss extensions and alternatives to neoclassical economics whenever they are helpful in understanding the important economic issues of our day.

Summary

1. **What is the basic structure of economic theory?** Economic theories are built from statements about people's objectives, aims, and preferences; statements about the constraints on available opportunities; and statements about how people choose among the available opportunities so as best to meet their objectives.

2. **Why is rationality of central importance to economics?** To be rational means to act purposefully to achieve one's objectives, given the available opportunities. In some cases, economists assume *full rationality*, which means that they assume that people make full use of all available information in calculating how best to meet their objectives. In other cases, they assume *bounded rationality*, which means that they assume that people intend to make the choices that best serve their objectives, but have limited ability to acquire and process information. The assumption of rationality is sometimes further modified to allow for other-regarding as well as self-regarding preferences.

3. **What is the meaning of market performance and market failure?** *Market performance* refers to how efficiently markets do their job of providing arrangements for mutually beneficial trade. Ideally, markets would make it possible to carry out every possible mutually beneficial trade, in which case they would operate perfectly efficiently. Sometimes, however, *market failure* occurs, in which case markets fail to carry out their job efficiently. *Externalities, public goods,* and insufficient competition (leading to *monopoly*) are among the most widely discussed sources of market failure.

4. **What are some alternative theories of the economic role of government?** According to the market failure theory of government, we should leave everything to markets that they can do efficiently. Government should intervene only to correct market failures, whether narrowly or broadly defined. *Public choice theory* maintains that many government policies are not efforts to correct market failure but result from *political rent seeking* instead. Rent seeking refers to the process of seeking payments in excess of opportunity costs.

Key Terms   Page

Problems and Topics for Discussion

1. **Alternative path theories**   The chapter proposes a simple theory to explain the existence of a path across a grassy area on a certain college campus. Here is another theory that might also explain the path: "Economics lectures are so boring that students prefer to be late to them. However, near the sidewalk on one side of the quad there is a beehive, and many students have suffered stings; and on the other side of the quad is the chemistry building, which smells bad when the wind blows a certain way. Sometimes if you cut across the middle of the quad, you find four-leaf clovers that give you good luck on your exams. Those are the reasons that there is a path across the quad." Applying the principle of Ockham's razor, which theory do you think is better? Why? Would you reject the more complex theory out of hand, or would you first want to make some observations? What observations would you make?

2. **Italians in America**   According to a theory suggested in the chapter, people drive smaller cars in Italy than in the United States not because of different preferences but because they face different constraints on their opportunities—higher gasoline prices, narrower streets, and so on. On the basis of that theory, what prediction would you make about the cars driven by Italians who move to the United States? What kind of observations would you suggest to test whether preferences or constraints are the key factor in the choice of car size?

3. **What makes a fair offer?**   J. B. is a woman of limited income and almost no savings who faces a sudden financial emergency. The only way she can think of to raise the money she urgently needs is to sell her car. She has little experience in the used car market, so she offers her car to a nearby dealer, the first one she can think of. The dealer, R. S., thinks he can resell the car for about $3,000. Normally he would offer about $2,000, which would leave him enough margin to cover the costs and risks of his business plus some profit. He might even raise his offer a bit if the seller were a hard bargainer. However, R. S. quickly sees that J. B. is desperate for cash and that she does not know of any other way to find a buyer quickly. He sees that he is in a position to offer an ultimatum, so he offers $600 in cash for the car, immediate sale, take it or leave it.

Answer the following questions:

   a. Put yourself in J. B.'s position. Even though you are an unsophisticated seller, you realize that $600 is a low offer. Would you be tempted to reject the offer even if you know of no other immediate buyer and even if the $600 is enough solve your immediate financial emergency? Discuss your reasoning.

   b. Put yourself in R. S.'s position. Would you offer more than $600 for the car? Why or why not? Discuss your reasoning.

   c. Put yourself in the position of J. B.'s neighbor. J. B. accepts the offer and later, when it is too late for you to advise her or offer her financial help (if you are able to do so), she tells you the story. You go to R. S. and demand an explanation of why he made such a low offer. He candidly tells you that he would have offered more if he thought she had any alternative and if she were not so desperate for cash. He points out that J. B. must have believed that she was better off with the $600 than without it; otherwise she could have refused the offer. Accepting that J. B.'s conduct was entirely legal, do you think it was ethical? Discuss.

4. **The economics of voting**   Did you vote in the most recent state or national election? If so, did your objectives and constraints influence your choice of a candidate? If you did not vote, did objectives and constraints influence that decision? Do you think your choice of a candidate (or your choice not to vote) was a rational one? Discuss.

5. **Government failure versus market failure**   When the possibilities of both government failure and market failure are taken into account, does the fact that a government policy causes inefficiency necessarily mean that abolishing the policy would result in greater efficiency? Does the fact that a certain market fails to work efficiently necessarily mean that intervention by government would improve the situation?

Case for Discussion

A Price That's Too Good May Be Bad

Almost any aisle of any supermarket is a battleground in the never-ending war between house brands and national brands. The weapons of the national brands are advertising, reputation, and brand recognition. The big gun on the side of the house brands is price. One day recently, for example, shoppers at a Virginia Safeway store could take their choice of Johnson & Johnson baby powder for $3.29 or a can of the Safeway brand at $2.59, of Kellogg's cornflakes at $1.97 per box or the house brand at $1.59, of Wesson vegetable oil at $4.59 per bottle or Safeway's product at $3.39 per bottle, or of Heinz distilled vinegar at $1.93 per quart with Safeway's Townhouse brand at $1.23.

What logic lies behind this competition? One's first thought might be that it all depends on the law of demand. If so, one would think, the lower the price of the house brand, the higher its sales relative to the national brand. Marketers of consumer products have found that the law of demand applies only up to a point in the competition between house brands and national brands. Paradoxically, a price that is too low can actually hurt the sales of the house brand.

Consider the case of Pathmark supermarkets' Premium All Purpose cleaner. Pathmark designed this house brand product to compete head-to-head with Fantastik, the leading national brand. The two products were chemically identical. The house brand's packaging mimicked that of the national brand; and Pathmark's product carried a price of at just $.89, versus $1.79 for Fantastik.

Yet, from its first introduction, Premium All Purpose cleaner was a slow seller. Frustrated Pathmark marketers even added a sticker to the label that said, "If you like Fantastik, try me!" The sticker did not help. Finally, Pathmark decided to drop the product.

What went wrong? Interviewed by *The Wall Street Journal,* Robert Wunderle, a representative of Supermarket General Corporation, Pathmark's corporate parent, blamed the failure on a price "so low that it discredited the intrinsic value of the product."

Many retailers consider it risky to price their house brands more than 20 to 25 percent below the national brand. There are exceptions, however. If the product is so simple and familiar that consumers believe there can be no quality difference, it is safe to establish a bigger discount. Thus, for example, Safeway puts a bigger discount on its house brand vinegar and vegetable oil than on its house brand baby powder or cornflakes.

Peter Schwartz, president of Daymon Associates, Inc., a private-label research and marketing firm, explains the problem this way: "The further the distance from the national brand, the higher the credibility problem for consumers. Once you get outside the customer's comfort zone, the consumer psychology becomes, 'Gee, they must have taken it out in quality.' "

Source: Based in part on Alix M. Freedman, "A Price That's Too Good May Be Bad," *The Wall Street Journal*, November 15, 1988, B1.

Questions

1. Would you characterize the behavior of consumers who buy Fantastik brand cleaner instead of Pathmark's Premium All-Purpose cleaner as full rationality, irrationality, or bounded rationality? Explain.

2. The case suggests that in choosing among alternative brands of goods, consumers sometimes rely on the rule of thumb that higher prices tend to be associated with higher quality. From your own experience as a shopper, how valid do you think that this rule of thumb is on the average: valid always or rarely valid? Give examples.

3. A consumer who followed the assumptions of bounded rationality would be most likely to apply the preceding rule of thumb, rather than seeking independent information on product quality, in purchasing which kinds of goods?

    a. Major purchases such as automobiles

    b. Goods that people buy frequently and can easily be inspected, such as clothing

    c. Goods like household cleaners that people buy infrequently and constitute a small part of the consumer's budget and cannot easily be inspected or tested before purchase

4. Discuss why the rule of thumb is more reasonable in some cases than others and give additional examples of each case.

Endnotes

1. Thorstein Veblen, "In Dispraise of Economists," in *The Portable Veblen,* ed. Max Lerner (New York: Viking Press, 1958), 232–233.

2. See Richard H. Thaler, "From Homo Economicus to Homo Sapiens," *Journal of Economic Perspectives,* Volume 14, No. 1 (Winter 2000): 133–141.

3. For a representative collection of papers on the theory of rent seeking, see James M. Buchanan, Robert D. Tollison, and Gordon Tullock, eds., *Toward a Theory of the Rent-Seeking Society* (College Station: Texas A&M Press, 1980).

Chapter 5

Understanding *the* Choices Consumers Make

After reading this chapter, you will understand the following:

1. The key elements that influence consumer choice

2. How consumers balance their choices to achieve equilibrium

3. How price changes affect quantities of goods demanded

4. Why demand curves have negative slopes

5. Why both consumers and producers gain from exchanges

6. Why the burden of a tax exceeds the revenue raised by government

Before reading this chapter, make sure you know the meaning of the following concepts:

1. Substitutes and complements

2. Normal and inferior goods

3. Incidence of a tax

Of all the many economic choices that people make every day, those they make as consumers are the most important. Consumers buy about 70 percent of all goods and services produced in the U.S. economy. Beyond the things they shop for, they make other economically important choices—whether to marry or have children, whether to buckle their seatbelts—that don't involve buying things. This chapter will introduce a set of tools that economists use to think about consumer choice.

5.1 Utility and the Rational Consumer

As we saw in the preceding chapter, economists think about the choices in terms of objectives and constraints. Studying consumer choice gives us a chance to fill this generalization with some specific content.

Utility

We begin with consumer *objectives*—why is it that people consume goods and services at all? The usual answer is that consumption of goods and services is a source of pleasure and satisfaction. A dish of pasta to eat, a warm bed to sleep in, a movie to view—each serves a particular consumer want or need.

Utility

The pleasure, satisfaction, or need fulfillment that people obtain from the consumption of goods and services

Economists refer to the satisfaction people get from the things they consume as **utility**. The term goes back some two hundred years to the work of the eccentric English social philosopher Jeremy Bentham (1748–1832). Bentham was obsessed with reforming social institutions in a way that would bring about the "greatest good for the greatest number." He thought ordinary words such as *pleasure, satisfaction,* or *happiness* were too weak to convey the power of his vision of maximum bliss, so he coined the new word *utility* and established a movement called utilitarianism to promote the idea. Over the centuries, the term *utility* has lost the mystical overtones that it had for Bentham and his followers, but economists still use it when they refer to the objective that consumers pursue when choosing among goods and services.

Constraints on Opportunities

The constraints that shape the opportunities available to consumers are the next component of the theory of consumer choice. Those constraints include everything that prevents people from consuming all they want of everything they want.

The most important constraints are limits on the kinds of goods available, the prices of those goods, and the size of the consumer's budget. A restaurant menu provides a simple example. Suppose you have $10 to spend on lunch. You may want Caesar salad with grilled chicken, but it is not on the menu. Crab cakes are the special of the day; you love them, but they cost $19.95. In the end, you settle for a cheeseburger.

To be sure, there are situations in which constraints other than budgets and market prices may be the most important ones. In choosing how fast to drive your car, the "price" (opportunity cost) of greater safety may be taking more time to get where you are going. In choosing a spouse, one constraint is a law that says you can be married to only one person at a time. *Economics in the News 5.1* gives further examples of the many considerations, in addition to prices and budgets, which shape our choices as consumers.

In constructing a theory of the way consumers maximize utility within their budget constraints, we will proceed in two steps. First, we look at a traditional version of the theory based directly on the notion of utility; then we look at a more modern version in which utility plays a less explicit role.

Economics in the News **5.1**

What Makes Us Choose?

Economic theory has long focused on prices and consumer budgets as the two biggest factors that shape consumer choices. Certainly, no one thinks that those constraints are unimportant. However, the rapidly expanding field of behavioral economics calls attention to many other factors that lie behind our choices.

Consider popcorn. How much popcorn you eat at a movie is entirely a rational choice, depending on the price, your budget, and maybe on how hungry you are, right? Wrong!

According to Brian Wansink, Cornell Professor and author of the book *Mindless Eating*, rationality has little to do with it. To make his point, Wansink gave away free popcorn in a suburban Chicago movie theater. The popcorn wasn't even very fresh, but that didn't seem to matter. What did matter was the size of the container. Some moviegoers got huge buckets of popcorn, while others got truly colossal buckets. Although both sizes held more than a normal person could eat, those with the colossal buckets ate more than those with the merely huge ones. After the experiment was over, the subjects had a hard time believing the results. "Things like that don't fool me," one said.

In other experiments Wansink showed that big dinner plates make people eat more; short, fat glasses that hold exactly the same amount of liquid as tall, skinny ones make portions look smaller and encourage people to drink more; and kitchen cabinets with glass doors, or no doors, cause people to eat more than cabinets that keep the food out of sight. Even the choice of how to arrange items inside refrigerators can influence how much we eat.

John A. Bargh, a professor of psychology at Yale, explains some of the choices we make in terms of the role of the unconscious mind. He sees the unconscious mind as constantly at work making suggestions about choices before our conscious mind takes up the job of making the choice. In one experiment, a stranger, whose hands are full with a clipboard, books, and other items, asks a student to help by holding a cup of coffee for a moment. Sometimes it is hot coffee and sometimes iced coffee. When the experimenter asks students to rate a hypothetical individual's personality a few minutes later, those who have recently handled hot coffee described a warm, friendly personality while those who have handled the iced coffee saw the individual as colder and more selfish.

Marketers take practical advantage of the power of context to influence our decisions. Have you ever wondered who on earth would buy the $14,000 Ralph Lauren handbag or the $6,900 Beefeater barbeque grill? According to Swarthmore College professor Barry Schwartz, luxury goods makers can profit from displaying those items even if no one buys them. Their real purpose is to set a context in which other items that cost a lot, but not quite as much, fall into the category of "affordable luxury." Schwartz himself

(Continues)

admits to having once bought an $800 suit he didn't need just because it looked reasonable next to others that cost $3,000. "I got sucked in. And I knew what was happening," he says.

Sources: For Wansink's work, David Leonhardt, "Your Plate is Bigger than your Stomach," *The New York Times*, May 2, 2007; for Bargh's, Benedict Carey, "Who's Minding the Mind," *The New York Times*, July 31, 2007; for Schwartz's, Christina Binkley, "The Psychology of the $14,000 Handbag," *The Wall Street Journal*, August 9, 2007.

Diminishing Marginal Utility and Consumer Choice

Jeremy Bentham's notion of "the greatest good for the greatest number" was anything but scientific. In the late nineteenth century, economists took a major step forward in their understanding of consumer choice—an episode now known as the "marginal revolution." The British economist William Stanley Jevons was the first economist to put the new theory into print, but he shares credit with at least three others who were working along the same lines simultaneously: the Austrian Carl Menger, the Swiss Leon Walras, and the Englishman Alfred Marshall.

The central insight of the theory of marginal utility is that most choices are not all-or-nothing matters, such as whether to take up smoking or to swear off smoking forever. Instead, they are incremental decisions, such as whether to order a tall or a grande cappuccino. Whenever economists refer to the effects of doing a little more or a little less of something, they apply the adjective *marginal*. Thus, the **marginal utility** of a good is the amount of added utility that a consumer gains from consuming one more unit of that good, other things being equal.

The most important principle that Jevons and others developed is **diminishing marginal utility**: the greater the quantity of any good consumed, the less the marginal utility derived from consuming one more unit of that good.

Let's apply the principle of diminishing marginal utility to an everyday situation. Assume that you have just sat down at a lunch counter that is selling pizza at a price of $2 for a rather skimpy slice and lemonade at a price of $1 for a small glass. You have $10 to spend on lunch. What will you order?

Your objective is to choose a lunch that will give you the greatest possible utility. Will you spend all your money to buy five pieces of pizza? Probably not. However much you like pizza, you will not get as much satisfaction out of the fifth piece as the first—at least not according to the principle of diminishing marginal utility. Probably you will be willing to pass up the fifth piece of pizza to have a couple of glasses of lemonade with which to wash the first four down. Doing so will increase your total utility because the first two lemonades will give you a lot of satisfaction and the last piece of pizza only a little. How about the fourth piece of pizza? Maybe you will be willing to give up half of it for one more glass of lemonade. As you cut back on pizza and increase your consumption of lemonade, the marginal utility of

Marginal utility

The amount of added utility gained from a one-unit increase in consumption of a good, other things being equal

Principle of diminishing marginal utility

The principle that the greater the consumption of some good, the smaller the increase in utility from a one-unit increase in consumption of that good

pizza rises and that of lemonade falls. Finally, you get to the point at which you cannot increase your utility by spending less on one good and more on the other within a given budget. You have reached a point of **consumer equilibrium**.

You reach consumer equilibrium when the marginal utility you get from a dollar's worth of one good equals the marginal utility you get from a dollar's worth of the other. Another way to say it is that the ratio of the marginal utility of a good to its price must be the same for all goods:

Consumer equilibrium

A state of affairs in which a consumer cannot increase the total utility gained from a given budget by spending less on one good and more on another

$$\frac{\text{Marginal utility of good A}}{\text{Price of good A}} = \frac{\text{Marginal utility of good B}}{\text{Price of good B}}$$

We can apply this formula using an imaginary unit of utility, the "util." Suppose, for example, that you have adjusted the quantities of pizza and lemonade you buy so that you get 10 utils from another slice of pizza at a price of $2 per slice and 5 utils from another glass of lemonade at a price of $1 per glass. At these ratios, you get no more added satisfaction from an extra dollar's worth (one half-slice) of pizza than from an extra dollar's worth (one glass) of lemonade. It is not worthwhile to trade off some of either good for some of the other. You are in consumer equilibrium.

On the other hand, suppose you get 18 utils from another slice of pizza (9 utils per half-slice) and 4 from another glass of lemonade, still given the same prices. Now you are not in consumer equilibrium. Cutting back by one lemonade would lose you just 4 utils. You could then use the dollar you saved to buy another half-slice of pizza, thereby gaining 9 utils. By making this adjustment in your consumption pattern, you would not only gain total utility but also move closer to consumer equilibrium, because the marginal utility you would get from pizza would fall slightly as you consumed more and the marginal utility you would get from lemonade would rise a little as you consumed less.

Attaching numbers to things in this way helps explain the principle involved. Remember, in practice consumer choice is a much more subjective process. Some people count calories when they sit down to lunch; some count the pennies in their pockets; but no one counts "utils"—they cannot really be counted. Utility is something we feel, not something we think about. Because some people feel differently about what they eat than others do, they make different choices. Perhaps you would rather have a calamari salad and a glass of San Pellegrino than either pizza or lemonade. Whatever your choice, the logic—the balancing of utilities, the concept of equilibrium—is the same.

From Consumer Equilibrium to the Law of Demand

We can use the concepts of consumer equilibrium and diminishing marginal utility together to explain the law of demand. Suppose you have adjusted your pattern of consumption until you have reached an equilibrium in which, among other things:

$$\frac{\text{MU of pizza}}{\$2} = \frac{\text{MU of lemonade}}{\$1}$$

As long as this equality holds, you will not benefit from increasing your consumption of pizza; doing so would soon push down the marginal utility of pizza. The marginal utility per dollar's worth of pizza would drop below the marginal utility per dollar's worth of lemonade, making you better off if you switched back to more lemonade.

What if the price of pizza were to drop to, say, $1.50 per slice, upsetting the equality just given? To make the two ratios equal again, given the new price of pizza, either the marginal utility of lemonade would have to rise or that of pizza would have to fall. According to the principle of diminishing marginal utility, one way to get the marginal utility of pizza to fall is to consume more pizza, and one way to get the marginal utility of lemonade to rise is to consume less lemonade. Perhaps you would do a little of both—that is, cut back a little on lemonade and consume a little more pizza. In so doing, you would be acting just as the law of demand would predict: A decrease in the price of pizza would have caused you to buy more pizza.

This line of reasoning connects the law of demand with the principle of diminishing marginal utility in a way that appeals to common sense. However, that is not good enough for all economists. In the next section, we will look at an alternative line of reasoning.

5.2 Substitution and Income Effects

Many economists view the whole concept of utility as suspect because it is impossible to measure objectively. Instead, they favor an explanation of the law of demand that avoids measurement of utility by using the concepts of substitution and income effects.

The Substitution Effect

Substitution effect

The part of the increase in quantity demanded of a good whose price has fallen that is the result of substitution of that good for others that are now relatively more costly

One reason people buy more of a good whose price falls is that they tend to substitute a good with a lower price for other goods that are relatively expensive. Earlier, we looked at the effects of a decrease in the price of pizza. The change in price will cause people to substitute pizza for other foods that they might otherwise have eaten—hamburgers, nachos, whatever. Broader substitutions are also possible. With the price of pizza lower than before, people may substitute eating out for eating at home, or a pizza party for an evening at the movies. The part of the increase in the quantity demanded of a good whose price has fallen that is caused by the substitution of that good for other goods that are now relatively more costly is known as the **substitution effect** of a change in price.

The Income Effect

A second reason that the change in a good's price will cause a change in the quantity demanded has to do with the effect of price changes on real income.

Economists use the term *nominal* to refer to quantities measured in the ordinary way, in terms of the dollar prices at which transactions actually take place. They use the term *real* to indicate quantities that have been adjusted to take into account the effects of price changes. The distinction between real and nominal income is a typical application of these terms: If your monthly paycheck is $1,000, that amount is your nominal income—the number of dollars you earn. If your nominal income stays at $1,000 while inflation doubles the average prices of all goods and services, your *real* income—your ability to buy things taking price changes into account—will fall by half. If your nominal income stays at $1,000 while the average prices of goods and services drop by half, your real income will double.

Macroeconomics uses the distinction between real and nominal income when discussing inflation, when the prices of many goods are changing at once. We can also apply the distinction in microeconomics when we look at the effects of a change in the price of just one good. The reason is that if the price of even one good changes, while the prices of other goods remain constant, there will be some effect on the average price level and, hence, on real income.

With this in mind, let's return to our example. Again, suppose that the price of pizza falls while your nominal income and the prices of all other goods and services stay the same. Although pizza has only a small place in your budget, a fall in its price means a slight fall in the average level of all prices and, hence, a slight rise in your real income. If you continued to buy the same quantity of pizza and other goods and services as before, you would have a little money left over. For example, if the price of pizza goes down by $.50 a slice and you usually buy ten slices a month, you would have $5 left over after making your usual purchases. That is as much of an increase in your real income as you would get if your paycheck were increased by $5 and all prices remained constant.

The question now is: What will you spend the $5 on? The answer: You will use it to buy more of things that are normal goods. If pizza is a normal good, one of the things you will buy with your increased real income is more pizza. The portion of the change in quantity demanded of a good whose price has fallen that is caused by the increase in real income resulting from the drop in price is known as the **income effect** of the price change.

BVT *Lab*

Flashcards are available for this chapter at www.BVTLab.com.

Income effect

The part of the change in quantity demanded of a good whose price has fallen that is the result of the increase in real income resulting from the price change

Income and Substitution Effects and the Demand Curve

If we are dealing with a normal good, the income effect is a reason for buying more when the price falls. With both the income and substitution effects causing the quantity demanded to increase when the price falls, the demand curve for a normal good is certain to have a negative slope. We can reach this conclusion with no reference to the awkward concept of utility. So far, so good.

If we are dealing with an inferior good, the situation is a little different. Let's say that hot dogs are an inferior good for you. You eat them if you are hungry and they are all you can afford; but if your income goes up enough to buy pizza, you phase out hot dogs. What will happen if the price of hot dogs goes down while the prices of all other goods and services remain constant?

First, there will be a substitution effect. Hot dogs now are cheaper compared with lemonade, pizza, pretzels, haircuts, or whatever. Taken by itself, the substitution effect will cause you to buy more hot dogs. Other things (including real income) being equal, the rational consumer will always buy more rather than less of something when its opportunity cost (in this case, its price relative to other goods) goes down; but here other things are not equal. At the same time that the decrease in the price of hot dogs tempts you to substitute hot dogs for other things, it also raises your real income slightly. Taken by itself, the increase in real income would cause you to buy fewer hot dogs because hot dogs are an inferior good for you. Thus, in the case of an inferior good, the substitution and income effects work at cross-purposes.

What, then, is the net effect of a decrease in the price of hot dogs? Will you buy more or fewer of them than before? In the case of a good that makes up only a small part of your budget, such as hot dogs, it is safe to assume that a lower price will cause you to buy more and a higher price to buy less. That is because a change in the price of something you don't buy much of will have only a small income effect. In that case, the substitution effect will outweigh the income effect. Thus, when the substitution effect is larger than the income effect, the demand curve for an inferior good still has a negative slope.

However, there is a theoretical possibility that the demand curve for an inferior good might have a positive slope. For this to be the case, the good would have to make up a large part of a person's budget so that the income effect would be large. Imagine, for example, a family that is so poor that they spend almost all of their income on food, and almost the only foods they can afford to buy are bread and oatmeal. They eat bread as a special treat on Sunday, but the rest of the week they must make do with inferior-tasting but cheaper oatmeal. One day the price of oatmeal goes up, but not by enough to make it more expensive than bread. The rise in the price of oatmeal is devastating to the family's budget. It forces them to cut out their one remaining luxury: They give up their Sunday loaf of bread and replace it with oatmeal. The paradoxical conclusion, then, is that a rise in the price of oatmeal causes this family to buy more, not less, oatmeal. The family's demand curve for oatmeal has a positive slope. An inferior good that has a positively sloped demand curve because the income effect outweighs the substitution effect is called a **Giffen good** after a nineteenth-century English writer, Robert Giffen, who supposedly mentioned the possibility.

The conditions required for a positively sloped demand curve—an inferior good that makes up a large portion of the consumer's budget—are very special. People rarely encounter those conditions. If you are in the pizza business—or even in the oatmeal business—you can be virtually certain that, taking the world as it really is, raising the price of any good or service will cause people to buy less of it and cutting the price will cause them to buy more of it. Economists have demonstrated the Giffen-good phenomenon under carefully controlled experimental circumstances, however, as reported in *Applying Economic Ideas* 5.1. Nothing in the pure logic of rational choice disproves the possibility of such a situation occurring in an actual market.

Giffen good

An inferior good accounting for a large share of a consumer's budget that has a positively sloped demand curve because the income effect of a price change outweighs the substitution effect

Applying Economic Ideas **5.1**

Testing Consumer Demand Theory with White Rats

Traditionally, most empirical work in economics uses observation of market behavior as its data source. In recent years, however, a growing number of economists have engaged in laboratory experimentation. Many of the experiments involve students as their subjects. For example, a group of students might simulate the operation of a stock exchange, with shares of stocks exchanged for tokens or pennies.

The use of human subjects has its limits, however. For one thing, it is hard to get subjects to agree to take part in long-term experiments that might change their whole way of life. Moreover, human subjects are usually aware that they are part of an experiment. That awareness might affect their behavior. To get around these drawbacks, economists John Kagel of the University of Houston and Ray Battalio of Texas A&M seized on the idea of using animal subjects in economic experiments. Their pioneering experiments have borne out many of the predictions of consumer choice theory in the laboratory.

For example, in one experiment, they placed two white rats in standard laboratory cages with food and water freely available. At one end of each cage were two levers that activated dipper cups. One dipper cup

John Kagel and Ray Battalio used rats to test theories on consumer choices.

(Continues)

provided a measured quantity of root beer when a rat depressed its lever; the other provided a measured quantity of a different non-alcoholic soft drink, Collins mix. Previous experimentation had shown that rats prefer both to water.

Within this setup, the experimenters could give each rat a fixed "income" of so many pushes on the levers per day. The rats could distribute the pushes in any way between the two levers. Experimenters could also control the "price" of root beet and Collins mix by determining the number of pushes the rat had to "spend" to obtain one milliliter of liquid.

In an initial experimental run lasting two weeks, the rats received an income of three hundred pushes per day, and both drinks required twenty pushes per milliliter. Under those conditions, Rat 1 settled down to a pattern of drinking about eleven milliliters of root beer per day and about four milliliters of Collins mix. Rat 2 preferred a diet of almost all root beer, averaging less than one milliliter of Collins mix per day.

Once the initial conditions were established, the experimenters were ready to see how the rats would respond to changes in prices and incomes. First, they doubled the price (in pushes per milliliter) of root beer and cut the price of Collins mix in half. At the same time, they adjusted each subject's total income of pushes to make it possible for each to afford to continue the previous consumption pattern. (That adjustment eliminated any possible income effect of the price change, so that the substitution effect alone determines the outcome.) Economic theory predicts that under the new conditions the rats would choose to consume more Collins mix and less root beer than before, even though their income was enough to maintain the original pattern if they chose to do so.

The rats' behavior exactly fitted these predictions. In two weeks of living under the new conditions, Rat 1 settled down to a new consumption pattern of about eight milliliters of root beet and seventeen milliliters of Collins mix per day. Rat 2, which had chosen root beer almost exclusively before, switched over to about nine milliliters of root beer and twenty-five milliliters of Collins mix.

Another experiment focused on income effects. In this case, the two liquids chosen were root beer, which rats love, and quinine water, which they are more reluctant to drink. At the beginning of the experiment, the price of root beer was set at twice the price of quinine water. If the rats' income of pushes per day remained low, they would drink some of the relatively cheap quinine water along with some of the more expensive root beer. As their income rose, they would switch away from quinine water toward more root beer. The conclusion: For rats, root beer is a normal good and quinine water an inferior good.

Having established that quinine water was an inferior good, Kagel and Battalio set out to see if they could demonstrate the Giffen-good effect. That effect requires an inferior good that also accounts for a large part of the subject's total expenditures. To produce these conditions, the experimenters kept the rats in "poverty." Their budget was so low that without drinking a fair amount of quinine, they would become dehydrated.

Without changing the total budget of pushes, the experimenters then reduced the price of quinine water. If the rats maintained their previous consumption pattern, they would have pushes left over. What would they spend the extra pushes on? Root beer, of course. Being able to afford more root beer, the rats could now cut back on their consumption of quinine without risking dehydration. The net result: Cutting the price of quinine with no change in nominal income (pushes per day) caused the rats to drink less quinine. For impoverished rats, quinine water is a true Giffen good.

Sources: The root beer–Collins mix experiment is reported in John H. Kagel and Raymond C. Battalio, "Experimental Studies of Consumer Demand Behavior," Economic Inquiry 8 (March 1975): 22–38, *Journal of the Western Economic Association*. Reprinted with permission. Kagel and Battalio's root beer–quinine experiment is summarized in Timothy Tregarthen, "Found! A Giffen Good," *The Margin* (October 1987): 8–10.

Applications of Income and Substitution Effects

We can apply the theory of consumer choice to any situation in which a consumer seeks to maximize utility in the face of given alternatives and constraints. That is true even when the "goods" in question are not "for sale," and even when constraints and the opportunity costs of the available alternatives do not take the form of money. This section will look at some of the wider applications of the theory of consumer choice.

The Demand for Safety

Let's begin with an example from the field of automobile safety. When you get into a car to go somewhere, you face a trade-off between travel time and safety. A quick trip is good, but so is a safe one. Making the trip safer by driving more slowly, stopping for yellow lights, and so on has an opportunity cost in terms of time. Cutting travel time by driving faster and going through yellow lights has an opportunity cost in terms of safety.

If the opportunity costs change, the choices drivers make also tend to change. For example, suppose there is snow on the road that makes the road less safe and raises the opportunity cost of speed. When it snows, then, drivers slow down and shift their choices away from speed in the interest of safety, just as the substitution effect would predict.

A change in the design of cars to make them safer, for example by adding seat belts as was done starting in the 1960s and air bags as in the 1990s, also changes the opportunity cost of speed relative to that of safety. Cutting travel time by speeding up and running yellow lights entails giving up less safety in a car with seat belts or air bags than in one without those devices. Because the opportunity cost of speed is lower in a safer car, logically the substitution effect would cause people to drive faster and less carefully. Does this really happen? In a classic 1975 study, economist Sam Peltzman reported evidence that it does. In a stunning example of the law of unintended consequences, he reported that while drivers who wore seat belts increased their own safety, they drove faster and less carefully. As a result, they killed more pedestrians and bicyclists. Since the time of Peltzman's initial work, numerous other studies have confirmed that "offsetting behavior," as it is called, in response to improved risk-avoidance technology is widespread, although it is not always so strong that new safety devices or regulations are completely ineffective.

Adding seat belts to cars may change the behavior of drivers.

Some studies have found an income effect as well as a substitution effect on driving behavior. Robert W. Crandall and John D. Graham suggest that safety is an inferior good. It seems that as people's incomes go up, they begin to feel that their time is too valuable to spend in a car. Perhaps they speed up so they can get to their high-paying jobs or fashionable parties more quickly. If they decide to run a greater risk of killing themselves and others along the way—well, that is part of the logic of consumer choice. Maybe people with less exciting destinations have less reason to be in a hurry.

Children as Durable Consumer Goods

University of Chicago economist Gary Becker, winner of the 1992 Nobel Memorial Prize in Economic Sciences, has made his reputation by applying economic reasoning to areas of choice that many people think of as non-economic. Some of his best-known research concerns choices made within the family. As an example, consider Becker's analysis of the number of children a family chooses to have.

Gary S. Becker, left, from the University of Chicago, receives the 1992 Nobel Economics Prize form Sweden's King Carl Gustav in Stockholm, Sweden.

Children, in Becker's view, are durable consumer goods. They return benefits to parents over many years through love, family pride, and mowing the lawn; but there are also, opportunity costs associated with having children. Those costs include the goods and services forgone to pay the extra grocery bills, clothing bills, and doctors' bills for the children. In Becker's view, the biggest opportunity cost of having children is the time parents spend caring for them. They could use that time instead to earn income. Thus, the higher the parents' earning power, the greater the opportunity cost of having children.

What does that imply about the number of children a family chooses to have? In societies around the world, as family income rises, the number of children per family tends to fall. Does that mean that children are inferior goods? Not at all, says Becker. Children are normal goods; other things being equal, the income effect would cause a family to want more children as its income increases. But other things are not equal. As Becker notes, there is also a substitution effect. If the higher income reflects a higher hourly wage, it increases the opportunity cost of each hour spent caring for children. On the average, the substitution effect outweighs the income effect, so higher-income families end up having fewer children.

As confirmation, Becker notes that it is possible to distinguish the income and substitution effects, at least in part, by looking separately at the effects of changes in the incomes of men and women. Traditionally, women perform a greater proportion of childcare than men. In a family where that is the case, an increase in a woman's income would have a stronger substitution effect than an increase in a man's income. The reason is that, in such a family, a woman with a high income would encounter a high opportunity cost for each hour taken off from work to devote to childcare. By assumption, the man would take few hours off for childcare regardless of his income. Empirical data, in fact, reveal such a pattern to be prevalent: Birth rates tend to vary directly with incomes earned by men because the income effect outweighs the relatively weak substitution effect. Birth rates vary inversely, however, with incomes earned by women, who experience a relatively stronger substitution effect.

What is it that parents substitute for a greater quantity of children when their incomes rise? Some, no doubt, substitute ski vacations in Austria, BMWs, and other luxuries. Yet, Becker notes, they have another reaction as well, one that is consistent with the theory of consumer choice. In place of a greater number of children, he says, upper-income families substitute investment in higher-quality children: piano lessons from the age of five, tutors to help cram for SAT exams, tuition payments to Yale Law School. It's all so *rational*, says Becker.

5.3 Consumer Surplus

This chapter looked at consumer choice and the demand curve from two perspectives—that of utility theory and that of income and substitution effects. In both cases, the demand curve was viewed as answering the question. How much of a good will consumers wish to purchase at any given price? In this section, we turn to a different question to which the demand curve also can provide an answer: How much will consumers be willing to pay for an additional unit of a good, given the quantity they already have?

The Demand Curve as Willingness to Pay

Figure 5.1 shows a demand curve for apples for a college student, Hannah Lee. Lee stocks up on snack foods at a local supermarket and often includes apples in her purchases. The demand curve given in the figure shows that the number of apples she eats each month depends on their price. Currently the price of an apple is $.40. At this price, she buys ten per month. On other days, she substitutes an orange or a banana.

FIGURE 5.1   CONSUMER SURPLUS

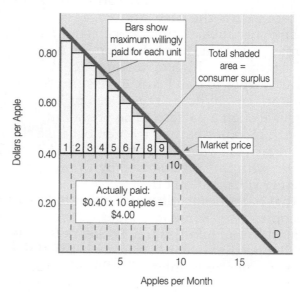

The height of a demand curve shows the maximum that this consumer would be willing to pay for an additional unit of a good. For example, she would be willing to pay up to $.85 for the first apple bought each month but only $.55 for the seventh. A vertical bar shows the maximum she would willingly pay for each unit. In this case, the market price is $.40; thus, she buys 10 apples a month, paying a total of $4.00. The difference between what she actually pays at the market price and the maximum she would have been willing to pay, shown by the shaded area, is **consumer surplus**.

The demand curve shows that $.40 is the most that Lee would be willing to pay for the tenth apple. If the price rose to $.45, she would substitute some other fruit for the tenth apple. However, she would not cut out apples altogether. Although $.40 is the most she is willing to pay for the tenth apple, she would not give up the ninth apple unless the price rose above $.45. Similarly, she would be willing to pay up to $.50 before giving up the eighth apple, up to $.55 before giving up the seventh, and so on. The height of the demand curve at each point (emphasized here by a vertical bar) shows the most that she would pay for each unit consumed. That maximum decreases as the quantity consumed increases, in accordance with the principle of diminishing marginal utility.

Measuring the Surplus

Figure 5.1 shows the most that Lee is willing to pay for various quantities of apples, but it also shows that she need not pay this amount. At the going price of $.40, she pays only a total of $4 for the ten apples she buys each month. Except for the last unit purchased, she gets each unit for less than what she would willingly have paid for it. We call the difference between the most she would have paid for each unit and the amount paid at the market price the **consumer surplus** for that unit. The figure shows the consumer surplus on each unit as the shaded portion of the corresponding vertical bar. For example, the surplus on the first apple, for which Lee would have paid up to $.85, but for which she actually paid only $40, is $.45. The total consumer surplus on all units purchased is the sum of the shaded portions of the bars. The area of the triangle between the demand curve and the market price provides an approximate measure of consumer surplus.

Consumer surplus

The difference between the maximum that a consumer would be willing to pay for a unit of a good and the amount that he or she actually pays

Consumer Surplus, Producer Surplus, and Gains from Exchange

We can extend the same reasoning to the producers' side of the market. Consider Figure 5.2, which shows supply and demand curves for a typical market. The intersection of the supply and demand curves shows the equilibrium market price. The demand curve, as we have seen, measures the maximum amount that most consumers would pay for each unit—for example, $1.50 for the one thousandth unit. Consumer surplus is the difference between the most that consumers would have been willing to pay and what they actually pay at the market price.

Now turn to the supply curve. The height of the supply curve at any point represents the lowest price that producers would accept for that unit. For example, producers would not accept less than $.75 for the one-thousandth unit sold. If they could not get at least that much, they would divert their resources to another use rather than produce the one thousandth unit of this product.

However, as the figure is drawn, producers receive the market price of $1 per unit for all units sold, including the one thousandth. On that unit, they earn a producer surplus of $.25. The **producer surplus** earned on each unit is the difference between the market price and the minimum that the producers would accept in exchange for that unit, for example, the difference between $1 and $.75 for the one thousandth unit. The total producer surplus earned on all units is the area between the supply curve and the market price.

Producer surplus

The difference between what producers receive for a unit of a good and the minimum they would be willing to accept

We see, then, that there is symmetry to the concept of market surplus. Consumers buy the goods, except for the very last unit, for less than the maximum amount they would have been willing to pay; and producers sell the goods, except for the very last unit, for more than the least they would have been willing to accept. The conclusion: *both buyers and sellers gain from exchange.* That is why markets exist. As long as buying and selling is voluntary, markets make everyone better off than they would be if they did not participate. Assuming an equilibrium at the intersection of the supply and demand curves, as in Figure 5.2, the total of the mutual gains from exchange—consumer surplus plus producer surplus—is equal to the entire shaded triangle between the supply and demand curves to the left of their intersection point.

FIGURE 5.2   GAINS FROM EXCHANGE

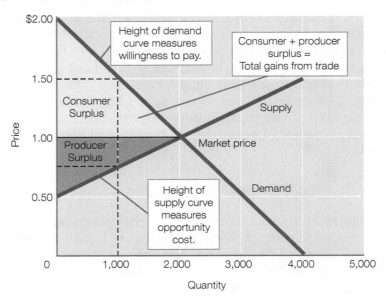

This figure shows that both consumers and producers gain from exchange. The equilibrium market price is $1 per unit. The demand curve shows the most that consumers would pay for each unit. The area between the demand curve and the market price shows the consumers' gains from exchange, in the form of consumer surplus. The supply curve shows the least that producers would accept rather than put their resources to work elsewhere. Producers earn a surplus equal to the difference between what they actually receive at the market price and the minimum they would have been willing to accept. The producer surplus corresponds to the area between the supply curve and the market price. Total gains from exchange are equal to the entire area between the curves up to their point of intersection.

Application: The Excess Burden of a Tax

Figure 5.3 uses consumer and producer surplus to analyze the effects of a price of a tax on gasoline. Imposing a $1.00-per-gallon tax on gasoline shifts the supply curve upward by $1.00 and raises the equilibrium price, including tax, from $2.00 to $2.80 per gallon. The price received by sellers, after tax, falls from $2.00 to $1.80 per gallon.

FIGURE 5.3   EXCESS BURDEN OF A TAX

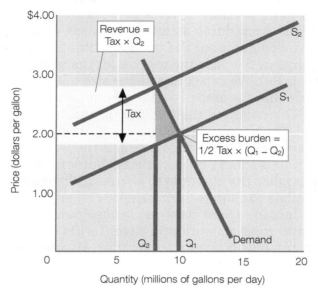

Imposing a tax of $1.00 per gallon on gasoline raises the equilibrium price from $2.00 to $2.80 per gallon. The price that sellers receive after they pay the tax falls to $1.80. Revenue collected by the government equals the tax times Q_2, the equilibrium quantity after tax. The economic burden of the tax falls partly on consumers and partly on producers. There is also an excess burden, which takes the form of the unrealized consumer and producer surpluses from the added units that would have been sold without the tax. The excess burden is equal to the area of the triangle between the supply and demand curves and between the pretax quantity, Q_1, and the after-tax quantity, Q_2.

To get a complete picture of the impact of the tax, we need to look beyond the price changes to the effects on consumer and producer surplus. Figure 5.3 shows that the tax brings in $8 million per day in revenue, equal to the after-tax quantity Q_2 (8 million gallons) times the amount of the tax ($1.00 per gallon). Part of that revenue comes from the surplus consumers would have captured by being able to buy 8 million gallons at $2.00 rather than at $2.80. Part comes from the producer surplus sellers would have earned by selling 8 million gallons at $2.00 rather than at $1.80. The sum of those two amounts equals the tax revenue collected by the government.

In addition, there is a further burden on consumers and producers that does not generate any revenue for the government. That part of the burden of the tax arises from the 2-million-gallon reduction in the quantity sold. The surplus that consumers would have received from that extra 2 million gallons is equal to the triangle above the pretax price of $2.00 between Q_1 and Q_2. Similarly, producers would have earned a surplus equal to the triangle below the pretax price between Q_1 and Q_2. We call the lost consumer-plus-producer surplus the **excess burden of the tax**.

Excess burden of the tax

The part of the economic burden of a tax that takes the form of consumer and producer surplus that is lost because the tax reduces the equilibrium quantity sold

The common sense behind this is that a tax imposes a burden on consumers and producers that is larger than the amount the government takes in as revenue. It does so because the tax discourages buyers and sellers from doing as much business with one another as they would have done without the tax. The potential mutual gain from pushing exchange in the gasoline market all the way out to 10 million gallons per day is lost. We can compute the size of the excess burden by applying the rule that the area of a triangle equals one-half of its height times its base. The height is the tax ($1.00), and the base is $Q_1 - Q_2$ (2 million gallons). Thus, the excess burden is $1 million per day. The total burden on consumers plus producers equals the $8 million collected by the government plus this $1 million excess burden, or $9 million.

We can generalize the example to all taxes. Virtually any tax causes firms or individuals to change their behavior by engaging in less of the taxed activity. Income taxes have an excess burden related to their reduction of incentives to work and save. Tariffs on imports have an excess burden related to the fact that they discourage international trade. The excess burden of a tax is just as much a part of the opportunity cost of the services that the government supplies as are the taxes actually collected by the government.

Summary

1. **What key elements influence consumer choices?** Consumers choose rationally when they set goals and make systematic efforts to achieve them. Their choices are influenced by objectives and constraints on opportunities. The objective is *utility*—the pleasure and satisfaction that people get from goods and services. The added utility obtained from a one-unit increase in consumption of a good or service is its *marginal utility*. The greater the rate of consumption of a good, the smaller the increase in utility from an additional unit consumed. Prices and incomes are the most important constraints on consumer choices.

2. **How do consumers balance their choices of goods and services to achieve equilibrium?** *Consumer equilibrium* occurs when consumers cannot increase the total utility they obtain from a given budget by shifting spending from one good to another. In equilibrium, the marginal utility of a dollar's worth of one good equals the marginal utility of a dollar's worth of any other good.

3. **How do price changes affect the quantities of goods demanded?** We can separate the change in quantity demanded caused by a given change in price into two parts. The part that comes from the tendency to substitute cheaper goods for more costly ones is the *substitution effect*. The part that comes from the increase in real income that results from a decrease in the price of the good, other things being equal, is the *income effect*.

4. **Why do demand curves have negative slopes?** For a normal good, the substitution and income effects work in the same direction. The demand curves for normal goods, therefore, have negative slopes. For inferior goods, the income effect and the substitution effect work in opposite directions. That means the demand curve for an inferior good will have a negative slope only if the substitution effect outweighs the income effect. In practice, this is almost always the case, although *Giffen goods* with positively sloped demand curves are a theoretical possibility.

5. **Why do both consumers and producers gain from exchange?** When consumers buy a product at its market price, they usually pay the same amount for each unit purchased. However, because of the *principle of diminishing marginal utility*, the first units purchased are worth more to them than the last ones they purchase. The difference between what consumers actually pay for a unit of a good and the most they would be willing to pay is the *consumer surplus* gained on that unit of the good. Similarly, the difference between what sellers actually receive for a good and the least they would have accepted is the *producer surplus*.

(Continues)

6. **Why does the burden of a tax exceed the revenue raised by government?** When the government puts a tax on a good or service, the equilibrium price including the tax rises while the equilibrium price net of the tax falls. As a result, the equilibrium quantity falls, making both consumers and producers forgo some surplus. We call the forgone surplus that is not captured in the form of tax revenue the *excess burden of the tax*. It is a burden on consumers and producers over and above what the government collects as tax revenue.

Key Terms   Page

Problems and Topics for Discussion

1. **Externalities of automobile safety**   The increase in deaths of pedestrians and bicyclists resulting from drivers' use of seat belts or air bags is an example of an *externality,* a concept introduced in Chapter 4. What could the government do to prevent this externality while still achieving the goal of increased driver safety? Bonus question: If you complete the appendix to this chapter, analyze the trade-off between speed and safety using an indifference curve diagram. How does the installation of seat belts in a car change the budget line?

2. **Can there be increasing marginal utility?**   Can there be increasing marginal utility in some cases? For example, suppose it would take eight rolls of wallpaper to decorate your kitchen. If someone gave you seven rolls of wallpaper, you would get only limited utility from them. An eighth roll, however, would give you great utility. Do you think this is a valid exception to the principle of diminishing marginal utility?

3. **Consumer equilibrium, marginal utility, and prices**   Martha Smith consumes two pounds of pork and five pounds of beef per month. She pays $1.50 a pound for the pork and $2 per pound for the beef. What can you say about the ratio of the marginal utility of pork to the marginal utility of beef, assuming that this pattern represents a state of consumer equilibrium for Smith? Is the ratio 3/4, 4/3, 5/2, 2/5, or none of these?

4. **Excess burden of a tax**   Figure 2.3 in Chapter 2 shows supply and demand curves for chicken. Using the approach outlined in this chapter, calculate the revenue raised by a $.50 per pound tax on chicken and the excess burden of the tax. How much of the excess burden is borne by consumers? How much by producers?

Case for Discussion

The Food Panic of 2010: Gone but Not Forgotten

World food prices are notoriously volatile, rising and falling with the weather and political developments, as well as from purely economic causes. Few recent years have seen as much instability as 2010, however. As the chart shows, the world food price index from the Food and Agriculture Organization rose more sharply in the second half of 2010 than in any recent year.

Increases in prices for some crops had specific causes. Wheat prices rose because of simultaneous droughts in Russia and Australia, two big producers. Corn prices rose, in part, because U.S. policy encouraged diversion of corn from food to ethanol production. What was remarkable, though, was that the price increases extended to all grains—including rice, a staple of millions in Asia, and even minor grains like barley and millet. Vegetable oils were also affected.

The political and social consequences were dramatic. Food riots occurred in countries as far apart as Mexico and Mozambique, as prices cut sharply into the budgets of poor families. Governments in some countries like India reacted with emergency laws prohibiting hoarding or blamed the increases on mysterious speculators in far-away financial markets.

An especially worrisome concern was the possibility that shortages would feed on themselves. Some food officials warned that high prices would force even middle-income families to move away from a healthy, diversified diet to one based almost entirely on staple grains. If that happened, high prices could actually lead to an increase in demand, making the crisis still worse.

The FAO world food price index hit a record high in early 2011, but then eased again as growing conditions improved. Food experts at international agencies warn that the crisis of 2010 shows an underlying fragility of the world food situation, in which one or two isolated crop failures can quickly spread throughout the world.

Source of chart: Food and Agriculture Organization, FAO Food price index, February 9, 2012 (http://www.fao.org/worldfoodsituation/wfs-home/foodpricesindex/en/).

Questions

1. Why do the prices of all grains tend to rise together? Does this give you any clue as to whether consumers treat the goods as complements or as substitutes?

2. Why would an increase in the price of a good like rice lead to hoarding? Do you think laws preventing hoarding will make things better for consumers in the short run? In the long run?

3. Why do food officials worry that an increase in the price of staple grains could cause an increase in consumption? Explain in terms of the income and substitution effects. What does this possibility suggest about the slope of the demand curve for rice?

4. Bonus question: Using tools introduced in the appendix, sketch a set of indifference curves and budget lines to illustrate the case in which an increase in the price of rice leads to an increase in the quantity demanded.

Endnotes

1. The positive slope of the demand curve for a Giffen good assumes a fully rational consumer. The Case for Discussion in Chapter 4 introduced the possibility that goods like house-brand supermarket goods may also have positively-sloped demand curves, but for a different reason. In the case of house-brand goods, consumers buy less of a product that is "too cheap" because bounded rationality causes them to rely on a rule of thumb that associates higher price with higher quality.

2. Sam Peltzman, "The Effects of Automobile Safety Regulation," *Journal of Political Economy* 83 (August 1975): 677–725. In a follow-up study, Robert W. Crandall and John D. Graham ("Automobile Safety Regulation and Offsetting Behavior: Some New Empirical Estimates," *American Economic Review* 74 (May 1984): 328–331) also found that safety regulation had unintended consequences on driving behavior.

3. An advanced microeconomics course would explain that for reasons associated with the income effect, the triangle does not provide a precise measure of consumer surplus. However, the approximation is close for goods that make up only a small part of consumers' total expenditures.

Appendix to Chapter 5:
Indifference Curves

The body of this chapter gives two versions of the theory of consumer choice—one based on marginal utility and the other on income and substitution effects. This appendix gives a third version, based on what economists call *indifference curves*. Indifference curves are not central to this book, but intermediate- and advanced-level economic writings often use them. Many students and instructors find it worthwhile to study them, even if briefly, as part of an introductory course. This appendix will serve their needs.

5A.1 Constructing an Indifference Curve

Begin by supposing that I am an experimenter and you are my subject. I want to find out how you feel about consuming various quantities of meat and cheese. It would be convenient if I had a utility meter, but I do not. Instead, to discover your attitudes toward the consumption of these goods, I offer you a number of baskets (two at a time) containing varying amounts of meat and cheese.

As I offer each pair of baskets, I ask: "Would you prefer the one on the left to the one on the right? Would you prefer the one on the right to the one on the left? Or are you indifferent between the two?" In this way, I hope to get a meaningful answer from you. I know I have a better chance of getting an answer this way than I would if I asked you how many utils you would get from each basket.

At some point in the experiment, I offer you basket A, which contains eight pounds of meat and three pounds of cheese, and basket B, which contains six pounds of meat and four pounds of cheese. I ask you the usual questions, and you answer that you are indifferent between the two baskets. You feel that the extra pound of cheese in basket B just makes up for the fact that it has two pounds less meat than basket A. This gives me a useful bit of information: It tells me that for you baskets A and B belong to an **indifference set**—a set of consumption choices each of which yields the same amount of satisfaction such that no member of the set is preferred to any other. Exploring the matter further, I find that two other baskets, C and D, also belong to the same indifference set, which now has the following four members:

Indifference set

A set of consumption choices, each of which yields the same utility so that no member of the set is preferred to any other

Basket	Meat (Pounds)	Cheese (Pounds)
A	8	3
B	6	4
C	5	5
D	4	7

Having thanked you for taking part in my experiment, I get out a piece of graph paper. First, I draw a pair of axes, as in Figure 5A.1. I put pounds of meat on the horizontal axis and pounds of cheese on the vertical axis. Each basket of goods corresponds to a point in the area between the two axes, as, for example, the points representing baskets A B, C, and D. Those points and all others that lie on the smooth curve joining them are members of the same indifference set. The curve itself is an **indifference curve**—a curve composed of points that are all members of the same indifference set.

Indifference curve

A graphical representation of an indifference set

FIGURE 5A.1   AN INDIFFERENCE CURVE

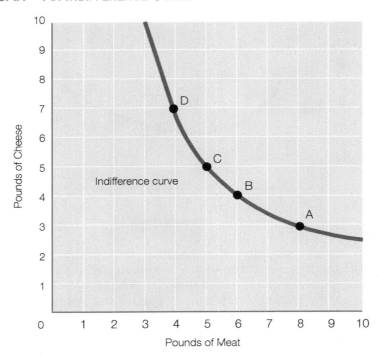

Each point in this diagram stands for a basket of meat and cheese. A, B, C, and D are baskets among which a certain consumer is indifferent. All give equal utility. Those points and all the others on a smooth curve connecting them form an indifference set. An indifference curve is a graphical representation of an indifference set.

5A.2 Some Characteristics of Indifference Curves

Indifference curves have characteristics that reflect certain regularities in patterns of consumer preferences. Five of these are of interest to us:

1. *Indifference curves normally have negative slopes.* For example, the curve in Figure 5A.2 is not possible if both meat and cheese are desired goods—that is, if the consumer prefers more to less, other things being equal. The basket shown by point A contains more of both goods than that shown by point B. This implies that if greater amounts of meat and cheese give greater satisfaction, A must be preferred to B; it cannot be a member of the same indifference set as B.

FIGURE 5A.2   INDIFFERENCE CURVES HAVE NEGATIVE SLOPES

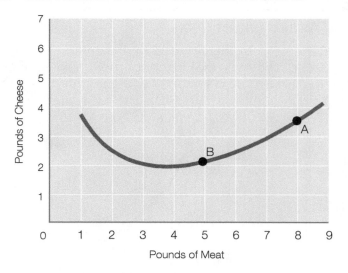

Indifference curves normally have negative slopes. The positively sloped portion of the indifference curve shown here is impossible if both goods give increased satisfaction with increased quantity. A has more of both goods than B. Therefore, point A should be preferred to point B and, hence, could not lie on the same indifference curve.

---

2. *The absolute value of the slope of an indifference curve at any point is the ratio of the marginal utility of the good on the horizontal axis to the marginal utility of the good on the vertical axis.* For example, look at Figure 5A.1. Between D and C, the slope of the curve is approximately –2 (or simply 2 when we take out the minus sign to give the absolute value). This shows that the marginal utility of meat is approximately twice that of cheese when the amounts

consumed are in the region of baskets C and D. Because the marginal utility of meat is twice that of cheese in this region, the consumer will feel neither a gain nor a loss in total utility in trading basket D for basket C, that is, in giving up two pounds of cheese for one extra pound of meat. Because it shows the rate at which a consumer can substitute meat for cheese without a gain or loss in satisfaction, we call the slope of the indifference curve the **marginal rate of substitution** of meat for cheese.

3. *Indifference curves are convex; their slopes decrease as one moves downward and to the right along them.* This implies that the ratio of the marginal utility of meat to the marginal utility of cheese (or the marginal rate of substitution of meat for cheese) decreases as one moves downward and to the right along the curve. Look once more at Figure 5A.1. In the region between D and C the slope of the curve is approximately –2, indicating that the ratio of the marginal utility of meat to that of cheese is approximately 2:1. By comparison, in the region between B and A the slope is only about –1/2. The substitution of meat for cheese has caused the ratio of the marginal utility of meat to the marginal utility of cheese to fall to approximately 1:2.

4. *We can draw an indifference curve through the point that represents any basket of goods.* In Figure 5A.3 we show the same indifference curve as in Figure 5A.1, now giving it the label I_1. Point E, which represents a basket containing seven pounds of meat and five pounds of cheese, is not a member of the indifference set represented by this curve. Because it lies above and to the right of point B and has more of both products than B, it must be preferred to B. Other points, such as F and G, have more cheese and less meat than E and, on balance, give the same satisfaction as E. The consumer is indifferent among E, F, G, and all other points on curve I_2 and prefers all of these points to any of those on I_1.

Any point taken at random, along with the other points that happen to give the same amount of satisfaction, can form an indifference curve. Several other (unlabeled) curves also appear in Figure 5A.3. Were all possible curves drawn in, they would be so close together that the lines would run into a solid sheet, completely filling the space between the axes. We call a selection of indifference curves showing their general pattern but leaving enough space to make the graph easy to read an **indifference map**.

Marginal rate of substitution

The rate at which a consumer can substitute one good for another with no gain or loss in satisfaction

Indifference map

A selection of indifference curves for a single consumer and pair of goods

FIGURE 5A.3   MULTIPLE INDIFFERENCE CURVES

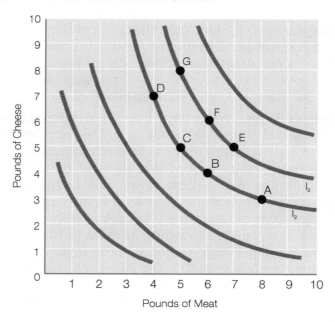

We can draw an indifference curve through any point. Here curve I_1 represents an indifference set containing points A, B, C, and D, and I_2 represents a set including points E, F, and G. All points on I_2 are preferred to all points on I_1. We call a representative set of indifference curves like these an indifference map.

Transitivity

The principle that if A is preferred to B and B is preferred to C, A must be preferred to C

5. *Indifference curves do not cross.* Consumer preferences have the property of **transitivity**, meaning that if you prefer A to B and B to C, you will prefer A to C. Looking at Figure 5A.4, you can see that crossed indifference curves are not possible. Consider points A, B, and C. A and B lie on the same indifference curve, I_1; hence, the consumer is indifferent between them. A and C both lie on I_2; thus, the consumer is indifferent between them, too. Because consumer preferences are transitive, if B is as good as A, and A is as good as C, then C is as good as B. But C lies above and to the right of B. It represents a mix of goods that contains more of both meat and cheese. If more is better, the consumer must prefer C to B. Because crossed indifference curves imply a contradictory set of preferences, we must conclude that they cannot cross.

FIGURE 5A.4   INDIFFERENCE CURVES CANNOT CROSS

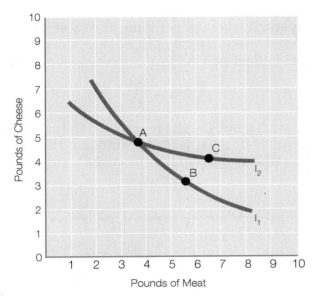

Because consumer preferences are transitive, indifference curves cannot cross. The impossible curves shown here represent contradictory preferences. A and B are both on I_1; therefore, the consumer must be indifferent between them. A and C are both on I_2; hence, the consumer must be indifferent between them as well. Transitivity implies that the consumer is indifferent between B and C, but this is impossible because C contains more of both goods than B does.

5A.3 The Budget Line

The range of choices open to a consumer with a given budget and with given prices can be shown on the same kind of graph we have used for indifference curves. Figure 5A.5 shows how to do it. Suppose you have a food budget of $10 per week, the price of meat is $2 a pound, and the price of cheese is $1 a pound. If you spend all your money on meat, you can have up to five pounds of meat; if you spend all your money on cheese, you can have up to ten pounds of cheese. Combinations such as two pounds of meat and six of cheese or four pounds of meat and two of cheese are also possible. Taking into account the possibility of buying a fraction of a pound of meat or cheese, we show these choices on the graph as a diagonal line called a **budget line** running from 10 on the cheese axis to 5 on the meat axis.

Using m to stand for amount of meat and c for amount of cheese, the equation for the budget line is

$$2m + 1c = 10.$$

Budget line

A line showing the various combinations of goods and services that consumers can buy at given prices with a given budget

This equation simply says that the number of pounds of meat bought times the price of meat plus the number of pounds of cheese bought times the price of cheese must add up to the total budget if all the money is spent. In more general terms, the equation for a budget line for goods x and y—with P_x the price of x, P_y the price of y, and B the consumer's total budget is:

$$P_xX + P_yY = B.$$

The slope of such a budget line is $-P_x/P_y$. In the case shown in Figure 5A.5, where the price of meat is $2 a pound and the price of cheese is $1 a pound, the slope of the budget line is –2.

FIGURE 5A.5   THE BUDGET LINE

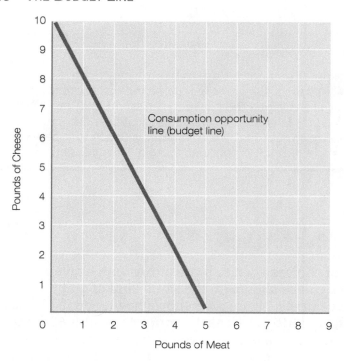

Suppose you have a food budget of $10 per week. You can spend your money on meat at $2 a pound, on cheese at $1 a pound, or on some mix of the two. The consumption opportunity line (budget line) shows all the possible combinations given these prices and your budget.

5A.4 A Graphic Representation of Consumer Equilibrium

Indifference curves and the budget line give a useful graphic representation of consumer equilibrium. Figure 5A.6 shows the budget line from Figure 5A.5 superimposed on an indifference map like the one shown in Figure 5A.3. In this way, we can easily compare consumer preferences and consumption choices. For example, point B is preferred to point A because it lies on a "higher" indifference curve (one that at some point, such as C, passes above and to the right of A). By similar reasoning, point B is preferred to point D. Of all the points on or below the budget line, it is clear that point E, which represents two and a half pounds of meat and five pounds of cheese, is the most preferred, because all the other points on it lie on lower indifference curves. Every point that is better (like F) lies outside the range of consumption choices.

FIGURE 5A.6   CONSUMER EQUILIBRIUM

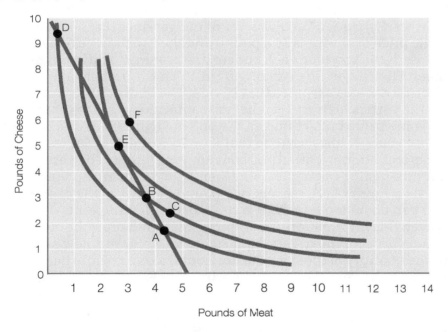

E is the point of consumer equilibrium given the indifference curves and budget line shown. All points that are better than E (such as F) lie outside the budget line. All other points for goods that the consumer can afford to buy (such as A and D) lie on lower indifference curves than E and hence are less preferred.

Because E is the point that gives the greatest possible satisfaction, it is the point of consumer equilibrium. At E, the relevant indifference curve is just tangent to the budget line; this means that the slopes of the curve and the budget line are the same at that point. The slope of the indifference curve, as shown earlier, equals the ratio of the marginal utility of meat to the marginal utility of cheese. The slope of the budget line equals the ratio of the price of meat to the price of cheese. Thus, it follows that in consumer equilibrium,

$$\frac{\text{Marginal utility of meat}}{\text{Marginal utility of cheese}} = \frac{\text{Price of meat}}{\text{Price of cheese}}$$

This is a restatement of the condition for consumer equilibrium given in this chapter.

5A.5 Derivation of the Demand Curve

This appendix concludes with Figure 5A.7, which shows how to derive a demand curve for meat from a set of indifference curves. Along with the curves, Figure 5A.7 shows a set of budget lines. Each line assumes that the price of cheese is $1 a pound and the consumer's budget is $10, as before. Now, however, each budget line assumes a different price, P_m, of meat. The budget line running from 10 on the vertical axis to 2.5 on the horizontal axis assumes that P_m = $4. The budget line running from 10 on the vertical axis to 5 on the horizontal axis assumes that P_m = $2. (This is the same budget line as the one in Figures 5A.5 and 5A.6.) The other two budget lines assume that P_m = $1.50 and P_m = $1, respectively.

The equilibrium pattern of consumption differs for each price of meat, other things being equal. When P_m = $4, point A, which represents six pounds of cheese and one pound of meat, is the best the consumer can do; when P_m = $2, B is the most preferred point.

Given this information, it is a simple matter to draw the consumer's demand curve for meat. Part (b) of Figure 5A.7 shows a new set of axes, with the quantity of meat on the horizontal axis as before but the price of meat on the vertical axis. From Part (a) of Figure 5A.7 when P_m = $4 the consumer chooses combination A, which includes one pound of meat. In Part (b), therefore, we mark point a as the quantity of meat demanded at a price of $4; then we add point b, which corresponds to point B in Part (a); and so on. Drawing a smooth line through points a, b, c, and d gives the consumer's demand curve for meat. As expected, it has the downward slope predicted by the law of demand.

FIGURE 5A.7   DERIVATION OF A DEMAND CURVE

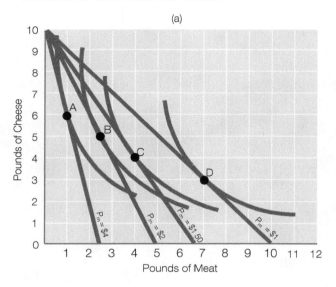

(a)

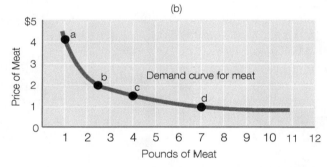

(b)

Part (a) of this figure shows a consumer's indifference map for meat and cheese and a set of budget lines. Each budget line corresponds to a different price, P_m, of meat. All four budget lines assume the price of cheese to be $1 and the total budget to be $10. Points A, B, C, and D in Part (a) show the choices the consumer makes at meat prices of $4, $2, $1.50, and $1. Part (b), plots the data on meat consumption at the various prices on a new set of axes. The smooth line connecting points a, b, c, and d is the consumer's demand curve for meat.

Chapter 6

The Economics *of* Climate Change *and* Environmental Policy

After reading this chapter, you will understand the following:

1. How we can understand the problem of climate change and other environmental issues in terms of externalities

2. How property rights and private negotiation can help control externalities

3. What government policies are available to control externalities

4. How we can apply public choice theory to environmental issues

Before reading this chapter, make sure you know the meaning of the following concepts:

1. Positive and normative economics

2. Externalities

3. Property rights

4. Market failure and government failure

5. Transaction costs

6. Public choice theory

Externalities, as we learned in Chapter 4, are effects that production or consumption activities have on third parties. Pollution is one of the most important kinds of externality. It undermines the efficiency of the price system because the harm to pollution victims does not enter into market prices. As a result, users of any product that causes pollution receive a false signal that tells them "use more," when a price equal to the true opportunity cost would tell them "use less."

For example, when you fill the gas tank of your car, the price at the pump reflects costs of pumping crude oil out of the ground, transporting it, refining it, and distributing it through the retail network. However, the price does not fully reflect the environmental damage done either in production (drilling, refining, transporting) or in end use (the pollutants emitted through your tailpipe).

Some forms of pollution from the production and use of oil and other forms of energy have been sources of concern for years. The smog that used to choke the air of Los Angeles and is still present in many third-world cities is an example. More recently, climate change has become the most talked-about environmental issue. According to widely used scientific models, greenhouse gasses from industrial and consumer sources trap heat within the earth's atmosphere. That causes a gradual warming of the planet, which in turn has the potential to trigger changes not just in temperature but also in rainfall patterns, storm tracks, ocean currents, and so on. On balance, the changes in climate appear more likely to be harmful than helpful.

This chapter takes a closer look at the problem of climate change and other pollution issues, and at policy changes that could help restore the efficient working of price systems.

6.1 Pollution Abatement as a Problem of Scarcity

Pollution, says the *American Heritage Dictionary*, is "the contamination of soil, water, or the atmosphere by noxious substances." That is a fine definition—from the victim's point of view. To understand pollution as an economic problem, however, we must consider the polluter's point of view as well. People do not—at least we hope they do not—pollute the environment just for the fun of it. Instead, they do so because it is an inexpensive way of getting rid of wastes. Seen from this perspective, it is clear that pollution is a problem of scarcity. The earth's scarce air, water, and other resources cannot absorb unlimited waste without serious harm.

The Costs of Pollution Abatement

The types of pollution that are most in the news involve noxious gases, toxic chemicals, and bulky solids that are by-products of commercial activities. Polluters, left to their own devices, have an incentive to choose the lowest-cost method of getting rid of these by-products; this often means discharging by-products directly into the environment. *Pollution abatement* means taking measures to reduce the open discharge of harmful wastes through changes in production methods, recycling, capture and storage, or other methods. Abatement reduces the impact on the environment; but, at the same time, it increases the cost to the polluter of waste disposal.

Figure 6.1 uses the example of carbon dioxide (CO_2) emissions from a coal-burning power plant to illustrate the cost of pollution abatement. The label "business as usual" shows amount of CO_2 emitted by the plant if the firm makes no abatement efforts. Beginning from that point, the plant could reduce emissions using several strategies. For example, the least expensive approach might be to improve the efficiency of the generating equipment. All of the CO_2 from burning the coal would still go into the air, but the plant would not have to burn as much coal per kilowatt-hour of electricity. The approach could eliminate perhaps a third of the CO_2, at a cost of less than $10 per ton. If the plant wanted to reduce CO_2 pollution still more, it could switch its fuel from coal to natural gas. The figure suggests that doing so could eliminate about half of the remaining pollution, but at a higher cost—around $15 per ton of CO_2 avoided.

The lowest-cost method of getting rid of by-products often means discharging them directly into the environment.

Finally, using still-experimental technology to capture and store the CO_2 instead of releasing it into the air could theoretically eliminate nearly all of the CO_2. The figure shows that doing so might cost from $20 to $40 per ton of avoided CO_2, or even more.

FIGURE 6.1   COST OF POLLUTION ABATEMENT

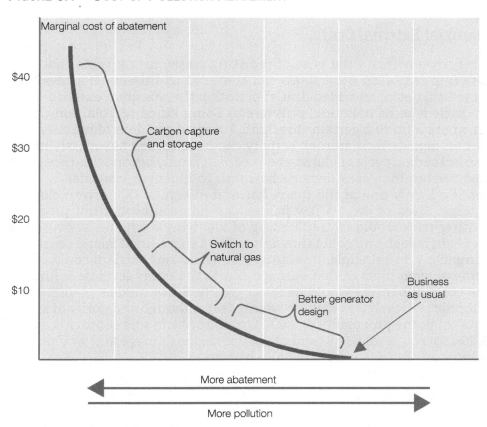

This graph shows the hypothetical costs of reducing carbon dioxide from a coal-fired electric power plant. With no pollution control, emissions would be at the "business as usual" level. The cheapest method of pollution abatement, improving the efficiency of the generating equipment, could eliminate about a third of the pollution at a cost of less than $10 per ton. Switching to natural gas would eliminate even more pollution, and using still-experimental carbon capture and storage technology could eliminate almost all of it. Decreasing pollution still more requires progressively more expensive abatement technologies. For that reason, as the amount of pollution decreases, the marginal cost of abatement increases.

The numbers in the figure are only illustrative. The costs would vary from one source to another and would change as technology and costs of alternative fuels changed. However, they suggest a principle that

Marginal cost of abatement

The cost of reducing waste discharged into the environment by one unit

applies to nearly every source of pollution: The cost of reducing pollution by one more unit, known as the **marginal cost of abatement**, increases as the degree of abatement increases. Since the diagram shows increasing pollution from left to right and increasing abatement from right to left, the principle of increasing marginal cost of abatement is shown by a negatively-sloped curve that becomes steeper as it approaches the vertical axis.

Marginal External Cost

Marginal external cost

The total additional cost to all affected parties of an added unit of pollution

We turn now from the cost of reducing waste to the costs that pollution imposes on others. We call the total additional cost to all affected parties of an added unit of pollution the **marginal external cost**.

Each type of pollution is different. Some kinds of pollution do no harm at all up to a certain threshold. For example, a certain amount of carbon dioxide from human activity can be absorbed harmlessly in the natural carbon cycle of plants and oceans. It is only beyond this threshold that further increases become harmful. To illustrate, consider a rising sea level, only one of the many harmful effects of CO_2-driven climate change. Rises of even a few inches can damage beachfront property. Further rises would cause flooding of low-lying farmland in countries like Bangladesh and could threaten to flood some small island countries completely. In principle, investment in dykes and barriers could offset some or even most of that damage; but as the ocean level rises further, the costs of barriers would increase greatly. Some models predict catastrophic sea level rises of up to twenty feet, although a majority of scientists think the probability of such a catastrophe in this century is small. A 20-foot sea-level rise would cause enormous damage and would overwhelm any human efforts to build barriers.

The same pattern appears when we consider other types of harm from climate change—damage from changes in rainfall, from extreme weather events, from reduction in biodiversity, and so on. In short, studies of many different effects of climate change suggest that as the earth's temperature rises, the harm done by an additional degree of warming—the marginal external cost—increases.

The Optimal Quantity of Pollution

Figure 6.2 combines a marginal cost of abatement curve similar to that in Figure 6.1 with a positively sloped curve representing marginal external cost. This time, the figure represents not the CO_2 emissions from a single plant but emissions for the world as a whole. The horizontal axis shows gigatons (billions of tons) of carbon dioxide equivalent or CO_2E. (CO_2E is a measure of greenhouse gasses that includes not only CO_2 but also other gasses like methane and nitrous oxide.)

FIGURE 6.2   THE OPTIMAL QUANTITY OF POLLUTION

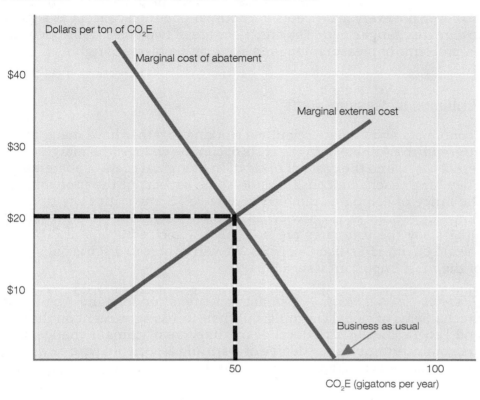

This figure shows a positively sloped curve for the marginal external cost of greenhouse gas emissions and a negatively sloped curve for the marginal cost of abatement. (To simplify the diagram, both curves are straight lines.) The intersection point is the economically optimal quantity of pollution. To the right of that point, the harm done by pollution exceeds the cost of eliminating it. To the left of that point, the cost of abatement is greater than the harm done by pollution.

The intersection point of the curves shows the economically optimal quantity of pollution. To the right of the intersection in Figure 6.2, it would be worthwhile to undertake additional abatement efforts because the external costs saved would be less than the cost of reducing greenhouse gas emissions. To the left of the intersection, the marginal cost of abatement exceeds the marginal external cost. For quantities of pollution below the optimal amount, further abatement is not cost effective. The relatively small amount of avoided harm is not enough to offset the scarce resources used to further reduce pollution.

To economists, the logic of the optimal quantity of pollution is no different from that underlying the choice of the least-cost method of producing running shoes or the choice of the optimal location for a new warehouse. Clearly, cleaning up the environment entails costs and trade-offs. Few people would advocate choosing either of the extremes—the whole world as an uninhabitable sewer or a pristine wilderness from which all humans have been eliminated. If we reject both extremes, says the economist, there must be an optimal point between them. However, not everyone accepts the optimal-pollution concept as a guide to climate change policy. The criticisms are of two types, some focusing on problems of measurement and some on problems of rights.

Problems of Measurement

Economists and climate scientists working together have made many attempts to estimate both the costs of climate change (the marginal external costs) and the costs of mitigation (marginal costs of abatement). They have reached a consensus on some aspects of the problem, but the range of estimates remains very wide[1]. Some critics say that the range of estimates is so wide as to offer no useful guidance at all. Others say the estimates are not only imprecise but are also biased toward business-as-usual policies. We will be able to discuss only a few of the most important issues here.

Scientific Uncertainties   Climate scientists understand the basic mechanisms of global warming, but there is less agreement on the size and geographical distribution of the impacts of climate change. One area of uncertainty is the degree of warming associated with any given increase in greenhouse gasses in the atmosphere. For example, ac-

cording to the Intergovernmental Panel on Climate Change (IPCC), the amount of additional warming associated with stabilizing CO_2 concentrations at 550 parts per million (well below the business-as-usual level) could be anywhere from 1 to 3.5 degrees centigrade. The effects of any given amount of warming are also uncertain. For example, two degrees of additional warming could produce anywhere from six inches to as much as three feet of additional sea level rise. Another problem is that increases in the average global temperature do not produce uniform changes in climate. Temperatures tend to change more near the poles and less near the equator. Storm tracks, rainfall patterns, and other details of climate change are still harder to predict, even though exactly those details may be critical to calculating damages. Complex climate feedback loops cause great difficulties, especially in forecasting climate change. For example, warming increases the release of methane from permafrost, which in turn causes additional warming; but warming also may increase cloud cover, which would reflect some solar energy back into space and slow warming.

Market and Nonmarket Damages   Once climate scientists have done their best to forecast the degree of future warming and the details of its effects on the climate, economists have to convert the costs and benefits into dollar terms. Market damages are all costs to which we can, in principle, assign a monetary value. For example, economists try to estimate the value of damage to crops. Many regions, especially near the tropics, will suffer a loss in farm productivity; but farm output in some northern regions will probably increase, at least with moderate degrees of warming. It is also possible to calculate market damages for sea level rise, increased storm intensity, and changes in energy used for heating and cooling. Nonmarket damages are harder to convert to monetary terms. Examples include health effects from the spread of malaria or changes in death tolls from heat and cold. It is harder still to measure damages to biodiversity and the recreational value of natural areas.

The Interaction of Economic Growth and Climate Change   The complex interaction between economic growth and climate change raises special problems. On the one hand, economic growth is the root cause of increased greenhouse gas emissions. The global warming forecasts of the IPCC, the IMF, and others assume continued economic growth in both advanced and developing market countries. For example, the IMF estimates that by the middle of the twenty-first century, the level of real income (that is, income expressed in today's dollars to eliminate the effect of inflation) will be about three times what it is now in the United States and about six times what it is now in developing countries. The IPCC forecasts that by 2100, world GDP per capita will be four to twenty times higher than it is today. In that case, the world average level of per capita income, including even the poorest countries, would be higher than that of the United States today. It is this enormous projected increase in economic activity that is the main driver of the expected, and feared, increase in global average temperatures.

Feedback mechanisms complicate the relationship between economic growth and climate change. For example, although growth contributes to climate change, climate change, in turn, tends to slow growth. According to estimates by the IMF, climate change is likely to cause world GDP at the end of the twenty-first century to be 1 to 7 percent below what it otherwise would be[2]. By the end of the twenty-second century, the loss could be from 3 to 35 percent. Keep in mind, however, that these losses are relative to the baseline. They do not mean that people living in 2100 will be 1 to 7 percent poorer than those living today because the baseline projections call for a very large increase. On the average, the world level of income for a family of four in 2100 (stated in today's U.S. dollars) could easily be as high as $100,000 without climate change, far above today's world average of about $16,000. If so, warming would reduce that from $100,000 per family to something like $93,000 to $99,000.

Costs of Abatement   Just as there are difficulties in measuring external costs of greenhouse gas pollution, it is also hard to measure costs of pollution abatement. Uncertainties regarding the relative future prices of carbon-based and renewable energy provide one reason. Price and income elasticities of demand for energy are also hard to estimate. Most difficult of all to forecast is the rate at which

BVT *Lab*

Flashcards are available for this chapter at www.BVTLab.com.

new technologies will come on line. Taking all of these uncertainties into account, the best estimate of the cost of stabilizing the atmospheric CO_2 level at 550 parts per million (above today's level but well below business as usual) appears to be about 1 to 2 percent of world GDP. Again, this means a reduction from a growing baseline level of GDP, not from today's level.

Comparing the Present and the Future   Probably the biggest difficulty of all in measuring the external costs and abatement costs is that of comparing costs that occur now with those that will occur in the distant future. Climate change is a process that plays out over a time frame of centuries. Even in the impossible event that we could reduce greenhouse gas emissions to zero tomorrow, the earth would continue to warm gradually and the ocean would continue to rise for hundreds of years, although more slowly than otherwise, before reaching equilibrium.

As a result, climate policy requires trading off costs that occur now to obtain benefits not only for the children and grandchildren of those living today, but also for tens of generations in the future. How can we compare the value of a dollar taken from consumption or production today with increased health or welfare of someone living one hundred years from now? Different methods of answering this question are the single greatest source of disagreement in estimating the net costs and benefits of policies to slow climate change. The appendix to this chapter more fully discusses the comparison of costs and benefits over time.

Problems of Rights

In addition to the problem that we can measure neither external costs nor abatement costs accurately, the optimal-pollution concept encounters a second criticism, arising from the notion that pollution is a violation of the rights of its victims[3]. In that regard, pollution is similar to the crimes of theft, vandalism, or assault. We are not guided solely by economic trade-offs in our treatment of those crimes, nor should we be in the case of pollution.

Suppose, for example, that a vandal breaks into a person's home and slashes a valuable painting. How should a court decide the case? Should it listen to testimony from the owner about the painting's value, hear testimony from the vandal about the thrill of slashing it, and then weigh the vandal's thrill-value against the owner's artistic sensibility? Such an approach would outrage most people. They would say that the vandal violated the owner's right to enjoy the painting and that the vandal's thrills from the slashing should count for nothing. Similarly, people who take the rights-based approach to pollution argue that no possible saving of abatement costs can negate the polluter's duty to respect the rights of victims. Unless the polluter gets permission from the victim, or pays full compensation for harm caused (including subjective, non-economic harm), pollution should cease, regardless of the relative levels of abatement costs and external costs.

The discussion that follows employs the optimal pollution concept, but the reader should keep in mind that it is not the only possible point of view.

6.2 Controlling Externalities Through Voluntary Exchange

In Chapter 1, we viewed markets as ways to coordinate plans among producers and consumers. Under proper conditions, we can count on markets to provide us with shoes, cars, and lawn care services in something close to the optimal quantities and to use scarce resources efficiently in doing so. Now we ask under what conditions markets can provide efficient control of externalities.

Markets Without Transaction Costs

We can begin by seeing how voluntary exchange would handle the problem of pollution in a world without transaction costs. In such a world, technical information about the causes and effects of pollution is available to everyone at no cost. Also, people do not behave opportunis-tically. They honestly share information about how much it would be worth to escape the effects of pollution, and they voluntarily abide by any agreements they reach.

To keep things simple, we will first look not at the complex issue of climate change but at a smaller, more local problem. We will suppose that there is a steel mill owned by John Miller, and downwind from it a forest owned by Joan Forester. Noxious fumes from the steel mill are killing the trees in the forest. How can Forester and Miller resolve the problem?

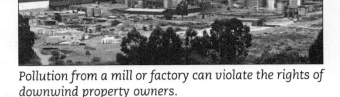

Pollution from a mill or factory can violate the rights of downwind property owners.

Property Rights   To know how the situation will be handled, we first need to know the property rights of Miller and Forester, especially as property rights affect use of the air. There are two possibilities. One is that the owner of the forest has a right to prevent pollution of the forest air. The other is that the owner of the mill has a right to dump wastes into the air regardless of where they end up. Why does it matter?

First, suppose that the air rights belong to Forester. Acting on the basis of those rights, she goes to Miller and tells him her trees are being damaged by pollution from his mill. He agrees he must do something. After an open and honest discussion, they agree on one of these three solutions:

1. Miller agrees to stop the pollution. He does so either by installing pollution-control equipment or by shutting down the mill, whichever is less costly to him.

2. Miller agrees to compensate Forester for the value of the trees killed by pollution. This alternative will be better for both parties if the value of the trees killed by the pollution is less than the cost of pollution abatement.

3. Miller agrees to buy the forest at a price acceptable to Forester. He then manages the combined steel and forestry enterprise in an efficient manner, installing whatever pollution control equipment, if any, he finds to be cost-effective.

Suppose instead that the air rights belong to Miller. In that case, when Forester approaches him to discuss the pollution damage, he will not have to do anything unless she offers him something of value in return. In that case, the parties are likely to reach one of different agreements:

1. Forester pays Miller an agreed-upon amount to stop the pollution, which he does either by installing control equipment or shutting down the mill, whichever is less costly.

2. Forester buys the mill at a price acceptable to Miller and then manages the combined enterprise in an efficient manner.

3. The parties agree that the value of the trees killed by the pollution is less than the cost of pollution abatement, in which case they take no action.

The Coase Theorem   We can draw several generalizations from the example of the forest and the steel mill. First, negotiations between the parties will always result in an optimal quantity of pollution, in the sense that they will reduce pollution up to, but not beyond, the point that the marginal cost of abatement is less than the damage it does to the trees. Second, the parties will choose the most efficient means of abatement—installing control equipment, shutting the mill, or whatever. Finally, the parties will achieve these results regardless of the initial assignment of property rights. Whether the air rights belong to the owner of the forest or to the owner of the steel mill will determine who must compensate whom, but will not affect the degree of pollution abatement or the means used to achieve it. For example, if it is cost-effective to install control equipment, the initial property rights will determine whether Forester or Miller pays for it; but in either case, they will install it.

The idea that, in the absence of transaction costs, private agreements will efficiently resolve problems of externalities, regardless of the initial assignment of property rights, is commonly known as the **Coase theorem**, after Ronald A. Coase.[4]

Coase theorem

The proposition that private agreements will efficiently resolve problems of externalities, regardless of the initial assignment of property rights, provided that there are no transaction costs

Market Resolution of Externalities in Practice

Transaction costs are never zero in the real world, but they are sometimes low enough to allow externalities to be resolved through voluntary exchange. *Economics in the News 6.1* provides one example.

Economics in the News **6.1**

Using Property Rights to Protect the Land

The Brazilian Amazon with its vast adjacent forest known as the Mato Grosso is one of the world's environmental battlegrounds. Every year, deforestation adds millions of tons of carbon dioxide to the earth's atmosphere and further reduces habitat for endangered species.

The Brazilian government is well aware of the threat. It has passed laws that restrict deforestation and require ranchers to keep up to 80 percent of their land in forest. If they

Every year deforestation adds millions of tons of carbon dioxide to the earth's atmosphere

have previously cleared too much, they must replant. The laws, unfortunately, are not always enforced. Corrupt local officials sometimes turn a blind eye to violations. Land speculators team up with gangs of illegal land invaders who burn first and then stake claims to the devastated land. Police are sometimes afraid to go into the forest to confront the heavily armed gangs.

John Cain Carter is one rancher who has had enough of the lawlessness and destruction. A transplanted Texan with a Brazilian wife, he founded the Aliança da Terra (Land Alliance), an organization that builds alliances between farmers and environmentalists, while finding incentives that use market forces to protect the environment. In comments published on the web site Amazônia, Carter says, "People think farmers in the Amazon are bandits, so we're trying to show there are good people who are trying to make a difference and reduce their impact .... We're turning the system on its head, adding transparency and credibility to turn it into a worldwide example of good land stewardship."

Carter's organization sends environmental engineers and agronomists to help ranchers improve land management practices by replanting forests, protecting fragile waterways from damage done by cattle, and limiting erosion and pollution. Their reward comes not just in terms of increased self-respect but in increased profits, too. Some of the profits come from payments for carbon reduction credits when land is reforested. Another source of profit is the sale of beef and soy that the organization certifies. McDonald's, Burger King, and other big buyers are willing to pay premium prices for these products to show that their businesses are environmentally friendly.

Not-for-profit groups like the World Wildlife Fund have supported the efforts of the Land Alliance and other local groups, like the Roundtable on Responsible Soy Association. In 2011, the Botanical Research Institute of Texas gave Carter their International Award for Excellence in Conservation. Not all environmentalists are enthusiastic. Some shun

(Continues)

alliances with farmers and ranchers in favor of activities like eco-tourism and gathering forest products for sale. However, speaking to the Washington Post, Christopher Wells, head of the soy producers' group, sees cooperation of business and environmentalists as essential. Unless everyone works together, he says, "We'd go back to a world of bitter debate between NGOs and big industry. That's where we were five years ago. I don't see any other way other than this."

Sources: Jonathan Wheatley, "Edge of Destruction," *Financial Times*, April 26, 2008, Life and Arts p. 1; Monte Reel, "Applying Capitalism to Protect Dwindling Brazilian Forestland," *Washington Post*, April 25, 2008 (http://www.washingtonpost.com/wp-dyn/content/article/2008/04/24/AR2008042403392_pf.html); "Land Invasions Undermine Amazon Forest Law," Amazonia, April 3, 2008 (http://www. amazonia.org.br/english/noticias/noticia.cfm?id=265626); "Amazon Rainforest Conservationist to Receive BRIT Award," Botanical Research Institute of Texas, Dec. 7, 2010, http://www2.brit.org/newsroom/current-news/john-cain-carter-will-receive-2011-international-award-of-excellence-in-conservation/

There is no need to go as far as the Amazon to find cases where markets serve to protect the environment. Restrictive covenants and conservation easements are used to promote environmental values in many communities in the United States. Easements and covenants are legally binding agreements that limit what owners can do on their property. For example, Ducks Unlimited (DU) uses conservation easements to protect more than 12 million acres of wetlands in Canada, the United States, and Mexico. DU negotiates terms of the agreements with farmers and other landowners, and monitors them annually to ensure compliance with their terms.

Covenants often resolve small-scale externalities in residential communities. Left to their own devices, people do many things that annoy their neighbors. They hold loud parties, leave bright outdoor lights on all night, park boats or junked cars in their front yards, and leave garbage uncollected. Real estate developers have found that many people will pay a premium price for a home in a neighborhood where they know their neighbors will not do those things. Accordingly, when they subdivide a tract of land for a new neighborhood, they add restrictive covenants to the deeds. When home buyers sign the deeds, they agree to a list of restrictions on loud parties, lights, boats, garbage, and so on. In most cases, neighbors comply with the covenants voluntarily because they find it mutually beneficial to do so, but the injured parties can enforce the covenants in court if necessary.

Still another example concerns the pollination of crops by honeybees. Although most of the examples discussed in this chapter focus on harmful externalities, this one is a beneficial externality. Farmers pay fees to beekeepers to place their hives near their apple orchards, blueberry farms, or whatever. For farmers, the fees, which total tens of millions of dollars a year in the United States, are more than offset by the increase in crop yield. Beekeepers, for their part, gain a second source of revenue, in addition to sales of honey.

Without such a market, beekeepers would limit the number of hives to the quantity justified by sales of honey alone. The external benefit to fruit growers would not enter into their calculations. When they can earn extra revenue by selling pollination services, they keep more hives. That is good not only for beekeepers and fruit growers but also for consumers, who get more of both honey and fruit.

Transaction Costs as Barriers to Voluntary Resolution of Externalities

Although there are many examples where private negotiations resolve problems of externalities, they do not always work. The reason is that transaction costs are often far from zero. To see why, we will move away from small, local externalities, like those of land use and bee-keeping, and resume our earlier discussion of climate change.

Scientific Uncertainties   To resolve a dispute through private negotiations, one must know the source of the pollution and the extent of the damage. The global nature of climate change makes that impossible. There is a broad scientific consensus that emissions of CO_2 and other greenhouse gasses are changing the climate, but beyond that, there are many scientific uncertainties. We do not know exactly where the greatest damages will occur. We cannot trace the damage in a certain place (for example, coastal flooding of farmland to the land of a farmer in Bangladesh) to any one source of pollution (for example, an electric power plant in Illinois). As a result, victims of climate change cannot know with whom to negotiate. Also, because we do not know exactly how much a given amount of CO_2 will raise the sea level (or otherwise cause harm), we cannot know how much harm would be avoided by any given reduction in emissions. That means that victims would not know how much compensation to ask for, even if they knew from whom to ask it.

Effectiveness of the Legal System   Resolving disputes over environmental property rights depends, in part, on the effectiveness of tort law—the area of civil law concerned with harms (torts) done by one person to another. Lawsuits involving accidental personal injury, product defects, and damage to property through negligence are familiar examples of tort law in action.

The areas of tort law that touch most directly on pollution are *nuisance* and *trespass*. The law of nuisance protects people against externalities such as noise from an airport or a neighbor's parties. Trespass traditionally covers one person's entry onto another person's land; it can also include harmful invasions by smoke, chemical leakage, and other forms of pollution. Some examples of pollution raise issues of both nuisance and trespass.

Tort law works best to resolve environmental disputes where the initial distribution of property rights is clearly established, and where there is a court willing to rule on disputes. In practice, environmental property rights are often unclear, and there are often no courts with the needed authority. In the case of climate change, industries in developed countries may claim a right to emit greenhouse gasses on the grounds that they complied with all pollution regulations in force at the time their plants were built. The government of a low-income country like China may counter that industry in developed countries has already used more than its fair share of the limited capacity of the earth's atmosphere to absorb pollution. The advanced countries should start cleaning up their act now, while low-income countries get their chance to catch up. There are no global legal codes or courts to resolve disputes of this kind. Without the ability to appeal to effective courts, private negotiations among citizens living in different countries have small chance of succeeding.

Costs of Negotiation Among Many Parties The large number of parties involved in many environmental disputes is still another factor that increases transaction costs. When there are many parties, negotiating and enforcing an agreement to resolve an externality could be prohibitively expensive even if there were no legal or scientific uncertainties. For climate change, the parties include millions of businesses and billions of individuals throughout the world. It is hard to imagine successful private negotiations on such a scale.

In sum, we cannot always rely on private negotiations, backed by an appeal to tort law, for large-scale environmental problems, however useful they may be on a local scale. We turn next to the alternative of controlling pollution through regulation.

6.3 Controlling Externalities Through Regulation

As awareness of environmental problems increases, governments everywhere feel increasing pressure to do something. They have responded with many kinds of laws and regulation. This section looks at three categories of environmental regulation: command and control, emission charges, and cap-and-trade systems.

Command and Control

The command and control approach is illustrated by many of the U.S. government's early efforts to control pollution—for example, the Clean Air Act, the Clean Water Act, the National Environmental Policy Act, and the Noise Control Act—all of which date to the 1970s. Command-and-control laws often require use of a specific pollution control technology without comparing its cost to alternative methods. In other cases, rules set a goal, such as 90 percent cleanup, for all pollution sources without considering differences in cost of abatement. Sometimes, in areas in which pollution is especially bad, regulations ban new pollution sources entirely.

The early command-and-control regulations had some success in reducing air and water pollution. Still, they are open to the criticism that requiring specific cleanup technologies reduces the incentive to discover new, lower-cost methods. If regulations pay no attention to balancing marginal abatement costs among cleanup technologies, sources, and kinds of pollution, the total cost of achieving any given goal is higher than it needs to be. High costs give rise to political pressure to cut back on pollution control in general. In the end, excessive reliance on command-and-control can be self-defeating.

Today economists see command-and-control as the wrong response to most environmental problems. At best, the approach makes sense for cases where zero emissions are an appropriate goal, for example, banning DDT or lead additives for gasoline. For cases where zero emissions are not appropriate, other approaches are likely to be both more cost effective and more politically feasible.

Emission Charges (Pollution Taxes)

Economic approaches to pollution control work by bringing external costs to bear on the pollution source. Polluters then face an incentive to balance marginal abatement costs against marginal external costs and move toward an optimal level of pollution. One simple thing that can be done is to impose an emission charge, or pollution tax, of a fixed amount per unit of waste. For example, all sources of sewage might be required to pay a charge of $40 per ton of discharge into lakes and rivers. For climate change, a carbon tax could impose a charge per ton of carbon dioxide (or CO_2 equivalent) released into the atmosphere.

Figure 6.3 shows how a carbon tax would work. As discussed earlier, the optimal quantity of pollution corresponds to the intersection of the curves for marginal cost of abatement and marginal external cost of pollution. With a carbon tax in force, polluters will prefer to reduce emissions rather than pay the charge whenever the marginal cost of abatement is less than the charge. In Figure 6.3, that would be the case for levels of pollution greater than fifty gigatons per year. For levels of pollution less than fifty gigatons per year, polluters would prefer to pay the tax. If, as in the figure, the tax is set exactly at the level where the marginal abatement cost and marginal external cost curves intersect, the result will be the optimal level of pollution.

An emission charge of a fixed amount per ton gives polluters an economic incentive to keep the air clean.

Of course, it is possible that the charge would be set too low or too high. Measurement problems may make it hard to tell just where the curves intersect. Even if the tax is initially set at the optimal level, changing conditions may shift one or both of the curves, in which case the old tax will be too high or too low. However, even if the chosen rate were not optimal, a carbon tax would encourage the use of efficient techniques to achieve any given level of emissions. That is so because a uniform charge would exert equal pressure on all polluters to cut back on their output of wastes. It would encourage them to eliminate pollution first from the sources they can control most cheaply. It would avoid the problem that occurs under command-and-control, in which all sources are subject to the same regulations even though some sources cause less harm than others.

FIGURE 6.3   EFFECT OF A CARBON TAX

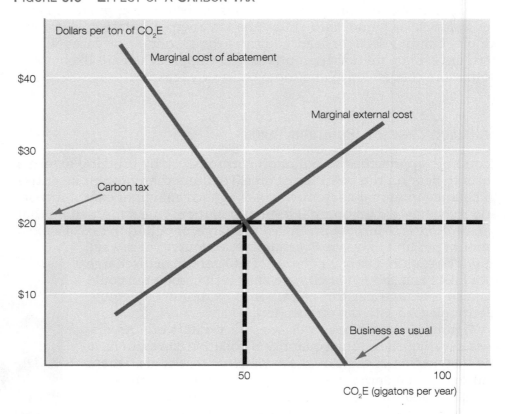

This figure shows the effect of a carbon tax. For levels of pollution above 50 gigatons per year, marginal abatement cost is less than the tax; thus it would be more profitable for polluters to reduce CO_2 output than to pay the tax. For levels less than 50 gigatons per year, it would cost less to pay the tax than to make further reductions in emissions. To achieve the optimal level of emissions, the carbon tax is set at a level equal to the intersection of the marginal abatement cost and marginal external cost curves. A tax that was too high, too low, or that did not apply equally to all pollution sources would still result in a reduction of pollution relative to the business-as-usual level, but it would not be fully efficient.

For example, a command-and-control approach to CO_2 emissions might impose strict mileage standards on cars regardless of the number of miles per year the car is driven or the purpose for which it is used. In contrast, a carbon tax that raised the price of gasoline would give people who drove the most the greatest incentive to buy a low-carbon vehicle.

The control of chlorofluorocarbons (CFCs) under the 1987 Montreal Protocol is one example of the successful use of emission charges. Those chemicals, once used for items ranging from hair products to refrigerators, damage the earth's protective ozone layer. To meet its initial commitment to reduce emissions of CFCs under the Montreal Protocol, the U.S. government imposed a heavy tax. Later, after less harmful substitutes became available, regulators replaced the tax with an outright ban on CFCs.

Cap and Trade

Emission charges are one way of using market incentives. Another market-based approach uses tradable waste-discharge permits, commonly known as "cap and trade."

Figure 6.4 shows how a cap-and-trade scheme works. The vertical line in the diagram corresponds to the "cap," that is, the overall limit on the amount of pollution allowed from all sources in the affected area—as broad an area as possible in the case of climate change, but for other pollutants, a region or a single city. Ideally, the cap corresponds to the optimal quantity of pollution.

After regulators set the overall emission limit, they divide it into a fixed number of permits and distribute them among pollution sources. The permit holders can then buy and sell them as they see fit. Polluters whose marginal cost of abatement is relatively high become buyers of permits, and those with relatively low marginal abatement costs become sellers. As the market for permits approaches equilibrium, the marginal cost of abatement approaches an equilibrium value that is the same for all sources. The uniform equilibrium permit price provides an incentive to use efficient means to achieve the target level of pollution, just as a uniform emission charge does.

The largest cap-and-trade scheme in operation today controls carbon emissions in the European Union. Australia and California have announced smaller-scale programs that they plan to implement in coming years. We will return to some of the practical and political problems of cap and trade later in the chapter.

6.4 Environmental Policy and Public Choice

Up to this point, we have focused on the best way of designing environmental policy in order to overcome possible market failures arising from externalities. This section draws on concepts from public choice theory to explain why real-world policies often depart from the ideal, and why the political process sometimes leads to government failure.

FIGURE 6.4 EFFECT OF EMISSIONS TRADING

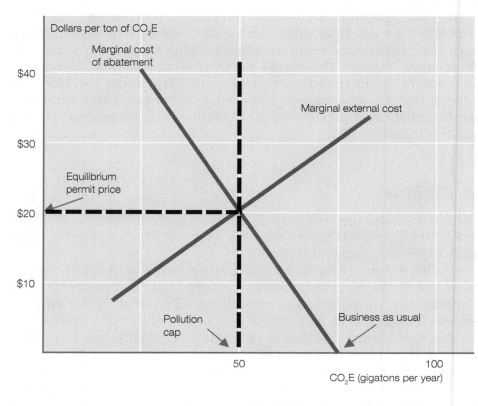

This figure shows the effect of a policy of a cap and trade regulation strategy applied to greenhouse gas emissions. The total allowable amount of CO_2 equivalent is limited by the number of permits issued, in this case 50 gigatons. Permit holders can trade them as they see fit. Those with higher marginal abatement costs will buy permits from those with lower costs. The market will reach equilibrium when the marginal cost of abatement is equal for all pollution sources. The equilibrium price of a permit corresponds to the intersection of the marginal cost of abatement curve with the line representing the number of permits.

Environmental Policy in a Democracy

Public choice theory looks at environmental policy in terms of the way people pursue their economic interests through the political process. In a democracy, that means focusing on political choices made by voters and their elected representatives.

One of the simplest models in public choice theory is the **median voter model**. According to that model, political choices in a democracy reflect the interests of voters whose preferences lie near the middle of the range represented in the community. To use a simple example, consider a town where citizens gather once a year to vote on important

Median voter model

A model showing that there is a tendency for decisions in a democracy to reflect the interests of voters whose preferences lie near the middle of the scale

issues. This year the big issue is whether the town should use tax revenue to improve its schools or give a tax break, instead, to an organization that wants to construct an assisted living facility for elderly residents. Young parents are more likely to vote in favor of schools, while older voters are more likely to favor tax breaks for assisted living. According to the model, the outcome of the vote will depend on the age of the *median* voter—that is, the voter whose age is such that exactly half the citizens are older and half are younger. In a community where the median age is young, families that favor schools are likely to be in the majority. In a community where the median age is older, assisted living is more likely to win.

It is not hard to find examples in which environmental policy appears to be consistent with the median voter model. For example, California, under both Republican and Democratic governors, has long been a leader among states in its environmental regulation. Very likely, that happens because the median California voter is more concerned about the environment than voters in other parts of the country. Political support for environmental policy varies over time, as well as from place to place. Economists consider environmental quality to have a relatively high income elasticity of demand. As a result, as growth raises the income of the median voter, we would expect stronger political support for policies that promote clean air, opportunities for outdoor recreation, and protection of other environmental values. That is just what democratic political systems have produced in most high-income countries.

Vote Trading and Special Interests

Although the median voter model does appear to explain some trends in environmental policy, it is by no means a complete theory. Public choice economists have modified the median voter model to account for the frequently disproportionate influence of small groups that share intensely felt interests. They identify two features of political systems that are especially important in amplifying the voice of special interests, even when they represent a small minority of voters.

Costs of Lobbying and Political Expression   Like everything we do, participation in democratic politics has opportunity costs. Those costs are not limited to making the effort to vote once a year in an election. Other forms of political action, like writing to elected representatives, calling in to local talk shows, attending meetings, tweeting political slogans, or marching in demonstrations also take time and effort. Making campaign contributions or employing professional lobbyists cost not just time but also money. Finally, there is a large opportunity cost just to keep informed about what goes on in the political world and how it affects your own life.

When you are a member of an organized group that has a common interest in some policy, you can often share the opportunity costs of political action. You can keep informed through a web site or newsletter supported by your organization. Your job or your leisure interests naturally keep you in touch with like-minded people. Your organization may use dues or a special fund-raising drive to sponsor lobbyists or political ads. Because sharing lowers opportunity costs of political action for each member, organized groups tend to speak with a louder voice, relative to their numbers, than do unorganized individuals.

Small, well-organized groups also have another source of strength. Political action by a group has the property of a public good: All members benefit whether they contribute or not. As explained in Chapter 4, the *free rider problem* often hampers production of public goods. Group members would like to gain from the group's political activities without bearing their fair share of the costs. Small, well-organized groups have ways of overcoming the free-rider problem. Some, like labor unions and professional associations, may have compulsory dues. Others, like churches or parent-teacher groups, may bring social pressures to bear on group members that would otherwise be unwilling to do their fair share. In contrast, the free rider problem makes it nearly impossible to mobilize large groups in pursuit of shared interests that are not central to the life of each member.

Logrolling   Representative democracy is a second factor that increases the political impact of small groups that share intense interests. Direct voting by individual citizens, as in referendums or town meetings, is the exception rather than the rule in most democratic systems Instead, citizens usually express themselves in a two-stage process: First they vote for representatives such as senators, members of Congress, and state legislators. Then the representatives they elect vote on each issue.

Representative democracy adds an important element to the political process—vote trading, or **logrolling** as it is often known. Logrolling is possible because voting in legislatures differs in two important ways from voting in general elections. First, legislative voting almost never takes place by secret ballot. Second, legislators vote frequently on specific issues, rather than only now and then on more general issues. Those features make it possible for one representative to promise her vote on issue A in exchange for a promise that her colleague will provide his vote on issue B.

Logrolling often allows strongly felt interests to prevail even when only a minority of the population favors them. For example, as detailed in the case for discussion at the end of this chapter, Senators from corn-growing states can build a coalition to support subsidies for corn-based ethanol by trading away votes on issues like flood control or urban transit systems that are important to voters in other states. Although logrolling serves the narrowly economic interests of groups like corn farmers, it can be useful in promoting non-economic interests of any minority group. For example, logrolling has helped pass civil rights laws and protections for disabled persons, causes that might have been slow to win majority support if every issue were decided according to the preferences of the median voter.

Logrolling

The practice of trading
votes among members of a
legislative body

Special Interests and Environmental Policy   When it comes to environmental policy, majority interests, expressed through the influence of the median voter, and special interests, expressed through small-group action and logrolling, can interact in complex ways. The case of regulations controlling sulfur dioxide (SO_2) emissions from coal-fired electric power plants provides a case in point.

A number of different technologies are available for reducing SO_2 emissions. Typically, switching to a low-sulfur coal is the cheapest alternative, and scrubbing the sulfur from combustion gases is the most expensive. Nonetheless, in its 1977 amendments to Section 111 of the *Clean Air Act*, Congress required that any newly constructed electric power plant meet the emissions limit by scrubbing. That requirement applied to all plants, regardless of how clean or dirty their fuel or combustion technology was. In contrast, existing plants, including some of the dirtiest ones that burned the most sulfurous midwestern coal, did not have to scrub. Instead, they were allowed to build tall smokestacks—up to one thousand feet high—that keep the air in surrounding communities fairly clean but do nothing to limit total emissions. The resulting pollution, injected into the upper atmosphere by the tall stacks, worsened the problem of acid rain hundreds of miles downwind.

To meet local pollution standards and avoid installing scrubbers, some smoke stacks where built up to 1,000 feet high.

Why did Congress choose this approach to controlling sulfur dioxide emissions? The answer appears to lie in the coalition that passed the *Clean Air Act*, which included the following:

- Coal-mining interests in the high-sulfur areas of Ohio, Illinois, West Virginia, and elsewhere wanted to strengthen demand for their product. Both unions and mine owners were afraid that changing fuels would result in the loss of coal production jobs to western states that mine low-sulfur coal.

- Industrial and labor interests from eastern and midwestern states wanted to protect profits by stopping the flight of industry to western and southern states. By focusing control efforts on newly built plants, the *Clean Air Act* gave old, dirty plants a few more years of life. Moreover, by focusing on scrubbing rather than changing fuels, the act ensured that coal-burning plants in the South and West are unable to exploit the cost advantage of a location close to sources of low-sulfur coal.

- Environmentalists, who were unable to obtain a majority in Congress by themselves, were willing to enter an "unholy alliance" on the theory that any pollution control measure was better than none.

After the passage of the 1977 Clean Air amendments, environmentalists became dissatisfied with the deal. Pollution did not decrease as rapidly as they had hoped, partly because scrubbers are not always reliable and partly because the regulations slowed the replacement of

Applying Economic Ideas **6.1**

Cap and Trade for Acid Rain

In the 1980s, before climate change began to make the headlines, acid rain was the most widely discussed environmental problem in the United States. Acid rain occurs when sulfur dioxide (SO_2) and other pollutants, mainly from coal-fired power plants, rise into the atmosphere and undergo chemical reactions that increase the acidity of rain that falls downwind. Steadily increasing acidity of rain was destroying forests, damaging crops, and creating a constant haze throughout the Eastern United States. Early environmental legislation took a command-and-control approach by mandating stack scrubbers and other technology for midwestern power plants. However, those controls turned out to be insufficient, and damage from acid rain continued to increase.

By 1990, it was time to try a new approach. A set of amendments to the Clean Air Act permitted the Environmental Protection Agency (EPA) to try a cap-and-trade approach to control of SO_2 emissions. There were many skeptics. Some environmentalists feared that the incentives of cap-and-trade would be too weak to persuade industry to cut back on pollution. Industrial interests claimed that the controls would be too tight and that the market price of permits would soar to unaffordable levels. However, despite the many doubts, the EPA went ahead with its program.

The result surprised almost everyone. Cap-and-trade for acid rain control became one of the greatest environmental success stories of recent time. SO_2 emissions fell by more than half over the next decade; and the cost of the program was far below projections. Rather than rising to a range of $500 to $2,000 per ton, as had been projected by some critics, the equilibrium price of permits fell steadily. By 2003, it was only $150 per ton. The acidity of rain in the Adirondacks and New England fell by 25 to 50 percent. Forests and streams began to recover their ecological health. The success of the acid rain program became one of the strongest arguments in favor of using a cap-and-trade approach to the problem of climate change.

The old Bavarian Forest around Lusen mountain suffered as a result of acid rain and the bark beetle in 1996; now a new forest is growing.

Unfortunately, the story does not have a happy ending. In 2010, the sulfur dioxide trading program fell apart. The reasons were more legal than economic. Although the program had operated successfully for many years, its complexity left it open to challenge in court. When courts ruled against some provisions of the program, the Environmental Protection Agency changed the rules of the game in ways that caused outstanding permits to become worthless. Some sources, including some categories of coal-fired power plants, were subjected to new command-and-control rules requiring greater emission reductions than under permit trading. At the same time, other sources lost all incentive to clean up, since the permits they could earn by doing so no longer had any market value.

The EPA set to work to rewrite the rules for SO$_2$ trading in a way that would meet the legal challenges. In mid-2011, it issued a new Cross State Air Pollution Rule (CASPR). The new rule attempted to correct the legal flaws of the earlier version, even at the expense of some compromises that might limit its effectiveness. Despite the changes, CASPR also came under challenge. On December 30, less than forty-eight hours before it was to take effect, the U.S. Court of Appeals for Washington, DC stayed its implementation, pending further arguments on the merits of the rule.

It is too early to know what the outcome of the latest court battle will be, or what will be the long-run impact will be on acid rain levels. There is no doubt, though, that the whole episode is great disappointment to supporters of cap and trade.

Sources: Environmental Defense Fund, "The Cap-and-Trade Success Story," www.edf.org/page.cfm?tagID=1085; Environmental Protection Agency, "Cap and Trade: Acid Rain Program Results", www.epa.gov/airmarkets; Edwin G. Dolan, TANSTAAFL: A Libertarian Perspective on Environmental Policy, Searching Finance (2011). For details of the legal battle, see "Court's Latest Stay of Clean Air Regulations Shows the Best Can Be the Enemy of the Good," Ed Dolan's Econ Blog, January 12, 2012 (http://www.economonitor.com/dolanecon/2012/01/12/court%E2%80%99s-latest-stay-of-clean-air-regulations-shows-the-best-can-be-the-enemy-of-the-good/).

old, dirty facilities by new, cleaner ones. These changes gave rise to a new coalition that, in 1990, passed a set of amendments to the *Clean Air Act*. This time, environmentalists broke with the midwestern coal and industrial interests and supported the use of a cap-and-trade strategy. As discussed in *Applying Economic Ideas* 6.1, the new approach turned out to be much more effective, although it, too, eventually fell victim to changing circumstances.

Alternative energy resources are another area in which economics, science, and politics clash. Each form of alternative energy—wind, solar, biomass and others—has supporters and critics. Given a level playing field, we might hope that the forms of alternative energy that produce the greatest environmental benefits at the lowest costs would emerge most rapidly. A simple way to do that would be to impose a carbon tax or cap-and-trade scheme that would raise the price of carbon-based energy, thus making alternatives more attractive, over time. However, politicians and regulators have not done that. Instead, they are subject to constant lobbying to subsidize some momentary favorite with little attention to cost efficiency. In addition, energy sources promoted on environmental grounds must compete in the political arena with dirtier energy sources that claim national security benefits, for example, the substitution of fuel from Canadian oil stands for oil imported from less friendly or stable countries.

The examples given help explain why government policies do not always resolve environmental issues in an efficient manner. The insights of public choice theory suggest the evaluation of policy alternatives comes down to a matter of balancing market failures, on the one hand, against government failures, on the other.

Summary

1. **How can pollution and other environmental issues be understood in terms externalities?** Pollution occurs when firms (or sometimes consumers) discharge wastes into soil, water, or the atmosphere. The optimal quantity of pollution is the quantity beyond which the marginal external cost of pollution exceeds the marginal cost of abatement.

2. **How can property rights and private negotiation help control externalities?** In a world without transaction costs, it would be possible to resolve problems of externalities through voluntary negotiation. In such a world, according to the Coase theorem, voluntary exchange would result in efficient resource allocation regardless of the initial assignment of property rights. In practice, high transaction costs limit the power of negotiations to resolve environmental problems.

3. **What policies are available to control pollution?** Early pollution control policies in the United States followed a command-and-control approach. Economists have criticized the command-and-control approach for poor performance in terms of efficiency because it often does not consider marginal abatement costs and does not provide incentives to employ the least-cost abatement technology. One alternative to the command-and-control approach is to impose emission charges (pollution taxes), which would require a per-unit fee for the discharge of wastes into the environment. Another is the cap-and-trade approach using tradable waste-discharge permits. Economists favor these approaches because they include incentives to meet a given pollution control target in an efficient manner.

4. **How can we apply public choice theory to environmental issues?** Public choice economics can help explain what environmental policies are politically successful. According to the median voter model, the relatively high income elasticity of demand for environmental quality explains more attention to pollution control in high-income countries. Public choice theory can also help explain why the pollution control policies adopted by government are not always the most efficient ones. One reason is the tendency of small, well-organized interest groups to exercise disproportionate influence in a democracy. Environmental policy sometimes gives rise to government failure rather than correction of market failure.

Key Terms   Page

Problems and Topics for Discussion

1. **Environmental rights**   "Pollution is garbage. Just as no one has a right to dump garbage on his/her neighbor's property, no one has a right to pollute the planet. A pollution-free environment is a basic human right." Do you agree, disagree, or agree only in part? What are the economic implications of your position? Discuss.

2. **Beneficial externalities and property rights**   Beekeepers need flowers to produce honey, and farmers need bees to pollinate crops. At present, beekeepers have the right to place hives where their bees will fly onto neighbors' property, and the neighbors do not have the right to exclude the bees. Suppose instead that the law treated invasion by bees as a form of trespass, so that property owners could sue beekeepers that allowed the insects to fly onto their land without permission. How would this alter the economic relations between farmers and beekeepers? Do you think that it might lead to a situation in which beekeepers have to pay farmers for access to the blossoms of their crops? Discuss in terms of the Coase theorem and the Miller-Forester example.

3. **Smoking in restaurants**   Smoking results in externalities that are unpleasant for nonsmokers. Given this fact, why would a restaurant find it profitable to establish smoking and nonsmoking areas? Do you think that government policies should try to resolve the problem of smoking in restaurants through voluntary market incentives, or should there be a government policy mandating (or preventing) designated smoking areas in restaurants, or prohibiting smoking in restaurants altogether? Do you think that the same conclusions apply to smoking on airplanes? In a government office? Discuss.

4. **Automobile pollution**   One way to control automobile pollution is by the use of catalytic converters and other devices that limit pollution to a certain quantity per mile driven. For comparison, imagine a system in which drivers had to pay an annual tax based on the total pollution emitted by their cars. The tax would be calculated by measuring the quantity of pollution per mile, using a testing device such as those now used for vehicle inspections, and multiplying that figure by the number of miles per year shown on the car's odometer. People could choose to buy catalytic converters, more expensive and more effective devices, or no control devices at all. What considerations would determine the type of pollution control device purchased? Do you think that the tax system would be more efficient than the current system, which directly regulates the average fuel economy of vehicles, regardless of how much they are driven? Would it be as effective in reducing pollution? Would it be as fair? Discuss.

Case for Discussion

Fill It Up with Ethanol?

Stand on any street corner in Rio de Janeiro, and you will notice a faint aroma reminiscent of a camping trip or a fondue feast—the aroma of burning alcohol. Nearly all cars in Brazil run on alcohol—more exactly, ethanol produced from sugar cane. Brazilians can buy gasoline at their local filling station if they must, but the price is higher, even taking into account the fact that gasoline has higher energy content than ethanol and, accordingly, produces better mileage.

Ethanol-based motor fuel is growing in popularity in the United States, as well. Unlike the case in Brazil, few U.S. cars can run on pure ethanol, but blends containing anywhere from 10 percent to 85 percent ethanol are being promoted as a solution to the national "addiction" to imported oil. Since U.S. farmers grow little sugarcane, most ethanol producers there use corn. In late 2007, Congress passed new energy legislation that further increased already generous subsidies for ethanol production. Does it make economic or environmental sense?

Among the first scientists to cast suspicion on the case for corn-based ethanol were Cornell University's David Pimentel and Tad Patzek of the University of California, Berkeley. Their research showed that corn-based ethanol consumes about 30 percent more energy than the fuel yields. Furthermore, much of the energy used to drive tractors and fuel ethanol plants is petroleum based. Far from being a solution to the energy crisis, corn-based ethanol makes it worse. The corn lobby soon struck back with new research sponsored by the U.S. Department of Agriculture. Those studies said that Pimentel and Patzek based production costs on average technology, which included some now-obsolete plants, not the most efficient technology embodied in the newest plants. They also failed to include the energy-saving value of ethanol by products like high-protein cattle feed. When these and other considerations are added, corn-based ethanol appeared to produce a small but positive net gain to the nation's energy balance. Still more recent research, published in Science in early 2008, argues that all of the earlier studies failed to include the effects of land use. As farmers in the U.S. and around the world plow up previously unfarmed land for crops, they release massive amounts of CO_2 and other greenhouse gasses into the air. When we take land use effects into account, corn-based ethanol and most other biofuels unambiguously do more harm than good to the environment.

(Continues)

If food-based biofuels are such a bad idea, why are they so heavily subsidized? It is best to seek the answer not in economics but in politics. Midwestern corn farmers are delighted to see the demand for their product grow as more and more subsidized ethanol plants come on line. Use of corn to make ethanol drives up world food prices, but hungry people in Africa and Asia do not vote in U.S. elections. U.S. consumers (at least this is what members of Congress seem to hope) can be easily fooled into believing that, when they fill up their tank with ethanol, they are helping make the world a better place to live in.

Questions

1. Suppose that each gallon of gasoline consumed results in $.50 of harmful externalities while each gallon of ethanol results in just $.15 of harmful externalities. If ethanol costs $.35 cents more per gallon to produce, would it be efficient to encourage ethanol-based fuels? Why or why not? What if, when land-use effects are taken into account, the externalities from corn-based ethanol are the same as those from gasoline? Discuss in terms of concepts from this chapter.

2. In order to persuade motorists to use ethanol as fuel, the price of ethanol (adjusted for its lower energy content) must be the same as or lower than gasoline. Do you think it would be better to encourage use of ethanol by putting a tax on gasoline or by subsidizing production of ethanol? Which would result in the greater total saving in gasoline use? Why? What political considerations might affect the choice between tax and subsidy?

3. If there are fewer corn farmers than motorists, why has Congress blocked imports of Brazilian ethanol, which is much cheaper than that produced in the United States, rather than encouraging such imports? Discuss in terms of concepts from public choice theory.

Endnotes

1. For an overview of the issues involved in measuring the impacts of climate change and the costs of mitigation, consult one or both of the following studies: Intergovernmental Panel on Climate Change, Climate Change 2007 Synthesis Report, Summary for Policymakers, http://www.ipcc.ch/, or International Monetary Fund, World Economic Outlook, April 2008, Chapter 4: Climate Change and the Global Economy, http://www.imf.org/external/pubs/ft/weo/2008/01/index.htm.

2. IMF, *World Economic Outlook,* April 2008, Chapter 4.7

3. For a more extended discussion of the issues raised in this section, see Edwin G. Dolan, "Science, Public Policy, and Global Warming: Rethinking the Market Liberal Position," *Cato Journal,* Fall 2006, http://www.cato.org/pubs/journal/ cj26n3/cj26n3-3.pdf.

4. The theorem is implicit in Ronald Coase, "The Problem of Social Cost," *Journal of Law and Economics* (October 1960): 1–44. Coase's colleague, George Stigler, first used the term "Coase theorem" for this proposition. Since then, there has been a long controversy regarding how the theorem should be interpreted. For a thorough review, see Glenn Fox, "The Real Coase Theorems," *Cato Journal,* Fall 2007

Appendix to Chapter 6:
Valuing Costs and Benefits Over Time

Business managers often face situations that require the comparison of costs and benefits that occur at different points in time. For example, should a trucking company improve its service by building a new warehouse? Doing so would require an investment now and would produce cost savings and service improvements over many years in the future. If the company builds the warehouse, how much insulation should it put in the roof? More insulation would increase the immediate construction cost but save future heating costs.

Discounting   The standard method for comparing costs and benefits that occur at different points in time is known as discounting. To understand discounting, begin by imagining a firm that has surplus funds available for investment. If it puts them to work earning interest (say, by placing them in a bank account, making a loan, or buying a security), the original sum it invests will grow year by year. At 10 percent interest per year, $100 invested today will be worth $110 a year from now. After two years, it will be worth $121—the $11 gain in the second year reflects interest of $10 on the original principal and $1 interest on the $10 interest earned in the first year. Generalizing from this example, we can say that the value V of $1 invested for t years at a rate of interest of r percent per year is given by the formula $Vt = (1 + r)^t$.

In a world where people can loan funds out at interest, it is always advantageous to receive a payment earlier rather than later. The opportunity cost of receiving a sum later rather than sooner is the interest that the funds could otherwise have earned. Consider, for example, the cost of receiving $100 a year from now rather than today, assuming an interest rate of 10 percent per year. Delaying receipt of the sum would mean forgoing a year's interest. Rather than give up that interest, a firm would be just as well off to receive a smaller sum now as to receive the $100 a year from now. To be precise, it would be just as good to get $91 now as $100 a year from now because the $91 placed for a year at 10 percent would grow to $100 (give or take a few cents). Similarly, $100 payable two years from now is equivalent to about $83 today, assuming 10 percent interest; $100 three years from now is worth about $75 today; and so on.

We can generalize this kind of example to any period of time and any interest rate. Let V_p be the sum of money that, if it is invested today at r percent interest, will grow to the sum V_t after t years. V_p is known as the **present value** of the sum V_t, payable t years from now, discounted at r percent per year. The formula for calculating the present value of any future sum is

$$V_p = \frac{V_t}{(1 + r)^t}$$

Present value

The value today of a sum payable in the future (In mathematical terms, the present value of a sum V_p, payable t years in the future, discounted at r percent interest, would grow to the value V_t in t years; the present value formula is $V_p = V_t/(1 + r)^t$.)

An Example   Suppose you own a chain of stores selling hiking shoes. You think your customers will react favorably if you "go green" by converting your stores to a carbon-neutral source of electric power. A supplier gives you a choice of two technologies: a solar-electric panel or a bio-diesel generator. For the sake of discussion, we will consider the environmental benefits of the two methods to be equal.

The economic costs and benefits are not the same, however. The solar panel will cost $25,000 to install, but it has very low operating cost. It requires no fuel and just $100 per year for routine maintenance. The bio-diesel generator is much less expensive to install—just $10,000. However, it will require annual costs of $2,000 per year for fuel and maintenance. Both installations have an expected lifetime of ten years. Which is better?

If we just add up total expenses over the ten-year period, the solar solution wins hands down. It has a total cost of just $26,000, compared to $30,000 for the bio-diesel alternative. However, that comparison is misleading. The major cost of the solar electric panel occurs immediately, while the high fuel costs of the bio-diesel generator occur later. If future dollars are worth less than present dollars, a full comparison requires the use of discounting.

Table 6A.1 presents the complete analysis of the problem. There, in addition to the undiscounted information on costs and benefits, additional columns give the discounted value of future costs and benefits at two possible discount rates, 4 percent per year and 6 percent per year. For example, we can use the table to determine that the present value of the $2,000 that will be spent on diesel fuel in year 5 is $1,494.52 if we use a 6 percent discount rate ($2000 \times 1.06)^5$) and $1,643.85 if a 4 percent discount rate is used ($2000 \times (1.04)^5$).

TABLE 6A.1   COST COMPARISON

Year	Solar-Electric Panel			Bio-Diesel Generator		
	Undiscounted Expense	Discounted at 6%	Discounted at 4%	Undiscounted Expense	Discounted at 6%	Discounted at 4%
0	25,000	25,000	25,000	10,000	10,000	10,000
1	100	94	96	2,000	1,887	1.920
2	100	89	92	2,000	1,780	1,849
3	100	84	89	2,000	1,679	1,778
4	100	79	85	2,000	1,584	1,710
5	100	75	82	2,000	1,495	1,644
6	100	70	79	2,000	1,410	1,581
7	100	67	76	2,000	1,330	1,520
8	100	63	73	2,000	1,255	1,461
9	100	59	70	2,000	1,184	1,405
10	100	56	68	2,000	1,117	1,351
Total	26,000	25,736	25,811	30,000	24,720	26,219

Looking across the bottom row, we see that the total present value of installation costs plus future operating costs, discounted at 6 percent, is $25,736.01 for the solar installation compared to just $24,720.17 for the bio-diesel option. At that interest rate, the benefit of postponing some expenses to a future date outweighs the fact that total undiscounted expenses are greater. However, discounted at a 4 percent discount rate, the solar electric option is less expensive by a small margin.

It turns out, then, that the choice between solar electric and bio-diesel depends not just on the pattern of costs over time but also on the discount rate used. For the case under discussion, it is not hard to determine the proper discount rate. The discount rate used should be the opportunity cost of funds for the firm. If the firm must borrow money to install the equipment, the opportunity cost is the interest rate charged on the loan. If it has spare cash that it can use for the project, the opportunity cost is the next-best alternative investment, for example, using the cash to buy government bonds.

Applying Discounting to Climate Change   The problem of deciding how much to spend now to mitigate future climate change is similar in some ways to the problem of deciding between alternative methods of generating electricity. In both cases, costs and benefits occur over time. In both cases, costs are concentrated more heavily in the near future while benefits accrue over the more distant future. In both cases, the method of discounting is the proper way to compare the present value of costs and benefits that occur at different times.

The main difference is that the costs and benefits of climate change policy occur over a vastly longer time horizon. Decisions made now to slow emissions of greenhouse gasses will affect atmospheric concentrations of gasses, global temperatures, and sea levels for centuries to come. Applying the discount formula over such long periods tells us that costs and benefits in the far distant future have very little value today. For example, the present value of $1,000, discounted at 4 percent for 100 years, is less than $20. Discounted for three hundred years at 4 percent, the present value of $1,000 is only about one cent. Translated into everyday language, the discount formula seems to tell us that we should hardly care at all about something that will not happen for one hundred years and that we should be almost completely indifferent even to huge catastrophes if we think they will not happen for three hundred years.

Many people, confronted with the mathematics of discounting over long periods, reject the results out of hand. Forget the math, they say—we do care! We like our little planet; it's the only one we have! We do not want to destroy it—not tomorrow and, just as certainly, not 100, 300, or even 1,000 years from now!

Economists who study climate change react to these protests in different ways. Some brush them aside, saying, in effect, that it is not rational to care much about the distant future. Others attempt to reconcile the protests with the discounting method by reconsidering what the proper interest rate should be. Perhaps the market-based interest rates in the range of 3 to 5 percent, which is appropriate for ordinary commercial decisions and short-term policymaking, are not the right ones to use when thinking about the distant future. Perhaps instead, we should use a much smaller interest rate or one that starts at a market-based rate for the near future and falls over time.

It turns out that for the question of how much to do now to mitigate climate change, the choice of a discount rate makes more difference than any other consideration. One way to compare policy recommendations is to frame them in terms of a carbon tax. A strong policy recommendation is equivalent to a high tax (or a strict cap-and-trade policy that would produce a high price for carbon permits). A weak policy recommendation is equivalent to a low tax, or even none. Policy makers often express their idea of the proper level of a carbon tax in dollars per ton. In more familiar terms, a carbon tax of $1 per ton is equivalent to a tax of about one cent per gallon of gasoline.

William Nordhaus of Yale University is one of the best known among economists who applies the standard discounting approach to climate change. In some of his early work, he used a discount rate that started with a market-based rate of about 4 percent, gradually decreasing to about 2 percent for the distant future. Based on those discount rates, Nordhaus calculated that an optimal carbon tax (or equivalent cap-and-trade permit price) would be about $35 per ton, as of 2008. That would be close to the market price for carbon permits that prevailed in the European Union as of mid-2008. In consumer terms, such a tax would add about $.35 per gallon to the cost of gasoline. In more recent work, Nordhaus has revised his recommended carbon tax upward a little, while some other economists who use market-based discount rates have come up with even lower recommendations.

On the other hand, economists like Nicholas Stern, author of a widely-cited climate change study sponsored by the British Treasury, advocates using a much lower discount rate based on the ethical principle that human life has equal value regardless of the century in which people are born. As a result of applying a low discount rate, Stern estimates the optimal carbon tax to be more than $300 per ton, almost ten times as high as Nordhaus's recommendation. A carbon tax of that level would impose much higher costs on consumers and businesses, and would be equivalent to a much stricter cap-and-trade program than that implemented by the European Union, currently the world's strictest policy.

Who is right? Economics, in this case, simply cannot supply the answer. Either we care about the distant future, or we do not. Either we believe that human life has equal value regardless of a person's century of birth, or we believe current life has greater value than future life. The most economics can do is to help us understand the consequences of whatever policy choices we make.

Chapter 7

Global Trade
and Trade Policy

After reading this chapter, you will understand the following:

1. How we can apply the principle of comparative advantage to international trade

2. The relationship of competitiveness to comparative advantage

3. The trend of international trade policy in recent years

4. How international trade affects income distribution within each country

5. How public choice theory can help in understanding protectionist policies

Before reading this chapter, make sure you know the meaning of following concepts:

1. Opportunity cost

2. Comparative advantage

3. Political rent seeking

4. Public choice theory

Markets are not confined to national borders. They are world wide, and global trade is changing the world economy. Not a day goes by without a top story about trade in the news. Is China playing fair with its currency? Is it monopolizing the supply of rare earth metals or undercutting U.S. solar panel makers? Will troubles in the euro area spread to the United States by way of close trade links? Will buying more oil from Canada rescue the United States from dependence on energy from hostile foreign sources, or will it add to environmental destruction? To understand any of these stories, we have to know why countries trade with one another and how that trade affects their domestic economies.

During the second half of the twentieth century, the volume of world trade increased by a factor of 17, compared with a six-fold growth of output; and the growth of trade continues. Figure 7.1 shows shares of the biggest players in terms of imports and exports of merchandise. Not surprisingly, the United States is the world's largest importer both of goods and services. The United States is also the third-largest merchandise exporter.

Figure 7.1 shows only the raw data of trade. The most interesting questions will require digging beneath the surface. How do choices made by consumers and firms interact to determine who exports to whom and who imports from whom? Does the growth of imports and exports make markets more efficient? Does it make people better off or worse off? How are trade patterns affected by national and international trade policy; and what forces, in turn, determine trade policy? The rest of the chapter will explore these issues.

FIGURE 7.1 WORLD EXPORT AND IMPORT LEADERS

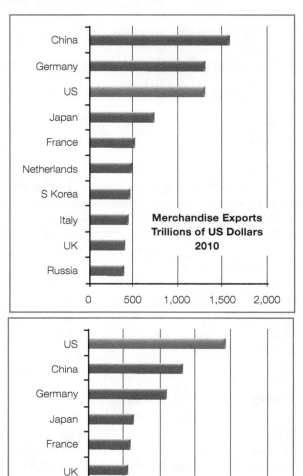

This figure shows the global top 10 exporters and importers of merchandise, based on 2010 estimates. If the European Union were considered as a single economy, it would be the largest exporter and second-largest importer.

Data Source: *CIA World Factbook*

7.1 The Theory of Comparative Advantage: Review and Extensions

The explanation of who trades with whom begins with *comparative advantage*, a concept first introduced in Chapter 1. We will begin our discussion of international trade by reviewing this theory, first using a numerical example and then a graphical approach.

Numerical Approach

To keep things simple, we will start with a world that has just two countries—call them Norway and Spain. Both have farms and offshore fishing grounds, but Spain's moderate climate makes both the farms and the fishing grounds there more productive. Spain can produce a ton of fish with four hours of labor and a ton of grain with two hours of labor. Norway needs five labor hours to produce a ton of fish and five labor hours to produce a ton of grain. We will consider only labor costs in this example and assume constant per-unit labor costs.

Because it takes fewer labor hours to produce both fish and grain in Spain, we say that Spain has an **absolute advantage** in both goods. However, absolute cost differences do not matter all that much for international trade. Differences in opportunity costs between the two countries matter much more. In Norway, producing a ton of fish means forgoing the opportunity to use five labor hours in the fields. A ton of fish thus has an opportunity cost of 1 ton of grain there. In Spain, producing a ton of fish means giving up the opportunity to produce 2 tons of grain. In terms of opportunity costs, then, fish is cheaper in Norway than in Spain and grain is cheaper in Spain than in Norway. We say that the country with lower opportunity cost for a given good has a *comparative advantage*.

Absolute advantage
The ability of a country to produce a good at a lower cost, in terms of quantity of factor inputs

If we looked only at labor costs and absolute advantage, mutually beneficial trade between Spain and Norway might not seem possible. Norwegians might like to get their hands on some of those cheap Spanish goods, but why would the Spanish be interested? After all, couldn't they produce everything at home more cheaply for less than the cost of producing it abroad? If so, how could they gain from trade? We can see why trade is worthwhile after all only by looking at comparative advantage.

A country with lower opportunity cost for a given good, such as fish, has a comparative advantage in international trade.

A country has an absolute advantage in producing a good if it uses fewer factor inputs.

Imagine, for example, that a Norwegian fishing boat decides to sail into a Spanish port with a ton of fish. Before the Norwegians' arrival, Spanish merchants in the port will be used to exchanging 2 tons of locally produced grain for a ton of fish, while the Norwegians will be used to getting only 1 ton of Norwegian grain for each ton of Norwegian fish. Thus, any exchange ratio between 1 and 2 tons of grain per ton of fish will seem attractive to both parties. For instance, a trade of 1.5 tons of grain for a ton of fish will make both the Spanish merchants and the Norwegian fishers better off than they would be if they traded only with others from their own country.

The profit made by the first boatload of traders is only the beginning of the story. Additional benefits come as each country begins to specialize in producing the good in which it has a comparative advantage. Norwegians will discover that instead of working 5 hours to raise a ton of grain from their own rocky soil, they can fish for five hours and trade their catch to the Spaniards for 1.5 tons of grain. In Spain, people will find that it is no longer worth their while to spend four hours catching a ton of fish. Instead, if they work just three hours in the fields, the 1.5 tons of grain that they grow will get them a ton of fish from the Norwegians. In short, the Norwegians will find that it pays to specialize in fish, and the Spaniards in grain.

Now suppose that trade continues at the rate of 1.5 tons of grain per ton of fish until both countries have become completely specialized. Spain no longer produces any fish, and Norway no longer produces any grain. Norwegians catch 200 tons of fish, half of which they export to Spain. The Spanish grow 500 tons of grain, 150 tons of which they send to Norway. Table 7.1 compares this situation with a nonspecialized, pretrade situation in which each country produces some of both products.

The comparison reveals three things. First, the Norwegians are better off than before; they have just as much fish to eat and 50 tons more grain than in the pre-trade equilibrium. Second, the Spaniards are also better off; they have just as much grain to consume as ever—and more fish. Looking at both countries together, we see that total world output of both grain and fish has risen because of trade. Everyone is better off, and no one is worse off.

TABLE 7.1   EFFECTS OF TRADE ON PRODUCTION AND CONSUMPTION

	Spain	Norway	World Total
Before Trade			
Fish			
Production	75	100	175
Consumption	75	100	175
Grain			
Production	350	100	450
Consumption	350	100	450
After Trade			
Fish			
Production	0	200	200
Consumption	100	100	200
Grain			
Production	500	0	500
Consumption	350	150	500

All figures represent tons produced or consumed.

This table shows production and consumption of fish and grain in Spain, Norway, and the world as a whole before and after trade. The example assumes that each country specializes in the product in which it has a comparative advantage and that they trade fish for grain at the rate of 1.5 tons of grain per ton of fish.

Graphical Presentation

We can illustrate comparative advantage graphically using a set of production possibility frontiers based on the Spanish-Norway example. Figure 7.2 does so using three production possibility frontiers.

FIGURE 7.2 A GRAPHIC ILLUSTRATION OF COMPARATIVE ADVANTAGE

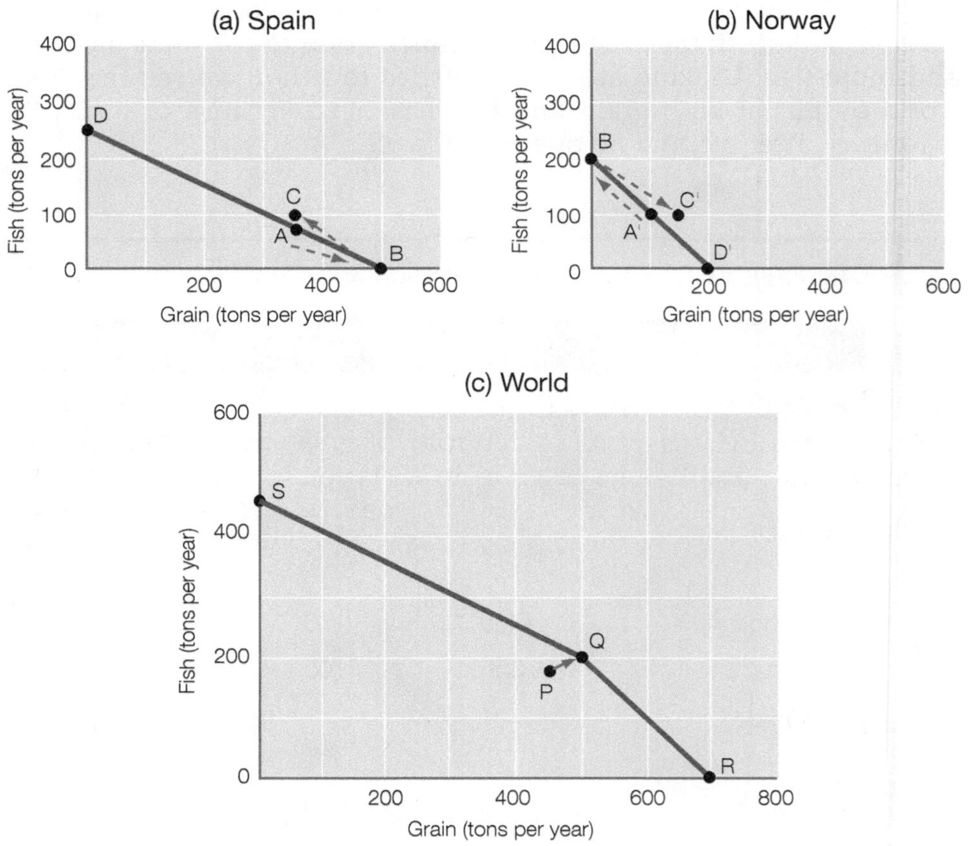

This figure shows production possibility frontiers for Spain, Norway, and the two countries combined. Before trade, Spain produces and consumes at point A and Norway at point A'. Together these correspond to world consumption point P, which is inside the world production possibility frontier. After trade begins, Spain specializes in producing grain (point B) and trades part of the grain for fish, moving to consumption point C. Norway specializes in producing fish (point B') and reaches consumption point B' through trade. As a result, world efficiency improves, allowing the global economy to reach point Q on the world production possibility frontier.

Part (a) is the production possibility frontier for Spain. Given one thousand available labor hours and a cost of two labor hours per ton of grain, Spain can produce up to 500 tons of grain per year if it produces no fish (point B'). If it produces no grain, Spanish fishers can catch up to 250 tons of fish at a cost of four hours per ton of fish (point D'). The line running from B to D represents the combinations of grain and fish that Spain can produce.

Part (b) shows the production possibility frontier for Norway. In Norway, fish and grain both take five labor hours per ton to produce. If Norwegians devote all their time to fishing, they can catch up to 200 tons of fish per year (point B'). If they devote all their time to farming, they can grow up to 200 tons of grain (point D'). The line between B_1 and D_1 represents Norway's production possibility frontier.

According to Figure 7.2, before trade begins, Spain produces and consumes 350 tons of grain and 75 tons of fish, corresponding to point A on Spain's production possibility frontier. Norway produces and consumes 100 tons each of fish and grain, corresponding to point D' on Norway's frontiers.

BVT *Lab*

Flashcards are available for this chapter at www.BVTLab.com.

The World Production Possibility Frontier

Part (c) of Figure 7.2 shows how we can construct a production possibility frontier for the world as a whole (which has just these two countries in our example). First, assume that both countries devote all their labor to grain. That results in 500 tons of grain from Spain plus 200 from Norway, or 700 tons of grain in all (point R in Part (c) of Figure 7.2). Starting from there, assume that the world begins to increase its output of fish. For efficiency, Norwegian farmers should be the first to switch to fishing because the opportunity cost of fish is lower in Norway (1 ton of grain per ton of fish) than in Spain (2 tons of grain per ton of fish). As Norwegians switch to fishing, then, world production moves upward and to the left along the line segment RQ.

When all Norwegians have abandoned farming for fishing, the world will have arrived at point Q–500 tons of grain (all Spanish) and 200 tons of fish (all Norwegian). From that point on, the only way to get more fish is to have Spanish farmers switch to fishing. At the opportunity cost of 2 tons of grain per ton of fish, this moves the economy along the line segment QS. When all Spanish farmers are fishing, the world arrives at point S, where world output is 450 tons of fish and no grain. The production possibility frontier for the world as a whole, then, is the kinked line RQS.

Effects of Trade

The pre-trade production point for the world as a whole lies inside the world production possibility frontier. Adding together the quantities of fish and grain from A and A', we arrive at point P in Part (c) of Figure 7.2—450 tons of grain from 175 tons of fish. This is inefficient; the world economy as a whole could produce more of both goods. To increase efficiency, both countries must specialize.

Suppose that Spain shifts its production from 350 tons of grain and 75 tons of fish (point A) to 500 tons of grain and no fish (point B). It then trades the extra 150 tons of grain for 100 tons of Norwegian fish. Spain's consumption ends up at point C, while its production remains at B. At the same time, Norway shifts production from A' to B', that is, it specializes entirely in fish. The extra 100 tons of fish are traded for the 150 tons of Spanish grain, moving Norwegian consumption to point C'.

Through specialization plus trade, then, both Spain and Norway move to points that lie outside their own production possibility frontiers. As they do so, the world as a whole moves from point P inside its production possibility frontier to point Q on the frontier. In this way, specialization improves the efficiency of the world economy as a whole, increases production of both goods, and leaves both countries better off than they would be if they did not trade.

Does Comparative Advantage Really Work?

Ricardo's theory of comparative advantage suggests that each country will export goods for which its labor is relatively productive compared with that of its trading partners. A number of economists have put this simple version of the theory to empirical tests.

One of the first to do so was G. D. A. MacDougal. In 1951, MacDougal published a study of U.S.-British trade, using data from 1937.[1] He compared a number of industries in terms of relative labor productivity in the two countries with the ratio of their exports of the products of those industries. The results strongly supported the Ricardian theory. Labor productivity was higher in the United States than in the United Kingdom for all of the industries studied, indicating that the United States had a Ricardian absolute advantage in all of the products. As predicted by the theory, however, the United Kingdom was relatively successful in exporting the goods in which its labor productivity disadvantage was smallest. British exports were greater than U.S. exports for all the industries in which British labor was more than half as productive as U.S. labor (for example, woolen cloth, footwear, hosiery). U.S. exports exceeded British exports for all the industries in which U.S. labor was more than twice as productive as British labor. Later studies using different sets of data have tended to confirm this result.

Comparative Advantage with Multiple Factors of Production

The Ricardian model of comparative advantage focused on a single factor of production: labor. Studies such as MacDougal's indicate that the single-factor version of the theory has considerable explanatory power. Even better, we can extend it to take more than one factor of production into account.

The Heckscher-Ohlin Theorem   Early in the twentieth century two Swedish economists, Eli Heckscher and Bertil Ohlin, developed a model that included two factors of production: capital and labor. They reasoned that countries with abundant supplies of labor and little capital would have a comparative advantage in labor-intensive goods, while countries with abundant capital and relatively less labor would have a comparative advantage in capital-intensive goods. The proposition that countries would tend to export products that use their relatively more abundant factor more intensively has come to be known as the **Heckscher-Ohlin theorem**. For example, just as the theorem would predict, the United States exports capital-intensive aircraft to China in exchange for labor-intensive clothing.

Heckscher-Ohlin theorem

The proposition that countries tend to export goods that make intensive use of the factors of production that the country possesses in relative abundance

The Importance of Demand

Both single-factor and multiple-factor versions of the theory of comparative advantage focus on supply conditions as the explanation of trade patterns. They implicitly assume that the consumer preferences are identical in all countries. In practice, though, patterns of trade contain some features that we can explain only by considering demand.

One such feature is a tendency of countries to trade most with others at a similar level of economic development. That runs against what we would expect from the simple Ricardian theory, which suggests that trade would be most profitable between countries that differ the most from one another. For example, simple comparative advantage would suggest that the United States would have more trade with Mexico, structurally a very different economy, than with Canada, which not only has a much smaller population than Mexico but also is more similar in many ways to the United States. Instead, Canada turns out to be the largest U.S. trading partner, and several distant countries, including Germany and Japan, rank close to nearby Mexico.

A closely related puzzle is the fact that countries often both import and export the products of a given industry. For example, the United States is both a major importer and exporter of motor vehicles, textiles, computers, foodstuffs, and footwear.

Comparative advantage can explain these trade patterns only at the expense of trivializing the concept—by saying, for example, that Germany has a comparative advantage in producing Audis and the United States has a comparative advantage in producing Cadillacs. A better explanation is that such trade patterns reflect the influence of demand and tastes. Firms in developed countries sell where the demand for their products is greatest—in other developed countries. Cross-trade within product categories reflects patterns of tastes: Although U.S. automakers pattern their cars to fit the tastes of a majority of domestic consumers, some U.S. drivers share Euro-style tastes for Audis and BMWs. The Ricardian theory and its modern variants, which look only at production costs, do not consider these demand-side influences.

Comparative Advantage and "Competitiveness"

According to the data in Figure 7.1, the United States is one of the world's biggest exporters, and its exports have been growing steadily. However, as U.S. exports have set records, its imports have grown even more rapidly. In the first decade of the twenty-first century, the *trade deficit*—the amount by which imports exceed exports—reached an all-time high. That became a major cause of national concern. News reporters, editorialists, and politicians feared that the United States was no longer "competitive" in the world economy. Competitiveness means different things to different people, but at the heart of it is a concern that foreign workers work harder and foreign business managers have become smarter than their U.S. counterparts. "Soon the Chinese, the Koreans, and the Europeans will be better at everything than we are," people have said. "Eventually we won't be able to export anything at all!"

Some aspects of U.S. trade trends are a legitimate cause for concern. However, the theory of comparative advantage casts doubt on the notion that a country can reach a point at which it imports everything and exports nothing. In fact, classical trade theory, as shown by our earlier Spain-Norway example, maintains that a country always has a comparative advantage in producing something even when it has an absolute disadvantage (in terms of labor hours or other factor inputs) for all goods. In terms of comparative advantage, then, a country must always be "competitive" in producing something.

Still, comparative advantage does not guarantee an exact match between the value of a country's exports and the value of its imports. The numerical examples given earlier, which suggest that must be the case, omit two important details. First, they leave out international financial transactions—purchases and sales of corporate stocks, government bonds, and other securities, bank loans, and more complex transactions like swaps and futures contracts. Second, they assume that trade takes the form of barter, whereas in practice most international trade uses money as a means of payment. Let's look briefly at these financial considerations.

Financial Transactions and the Balance of Trade   Without financial transactions, a country could not import more goods and services than it exports, or to export more than it imports, in a given year. To take a simple case, suppose that U.S. consumers decide to buy $100 million worth of flat-screen TVs from Korean firms. What will the Korean firms do with the $100 million they receive? They can use it to buy airliners built in the United States, in which case trade in goods between the United States and Korea will balance. However, they can instead use it to buy U.S. government bonds or make deposits in U.S. banks. In that case, the United States will export no goods in the current year to balance the imports of TVs. The Korean owners of the bonds or bank deposits have a claim on future exports from the United States; they can cash in their financial assets and spend them any time they like. Meanwhile, despite the U.S. comparative advantage in producing airliners, the U.S. trade accounts will show more imports than exports.

Could we say, then, that recent U.S. balance-of-trade deficits reflect a comparative advantage for the United States in the production of financial assets? That would certainly be one way to look at it. We could also say that Korean buyers simply prefer future U.S. airliners to current ones. That would be closer to the truth. A large part of the current U.S. trade deficit can be explained by the fact that many other countries, especially in Asia, have much higher savings rates than the United States, something that does indicate a preference for future consumption over current consumption. Looked at in this light, we should be cautious about assuming that the imbalance in merchandise trade reflects a loss of "competitiveness" in the sense of lost comparative advantage. It may just mean that U.S. consumers want goods now, whereas Asian consumers are more farsighted.

Exchange Rates and Competitiveness　　To understand international trade fully, we must also take into account the fact that it is conducted using money. However, there is no world money. Some countries use dollars, others use euros, and some have used strange-sounding currencies like the xu that you are unlikely ever to have heard of unless you play word games. Usually, then, before you can buy goods, services, or financial instruments from abroad, you must first trade your own currency for the currency of the country from which you want to buy. We call the institutions for making those trades *foreign-exchange markets.* The windows at international airports where tourists can use dollars to buy euros or yen are a tiny part of these markets. Most foreign exchange transactions take place through banks in New York, London, Tokyo, and other world financial centers.

Before buying goods or services from abroad you must first trade your own currency for the currency of the country from which you want to buy.

In many cases, exchange rates between currencies vary from day to day according to supply and demand conditions. For example, during 2011, the value of the euro varied from a low of $1.31 to a high of $1.47. As exchange rates vary, so do the prices of countries' imports and exports. At 1.40 euros to a dollar, an American importer would have to spend almost $100 to buy a bottle of champagne that had a price, in France, of 71 euros. If the exchange rate were 1.30 euros per dollar, the same bottle would cost only about $92. We see, then, that the ability of U.S. exporters to compete in world markets—and the ability of U.S. firms to compete against imports in their home markets—depends not only on Ricardian comparative advantage but also on exchange rates.

Not all countries allow the exchange rates of their currencies to move freely in response to supply and demand. Some countries permanently fix the value of their currency relative to that of a major trading partner. For example, Hong Kong holds the exchange rate of the Hong Kong dollar at a fixed value of about U.S. $0.13, and Latvia holds the exchange rate of its currency, the lats, at .7 lats per euro. It is rarely a matter of controversy when small countries set a fixed value for their currencies relative to a major currency like the dollar or euro. When large countries intervene in exchange rate determination, the result can be much more controversial.

China is a leading example of a country that actively manages its exchange rate without maintaining a completely fixed value. In recent years, China has regularly kept the value of its currency, the yuan (also known as the renminbi), at a level that makes Chinese exports more competitive than they would be if market forces alone set the exchange rate. That has led to accusations that China is unfairly harming the interests of U.S. firms that would like to export more goods to China, and firms that produce goods in the United States that compete with imports from China. A full exploration of Chinese currency policy raises macroeconomic issues that lie beyond the scope of this chapter.

7.2 Trade Policy and Protectionism

Up to this point we have pictured a world in which Norwegian fishers and Spanish farmers are free to trade as dictated by comparative advantage. In practice, however, governments are deeply involved in the regulation and promotion of trade, not just in their policies toward exchange rates, but in many other ways as well. This section examines government policies toward international trade.

Moves toward Freer Trade since World War II

The post–World War II period saw a broad movement toward freer trade aided by several new international organizations. The International Monetary Fund, established in 1944, maintains a stable financial climate for trade. In the General Agreement on Tariffs and Trade (GATT), major trading nations came together to combat **protectionism**—policies that shield domestic industries from competition by imports. In 1995, the World Trade Organization (WTO), which is now the world's principal authority overseeing international trade, replaced GATT.

Protectionism

Any policy that shields domestic industries from import competition

Tariff

A tax on imported goods

WTO rules permit taxes on imports, known as **tariffs**, but restrict their use. Under the most-favored-nation principle, WTO member nations are supposed to charge the same tariff rates for imports from all WTO countries. A series of multinational negotiations sponsored by the WTO succeeded in lowering the average level of tariffs from 40 percent at the end of World War II to less than 10 percent today. Throughout this period, as noted earlier, the volume of world trade grew consistently faster than the volume of world output. Also, the WTO has tried, with far from complete success, to discourage the use of **import quotas**—restrictions on the quantity of a good that can be imported during a given period.

Import quotas

A limit on the quantity of a good that imported over a given period

Regional Trading Blocs   In addition to the activities of the WTO, there have been efforts to set up regional trading blocs in several parts of the world. The best known of these is the European Union (EU). A key aim of the EU has been to eliminate all barriers to trade among the major European countries, eventually leading to a situation in which trade among these countries is nearly as free as trade among the states of the United States.

Applying Economic Ideas 7.1

The Korea-U.S. Free Trade Agreement, Five Years in the Making

In January 2012, a major bilateral free trade agreement known as KORUS FTA came into effect. The pact, which will boost the already-large volume of trade between the United States and South Korea, its seventh-largest trading partner, illustrates both the promise and the problems of free trade agreements.

The initial negotiations leading to KORUS FTA took place in 2006. The agreement covers trade in manufactured goods like cars and electronics; agricultural products like beef; and services, including parcel delivery, business services, and others. In economic terms, it appears to be a clear win-win deal. Both sides will lower tariff and nontariff barriers to trade. Korea, which had higher tariffs and more stringent nontariff import regulations to begin with, will have to make even greater changes than the United States under the terms of KORUS FTA.

Despite its promised economic advantages, political problems stalled ratification of the agreement for more than five years. In two ways, the political trade game follows different rules than the economic game. First, whereas economists tend to focus on net gains, politics is very sensitive to the fact that any change in trade policy produces some losers along with the winners. Second, the political influence of winners and losers is not necessarily proportional to the magnitude of their economic gains or losses. Instead, well-organized groups—like corporations, farm groups, and unionized workers—have disproportionate political power compared to poorly organized groups like consumers and non-unionized workers.

KORUS FTA provides a perfect illustration of the political economy of free trade. The strongest opposition to the original treaty came from the Big Three automakers and their unions, which controlled enough Democratic votes in Congress to block ratification. Opponents claimed that U.S.-Korean automobile trade is inherently unfair because Korea exports seven hundred thousand cars a year to the United States while importing one hundred times fewer U.S. cars. Little attention was paid to the fact that KORUS FTA would lower Korean auto tariffs by more than U.S. tariffs would be lowered, or that Korean and U.S. automakers each produce many cars in the others' country, which do not show up in import figures, or that trade in auto parts is closer to balance than trade in finished cars. In the end, an agreement was reached that both sides would lower barriers to trade in automobiles, but those in the United States would be phased in over a longer period.

Additional opposition came from U.S. beef producers. Korea has blocked U.S. beef imports, alleging risks of mad cow disease. That infuriated Senator Max Baucus (D-Mont.), Chairman of the Senate Finance Committee, which was a key gateway for ratification. Many observers think Korean health concerns are bogus; but whatever the science behind them, they are political reality. Breaking down the Korean barriers took months of hard negotiation.

Although the governing party in South Korea favored ratification of KORUS FTA, fierce opposition from farm interests slowed ratification there. In a last ditch effort to derail the final vote of approval held in December 2011, an opposition lawmaker threw a teargas canister in the Korean parliamentary chamber. Despite that disturbance, the Korean parliament ratified the agreement, clearing the way for it to come into force at the beginning of 2012.

Source: Based in part on material from Ed Dolan's Econ Blog (www.dolanecon.blogspot.com), used with permission.

The EU has not achieved all of its goals in full. Differences in levels of economic development among the countries of the EU, which are greater than those among the states of the United States, have been a recurring source of problems. Also, the goal of a single currency for Europe has proved more difficult to achieve than many had hoped. Nonetheless, after its expansion to twenty-seven countries in 2007, the EU, with a population of nearly 500 million, can fairly be considered the world's largest unified economic zone in most respects.

On the other side of the Atlantic, progress was under way toward the formation of an even larger trading bloc. The first step toward forming this bloc was a 1989 agreement between the United States and Canada, its largest trading partner, to eliminate nearly all barriers to trade over a ten-year period. The next step took place in 1994, when the North American Free Trade Agreement (NAFTA) added Mexico, the third-largest U.S. trading partner. Since NAFTA came into force, trade among the U.S., Canada, and Mexico has more than doubled. In 2011, the U.S. Congress ratified three more bilateral trade agreements, with South Korea, Colombia, and Panama. *Applying Economic Ideas 7.1* discusses the Korean agreement, which is the largest of the three. Other examples of regional trading blocs include the ASEAN Free Trade Area (AFTA), which unites six Asian countries—Thailand, Philippines, Malaysia, Brunei, Singapore, and Indonesia—with a total population of 320 million people. A similar regional trading block, known as MECCSUR, links several of the largest economies in Latin America.

Despite their advantages, there is a downside to regional free trade blocs. That is the tendency of such blocs to raise protectionist barriers against outsiders. For example, NAFTA contains provisions protecting North American (mainly U.S.) firms against competition from Asian and European rivals. The EU is notorious for shielding its farmers from outside competition. Serious worries remain about the possibility of open trade war between the blocs. AFTA, on the other hand, is composed of relatively poor nations that cannot afford to cut themselves off from world trade. Their bloc adheres to the principle of "open regionalism" that will lower barriers within the group without raising them against outsiders.

Countertrends: Other Forms of Protectionism

Spurred by the strengthening of free-trade institutions, the volume of world trade has increased greatly in recent decades. However, GATT and the WTO did not end protectionism. In addition to the continued use of traditional tariffs and quotas, especially in agriculture, new types of protectionism sprang up. The new protectionism included devices such as "orderly marketing agreements" and "voluntary export restraints." These involve the use of political pressure—usually backed by the threat of a tariff or quota—to restrain trade in a particular good.

The Multifiber Arrangement (MFA), formally adopted in 1974, was an example of this new kind of protectionism.[2] The arrangement, which began as a temporary restriction on imports of Japanese cotton textiles into the United States, grew into a vast web of quotas that all major trading countries used to manage trade in textiles and apparel. It was a serious violation of the spirit and, sometimes, the letter of WTO principles, not only in its emphasis on quotas, but also in its open discrimination among exporting nations. By imposing much more stringent limits on imports from developing countries than from industrialized exporters in the EU and elsewhere, the MFA undermined not only the most-favored-nation principle but also stated U.S. policy of promoting economic development in low-income countries.

Several developing countries complained that unfair treatment by MFA restrictions cost them as much as 20 million jobs each year. Those complaints led to the termination of the MFA at the end of 2004. The end of the MFA helped rationalize patterns of international textile trade, but there were some painful effects in the short run as production shifted to the lowest-cost producers like China and Bangladesh.

Some elements of protectionist agreements are nominally voluntary, but their effects on consumers scarcely differ from those of a compulsory tariff or quota. Prices go up and reductions in efficiency occur as production moves against the direction of comparative advantage. For example, according to one estimate, the cost of the Multifiber Arrangement to U.S. consumers was more than $20 billion per year or about $238 per U.S. household at its height in 1986.

Antidumping rules are another aspect of the new protectionism. A country "dumps" its goods when it sells them in a foreign market for less than the price at which it sells them at home or for less than the cost of producing them. Under certain provisions of U.S. law, domestic producers facing competition from imports that have been "dumped" on the U.S. market can seek tariffs. For example, in 2011, U.S. makers of solar panels filed an antidumping complaint that, if successful, would result in the imposition of tariffs of from 50 to 250 percent on imported panels. Users of solar panels have protested strongly, saying that such tariffs would be a significant setback to the green energy movement in the United States. The International Trade Commission may issue a final ruling as soon as 2012.

Understanding Protectionism: Impacts of Trade on Income Distribution

Why is it that protectionism is so widespread, despite the potential economic efficiency gains of free trade? One explanation is the way trade affects the distribution of income within countries. We can illustrate some of the main ideas by modifying the Spain-Norway example to include more than one factor of production.

Suppose that fishing requires a large capital investment per worker, in the form of expensive boats, nets, and navigation equipment, while farming requires a smaller investment in tractors and plows. If so, we say that fishing is capital intensive and farming is labor intensive.

In 2011, U.S. makers of solar panels filed an antidumping complaint that would result, if passed, in the imposition of tariffs on imported panels.

Suppose also, as before, that without trade the opportunity cost of fish is higher in Spain than in Norway, so that Spain has a comparative advantage in grain and Norway has a comparative advantage in fish. In this two-factor world, as in our earlier single-factor example, international trade allows total world production of both fish and grain to increase, and also increases the quantities of both goods available in both countries. Now, however, a new question arises: Who will receive the gains from trade within each country?

To answer that question, we must look at how trade affects factor markets as it brings about increasing specialization in each country. In Norway, production shifts from farming to fishing. As grain production decreases, Norwegian farming releases large quantities of labor and smaller quantities of capital. At the same time, the expanding fishing industry requires lots of capital but relatively little labor. The shift in production thus creates a surplus of labor relative to capital. Factor markets can return to equilibrium only when wages fall relative to the rate of return on capital. Only then will fisheries adopt more labor-intensive production methods. Meanwhile the opposite process occurs in Spain where the shift from fishing to farming depresses the rate of return on capital and raises the wage rate.

These changes in relative factor prices determine the distribution of the gains from trade within each country. Spanish workers and Norwegian boat owners will gain doubly from trade—first because trade increases the size of the pie (the total quantity of goods), and second because the shifts in factor prices give them a larger slice of that pie. For Norwegian workers and Spanish owners of agricultural capital, in contrast, one of these effects works against the other. Those groups still benefit from the growth of the economic pie, but they get a smaller slice of it than before. Trade may or may not end up making them better.

Suppose that the comparative advantage in the pre-trade situation is large and the difference in factor intensity between the two countries is small. If so, Norwegian workers and owners of Spanish farms will still receive absolute gains from trade, even though they will lose ground relative to others in their own country. If conditions are less favorable, however, they can end up worse off than they were before trade began. Who gains and who loses depends partly on the degree of specialization of factors of production.

So far, we have looked at matters only in terms of broadly defined labor, as if workers could move from job to job without cost. However, suppose instead that we think not in terms of labor in general but in terms of people with farming skills and people with fishing skills. When we take specialized skills and other specifics into account, the effects of trade include not only changes in relative wages but also periods of unemployment and costs of retraining. The uneven impact of changes in trade patterns on the lives and jobs of specific categories of workers turns out to be one of the main sources of political support for protectionism.

Protectionism and Public Choice

International competition, like competition within a country, tends to drive wages and returns to other factors of production toward the level of opportunity costs. Protection against foreign competition relieves the pressure and permits the protected firms and workers to earn profits and wages in excess of opportunity costs, or rents, as we called them in Chapter 4. We can analyze the political process that results in trade restrictions in terms of public choice theory and rent seeking.

Consider, for example, the costs and benefits of U.S. trade restrictions on imported sugar. Historically, the United States produced about half of the sugar it consumed and imported the rest.[3] By the early 2000s, as a result of trade restrictions, it was importing only about 12 percent of its sugar. As a result, sugar prices in the United States approached double the world price, ranging from two to three times the world price, at a cost to U.S. consumers of billions of dollars per year. The United States not only maintains barriers to direct imports of sugar but also has a high tariff on the indirect import of sugar in the form of ethanol distilled from sugar cane in Brazil and other countries. That not only helps keep the U.S. price of sugar high but also raises the price of corn, as well, since in the United States ethanol comes mainly from corn rather than sugar cane.

What explains the willingness of U.S. consumers to pay high prices for sugar? It is, apparently, a classic case of the disproportionate political influence of small, well-organized interest groups. The benefits of restrictions on sugar imports are concentrated on producers, who

The United States not only maintains barriers to direct imports of sugar but also has a high tariff on the indirect import of sugar in the form of ethanol distilled from sugar.

are few in number. Large companies like Flo-Sun and U.S. Sugar contribute hundreds of thousands of dollars to candidates of both major parties during each election cycle. On the other hand, the cost of sugar quotas to consumers are as little as $6 per person, according to one some estimates. For consumers, then, sugar policy is an insignificant consideration in making political choices.

Sugar policy also has an impact on jobs. Only about sixteen thousand U.S. workers work in sugar production and refining in the United States, and an end to quotas would threaten the jobs of only about three thousand of those. Production of corn sweetener, which benefits indirectly from high sugar production, employs more workers, perhaps as many as two hundred fifty thousand; but the threat to those jobs is also less direct. If sugar quotas ended, the chief employment benefit would be creation of new jobs in the food processing industry, which already employs far more workers, more than five hundred thousand. The political impact of changes in the job market, however, is not proportional to the number of jobs affected. The key consideration is that workers in sugar production know who they are and understand that their jobs are under threat from a policy change. Potential new workers in food processing, currently employed elsewhere or unemployed, do not specifically identify sugar policy as a factor affecting their welfare. As a result, sugar workers are politically active on the issue and potential new food processing workers are not.

We could repeat this kind of analysis for any protected market. For example, one study estimated the cost to consumers of each job saved in the apparel industry by the MFA at $46,000 per year, compared with average earnings of just $11,000 per year for textile workers.[4] Studies of tariffs and quotas on peanuts, books, ceramic tile, and other products give similar results. In each case, economic investigators have found that total gains to producers fall short of total costs to consumers, with the benefits concentrated on compact, politically active groups and the costs spread among millions of households.

A Race to the Bottom?

Often opponents of free trade speak a simple language of self-interest, using money and political power to advance their positions regardless of effects on others. However, some opponents of global trade who live in high-income countries have a real concern that trade may harm people in their low-income trade partners.

One such concern is that free trade leads to a "race to the bottom" in global labor standards. Trade based on comparative advantage is all well and good, they would say, if a country does have a genuine advantage in producing something at a low cost. They would hardly want Iceland to be self-sufficient in coffee or expect the city-state of Singapore to have to produce all its own rice. Still, they say, some kinds of cost advantage are not a legitimate basis for trade. In particular, critics argue that countries should not be encouraged to lower health and safety protections for workers to gain a comparative advantage based on lower labor costs.

In evaluating concerns about labor standards, it is helpful to distinguish between "cash standards" and "core standards." Cash standards mean wages and non-wage labor benefits like employer-paid health care or paid vacation. To insist that those workers in poor countries earn the same pay and benefits as those in rich ones could be to cut them off from the possibility of trade-based growth. Refusing to buy anything from people who are poor seems like a strange way to help them become rich. Experience shows, instead, that countries like Korea or Taiwan, which were relatively open to trade during their early years as low-wage countries, grew rapidly and eventually reached high average wage levels without extremes of inequality. In China today, changing patterns of trade are increasingly forcing out relatively primitive textile and footwear factories, which thrived when wages were $2 per day or less. Workers are, instead, moving to more modern factories producing photovoltaic panels or computer chips, where wages are $10 per day or more. Those wages are still very low by U.S. or European standards, and income distribution in China is less equal than in the earlier generation of "Asian tigers." However, for the workers involved, $10 a day represents an important step from poverty to economic security.

Core labor standards, on the other hand, are more a matter of universal human rights than simply of labor costs. Meeting core labor standards requires doing away with forced labor and abusive child labor, while guaranteeing the right for workers to bargain collectively and ending discrimination in employment. A true "race to the bottom" would occur if policies encouraged production to move to the countries that most flagrantly ignored core labor standards.

There is a similar concern that global trade could lead to a "race to the bottom" in environmental standards. As we saw in Chapter 6, sustainable waste disposal practices are typically more costly for producers than dumping untreated wastes into the environment.

To some extent, lower environmental standards in low-income countries may reflect an unwillingness of people in low-income countries to sacrifice as much material consumption for a given improvement in local air or water quality as those in high-income countries. Environmental quality is a "normal good" as we defined it in Chapter 5. As incomes rise, people are willing to "buy" more environmental quality. For that reason, levels of many (but not all) kinds of pollution tend to follow an inverted-U pattern over time. Pollution is low in countries that have hardly any industry at all, greatest in newly industrializing countries and lower again in wealthy industrial countries that choose to invest heavily in pollution control. Increasing levels of air pollution in Beijing over recent decades while Los Angeles air has become cleaner illustrate this trend.

On the other hand, sometimes companies or even entire countries can be tempted to cut costs by opposing or violating environmental regulations. Suppose, for example, that two countries both have well-intended environmental laws. However, in one the laws are enforced, and in the other corrupt inspectors take bribes to turn their backs on violations. Would it be right to say that the latter country had a comparative advantage based on lower costs? Economic analysis says that it would not. Total costs of production, including both internal and external costs, are likely to be higher, not lower, in the country where externalities go uncontrolled. Costs only appear lower because lax enforcement allows producers to impose the costs on their neighbors. If the pollution in question has a cross-border nature, like emissions of greenhouse gasses or the chemicals that destroy the earth's protective ozone layer, it is even harder to argue that world efficiency gains when trade moves production to high-pollution countries.

Summary

1. **How can we apply the principle of comparative advantage to international trade?** A country has a comparative advantage in the production of a good if it can produce it at a lower opportunity cost than its trading partner can. When each country exports goods in which it has a comparative advantage, total world production of all goods and services, as well as total consumption in each trading country, can increase. The Heckscher-Ohlin theorem proposes that countries will tend to have a comparative advantage in goods that make intensive use of the factors of production that are relatively abundant in that country.

2. **What is the relationship between competitiveness and comparative advantage?** In recent years, U.S. imports have expanded more rapidly than exports, leaving the country with a record trade deficit. Some observers interpreted that situation as indicating a loss of competitiveness, implying that U.S. firms were no longer capable of producing goods that other countries wanted. However, financial transactions and exchange rates also influence trends in imports and exports. When considering those factors, a country that is "competitive" in the sense that it produces high quality goods using state-of-the-art management and technology can still import more than it exports.

3. **What has been the trend of international trade policy in recent years?** The general trend in international trade policy has been toward a reduction of traditional tariff and quota barriers to trade. Another important trend has been the growth of regional and bilateral trade agreements like the European Union, NAFTA, and the new Korea-U.S. free trade agreement. On the other hand, protectionist practices, including both traditional kinds and new ones such as orderly marketing agreements, voluntary quotas, antidumping laws, and restrictive product standards, have by no means disappeared.

4. **How does international trade affect income distribution within each country?** In a world with two or more factors of production, trade tends to increase the demand for factors that export industries use relatively intensively and decrease demand for those that import-competing sectors use intensively. As a result, although trade benefits a country as a whole, it may not benefit owners of factors that are specialized for producing goods that compete with imports.

(Continues)

5. **How can we understand protectionist policies in terms of public choice theory and rent seeking?** Because protectionist policies shield firms and factory owners from international competition, those firms can earn rents, that is, payments in excess of opportunity costs. Often those who benefit from these rents are small, well-organized groups that have political influence out of proportion to their numbers. Although the overall costs of protectionism tend to outweigh the benefits, the consumers share the costs widely, whereas the gains from trade barriers accrue to small but well-organized groups of firms and workers in protected industries.

Key Terms   Page

Problems and Topics for Discussion

1. **NAFTA and comparative advantage**   Under NAFTA, the U.S. has exported larger quantities of high-tech goods (for example, advanced construction equipment) to Mexico, while importing more low-tech goods (for example, vacuum cleaners) from Mexico. What does that suggest about U.S. versus Mexican comparative advantage in the production of construction equipment? Of vacuum cleaners? Could such examples be consistent with the Heckscher-Ohlin theorem? What are the potential benefits and costs of NAFTA for U.S. and Mexican workers? Consumers? Owners of productive resources other than labor?

2. **A change in costs and comparative advantage**   Using the hypothetical numbers of the example in this chapter, suppose that Norway introduces new, high-yield grains and that the number of labor hours needed to grow a ton of grain there falls from 5 hours to 2.5 hours. What will happen to trade between Norway and Spain? If the number of labor hours needed to grow a ton of grain in Norway falls all the way to 2, what will happen to the pattern of trade?

3. **Competitiveness**   Consider the following statement: "The United States may still be number one, but I don't think we will be much longer. China, India, Brazil, and other emerging market countries are catching up. Soon it will no longer be economical for us to produce anything." On the basis of what you have learned about the principle of comparative advantage, do you think it is possible to reach a point at which it is no longer worthwhile to produce anything—that is, a point at which it becomes economical to import all goods? Discuss.

4. **Trade bargaining**   If you were a strong supporter of free trade and in charge of U.S. international trade policy, would you cut tariffs and quotas, or would you negotiate with the nation's trading partners, maintaining trade barriers unless they lowered theirs also? Discuss.

5. **The globalization debate**   Do a Web search for recent commentary on globalization and environmental standards (or labor standards). Reading pro- and anti-globalization sources, can you identify "economic" issues and "core" issues? Can you identify any cases in which it appears that parties to the debate are using altruistic rhetoric to defend simple self-interest?

Case for Discussion

Has the Brazil-U.S. Cotton Dispute Finally Been Resolved?

In 2002, Brazil initiated a case (DS267) within the WTO's dispute resolution mechanism. The complaint claimed that the United States had violated its WTO obligations by providing subsidies of $12.5 billion to U.S. cotton growers between 1999 and 2002, boosting U.S. exports and depressing prices at the expense of Brazilian cotton growers and other producers. The United States is the second-largest producer of cotton and the largest exporter.

In due course, in 2004, the WTO issued a ruling in Brazil's favor. The following year, in response to the ruling, the United States made several modifications to its cotton subsidy program. Brazil argued that the changes were inadequate and renewed its complaint. Over the next several years, the WTO issued additional rulings, all in favor of Brazil. Finally, in 2010, Brazil announced that it would take action by imposing tariffs on more than $800 million in goods imported from the United States.

U.S. negotiators appeared backed into a corner by the fact that no fundamental changes to its cotton subsidies would be possible before the next comprehensive review of farm legislation, scheduled for 2012. In the meantime, the two countries reached a temporary agreement. Under its terms, the United States would pay almost $150 million to a special fund created to benefit the Brazilian cotton industry and would make short-term administrative changes to the cotton subsidy program.

At this writing, it is still uncertain whether the 2012 farm bill review will lead to fundamental changes in U.S. cotton policies. Cotton farmers continue to resist any such changes, while U.S. consumers and Brazilian exporters are hoping the protectionist cotton regime will finally end.

Sources: Jonathan Wheatley, Edward Alden, and Frances Williams, "Brazil Victory Could Prompt Subsidies Cases," *Financial Times,* April 28, 2004, p. 8; Penny Hill Press (Congressional Research Service), "Brazil's WTO Case against the U.S. Cotton Program," January 18, 2011, http://international-trade-reports.blogspot.com/2011/01/brazils-wto-case-against-us-cotton.html

Questions

1. A subsidy on exports is, in a sense, the opposite of a tariff on imports. If a tariff lowers efficiency, would you expect a subsidy to increase efficiency or lower it? How do tariffs and subsidies compare in the way they distort trade according to comparative advantage?

2. Who gains and who loses from U.S. cotton subsidies? Consider each of the following groups: U.S. producers, U.S. taxpayers, Brazilian producers, and consumers in both countries? Do you think total gains exceed or fall short of total losses?

3. How could you explain the expenditure of billions of taxpayer dollars to subsidize a relatively few, highly prosperous U.S. cotton producers? Do the categories of public choice theory help here?

4. Use your Internet research skills to learn whether there have been any further changes to U.S. cotton policy since 2011.

Endnotes

1. G. D. A. MacDougal, "British and American Exports: A Study Suggested by the Theory of Comparative Costs," *Economic Journal* (December 1951).

2. For a thorough discussion of the MFA, see Thomas Grennes, "The Multifiber Arrangement and the Management of International Textile Trade," *Cato Journal* (Spring/Summer 1989): 107–131.

3. Information on sugar policy and its effects based on Mark A. Groombridge, "American's Bittersweet Sugar Policy," Cato Institute Center for Trade Policy Studies, December 4, 2001.

4. See Grennes. The comparison of consumers' costs to workers' wages actually understates the true cost-benefit ratio because the MFA's cost to consumers continued year after year, whereas displaced apparel workers are out of work less than six months, on the average. Estimates that consider this fact indicate that consumers bear $31 in costs through higher apparel prices for each $1 benefit to apparel workers.

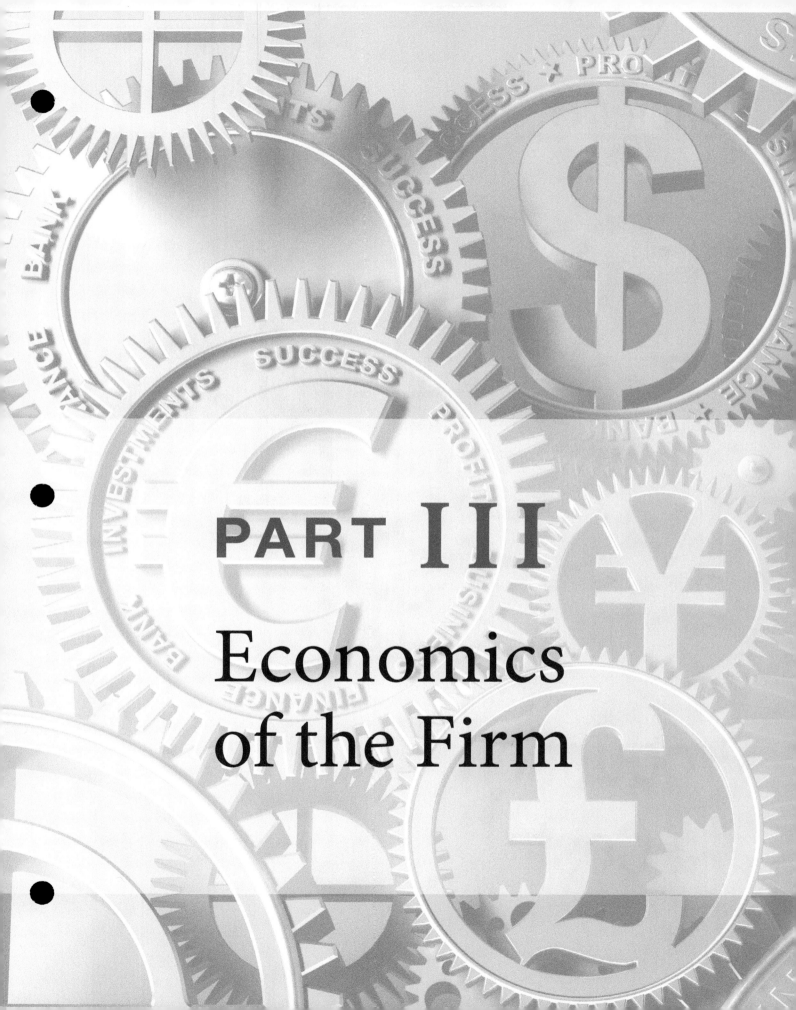

PART III

Economics of the Firm

Chapter 8

Production
and Cost

After reading this chapter, you will understand the following:

1. How economists view the concepts of cost and profit

2. The distinction between short-run and long-run time horizons

3. How costs vary in response to changes in the quantity of a variable input

4. The graphical representation of production costs

5. The choices a firm faces in the course of long-run expansion

Before reading this chapter, make sure you know the meaning of the following concepts:

1. Opportunity cost

2. Entrepreneurship

3. Economic rent

4. Rational choice

Business firms are among the most visible features of a market economy. Some of them are giants like Google that seem to reach into every corner of our lives. Others are small local operations like a lawn service or espresso stand. As consumers we count on business firms for the goods and services we buy, workers count on them to provide jobs, and governments count on them to pay taxes. The chapters in this section look at firms from several perspectives. This chapter looks at the way they transform inputs of labor, capital, and natural resources into useful goods and services. Chapters 9, 10, and 11 look at how firms compete with one another in the effort to earn profits and avoid losses. Chapter 12 looks at issues in public policy that arise when competition does not work smoothly. By the time we have put the whole picture together, we will see just why firms are one of the basic units of a market economy.

8.1 Costs and Profits

As we did in the case of consumer choice, we will begin our discussion of firms by looking at the objectives and constraints that shape their choices. For most firms, earning profits and avoiding losses is a key objective. The main constraints on a firm's opportunities are its costs of production and demand for its output. This chapter will focus on profits and costs. The next chapter will introduce demand.

The Profit Motive

The idea that firms are in business to maximize profits is familiar, but not without controversy. It is open to an objection similar to that raised against the rationality in consumer choice. It implies too narrow a view of human nature, its critics say; profit is important, but it is hardly the only thing businesses are interested in. Managers of some firms seem to display other-regarding preferences. They spend large amounts on supporting the arts or aiding the homeless and exhibit concern for their workers, their customers, and the environment beyond any level that might increase profits by enhancing the firm's public image. Other firms are led by egotists who will risk all, including profit itself, in pursuit of building a personal empire. Still others are run by people who are content to earn a minimum profit required for survival and, if things go well, to take Wednesday afternoons off for a game of golf or a trip to the mountains rather than toil away for a few extra dollars.

After the discussion of rational choice in Chapter 4, it should not be hard to guess how economists answer objections to the profit maximization assumption.

One defense of assumption is that economists do not mean profit maximization as a complete description of the motives of business managers. Rather, it is a simplification that has the purpose of giving a sharper structure to theories about the way changes in costs or demands affect decisions. Following the principle of Ockham's razor, we should discard a simple theory for a more complex one only when the simple theory fails to explain behavior observed in the real world. In practice, theories based on profit maximization explain a great deal of what firms do. In some special situations, we can improve the theories by considering objectives other than profit, but we do not always need to do so.

The *survivorship principle* is a second defense of the profit maximization assumption. Imagine that ownership of firms is at first distributed randomly among people who are inclined to pursue the objective of profit and others who favor the objectives of benevolence, ego satisfaction, or the easy life. Over time, the firms that maximized profit would increase their capital and grow steadily through reinvestment or acquisition. Those that pursued other objectives would at best have fewer profits to invest in expansion and at worst go out of business because of losses. Over time, those firms that survived in the market would be more likely to be the profit maximizers.

The Nature of Costs

Profit is the difference between revenue and costs, so we cannot get far in discussing profits without looking at costs. As we learned in Chapter 1, economists think first and foremost in terms of *opportunity cost*, without which no production can take place. There are never enough resources to satisfy all wants, so the decision to produce any one thing implies the need to forgo using the same resources to produce something else. The opportunity costs of production are a fundamental constraint on a firm's ability to maximize its profits. In this section, we will explore several aspects of production costs and explain their relationship to one another.

Implicit and Explicit Costs   There are several components to the opportunity costs of production. They include whatever the firm pays—to workers, investors, and owners of natural resources in order obtain the basic factors of production—and also payments to suppliers of intermediate goods, such as parts, semi-finished materials, and business services. We can classify those costs in several ways. We begin with the distinction between explicit and implicit costs.

Explicit costs are opportunity costs that take the form of explicit payments to suppliers of factors of production and intermediate goods. They include workers' wages, managers' salaries, salespeople's commissions, payments to banks and other suppliers of financial services, fees for legal advice, transportation charges, and many other things.

Not all opportunity costs take the form of explicit payments to parties outside a firm, however. Most firms also incur **implicit costs**, which take the form of opportunity costs of using resources that a firm's owners (or the firm itself as a legal entity) contribute without receiving explicit payment.

Consider, for example, the owner of a small firm who works along with the firm's hired employees without receiving a salary. By doing so, he or she gives up the opportunity to work for someone else. The correct measure of the opportunity cost of the owner's labor would be the wage or salary available from the next-best employment opportunity. In addition to supplying their own labor, small-business owners often invest their savings in their firms without receiving any explicit interest payment. The opportunity cost of capital for such a firm is the interest or dividend available from investing the same capital elsewhere. Firms normally do not record implicit costs in their accounts, but this does not make those costs any less real.

For a publicly traded corporation, the most important implicit cost is the opportunity cost of capital contributed by shareholders. Shareholders will not buy a corporation's stock unless they expect adequate compensation through dividends or through increases in the market price of their shares. The minimum rate of return needed to attract investors stock will vary from one company to another, depending on risks, taxes, and other considerations.

Explicit costs
Opportunity costs that take the form of explicit payments to suppliers of factors of production and intermediate goods

Implicit costs
Opportunity costs of using resources that firm's owners (or the firm itself as a legal entity) contribute without receiving explicit payment

A small business incurs an implicit cost when its owner works alongside employees without receiving a salary.

Pure economic profit

The sum that remains when we subtract both explicit and implicit costs from total revenue

Accounting profit

Total revenue minus explicit costs

Normal profit (normal return on capital)

The implicit opportunity cost of capital contributed by the firm's owners (equity capital)

Costs and Profits   The distinction between explicit and implicit costs is important for understanding the meaning of the term *profit*. Economists use the term **pure economic profit** to mean the difference between a firm's total revenue and all of its opportunity costs, including both explicit and implicit costs. It is important to distinguish pure economic profit from two other uses of the term profit.

First, in the business world, we often use *profit* to mean revenue minus explicit costs only, without considering implicit costs. Economists call that concept **accounting profit** because it considers only the explicit payments that appear in the firm's written accounts.[1] The relationship between accounting profit and pure economic profit is as follows:

$$\text{Pure economic profit} = \text{Accounting profit} - \text{Implicit costs}$$

or alternatively

$$\text{Accounting profit} = \text{Pure economic profit} + \text{Implicit costs}$$

Second, pure economic profit needs to be distinguished from so-called normal profit, a term that refers to the opportunity cost of capital contributed by the firm's owners (*equity capital*, in financial terminology). **Normal return on capital** is a more exact term for normal profit. Suppose, for example, that you use $200,000 of your own savings as capital for a new business. You could, instead, invest in securities that pay a 10 percent rate of return, or $20,000 per year. That $20,000 would be your opportunity cost of capital. It represents the return your funds would have earned in the best alternative use. The same reasoning would apply if outside shareholders contributed the capital, rather than an entrepreneur who actively participated in managing the business.

To understand why we call the opportunity cost of owners' capital normal profit, consider a firm that has no other implicit costs. In order for such a firm to earn zero economic profit, its accounting profit would have to be equal to its implicit opportunity cost of capital. We could call that rate of accounting profit "normal" in the sense that it is just enough to make it worthwhile for owners to invest their capital in this firm, rather than in the next best line of business available. Lines of business that earned more than this (that is, a positive pure economic profit) would be "abnormally" profitable and would swiftly attract new investors and competitors. Those that earned less would be less than "normally" profitable and would tend to shrink as investors channeled their capital elsewhere.

If a firm has other implicit costs in addition to those of owners' capital, its accounting profit must be sufficient to cover them, too, in order to earn zero economic profit. We can express this idea in terms of any of the following equations:

Accounting profit = Pure economic profit + Implicit costs

= Pure economic profit + Implicit cost of capital
+ Other implicit costs

= Pure economic profit + Normal profit
+ Other implicit costs

An Example   At several points in this chapter and the next, it will be convenient to use an imaginary business as a basis for numerical examples of concepts that we introduce. We will call our imaginary business Fieldcom, Inc. It is a small business started by a couple named Ralph and Andrea Martin. The Martins buy commonly available computer parts and assemble them into special-purpose smartphones that are "ruggedized" so that they can be used not only in an office or on a commuter train, but also in stressful environments like a desert oil field, a tropical mining site, or aboard an ocean racing yacht.

Figure 8.1 uses Fieldcom, Inc. to illustrate the concepts of pure economic profit, accounting profit, and normal profit. The figure shows Fieldcom as having earned total revenues of $600,000 in the past year. Explicit costs—salaries paid to employees and materials purchased—came to $400,000. That left an accounting profit of $200,000. The explicit costs do not include all of the firm's opportunity costs, however. Both Andrea and Ralph Martin gave up high-paying jobs to start the firm. Figure 8.1 lists their combined former income of $160,000 as an implicit cost of production. Another implicit cost is the $20,000 of forgone annual income that the Martins could have earned on $200,000 of personal savings if they had invested it elsewhere instead of in their business. This is the firm's opportunity cost of capital—the normal profit or normal return on capital required to attract capital to this use rather than to the best alternative use. When we subtract both explicit and implicit costs (including normal profit) from revenue, the firm has a pure economic profit of $20,000.

FIGURE 8.1   ACCOUNTS OF FIELDCOM, INC.

Total Revenue	$600,000
Less explicit costs:	
Wages and salaries	300,000
Materials and other	100,000
Equals accounting profit	$200,000
Less implicit costs:	
Forgone salary, Andrea Martin	80,000
Forgone salary, Ralph Martin	80,000
Opportunity cost of capital	20,000
Equals pure economic profit	$20,000

This figure shows the implicit and explicit costs of the imaginary firm Fieldcom, Inc., owned by entrepreneurs Ralph and Andrea Martin. Total revenue minus explicit costs equals accounting profit. Subtracting implicit costs from this quantity yields pure economic profit. Other terms for the opportunity cost of capital contributed by the Martins are "normal profit" or "normal return on capital."

Costs Are Subjective   A final word is in order regarding costs. Comparing the theory of consumption in Chapter 5 to the theory of production costs, it may at first appear that we are moving from an area of economics governed by *subjective* valuations to one of *objective* valuations; but that is true only in part, if at all.

What is true is that business managers and their accountants do try to record costs using consistent methods that are as free as possible from wishful thinking and intentional bias. In that sense, cost accounting is objective.

In a deeper sense, though, the theory of cost is just as subjective as is the theory of consumer choice. All costs are *opportunity costs* that reflect the value that a firm would have earned by putting resources to their best alternative use, a value that, in turn, depends on the demand for alternative products. For that reason, there can be no clear line between "objective" determinants of cost and "subjective" determinants of demand.

Furthermore, opinions can differ as to what is the best alternative. For example, just what is the opportunity cost to the Martins of investing their $200,000 savings in their firm? Ralph might think that the best alternative use would have been to purchase a portfolio of blue-chip stocks paying a 5 percent rate of return. Andrea might think the best alternative use would have been to buy shares in an aggressive hedge fund, a riskier use of their savings, but one yielding an expected return of 15 percent. Who is to say which one is right? Which alternative use of the $200,000 is best depends not only on subjective estimates of the likely return from alternative investments but also on the subjective attitude toward risk of the person making the investment.

The same is true of the opportunity costs of resources other than capital. For example, estimating the opportunity cost of assigning a worker to one task must take into account not only the worker's pay but also what he or she could have contributed by doing another task instead. A manager will not always be able to measure the worker's productivity objectively in both tasks, so the decision will rest on a subjective judgment. In short, because choices are subjective, costs are subjective, too.

Profit, Rents, and Entrepreneurship

Pure economic profit, as we have defined it, is the difference between what a firm receives for the products it sells and the opportunity cost of producing them. We first introduced the notion of payments in excess of opportunity costs in Chapter 4, where we called them *economic rents*. Pure economic profit, then, is a type of economic rent, but the two terms are not fully interchangeable.

For one thing, economic rent is a broader notion than profit. We usually use *profit* when discussing the net income of business firms, but it is possible for any factor of production to earn *rents*. Consider, for example, the income of rock stars, sports professionals, and other people with exceptional talents. Their opportunity cost of pursuing their chosen line of work may be low, in the sense that their income from their best-paying alternative occupation (say, selling insurance or working as a lifeguard) may be far lower than what they now earn. The amount by which their extraordinary income as a rock star, sports professional, or whatever exceeds their income from their best alternative occupation is economic rent, but we would not usually call it profit.

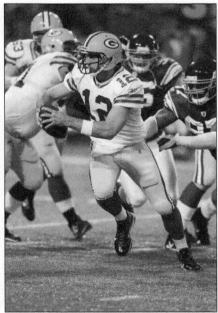

The income of professional athletes often include a large share of economic rent.

We can also make a distinction between *profit seeking* and *rent seeking*. Profit seeking is what entrepreneurs do when they look for ways to create goods and services that are worth more than the inputs they require. Henry Ford, Steve Jobs, and Sam Walton are examples of people who devoted their lives to finding new ways of satisfying customer needs. *Profit seeking*, then, means finding ways to create new value.

On the other hand, some firms try to increase their revenues by seeking restrictions on competition, not through innovation and cost reduction. For example, the U.S. cotton and sugar farmers have increased their business earnings not so much by cutting costs or improving their products as by persuading Congress to restrict imports. We can best think of doing so as being the result not of profit seeking but of political rent seeking.[2]

U.S. cotton farmers have increased their business earnings by persuading Congress to restrict imports.

The distinction between profits and rents is certainly not watertight. In both cases, we are dealing with revenues that exceed opportunity costs. Data like those presented in Figure 8.1 do not tell us all we might want to know about the origin of the $20,000 of pure economic profit. Did the Martins earn that $20,000 by creating a superior new product or by lobbying Congress to obstruct the efforts of competitors? It is not always possible to tell by looking at the kind of cost and revenue data that we deal with in this chapter and the one that follows.

Fixed Costs, Variable Costs, and Sunk Costs

Variable inputs

Inputs that can be varied within a short time in order to increase or decrease output

Variable costs

The explicit and implicit costs of providing variable inputs

Fixed inputs

Inputs that cannot be increased or decreased in a short time in order to increase or decrease output

Fixed costs

The explicit and implicit opportunity costs associated with providing fixed inputs

Short run

A time horizon within which a firm can adjust output only by changing the amounts of variable inputs it uses while fixed inputs remain unchanged

Long run

A time horizon that is long enough to permit changes in both fixed and variable inputs

The implicit-explicit distinction is not the only way to classify costs. Another approach focuses on the time horizon for production decisions.

The amounts of inputs a firm uses vary as the amount of output changes. It is possible to adjust the amount of some inputs quickly. For example, a firm can increase inputs of electricity instantly by flipping a switch. Raw materials and hourly labor are other examples of inputs that the firm can adjust quickly. We call them **variable inputs** and the costs of obtaining them **variable costs**. Other inputs take longer to adjust. For example, building a new office building takes many months. In general, inputs that take longer to adjust are those that define the size of the firm's plant, including structures and production equipment. We call them **fixed inputs**, and we call the cost of providing them **fixed costs**.

Which inputs are fixed and which are variable depends not so much on the physical properties of the inputs themselves as on context of decisions about them. For example, a firm that hires workers on an hourly basis may treat wages as a variable cost. Another firm that hires workers on a yearly contract, subject to a "no layoff" agreement with its labor union, would treat wages as a fixed cost. Public policies may also affect what is a fixed or variable cost. For example, in the United States, most firms follow the principle of *employment at will*, meaning that they can lay off workers whenever they think doing so would improve their profits. That makes wages a variable cost. In contrast, many European countries have strong labor protection laws that require advance notice, complex paperwork, and large severance payments when a firm lays off workers. That makes wages more of a fixed cost.

Fixed and variable inputs, in turn, are the basis for a distinction between two time horizons: the short run and the long run. Those terms are operational concepts, not periods of calendar time. The **short run** is a length of time in which the firm can vary output by using more or fewer variable inputs, but one that is too short for changes in the size of a firm's plant (that is, its fixed inputs). The **long run** is a time horizon long enough to change fixed as well as variable inputs. For example, an automaker can vary output from month to month by adding extra shifts of workers without adding or expanding plants. That is the short run. Over a period of a few years, the same firm can increase capacity to meet expected growth of demand by building new plants or expanding old ones.

Implicit and Explicit Fixed Costs   In all cases, cost means opportunity cost, including both implicit and explicit costs. Implicit fixed costs deserve special attention.

Fixed costs, by their nature, do not vary with the firm's rate of output. They must be borne by the firm as long as it stays in business regardless of how much it produces in the short run. Some fixed costs take the form of periodic payments, which means they are explicit fixed costs. Implicit fixed costs are opportunity costs associated with facilities owned by the firm itself, but not reflected in ongoing payments.

The distinction between explicit and implicit fixed costs will be clearer if we consider an example. Consider a trucking firm that cannot operate without a warehouse. The warehouse is a fixed cost because, within wide limits at least, the firm needs it regardless of how much freight it hauls in a given month. The cost of the warehouse could be either explicit or implicit depending on who owns it. The firm might lease the warehouse for an annual payment of $12,000 in installments of $1,000 per month. The lease payments would be an explicit fixed cost. Instead, it might use cash reserves to buy the warehouse for a price of $120,000. The $120,000 used to buy the warehouse could have been used for some other purpose—say, to buy securities yielding 10 percent interest. The income ($12,000 a year or $1,000 a month) that could have been earned with those funds if they had not been used to buy the warehouse is an opportunity cost of owning the warehouse—an implicit fixed cost.

A warehouse is a fixed cost for a trucking firm that cannot operate without it.

Whether the warehouse cost is explicit (as under a lease) or implicit (as under ownership), it continues as long as the firm stays in business, even if it goes a month without carrying any freight at all. However, if the firm decides to quit the trucking business, it no longer needs a warehouse. If the firm rents the warehouse, it can terminate the lease; if it owns the warehouse, it can sell it and recover the $120,000 for use elsewhere. Either way, it would cease to bear the $1,000-a-month fixed cost of the facility.

Sunk Costs   It is important not to confuse fixed costs, especially implicit fixed costs, with **sunk costs**. Sunk costs reflect once-and-for-all expenditures that a firm cannot recover even if it leaves its line of business. For example, the trucking firm in our example might have paid $1,000 to have "Taylor Trucking" painted on the wall of its warehouse. That is a sunk cost. If the firm sells the warehouse (or terminates its lease), the sign becomes worthless. There is no way to recover the $1,000 because the next owner or tenant will want a different sign.

Sunk costs

Once-and-for-all costs that a firm cannot recover once it incurs them

Are sunk costs opportunity costs? That depends on circumstances. If a firm is entering a new line of business or expanding its operations, the sunk costs of doing so are an opportunity cost. For example, if our trucking firm is considering service to a new city, it must think, "opportunity cost of entering the new market equals $120,000 to buy a warehouse plus $1,000 to paint the sign." On the other hand, once the firm has incurred a sunk cost, it is no longer an opportunity cost relevant to any future decision because it has, once and for all, lost the opportunity to do anything else with the funds in question. If the firm later considers abandoning service to the city in question, it should think only, "We could get $120,000 by selling the warehouse." The $1,000 paid for the sign is irrelevant. Experienced managers often express the irrelevance of sunk costs to ongoing operations with the phrase "bygones are bygones."

The remainder of this chapter will be concerned only with firms' ongoing fixed and variable costs of doing business. Sunk costs will come back into the picture in later chapters.

8.2 Production and Costs in the Short Run

Now that we have pinned down the meaning of cost, our next job is to build a theory to explain how a firm's costs vary with its level of output. A firm's cost of production is one of the basic constraints that shape a firm's decisions (along with demand, which we will take up in the following chapter). We will divide the discussion of cost theory into two parts, short run and long run.

Production with One Variable Input in the Short Run

Although most firms can vary any of several inputs in the short run, we will keep things simple at the outset by considering the case in which there is only one variable input—the quantity of labor. To do so, we will turn once again to our imaginary firm Fieldcom.

Total physical product

The total output of a firm, measured in physical units

Figure 8.2 shows what happens to daily units of output, or **total physical product**, as the firm varies the number of workers from zero to eight. If it employs no one, or just one worker, it cannot produce anything because some parts of the job require at least two people working together. Two workers can get production moving; but because they use a lot of time setting up jobs and changing from one job to another, they are able to produce at a rate of only one smartphone per day. When a third worker joins them, specialization becomes possible and production increases to three units a day. A fourth worker gets things moving really smoothly, and output goes up to seven units a day. Adding workers five, six, and seven boosts the plant's output to its maximum of thirteen units a day. Beyond that point, it does no good to add more workers; all the tools and equipment are in use, and any extra workers would have to stand around waiting for a turn to use them.

In practice, the firm could increase output beyond thirteen units per day by adding other inputs along with more workers—more assembly tables, more testing equipment, and so on. For the moment, however, we are looking at the effects of increasing labor alone, other things being equal.

FIGURE 8.2   RESPONSE OF OUTPUT TO CHANGES IN ONE VARIABLE INPUT

(a)

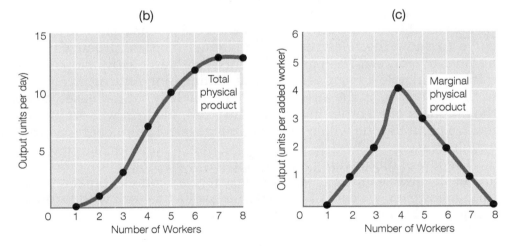

(1) Input (Workers per Day)	(2) Total Physical Product (Units per Day)	(3) Marginal Physical Product (Units per Worker)
0	0	0
1	0	1
2	1	2
3	3	4
4	7	3
5	10	2
6	12	1
7	13	0
8	13	

This figure shows how Fieldcom, Inc., responds to changes in labor inputs. All other inputs remain constant while the number of workers is varied. One worker can produce nothing. After that, output increases as more workers are used. After seven workers are on the job, more workers add nothing to output. Column 3 of Part (a) and the chart in Part (c) show the amount of output added by each worker, a quantity we call the marginal physical product of the variable input.

Marginal Physical Product   The chart in Part (b) and columns 1 and 2 in Part (a) of Figure 8.2 show the relationship between labor inputs and daily output. In the range of one to seven workers, output rises as labor input increases, but not at a constant rate. Column 3 of the table and the chart in Part (c) of the figure show how much output changes for each added worker. We call the change in output produced by an added unit of a variable input the **marginal physical product** of that input. (As elsewhere, the adjective *marginal* refers to the effect of a small change in a quantity.)

In our example, the marginal physical product is one unit of output when labor input increases from one unit to two; from two to three workers, marginal physical product rises to two units; and so on. The step from three workers to four gives the greatest boost to output. After that, output increases at a diminishing rate with each added worker. Once the staff reaches seven workers, the marginal physical product drops to zero.

The Law of Diminishing Returns   Our example shows a pattern that economists consider typical for the marginal product of a single variable input. At first, marginal product increases as the firm adds workers. Increasing marginal product reflects the advantages of cooperation, the superiority of team production, and the benefits of specialization by comparative advantage. After a point, however, marginal product stops rising and begins to fall. In the case of a single variable input, the principal reason for the eventual decline in marginal physical product is the overcrowding of complementary fixed inputs—in our example, such things as workspace, tools, and testing equipment.

Part (c) of Figure 8.2 uses a graph called the *marginal physical product* curve to show the relationship of marginal physical product to the number of workers. The part of the curve with a negative slope illustrates a principle known as the **law of diminishing returns**. According to that principle, as the amount of one variable input increases while the amounts of all other inputs remain fixed, the firm will eventually reach a point beyond which the marginal physical product of the input will decrease.

The law of diminishing returns applies to all production processes and to all variable inputs. The example just given comes from manufacturing; however, we could illustrate the law just as well with farming, using fertilizer as the variable input. Applying more fertilizer increases output, but beyond some point the gain in output from one more ton of fertilizer tapers off. (Too much fertilizer could even poison the plants, in which case marginal physical product would become negative.) Oil refineries, power plants, barber shops, government bureaus—indeed, *all* production processes—are subject to the law of diminishing returns.

From Marginal Physical Product to Marginal Costs

The relationship between inputs and output in terms of physical units is an important constraint on a firm's profit-maximizing activities.

Marginal physical product

The amount by which output, expressed in physical units, increases as a result of adding one unit of a variable input, other things being equal

Law of diminishing returns

The principle that as one variable input increases while all others remain fixed, a the firm will eventually reach a point beyond which the marginal physical product of the variable input will begin to decrease

However, many business decisions a focus not on physical units but on money. Our next step, then, is to restate the constraint information given in the marginal physical product curve in money terms by asking how much each added unit of output costs.

FIGURE 8.3   Cost and Output with One Variable Input

(a)

(1) Output (Units per Day)	(2) Labor Input	(3) Total Labor Cost (Dollars per Day)	(4) Marginal Cost (Dollars per Unit)
0	0	0	
			200
1	2	200	
			50
3	3	300	
			25
7	4	400	
			33
10	5	500	
			50
12	6	600	
			100
13	7	700	

(b)

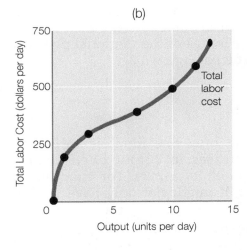

(c)

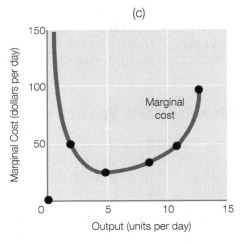

This figure shows how the cost of production at Fieldcom, Inc., changes as output varies. The table and graphs use data from Figure 8.2; however, here we recast them to stress cost, assuming a daily wage of $100 per worker. Column 3 of the table and the chart in Part (b) show total labor cost for various output levels. Column 4 of the table and the chart in Part (c) show marginal cost— the amount by which cost increases per added unit of output. For example, increasing the number of workers from three to four raises output by four units, from three to seven units per day. Over this range, then, the cost of each added unit is one-quarter of a day's wage, or $25.

Marginal cost

The increase in cost required to increase the output of some good or service by one unit

We call the change in cost associated with a one-unit change in output **marginal cost**. Here is how we can make the transition from marginal physical product to marginal cost, still using the Fieldcom example. First, we rearrange the data given in Figure 8.2 in terms of input per unit of output, as in Figure 8.3. The table in Part (a) of the figure reverses the order of the first two columns. Also, we have flipped the charts in Parts (b) and (c) around so that they now have units of output, rather than units of labor input, on the horizontal axis.

The next step is to convert physical units of input into costs. To do so, we need to know the cost per unit of input. For our example, we will assume that the cost of hiring one worker is $100 per day. Multiplying the labor inputs in column 2 of the figure by the $100-per-day wage yields total labor costs, which appear in column 3. Those data then form the basis for the total labor cost curve in Part (b) of the figure. Taking the rearrangement of the axes and the change in units into account, we can recognize the total labor cost curve as the mirror image of the total physical product curve.

Finally, column 4 of the table in Figure 8.3 shows marginal cost, that is, the change in cost for each added unit of output. Increasing output from zero to one requires adding two workers, so the added cost per unit in that range is $200; increasing output by two more units (from one to three) requires one more worker, so the cost per added unit of output in that range is $50; and so on. The marginal cost curve shown in Part (c) of the figure comes from columns 1 and 4 of the table. Again, considering the change in units and rearrangement of the axes, Part (c) of Figure 8.3 looks much like a mirror image of the marginal physical product curve that was shown in Part (c) of Figure 8.2.

More Than One Variable Input

The Fieldcom example assumes that only one input is varied. In practice, short-run increases or decreases in output often involve changes in many—although not all—of its inputs. For example, if Fieldcom wanted to raise its output, it might not only have to hire more workers but also use more fuel to keep the shop heated longer each day and double the rate at which it orders parts.

The appendix to this chapter outlines a way of analyzing changes in two or more variable inputs. Without going into detail, we can say that as long as at least some inputs remain fixed, the law of diminishing returns continues to apply. Also, a region of increasing marginal physical product will often exist at low levels of output. Together, those features tend to give total cost curves with a reverse-S shape and U-shaped marginal cost curves, even when there is more than one variable input, just as in the case of the simpler one-input example.

A Set of Short-Run Cost Curves

Figure 8.4 shows a complete set of short-run cost curves for the firm in our example, together with a table showing the data used in drawing the curves. Part a of the figure shows three total cost curves. The first is a total variable cost curve similar to the one shown earlier in Figure 8.3. The second curve shows total fixed costs, which we assume to be $2,000 per day. These include all the costs of office staff, testing equipment, rent, and so on that are the same regardless of the firm's level of output. Adding columns 2 and 3 gives the third curve, total cost. The total cost and total variable cost curves parallel. The vertical distance between them equals total fixed cost.

FIGURE 8.4   A SET OF SHORT-RUN COST CURVES

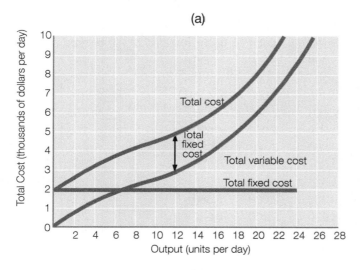

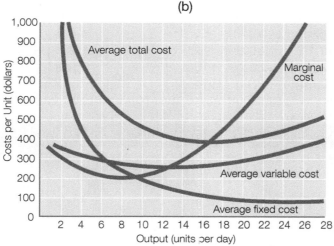

(Continues)

FIGURE 8.4   A SET OF SHORT-RUN COST CURVES (Continued)

(c)

Quantity of Output (Units per Day) (1)	Total Variable Cost (Dollars per Day) (2)	Total Fixed Cost (Dollars per Day) (3)	Total Cost (Dollars per Day) (4)	Marginal Cost (Dollars per Unit) (5)	Average Variable Cost (Dollars per Unit) (6)	Average Fixed Cost (Dollars per Unit) (7)	Average Total Cost (Dollars per Unit) (8)
0	$ 0	$ 2,000	$ 2,000		—	—	—
				$ 380			
1	380	2,000	2,380		$ 380	$ 2,000	$ 2,380
				340			
2	720	2,000	2,720		360	1,000	1,360
				305			
3	1,025	2,000	3,025		342	667	1,009
				275			
4	1,300	2,000	3,300		325	500	825
				250			
5	1,550	2,000	3,550		310	400	710
				230			
6	1,780	2,000	3,780		296	333	629
				215			
7	1,995	2,000	3,995		285	286	571
				205			
8	2,200	2,000	4,200		275	250	525
				200			
9	2,400	2,000	4,400		266	222	488
				205			
10	2,605	2,000	4,605		260	200	460
				215			
11	2,820	2,000	4,820		256	181	437
				230			
12	3,050	2,000	5,050		254	169	421
				250			
13	3,300	2,000	5,300		254	154	408
				275			
14	3,575	2,000	5,575		255	143	398
				305			
15	3,880	2,000	5,880		259	133	392
				340			
16	4,220	2,000	6,220		264	125	389
				380			
17	4,600	2,000	6,600		271	118	389
				425			
18	5,025	2,000	7,025		279	111	390
				475			
19	5,500	2,000	7,500		289	105	394
				530			
20	6,030	2,000	8,030		302	100	402
				590			
21	6,620	2,000	8,620		315	95	410
				655			
22	7,275	2,000	9,275		331	91	422
				725			
23	8,000	2,000	10,000		348	87	435
				800			
24	8,800	2,000	10,800		367	83	450

(d)

Common Abbreviations	Useful formulas:
Q Quantity of output	$TC = TFC + TVC$
TC Total cost	$MC = \dfrac{\text{Change in TC}}{\text{Change in Q}} = \dfrac{\text{Change in TVC}}{\text{Change in Q}}$
TFC Total fixed cost	
TVC Total variable cost	$AVC = \dfrac{TVC}{Q}$
MC Marginal cost	
AVC Average variable cost	$AFC = \dfrac{TFC}{Q}$
AFC Average fixed cost	
ATC Average total cost	$ATC = \dfrac{TC}{Q}$

We can derive a whole set of short-run cost curves from data on fixed and variable costs, as this figure shows. The figure presents the data in the form of a table and a pair of graphs. The figure also lists a number of useful abbreviations and formulas.

Some Geometric Relationships

Parts (a) and (b) of Figure 8.4 illustrate some important geometric relationships among the cost curves. First, notice that the minimum point of the marginal cost curve corresponds to the inflection point of the total variable cost curve, that is, the quantity of output where it stops flattening out and starts getting steeper. That relationship holds because the slope of the total variable cost curve—that is, the rate at which total variable cost changes as output changes—is equal to marginal cost. Another way to express the relationship is to say that the height of the marginal cost curve equals the slope of the total variable cost curve.

Next, notice that the marginal cost curve intersects both the average variable cost and the average total cost curves at their lowest points. That relationship reflects the **marginal-average rule**. To understand the rule, ask what the cost of making one more unit of output will be, starting from any point. The answer is equal to the marginal cost of that unit. Then ask whether that cost is more or less than the average cost of all units produced up to that point. If the added cost of the next unit produced is less than the average cost of all the previous units, adding it will have the effect of pulling down the average. If the next unit costs more, adding it will pull the average up. It follows that whenever marginal cost is below average variable cost, the average variable cost curve must be falling (negatively sloped); and whenever marginal cost is above average variable cost, the average variable cost curve must be rising (positively sloped). That, in turn, implies that the marginal cost curve cuts the average variable cost curve at its lowest point. The same reasoning holds for the relationship between marginal cost and average total cost.

The marginal-average rule is not unique to economics; we encounter it in many everyday situations. Consider, for example, the effect of your grade in this course on your grade point average. You could call your econ grade your "marginal grade" because it represents the grade points earned by taking this particular additional course. If your econ grade is higher than your previous average, it will pull your average up. If you do worse than average in this course, your grade point average will fall. The relationship between your marginal grade and your cumulative grade point average is the same as that between marginal cost and average cost.

Finally, Part (d) of Figure 8.4 summarizes the relationships among the various cost concepts as simple formulas. Part (d) gives some common abbreviations that are useful for note taking.

Marginal-average rule

The rule that marginal cost must equal average cost when average cost is at its minimum

8.3 Long-Run Costs and Economies of Scale

Up to this point, we have focused on short-run decisions, for example, how many smartphones to produce in Fieldcom's workshop or how much corn to grow on a certain piece of land. These short-run decisions involve changes in variable inputs only. They correspond to movements along a firm's short-run cost curves.

Now we turn our attention to decisions regarding a lasting expansion or contraction of the firm's stock of fixed inputs. For example, farmers might adjust to new subsidies for corn-based ethanol by buying additional land or farm equipment. Such decisions bring about changes in long-run costs. For the time being, we consider only fixed costs that are recoverable in the event that the firm leaves its line of business or permanently scales back its operations. We assume that there are no sunk costs.

Planning for Expansion

Put yourself in the position of an entrepreneur about to set up a small firm. Like many startups, you are going to start small, working in your own garage, but you want to do some long-range planning, too. In consultation with specialists, you put together plans for plants of five possible sizes, each of which could represent a stage in the future growth of your firm. Figure 8.5 shows short-run average total cost curves for each of the plants. The first one shows short-run average total costs at various outputs that you could produce in your first plant, the garage. The second curve corresponds to a slightly larger plant, and so on.

Choosing a plant of a certain size does not commit a firm forever, but the choice is not a trivial one. A small firm cannot afford to take on the costs of a permanently larger plant just to fill a single order. It will not make sense to expand the size of your plant unless you can spread fixed costs over a large enough total output. For example, in the 1950s, Sony Corporation was a tiny firm just starting to produce transistor radios. A buyer for a large American retail chain asked for prices on quantities ranging from ten thousand to one hundred thousand radios. Akio Morita, Sony's chairman, surprised the buyer by giving a higher price per unit on the larger order. He explained that one hundred thousand units exceeded the company's plant capacity. It would be a big risk to invest in a larger plant just for one large order. The buyer ended up placing an order for ten thousand radios, which was just right for them at the time.[3] The moral of the story: Only when the firm expects a sustained long-term increase in its output should it move from one of the short-run curves shown in Figure 8.5 to the next.

In the 1950s, Sony was a tiny firm producing transistor radios.

FIGURE 8.5 SHORT- AND LONG-RUN AVERAGE COST CURVES

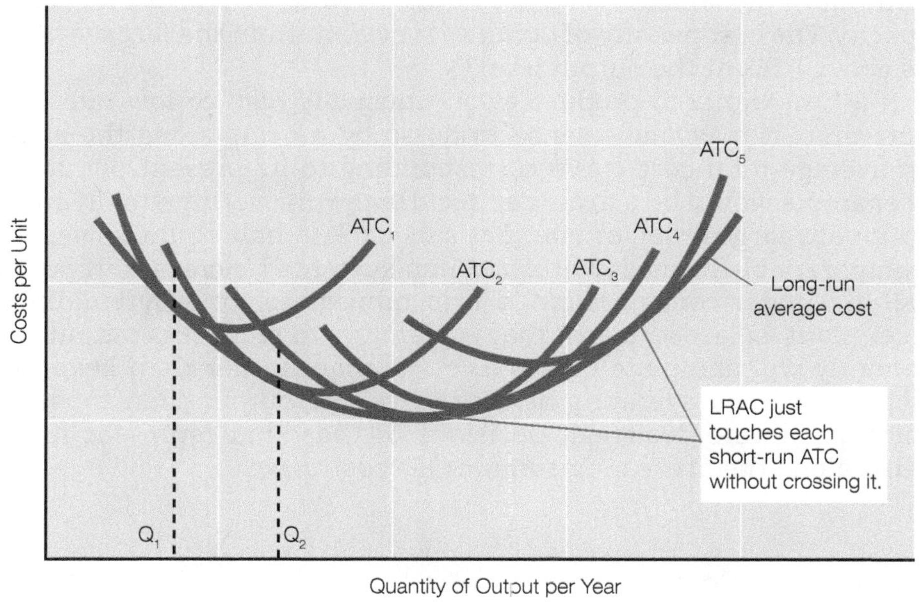

The position of the short-run average total cost curve for a firm depends on the size of its plant. In the long run, the firm has a choice of operating with any size of plant it chooses. Each plant size corresponds to a different U-shaped, short-run average total cost curve. This graph shows five such curves. A new firm might begin in the owner's garage, corresponding to short-run average total cost curve ATC_1. Then, as demand for its product expands, the firm might move to one of those farther to the right. Its long-run average cost curve is the "envelope" of these and other possible short-run average total cost curves; that is, it is a smooth curve drawn so that it just touches the short-run curves without intersecting any of them.

The five short-run cost curves in the figure represent only a sample of possible plant sizes. Taking into account the short-run curves that correspond to plants of sizes between those in the figure, we can draw a long-run average cost curve as the "envelope" of all the possible short-run average cost curves. By that, we mean the *long-run average cost curve* just touches each of the possible short-run curves without crossing them. The optimal size of plant for any given level of output in the long run will have a short-run average total cost curve that is just tangent to the long-run average total cost curve at the chosen level of output.

It may be possible to produce a given level of output in a plant larger or smaller than the optimal one, but doing so would carry a penalty in terms of cost per unit. For example, in Figure 8.5 the firm can produce output level Q_1 at least cost in a plant of the size corresponding to the short-run curve ATC_1. It could instead produce the same level of output in the larger plant corresponding to ATC_2, but only at a higher cost per unit. On the other hand, the larger plant shown by ATC_2 is the best plant size for output Q_2. Producing that larger quantity of output in the smaller plant would mean running it above its design capacity. The cost penalty of doing so is evident from the fact that ATC_1 lies above ATC_2 at the output level Q_2.

If a firm wants to produce at an unusually high or low rate for a short time, it may make sense to do so by moving along the short-run average total cost curve corresponding to its present plant size. An example would be a firm that decides to run overtime to fill an exceptionally large order, or one that cuts back to half-shifts to weather a temporary business downturn. When sustained increases in output level are under consideration, a firm minimizes costs by building a larger plant. Likewise, a firm that is planning to reduce its output permanently will eliminate or downsize its plant rather than keep production facilities operating at lower levels of output than those for which they were designed. Decisions of that kind represent movements along the firm's long-run average cost curve.

Economies of Scale

We call movements along a firm's long-run average cost curve, during which it is free to adjust quantities of all the inputs it uses, changes in the *scale* of production. Some special terminology applies to the way long-run average cost changes as the scale of production changes. In any output range in which long-run average cost *decreases* as output increases, the firm experiences **economies of scale**. In any output range in which long-run average cost *increases*, the firm it experiences **diseconomies of scale**. Finally, if there is any range of output for which long-run average cost does not change as output varies, it experiences **constant returns to scale** in that range.

The long-run average cost curve in Figure 8.5 is smoothly U-shaped, so there is no range of constant returns to scale. However, empirical studies suggest that the long-run cost curves of actual firms may have long flat sections in a middle range of output over which average cost changes little as output changes. Economies of scale for such a firm appear only at very low outputs, and diseconomies appear only at very high outputs. For a firm with such a long-run average cost curve, the level of output at which economies of scale end and constant returns to scale begin is the firm's **minimum efficient scale**.

Sources of Economies of Scale   Where do economies of scale come from? If firms grew simply by increasing fixed and variable inputs in exact proportion, so that a large plant amounted to nothing more than a lot of small plants built side by side, we might expect changes in scale to have no effect on average cost. That is not the way firms expand, however. As they grow, they tend to change the technologies they use and their methods of internal organization to take advantage of new opportunities offered by higher output levels.

Economies of scale

A situation in which long-run average cost decreases as output increases

Diseconomies of scale

A situation in which long-run average cost increases as output increases

Constant returns to scale

A situation in which there are neither economies nor diseconomies of scale

Minimum efficient scale

The output level at which economies of scale cease

In part, economies of scale stem from human factors like the advantages of team production and specialization according to comparative advantage. A firm can get very large before it completely exhausts the possibilities for cooperation and specialization. In a small firm, for example, the marketing function may be something the owner does from 3:00 p.m. to 4:00 p.m., after touring the plant floor and perhaps taking a turn running a machine. A somewhat larger firm can afford to hire a marketing manager who devotes full time to the job. In a still larger firm, subspecialties develop—a sales manager, a director of market research, an advertising specialist—all under the direction of the marketing manager.

Other economies of scale have origins in technology. In many lines of production, for example, a machine that is capable of doing twice the work of a smaller one costs less than twice as much to build and operate. A pizza oven that is big enough to bake sixty pizzas an hour costs less than twice as much as a thirty-pizza-per-hour model and takes less than twice the energy to operate. A tractor that can plow fifty acres a day costs less than twice as much as one that can plow only twenty-five acres, and the large model still requires only one driver. For a firm that is too small to make full use of a large piece of equipment, the smaller model can be the appropriate choice. As the firm grows, however, technological economies lower its average costs.

What is more, growth of a firm does not just mean constant expansion of a single plant. Operation of multiple plants can yield further economies of scale even after each plant reaches the minimum efficient scale where technical economies are exhausted. The McDonald's hamburger chain provides an example. The minimum efficient scale for a single plant (restaurant) is very small in the fast-food industry. Yet McDonald's gains some important economies by running a large number of restaurants as a system. Some of those are production economies. Individual food items and ingredients can be made in central kitchens, managers can be trained at "Hamburger University", and so on. A multi-plant firm such as McDonald's also realizes economies of scale in such areas as finance and marketing.

Sources of Diseconomies of Scale   Sources of economies of scale are not limitless. As a firm expands, it encounters diseconomies of scale as well as economies. Sometimes a firm can avoid purely technological sources of diseconomies. For example, as an airline grows, it may, at first, buy larger and larger planes; however, beyond a point, it starts buying more and more planes of optimal size. In other lines of business, firms can avoid potential technical diseconomies by building multiple plants of optimal size.

The most important diseconomies of scale are organizational. As a firm grows, it finds itself depending more and more on hierarchical means of coordinating its employees' activities. As a hierarchy grows, the

An airline may, as it grows, at first buy larger planes; but later it will change strategy and start buying more planes of optimal size.

BVT *Lab*

Visit www.BVTLab.com
to explore the student
resources available for
this chapter.

cost of channeling information to key decision makers tends to rise. Moreover, individual incentives become hard to maintain in a large hierarchical organization. More and more managerial skill has to be devoted to employee loyalty and motivation. There is an increasing risk that departments and divisions will pursue parochial interests that diverge from those of the firm as a whole.

In some lines of business, firms can grow to a very large size before the diseconomies start to outweigh the economies. Huge firms, such as Wal-Mart, Toyota, and Exxon Mobil, successfully manage hierarchies that are bigger than the governments of many countries. However, such corporate giants are always vulnerable to smaller, more aggressive rivals. It is easy to think of companies like IBM, AT&T, and General Motors that have lost market share to smaller rivals.

In other lines of business, comparatively small firms seem to have the edge. In farming, services, and many sectors of retail trade, small units predominate. Still other industries use franchising to combine economies of scale in a few functions such as marketing and product development with the operating flexibility of small-units.

Summary

1. **How do economists view the concepts of cost and profit?** *Explicit costs* are opportunity costs that take the form of explicit payments to suppliers of factors of production and intermediate goods. *Implicit costs* are the opportunity costs associated with using resources contributed by the firm's owners (or owned by the firm itself as a legal entity) that are not obtained under contracts calling for explicit payments. Implicit costs include the opportunity cost of capital needed to attract owners' capital to the firm. Revenue minus explicit costs gives accounting profit. Revenue minus all costs, both implicit and explicit, gives *pure economic profit*.

2. **What is the distinction between short-run and long-run time horizons?** *Fixed inputs* cannot be increased or decreased in a short time. We call the costs of those inputs *fixed costs*. *Variable inputs* are those that firms can add or reduce quickly in order to increase or decrease output; they include hourly labor, energy, and raw materials. Those inputs give rise to *variable costs*. *Sunk* costs are once-and-for-all expenditures that a firm cannot recover once it has made them. The *short run* is a period within which a firm can adjust only variable inputs. In the *long run,* a firm can make changes in fixed inputs, thereby changing its plant size.

3. **How do costs vary in response to changes in the quantity of a variable input?** When the amount of one input to a production process increases while the amounts of all other inputs remain fixed, output will increase, at least over some range. The amount that each one-unit increase in the variable input adds to output is the *marginal physical product* of that input. According to the *law of diminishing returns*, as the amount of one variable input increases (with the amounts of all other inputs remaining fixed), beyond some point the amount of output added per unit of added variable input (that is, the marginal physical product of the variable input) will begin to decrease.

4. **How can we represent a firm's cost structure geometric terms?** We can construct a whole set of cost curves for a firm from data on its fixed and variable costs: Total cost, total fixed cost, total variable cost, average fixed cost, average variable cost, average total cost, and marginal cost. According to the *marginal-average rule*, the marginal cost curve intersects the average variable cost and average total cost curves at their lowest points.

(Continues)

5. **What choices does a firm face in the course of long-run expansion?** In the long run, a firm can adjust the amounts of fixed inputs that it uses by expanding or reducing its plant. Each possible plant size has a U-shaped short-run average total cost curve. The firm's long-run average cost curve is the envelope of its short-run curves. When long-run average cost decreases as output increases, the firm experiences *economies of scale*. When long-run average cost increases as output increases, it experiences *diseconomies of scale*. If there are neither economies nor diseconomies of scale, the firm has *constant returns to scale*.

Key Terms   Page

Problems and Topics for Discussion

1. **Entrepreneurship and risk**   One of the opportunity costs borne by anyone who starts a new business, whether it is Akio Morita of Sony or our imaginary Ralph and Andrea Martin, is that of exchanging the secure life of employees of large firms for the risky life of entrepreneurs. Would you be willing to make that transition if you expected to earn no more than your previous salaries plus a "normal profit" on the capital you invested in your firm? Would you require some pure economic profit as compensation for the risks and responsibilities of being an entrepreneur? Or would the freedom of running your own business be so attractive you would do it even if your total income were less than what you could earn working for someone else? Discuss.

2. **Implicit and explicit costs**   List the basic costs of owning and operating an automobile. Which are explicit costs? Which are implicit costs? Does driving an automobile impose any external costs on the economy as a whole that do not show up on your list as either implicit or explicit costs? If so, what are they?

3. **Fixed and variable costs**   Divide the costs of owning and operating an automobile into fixed and variable costs. Suppose that you were deciding whether to drive to a football game at a nearby college or to take the bus instead. Would you consider both fixed and variable costs? Suppose that you were deciding whether to buy a house in a neighborhood where you could walk to work or a house in a neighborhood where you would have to buy a second car to drive to work every day. Would you consider both fixed and variable costs of the second car? Explain the difference between the two situations.

4. **Economies and diseconomies of scale**   Do you think the business of running a college is subject to economies or diseconomies of scale? Which parts of the college's operation (such as library, dormitories, faculty salaries, moving students between classes, and so on) are subject to economies of scale, diseconomies of scale, or constant returns to scale?

5. **Total cost curves**   Draw a set of coordinate axes on a piece of graph paper. Label the x axis "Output" (0 to 20 units) and the y axis "Cost" (0 to 20 units). Plot the following (x, y) points on your graph: (0, 4); (2, 6); (4, 7); (7, 8); (9, 9); (11, 11); (13, 14). Connect these points with a smooth curve and label it "total cost." Working from this curve, construct a total fixed cost curve and a total variable cost curve for the same firm.

(Continues)

6. **Marginal and average cost curves**   Draw a second set of coordinate axes on another piece of graph paper. Label the horizontal axis "Output" (0 to 20 units) and the vertical axis "Cost per Unit" (0 to 2 units, in tenths of a unit). Using as a basis the total cost, total variable cost, and total fixed cost curves you drew for problem 5, construct the following curves on your new graph: marginal cost, average total cost, average variable cost, and average fixed cost.

7. **Relating the long- and short-run cost curves**   Turn to Figure 8.5 and copy the diagram onto a sheet of graph paper, drawing the long-run average total cost curve and one of the short-run average total cost curves. Use these curves to construct the corresponding long- and short-run total cost curves. Both total cost curves should be reverse-S shaped and tangent to each other at the same output level for which the average total cost curves are tangent.

8. **Diminishing returns**   Suppose that you examine the relationship between the amount of coal burned per week in a certain power plant and the amount of electricity generated per week. You find that for small amounts of coal—too small even to bring the boiler up to the temperature needed to make steam—no electricity can be produced. After burning a certain minimum amount of coal, the plant begins to operate. From that point on, the added amount of electricity generated per added ton of coal burned is constant over a wide range. Then after a point, burning more coal produces no more electricity. Sketch the total physical product curve for this plant, and draw a graph showing how marginal physical product varies as output changes. Does this production process obey the law of diminishing returns?

9. **More on diminishing returns**   "If not for the law of diminishing returns, all the food that the world needs could be grown in a flowerpot." Do you agree, disagree, or agree in part? Suggestion: Think of land as the only fixed factor and fertilizer as the only variable factor. How much food could you grow in the flowerpot if the marginal physical product of fertilizer were constant regardless of the amount per unit of land?)

Case for Discussion

Tennis at the Grand Slam

The Grand Slam Sport and Health Club is a large, modern facility in the suburbs of a medium-sized American city. The club offers many activities, including swimming, weight training, and aerobics; but its leading attractions are its excellent indoor tennis courts. Members may play on clay or two types of hard-surface courts. To add to members' enjoyment, the club offers private and group lessons; tournament, ladder, and team competitions; and numerous other social events.

To join the club, a single individual pays a $1,000 nonrefundable initiation fee. In addition, there is an $88 monthly membership charge, which members must pay whether or not they use the facilities. Those two fees cover most of the club's costs, so it is able to keep the charge for actual playing time quite low. The fee for an hour's use of a court is only $2.

When it first started operation, the low hourly court fee created a problem for the club. The fee was so low that members would not bother to call to cancel a court reservation if they changed their minds about playing. Other members would then think that there was no space to play, when in fact the courts stood empty.

To overcome that problem, the club introduced a new rule: Members who make reservations and use the court pay the usual $2 per hour, but a member who makes a reservation and does not show up pays a penalty rate of $10 per hour for the unused time. A member may cancel a reservation nine hours or more in advance with no charge at all. The new rule has proved successful in reducing abuses of the reservation system and making court time more readily available to all members.

Questions

1. Classify the costs of membership in the Grand Slam as fixed, variable, and sunk.

2. Suppose that you are thinking about joining the Grand Slam to play indoor tennis. Which of the costs of membership are opportunity costs that would be relevant to your decision?

3. Suppose you are a member of the Grand Slam but consider dropping your membership so that you can afford to do other things. Which of the costs of membership in the club are opportunity costs that would be relevant to your decision?

4. Suppose that you are a member of the club and are deciding whether to spend next Saturday afternoon playing tennis there. Which of the costs of membership are opportunity costs that would be relevant to your decision?

5. Suppose that it is noon on Saturday. You have made a reservation for an hour of court time at 5:00 p.m. A friend asks you to join a pickup basketball game at that time instead. What is your opportunity cost of abandoning the tennis reservation to join the basketball game? How would the answer be different if you had received the basketball invitation the afternoon of the day before your court reservation?

Endnotes

1. If you have studied accounting, you will recognize that this description of "accounting profit" is somewhat oversimplified. Accountants and economists have different objectives in analyzing the operations of a business firm. As a result, their concepts of costs and profits do not always allow precise comparison. Although the comparison is not exact, what economists call "accounting profit" most closely corresponds to what corporate accountants would call "net operating profit after taxes" (NOPAT) plus interest expense.

2. See James M. Buchanan, "Rent Seeking and Profit Seeking," in *Toward a Theory of the Rent-Seeking Society*, eds. James M. Buchanan, Robert D. Tollison, and Gordon Tullock (College Station: Texas A&M University Press, 1980), 3–15.

3. The anecdote is told by Akio Morita in "When Sony Was an Up and Comer," *Forbes*, October 6, 1986, 98–102.

Appendix to Chapter 8:
Cost and Output with Two Variable Inputs

In the body of this chapter we looked at the relationship between cost and output when just one input is varied and all other inputs are kept constant. Now, in this appendix, we extend the theory to the case of more than one variable input.

8A.1 Substitution of Inputs

Having more than one variable input raises the possibility of substituting one input for another. Consider the case of Henry Hathaway, a farmer who grows corn. Hathaway spends all his time working on his farm and does not hire anyone to help him. For him, the amount of labor used in growing corn is a fixed input, and the machinery he owns is also a fixed input. In addition to those, he uses two variable inputs, fertilizer, which he buys by the ton, and land, which he leases by the acre from a landowner near his home.

Hathaway can grow a given quantity of corn—say, two hundred bushels—in many different ways. Figure 8A.1 shows some of the possibilities. One way to grow two hundred bushels of corn is to use 2.5 tons of fertilizer and 10 acres of land, corresponding to point P on the graph. If Hathaway wants to grow the same amount of corn on less land, he can substitute fertilizer for land. For example, at point Q he can grow two hundred bushels of corn on 5 acres by using 5 tons of fertilizer. By substituting still more fertilizer for land, he can move to point R, where the two hundred bushels are grown on just 2.5 acres using 10 tons of fertilizer.

FIGURE 8A.1   AN ISOQUANTITY LINE

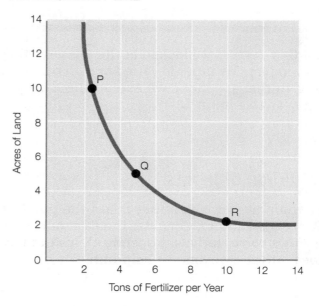

This graph shows an isoquantity line, or isoquant, for the production of 200 bushels of corn. The variable inputs are land and fertilizer; the other inputs, labor and machinery, are fixed. Points P, Q, and R represent various ways of growing the given quantity of corn. A movement downward along the isoquant represents the substitution of fertilizer for land while maintaining output at 200 bushels per year. As more and more fertilizer is used and less land, the isoquant becomes flatter because of diminishing returns.

8A.2 Diminishing Returns in Substitution

In this chapter, we defined the law of diminishing returns as it applies to a situation where one input varies while all others remain constant. In such a case, beyond some point, the amount of the variable input needed to make an extra unit of output increases. (That is another way of saying that the marginal physical product of the variable input decreases.) A similar principle applies when one input is substituted for another in such a way as to keep output at a constant level: As the amount of input x is increased, the amount of x needed to replace one unit of y increases.

Figure 8A.1 illustrates this principle. In moving from point P to point Q, 2.5 tons of fertilizer replaces 5 acres of land while output stays constant at two hundred bushels. In moving from point Q to point R, however, we must apply 5 more tons of to replace just 2.5 acres of land.

Because of diminishing returns in substituting one input for another, the curve connecting points P, Q, and R becomes flatter as one moves downward and to the right along it. That reflects the decreasing ratio of the marginal physical product of fertilizer to the marginal physical product of land as more fertilizer and less land are used.

8A.3 Choosing the Least-Cost Production Method

We call the line connecting points P, Q, and R in Figure 8A.1 an **isoquantity line**, or isoquant, because it shows the combinations of inputs that are sufficient to produce a given amount of output. (The prefix *iso* comes from a Greek word meaning "equal.") Although all the points on the isoquant are equal in terms of output, they are not equal in terms of cost. To see how a producer can choose the least-cost method of producing a given level of output, we need to know the prices of the inputs.

In the appendix to Chapter 5, we used budget lines to indicate the prices of consumer goods. Figure 8A.2 shows how we can use the same technique to represent the prices of inputs. The graph assumes a cost of $50 a ton for fertilizer and a rental price of $50 per year for land. At those prices, $400 can buy eight tons of fertilizer and no land, eight acres of land with no fertilizer, or any of the other points on line A; $500 will buy ten tons of fertilizer, ten acres of land, or any of the other points on line B; and so on.

Isoquantity line (isoquant)

A line showing the various combinations of inputs that are sufficient to produce a given quantity of output

---

FIGURE 8A.2   FINDING THE LEAST-COST PRODUCTION METHOD

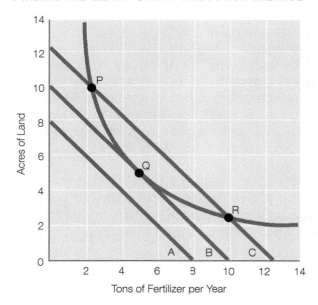

This graph shows how to find the least-cost method of production on an isoquant, given the input prices. In this example, the price of fertilizer is $50 a ton and the rental price of land $50 per year. The figure shows three budget lines representing various levels of spending on inputs. Line A, which corresponds to a total variable cost of $400, does not provide enough inputs to produce two hundred bushels of corn. Line C, which corresponds to a total variable cost of $625, provides enough inputs to grow two hundred bushels of corn using methods P or R. Line B, which corresponds to a total variable cost of $500, gives the least costly method of growing two hundred bushels, using method Q.

When we add the isoquant for two hundred bushels of corn to the set of budget lines, it becomes easy to find the least-cost method of production, namely, the method that uses 5 tons of fertilizer and 5 acres of land. That corresponds to point Q on the graph, where the isoquant just touches budget line B. Points P and R are possible ways of growing two hundred bushels of corn, but they lie on budget line C, which has input costs of $625. Note any budget of less than $500 (say, $400, as shown by budget line A) is not enough to reach the 200-bushel isoquant no matter how much goes to fertilizer and how much to land.

8A.4 Responses to Changes in Input Prices

If input prices change, the least-cost combination of inputs will change as well. Suppose that suburbs begin to expand in the direction of Hathaway's farm, driving up the price of land. Land that used to rent for $50 per acre per year now costs $200 per acre. The price of fertilizer remains unchanged at $50 a ton.

Figure 8A.3 shows the effects of the higher price of land. Now $500 is not enough to buy the combinations of inputs that fall along budget line B. Even if Hathaway spends all the money on land, he can rent only 2.5 acres. The new $500 budget line is C, which does not reach the 200-bushel isoquant at any point.

To grow two hundred bushels, Hathaway must now spend more than $500. As he increases his spending on land and fertilizer, the budget line shifts upward but stays parallel to C. When the budget line reaches D, which corresponds to spending $1,000 on inputs, it just touches the isoquant at R. We see that now $1,000 is the lowest cost for growing two hundred bushels of corn, given a price of $50 a ton for fertilizer and $200 an acre for land. With those prices, R is the least-cost combination of inputs.

Notice that the increase in the price of land not only increases the cost of producing a given quantity of corn but also causes a substitution of fertilizer for land. We will return to this topic of substitution among factors of production in later chapters.

FIGURE 8A.3 EFFECTS OF A CHANGE IN INPUT PRICES

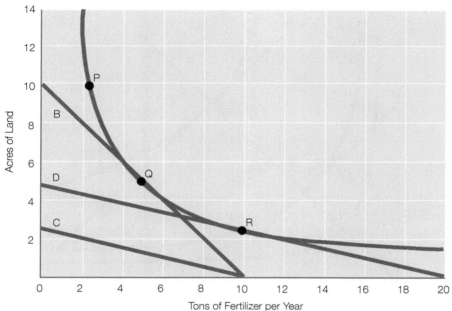

If the rental price of land increases from $50 to $200 per year while the price of fertilizer remains fixed at $50 a ton, it is no longer possible to produce 200 bushels of corn for $500. The $500 budget line shifts from position B to position C and now falls short of the 200-bushel isoquant. Increasing the amount spent on variable inputs to $1,000 shifts the budget line up to position D, where it just touches the isoquant at point R. The increase in the price of land not only raises the total variable cost of growing 200 bushels of corn but also causes a substitution of fertilizer for land, which is now relatively more costly.

8A.5 Varying Output

So far, we have assumed a fixed level of output. We can extend the iso-quant technique to analyze variations in output. Part (a) of Figure 8A.4 shows three isoquants, each corresponding to a different level of output. Points P, Q, and R represent three ways of growing two hundred bushels of corn; points S, T, and U three ways of growing one hundred bushels, and points V, W, and X three ways of growing three hundred bushels.

FIGURE 8A.4 EXPANSION OF OUTPUT AND TOTAL VARIABLE COSTS

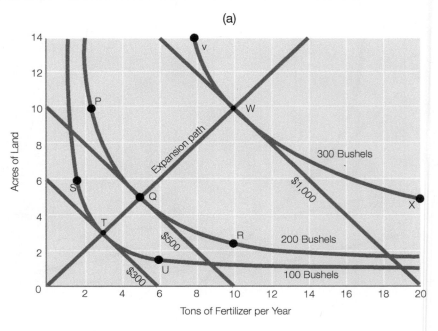

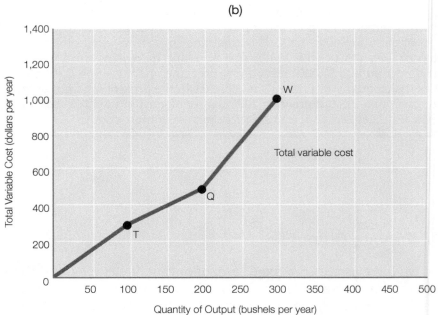

Part (a) of this figure shows three isoquants for the production of corn corresponding to outputs of 100, 200, and 300 bushels per year. Assuming input prices of $50 an acre for land and $50 a ton for fertilizer, we can draw budget lines to show the minimum total variable cost for each output level. As output expands, the firm will move from T to Q and then to W along a line that we call an expansion path. Part (b) of the figure plots the amount of output and the total variable cost for points along the expansion path. The result is a reverse-S-shaped total variable cost curve that shows diminishing returns for output levels above 200 bushels per year.

In this example, we return to prices of $50 an acre for land and $50 a ton for fertilizer. Using those prices, we draw a set of budget lines, corresponding to total variable costs of $300, $500, and $1,000.

There is a least-cost method for producing each output level given these prices. Point T is the best way to produce one hundred bushels, Q is best for two hundred bushels, and W is best for three hundred bushels. If we added more isoquants, we could show the least-cost production points for other output levels. All of them would lie along the line drawn from the origin through points T, Q, and W. We call such a line the firm's **expansion path**. As the firm moves along its expansion path, it uses more of both the variable inputs, while holding fixed inputs (labor and machinery, in our example) constant.

Expansion path

A line on an isoquant diagram showing the least-cost production points for various levels of output

8A.6 Deriving a Cost Curve from the Isoquant Map

Once we have found the expansion path, we can easily construct a total variable cost curve for the firm. Part (b) of Figure 8A.4 shows how we can do that. At the origin, both output and total variable cost are zero. At point T, output is one hundred bushels per year and total variable cost is $300 per year; at Q, we have two hundred bushels and $500; and at W, three hundred bushels and $1,000. The firm's total variable cost curve is a line connecting those points.

Note that the cost curve has the reverse-S shape discussed earlier in the chapter. That shape is a result of the law of diminishing returns, as applied to the case in which two inputs vary while all others remain fixed. Beyond point Q, the amounts of inputs needed to produce each added unit of output begin to rise, just as they did in the case of just one variable input. Only if all inputs vary while none remains fixed can a firm escape the effects of the law of diminishing returns.

Chapter 9

Supply *under* Perfect Competition

After reading this chapter, you will understand the following:

1. Characteristics that define the structure of a market

2. How a perfectly competitive firm determines its profit-maximizing output level in the short run

3. Under what conditions a firm will continue to operate even if it sustains a loss

4. The relationship of a firm's short-run supply curve to its cost curves

5. The conditions for long-run equilibrium in a perfectly competitive industry

6. The determinants of the shape of the long-run supply curve for a perfectly competitive industry

7. How efficiently markets perform under perfect competition

Before reading this chapter, make sure you know the meaning of the following concepts:

1. Entrepreneurship

2. Efficiency

3. Theories and models

4. Perfectly elastic demand

5. Objectives, constraints, and choices

6. Market performance

7. Monopoly

8. Short- and long-run costs

In a market economy, competition is everywhere. Competition may take the form of giants such as Boeing and Airbus struggling to dominate a market through sales efforts and product innovations. Sometimes it takes the form of intense rivalry between small firms for purely local markets—for example, two espresso stands on opposite sides of a busy road. Sometimes it takes the less visible form of small producers selling products like wheat or sugar that are nearly identical for all firms in the market. In this chapter and the two that follow, we will examine all of these varieties of competition.

Market structure

The key traits of a market, including the number and size of firms, the extent to which the products of various firms are different or similar, ease of entry and exit, and availability of information

Perfect competition

A market structure in which there are a large number of small firms, a homogeneous product, freedom of entry and exit, and equal access to information

Economists refer to the conditions that shape the competition in a market as **market structure**. Market structure depends on the number and size of firms, the nature of the product, ease of entry and exit, and availability of information.

In this book, we will look at four market structures that neoclassical economics has traditionally emphasized. The first, to which this chapter is devoted, is **perfect competition**. The defining characteristics of perfect competition are the presence of many firms, none with a significant share of the market; a product that is homogeneous; easy entry into the industry and easy exit from it; and equal access to information by buyers and sellers.

In saying that no firm has a "significant" share of the market, we mean that each firm is so small that its actions, alone, have no noticeable effect on the market price. By a "homogeneous product," we mean that the various firms' products are so nearly alike that they are perfect substitutes in the eyes of buyer. By "ease of entry," we mean that firms that are just starting to produce the product can do so on an equal footing with existing firms in terms of the prices paid for inputs, availability of technology, access to government permits or licenses, and so on. By "ease of exit," we mean that firms face no legal barriers to leaving the market and are able to find buyers or other uses for their fixed inputs. Finally, by "equal access to information," we mean that all buyers and sellers have complete information about the price of the product and of the inputs used to produce it, that buyers know all they need to know about product characteristics, and that all producers have equal knowledge of production techniques.

A second market structure, *monopoly*, is the opposite extreme from perfect competition. In a monopoly, a single firm accounts for 100 percent of sales of a product that has no close substitutes. We first encountered monopoly in Chapter 4. We will look at it in detail in the next chapter.

Perfect competition and monopoly are "ideal type" market structures. Few, if any, markets exactly fit the definitions although many approximate them. The next two market structures are more descriptive. **Oligopoly** means a market with only a few firms, at least some of which have a significant share of the market. The product may be either homogeneous or differentiated, there may or may not be significant barriers to entry, and buyers and sellers need not have equal access to all kinds of information. Most familiar markets for branded products, from automobiles to toothpaste, fit in this category. **Monopolistic competition** resembles perfect competition in that there are many small firms and easy entry and exit, but under monopolistic competition the various firms' products differ from one another. Many sectors of retail trade and services fit this category.

Oligopoly

A market structure in which there are only a few firms, at least some of which are large in relation to the size of the market

Monopolistic competition

A market structure in which there are many small firms, a differentiated product, and easy entry and exit

TABLE 9.1   MARKET STRUCTURES

	Number and Size of Firms	Nature of Product	Entry and Exit Conditions	Information Availability
Perfect Competition	Many firms, all small	Homogenous	Easy	Equal access to all information
Monopolistic Competition	Many firms, all small	Differentiated	Easy	Some restrictions
Oligopoly	Few firms, at least some of them large	Differentiated or homogeneous	May have some barriers to entry	Some restrictions
Monopoly	One firm	Unique product	Barriers to entry are common.	Some restrictions

Market structure means the conditions under which firms compete—the number and size of firms in a market, the nature of the product, the ease of entry and exit, and the availability of information. Perfect competition and monopoly are "ideal" types of structures. Few—if any—markets fit them perfectly. Monopolistic competition and oligopoly are more descriptive of markets found in the real world

9.1 Perfect Competition and Supply in the Short Run

Our first task in this chapter will be to build a simple model that fits the market structure of perfect competition. That model will help us understand how the profit-maximizing decisions of individual firms determine the quantity they will supply at various prices, and how the decisions of many firms together give rise to market supply curves. We will look first at the short run and then at the long run.

The Constraints

As discussed in the preceding chapter, neoclassical economic models assume that firms pursue the objective of maximizing profits. That assumption holds for all four of the market structures we will look at. The differences in the choices that firms make under various market structures arise from differences in the constraints they face rather than from differences in objectives.

Cost Constraints   Costs form one set of constraints, as explained in the preceding chapter. For our model of perfect competition, we make three special assumptions about costs:

1. All firms in the market have access to the same technology and know where to buy inputs at the same prices. These conditions follow from the assumptions of a homogeneous product and equal access to information by all firms. It follows that all firms have identical, long- and short-run cost curves.

2. Economies of scale cease at a small level of output relative to the quantity demanded by the whole market. That means there is room in the market for many firms each of which produces at the minimum long-run average cost.

3. There are no sunk costs. Firms that leave the market are able to recover implicit fixed costs by selling their plant and equipment to other firms. This is part of the requirement of free entry and exit.

Demand Constraints: The Firm as Price Taker   Demand is the other principal constraint on the choices made by a profit-maximizing firm. Under perfect competition, the demand constraint has a special form. Because all firms are small and have identical products, each firm is a **price taker**. For a price taker, supply and demand conditions in the market as a whole, beyond the control of any one firm, determine the price at which it can sell its output. If any one firm were to raise its price even a fraction above that prevailing in the market, it would lose all of its customers. Equally, there would be no point in lowering its price even a fraction below the prevailing market price. If it did so, it would receive more orders than it could possibly fill. As a result, each firm in a perfectly competitive market faces a horizontal demand curve, as in Figure 9.1.

Part (a) of Figure 9.1 shows hypothetical supply and demand curves in the market for chicken. The equilibrium price is $2.00 per pound, and the equilibrium quantity is 2 billion pounds per year. Part (b) shows how the market looks from the viewpoint of an individual producer. Any one firm can vary its output only over a range of thousands, not billions of pounds. That range is so small relative to the total quantity demanded that whether the firm produces 10,000, 20,000, or 40,000 pounds a year would not perceptibly affect the market price. A 10,000-pound movement is too small even to see on the scale of the market supply and demand curves. As far as the individual firm is concerned, then, the demand curve appears to be horizontal (perfectly elastic) at the market price, even though, when viewed from the perspective of the market as a whole, the demand curve has the usual negative slope.

We have used the term *marginal cost* to mean the amount by which total cost changes when output changes by one unit. Now we can introduce a similar term, **marginal revenue**, to mean the amount by which total revenue changes when output changes by one unit. Recall that revenue means price times quantity sold. For a firm with a perfectly elastic demand curve, marginal revenue is equal to price.

Price taker

A firm that sells its output at prices determined by forces beyond its control

Marginal revenue

The amount by which total revenue changes when output changes by one unit

For example, if the price of chicken is $2 per pound, the firm will receive revenue of $200 from the sale of 100 pounds of chicken and revenue of $202 from the sale of 101 pounds. A 1-pound increase in output yields a $2 increase in revenue, equal to the product's price. (Although marginal revenue and price are equal for a perfectly competitive firm, we will see in the next chapter that the same is not true for all market structures.)

FIGURE 9.1

MARKET DEMAND AND DEMAND FOR THE PERFECTLY COMPETITIVE FIRM

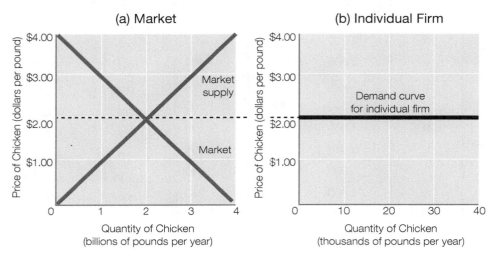

The perfectly competitive firm is a price taker. It is so small relative to the market as a whole that its decisions do not significantly affect the market price. In this example, the market equilibrium price is $2.00 per pound. The price will not be much affected if the individual firm shown in Part (b) produces 20,000 rather than 40,000 pounds out of the billions of pounds that in the market as a whole supplies. Because the individual competitive firm is a price taker, the demand curve it faces is perfectly elastic. As a result, marginal revenue equals price.

Short-Run Profit Maximization for the Firm

How does any one firm in a perfectly competitive market maximize profits, given the constraints of its cost and demand curves? A simple numerical example based on the same imaginary firm, Fieldcom that we used in the preceding chapter, will help us answer this question.[1] Part (a) of Figure 9.2 shows short-run cost data for Fieldcom. It also shows the revenue Fieldcom earns from the sale of each quantity of output, assuming a market price of $500 per unit.

FIGURE 9.2
SHORT-RUN PROFIT MAXIMIZATION UNDER PERFECT COMPETITION

(a)

Quantity of Output (1)	Total Revenue (2)	Total Cost (3)	Total Profit (2) − (3) (4)	Marginal Cost (5)	Marginal Revenue (6)
0	$ 0	$ 2,000	−$ 2,000		
				$ 380	$ 500
1	500	2,380	−1,880		
				340	500
2	1,000	2,720	−1,720		
				305	500
3	1,500	3,025	−1,525		
				275	500
4	2,000	3,300	−1,300		
				250	500
5	2,500	3,550	−1,000		
				230	500
6	3,000	3,780	−780		
				215	500
7	3,500	3,955	−495		
				205	500
8	4,000	4,200	−200		
				200	500
9	4,500	4,400	100		
				205	500
10	5,000	4,605	395		
				215	500
11	5,500	4,820	680		
				230	500
12	6,000	5,050	950		
				250	500
13	6,500	5,300	1,200		
				275	500
14	7,000	5,575	1.425		
				305	500
15	7,500	5,880	1,620		
				340	500
16	8,000	6,220	1,780		
				380	500
17	8,500	6,600	1,900		
				425	500
18	9,000	7,025	1,975		
				475	500
19	9,500	7,500	2,000		
				530	500
20	10,000	8,030	1,970		
				590	500
21	10,500	8,620	1,880		
				655	500
22	11,000	9,275	1,725		
				725	500
23	11,500	10,000	1,500		
				800	500
24	12,000	10,800	1,200		

This figure shows the profit-maximizing level of output chosen by a perfectly competitive firm, Fieldcom, Inc., given a market price of $500 per unit. We can find that level of output by comparing total cost and total revenue, as shown in Parts (a) and (b), or by comparing marginal cost and marginal revenue as in Part (c). Because the firm is a price taker, marginal revenue is equal to price. Profit increases up to the point at which rising marginal cost begins to exceed marginal revenue; after that point, it decreases. Regardless of the approach used, the profit-maximizing output is 19 units per day and the maximum profit per day is $2,000.

(Continues)

FIGURE 9.2
SHORT-RUN PROFIT MAXIMIZATION UNDER PERFECT COMPETITION *(Continued)*

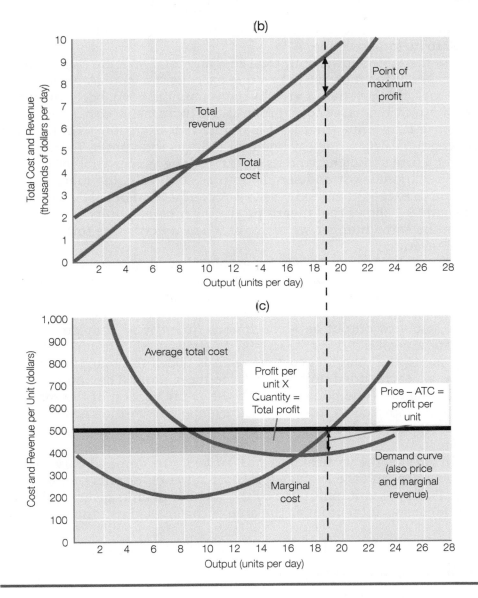

Subtracting total cost in column 3 from total revenue in column 2 yields the total profit the firm earns at each output. Profit reaches a maximum at nineteen units per day, where the firm earns $2,000 per day. Part (b) of the figure shows the profit-maximizing output level graphically. There the distance between the total revenue and total cost curves indicates the firm's total profit. That distance is greatest at nineteen units of output.

Instead of comparing total cost and total revenue, we can find the profit-maximizing output level by comparing marginal cost and marginal revenue. Look first at columns 5 and 6 of Part (a) of Figure 9.2.

Column 5 gives data on marginal cost. (Marginal cost data appear on lines between the entries in the first four columns to show that marginal cost is the change in cost as output moves from one level to another.) Column 6 shows marginal revenue, which, as explained, is equal to the product's price. Each smartphone that Fieldcom sells adds $500 to its total revenue.

As the table shows, both total cost and total revenue rise as output increases. If the increase in revenue exceeds the increase in cost (that is, if marginal revenue is greater than marginal cost), boosting output by one unit increases total profit. If the increase in cost exceeds the increase in revenue (that is, if marginal cost is greater than marginal revenue), raising output by one unit reduces total profit. To maximize profit, a firm should expand its output as long as marginal revenue exceeds marginal cost and should stop as soon as rising marginal cost begins to exceed marginal revenue. A comparison of columns 5 and 6 of Figure 9.2 shows that means producing nineteen units of output per day—the same number we arrive at when we compare total cost and total revenue.

Part (c) of Figure 9.2 gives the graphical version of the marginal approach to short-run profit maximization. Up to about nineteen units of output, the marginal cost curve lies below the marginal revenue curve, so each added unit of output increases profit. (The graph, unlike the table, pictures output as a continuous quantity so that profit maximization need not occur exactly at an even number of units.) Beyond that point, the marginal cost curve rises above the marginal revenue curve, so each added unit of output reduces profit. The point of profit maximization—the point at which the rising section of the marginal cost curve intersects the marginal revenue curve—matches the point in Part (b) at which the spread between total revenue and total cost is greatest.

In Part (c), the vertical distance between the demand curve, which shows price, and the average total cost curve represents the profit per unit. Profit per unit multiplied by the number of units gives total profit. Part (c) shows total profit as the area of the shaded rectangle.

Minimizing Short-Run Losses

In our example, Fieldcom was able to make a profit at a price of $500. However, market conditions might not always be so favorable. Suppose, for example, that the market price drops to $300. A lower market price means a downward shift in the firm's perfectly elastic demand curve. Being a price taker, the firm can do nothing about the price and will have to adjust its output as best it can to meet the new situation. Figure 9.3 shows the needed adjustments.

FIGURE 9.3
MINIMIZING SHORT-RUN LOSSES UNDER PERFECT COMPETITION

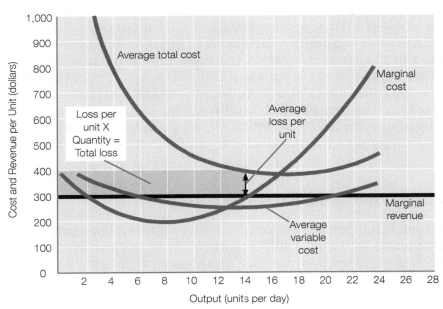

If the product's market price is too low to permit earning a profit, the firm must try to keep its losses to a minimum. For Fieldcom, Inc., given a price of $300 per unit, the point of minimum loss is 14 units of output per day. The marginal cost curve intersects the marginal revenue curve at a point higher than average variable cost but lower than average total cost. Each unit of output sold earns more than its share of variable cost but not enough to pay for its share of total cost when its share of fixed cost is included.

Notice that no output level allows Fieldcom to earn a profit when the price is $300. Instead, the firm must focus on keeping its losses to a minimum. In this case, that happens at fourteen units of output, the output level beyond which marginal cost rises above the price.

Note that the point where the rising section of the marginal cost curve intersects the marginal revenue curve lies between the average total cost and average variable cost curves.[2] Because the demand curve is below the average total cost curve, there is a loss on each unit sold. The total loss is equal to the shaded rectangle (loss per unit times quantity of output). At the same time, the demand curve lies above the average variable cost curve. That means revenue per unit is more than enough to cover variable cost, so that each unit sold makes at least some contribution toward fixed cost. For that reason, losses are smaller than they would be if the firm shut down, because it would have to pay fixed costs even if output were zero.

To help understand the logic of the loss-minimizing decision, suppose for a moment that wages are the firm's only variable cost and that rent on its building is its only fixed cost. At the point shown, the firm is bringing in more than enough revenue to pay its wage bill (variable costs); the remainder will help pay the rent. If the firm shuts down temporarily, it will have to pay the rent with no help at all from current revenue. That would mean a loss equal to fixed cost—even more of a loss than at fourteen units of output per day.

The idea of continuing operations in order to minimize losses only applies in the short run, when the fixed inputs must be paid for regardless of how much output is produced. A firm would not continue to operate indefinitely at a price below average total cost. In the long run, a firm can free itself of fixed costs by selling its equipment, allowing long-term leases to expire, and so on. We will return to the conditions under which firms will leave the industry later in the chapter.

Shutting Down to Cut Short-Run Losses

What would happen to Fieldcom if the price of smartphones dropped even lower than $300? Would it still be worthwhile for the firm to continue production in order to minimize loss? The answer, as Figure 9.4 shows, is no.

FIGURE 9.4   SHUTTING DOWN TO MINIMIZE SHORT-RUN LOSS

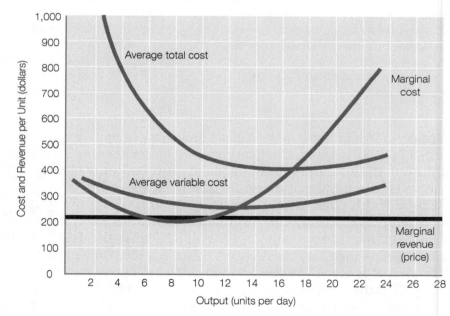

The price of a firm's output may drop so low that the firm must shut down in order to keep short-run losses to a minimum. As this figure shows, that would be the case for Fieldcom at a price of $225 per unit. Marginal cost rises above marginal revenue at about 11 units of output. That output yields a smaller loss ($2,345) than those slightly greater or lower. However, the firm can reduce its loss to just $2,000 a day if the firm shuts down.

The figure assumes a price of $225 per unit. With such a low price, the firm cannot make a profit at any output level; however, this time the best thing for the firm to do in the short run is to shut down. As illustrated by *Economics in the News* 9.1, temporary shutdowns are a normal way of adapting to changing supply and demand conditions. A short-run shutdown is not at all the same as going out of business. If the outlook for the future is good, it makes sense for a firm to keep its plant intact, pay its rent, and even continue some benefits for employees to ensure that they will be ready to come back when called. For that reason, a firm does not escape its fixed costs during a short-run shutdown. When market conditions improve, the firm can resume operations. Only if market conditions are never expected to improve will the firm consider winding up its affairs and going out of business.

Economics in the News **9.1**

Changing with the Seasons

Croatia is a small country that must make the most of its resources as it gets ready to join the European Union. One asset that will help it do so is a stunning Adriatic coastline with brilliant sun, sparkling clear water, and hundreds of islands, perfect for get-away weekends by Parisians or Berliners.

In the opinion of many, the crown jewel among the Croatian islands is Hvar. The tiny port of Hvar Town is a tourist paradise of ancient red-roofed houses cascading down a steep hill from an old fort at the top to a quaint fishing harbor below. Taking advantage of some fine, clear weather in mid-March, a recent visitor found the streets of Hvar Town lined with hotels, restaurants, and souvenir shops—all of them closed! Although it has facilities to serve thousands of tourists in the summer, all but one hotel and all but three or four restaurants close for the season each winter, to open again in the late spring.

The ancient harbor on the island of Hvar, Croatia

(Continues)

At first, it seems like such a waste. All that natural beauty is still there and the water is just as clear, even if the air is a few degrees cooler. Why don't the hotels and restaurants just offer low, off-season rates in order to stay busy all winter? With a little thought, though, the economic logic of the winter shutdown becomes clear. Hotel and restaurant owners have to take a close look at their costs when deciding whether to operate on a year-round or seasonal basis. They can't avoid some costs, such as property taxes and interest on bank loans, even if they temporarily shut down. On the other hand, they can eliminate others, especially labor costs for clerks and kitchen staff, by closing for the season. Up to a point, it pays to stay open by offering lower, off-season rates; but when those rates fall so low that they don't even cover the wages of the cooks and cleaners, it is time to close the shutters and wait for spring.

What about the one hotel that stays open in the winter? Is the owner just ignorant of economics? No, there's an economic logic behind the holdout strategy, too. If just one hotel stays open while all others shut, the few visitors to the town are enough to push its revenues above the break-even point. It's all an example of competition in action.

When a temporary shutdown is called for, it can be misleading to follow the rule of expanding output until marginal cost begins to exceed marginal revenue. With the price at $225, our firm Fieldcom reaches that point at about eleven units of output per day. That output level does give the firm a lower loss than a level slightly higher or slightly lower, but the firm incurs an even smaller loss by not producing at all.

To understand why an output of eleven units does not minimize loss, notice that the demand curve lies below the average variable cost curve at that point. Suppose again that wages are the firm's only variable cost and rent is its only fixed cost. At eleven units of output, revenue is not enough even to meet the firm's payroll. The firm will do better to send its workers home and save the cost of wages—even though when it does so, the owners will have to pay the entire rent from reserves without any help from current sales revenue.

The Firm's Short-Run Supply Curve

Taking all of these examples together, we get the information needed to draw a short-run supply curve for a perfectly competitive firm. Let's work through an example like the one shown in Figure 9.5, starting with a price of $500. As we saw earlier, Fieldcom will turn out nineteen devices a day at that price. Point E_1 of the firm's short-run marginal cost curve thus is a point on its supply curve.

FIGURE 9.5   DERIVATION OF THE SHORT-RUN SUPPLY CURVE

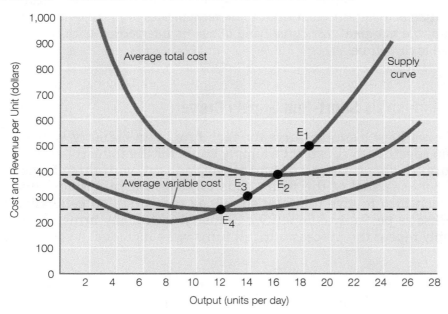

This graph shows how we can derive a short-run supply curve for Fieldcom, Inc. from its cost curves. When the price and marginal revenue is $500, the firm will produce at point E$_1$. As the price falls, the firm will move downward along its short-run marginal cost curve as shown by points E$_2$ and E$_3$. The firm will continue to produce at the point at which price equals marginal cost until marginal cost falls below average variable cost. E$_4$ thus is the lowest point on the firm's supply curve. Below that price, the firm will shut down.

Now, suppose that the demand for smartphones slackens and the market price begins to fall. As it does so, the point at which marginal revenue equals marginal cost moves downward along the firm's marginal cost curve. Soon the firm reaches point E$_2$, where marginal cost and average total cost are equal. That occurs at an output of about seventeen units and a price of about $385. At that price, the best the firm can do is break even; either a greater cost or a smaller output will result in a loss.

If the price falls still lower, the firm's objective becomes one of keeping its loss to a minimum. At a price of $300, for example, the firm minimizes its loss by making fourteen units (point E$_3$). In the range of prices between minimum average total cost and minimum average variable cost, the supply curve continues to follow the marginal cost curve.

At about $250, the price reaches the lowest point on the average variable cost curve. There the firm is just on the edge of shutting down—it is covering its variable costs with nothing to spare. Its loss is equal to its fixed costs. At any lower price, the firm will minimize its losses by shutting down. Thus, point E$_4$ is the lowest point on the marginal cost curve that is part of the firm's supply curve.

We can summarize the preceding discussion of the firm's short-run supply decision: *The short-run supply curve of a profit-maximizing firm operating in a perfectly competitive market coincides with the upward sloping part of the marginal cost curve lying above its intersection with the average variable cost curve.*

The Industry's Short-Run Supply Curve

Once we have a supply curve for each firm in an industry, we can add them together to construct a supply curve for the industry as a whole. Figure 9.6 shows the procedure for an industry with three firms. The right-most panel of the figure adds together the quantities supplied by each firm to give the total supply at each price. To generalize the process to perfectly competitive industry with many firms, we would simply repeat the process until all firms were included.

FIGURE 9.6 DERIVATION OF A SHORT-RUN INDUSTRY SUPPLY CURVE

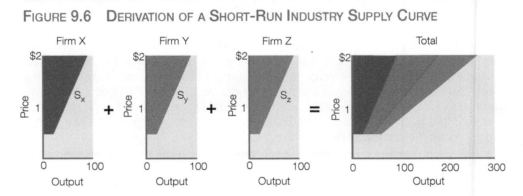

We can construct a short-run industry supply curve by summing the supply curves of individual firms. This figure shows the method for an industry with three firms. Getting a supply curve for a perfectly competitive industry with many firms would require adding the supply curves of more firms in the same way.

The procedure just shown for constructing an industry supply curve assumes that input prices do not change as output expands. For a small firm in a perfectly competitive industry, that is a realistic assumption. However, if all firms in an industry try to grow at the same time, the assumption may not hold. Input prices will rise when industry output expands unless the short-run supply curves for inputs to the industry are perfectly elastic. If input prices rise as the industry's total output grows, each firm's cost curves will shift upward as the outputs of all firms increase. That will make the short-run industry supply curve somewhat steeper than the sum of the individual supply curves.

9.2 Long-Run Equilibrium under Perfect Competition

Up to this point, we been concerned with the way firms change their output in response to price changes. Now we turn to another aspect of a competitive industry's response to changes in demand: entry and exit.

Changing the focus to entry and exit moves us from the short run to the long run. In the preceding chapter, we distinguished the long run, when firms can vary all inputs, from the short run, when some inputs are fixed.

The ability to vary all inputs in the long run—even durable inputs such as land, structures, and capital equipment—allows firms to enter a market for the first time, starting with a new plant and work force. It also means that they can leave a market for good, releasing all their employees and selling their plant and equipment. Sometimes firms leave voluntarily, with the owners selling the firm's assets and dividing the proceeds. Other times they leave the market only when forced to do so, as when creditors petition a bankruptcy court to force a sale of the firm's assets in order to pay its debts. Typically, as an industry expands and contracts, many firms enter and leave it.

Free entry and exit of firms is one of the basic traits of a perfectly competitive market. Entry is not free in the sense that firms can enter at no cost. They may have to pay a great deal to purchase equipment, hire key employees, and so on. Free entry simply means that if new firms are willing to make the necessary investment, they are free to compete with existing ones on a level playing field. There are no major barriers in the form of patents, licenses, permits, trade secrets, collusion by firms already in the industry, or lack of access to raw materials to keep them out. Likewise, free exit means that firms face no legal barriers to shutting down or moving if they find that they cannot make a profit. Strictly interpreted, free exit also means that firms have no sunk costs. When they leave the industry, they can put fixed assets to other uses or find buyers for them.

Free entry and exit did not play a direct role in our discussion of a firm's short-run supply decision. However, as we will now see, it is crucial to understanding how a competitive market works in the long run.

Long-Run Equilibrium for a Competitive Firm

We have often used the term equilibrium to refer to a state of affairs in which economic decision makers have no incentives to change their plans. Three conditions are required for a perfectly competitive firm to be in equilibrium in the long run:

1. The firm must have no incentive to produce a larger or smaller output given the size of its plant (that is, the amount of fixed inputs it uses). That requires short-run marginal cost to be equal to short-run marginal revenue, which in turn means that the short-run equilibrium condition is also a condition for long-run equilibrium.

2. Each firm must have no incentive to change the size of its current plant (that is, the amount of fixed inputs it uses).

3. There must be no incentive for new firms to enter the industry or for existing firms to leave it.

Figure 9.7 shows a perfectly competitive firm that meets these three requirements. First, short-run marginal cost equals price at twenty-five units of output per day, which is the level of output the firm will choose in order to make the maximum profit. Second, the firm has a plant that is just the right size to make short-run average total cost equal to the lowest possible long-run average cost at the chosen output level. The short-run average total cost curve for a plant of any other size would give a higher average total cost for the chosen output. Third, both long-run average cost and short-run average total cost are equal to price at the equilibrium level of output. That guarantees there is no incentive for entry or exit. As always, average total cost comprises both explicit and implicit costs, including the opportunity cost of capital, or "normal profit." When price equals average total cost, then, firms are earning zero economic profit. Any positive economic profit would attract new firms into the industry, whereas negative economic profits (economic losses) would cause firms to leave the industry.

FIGURE 9.7 A PERFECTLY COMPETITIVE FIRM IN LONG-RUN EQUILIBRIUM

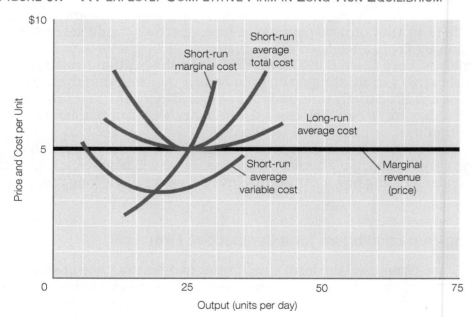

Long-run equilibrium in a perfectly competitive industry requires that the typical firm (1) have no short-run incentive to change the level of its output, (2) have no long-run incentive to change the size of the plant used to produce its output, and (3) have no long-run incentive to enter or leave the industry. That requires that price, short-run marginal cost, short-run average total cost, and long-run average cost all have the same value in equilibrium, as shown here.

The following equation summarizes the three conditions for long-run equilibrium:

$$\text{Price} = \text{Marginal cost} = \text{Short-run average total cost}$$
$$= \text{Long-run average cost}$$

If any part of this equation does not hold, firms will have a reason to change their plans. If price does not equal short-run marginal cost, they will have an incentive to change their output levels by changing the quantity of variable inputs used—even if they cannot, in the short run, change the size of their plants. If short-run average total cost does not equal long-run average cost, their current plant is too large or too small to produce their current level of output at the least possible cost. They will want to change the size of the plants they are using, so that their plant will be the ideal size to produce their current output. If price is lower than long-run average cost, firms now in the industry will want to leave it; if price is above long-run average total cost, firms will want to enter the industry from outside.

Industry Adjustment to Falling Demand

A state of long-run equilibrium like that shown in Figure 9.7 exists only as long as outside conditions do not change. Suppose that those conditions do change—for example, there is a long-run decrease in the market demand for the firm's product. Figure 9.8 shows what will happen.

Part (a) of Figure 9.8 shows a set of cost curves for a typical firm. Part (b) is a supply-and-demand diagram for the market as a whole. The short-run industry supply curves shown are the sum of those of the individual firms (see Figure 9.6). The demand curves in Part (b) are market demand curves.

Suppose that initially the short-run market supply and demand curves are in the positions S_1 and D_1. The equilibrium price is $5. Each firm takes this price as given and adjusts its output on that basis, producing twenty-five units. At that price and output, a typical firm would just break even. (Remember, though, "breaking even" in the economic sense means earning enough to cover all costs, including the opportunity cost of capital.)

Now something happens—say, a change in consumer tastes or incomes—that shifts the demand curve to a new position, D_2. The short-run effect is a decrease in the market price to $4. Each firm, being a price taker, will view the decrease in price as beyond its control and will adjust to it as best it can. As Part (a) of Figure 9.8 shows, that means cutting back output slightly in order to keep losses to a minimum, but not shutting down completely. Each firm's movement downward along its short-run marginal cost curve is what causes the movement of the market as a whole downward and to the left along the short-run supply curve.

BVT *Lab*

Improve your test scores. Practice quizzes are available at www.BVTLab.com.

FIGURE 9.8   LONG-RUN ADJUSTMENT TO DECLINING DEMAND

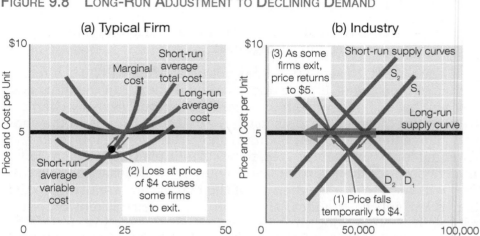

Part (a) represents a typical firm in a perfectly competitive industry; Part (b) represents the industry as a whole. At first, both the firm and the industry are in long-run equilibrium at a price of $5. Then something happens to shift the market demand curve leftward from D_1 to D_2. In the short run, the price falls to $4 at the intersection of D_2 and S_1. The firm's short-run response is to move downward along its marginal cost curve. Because the price is still above average variable cost, the firm does not shut down. After a while, some firms (not the one shown) get tired of taking losses and leave the industry. This causes the market supply curve to shift toward S_2 and the market price to recover. The typical firm returns to the break-even point. The market has traced out part of its long-run supply curve as shown by the large arrow.

The new short-run equilibrium cannot last because each firm is operating at a loss. The firms' owners are not earning a normal rate of return, that is, they are not earning enough to cover the opportunity costs of keeping their capital invested in the industry. If the market demand curve shows no hope of shifting back to the right, some owners will pull their capital out of the industry. They may go bankrupt, abandoning their fixed assets to their creditors. They may sell their plant and equipment and get out while they can, or they may keep their firms running but convert their plants to make goods for other, more profitable markets.[3]

For the sake of the example, suppose that the typical firm shown in Figure 9.8 is not one of the first to leave. As some other firms withdraw, industry output falls by the amount of their output. The short-run market supply curve, which now comprises fewer individual supply curves, shifts to the left toward S_2. As it does so, the market price begins to move upward along demand curve D_2. When the price gets all the way back to $5, the firms remaining in the industry will no longer be losing money. Firms will stop leaving the industry, and the market will have reached a new long-run equilibrium. At the new equilibrium price, short-run marginal cost, short-run average total cost, and long-run average cost will once again be equal.

This sequence of events has traced out a portion of the industry's *long-run supply curve*, as shown by the large horizontal arrow. A long-run supply curve for an industry shows the path along which equilibrium price and quantity move when there is a lasting change in demand. Movement along this curve requires enough time for firms to adjust the sizes of their plants, or to enter or leave the market.

Industry Adjustment to Rising Demand

When there is a long-run increase in demand, freedom of entry plays the same role that freedom of exit plays when demand falls. Figure 9.9 shows that case. The starting position is the same as in Figure 9.8. Short-run supply curve S_1 and demand curve D_1 give an equilibrium price of $5. Each individual firm breaks even at an output of twenty-five units. Now watch what happens as the demand curve shifts to the right, to D_2. In the short-run, the market price increases to $6. The typical firm adjusts to the new price by moving up along its short-run marginal cost curve. As all firms do this, the market moves up and to the right along short-run supply curve S_1.

FIGURE 9.9   LONG-RUN ADJUSTMENT TO AN INCREASE IN DEMAND

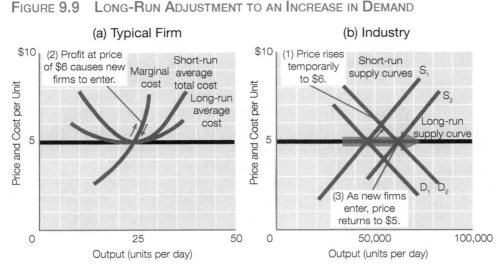

In this figure, both the firm and the industry start out in equilibrium at a price of $5. Then something happens to shift the market demand curve rightward to D_2. In the short run, the price rises to $6 at the intersection of D_2 and S_1. Each firm responds in the short run by moving upward along its marginal cost curve, earning better-than-normal profits. After a while, the high profits attract new firms into the industry. As those firms enter, the market supply curve shifts toward S_2. Profits for the typical firm return to zero, and new firms stop entering the industry. Again, the market has traced out part of its long-run supply curve as shown by the large arrow.

As before, the short-run position is not the new long-run equilibrium because now all firms are making an economic profit. Entrepreneurs will soon spot this healthy, growing market as a good one in which to invest. Some of them may start new firms in this market; others may shift the plant and equipment from making something else to making goods for this industry. Whether the entry is by new firms or by existing ones that are producing for this market for the first time, new entries will cause the supply curve to shift to the right, toward S_2.

As the short-run market supply curve shifts to the right, the price falls. It does not fall far enough to drive the new entrants out of the market, but it does fall far enough to drive pure economic profits back to zero. Entry of firms into the market will stop, and the market will reach a new long-run equilibrium at the intersection of S_2 and D_2.

Once again, the large horizontal arrow in Figure 9.9 traces out a portion of the long-run supply curve for the industry. Once again, the long-run supply curve is perfectly elastic. A rightward shift in the demand curve has, in the long run, produced an increase in quantity supplied but no change in price.

As a final detail, note the importance of the assumption that there are no sunk costs in the industry. If entering the industry required specialized investments that could not be recovered later, firms would view them as opportunity costs when deciding whether to enter. They would not enter unless the price was high enough (and was expected to stay high enough) to give them a normal rate of return on the non-recoverable investments. Once in the industry, however, those sunk costs would no longer affect decisions, according to the "bygones are bygones" principle. They would not count as part of the fixed (but not sunk) costs that the firm must cover to make continued operation worthwhile. In that case, existing firms might stay in business indefinitely even if the price fell somewhat below a level that would attract new firms. When sunk costs are present, then, the industry supply curve is no longer a two-way street. In effect, an industry with sunk costs would follow one supply curve when expanding—and a different, lower one when contracting.

Although the theoretical model of perfect competition does not allow for sunk costs, such costs are common in the real world. Consider the history of that uniquely American entertainment establishment, the drive-in theater. In the early years after World War II, drive-in theaters were a growing business. With demand high, many entrepreneurs entered the industry. Later, demand for that form of entertainment decreased. Even when market demand dropped well below the level needed to make it worthwhile to construct new drive-ins, existing operators stayed in business. They did so even

The drive-in theater, a uniquely American entertainment establishment, was a growing business after World War II.

though they were no longer earning enough to cover the original sunk cost of their screens and projection houses because they could neither move those facilities nor convert them to any other use. Only when demand fell still lower, so that revenues no longer covered variable costs (such as wages, electricity, and film rentals) plus recoverable fixed costs (such as the cost of land), did drive-in theater operators finally leave the market.

The Elasticity of Long-Run Supply

In Figures 9.8 and 9.9, the long-run industry supply curve is perfectly elastic. As a result, a change in demand affects only the equilibrium quantity, not the price, in the long run. However, that is not the only possible case. Positively sloped, negatively sloped, and U-shaped supply curves are also possible.

The shape of the long-run industry supply curve depends mainly on what happens in the long run to the industry's input prices as output expands. If the long-run supply of all inputs to the industry is perfectly elastic, the prices of those inputs will not change as the quantities demanded by the industry increase. It may also be that the industry uses such a small part of the total supply of each input that any change in input prices that does occur will be slight. For example, cookie stores use such a small part of the total supply of flour that expansion or contraction of such stores will have no perceptible effect on its market price. Industry output can, therefore, expand without affecting the costs of the individual firms and the supply curve will be perfectly elastic.

Suppose, though, that the industry is a heavy user of a relatively specialized input whose output can rise only at an increasing cost. Take the home construction business, for example, which uses a large share of all lumber produced. A long-run increase in home construction will exhaust the lowest-cost stands of trees and cause suppliers to begin harvesting higher-cost timber. The home construction industry also employs a large share of all carpenters in the country. If the industry expands, carpenters' wages may have to rise relative to those of, say, auto mechanics in order to attract additional workers into the occupation.

Figure 9.10 shows what happens in such an industry as a permanent increase in demand causes output to expand. As in earlier examples, the shift in demand first pushes price up along the short-run supply curve. New firms enter the market. Now, though, the expansion of the industry raises input prices. Each firm's short-run marginal cost and average total cost curves shift upward from MC_1 to MC_2 and from ATC^1 to ATC_2. As a result, the new long-run equilibrium is at a higher price than the initial equilibrium. The long-run industry supply curve, drawn through the two points of short-run equilibrium, therefore has a positive slope.

FIGURE 9.10   A POSITIVELY SLOPED LONG-RUN INDUSTRY SUPPLY CURVE

(a) Typical Firm

(3) As industry expands, cost curves shift upward.

MC₂

MC₁ ATC₂

ATC₁

(2) Profit at price of $7 causes new firms to enter.

Price and Cost per Unit — $10 ... 5 ... 0

Output (units per day) — 25 ... 50

(b) Industry

(1) Price rises temporarily to $7.

Long-run supply curve

D₂

D₁

S₁ S₂

(4) With higher costs, new equilibrium price is $6.

Price and Cost per Unit — $10 ... 5 ... 0

Output (units per day) — 50,000 ... 100,000

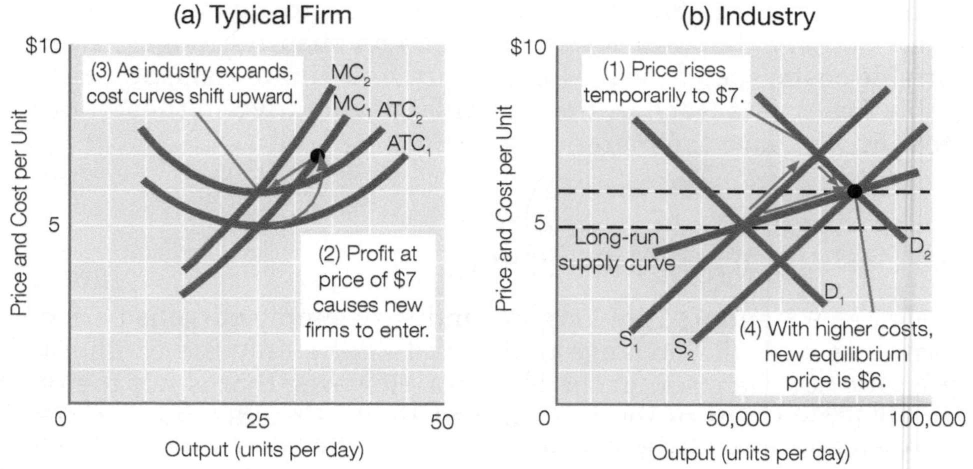

In Figures 9.8 and 9.9, we assumed that input prices do not change as industry output expands. This pair of diagrams shows what happens if industry expansion causes input prices to rise. As output expands, rising input prices push up the firm's marginal cost curve from MC_1 to MC_2 and its average total cost from ATC_1 to ATC_2. The result is a new long-run equilibrium price that is higher than the initial price. The long-run industry supply curve now has a positive slope.

It is also possible for the price of an input to decrease as the industry's total output increases. For example, as sales of electronic equipment expand, the firms that make components for such equipment may be able to use cheaper production methods. If that occurs, the short-run cost curves for all firms will drift downward as new firms enter the industry. The long-run supply curve then will be negatively sloped.

Finally, it is possible for these various forces to operate together. At first long-run supply is influenced by the falling price of one special input, but beyond a certain point, some other special input becomes a limiting factor that causes the long-run supply curve to bend upward. The long-run industry supply curve then becomes U-shaped.

As we have seen, many variations are possible. Only through direct observation of the industry in question can we tell which possibility applies.

9.3 Market Performance under Perfect Competition

In Chapter 4, we introduced the notion of *market performance* to indicate how efficiently markets do their job of allowing buyers and sellers to capture mutual gains from trade. Perfectly competitive markets have long earned high marks for several aspects of performance. In this section, we look at market performance under perfect competition under the headings of *what* to produce and *how* to produce it.

What to Produce?

We first introduced the concept of market performance using a diagram like Figure 9.11, which shows hypothetical data for the market for peaches. The height of the demand curve at any point shows how much consumers are willing to pay for one more pound, that is, the marginal benefit they get from the good. The height of the supply curve shows how much suppliers need in order to cover the opportunity cost of supplying the marginal pound. As long as the demand curve is higher than the supply curve, producing and selling one more unit at any price between the two curves can benefit both parties. Opportunities for mutually beneficial trades are exhausted (and efficiency is achieved) only when enough is produced to reach the intersection of the two curves. Output beyond the intersection is neither efficient nor mutually beneficial.

FIGURE 9.11   EFFICIENT OUTPUT UNDER PERFECT COMPETITION

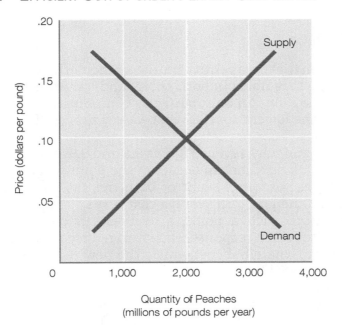

This figure shows supply and demand curves for a perfectly competitive market for peaches. Under perfect competition, each firm's efforts to keep marginal cost equal to marginal revenue ensure that the industry will produce at some point on the supply curve. Equilibrium for the market as a whole can occur only at the point where the supply and demand curves intersect.

This chapter has shown how a perfectly competitive market guides supply and demand toward the efficient equilibrium by establishing a price at the intersection of the supply and demand curves. If the equilibrium is disturbed, the market will adjust in a way that returns it to the efficient point. For example, suppose a shift in the supply or demand curves leaves the market temporarily with a price that is higher than the intersection of the supply and demand curves. In that case, a surplus (excess quantity supplied) develops. Unplanned accumulation of inventory causes the price to fall. As the price falls, firms move down along the supply curve to keep marginal cost equal to marginal revenue. Similarly, a price that is lower than the intersection of the supply and demand curves results in a shortage. Depletion of inventories causes the market price to rise. Firms move up along the supply curve to keep marginal cost and marginal revenue equal.

Generalizing, we can see that an economy where all markets were perfectly competitive and there were no externalities would produce the efficient quantity of every good. The result would be an efficient answer to the question of what to produce—how many peaches, apples, tomatoes, and so on. Starting from equilibrium in such an economy, we could not substitute any good for another (say, by producing more peaches instead of using the same resources to produce apples) in a way that would make any person better off without making at least one other person worse off.

How to Produce

The conclusion that competitive markets efficiently solve the problem of what to produce holds in both short- and long-run equilibrium. In addition, in the long run only, perfectly competitive markets produce each good at the lowest possible cost—a key aspect of the question of how to produce.

To understand why, review Figures 9.8 and 9.9. In those figures, the point of long-run equilibrium occurs at the point where a typical firm operates at the minimum point of both the short-run average total cost curve and the long-run average cost curve.

Starting from such a point, a decrease in demand causes the market price to fall. In response, each firm reduces output to the point where short-run marginal cost equals the new price. Although short-run marginal cost is lower at that output, short-run average total cost is higher because the firm moves up and to the left along the average total cost curve as output falls. At that stage in the adjustment to falling demand, then, the economy is not producing the given level of output at the lowest possible cost. That is inefficient.

However, the inefficient situation does not last. Because short-run average total cost exceeds the market price, the firms suffer an economic loss and some of them will leave the industry. If there is no further change in demand, as the number of firms in the industry decreases, each firm is able to increase its output and move back toward its point of least-cost production. Much the same is true of the expansion of industry output after an increase in demand.

Under perfect competition, firms not only produce at the lowest possible short-run average total cost, given the size of their plants, but also select the correct plant size to minimize average cost in the long run. To see why, suppose that one firm had a plant that was not the optimal size. As we saw in the last chapter, the short-run average total cost curve for such a firm would be tangent to its long-run average cost curve at a point above and to the right of the point of long-run minimum cost (if the plant were too large) or above it and to the left (if the plant were too small). The firm with the wrong size plant would be at a cost disadvantage relative to its competitors. As competition drove the market price toward minimum long-run average cost, the firm would either adjust the size of its plant to the cost-minimizing level or leave the industry because of economic losses.

Other Aspects of Market Performance

The tendency of perfectly competitive markets to produce the efficient quantity of each good at the lowest cost is an important strength of that market structure. In Chapter 13, we will apply similar reasoning to perfect competition to factor markets. When we do so, we will see that perfectly competitive markets perform efficiently with regard to the questions of *who* and for *whom* as well as those of *what* and *how*. In those respects, long-run equilibrium in perfectly competitive markets sets a standard against which to judge the performance of other market structures.

Still, it would be claiming far too much to say that perfect competition has the best possible market performance under all conditions, and it would be premature to condemn all real-world markets that depart from the structural characteristics of perfect competition. Before we write off all markets that are not made up exclusively of small firms, all markets in which products are not homogeneous, all markets in which newly entering firms encounter entry barriers or incur sunk costs, or all markets in which some participants know things that others do not, many questions must be asked. Among them are the following:

- Is it possible that other markets equal or come close to the efficiency of perfect competition despite structural differences?

- How do alternative market structures perform when we focus on innovation and entrepreneurship rather than on equilibrium with unchanging technology?

- When markets fail to perform efficiently, what public-policy options are available? How should we weigh the dangers of government failure against the dangers of market failure?

Only when we have explored those further questions will we be in a position to make a balanced judgment of market performance under various market structures.

Summary

1. **What characteristics define market structure?** *Market structures* differ in terms of the number and size of firms, the nature of the product, ease of entry and exit, and availability of information. In a *perfectly competitive market* (1) there are many buyers and sellers, each of which is small relative to the market as a whole; (2) the product is homogeneous; (3) it is easy to enter or leave the market; and (4) all buyers and sellers have equal access to information. Other market structures we will study in this course include *monopoly, oligopoly,* and *monopolistic competition.*

2. **What determines the profit-maximizing output level in the short run for a perfectly competitive firm?** In the short run, the firm should expand output up to, but not beyond, the point at which marginal cost rises to the level of *marginal revenue*, if marginal revenue is at least equal to average variable cost at that point.

3. **Under what conditions will a firm continue to operate even if it sustains a loss?** If marginal revenue is below average total cost at the point where marginal cost and marginal revenue are equal, the firm cannot earn a profit. It will minimize loss in the short run by staying open if marginal revenue is above average variable cost. If marginal revenue is below average variable cost at the same point, the firm will minimize loss by shutting down.

4. **What is the relationship between a firm's short-run supply curve and its cost curves?** The short-run supply curve for a perfectly competitive firm is the upward-sloping part of the marginal cost curve lying above its intersection with the average variable cost curve.

5. **What are the conditions for long-run equilibrium in a perfectly competitive industry?** Long-run equilibrium in a perfectly competitive industry requires (1) that price be equal to short-run marginal cost so that firms are content with the level of output they are producing; (2) that short-run average total cost be equal to long-run average cost so that firms are satisfied with the size of their plants, given their output rate; and (3) that price be equal to long-run average cost so that there is no incentive for new firms to enter the industry or for existing firms to leave it.

6. **What determines the shape of the long-run supply curve for a perfectly competitive industry?** A perfectly competitive industry adjusts to long-run changes in demand through exit of firms (in the case of a fall in market demand) or entry of new firms (in the case of a rise in market demand). If input prices do not change as the industry's output changes, the industry's long-run supply curve will be perfectly elastic. If input prices rise, the long-run supply curve will have a positive slope; if they fall, it will have a negative slope.

7. **How efficiently do markets perform under perfect competition?** Under conditions of equilibrium, a perfectly competitive market produces an output that corresponds to the intersection of the market's supply and demand curves. An economy where all markets are in perfectly competitive equilibrium and there are no externalities thus answers the question of what to produce efficiently. Also, in long-run equilibrium, a perfectly competitive market produces at the lowest possible cost. That means it also provides an efficient answer to the question of how to produce.

Key Terms   Page

Marginal revenue	270
Market structure	268
Monopolistic competition	268
Oligopoly	268
Perfect competition	268
Price taker	270

Problems and Topics for Discussion

1. **Market structures**   Give examples (other than those in the text) of industries that fit, or approximate, the market structures of perfect competition, monopoly, oligopoly, and monopolistic competition.

2. **Buyers as price takers**   Price taking can apply to buyers as well as to sellers. A price-taking buyer cannot influence prices by changing the amount purchased. Are you a price taker for the goods you buy? Can you give an example of a firm that might not be a price taker in the market in which it buys one or more of its inputs?

3. **Changes in fixed cost and the supply curve**   Suppose Fieldcom buys some automated equipment to speed up production of its smartphones. The equipment adds $500 per day to the firm's fixed costs, but it saves $50 per unit in variable costs. Rework the graph in Figure 9.5 to show how the new equipment affects Fieldcom's supply curve. (You may want to rework Part (a) of Figure 9.2 as a basis for the new supply curve.) What is the minimum price the firm must now charge to continue operating in the short run? What is the lowest price at which it can break even?

4. **Long- and short-run elasticity of supply**   Chapter 3 asserted that, other things being equal, the elasticity of supply of a good tends to be greater the more time firms have to adjust to new market conditions. Explain the basis for that assertion using the theory of perfect competition.

5. **Long-run supply with falling input prices**   Figure 9.10 shows the long-run adjustment of a competitive industry to an increase in demand for the case where input prices rise as industry output increases. Assume, instead, that input prices fall as output rises. Draw a new set of diagrams to show how a typical firm and the industry as a whole would respond to an increase in demand.

Case for Discussion:

Independent Truckers as a Perfectly Competitive Industry

The next time you are out on the highway, take a look at the trucks that are passing you. You will see many that belong to large firms, such as FedEx, that haul large numbers of small shipments all over the country on regular schedules. You will also see trucks that bear the names of companies for which transportation of their own products is a small part of their total operations.

If you look closely, you will also see that about one truck in four looks different. The tractors, many of which are brightly painted and highly chromed, often have sleepers attached to them. The trailers, often refrigerated, are likely to full of farm produce moving to market. These are the trucks of independent owner-operators, who move much of the nation's output of farm goods and some manufactured goods. Each firm in this market consists of a person who owns and drives just one truck. There are tens of thousands of owner operators—just how many is hard to count.

From the shipper's point of view, one refrigerated truck is about as good as another as long as it is heading in the right direction; and most independent truckers will go wherever their loads take them.

Entry into the market is easy. Some people go into business with a used truck and as little as $5,000. Most operators buy their trucks on credit. Exit is also easy—too easy, some say. Many independent truckers go broke every year, and the number of firms rises and falls with the state of the economy.

Information is the lifeblood of the owner-operator. Truckers cannot make money unless they can find loads. Empty return runs after making a delivery are deadly to profitability. In the past, truck stop payphones and gossip over a cup of coffee were the main information channels, but the Internet has revolutionized the flow of information among shippers and truckers. Several competing web sites—some of which are free, others of which charge brokerage fees—match truckers to loads.

People who run the giant trucking companies that haul manufactured goods often look down their noses at the independent truckers with their loads of apples and potatoes. They call them gypsies or worse. This system, however, succeeds in putting fresh produce on dinner tables in every town every day.

Questions

1. In what ways does the independent trucking industry approximate the requirements of perfect competition? Are there any ways in which it does not meet those requirements?

2. On the average, the firms in a perfectly competitive industry earn no pure economic profits. However, average conditions do not always apply. What would you expect to happen to the profits of independent truckers when the economy enters a recession? When it enters a period of prosperity? What do you think would happen to the number of firms in the industry at such times?

3. Diesel fuel is a major input for independent truckers. What would you expect to happen to the profits of independent truckers and the number of firms in the industry as the price of fuel rises and falls? Outline the sequence of events in each case. (Drawing a graph may help.)

Endnotes

1. Bear in mind that in the real world, it is hard to find firms that exactly fit the ideal type of perfect competition. For example, the description of Fieldcom in Chapter 8 implied that the firm's smartphones had special qualities of "ruggedization" that set them apart from others. That would violate the assumption of product homogeneity. For the purposes of this chapter, imagine that the idea of "ruggedized" smartphones did not work out but that the Martins, and many other small producers as well, have discovered that they can survive by making "generic" smartphones that function just like others on the market.

2. This graph shows why we emphasize that profit maximization occurs where the rising section of the marginal cost curve intersects the marginal revenue curve. Sometimes there is also an intersection of the falling section of the marginal cost curve with the $300-per-unit marginal revenue curve, as is the case at about two units of output in Figure 9.3. That intersection is *not* a point of profit maximization but rather one of loss maximization.

3. The discussion of exit from a perfectly competitive market seems to pose a paradox: If all firms are exactly alike, why don't they all stay in the market as long as conditions are favorable, and then all leave the market at the same instant when conditions become unfavorable? However, real-world markets only approximate the conditions of perfect competition. In such markets, small differences in firms' circumstances of cost or demand, or in the temperaments of their owners, will cause some to leave the market before others do.

Chapter **10**

The Theory
of Monopoly

After reading this chapter, you will understand the following:

1. How monopolies can exist

2. How to determine the profit-maximizing price and output for a monopoly

3. The conditions for long-run equilibrium under monopoly

4. The kinds of pricing strategies used by monopolies

5. How monopoly affects market performance

Before reading this chapter, make sure you know the meaning of the following concepts:

1. Market performance and market failure

2. Rent seeking

3. Consumer and producer surplus

4. Market structure

A monopoly is a market structure in which a single firm is the sole supplier of a product that has no close substitute. Few markets meet the definition literally. Is Microsoft a monopolist in the market for operating systems? No, it has a large market share, but Linux users would deny a lack of substitutes. Does the U.S. Postal Service have a monopoly on delivery of mail? Yes, if narrowly defined as first-class postal mail, but Federal Express, e-mail, and fax are close substitutes. Does your local electric company have a monopoly? Probably yes, if you mean delivery of electric power by wire, but industrial users of co-generation equipment and green consumers with off-the-grid systems are examples of substitutes.

Still, we can learn much from studying monopoly as a market structure, even if we have a hard time finding perfect real-world examples. One reason is that many features of the model of monopoly apply to all firms that are not price takers, even if they are not pure monopolists. Also, we will learn much about real world markets by asking why monopoly in its pure form is rare and, where it exists, why it does not last forever.

10.1 Varieties of Monopoly

We can begin by looking at three situations in which a single firm can be sole supplier to a market.

Closed monopoly

A monopoly that enjoys the protection of legal restrictions on competition

1. A **closed monopoly** has the protection of legal restrictions on competition. For example, state law in Washington prevents anyone from offering competing car ferry service to islands served by the Washington State Ferry System. Patents and copyrights also create closed monopolies. For example, no one but Pfizer can make the top-selling cholesterol-reducing drug Lipitor. Note, however, that these closed monopolies do not prevent sale of substitutes, for example, air service to Washington islands or drugs that use other metabolic mechanisms to control cholesterol.

Natural monopoly

An industry where long-run average cost is at a minimum when only one firm serves the market

2. A **natural monopoly** is an industry in which long-run average cost is at a minimum when just one firm serves the market. Distribution of natural gas to residential customers is an example. In such an industry the minimum efficient scale of production for a good is close to (or even larger than) the quantity demanded at any price high enough to cover costs. For that reason, dividing production between two or more firms (for example, running two sets of gas pipes down every street) would mean an inefficiently high cost per unit for each. Other natural monopolies are based on ownership of a unique natural resource. For example, for many years ownership of a uniquely productive mine in Utah gave the Brush Wellman Company a near monopoly over production of beryllium, an ultra-light metal used in aerospace applications.

Open monopoly

A monopoly where one firm temporarily becomes the sole supplier of a product but has no special protection from competition

3. An **open monopoly** is a market where a firm becomes, at least for a time, the sole supplier of a product without having the special protection against competition of a closed or natural monopoly. The first firm to venture into the market for a new product often finds itself in such a position, although other competitors may enter later. An example is Apple's iPhone, which had a monopoly in the market for touch-screen cell phones until competitor Blackberry, followed by others, introduced similar products.

The classification of monopolies into these three categories is a loose one. Some firms may belong to more than one category. For example, local utilities like electric and gas companies may be both natural monopolies (because of economies of scale) and closed monopolies (because of regulatory barriers to competition). Also, the classification may depend on the time horizon in question. For example, patent protection may give a firm a closed monopoly in the short run. However, patents eventually expire and competitors are able to invent new products that circumvent them, so the markets are open monopolies in the long run. Patented pharmaceuticals are an example. *Economics in the News 10.1*, which discusses China's monopoly of rare earth metals, illustrates some of the considerations that go into classifying a monopoly as closed, natural, or open.

Economics in the News 10.1

China's Fragile
Rare Earth Monopoly

In September 2010, a Chinese fishing boat collided with a Japanese Coast Guard vessel near a group of disputed islands in the East China Sea. The collision sparked a chain of events that led to an apparent cutoff of China's shipments to Japan of rare earth elements (REEs). REEs are a group of seventeen elements with exotic names like neodymium and yttrium that are vital ingredients in many high-tech products. Suddenly the world became aware that China, home to some 95 percent of global REE production, held an alarming strategic monopoly.

How did China become the world's leading producer of REEs? Did the 95 percent market share it held in 2010 represent a true natural monopoly? Will its dominance last? Some basic economic ideas can help us find the answers.

We can begin by revealing what everyone already seems to know: Rare elements are not really rare. All seventeen rare earth elements are more abundant in the earth's crust than gold, and some of them are as abundant as lead. The thing that makes them hard to mine is the fact that they do not occur in highly concentrated deposits like gold and lead. Even the best REE ores have very low concentrations. On the other hand, such ores exist widely throughout the world. Until the 1960s, India, Brazil, and South Africa were the leading producers. From the 1960s to the 1990s, the Mountain Pass Mine in California was the biggest source. China's dominance of REE production dates only from the late 1990s.

So, what explains China's big market share? Good ore deposits, but not uniquely good, are one factor. Second, low labor costs help China's REE mines just as they help its toy factories. A third consideration may have been most important of all: Mining of REEs can produce very nasty waste products. Up until recently, Chinese authorities were willing to turn a blind eye to environmental devastation caused by primitive, often illegal, but low-cost small-scale mines. Meanwhile, environmental problems were a major factor leading to the shutdown of the Mountain Pass Mine. Following a big spill of radioactive waste, U.S. authorities demanded new environmental safeguards. Already facing low-cost Chinese competition, the mine closed rather than undertake the needed investments.

The abundance of REE ores suggests that China's 95 percent market share does not represent a true natural monopoly, that is, one based on ownership of unique resources. However, that does not mean it lacks short-run monopoly power. In the short run, supply of REEs is much less elastic than in the long run. Any short run increase in supply can only come from mines that are already open or, to a very limited extent, come from "urban mining"—that is, recycling of REEs from scrapped computers and the like.

Short-run demand is also inelastic. High-tech production lines are set up to produce hybrid cars and computer hard drives using well-tested but REE-dependent technologies. You can't just substitute nickel for the neodymium in a magnet and expect the product still to do its job.

(Continues)

In the long run, though, all evidence points to much greater elasticity of both supply and demand. After the 2010 run-up in REE prices, the U.S. mining company Molycorp quickly obtained a permit to reopen California's Mountain Pass Mine; it expects to be filling customer orders by 2012. Also in 2012, Australia, a supplier of nearly every other mineral, received an initial operating license to begin refining REE ores at a plant in Malaysia. Looking farther ahead, Germany signed an agreement with Kazakhstan that will permit joint development of REEs in the latter country.

China is the world's leading producer of rare earth elements.

On the demand side, it is not quite true to say that REEs are irreplaceable ingredients of today's high-tech products. At least in many cases, producers use REE-dependent technologies not because they are the only way to do something but because they are a good way to do it given reasonable prices and reliable availability of the raw materials. Japanese, Korean, and U.S. companies are already developing alternative technologies for electric motors, computer hard drives, and other REE-dependent products.

The bottom line: China has a big market share, but no natural monopoly. Any efforts it makes to exploit its advantage based on low short-run elasticities only accelerate the development of alternative sources and new technologies.

Source: Based in part on "China's Fragile Rare Earth Monopoly," Ed Dolan's Econ Blog (http://dolanecon. blogspot.com), October 24, 2010, reproduced by permission.

In the end, we can probably consider all monopolies to be open. Technologies change and the legal restrictions that protect closed monopolies from competition are subject to challenge in legislatures and courtrooms. Long-distance telephone service, on which AT&T once held a monopoly, is a case in point. Polaroid's once-lucrative monopoly on instant-film cameras became nothing but a technological curiosity with the rise of digital photography. All monopolists face competition by substitutes for the products they produce.

10.2 Simple Monopoly

The model of monopoly, like that of perfect competition, aims to explain firms' behaviors in terms of objectives and constraints. The objective, profit maximization, is the same in both cases. The differences in market outcomes, between monopoly and perfect competition, stem from differences in the constraints that limit the set of opportunities.

Constraints Faced by Monopoly

A monopolist's ability to earn a profit, like that of other firms, is constrained in part by its production costs. The model presented here has its basis in the theory of cost presented in Chapter 8. The special restrictions imposed in perfect competition (a minimum efficient scale that is small relative to the size of the market and no sunk costs) do not apply to monopoly.

The other principal constraint on the monopolist's profit-making opportunities is the demand for its product. Because a monopolist is, by definition, the only firm in its market, the demand curve it faces is that for the entire market. Unlike the perfect competitor's horizontal demand curve, then, the monopolist's demand curve has a negative slope. A monopolist can sell more output only by lowering its price

A monopolist, then, is not a price taker. Instead, its demand curve is a menu of price-quantity combinations from which it selects the one that will produce greatest profit. Because it searches for the most profitable price in a range of prices along the demand curve, we can say that a monopolist is a **price searcher**.

This section begins with a version of the monopoly model that adds one more constraint: We assume that the firm offers its product at the same price to all customers and allows them to buy as much or as little as they want at that price. We will call a monopoly that follows this pricing strategy a **simple monopoly**. We will turn to other pricing strategies later in the chapter.

Price searcher

A firm that faces a negatively sloped demand curve for its product

Simple monopoly

A monopoly that offers its output at the same price to all customers and allows them to buy as much or as little as they want at that price

Output, Price, and Marginal Revenue under Simple Monopoly

For all points on the demand curve, revenue equals price multiplied by quantity. The relationship between price and revenue as a firm moves along its demand curve depends on elasticity. When demand is *elastic*, a decrease in price causes total revenue to increase because the percentage change in quantity is greater than the percentage change in price. When demand is *inelastic* revenue decreases when the price decreases. As we saw in Chapter 3, elasticity varies along a demand curve that is a straight line. Figure 10.1 provides a detailed view of the relationship between price and revenue for a straight-line demand curve.

Figure 10.1 shows the relationship of price to revenue in three ways. Part (a) gives the data in numerical form. Part (b) shows a graph with price on the vertical axis and quantity on the horizontal axis. Part (c) shows a graph with total revenue, rather than price, on the vertical axis. Because the demand curve in Part (b) is elastic in its upper range and inelastic in its lower range, revenue first increases

FIGURE 10.1
DEMAND, TOTAL REVENUE, AND MARGINAL REVENUE UNDER SIMPLE MONOPOLY

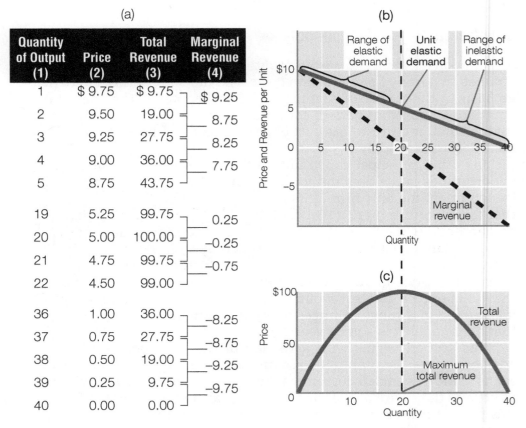

(a)

Quantity of Output (1)	Price (2)	Total Revenue (3)	Marginal Revenue (4)
1	$ 9.75	$ 9.75	
			$ 9.25
2	9.50	19.00	
			8.75
3	9.25	27.75	
			8.25
4	9.00	36.00	
			7.75
5	8.75	43.75	
19	5.25	99.75	
			0.25
20	5.00	100.00	
			−0.25
21	4.75	99.75	
			−0.75
22	4.50	99.00	
36	1.00	36.00	
			−8.25
37	0.75	27.75	
			−8.75
38	0.50	19.00	
			−9.25
39	0.25	9.75	
			−9.75
40	0.00	0.00	

This figure shows the relationship of demand, total revenue, and marginal revenue for a simple monopoly. Total revenue is the product of price multiplied by output at each point on the demand curve. Marginal revenue is the increase in total revenue caused by a one-unit increase in output. When demand is elastic, marginal revenue is more than zero and total revenue is increasing. When demand is inelastic, marginal revenue is less than zero and total revenue is decreasing. Marginal revenue is less than price at all levels of output.

and then decreases as output expands. That accounts for the shape of the "revenue hill" in Part (c).

The relationship between price and *marginal revenue* is especially important for understanding the model of simple monopoly. Marginal revenue, as we defined it in the preceding chapter, is the change in total revenue caused by a one-unit increase in a firm's output. Column 4 in Part (a) of Figure 10.1 shows marginal revenue for this firm as the difference between successive values of total revenue (column 3). Part

(b) gives the same information in graphical form. The firm's marginal revenue curve is above the horizontal axis when total revenue is increasing (elastic demand) and below it when total revenue is decreasing (inelastic demand). It intersects the horizontal axis at the point of maximum total revenue.

There is an easy rule that will allow you to sketch the marginal revenue curve corresponding to any straight-line demand curve: *The marginal revenue curve for a straight-line demand curve always cuts the horizontal distance from the demand curve to the vertical axis exactly in half.* Following that rule, place the point where the marginal revenue curve intersects the horizontal axis halfway between the origin and the horizontal intercept of the demand curve, that is, the point where the demand curve intersects the horizontal axis. (In Figure 10.1 the marginal revenue curve cuts the horizontal axis at 20, half of 40.) Next, mark the point where the marginal revenue intersects the vertical axis, which is the same as that for the demand curve. (The vertical intercept is at $10 in Figure 10.1.) Connect those two points with a straight line that extends on through the horizontal axis, as shown. The rule does not work for curved demand curves; to keep things simple, we will look only at linear demand curves in this chapter.

The marginal revenue curve is always below the demand curve. For a simple monopolist, the marginal revenue that the firm gets from the sale of one additional unit is less than the selling price, not equal to it as in perfect competition. To understand why, remember that the firm sells all units at the same price, which means it must cut the price on all units, not just on the last one, to increase the quantity sold. For example, if our monopolist wants to increase sales from nineteen units per period to twenty units, it must cut the price on all twenty units from $5.25 to $5. Although the firm gains $5 in revenue from the sale of the twentieth unit, its total revenue increases by only $.25, from $99.75 to $100. The added revenue from the twentieth unit is mostly offset by a revenue reduction of $.25 per unit ($4.75 in all) on the first nineteen units sold.

The fact that the marginal revenue curve for a monopolist lies below its demand curve illustrates the marginal-average rule discussed in the preceding chapter. The average revenue realized by the simple monopolist, as represented by the height of the demand curve for any given level of output, must be falling if marginal revenue is less than average revenue.

Finding the Point of Maximum Profit

Figure 10.2 adds the monopolist's cost curves to its demand and marginal revenue curves. We can use this chart to find the price-quantity combination that yields maximum profit.

Column 6 of Part (a) of Figure 10.2 shows total cost for the firm at various output levels. Subtracting total cost from total revenue

BVT *Lab*

Flashcards are available for this chapter at www.BVTLab.com.

FIGURE 10.2 PROFIT MAXIMIZATION FOR A MONOPOLIST

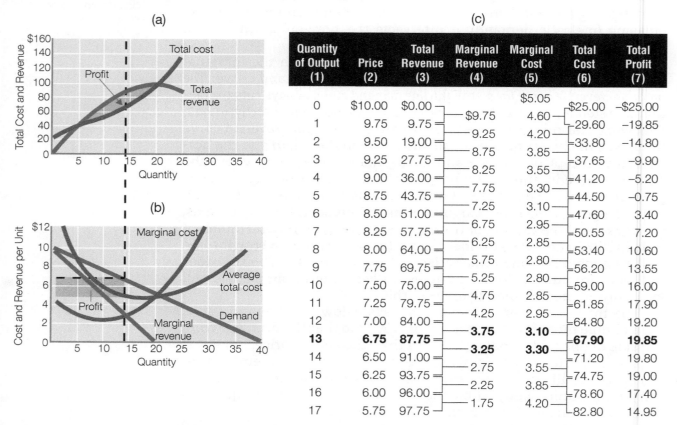

Quantity of Output (1)	Price (2)	Total Revenue (3)	Marginal Revenue (4)	Marginal Cost (5)	Total Cost (6)	Total Profit (7)
0	$10.00	$0.00		$5.05	$25.00	-$25.00
1	9.75	9.75	$9.75	4.60	29.60	-19.85
2	9.50	19.00	9.25	4.20	33.80	-14.80
3	9.25	27.75	8.75	3.85	37.65	-9.90
4	9.00	36.00	8.25	3.55	41.20	-5.20
5	8.75	43.75	7.75	3.30	44.50	-0.75
6	8.50	51.00	7.25	3.10	47.60	3.40
7	8.25	57.75	6.75	2.95	50.55	7.20
8	8.00	64.00	6.25	2.85	53.40	10.60
9	7.75	69.75	5.75	2.80	56.20	13.55
10	7.50	75.00	5.25	2.80	59.00	16.00
11	7.25	79.75	4.75	2.85	61.85	17.90
12	7.00	84.00	4.25	2.95	64.80	19.20
13	**6.75**	**87.75**	**3.75**	**3.10**	**67.90**	**19.85**
14	6.50	91.00	3.25	3.30	71.20	19.80
15	6.25	93.75	2.75	3.55	74.75	19.00
16	6.00	96.00	2.25	3.85	78.60	17.40
17	5.75	97.75	1.75	4.20	82.80	14.95

A monopolist maximizes profits by producing the output where marginal cost equals marginal revenue. The price it charges for the product is equal to the height of the demand curve (rather than the height of the marginal revenue curve) at the profit-maximizing output. Beyond 13 units of output, total revenue continues to rise for a while, but profit falls because total cost rises even more rapidly.

(column 3) gives total profit (column 7). A glance at column 7 shows that thirteen units is the profit-maximizing output level. The graphical version of the total revenue–total cost approach to profit maximization appears in Part (c) of the figure. Total profit equals the vertical gap between the total cost and total revenue curves. It reaches a maximum where the two curves are farthest apart. Part (b) and column 4 of Part (a) show the marginal approach. Marginal revenue is the amount by which total revenue increases when output rises by one unit, and marginal cost is the amount by which total cost increases. It follows that as long as marginal revenue exceeds marginal cost, one more unit of output adds more to total revenue than to total cost—thus, profit increases. Beyond thirteen units of output, marginal revenue falls below marginal cost, so more output reduces total profit. The logic here is the same as for a perfectly competitive firm, except that now marginal revenue is variable rather than constant.

Profits reach their maximum at the point where the positively sloped section of the marginal cost curve intersects the marginal revenue curve. Profit per unit at that point equals the vertical gap between the demand curve and the average total cost curve. The shaded rectangle gives total profit (profit per unit times quantity of output).

To avoid a mistake that many students make, note that the intersection of the marginal cost and marginal revenue curves gives the profit-maximizing *output* for the firm, but the profit-maximizing price is equal to the height of the demand curve for that level of output. For a monopolist, that price is always above marginal cost at the point of maximum profit. In our example, marginal cost at thirteen units of output is $3.10 per unit; but according to the demand curve, consumers are willing to pay $6.75 per unit for thirteen units of output. The monopolist clearly prefers to charge $6.75, not $3.10, for that quantity.

Profit Maximization or Loss Minimization?

If market conditions are unfavorable, a monopolist, like a perfectly competitive firm, may be unable to earn a profit in the short run. In such a case, it will try to minimize losses. Whether a profit is possible depends on the position of the demand curve relative to the firm's average total cost curve.

Figure 10.3 shows the case of loss minimization. Fixed costs are now higher than in our earlier example, so that the demand curve lies below the average total cost curve at all points. The monopolist might find itself in such a position as the result in the increase of the price of some fixed input. Following the usual rule, profit is maximized (or loss minimized) at the point where the marginal cost and marginal revenue curves intersect, still at about thirteen units of output. The demand curve shows that the firm cannot sell that much output for more than $6.75 per unit, but average total cost at ten units of output is now $8.30. At $6.75 per unit, then, the firm will lose $1.55 on each unit sold. The shaded rectangle shows the total loss.

FIGURE 10.3   A MONOPOLIST SUFFERING A SHORT-RUN LOSS

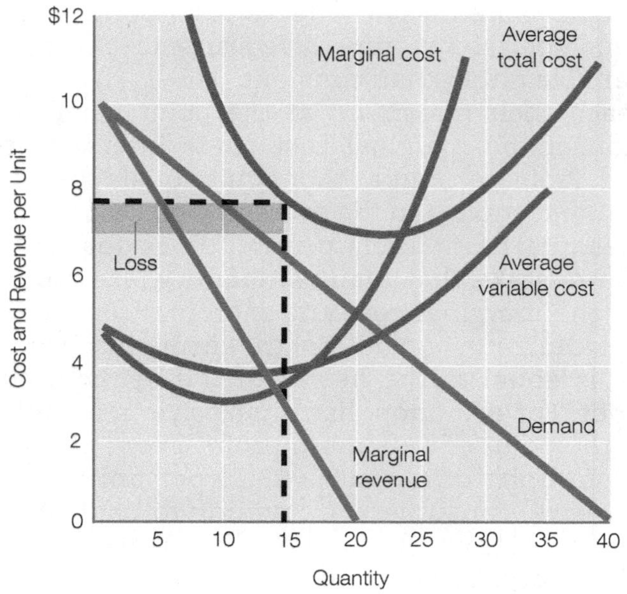

Sometimes costs may be too high in relation to demand to allow a monopolist to earn a profit. In this example, the demand curve lies below the average total cost curve at all points. The best the monopolist can do in the short run is to minimize loss by producing where marginal cost equals marginal revenue. If the demand curve were to shift downward even further, preventing the firm from obtaining a price that would cover average variable cost, the short-run loss-minimizing strategy would be to shut down.

Although the firm suffers a loss at three units of output, no other output will yield a smaller loss. In Figure 10.3, the price of $6.75 per unit is more than enough to cover average variable costs. A monopolist, like a perfect competitor, is better off staying in business in the short run, even at a loss, as long as its price is greater than the average variable cost.

We see, then, that being a monopolist does not guarantee a profit. If the loss-making situation shown in Figure 10.3 were only temporary, the firm would ride it out and wait for better times to return. Sometimes, however, a monopolist faces a permanent increase in cost or decrease in demand. A privately owned, profit-maximizing monopolist will then leave the industry, freeing itself of its fixed costs by selling its assets, terminating its long-term leases, and so on. Urban mass transit systems, which are the subject of the Case for Discussion at the end of this chapter, are a case in point. In many cities, they used to be privately owned closed monopolies. When the demand for mass transit services fell, the systems could no longer operate at a profit and might have disappeared entirely but for public subsidies.

10.3 Profit Maximization in the Long Run

The model of simple monopoly we have worked with up to this point is oriented toward the short run. This section turns to the long run. As we will see, the long run behavior of monopoly depends on the potential for entry of new direct competitors and on the extent of competition from substitute products.

Long-Run Equilibrium without Threat of Entry

The simplest situation is that of a monopolist that faces no threat of entry at all by competitors. For such a firm, a graph like Figure 10.2 can represent long-run as well as short-run profit maximization. Only the interpretation of the curves changes. The curve that is labeled average total cost in Figure 10.2 would now be interpreted as the firm's long-run average cost curve, allowing for free adjustment of fixed inputs. The marginal cost curve would be the corresponding long-run marginal cost curve, and the demand curve would be the long-run demand curve. The long-run equilibrium would occur at the output where long-run marginal cost equals long-run marginal revenue, and the long-run equilibrium price equal the height of the long-run demand curve at that point. Beyond what we have already said about the short run, three things are worth noting about the long-run equilibrium for a monopolist.

1. The firm must at least break even in the long-run equilibrium. The loss-minimizing situation shown in Figure 10.3 cannot be a long-run equilibrium because, unless it received a subsidy, the firm would leave the market if it could not at least recover its long-run average cost.

2. Unlike the case of perfect competition, long-run equilibrium under monopoly need not occur at the minimum point on the firm's long-run total cost curve. It could occur at an output less than the point of minimum long-run average cost (as shown in Figure 10.2) or at an output greater than the point of minimum long-run average cost (as would be the case if the demand curve in Figure 10.2 were to shift strongly to the right). Whatever its long-run equilibrium output, the monopolist will select the size of plant that is best suited to that level of output. Doing so would make the short-run average total cost curve tangent to the long-run average cost curve at the equilibrium output.

3. The price that will maximize long-run profit for the firm will be lower than the price that will maximize short-run profit if, as is usually the case, demand is more elastic in the long run than in the short run. Beginning from a point of long-run equilibrium, a monopolist could temporarily increase its profit by raising its price and cutting output to move up along its less-elastic

short-run demand curve. Given that higher price, customers would make long-run adjustments in their consumption patterns, reducing the quantity demanded until they were back on the long-run demand curve at a correspondingly lower level of output. The monopolist's profit at the higher price would then be less than at the original long-run equilibrium price.

Open Monopoly, Entrepreneurship, and Limit Pricing

In the cases we have examined so far, it is easy to identify a specific equilibrium point, but that is largely because we have made many simplifying assumptions. Among other things, we have assumed that technologies, consumer tastes, product characteristics, and legal constraints are unchanging. In the real world, entrepreneurial behavior by monopolies and potential competitors makes the situation more complex. Demand and cost curves can no longer be treated as given because any firm that earns a pure economic profit for any length of time is sure to attract the attention of someone with a new idea for getting a piece of the action.

Consider long-run equilibrium for an open monopolist. Such a firm is currently the sole supplier of its product, but it has no secure hold on its market like those provided by the decisive cost advantages of a natural monopoly or the legal barriers to entry of a closed monopoly. With little or no built-in protection from would-be rivals, what options does an open monopoly have?

One option is to push the price all the way up to the short-run profit-maximizing level, enjoy pure economic profits while they last, and accept the fact that sooner or later other firms will enter the market and take away part or all of those profits. Often that is just what firms do. The consumer electronics industry provides some familiar examples. The first firm to reach the market with a touch-screen cell phone, a flat-screen TV, or digital video recorder typically sets a high initial price. Soon other firms enter with products that closely imitate the original one. The market then becomes an oligopoly in which the first firm may still hold a significant market share, but with less pricing power. With luck, by the time pure economic profits disappear entirely, the firm's research department will come up with a new product from which the firm can again reap temporary monopoly profits. The hope of even short-lived monopoly profits can be a strong spur to innovation.

Another strategy is to set a lower price that yields somewhat less than the maximum short-run profit but at the same time makes the market a less attractive target for would-be competitors. We call such a strategy **limit pricing** because it limits short-run profits in the hope of limiting entry.

Limit pricing tends to be more attractive if the monopolist enjoys any cost advantage, even a small one, over potential entrants. For example, a new entrant may need to incur sunk costs, say, to recruit a network of

Limit pricing

A strategy in which the dominant firm in a market charges less than the short-run profit maximizing price in order to limit the likelihood of entry

dealers or acquaint consumers with a new brand name, or perhaps through "learning by doing" the first firm in the market has achieved lower production costs than another firm can achieve when it first enters the market. Given such a cost advantage, the first firm may be able to earn a pure economic profit at a price that is still low enough to deter other entrants.

There need not be an all-or-nothing choice between short-run profit maximization and limit pricing. A firm may set an intermediate price that merely slows entry without entirely preventing it. It may introduce its product at a high price and then "slide down the demand curve" as other firms enter. The variations are endless.

Consumer electronics are typically set at a high price when they initially enter the market.

As the firm's attention turns away from the marginal cost-marginal revenue calculus of the simple monopolist to strategic moves and countermoves against actual and potential rivals, the market structure that we have called open monopoly shades into oligopoly, which is a subject of another chapter.

Closed Monopoly and Rent Seeking

Let's turn now to the implications of entrepreneurship for a closed monopoly—one that is protected by a legal barrier, such as a government permit or a patent. If competition in any form is impossible, there is nothing to add beyond what we said earlier in the section on long-run equilibrium without threat of entry. However, few if any monopolies are that tightly closed. Instead, they face threats to their profits on two fronts: (1) the development of substitute products and (2) challenges to the legal barriers that seal the market off from competition.

First, consider substitute products. Although the market structure of monopoly assumes that the product has no "close" substitutes, closeness is a matter of degree. There is no such thing as a product with no substitutes whatsoever. Moreover, a monopolist must worry not only about existing substitutes but also about the development of new ones. If one firm has a monopoly on a patented drug, rival researchers will strive to develop other therapies for the condition in question. If a railroad charges a monopoly price on a route that has no competing rail service, it will encourage competition from pipelines, barges, and trucks.

Over time, then, the higher the price set by the monopolist and the longer it holds that price, the more rival entrepreneurs will try to supply varied and attractive substitutes. As they do so, they will push the monopolist's demand curve to the left.

Meanwhile, the same or other rivals will be at work on another front. A law may protect the closed monopolist's hold on the market, but lobbyists can persuade legislatures to change laws, and lawyers can find loopholes in them. The larger the profit the closed monopoly is earning, the more attractive it will be for potential rivals to invest in lawyers and lobbyists. To combat them, the monopoly will have to invest in lawyers and lobbyists of its own.

The efforts of firms to break into or protect closed monopolies are examples of rent seeking. The "rents" being sought in this case are the monopolist's pure economic profit, but rent seeking and defenses against rent seeking are costly. They require firms to hire lawyers, lobbyists, and researchers, and divert the time of their managers from other tasks. Those costs come on top of production costs, increasing total costs. In terms of our model, the costs of rent seeking and defenses against it push firms' cost curves upward.

Rent seeking is not always limited to rivals trying to enter the firm's market. A monopolist's own employees may get in on the act. Monopoly profits earned by a protected employer—say, a municipal transit company or a firm with a monopoly contract to collect a city's garbage—are an attractive target for labor unions. Unions do not always depend only on their own bargaining power. Sometimes they may seek legislative intervention in labor disputes. A monopolist's suppliers, and even its customers, may also undertake rent seeking.

A closed monopolist may end up squeezed from both sides. Entrepreneurs who develop substitute products push its demand curve to the left—and at the same time, the need to defend against rent seekers pushes its costs upward. Even if no rivals enter the monopolist's market directly, it will move toward a position like that in Figure 10.4, where it just breaks even. At that point, the price P that corresponds to the output where marginal cost equals marginal revenue is just enough to cover average total costs.

As an example of a monopolist caught in such a squeeze, consider the U.S. Postal Service. For two centuries, it has fought for and held on to its closed monopoly on delivery of first-class mail. Yet the postal service, far from being richly profitable, is not able even to break even. Part of the explanation is the vigorous expansion of substitutes (UPS, Federal Express, electronic transmission of documents) and the successful rent-seeking activities of postal employee unions.

To summarize, the life of a monopolist is not a bed of roses. True, extraordinary short-run profit opportunities may arise, but a monopolist must not be overly aggressive in exploiting them. New substitute products, newly entering firms, and rent-seeking—all pose threats. In real life, being a monopolist requires a lot more work than just finding the point where a couple of lines cross on a graph.

The U.S. Postal Service is an example of a closed monopoly being squeezed by expansion of substitutes, such as UPS and FedEx, and its employees' successful rent seeking activities.

FIGURE 10.4   THE BREAK-EVEN POSITION FOR A MONOPOLIST

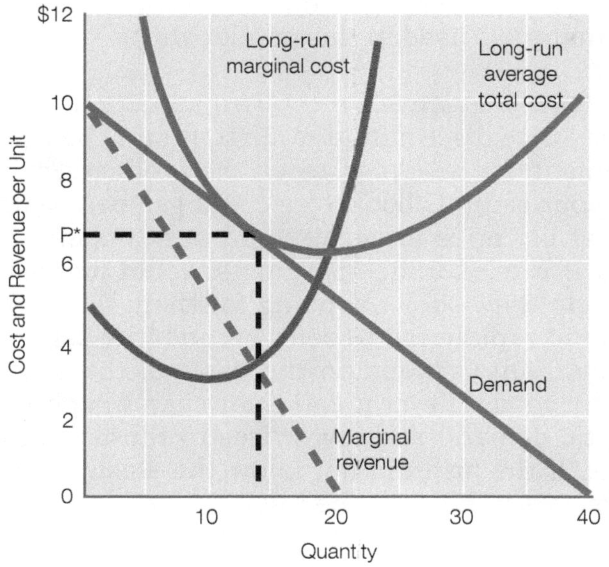

This exhibit shows a monopolist that is just breaking even. The firm earns enough revenue to cover all costs, including the opportunity cost of capital, but not enough to permit an economic profit. A closed monopoly can end up in this position through erosion of demand as substitutes are developed or by the costs of defending its monopoly position against rent seekers.

10.4 Complex Pricing Strategies

The model of simple monopoly assumes that the firm sells all units at a uniform price, with customers allowed to buy as much or as little as they want. Not all firms use that simple pricing strategy. In this section, we look at two common pricing strategies that are more complex than that of simple monopoly.

Price Discrimination

The first complex pricing strategy is one of charging different prices to different buyers for the same product. When the prices charged to different buyers do not simply reflect differences in the costs of serving them, we say the firm practices **price discrimination**. For example, a theater that charges $8 for an adult seat and $6 for a child's is practicing price discrimination because the cost of providing a seat to

Price discrimination

The practice of charging different prices for various units of a single product when the price differences are not justified by differences in cost

a child and to an adult is the same. However, a clothing maker that charges lower prices for children's sizes of T-shirts than for adult sizes is not practicing price discrimination, if the difference only reflects the lower cost of materials used in the smaller shirts.

Conditions for Price Discrimination   Two conditions must hold for a firm to practice price discrimination. First, it must be impossible, or at least inconvenient, for buyers to resell the product. For example, it is unlikely that your campus bookstore could get away with selling economics texts at list price to seniors and at a 25 percent discount to everyone else. If it tried to do so, seniors would just ask friends in a lower class to do their book shopping for them. The bookstore's list-price sales would rapidly fall to zero. Second, the seller must be able to classify buyers into groups on the basis of the elasticity of their demand for the good. The firm can then charge high prices to those with less elastic demand and low prices to those with demand that is more elastic. If the firm did not know the elasticities, it would not know which buyers to hit with the higher price.

Monopolists are not the only firms that can use price discrimination. The practice appears in other market structures, as well. Consider, for example, price discrimination by colleges and universities, which are price searchers but not monopolies. First, the school's business office sets tuition and fees at a level that it thinks is as high as anyone would be willing to pay. Next, the admissions office gives its approval to a certain number of qualified applicants. Finally, the financial aid office gives selective price rebates, called scholarships, to students who would be unwilling or unable to attend if they had to pay the full tuition.

A college or university is in an ideal position to practice price discrimination. For one thing, students cannot resell the product. If you gain admission to both Harvard and Dartmouth, and choose to attend Harvard, you cannot sell your place at Dartmouth to someone who did not get into either school. Also, schools insist that applicants supply a great deal of information on families' willingness and ability to pay. Because the demand for a good tends to be less elastic the smaller the share of income a family spends on it, rich families are likely to have less elastic demand for college education than poor families. Finally, an applicant's high-school grades and test scores also help in estimating his or her elasticity of demand. A student with higher grades probably has more alternatives and, hence, more elastic demand. A student with lower grades may be lucky to get into just one school. For that reason, it makes sense to charge lower prices (that is, give larger scholarships) to students with good grades.

Colleges and universities are in an ideal position to practice price discrimination.

In this case, as in others where markets can be divided into separate submarkets with distinct demand curves, the firm sets marginal cost equal to marginal revenue in each market.

The result is a higher equilibrium price for customers whose demand is less elastic.

Fairness and Price Discrimination

Many people, especially those who pay the higher prices, consider price discrimination unfair. They may be infuriated, for example, to learn that the person in the next seat on an airplane paid less than they did for a ticket on the same flight. In fact, many people think it is unfair for a firm to charge different prices to different customers even when the difference is justified by considerations of cost. An example is the practice of charging young men more than young women for automobile insurance. Insurance companies insist that different rates are justified by the fact that costs of insuring men are higher because they are involved in more accidents, but that does not end the perception that the difference in rates is unfair.

Economists tend to look more kindly on price discrimination. They not only see it as a practice that promotes efficiency but also as one that often promotes fairness as well. The example of college scholarships illustrates one of the reasons that price discrimination can be beneficial. That form of price discrimination makes it possible for some students to attend colleges that they otherwise could not afford while shifting part of the cost, in the form of high tuition, to students who can most afford to pay. Similarly, price discrimination makes it easier for parents to take young children to the movies. It makes it possible for students who are willing to buy tickets in advance and stay at their destinations over a Saturday night to fill airline seats that business travelers would leave empty.

10.5 Two-part Pricing

Two-part pricing is another strategy that departs from the model of simple monopoly. Under two-part pricing, customers first pay for the right to be a buyer and only then have the right to buy as much as they want at a fixed price. To give them general names, we can call the amount paid to be a buyer the **access fee** and the price per unit for buyers who have paid the access fee the **user charge**. The specific terms used vary from one application of this strategy to another.

Here are a few familiar examples of two-part pricing:

- Nightclubs often impose a cover charge (access fee) for admission and then sell food and drinks at prices (user charges) stated on a menu.
- Utilities such as electricity, telephone, and sometimes cell-phone service charge a flat monthly connection charge (access fee), which sometimes includes a fixed minimum amount of

Two-part pricing

A pricing strategy in which people must pay for the right to be a buyer before choosing how much to buy at a given price

Access fee

The part of a two-part pricing strategy paid for the right to become a customer

User charge

The per-unit price offered in a two-part pricing strategy to qualified customers who have paid the access fee

use, plus a charge per kilowatt-hour or minute of phone service (user charge) beyond any amount covered by the access fee.

- Country clubs charge large membership fees (access fees), sometimes reaching tens of thousands of dollars, for the right to join. Members then pay small "greens fees" (user charges) each time they play golf.

- The popular discount chain Costco charges an annual membership fee (access fee) for a card that gives admission to its stores. Members then pay low prices on merchandise (user fees).

A two-part pricing strategy helps a firm get around a dilemma that faces the simple monopolist. If the firm maximizes profit by setting a price where marginal revenue equals marginal cost, it must turn away some potentially profitable business—namely, the extra units it could sell at a price below the simple monopoly price but higher than marginal cost. Price discriminators get around the dilemma by cutting the price for some, but not all, units sold. Two-part pricing gets around the dilemma in a different way. Charging less than the simple monopoly price for all units "costs" it some revenue, but it recoups the "lost" revenue through the access fee.

Nightclubs are a familiar example of two-part pricing.

Customers are often happy with two-part pricing because it gives them lower prices (at the margin) than their price-searching competitors. For example, Costco, because of its membership fee, is often able to offer merchandise at a lower mark-up over cost than rival Wal-Mart, which has no membership requirement, and country clubs that require membership fees provide higher-quality, less-crowded courses and clubhouses compared with public golf courses that rely on greens fees alone.

Two-part pricing is especially common in markets where fixed costs are high and marginal costs are low. Electric power companies, telephone companies, and golf courses all fit that model. Without access fees, per-unit prices would have to be very high relative to marginal costs in order for the firm to break even. Sometimes fixed costs constitute almost all the cost of a service, and marginal costs are nearly zero. In that case, the access fee may provide all of the firm's revenue and the user fee may be set to equal zero (that is, equal to marginal cost). For example, in the early days of the Internet, most Internet service providers charged a monthly connection charge plus a fee per hour of use or per megabyte of data. Later, as server and pipeline capacities grew, the marginal cost of an added hour of service fell close to zero. Today, most providers rely on the monthly access charge alone for revenue and set the user charge at zero. This model is increasingly common for cell phone service, too.

10.6 Market Performance under Monopoly

In the last chapter, we looked at market performance under perfect competition. That market structure received high marks in two respects. First, we saw that in competitive equilibrium marginal cost is equal to market price. Production thus proceeds to the point beyond which no further mutual gains are possible for buyers and sellers. In that sense, an economy of competitive markets provides an efficient solution to the question of what to produce. Second, we noted that in long-run equilibrium a perfectly competitive firm produces at the lowest point on its long-run average cost curve. That is a key aspect of efficiency in the choice of how to produce.

Now we turn to market performance under monopoly. First, we compare simple monopoly with perfect competition in terms of the questions of what and how to produce. We then look briefly at the question of for whom goods to produce. Finally, we explore some unresolved issues.

What to Produce: Consumer and Producer Surplus

Figure 10.5 uses the concepts of consumer and producer surplus (introduced in Chapter 5) to compare market performance under monopoly and perfect competition.

Part (a) of the exhibit shows a perfectly competitive market. As we saw in Chapter 5, the height of the demand curve measures the maximum amount that consumers would willingly pay for any given quantity of output. The height of the supply curve measures the minimum amount that suppliers would willingly accept for the given output. Because the supply curve is the sum of the marginal cost curves of individual firms, its height reflects the opportunity cost of producing each additional unit. The equilibrium price is $20 and the equilibrium quantity is two hundred units. Consumers, who would be willing to pay more than $20 for all but the two hundredth unit, earn a consumer surplus equal to the area beneath the demand curve but above the market price. Producers, who produce all but the two hundredth unit at an opportunity cost of less than $20, earn a producer surplus equal to the area above the supply curve but beneath the market price. Together, the surpluses represent consumers' and producers' mutual gains from exchange.

We see, then, that a competitive market carries production to the point that exhausts all potential gains from exchange. Neither buyers nor sellers would gain from producing more than two hundred units. From the 201st-unit on, the opportunity cost of the unit to producers as measured by the supply curve exceeds its value to consumers as measured by the demand curve.

Now consider the situation under simple monopoly, as shown in Part (b) of the exhibit. To make the comparison easy, we assume the demand and marginal cost curves for the monopolist to be the same as the market demand and supply curves for the competitive industry.

FIGURE 10.5
MARKET PERFORMANCE UNDER MONOPOLY AND COMPETITION

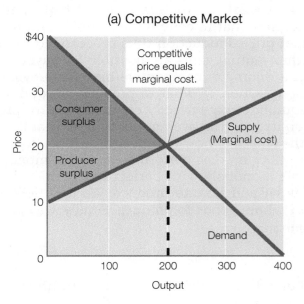

(a) Competitive Market

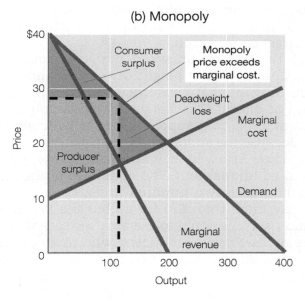

(b) Monopoly

Under perfect competition, Part (a), firms carry out production to the point where the price consumers are willing to pay for the last unit produced just equals the opportunity cost of producing it. Buyers and sellers realize all possible gains from trade in the form of producer and consumer surplus. Under monopoly, production stops short of that point. Consumer surplus is smaller and producer surplus larger than under competition, and the total is smaller. Some potential gains from trade go unrealized. The conclusion: simple monopoly causes market failure.

To maximize its profits, the simple monopolist must limit production to 120 units and charge a price of $28. Even at that price, consumers are better off than they would be if the good were entirely unavailable. They earn a surplus equal to the area beneath the demand curve but above the $28 price. The monopolist earns a producer surplus. The 120th unit, which it sells for $28, costs only $16 to produce, for a producer surplus of $12. Surpluses on earlier units, which cost less to produce, are even greater. The total producer surplus equals the shaded area above the marginal cost curve but below the $28 price, bordered on the left by the vertical axis and on the right by the profit-maximizing quantity.

Comparing competition with monopoly reveals three differences.

1. Consumer surplus is smaller under simple monopoly.

2. Producer surplus is larger under simple monopoly.

3. The total of producer and consumer surpluses is smaller under simple monopoly.

The third difference suggests that monopoly is inefficient, in the sense that buyers and sellers fail to realize some potential gains from exchange. Other things being equal, production of units 121 through 200 would provide benefits to consumers that exceed their costs. This would make both producers and consumers better off. The potential gains from trade that go unrealized are equal to the triangle lying between the supply and demand curves and bordered on the left by the monopolist's profit-maximizing quantity. That area represents a **deadweight loss**, that is, a loss to one party that is not offset by a gain to anyone else. (The excess burden of a tax, which we discussed in Chapter 5, is another example of a deadweight loss.)

Now we come to the key question: If producing another 80 units of output would make both buyers and sellers better off, why don't they do it? The answer lies in our assumption that a simple monopolist offers a single price per unit to all buyers. More complex pricing strategies can overcome the deadweight loss that arises from simple monopoly. A price-discriminating monopolist could sell the first 120 units at $28 and then sell units 121 through 200 at $20. If it did so, both the firm and at least some of its customers would benefit. A monopolist that used two-part pricing could set the price equal to the marginal cost of $20 and make up the lost revenue through an access fee. In either case, there would be no deadweight loss.

In contrast, a simple monopolist must sell all units at the same price, without charging an access fee. If it does so, it cannot cut the price on units 121 through 200 without also cutting the price on units 1 through 120. The intersection of the marginal cost and marginal revenue curves marks the limit of the simple monopolist's willingness to produce.

To summarize, the fact that a simple monopoly's price exceeds its marginal cost in equilibrium means that it produces too little of

Deadweight loss
A loss of consumer or producer surplus that is not offset by a gain to someone else

the good to realize all potential gains from trade. Simple monopoly is therefore inefficient compared with firms that charge prices closer to or equal to marginal cost. Perfect competition is one way to overcome this problem, but not the only way. In the real world, price-searching firms, including monopolies, monopolistic competitors and oligopolists, often use complex pricing strategies that keep prices closer to marginal cost than is possible under simple monopoly and avoid, or at least reduce, the deadweight loss implied by Figure 10.5.

How to Produce: Average Total Cost in Monopoly Equilibrium

As we saw in the preceding chapter, a second favorable trait of perfect competition is that it produces its long-run equilibrium output at the least possible long-run average cost. That need not be true for monopoly, for which the point of long-run equilibrium can occur anywhere along the long-run average cost curve. Many economists point to this difference as further evidence that monopoly is less efficient than perfect competition.

To see how serious the problem is likely to be, we need to consider three cases:

1. For a natural monopoly, equilibrium will typically be at an output where the firm is still subject to economies of scale. If so, dividing production between two or more firms would require each of them to operate at an even lower, even less efficient, level of output.

2. Empirical studies of cost suggest that many firms experience approximately constant returns to scale after reaching a minimum efficient scale. If there is enough demand for the product so that all producers are able to operate along the flat, constant-return segment of the cost curve, long-run average cost will be the same regardless of the number of firms in the market.

3. The equilibrium output may lie on the rising portion of the monopolist's average cost curve, where it encounters decreasing returns to scale. Dividing total output among two or more smaller firms would then decrease average total cost. However, a single firm could, at least to some extent, overcome the problem of decreasing returns to scale by operating several independent units each having a smaller, more efficient scale. For example, a hotel chain might serve a city with several units of reasonable size rather than trying to capture the whole market with a single, inefficiently large facility.

For Whom to Produce: Does Monopoly Promote Inequality?

Cartoonists draw monopolists as fat men with big cigars and long limousines. For good measure, they may show a child in rags watching the limousine drive by. Such cartoons reflect a common view that monopoly promotes inequality. To the extent that non-economists worry about monopolies at all, they are more likely to dislike monopolists because they see them as rich and powerful than because they are inefficient.

Sometimes monopoly does confer wealth and power. The "robber barons" that tried to monopolize the oil, steel, and tobacco industries at the turn of the century were a case in point. One of the richest people in the world today is Microsoft founder, Bill Gates. Although Microsoft's market is an oligopoly, its market share for some products is so large that people apply the term "monopoly" in popular discussion. Aside from such anecdotal evidence, does the theory of monopoly provide any reason to associate the market structure of monopoly with large private fortunes? Not necessarily.

Monopolists, often called robber barons, are drawn by cartoonists as fat men with big cigars.

For one thing, we must ask who owns the monopoly. If it is a corporation, insurance companies and union pension funds may own much of its stock, in which case its profits benefit widows and orphans as well as fat cats with big cigars. Other monopolies are small operations such as the only gas station or restaurant in an isolated small town. The owners may barely earn enough to cover costs. In still other cases, government owns monopolies. Amtrak, the retail liquor monopolies of many states, and the Tennessee Valley Authority's monopoly of electric power in an area covering several states are examples. Any profits those monopolies make go to finance other areas of government activity rather than creating private fortunes.

Finally, as we have seen, there is no guarantee that monopolists will earn pure economic profits in the long run. Competition from substitute products erodes the profits of some monopolies. Closed monopolies may spend potential profits on measures to fend off rent seekers. Open monopolies may limit their profits in order to deter other firms from entering the market.

There are, to be sure, large inequalities of wealth and income in a market economy, a subject to which we will return in Chapter 16. However, monopoly, as a market structure, is neither a necessary nor

BVT *Lab*

Visit www.BVTLab.com to explore the student resources available for this chapter.

a sufficient condition for inequality. There are poor monopolists, and there are people who grow rich under oligopoly, monopolistic competition, and even in markets that are close to perfect competition.

The Bottom Line

What is the bottom line regarding market performance under monopoly? What are its important failures? What, if any, are its strengths? The material presented in this chapter supports the following conclusions:

1. Simple monopoly can cause market failure by establishing an equilibrium price that exceeds marginal cost. However, strategies such as limit pricing, price discrimination, and two-part pricing often limit the extent of the market failure.

2. No monopolist is entirely free of competition from substitute products and potential entrants. In some cases, such competition may be sufficient in the long run to eliminate pure economic profit and significantly narrow the gap between price and marginal cost.

3. Closed monopolies pose the most serious threat of market failure. Legal protections shield them, at least partially, from competition by entrants and substitutes, and rent seeking costs cause further deadweight losses. However, there may be offsetting benefits. Monopolies based on patents and copyrights encourage innovation and creativity, and others, such as public transit systems, may help to offset deadweight losses from externalities of pollution and congestion.

4. Natural monopolies also pose a threat of market failure. Economies of scale protect them from the threat of entry by other firms unless new technology permits efficient small-scale production. We will discuss regulation of natural monopolies in Chapter 12.

5. Open monopolies pose the least threat of market failure. The threat of entry by potential competitors limits the ability of firms to earn pure economic profits in the long run. Limit pricing may keep prices close to the level of costs. A rapid pace of innovation may offset inefficiencies resulting from short-run monopoly pricing. We will return to the relationship between market structure and innovation in Chapter 12.

In short, there is more to say about the relationship between market structure and market performance. To take the next steps, we need to broaden the scope of our discussion to take into account the market structures of oligopoly and monopolistic competition that lie between perfect competition and monopoly. That is the task of the next chapter.

Summary

1. **How can a monopoly exist?** A monopoly is a firm that is the sole supplier of a product that has no close substitutes. Three classes of monopoly are *closed monopolies*, which have the protection of legal restrictions on competition; *natural monopolies*, which have the protection of economies of scale; and *open monopolies*, which have no special protections against the entry of potential competitors.

2. **What determines the profit-maximizing price and output for a monopoly?** A *simple monopoly* (one that does not practice price discrimination) earns a maximum profit at the quantity of output that makes marginal cost equal to marginal revenue. The price is equal to the height of the demand curve at the profit-maximizing output. If a monopoly cannot earn a profit in the short run, it will try to keep its loss to a minimum. If the loss-minimizing price is above average variable cost, the firm will continue to operate in the short run. If the loss-minimizing price is below average variable cost, it will shut down.

3. **What are the conditions for long-run equilibrium under monopoly?** In the long run, a monopoly that faces no threat of competition maximizes its profit at an output where long-run marginal cost is equal to long-run marginal revenue. Because demand tends to be more elastic in the long run, the long-run profit-maximizing price may be lower than the price that would maximize short-run profit. An open monopoly may discourage other firms from entering the market by using a *limit pricing* strategy, that is, by charging a price below that which would maximize short-run profit.

4. **What pricing strategies used by monopolies and other price-searching firms?** A monopolist or other firm that is not a price taker can practice *price discrimination* if buyers cannot resell its product and if it has some way of classifying buyers on the basis of elasticity of demand. Although price discrimination may seem unfair to buyers who pay higher prices, it may increase efficiency by allowing customers who value the product more than its marginal cost but less than the price that a simple monopolist would charge to buy the product. Another strategy is two-part pricing, which means charging an access fee for the right to become a customer plus a per-unit user fee.

(Continues)

5. **How does monopoly affect market performance?** Monopoly can cause market failure when the amount of output it produces is less than the amount that would make marginal cost equal to the price charged. As a result, some consumers who would be willing to pay a price that is higher than marginal cost are unable to buy from a monopolist. Because some gains from trade (consumer and producer surplus) are not as high as possible under a simple monopoly, there is a deadweight loss to the economy; however, strategies like limit pricing, two-part pricing, and price discrimination may reduce the deadweight loss. Finally, under long-run equilibrium conditions, a monopoly does not necessarily produce at the point of minimum long-run average cost.

Key Terms   Page

Access fee	315
Closed monopoly	300
Deadweight loss	319
Limit pricing	310
Natural monopoly	300
Open monopoly	300
Price discrimination	313
Price searcher	303
Simple monopoly	303
Two-part pricing	315
User charge	315

Problems and Topics for Discussion

1. **Charging any price you like**   "A monopolist can always make a profit because with no competition it can charge any price it likes." Do you think this statement is true? Suppose you own the only movie theater in a small town. Your corrupt uncle on the town's zoning board has promised you he will allow no competitors into the market. What factors might limit your ability to "charge any price you like"?

2. **Short-run shutdown for a monopolist**   Redraw the graph in Figure 10.3, shifting the demand and marginal revenue curves to illustrate the case in which a monopolist will shut down in the short run rather than continue to produce at a loss.

3. **Price discrimination**   Air travelers are sometimes annoyed to find that the price of a ticket for a short flight may exceed the price for a long flight. For example, a round-trip ticket from Washington, D.C., to Seattle on one airline cost $235, compared with the same airline's price of $278 from Washington, D.C., to Dayton, Ohio, less than a third of the distance. Travelers complain that such prices represent unfair discrimination against the residents of medium-sized cities such as Dayton. They say that airlines should charge prices that are proportional to the distance flown. The airlines answer that they can serve major city pairs, such as Washington, D.C.–Seattle, at a lower cost (with larger planes and fewer empty seats) than less frequently traveled city pairs, such as Washington, D.C.–Dayton. Do you see the airline's pricing policy in this example as true price discrimination? Discuss the merits of the current price structure and the proposed alternative in terms of fairness and efficiency.

4. **Two-part pricing for cell phones**   What cell phone carrier do you use? Does your carrier practice two-part pricing? Is there a fixed monthly fee that applies even if you do not use the phone? Are there any services for which the carrier charges by the minute or otherwise by the unit of use? What kinds are service does your carrier provide in unlimited quantity at zero user charge?

Case for Discussion:

Mass Transit as a Subsidized Monopoly

To many people, monopoly is synonymous with secure profits. Not all monopolies are profitable, however. The mass transit systems of most large U.S. cities are a case in point.

Until the 1960s, the majority of urban bus lines in the United States were private firms. Often there was more than one transit company in a city. Chicago had more than thirty at one point. The different companies did not compete head to head, however. City governments granted each firm a closed monopoly over the routes it operated, so that people often had only one way to get to any given destination.

In 1950, this largely private transit system carried some 17 billion passengers. Gradually, more commuters and shoppers begin to travel by car. By 1970, ridership on urban transit systems had fallen to just 7 billion. Along the way, the business became unprofitable for most private firms, despite their monopoly status. In 1963, for the first time, urban mass transit as a whole experienced an operating loss. It never regained profitability.

City governments could simply have let the private transit lines go out of business. In some cases, especially with trolley systems, they did so. However, cities bought out all subway and most urban bus systems and subsidized their continued operation.

City-owned monopoly transit systems, like private firms, must decide how to price their product. One possible rule would be to equate marginal cost and marginal revenue in order to minimize losses. Doing so would keep subsidies for the system to a minimum. However, several considerations have led many cities keep fares lower than equating marginal cost and marginal revenue would require. That means the required subsidies are larger than they would be if cities followed a simple loss-minimization strategy.

One consideration is efficiency. For commuters to choose efficiently between mass transit and driving their own cars, the transit fare should be equal to the marginal cost of providing an additional transit ride. A subsidy-minimizing price would be higher than marginal cost.

A second reason for keeping fares low is the desire to reduce traffic congestion. Congestion is a form of negative externality that causes inefficient use of transportation resources. A low fare that causes people to choose mass transit rather than travel by car helps offset the externality.

A final reason for keeping fares low is the desire to benefit low-income households, which tend to be heavy users of public transportation. Without affordable public transportation as a means of getting to work, some lower-income people would not be able to keep their jobs and, instead, would have to depend on welfare or unemployment payments.

In practice, then, most mass transit systems do not set fares to minimize subsidies. A better description of the pricing behavior of city governments would be to say that they leave transit fares low until taxpayers start complaining about the size of the subsidies. Then they raise fares to the point at which the strength of the marginal complaint from transit riders balances the marginal complaint from taxpayers.

Questions

1. Can you justify government subsidies to mass transit on a market-failure theory? Does public mass transit produce harmful externalities? Does it help to overcome harmful externalities? Is mass transit a public good? Discuss

2. Suppose that in the city of Metropolis, bus drivers for the city transit system earn much higher wages and benefits than drivers of privately operated tourist busses. Can you explain the difference in wages in terms of the theory of rent seeking? Why might the bargaining power of city transit drivers be higher than that of private tour bus drivers? Discuss in terms of efficiency and fairness.

3. On the basis of the theory of monopoly presented in this chapter, do you expect a profit-maximizing monopolist to reach equilibrium at a quantity of output where demand is elastic, inelastic, or unit elastic? Why? Now, suppose you hear on the morning news that your city's subway system has raised fares by 10 percent and that the system operators expect total revenue to increase as a result. What does that tell you about elasticity of demand? What does it tell you as to whether system managers are pursuing a subsidy-minimizing pricing strategy?

Chapter 11

Rivalry, Oligopoly, *and* Monopolistic Competition

After reading this chapter, you will understand the following:

1. The difference between competition and rivalry among businesses

2. Why oligopolistic firms sometimes collude to increase profits, and the problems they encounter when they do

3. The conditions that affect market performance under oligopoly

4. How small businesses compete with one another under monopolistic competition, and how well such markets perform

Before reading this chapter, make sure you know the following concepts:

1. Consumer and producer surplus

2. Economies of scale

3. Market structure

4. Types of monopoly

5. Limit pricing

What is the most competitive market in the world? Some people might say the market for commercial aircraft. Every order placed for large airliners comes down to a hard-fisted slugfest between two heavyweights, U.S.-based Boeing and EU-based Airbus. In 2001, Airbus edged out Boeing in the race for new orders and held the lead for five straight years. Then Airbus stumbled. Wiring problems and other difficulties set back delivery of its flagship A380 Superjumbo, designed to carry more than five hundred passengers. Meanwhile advance orders were brisk for Boeing's innovative 787 Dreamliner. In 2007, Boeing was back in the lead, but the American company again slipped to second place when it experienced its own problems meeting delivery schedules for the 787. Although it had not regained the lead in either orders or deliveries, by the end of 2011, Boeing did have the satisfaction of bagging its two largest-ever orders, fifty 777s to Emirates and one hundred-fifty smaller 737s to Southwest Airlines. The rivalry goes on.

The Boeing-Airbus example highlights the fact that the term *competition* has more than one meaning. In the phrase "perfect competition," it refers to *market structure*. A market is perfectly competitive if it has large numbers of small firms, the product is homogeneous, all firms share information equally, and it is easy to enter or leave the market. In contrast, competition in the form of Boeing versus Airbus refers to business rivalry. In this sense, "rivalry" refers to the activities of entrepreneurs, not just those of business managers who are responding to conditions that they accept as given.

In the market structure of *oligopoly*, to which much of this chapter is devoted, rivalry becomes a central issue. Rivalry is also an important issue for markets that border on oligopoly. At one end of the spectrum, oligopoly shades into what we have called open monopoly. In that market structure, a single firm, although it is the sole supplier of a product now, faces a threat of entry by potential rivals. At the other end, oligopoly shades into *monopolistic competition*, where many small firms compete to supply products that are not all alike. In monopolistically competitive markets, rivalry is likely to be strong among firms that are near neighbors. For example, rivalry among vendors on an urban street corner can be as sharp in its way as the rivalry between aircraft giants.

11.1 What Determines Market Structure?

What causes differences in market structure? Why are some markets, like aircraft or breakfast cereals, dominated by a handful of firms? Why are others, like restaurants and auto body shops, populated by many small firms that nevertheless engage in fierce rivalry? No single theory explains market concentration. Instead, we will look at several factors—including economies of scale, barriers to entry, and sunk costs—that influence the structure of individual markets.

Economies of Scale

A firm experiences economies of scale if its long-run average cost declines as its output increases. At one extreme is the case of natural monopoly, in which economies of scale are so strong that minimum-cost production requires that just one firm serve the entire market. In less extreme cases, the *minimum efficient* scale for a firm—the point at which the average total cost curve stops falling and begins to flatten out—is so large that only a few firms can efficiently coexist in the market.

Suppose, for example, that the minimum efficient scale for a single plant producing refrigerators is 20 percent of U.S. consumption. That would mean that no more than five firms of efficient size could exist in the market without forcing some firms to use plants that are too small to produce efficiently. However, empirical studies suggest that economies of scale at the *plant level* clearly are not enough to explain the observed degree of market concentration.

There are also sources of economies of scale above the plant level. Operating more than one plant may save transportation, research, finance, marketing, and administrative costs. Beyond economies of scale in the ordinary sense, which pertain to a plant's rate of output per unit of time, a firm with a larger market share can also carry out longer production runs at an efficient rate of output. To the extent that it can achieve cost savings through "learning by doing," a plant with a large market share benefits from greater experience with each product than does one with a small market share. Even when we define them broadly, economies of scale alone do not fully account for the degree of concentration found in many markets. Let's turn, then, to the role of barriers to entry.

Barriers to Entry

We can define a **barrier to entry** as any circumstance that prevents a new firm from competing on an equal footing with existing firms in a market.[1] In a market with neither large economies of scale nor high barriers to entry, growth will tend to occur mainly through the entry of new firms, leading to a decrease in concentration over time. With the presence of barriers to entry, the first firms in the industry may be able to maintain their market shares as the industry grows, even without the help of economies of scale.

Sometimes federal, state, or local governments deliberately create barriers to entry. The closed monopolies we encountered in Chapter 10 are examples, but governments often create what we might call closed oligopolies by letting more than one firm into a market without opening it to all competitors. For example, if you want to start a new federally chartered bank, you have to get permission from a federal agency, the Comptroller of the Currency. One factor in granting the permit is whether there are already enough banks in the area—in the judgment of the comptroller, not that of the market. The expense of applying for the permit and the risk that the application will not succeed are significant barriers to competition in the banking industry.

A second kind of barrier to entry is control of a nonreproducible resource. The market for rare earth elements (see *Applying Economic Ideas 10.1*) is a case in point. New entrants are beginning to make a dent in the former Chinese monopoly, but the scarcity of high quality ores acts as a barrier to entry, ensuring that the industry will never be more than an oligopoly.

Patents and copyrights, another class of barriers to entry, are important in both oligopoly and monopoly. A patent or copyright is in some ways like a restrictive regulation and in other ways like ownership of any other nonreproducible resource. In either case, patents and copyrights clearly can make entry difficult and contribute to market concentration. For example, in the early days of office copiers, patents held by Xerox Corporation slowed (but did not stop) entry of competing firms into the market.

As we use the term, a *barrier to entry* is something that keeps new firms from duplicating the performance of existing ones in terms of cost or product quality. It does not mean that every effort or expense that a firm must undertake to enter a market is a barrier to entry, by our definition. To start a new firm, an entrepreneur must take risks, find investors, recruit workers, attract customers, and so on. All of those activities are hard work—hard enough to discourage some people from making the effort—but the need for hard work is not a barrier to entry in the economic sense. When entrepreneurs are free to buy the building blocks for their new firms on the same terms as existing firms buy them, new entrants can penetrate even huge markets. Examples include Honda's entry into the automobile market, starting from the base of its motorcycle business, or the entry of Russia's Lukoil brand into the U.S. retail gasoline market via its purchase of Getty Petroleum Marketing.

Barrier to entry

Any circumstance that prevents a new firm in a market from competing on an equal footing with existing ones

Sunk Costs and Contestability of Markets

Sunk costs are another consideration that helps determine market structure. Entry into many industries requires major sunk costs. The new firm may need to purchase custom-made equipment with little resale value, construct a plant in a place where it would have no other obvious use, or spend heavily on advertising and promotion to establish a new brand name.

As we have defined the term, sunk costs are not necessarily barriers to entry if firms that are already in the market had to undertake the same expenses when they entered. In a market where demand for a product is growing and is expected to remain high enough to enable a new firm with at least the minimum efficient scale to cover all of its opportunity costs, including sunk costs, entry can take place just as it would in an industry in which there are no sunk costs.

The situation may be different in markets in which an increase in demand is only temporary. In such a market, sunk costs affect the feasibility of hit-and-run competition—entry by firms that expect to leave the market again once demand conditions return to normal. A firm will not enter such a market on a temporary basis unless it is sure it can recover its fixed costs when it leaves.

In some cases, firms will not be sure whether changes in demand conditions justify entry. In the face of uncertainty, firms will be bolder about entering if low sunk costs make it less costly to "test the waters" in a new market. For example, a greeting card retailer might rent a store in a new shopping center to test demand if it knows that it can terminate the lease if the store turns out to be unprofitable. Another category of retailer might have to build a special building that it could not use for anything else, so it would be more cautious about entering.

Contestable market

A market in which barriers to entry and exit are low

We call a market with low barriers to entry and with few or no sunk costs a **contestable market**. Such markets are open to hit-and-run competition. The airline industry is an example. Starting a whole new airline may entail sunk costs, but often the relevant market is a city pair, such as Baltimore–Miami. Entry into an established city-pair market by a carrier not previously operating there may require little more than renting a few gates and reassigning some airplanes and crews.

11.2 Interdependence and Collusion in Oligopoly

Earlier chapters presented simple models of profit maximization for perfect competition and monopoly. Those models were based on the analysis of rational responses of managers to cost and demand constraints. There is no similar general model of oligopoly. Instead, the theory of oligopoly consists of some broad principles that apply differently under the circumstances of particular markets.

Oligopolistic Interdependence

As in earlier chapters, we can begin with the constraints the firm faces in a market in which there are just a few rival firms. Oligopolists, like monopolists and perfect competitors, face the constraints of cost and demand conditions. In addition, they face another constraint that is absent from monopoly and perfect competition: the reactions of rival firms. When one firm changes its price, output, or product characteristics, the effect on its profits depends not only on how suppliers, workers, and customers respond (as is the case in the other market structures) but also on how its rivals respond. We call the linkage of each firm's choices to its rivals' reactions **oligopolistic interdependence**.

A simple example of street vendors will illustrate oligopolistic interdependence. Consider a hot-dog vendor named Suzy who sells hot dogs on the corner of 15th and L Streets. If she were the only vendor in the market, her profit-maximizing strategy would be based on calculations of marginal cost and marginal revenues—or if not actual calculations, at least on Suzy's seat-of-the-pants estimates of those variables. If there were enough firms in the market to sustain perfect competition, she would take prices as given and adjust output until the price equaled marginal cost.

Things are different, though, if Suzy faces competition from only three other vendors, one on each other corner at 15th and L. Suppose at first that all four vendors charge $2 per hot dog. Can any one of them gain by changing the price? That depends not only on each vendor's estimates of marginal cost and marginal revenue but also on each one's estimates of its rivals' actions. Suzy may decide to raise her price, say to $2.50, banking on the loyalty of her customers to slow any shift to her rival's cheaper products. Another vendor might try to undercut the market, charging $1.75 in the hope that the others' customers are not so loyal after all. Thus, the price charged and quantity produced in an oligopoly can change, not only as a result of changes in "objective" conditions, such as cost and demand, but also as a result of purely subjective estimates of human traits, such as stubbornness, loyalty, patience, and anger.

It follows that any model of oligopoly must begin by specifying how each firm expects its rivals to react to changing conditions. We can begin with the special case where rival firms agree to collude in the pursuit of profit.

Oligopolistic interdependence

The need to pay close attention to the actions of rival firms in an oligopolistic market when making price or production decision

Street vendors provide a simple illustration of oligopolistic interdependence.

Cartels

Oligopolistic interdependence may lead to collusion if all the firms in an oligopoly think they can jointly increase their profits by raising their price and working out an agreement for dividing the market among

Cartel

A group of producers that jointly maximize profits by fixing prices and limiting output

them. When *collusion* is open and formal and involves all or most of the producers in the market, we call the result a **cartel**.

A simple example will show how cartels work. Imagine an industry made up of one hundred small firms. Assume that marginal cost for all firms is a constant $1 per unit, regardless of the amount produced. Because marginal cost is constant, the marginal cost curve also serves as the long-run average cost curve and the long-run supply curve for the industry. Figure 11.1 shows such a perfectly elastic long-run supply curve, along with a demand curve for the industry.

FIGURE **11.1** PROFIT MAXIMIZATION FOR A CARTEL

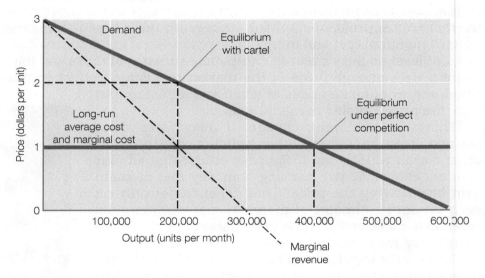

This graph shows an industry made up of one hundred firms, each producing at a constant long-run average and marginal cost. If the firms act like perfect competitors, the industry will be in equilibrium at the point where the demand and marginal cost curves intersect. If the firms form a cartel, they can jointly increase profits by restricting output to the point where marginal cost equals marginal revenue and raising the price from $1 to $2.

The industry's equilibrium price and level of output depend on how the market is organized. Initially, suppose that all firms act like perfect competitors. As we saw in Chapter 9, doing so will lead to an equilibrium where the market price is $1 per unit (equal to long-run average cost and long-run marginal cost) and total output is four hundred thousand units per month. In that equilibrium, firms earn no economic profit.

Now suppose that the heads of the one hundred firms meet to form a cartel. They elect a cartel manager, whom they ask to work out a production and marketing plan that will give the greatest possible total profit for the industry and will divide the profit fairly among the members.

The profit-maximizing problem that the cartel manager faces is the same as that of a monopolist. Industry profits are highest at the output where marginal revenue equals marginal cost—two hundred thousand units per month. If the firms limit output to that quantity, they can raise the price to $2 per unit. Doing so will yield $200,000 per month of pure economic profit.

To divide that profit among all the members, the cartel manager will give each firm an output quota of two thousand units a month, that is, half as much as each was producing before they formed the cartel. In that way, the member firms will reap the benefits of pure monopoly despite their small size and large number.

The Stability Problem   Although cartels are good for their members, they are not so good for consumers. For consumers, cartels mean a smaller supply of goods and higher prices. Fortunately for consumers, cartels have some built-in problems that make them hard to form and unstable when they do exist.

The first problem cartels face is control over entry. As we have seen, any industry where prices are higher than long-run average cost tends to attract new firms. Because the whole point of a cartel is to raise prices above cost, a cartel acts as a magnet for entrepreneurs. The entry of new firms into the market, however, does not increase the total amount that the cartel can sell at the profit-maximizing price. More firms only mean that it must divide the industry profit into smaller shares. It is not enough just to say that no new firms can join the cartel. If new firms enter the market independently, selling outside the framework of the cartel's market sharing agreement, they still depress the cartel's profits. Any cartel, then, needs to find a way to control entry if it is to serve the interests of its founding members.

A second problem that cartels face is enforcing output quotas. Each member of a cartel has an incentive to cheat. Cheating takes the form of producing output beyond its quota, and the reward, if the cheating is successful, is greater profit.

Take the cartel in Figure 11.1. As noted earlier, the quota for each of the one hundred members is two thousand units per month—just half of what each would produce under perfect competition.

What would happen if one firm cheated on its quota by stepping up its output while the others went on playing by the rules? The answer is simple: Producing an extra two thousand units would have only a small effect on the market price because it would represent only a 1 percent increase in total industry output. By producing four thousand units a month, the cheater would double its monthly profit, or nearly so, but only so long as other firms in the market did not cheat too.

What if ninety-nine firms cheated and stepped up their output to four thousand units while the one remaining firm stuck to its quota? With industry output at 398,000 units, the price falls close to the competitive level of $1. The firm that played fair would gain nothing for having done so.

The conclusion to which all this leads is that every member of a cartel will have an incentive to cheat if it expects other members to play fair—and it will also have an incentive to cheat if it expects others to cheat as well.

Oligopoly as a Game

As you have been reading the preceding paragraphs, it may have occurred to you that oligopoly is really a sort of a game—one in which, as in chess or poker, each player must try to guess the opponent's moves, bluffs, counter-moves, and counter bluffs as many moves ahead as

possible. Economists who specialize in oligopoly theory were excited by the appearance in 1944 of a thick, highly mathematical book entitled *The Theory of Games and Economic Behavior.*[2] Could it be that the authors, John von Neumann and Oskar Morgenstern, had at last solved the oligopoly puzzle?

Oligopoly is much like a game of poker in which each player has to guess the opponent's actions as many moves ahead as possible.

Clearly, Neumann and Morgenstern had taken a major step. Older oligopoly theories had often made some arbitrary assumptions about how one firm would react to others' moves, for example, by assuming that rivals would not react to their own price changes or that rivals would exactly copy every price change. Instead, Neumann and Morgenstern decided to ask, in effect, what optimal assumption each firm should make about its rivals' behavior.

A simple example will convey the spirit of the game theory approach. Imagine a market in which there are only two firms—Alpha Company and Zed Enterprises. It costs each of them $1 a unit to make their product. Each firm has a choice of setting its price at either $5 or $4. Which price will they choose?

Figure 11.2 shows the situation in more detail. The numbers are the profit each firm will earn under various combinations of prices. For example, if both firms set their price at $5 a unit, each will sell 100 units per month at a profit of $4 a unit, for a total monthly profit of $400. If both set the price at $4 a unit, each will sell 120 units at a profit of $3 a unit, for a total profit of $360. Clearly, $5 is the price that will maximize their joint profits; but under oligopoly, this price may not be a stable equilibrium. To see why, we must consider two other possible combinations of prices.

One is that Alpha will cut its price to $4 while Zed holds at $5. That would allow Alpha to take away a lot of Zed's customers and sell 180 units. Although its profit per unit would be lower ($3 instead of $4), the extra quantity sold would increase its total monthly profit to $540. Given this combination of prices, Zed would only retain its most loyal customers, selling 50 units for a total profit of $200. The final combination to consider is that Alpha holds its price at $5 while Zed cuts its price to $4. Then Zed will take away many of Alpha's customers earning $540 while Alpha earns only $200.

FIGURE 11.2 A SIMPLE OLIGOPOLY GAME

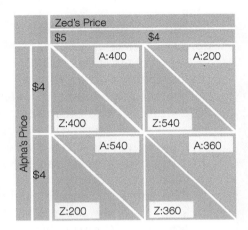

This figure shows the profits Alpha Company would earn under various pricing strategies for itself and its rival, Zed Enterprises. If both firms set their prices at $5, each will earn $400. If both lower their prices to $4, they will continue to split the market and each will earn $360. If Alpha lowers its price while Zed does not, Alpha will steal many of Zed's customers and earn $540 while Zed's profits fall to $200. If Zed lowers its price while Alpha's remains at $5, Zed will steal many of Alpha's customers, earning $50 and leaving Alpha with only $200.

What will happen depends on the assumptions that each firm might make about the other's behavior. If Alpha assumes that Zed will charge $5, Alpha will do best to charge $4. If Alpha assumes that Zed will charge $4, it will again do best to charge $4. It looks as though Alpha will do best to charge $4 regardless of what Zed does. Alpha will also be aware that Zed's view of the game is the mirror image of its own. After considering the likely effects of the different assumptions, each firm will see that it is rational to assume the worst, and the equilibrium price will be $4.

Economists call the situation shown in Figure 11.2 a **Nash equilibrium** after the American mathematician and game theorist John Nash. In a Nash equilibrium, each player's strategy is optimal given the strategy chosen by its rivals. Thus, neither player has an incentive to change strategies after finding out what strategy the other player has chosen.

The situation faced by the companies Alpha and Zed is highly simplified. Economists have explored other kinds of business games that have more complex pricing strategies. Even this simple game helps us understand an important point about oligopolies, however. Unless firms are able to reach an agreement to cooperate on prices and other aspects of their strategies, they are unlikely to earn the maximum possible combined profit. That, of course, will be good for their customers who will enjoy more goods at lower prices. But if the firms agree to form a cartel and enforce its rules successfully, prices will rise, the firms will prosper, but their customers will end up worse off.

Nash equilibrium

An equilibrium solution to a game in which each player's strategy is optimal given the other players' choice of strategy

Cartels in Practice   The problems of entry and cheating affect all cartels. The Organization of Petroleum Exporting Countries (OPEC) is a case in point. In 1973, OPEC controlled about 60 percent of the oil imports of the industrialized countries. Taking advantage of its market power, in the next eight years OPEC increased crude oil prices about tenfold, to a level approaching $40 per barrel (equivalent to over $100 a barrel in 2012 dollars). The oil ministers of the member countries met regularly to agree on how to set prices and divide output quotas. Saudi Arabia, the largest producer, had the greatest influence and the largest quota.

OPEC is an example of a practicing cartel.

The price increase brought the OPEC countries fabulous wealth in the short run. However, it also spurred output in non-OPEC areas, such as Alaska, the North Sea, and Mexico. Moreover, the demand for oil proved more elastic in the long run than in the short run as factories installed energy conservation equipment and consumers bought more fuel-efficient cars. As a result, over time, OPEC lost half of its former market share. At one point Saudi Arabia cut back its own output to less than 25 percent of capacity and tried to persuade smaller member countries to accept lower quotas as well. Cheating in terms of both price and quantity became widespread. At one point, the market price of oil plunged below $10 a barrel.

In the early years of the twenty-first century, prices rose again. One reason was a slowing pace of new discoveries. Another was booming oil demands in China and India. Most analysts agreed, however, that those peak prices had more to do with supply and demand conditions on the world market than with policy decisions by the OPEC cartel. For example, when prices plunged after a spreading global recession undermined demand toward the end of 2008, OPEC's attempts to stop the decline of prices with output cuts had little effect.

Coordination without Collusion

Formal cartels are relatively rare. They are uncommon partly because of their inherent instability, as explained in the preceding section. Also, as we will see in Chapter 12, cartels are often illegal. That leaves open the question of whether the firms in an oligopoly can, even without open collusion, tacitly coordinate their price and output decisions in a way that will jointly maximize their profit. To put it another way, will an industry in which there are only a few firms, but no formal cartel, perform more nearly like the model of perfect competition or like that of monopoly?

There have been a number of attempts to answer this question with formal models based on game theory, but their conclusions do not always fit the subtleties of real-world business behavior. Other economists have taken a less formal approach, based on conjectures about the conditions that tend to make cooperation by oligopolists easier or more difficult. Under conditions favorable to informal, tacit coordination, price and output may more closely resemble the results of a cartel. Under conditions that make informal coordination more difficult, price and output may more closely approximate the result of perfect competition. Here are some of the factors that make tacit coordination more or less difficult.

Number and Size of Firms   There is little doubt that the number and size of the firms in a market make a big difference. Tacit coordination is easier in a market with only two or three large firms of roughly equal size than in a market where a dozen equal-sized firms control half the market and smaller firms control the rest. If the number of firms is large enough and the size of the largest firms is sufficiently small, the market ceases to be an oligopoly. With a homogeneous product and easy entry and exit, it becomes perfectly competitive. With a differentiated product and easy entry and exit, it becomes monopolistically competitive, a case that we will analyze later in this chapter.

The relative size and number of the various firms in the market are important because cooperation is easier in an industry where there is one dominant firm that may be able to act as a price leader. Under the strongest form of **price leadership**, firms know how their rivals will react to price changes. The leader knows that the others will follow it, whether it raises or lowers the price. The others know that if they follow the leader, others will too, but not if they raise or lower prices on their own. When it works, this arrangement is tantamount to a cartel in that the dominant firm's efforts to maximize its own profit will also maximize those of the entire industry.

Price leadership

A situation in which price increases for all or most of the other firms in the market match decreases by a dominant firm in an oligopoly, known as the price leader

The Nature of the Product   The nature of the product also affects the ease or difficulty of coordination. A homogeneous product with a smooth flow of orders tends to make coordination easier; widely used steel products, such as railroad rails and wire, are examples. A variable product for which the flow of orders is irregular tends to make coordination more difficult; the ship building industry is a case in point. In such an industry, there are simply too many things to coordinate. It is not enough that all firms tacitly agree to sell at the same price; they must also agree on a set of price variations based on changes in quality, speed of delivery, size of order, and so on. Under these conditions an agreement to raise the price above the competitive level, even if sustained, is unlikely to lead to higher profits. It is more likely to lead to an outbreak of competition by firms offering higher quality, more convenient scheduling, volume discounts, and so on. Those factors will add to the cost of doing business or reduce revenue until excess profits disappear.

Growth and Innovation   The rates of growth and innovation in a market are another factor that affect the ease of coordination among rivals. In a market where product features, production techniques, and buyers' and sellers' personalities do not change from year to year, an agreement among firms, whether it is tacit or overt, will never have to be revised. In a market with rapidly changing elements, any agreement will soon become obsolete as conditions change or new buyers and sellers enter. Given the uncertainties of tacit agreements and the fact that overt ones are illegal, a faster pace of growth and change will make it harder for rival firms to coordinate their activities.

Ease of Entry and Exit   Barriers to entry play an important role in the price and output decisions of an oligopoly. Even if there are only a few firms in the market, the threat of entry by new firms may force existing ones to practice limit pricing in order to avoid attracting new rivals. Under such a strategy, as explained in Chapter 10, the price is set below the profit-maximizing level implied by short-run demand, marginal revenue, and marginal cost.

Barriers to entry are also important because they help determine how mergers will affect price and output decisions in an oligopoly. A merger within an oligopoly reduces the number of firms. By itself, the presence of fewer and larger firms would tend to make coordination easier, perhaps leading to a more cartel-like result. However, that outcome is less likely if low barriers to entry allow new firms to enter the market quickly and fill any gaps left by mergers. The publishing industry is an example of one where mergers of leading firms have taken place, but at the same time, new small firms have entered. Also, as pointed out earlier in the chapter, sunk costs can be as important as ease of entry in determining price and output decisions under oligopoly.

Market Performance under Oligopoly

Neither the formal approaches like game theory nor the informal rules of thumb just presented give conclusive answers to the question of market performance under oligopoly. Depending on the situation, some oligopolies may behave much like perfectly competitive markets, with prices equal or close to marginal cost. Others, with or without open collusion, may behave more like a monopoly, with prices higher than marginal cost and a resulting deadweight loss.

When they cannot answer questions about market performance by means of pure theory, economists turn to statistical methods. Ideally, one would like to measure the gap between price and marginal cost at the point of market equilibrium, but it is rarely possible to do so. In the absence of reliable data on marginal cost, an indirect approach may work. If firms in concentrated industries, on average, earn returns that exceed the opportunity cost of capital, we can infer that they are behaving more like monopolists than like perfect competitors. If, on the other hand, firms in concentrated industries earn only "normal profits"—that is, rates of return on capital that are no higher, on average, than those earned by firms in less concentrated industries—we can conclude that oligopolies perform about as well as more competitive industries. Following this reasoning, much of the debate about market performance under oligopoly focuses on rates of return.

The first person to try this approach in a systematic way was University of California professor Joe Bain. In 1951, Bain published the results of a study of forty-two selected industries for the years 1936 to 1940. According to Bain's analysis of the data, industries where the largest four firms controlled over seventy percent of the market earned higher profits than less concentrated ones. The link between profits and concentration was neither perfect nor strong, but it did exist.

During the 1950s and 1960s, many of Bain's students and followers repeated his studies for other industries and years. Most of them got the same results: a weak but persistent link between profits and concentration. Economists concluded that in general, the more highly concentrated an industry, the more it will tend to perform like a cartel or a monopoly. That appeared to be true even if there were no agreement among rivals to raise prices and divide markets.

As faith in this idea grew, economists tried as hard as they could to prove it. They used more advanced statistical techniques and better data that became available each year. Even so, the harder they tried, the more elusive the connection became. Some studies showed that adjusting the data for the size of firms in different markets caused the link between concentration and profits to disappear. Other studies showed that adjusting for differences in advertising expenditures caused the connection to evaporate. Still others suggested that results like Bain's hold only in periods of recession and disappear with the return of prosperity.

Moreover, as the link between concentration and profits was becoming more ambiguous, economists were growing less certain about how to interpret such a link, even they could confirm its existence. They found new reasons to explain why firms in more concentrated industries might appear to earn higher profits than firms in less concentrated ones. Those reasons had nothing to do with monopoly pricing or tacit coordination. For example, a concentrated industry that was growing rapidly might need to earn high profits to attract capital. Perhaps the high profits of the largest firms in each concentrated industry might simply reflect those firms' superior efficiency relative to smaller firms in the same industry. Finally, the higher profits that some concentrated industries appeared to earn might not be pure economic profits; they might merely reflect the fact that the categories used by accountants to record business transactions do not accurately reflect implicit costs.

BVT *Lab*

Improve your test scores. Practice quizzes are available at www.BVTLab.com.

11.3 The Theory of Monopolistic Competition

Up to now, we have looked at industries where many small firms produce a homogeneous product and at others where a few large firms make products that need not be alike. Those cases leave out a very large class of markets where there are many small firms, each of which makes a product that differs in at least some ways from those of its competitors, the market structure that we call *monopolistic competition*. Examples include restaurants, service stations, bakeries, some types of publishing companies, and countless others.

Profit Maximization under Monopolistic Competition

The most widely used model of monopolistic competition dates from work done in the 1930s by Edward H. Chamberlin and independently by Joan Robinson. As the name implies, it blends elements of the theory of monopoly and perfect competition. Like a monopolist, the monopolistically competitive firm is a price searcher that faces a negatively sloped demand curve. At the same time, like a perfectly competitive firm, the monopolistic competitor shares its market with many other small firms. Because there are many firms, the model of monopolistic competition ignores oligopolistic interdependence. It assumes that each firm in the market is so small that no one firm significantly affects what another one does.

Figure 11.3 shows short- and long-run equilibrium positions for a typical firm under monopolistic competition. The demand curve has a negative slope because each firm's product is a little different from its competitors' products. Because at least some customers care about differences in style, location, or other marketing advantages, each firm can raise its price at least slightly without losing all its customers. Given the negatively sloped demand curve, the short-run profit-maximizing position shown in Part (a) of the figure looks very much like that for a simple monopolist. The intersection of the marginal cost and marginal revenue curves determines the equilibrium level of output, and the height of the demand curve at that quantity determines the price.

However, this short-run equilibrium cannot also be long-run equilibrium under monopolistic competition. The reason is that monopolistically competitive markets are highly contestable, with easy entry and exit.

In the short-run position shown in Part (a) of Figure 11.3, the price exceeds average total cost so the firm is earning a pure economic profit. Profits attract new firms, and as new firms enter, two things happen. First, the demand curves of existing firms shift downward. That happens because the new firms' products, although not identical to those of the original firms, are close substitutes for them. Second, in response to the new competition, firms that are already in the market may step up their advertising, improve their product in some way, or take other steps to win back customers. Those efforts cause the firms' average total cost curves to shift upward. The downward shift in the original firms' demand curves or the upward shift in their cost curves, or both, continue until there are no more profits to attract new firms. The result is the long-run equilibrium position shown in Part (b) of Figure 11.3.

FIGURE 11.3
SHORT-RUN AND LONG-RUN EQUILIBRIUM UNDER MONOPOLISTIC COMPETITION

(a) The Short Run

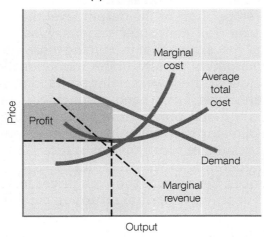

(b) The Long Run

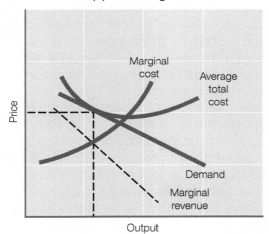

Under monopolistic competition, each firm is a price searcher with a negatively sloped demand curve. There are no barriers to entry by new firms. In the short run, a firm that produces at the point where marginal cost equals marginal revenue can earn pure economic profits, as shown in Part (a). In the long run, new firms are attracted to the market. That diverts part of the demand from firms that are already in the market and lowers each one's demand curve. Also, those firms may fight to keep their share of the market, using means that increase their costs. Entry by new firms will continue until the market reaches a long-run equilibrium where pure economic profit disappears, as shown in Part (b).

The Performance of Monopolistically Competitive Industries

Early developers of the model of monopolistic competition argued that the long-run equilibrium position shown in Figure 11.3 indicates poor market performance. One reason is that, as in the case of pure monopoly, each firm stops short of the output level that would maximize the sum of producer and consumer surplus. Also, the gap between price and marginal cost shows that producing more would benefit both the firm and its customers. Finally, under monopolistic competition a firm does not operate at the lowest point on its long-run average cost curve. If there were fewer firms, each producing a greater amount of output, the industry could provide the same quantity of goods at a lower total cost. Following this reasoning, the argument goes, monopolistic competition results in too many gas stations, supermarkets, and restaurants, each operating at less than full capacity and charging inefficiently high prices. Yet despite the high prices, each earns no pure economic profit, but only the normal return on capital it needs to stay in business.

The problem with this critique is that it places no value on the product variety that is the hallmark of monopolistic competition. It is beside the point to argue that prices would be a little lower if there were fewer barbershops, each somewhat less conveniently located; or fewer supermarkets, each a little more crowded; or fewer ice cream flavors, even if some people could not have their favorite. Would a move in that direction benefit consumers? Not necessarily, if consumers are willing to pay something for variety.

Furthermore, the model of monopolistic competition assumes that each firm practices simple monopoly pricing. In reality, though, strategies such as price-discrimination and two-part pricing are available to monopolistically competitive firms just as they are to monopolies and oligopolies. As explained in the last chapter, those strategies bring production closer to the point where marginal cost and marginal revenue are equal and improve the performance of the market.

When all is said and done, the modern view is that monopolistic competition and perfect competition are not all that different and that both serve customers reasonably well.

Summary

1. **How does rivalry among firms differ from perfect competition?** In a perfectly competitive market, there are so many firms that all are price takers. Products are alike, and output decisions by one firm have no effect on the decisions made by others. In oligopoly, there are only a few firms in the market, so each must pay attention to what other firms do. A change in price or quantity by one firm may induce others to react by making changes of their own. The fact that each firm's decisions depend on what others do, or might do, leads to a situation we can call rivalry to distinguish it from perfect competition.

2. **Why do oligopolistic firms sometimes collude to increase profits, and what problems do they encounter as a result?** A group of producers that jointly maximize profits by fixing prices and limiting output is a *cartel*. A cartel maximizes profits by setting output at the intersection of the marginal cost and marginal revenue curves for the industry as a whole. The chief problems encountered by cartels are controlling entry and preventing members from cheating on prices and output quotas.

3. **What conditions affect market performance under oligopoly?** Among the factors that affect market performance under oligopoly are the number and size of firms in the market, the presence or absence of price leadership, the nature of the product (homogeneous or varied), the pace of growth and innovation, and the ease or difficulty of entry and exit. If barriers to entry and exit are low, we say a market is contestable. Contestable markets appear to perform well even if they are highly concentrated.

4. **How is equilibrium achieved under monopolistic competition, and how well do such markets perform?** A monopolistic competitor maximizes profit at the output level at which marginal cost equals marginal revenue. In the long run, competition in such an industry results in equilibrium where price equals average total cost for each firm. In that equilibrium, price does not equal marginal cost, and production does not take place at the point of minimum average total cost; nevertheless, consumers enjoy the benefit of product variety.

Key Terms	Page #
Barrier to entry	331
Cartel	334
Contestable market	332
Nash equilibrium	337
Oligopolistic interdependence	333
Price leadership	339

Problems and Topics for Discussion

1. **Oligopolistic interdependence in action**   Look around your community for a case in which a firm is conducting a special sale or product promotion. To what extent, if at all, is the firm's action a response to something its rivals have done? To what extent, if at all, have its rivals reacted with their own sales or promotions?

2. **Barriers to entry**   "Barriers to entry are lower in the restaurant industry than in the airline industry because a restaurant requires only a few workers and a few thousand dollars in capital, whereas even a small airline requires many workers and millions of dollars in capital." Do you agree? Why or why not?

3. **The market for college education**   What market structure do you think best fits the market for college education? What factors do you believe affect the structure of the college education industry? How important are economies of scale? How important are barriers to entry and exit?

4. **Labor unions as cartels**   In what ways do labor unions resemble cartels? In what ways do they differ from cartels? Do you think labor unions ever suffer from the problems of instability that plague cartels?

Case for Discussion:

Hybrid Cars Star at Auto Show, but Not in Showroom

The 2012 Detroit Auto Shows saw a dazzling array of hybrid and all-electric vehicles. Toyota, which has led the sector to date with its Prius, added several new models to its line-up—including a smaller Prius C, a futuristic plug-in hybrid called the NS4 (not yet on sale), and a sports coupe from its Lexus luxury division. BMW and Acura also displayed luxury hybrids. The Chevy Volt and the Nissan Leaf, introduced last year, were on display, as well.

Many of the strongest reviews were going to a new hybrid model of the Ford Fusion. U.S. News Best Cars listing put the Fusion hybrid at the top of its list of nineteen affordable midsize cars. Reviewers were impressed not just with the Fusion's fuel economy (a respectable 41 m.p.g. in city driving) but also for its performance, a high-tech interior, and an all-around engaging driving experience. A plug-in model of the Fusion is to follow later in the year.

There is just one problem with the hybrid car market—a lack of buyers. Their share of the U.S. market in 2011 dropped to 2.2 percent from 2.4 percent in 2010 and is expected to stay flat in 2014. Slow sales stem from a price squeeze: Despite cutting margins, makers have had to price hybrids thousands of dollars above comparable all-gasoline models. At the same time, gasoline prices were running well below their peak level of $4 per gallon, reducing consumer enthusiasm. Reportedly, many consumers will not consider a hybrid unless they recoup the higher price through gas savings in a year or less.

The U.S. government is doing its best to boost hybrid and all-electric car sales. It offers tax rebates to buyers, and is raising fuel economy requirements toward the 50 m.p.g. level, unreachable except with hybrid or all-electric technology. The hoped-for leap in sales is still to come, however.

Sources: Based in part on information from Nick Bunkley, "Wanted or Not: Alternative-Fuel Cars Flood Auto Show," The New York Times, Jan. 9, 2012, and US News Best Cars, "Ford Fusion Hybrid: What the Auto Press Says," downloaded Jan. 18, 2012 from http://usnews.rankingsandreviews.com/cars-trucks/Ford_Fusion-Hybrid/.

Questions

1. How would you best characterize the market for hybrid autos: Perfectly competitive, oligopolistic, monopolistically competitive, or monopolistic? What information in this case supports your choice?

2. If the Fusion Hybrid enjoys strong demand, do you think that will allow Ford to charge a price higher than marginal cost? Why or why not?

3. The Toyota Prius broke open the market for hybrid cars. How did Toyota's rivals react to the introduction and success of the Prius? What evidence is there that Toyota has taken rivals' reactions into account when planning its marketing strategy?

4. What sunk costs does Ford encounter when bringing out a new car like the Hybrid Fusion? How are the sunk costs of introducing a new model relevant to the degree to which the automobile market is contestable?

Endnotes

1. Economists have struggled for decades to find consensus on the definition of "barrier to entry." For a survey of proposed definitions, see R. Preston MacAfee et. al., "What is a Barrier to Entry," American Economic Review, Papers and Proceedings (May 2004): 461–465.

2. John von Neumann and Oskar Morgenstern, *The Theory of Games and Economic Behavior* (Princeton, New Jersey: Princeton University Press, 1944).

Chapter 12

Regulating Markets

After reading this chapter, you will understand the following:

1. What business practices are illegal business practices under the antitrust laws

2. How economists' views on antitrust policy have changed over time

3. How the government regulates natural monopolies

4. Why the government regulates some industries despite their competitive structure

5. Current trends in health and safety regulation

Before reading this chapter, make sure you know the meaning of the following concepts:

1. Spontaneous order

2. Political rent seeking

3. Market failure

4. Public choice theory

5. Natural monopoly

6. Cartels

W hy regulate markets? If the principle of spontaneous order is such a good way of coordinating economic activity, why not just let markets do their job? Previous chapters have explored two motivations for regulation. One, based on the theory of market failure, explains regulation as an attempt to improve efficiency in circumstances where markets do not work perfectly. The other, based on public choice theory, explains regulation in terms of political rent seeing—the efforts of private parties to use the power of government for private gain. Chapters 6 and 7 showed how both points of view can help us understand environmental regulation and international trade policy. In this chapter, we turn our attention to additional areas of regulation, beginning with regulation of business behavior under monopoly and oligopoly.

12.1 Antitrust Laws and Policies

Antitrust laws

A set of laws that regulate market structure and the competitive behavior of firms

Antitrust laws are a set of laws that attempt to regulate market structure and the competitive behavior of firms. *Applying Economic Ideas 12.1* summarizes the main U.S. antitrust laws, some of which date back more than one hundred years. Today, most other countries also regulate market structure and competitive behavior in one way or another.

Applying Economic Ideas **12.1**

The Antitrust Laws

The Antitrust laws of the United States derive their name from the giant "trusts" of the nineteenth century, which were large industrial groups that established dominant positions in railroads, oil, steel, and other industries. The trusts aroused public opposition not so much because they were inefficient as because their wealth and power threatened the traditional livelihood of smaller-scale, traditional forms of business. As one judge of the period put it,

> [Large firms] may even temporarily, or perhaps permanently, reduce the price of the article traded in or manufactured, by reducing the expense inseparable from the running of many different companies for the same purpose. Trade or commerce under those circumstances may nevertheless be badly and unfortunately restrained by driving out of business the small dealers and worthy men whose lives have been spent therein and who might be unable to readjust themselves to their altered surroundings. Mere reduction in the price of the commodity dealt in might be dearly paid for by the ruin of such a class.[1]

The first of the antitrust laws was the **Sherman Antitrust Act** of 1890, which outlawed contracts, combinations, trusts, and conspiracies in restraint of commerce. It also declared conspiracies that monopolize or attempt to monopolize any area of commerce to be illegal. The law allows the government to break up monopolies (as it did in the cases of Standard Oil and American Tobacco in 1911, and AT&T in 1984); it also allows private antitrust lawsuits.

In 1914, Congress added two more antitrust laws. The **Clayton Act** focused on mergers, "tying contracts," under which the seller of a good prohibits the buyer from doing business with competitors, and interlocking directorates that allow individuals to control boards of several competing firms. The **Federal Trade Commission Act** of the same year broadly

The wealth and power of trusts such as the railroads, oil, and steel threatened smaller scale business.

outlawed "unfair methods of competition," without clearly defining the term, and established an independent agency, the Federal Trade Commission (FTC) to regulate business practices that it finds to be unfair.

In 1936, Congress amended the **Clayton Act** by passing the **Robinson-Patman Act**, which strengthened the law against price discrimination. It is often called the "Anti-Chain-Store Act" because its main purpose appears to have been to keep new, more efficient retailers like the A&P grocery chain from undercutting the prices of small local stores. In 1950, Congress passed a further set of amendments to the **Clayton Act**, known as the **Celler-Kefauver Act**, which strengthened provisions against mergers.

[1] *United States vs. Trans-Missouri Freight Ass'n.*, 166 U.S. 323 (1897).

Antitrust Policy

Economic abstractions like market failure and deadweight loss were not the original motivations for the antitrust laws. Those theoretical constructs did not yet exist in the 1890s. Later, however, economists attempted to reconcile the populist impulse behind the original antitrust laws with considerations of efficiency and market performance. The market-failure view of antitrust was expressed by the influential economist F. M. Scherer, who wrote that "the enforcement of antitrust laws is one of the more important weapons wielded by government in its effort to harmonize the profit-seeking behavior of private enterprises with the public interest."[2] Guided by this general concept, antitrust policy focused on several specific types of behavior.

Price Fixing   Economists have often singled out **price fixing** as one of the practices that most clearly violates the Sherman Act's strictures against "substantial lessening of competition." Competing firms are not to form cartels. They must make their pricing decisions on their own. Following this view, the courts and antitrust officials have tended to treat price fixing as a per se violation of the law, which means that only the fact of a price-fixing agreement need be proven in order to win a conviction. It is not necessary to prove that the price-fixing attempt was successful or that the prices set were unreasonable. Also, accused price fixers cannot defend themselves on the ground that their action might have had beneficial effects.

Besides making price fixing illegal, the law, as interpreted by the courts, applies to other forms of cooperative conduct that might affect prices indirectly. For example, courts have treated certain practices in which cartels engage, such as agreeing to restrict output or divide markets, just as severely as agreements on prices.

Mergers   After the Clayton Act was amended by the Celler-Kefauver Act in 1950, regulation of mergers become a major part of antitrust policy. In addition to opposing **horizontal mergers** (mergers of firms that compete in the same market), the government often challenged

Price fixing

Attempt by two or more firms to cooperate in setting prices

Horizontal mergers

Mergers of firms that compete in the same market

Vertical mergers

Mergers of firms with a supplier-purchaser relationship

Conglomerate mergers

Mergers of firms in unrelated markets

vertical mergers (mergers of firms with a supplier-customer relationship, such as an automaker and a spark plug manufacturer). **Conglomerate mergers** (mergers of firms in unrelated markets, for example, an oil company and a retail chain) were also frequent targets of antitrust enforcement.

Antitrust authorities never attempted to prohibit mergers altogether, however. Horizontal mergers, even between large firms, are permissible if the merger would increase efficiency, perhaps because one of the firms would fail without the merger, or because international competition is strong enough to ensure good market performance. For example, the 1987 merger of Chrysler with failing American Motors reduced the number of U.S. automakers by one, while creating a company that was supposed to be more able to compete with Japanese rivals. A subsequent 1998 merger of Chrysler with Germany's Damlier Motors gained approval based on similar hopes, but they proved unfounded. In 2007, Damlier sold Chrysler, leaving it once again independent but in a weaker competitive position than ever. Chrysler finally declared bankruptcy in 2009, after which it merged with Fiat. That merger, for the moment, appears to be working out much better than its earlier relationship with Damlier.

One of the largest company mergers was between AOL and Time Warner.

Other large mergers that have gained approval include several in the airline industry, the merger of Exxon with Mobil, and the merger of AOL with Time-Warner, which ultimately proved unsuccessful. Not all mergers meet with approval, however. For example, the government blocked a proposed merger of Coca-Cola with Dr Pepper, seeing no mitigating circumstances in that case. More recently, the government intervened to prevent a merger of defense giants Lockheed Martin and Northrop Grumman. More recently, in 2011, antitrust authorities expressed concern about a proposed merger of AT&T with T-Mobile. Concern about possible antitrust action was sufficient to cause AT&T to abandon the attempted merger without waiting for the government to issue an actual prohibition.

Vertical Restraints   Like vertical mergers, vertical restraints on trade involve agreements between a supplier and a customer. They are distinct from horizontal restraints, such as price-fixing, which involve agreements between direct competitors. Among the kinds of vertical restraints that antitrust authorities have challenged most often are resale price maintenance agreements, territorial restrictions, tying agreements, and exclusive dealing. Vertical restraints were at the heart of two of the antitrust suits filed against Microsoft Corporation in the 1990s by the U.S. Department of Justice and the European Commission. *Economics in News* 12.1 describes those suits.

Economics in the News 12.1

Microsoft versus the Trustbusters

Microsoft Corporation is one of the great entrepreneurial successes of our times. Founded in 1975 by Bill Gates and Paul Allen, it got its big break when it secured a license in 1981 to write an operating system for the new IBM PC. It used the success of the MS-DOS operating system it created for IBM to increase its market share among competing hardware makers until, by the end of the 1990s, it was selling more than 90 percent of all personal computer operating systems worldwide. In the process, Bill Gates became famous as the world's wealthiest individual.

Bill Gates, founder of Microsoft Corporation

Not surprisingly, a company with such a dominant position in the market became a target of antitrust investigations. In 1994, the U.S. Department of Justice brought a complaint against Microsoft based on the alleged illegal use of exclusionary contracts and predatory conduct to maintain its dominant market position. The heart of the case consisted of a series of allegations about the relationship between Microsoft's operating system and its Internet Explorer browser.

The government considered Microsoft's decision to "bundle" the browser together with the operating system to be an illegal exclusionary agreement. In addition, it considered the practice of giving away Internet Explorer without charge to be a form of predatory pricing. It saw both practices as having the principal objective of placing the rival Netscape browser at a disadvantage.

Microsoft countered that the software market was more competitive than the Justice Department claimed. Its 90 percent market share could be attributed to "network effects" that are at work in any market where there is an advantage for two users to share a product or standard. However, it saw its dominant position as constantly under threat of "catastrophic entry" by some new technology. As a result, Microsoft was driven to keep its prices low (just one-sixteenth of the theoretical profit maximizing price, by one estimate) and constantly innovate. Although it was a large firm, it argued that it served its customers well.

In 2004, after years of litigation, Microsoft reached a final settlement with the Department of Justice. The settlement did not prevent Microsoft from tying its browser to its operating system—the cornerstone of the government's original case.

It did require Microsoft to be more generous in providing information on the details of its operating system to rival software developers. The final result has hardly had an earth-shattering impact on the software market. Over time, Microsoft's dominance of the

(Continues)

browser market has faded away. By the end of 2011, rivals, including Firefox and Chrome, had taken over more than half of the market.

The settlement with the DOJ did not end Microsoft's antitrust troubles, however. While the U.S. suit was in progress, the European Commission, which has antitrust authority for the European Union, brought its own case. Although it focused on Microsoft's media player and its rivals rather than Internet browsers, in many ways it was similar to that of the U.S. Department of Justice.

On balance, the European Commission has been tougher on Microsoft than the U.S. government. By the time the parties finally settled the case, in December 2009, it had ultimately cost Microsoft more than $2 billion. One provision of the settlement required Microsoft to give users of its Windows operating system an easier way to opt out of using its Internet Explorer browser. Other provisions discouraged bundling of the media player and required greater sharing of information on software systems. Despite all the time and money spent on the litigation, it is not clear the antitrust action had any earth-shaking impact on the competitive structure of the software market in Europe.

Price Discrimination   The original Clayton Act listed price discrimination as an illegal practice, but the government did not actively enforce that section at first. Things changed in 1936. In that year, Congress amended the Clayton Act by passing the Robinson-Patman Act.

Many economists see the Robinson-Patman act as one that more closely fits the rent-seeking model than the market failure theory of antitrust law. The problem is that the act easily turns from a tool for promoting competition into a means by which a firm can shield itself from competition by its rivals. Large, efficient firms can face charges of price discrimination for selling at low prices even when the prices only reflect lower costs or other efficiencies. The government has again cut back its enforcement efforts against price discrimination in recent years.

Antitrust Reformers

In the mid-twentieth century, most economists accepted the view that any departure from perfect competition is a likely potential source of market failure. They saw antitrust policy as a tool for reshaping real-world markets to more closely resemble the textbook ideal. However, beginning in the 1980s, this began to change. More voices began to be heard that were skeptical of antitrust policy, at least as then practiced.

Many antitrust reformers criticized existing policy for its failure to consider transaction costs and the scarcity value of information. Increasingly, they saw many business practices that once seemed harmful to instead be harmless or even helpful. According to reformers, the main enforcement targets should be conspiracies to fix prices or divide markets, horizontal mergers that would create very large market shares, and predatory actions aimed at harming competitors (with predation carefully distinguished from mere rivalry). Enforcement actions should not overemphasize vertical restraints, nor should they focus on small horizontal mergers, or any vertical or conglomerate mergers, or on price discrimination.

In 1978, in setting forth a program for the reform of antitrust policy, Robert Bork wrote that these are "not prescriptions for the nonenforcement of the antitrust laws, but rather for their enforcement in a way that advances, rather than retards, competition and consumer welfare."[3] Beginning about that time, a number of academic critics of traditional antitrust policy left their universities for influential government posts. Among them were William Baxter, who headed the antitrust division of the Department of Justice during the first term of the Reagan administration, and James C. Miller III, who headed the Federal Trade Commission. Other critics—including Bork, Richard Posner, and Ralph Winter—received appointments to federal judgeships.

Meanwhile, trends in legal education were also having an effect on the thinking of antitrust lawyers. Legal education has long stressed learning from past cases and judicial opinions. Today, legal training also often includes a study of economics. As a result, students of antitrust law are encouraged to focus more closely on the questions of efficiency and consumer welfare raised by the cases with which they deal.

Entrepreneurship and Antitrust

Another group of critics, including representatives of the modern Austrian school, see a neglect of entrepreneurship as one of the fundamental problems of antitrust policy. Entrepreneurship, as defined in Chapter 1, is the activity of looking for new possibilities, making use of new ways of doing things, being alert to new opportunities, and overcoming old limits. In the world of business, the success or failure of a firm is critically dependent on its entrepreneurial abilities.[4]

The problem with traditional antitrust theory, say this group of critics, is that it focuses too much on **static efficiency**—the ability of an economy to get the greatest possible amount of consumer satisfaction with given amounts of resources and technology. Static efficiency measures how well the economy performs at a given time with given resources and technology; but the performance of an economy also depends on its **dynamic efficiency**—its success in increasing the rate of output per unit of resources. Dynamic efficiency is a measure of the rate at which the production possibility frontier shifts outward over time because of innovation and technological change. In the long run, dynamic, not static, efficiency is the engine of growth and prosperity.

If every feature of the economy that promoted static efficiency also contributed to dynamic efficiency, the distinction between the two would hardly matter. However, there are reasons to think that may not be the case. One key issue is the relationship between market structure and market performance. Much of traditional antitrust theory rests on the neoclassical view that perfectly competitive markets are the most efficient in the static sense, and monopoly is the least efficient. However, when we view efficiency in dynamic terms, the superiority

Static efficiency
The ability of an economy to get the greatest degree of consumer satisfaction from given amounts of resources and technology

Dynamic efficiency
The ability of an economy to increase consumer satisfaction through innovation and technological change

of perfect competition is not so clear. In fact, the traditional categories of market structure may be largely irrelevant to market performance measured in dynamic terms. That view goes by the name of the Schumpeter hypothesis, after the Austrian-born economist Joseph Schumpeter, who first brought it to widespread attention (see *Who Said It? Who Did It?* 12.1). Schumpeter and others suggested that in some cases large, oligopolistic firms might outperform small, perfectly competitive firms in dynamic terms.

Who Said It? Who Did It? **12.1**

Joseph Schumpeter on Competition and Entrepreneurship

Joseph Schumpeter was born in 1883 in a small city in what is now the Czech Republic, then part of the Austro-Hungarian Empire. He studied law at the University of Vienna and attended lectures by the leading economists of the day, including some of the founders of the Austrian school. He served briefly as Austrian minister of finance after World War I. In 1932, he left Austria for Harvard University where he wrote most of the works for which he is known today.

Schumpeter saw competition among entrepreneurs as the source of economic progress. In *Capitalism, Socialism, and Democracy*, he wrote,

> "The competition that counts is competition from the new commodity, the new technology, the new source of supply, the new type of organization ... competition which commands a decisive cost or quality advantage."

In Schumpeter's view, that kind of competition among entrepreneurs was the central dynamic force in capitalism, which he called "creative destruction." Sometimes creative destruction might mean literally driving a rival firm into bankruptcy, but that need not happen. More importantly, it destroys old ways of doing things and old products that do not serve customer needs so well. Schumpeter saw creative destruction as a state of perpetual market disequilibrium in which firms can survive only by constantly meeting the initiatives of rivals with new products and new production methods of their own.

In short, the capitalism of creative destruction that Schumpeter envisioned was a world away from the textbook model of perfect competition. "Perfect competition," he wrote, "is not only impossible but inferior and has no title to being set up as a model of ideal efficiency."

Source: Joseph Schumpeter, *Capitalism, Socialism, and Democracy* (New York: Harper & Row, 1942), 84–85, 105.

BVT *Lab*

Flashcards are available
for this chapter at
www.BVTLab.com.

According to Schumpeter, the source of innovation and technological change is competition—but competition among entrepreneurs, not the kind found in perfectly competitive markets. He saw two ways in which entrepreneurial competition promotes dynamic efficiency even when it leads, at least temporarily, to some degree of monopoly power.

First, Schumpeter points out, the hope of achieving monopoly power is often the entrepreneur's chief incentive for competition. The first firm to obtain new knowledge and put it to use is able to make pure economic profits because its new discovery gives it a temporary monopoly. If it introduced each new product at a price that just covered cost, or if it followed each cost-reducing innovation with a matching reduction in price, there would be little reason to innovate at all. If the first firm to adjust to changing conditions were unable to increase the gap between costs and revenues by doing so, there would be no incentive to be first. Competition among entrepreneurs is competition for monopoly power, at least in the short run. In this sense, monopoly is not the opposite of competition but, rather, a normal result of it.

Second, monopoly power acts to spur competition. That is true in the sense that an industry where monopoly profits are being made tends to attract entrepreneurs from the outside. Sometimes that means the entry of new firms. Other times, it means indirect competition by substitutes. The developments that led to the 2012 bankruptcy filing by Eastman Kodak Company provide a classic example. No one ever broke Kodak's dominance in production of photographic film. Instead, indirect competition from digital photography, a technology it once dismissed as little more than a toy, brought down the once invincible giant.

The Future of Antitrust Policy

Over the years, reformers succeeded in making a number of important changes in antitrust policy. In many respects, their once-radical ideas have become the new conventional wisdom. Does that mean that antitrust policy will play a permanently reduced role in economic affairs, with possible repeal of some of the more restrictive statutes? Perhaps, but perhaps not.

For one thing, outside the economics profession, the old populist view of antitrust remains alive. As one critic of reforms has put it, "antitrust [law] was intended also to further a social and moral vision of America. At the core of that vision was a conviction that the past greatness, and future potential, of the country depended on the kind of character—resourceful, practical, and determined—that only competitive individualism would foster."[5]

Consumer activist and former FTC Chairman Michael Pertschuk put it more simply when he characterized the proper focus of antitrust policy as a "Jeffersonian preference for dispersed power" applied not only to the dispersion of power among various branches of government but also to the dispersion of economic power among a multitude of relatively small firms.

12.2 Regulation of Natural Monopoly

The aim of antitrust policy is to prevent one firm, or a few firms acting in concert, from gaining control of a market. However, there are some cases, known as natural monopolies, in which there is no practical way to avoid the dominance of one firm. In this section, we examine policies intended to improve the performance of such markets, and also the unintended consequences the policies sometimes have.

The Policy Problem

A *natural monopoly* is an industry in which total costs are at a minimum when just one producer serves the whole market. Local gas, electric, cable TV, and water services are common examples. (But notice, in yet another example of Schumpeterian creative destruction, telephone service has fallen off the natural monopoly list.) It is easy for one such utility to hook up more customers once it has run its lines into their neighborhood, but it is wasteful and costly for a number of different companies to run lines down the same street.

The policy problem raised by a natural monopoly is how to keep the firm from taking advantage of its position to raise prices and restrict output. Figure 12.1 gives an example. That firm, an electric utility, has constant marginal costs and a negatively sloped long-run average cost curve. The demand curve intersects the long-run average cost curve at quantity Q_1, not far from the minimum efficient scale of production. If that output were divided between two firms, each of which produced half of quantity Q_1, the cost per unit would be a lot higher—and still more so if there were more than two firms.

If one unregulated firm operates in a market, it will act like a pure monopolist. Instead of producing Q_1 it will produce Q_2, which corresponds to the intersection of its marginal revenue and marginal cost curves. The price that corresponds to this output is P_2, which is far above marginal cost. This is too small an output and too high a price to permit efficient production.

The Regulatory Solution

It appears, then, that in a natural monopoly, competition by two or more firms and monopoly pricing by a single firm are both inefficient. The traditional way of trying to overcome the inefficiency is to allow just one firm to operate but to regulate its price. For example, regulators could limit the firm in Figure 12.1 to a price of no more than P_1, where the demand curve intersects the long-run average cost curve. The price ceiling would make the firm a price taker for output up to Q_1. Even if it kept output below Q_1, it would not be able to raise the price. With the price ceiling enforced, it earns the maximum profit by producing exactly Q_1 units. That is a lower price and a greater quantity than would result either from an unregulated pure monopoly or from competition between two or more firms.

FIGURE 12.1   REGULATION OF A NATURAL MONOPOLY

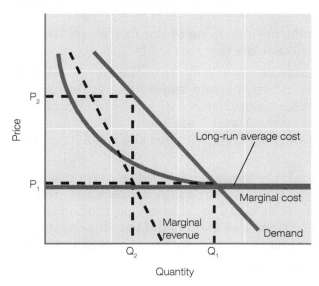

This graph shows the cost and demand curves for a natural monopoly such as an electric utility. As an unregulated monopolist, the firm would make the maximum profit by charging price P_2 and selling quantity Q_2. If regulators impose a maximum price of P_1, the firm will find it worthwhile to produce quantity Q_1.

For perfect efficiency, the price would have to equal marginal cost, which is slightly lower than P_1. At any price lower than P_1, however, the firm would suffer a loss. It could survive in the long run only if it received a subsidy. By allowing the firm to charge price P_1, which is high enough to just cover all costs, the regulators would avoid the need for a subsidy while giving up only a little efficiency.

Rate of Return as a Focus of Regulation   The correct regulated price is easy to identify in Figure 12.1 because the shapes and positions of the demand and cost curves are right there on the page. In the real world, though, regulators do not have full information about demand and cost. Lacking such information, they set the regulated price indirectly by focusing on the **rate of return** earned by the firm. The rate of return is the firm's accounting profit expressed as a percentage of its net worth.

To see why the rate of return is a useful focus, consider the implications of setting various prices. If the price is set equal to average total cost, the firm will earn a "normal profit," that is, a rate of return equal to the opportunity cost of capital. If the firm sets its price higher than average total cost, the firm will earn more than a normal profit, that is, enough to cover the opportunity cost of capital with some left over as economic profit. If it sets its price below average total cost, it will earn less than a normal profit. Because revenue is not enough to meet all opportunity costs, including that of capital, the firm will suffer an

Rate of return

A firm's accounting profit expressed as a percentage of its net worth economic loss. If the firm sets its price higher than average total cost, it will earn more than a normal profit.

Armed with this reasoning, the regulators proceed in five steps:

1. They measure the value of the firm's capital—say, $1.2 million. They call that the *rate base*.

2. They measure the average rate of return for similarly risky firms in other industries, and use that as an estimate of the normal rate of profit. Suppose it turns out to be 15 percent per year. (In practice, steps 1 and 2 are more difficult than they sound, but for our purposes, we will give the regulators the benefit of the doubt.)

3. They multiply the rate base by the normal rate of return to calculate the total cost of capital for the firm—in this case, $180,000 per year. That sum should be enough to both make interest payments on borrowed capital and to compensate the shareholders for their investment in the firm's common stock.

4. They ask the firm to propose a price or set of prices that it thinks will cover its capital costs.

5. As time goes by, they keep track of the firm's actual rate of return, holding the price down if the rate of return rises above the permitted normal rate and allowing price increases if the return falls below normal.

Limitations of Rate-of-Return Regulation   The objective of rate-of-return regulation is to achieve greater output at a lower price than unregulated natural monopoly, while allowing owners to earn a fair return on their investment. However, it may not always achieve that goal.

One reason, emphasized by economists of the public choice school, is regulatory capture. Sometimes regulated firms may "capture" the regulatory agency. They may do so by gaining control over the appointment of regulators or by tempting incumbent regulators to follow lax policies in the hope of finding well-paid "revolving door" jobs in the industry after their terms expire. In other cases, consumer interest groups succeed in capturing the regulators. They then seek the short-run gains that come from keeping rates low without regard for the regulated firms' long-run need to attract capital in order to maintain capacity and service quality.

Another possible problem is that even if regulators do not intentionally allow higher than normal returns, they may simply not know enough about the industry to set rates correctly. It is not easy to measure a regulated firm's stock of capital, its actual rate of return, or its opportunity cost of capital. The more regulators must rely on guesswork, the more likely they are to set rates that are inadvertently either too high or too low.

Serious problems may follow from rates that produce returns either higher or lower than the opportunity cost of capital. A study by Harvey Averch and Leland Johnson suggested that in the 1950s and

1960s permitted rates of return for electricity tended to be too high.[6] Doing so allowed the utilities to take advantage of their monopoly position. They could raise capital to build new plants, whether the plants were needed or not, and then add them into their rate base. The regulators, then, would allow them to raise their rates enough not only to pass along the costs of the new plants but also to earn a pure economic profit. The outcome—now known as the *A-J effect*—was wasteful over-investment in the regulated industry.

By the 1980s, the situation had changed. Some economists came to fear that rates of return had fallen too low. That would cause the A-J effect to operate in reverse. Utilities would avoid investing in new plants even when they would be justified from the consumer's point of view. Such a policy of "rate suppression" might keep rates low for consumers in the short run; but eventually, as old plants wear out and are not replaced or upgraded, the quality of service falls.

In short, either too high or too low an allowed rate of return is harmful. In their search for efficiency, regulators must walk a narrow line between these two kinds of errors.

12.3 Regulation of Competitive Industries

Natural monopolies are not the only industries to come under regulation. There are many others—transportation, banking, finance, and communications, to name just a few—that are subject to regulation even though their market structures are oligopolistic, monopolistically competitive, and in some cases, close to perfectly competitive. In this section, we look at the regulation of competitive behavior in such industries.

Historical Origins

Railroads first came under regulation in the late nineteenth century, but the big surge in regulation came in the 1930s. One tends to think of the Great Depression mainly in terms of high unemployment; however, another major feature of the Depression was low prices. Between 1929 and 1933, the consumer price index dropped about 25 percent. Today most economists would explain both the high unemployment and the falling prices in macroeconomic terms, blaming them on low aggregate demand, inappropriate monetary policy, and so on. At the time, however, people tended to blame the high unemployment levels on low prices. If only they could find a way to raise prices, business leaders said, it would be possible to put more workers on the payroll.

Many contemporary observers blamed low prices on excessive competition. Believing that too much competition was a barrier to economic recovery, Congress, in 1933, passed the National Recovery Act, which encouraged firms to use cartel-like methods to prop up prices.

The Supreme Court declared that particular act unconstitutional, but similar legislation that applied only to specific industries survived. Two of the most important industries where regulation limited competition were trucking, which came under the control of the Interstate Commerce Commission (ICC) in 1935, and airlines, which came under the regulation of the Civil Aeronautics Board (CAB) in 1938.

Rate and Entry Regulations in Transportation

The case of transportation regulation reveals some key differences between the regulation of competitive industries and that of natural monopolies. Two of the differences were a focus on limiting entry by new firms and a tendency to set minimum rather than maximum prices. The traditional argument for regulation of natural monopolies was that without regulation, prices would rise too high. In the case of airlines and trucking, the concern was that without regulation prices would fall too low.

Regulation of trucking and airlines did achieve the goal of raising prices and limiting the number of firms in those industries. As the years passed, however, many economists began to have second thoughts as to whether high prices and limited competition were the proper goals of government policy. With the advent of high inflation rates in the 1970s, the doubts about regulation grew stronger; economists turned almost unanimously against the regulation of entry and the setting of minimum rates in competitive industries.

Regulation and Political Rent Seeking

Critics of transportation regulation tended to view it as an example of political rent seeking. Regulation, in effect, allowed rival firms to form cartels, raise prices above opportunity costs, and earn excess profits.

In the preceding chapter, we saw that two major weaknesses of most cartels are inability to control entry and inability to keep members from cheating on price agreements. The laws that gave the ICC and the CAB authority over trucking and airlines dealt with those problems. Both agencies became highly restrictive in terms of entry by new firms. (The CAB did not let in a single new major airline for its first forty years, and the ICC was only slightly less restrictive.) Further, both agencies received, and used, the authority to prevent carriers from cutting prices below specified minimum levels, as well as the authority to regulate maximum rates.

A number of studies carried out in the 1960s and 1970s supported the cartel theory of regulation. Many of them compared regulated and unregulated markets. One study, for example, showed that unregulated intrastate airline fares in California and Texas were only about half of the regulated interstate fares for similar distances. Other studies compared regulated freight rates for industrial goods with those for agricultural produce, which were exempt from regulation. Again, the regulated rates seemed substantially higher.

Regulatory Reform

In the late 1970s, the government began to translate long-standing criticisms of transportation regulation into policy. New laws and newly appointed regulators began to ease restrictions on competition for passenger airlines, airfreight, trucking, and intercity bus service. Extensive deregulation also took place for railroad rates, and barriers to competition between railroads and motor freight relaxed. Congress abolished the CAB, giving a few of its functions, mostly related to safety, to the Federal Aviation Administration (FAA). The ICC stayed in business with a reduced staff and much more limited functions until 1995.

In addition to the reform of regulation in the transportation industries, there were significant changes in other industries. In communications, the breakup of AT&T and the rise of cell phones brought competition to the telephone industry, and the Federal Communications Commission changed the regulatory atmosphere in radio and television broadcasting. In the 1980s, financial deregulation removed regulations that had barred banks from competing by offering higher interest rates and new services. In 1999, Congress repealed key provisions of the Depression-era Glass-Stegall Act, which had separated commercial banking from investment banking.

Despite generally positive outcomes, deregulation has not always been an unqualified success. Finding the right balance between overly restrictive and overly permissive regulation has been especially difficult in the financial industry. Many critics have placed at least part of the blame for the financial crisis that began in 2007 on inadequate regulation of banks and other financial institutions, thus allowing them to take excessive risk while benefiting from an implicit promise of government bailouts in case of failure. In the aftermath of the crisis, the 2010 Dodd-Frank Act again tightened regulation of banking and finance. Whether or not the new laws and regulation have the balance right remains highly controversial.

12.4 Health and Safety Regulation

In the 1970s, as Washington was cutting back on some forms of regulation that dated from the Great Depression, it was expanding other areas of regulation. Among the agencies reflecting this trend were the Occupational Safety and Health Administration (OSHA), the Consumer Product Safety Commission (CPSC), the National Highway and Traffic Safety Administration (NHTSA), and the Environmental Protection Agency (EPA). In addition, some older agencies, such as the Food and Drug Administration (FDA), became more active than before. These agencies are not directly concerned with prices and competition; rather, their focus is on the kinds of goods that firms produce and how they produce them. Let's look at what economists have to say about some of the controversies surrounding health and safety regulation.

The U.S. cut back on some forms of regulation in the 1970s but expanded in others such as the Environmental Protection Agency (EPA).

Goals and Values

The goal of health and safety regulation is to make the world a safer, healthier, more pleasant place in which to live. The goal is hard to argue with—so why are the regulations designed to achieve it so controversial? Part of the answer is that even when we agree on goals, we can disagree about the best ways to pursue them. Also, although almost everyone believes that health and safety are good in themselves, they disagree about their relationship to other worthy goals. Two such disagreements about priorities often threaten to overshadow any consideration of the efficiency of health and safety regulation: the question of valuing health and safety and that of deciding whose values should shape policy when values differ.

Can We Assign an Economic Value to Health and Safety?   The first issue is whether we should even consider trade-offs between human health and safety, on the one hand, and material well-being, on the other. Many supporters of strong, strictly enforced health and safety regulations argue that there is no way to measure the value of human life. Regulators, therefore, should set rules without regard to economic trade-offs or cost-benefit ratios.

Others, however, do not share this view. They do not belittle the value of human life; rather, they see no point in condemning something that people do every day—that is, to risk their own health and safety in favor of other goals. People choose the convenience of car travel over the discomforts of bus travel, even though buses are many times safer than cars. They take high-paying jobs in cities rather than low-paying jobs in the country, even though they know country air is healthier than city air. They have medical checkups once a year but not twice a year or once a month because the gain in terms of health is not worth the sacrifice in terms of time and money.

Whose Values?   Even if we concede that we can apply cost-benefit analysis to health and safety, we still must face the question of whose values should govern any trade-offs. Should the guide for policy be the values of the people who receive the benefits and bear the costs, or should it be the judgment of experts? In practical terms, the question comes down to the one of when people should only be warned about health and safety hazards and when they should be forced to be safe and healthy whether they want to or not.

There is no unanimity among economists on this issue, but there is perhaps a bias toward the belief that it is reasonable to consider economic costs and benefits in making health and safety decisions and to allow well-informed people to make those choices for themselves. When economists discuss health and safety regulation with people who believe in health and safety at any cost, what is likely to take place is a fight rather than a rational debate. That is unfortunate because there are some things that economics as a science, or positive economics, can contribute to the controversy over health and safety regulation.

Benefits and Costs

One area on which economists and regulators should be able to agree is that once we choose regulatory goals, we should try to achieve them at the least cost. One way to do so is to issue regulations in the form of performance standards rather than engineering controls. Performance standards specify results, whereas engineering controls specify particular techniques that firms must use or equipment they must install. Chapter 6 discussed the trend in environmental regulation toward performance-based regulations, like cap-and-trade programs or emission charges, and away from measures that mandate specific engineering controls. Although perhaps not to the same extent, health and safety regulation has moved in the same direction.

Another issue on which economists can make a positive contribution is evaluating the benefits of a proposed regulation relative to its costs. For example, in 1984 the EPA issued a study that showed that banning lead in gasoline would have benefits totaling $1.8 billion. In the EPA's view, this would more than offset the cost, which it estimated at about $.02 per gallon of gasoline. Ethyl Corporation, which produced the lead additive that the EPA sought to ban, said that the agency had left out a major cost. According to Ethyl, banning lead would mean that older cars, designed before lead-free gasoline was widely available, would need valve repairs much more often. In Ethyl's estimate, the cost of those repairs would be $18 billion per year, far more than the benefits. In this case, cost-benefit analysis narrowed the grounds of the dispute over elimination of lead in gasoline and allowed progress toward agreement on terms of the phase-out.

Still another area of regulation in which economics can be helpful is tracing the unintended consequences of regulation. For example, Chapter 5 discussed auto safety regulation and its possible unintended effect of increasing hazards to pedestrians and bicyclists. Similarly, regulations requiring safety caps on aspirin bottles had the unintended effect of making it more likely that people would leave the caps off altogether—thus, in some cases, increasing hazards to children. A study by Richard L. Stroup and John C. Goodman detailed other cases in which well-intentioned health and safety regulations have had unintended effects that endanger health and safety.[7]

Summary

1. **Which business practices are illegal under the antitrust laws?** *Antitrust laws* seek to control market structure and the competitive behavior of firms. The oldest of the antitrust laws is the Sherman Act of 1890, which outlaws combinations and conspiracies in restraint of trade and makes any attempt to monopolize a market illegal. The Clayton and Federal Trade Commission Acts of 1914 seek to control unfair trade practices. The Clayton Act, together with the Celler-Kefauver Act of 1950, controls mergers. The Robinson-Patman Act of 1935 regulates price discrimination.

2. **How have economists' views on antitrust policy changed over time?** For many years, vigorous enforcement of antitrust laws had widespread support among economists. Then, in the 1970s, economists' views began to change. Reformers, armed with new views about the efficiency effects of business practices, now urge greater consideration for consumer welfare, fewer restrictions on all but the largest horizontal mergers, and less attention to vertical restraints and price discrimination. Public choice theorists see antitrust laws in terms of political rent seeking by small economic entities at the expense of large ones. Economists of the modern Austrian school see antitrust laws as damaging to entrepreneurship and innovations.

3. **What kinds of regulations apply to natural monopolies?** Natural monopolies, such as electric utilities, are subject to regulation that aims to prevent excessive *rates of return*. Regulation does not always work smoothly, however. If regulators set rates of return too high or too low, the regulated firm will face distorted investment incentives.

4. **What is the reason for regulation of some industries that have an inherently competitive structure?** Many industries come under regulation even though they are not natural monopolies. Some economists see such regulation as a form of rent seeking. In effect, regulation amounts to government imposition of a cartel. Firms, their workers, and their customers share the rents generated by regulatory "cartels."

5. **What are the current trends in health and safety regulation?** Regulation has been growing in the areas of health and safety at the same time that it has been decreasing in such industries as transportation, communication, and financial services. Disputes in these areas of regulation raise both normative and positive issues. The issues include the question of whether one can place an economic value on health and safety, as well as the issue of whose values should guide regulatory policy. In addition, there are questions of how to find ways to keep down the costs of regulation, compare its costs and benefits, and trace its unintended consequences.

Key Terms   **Page #**

Problems and Topics for Discussion

1. **Antitrust laws and economic rights**   "Everyone should have the unrestricted right both to sell goods and services in any market and to withhold goods or services from sale." Are the antitrust laws consistent with this statement? Why or why not?

2. **Public ownership of utilities**   Some city governments own utilities such as electric companies and gas distribution companies. What do you think are the advantages and disadvantages of public ownership of a natural monopoly compared with regulated private ownership? With unregulated private ownership?

3. **Value of trucking permits**   Before 1980 the ICC limited the number of trucking firms that could serve any given route. Often the only way a new firm could get permission to serve a route was to buy the "certificate" (permit) of a firm that already served that route. Some of those permits were worth hundreds of thousands of dollars. Why were the permits worth so much? After deregulation, the value of such permits fell to zero. Why do you think that happened?

4. **Regulation of taxis**   What regulations apply to taxis in the area where you live? Is there free entry into the market? Are minimum or maximum fares set? How easy is it to get a cab if you need one? Would you suggest any changes in regulatory policy for your area?

5. **Highway speed limits**   Highway speed limits vary widely from state to state and have also changed over time. In the 1970s and 1980s, highway speeds were limited to 55 miles per hour. Today many states allow much faster speeds. Some countries, notably Germany, do not have speed limits at all for their most modern roads. How would you go about judging whether a change in the speed limit is a good idea? Discuss.

Case for Discussion:

Tipping the Balance

As sport utility vehicles (SUVs) became more popular in the 1990s, an increase in rollover deaths began to draw the critical eye of government regulators. After the a highly publicized series of accidents involving Ford Explorers with Firestone tires, Congress required the National Highway Traffic Safety Administration (NHTSA) to test automobiles for rollover risk on a track. Prior to the increased fear of rollovers, the NHTSA used a mathematical formula to estimate a vehicle's star rating. For instance, a five-star rating meant that an automobile has a less than 10 percent chance of rollover in a single accident.

The NHTSA track tests were incorporated into safety ratings beginning with the 2004 models. Compared with prior years, the 2004 results showed improvement for a few SUVs. This added fuel to lobbyists' arguments against increased regulations targeting the SUV, such as gas mileage restrictions and subsidies for promoting the development of hybrids. "SUV Rollover Hysteria Appears Misplaced," said a news release from the lobbyist group Sport Utility Vehicle Owners of America.

Just how big a problem are rollovers? In 2004, the NHTSA estimated that only 2.5 percent of accidents involve a rollover. However, among drivers and passengers involved in a rollover accident, one-third of them die because of the accident. So, while rollovers are rare, the chances of surviving are less than comforting. According to statistics from the Insurance Institute for Highway Safety, SUVs had higher fatality rates compared with cars. Between 2000 and 2001, 1997–1999 model year cars weighing between 3,500 and 3,999 pounds had a fatality rate of 87 per million registered vehicles. That compared with a fatality rate of 160 for SUVs in the same weight class and model years.

By the mid-2000s, however, better design and increased use of electronic stability control (ESC) began to change things around. A 2011 study covering vehicles with model years from 2006 to 2009 found that the fatality rate for SUVs had fallen to half the rate for passenger cars. The new ESC technology became mandatory beginning with the 2012 model year. It is likely that fatalities will fall still more as a result.

Sources: Information from Danny Hakim, "The Tipping Point for Safety," The New York Times, February 22, 2004, and Paul A. Eisenstein, "Stability Control Systems Yielding Dramatic Drop in SUV Death Rates," The Detroit Bureau, June 9, 2011 (downloaded from http://www.thedetroitbureau.com/2011/06/stability-control-systems-yielding-dramatic-drop-in-suv-death-rate/, Jan 23, 2012).

Questions

1. Suppose that a court finds a company's vehicles to be unreasonably dangerous and orders it to pay $1 million per accident. Is that a reasonable figure? To put it in human terms, consider the following two ways of looking at the payment:

   a. Imagine yourself in a hospital following a near-fatal rollover accident that will leave you permanently disabled. A representative of the company enters the room and offers you a choice: You either can have $1 million or be restored to health. Which option would you take?

   b. Imagine that you are about to buy an SUV and that an ESC system is optional rather than required equipment. You expect to drive the car 100,000 miles before junking it. If the car has no stability control, the chance you will die in a rollover accident over that period are about 12 in 10,000. If it has a stability control system and you use it regularly, your chances of dying over the same period are about 2 in 10,000. If you value your life at $1 million, you should be willing to pay up to $1,000 for the stability control system. What is the maximum you would actually be willing to pay?

2. Setting aside the issue of whether $1 million is the "right" value for a human life, do you agree in principle that a cost-benefit formula is the proper framework for making the decision about modifying the stability design of SUVs, or do you feel that cost doesn't really matter? If you were an SUV manufacturer, would you install stability-control safeguards at a cost of, say, $500 per vehicle? If you were a consumer rather than a manufacturer, how much would you pay for an optional, stability package that would prevent a rollover accident—more than $500, or less?

3. Assume that ESC technology costs $500 per vehicle and cuts the risk of a rollover fatality in half, from 56 per million vehicle years to 28 per million vehicle years. Do you think automakers should give this information to consumers and then allow them to choose for themselves whether to buy ESC as an add-on, or should regulators require ESC on all vehicles? Discuss the reason for your answer.

Endnotes

1. *United States v. Trans-Missouri Freight Ass'n.*, 166 U.S. 323 (1897).

2. F. M. Scherer, *Industrial Market Structure and Economic Performance* (Chicago: Rand McNally, 1980), 491.

3. See Robert H. Bork, *The Antitrust Paradox* (New York: Basic Books, 1978), 405–406.

4. For a short exposition of Austrian antitrust views, see Armentano, "Efficiency, Liberty, and Antitrust Policy," *Cato Journal* (Winter 1985): 925–931. Those views are developed at greater length in *Antitrust and Monopoly: Anatomy of a Policy Failure* (New York: Wiley, 1982).

5. Robert A. Katzman, "The Attenuation of Antitrust," *Brookings Review* (Summer 1984): 24.

6. Harvey A. Averch and L. L. Johnson, "Behavior of the Firm under Regulatory Constraint," *American Economic Review* (December 1962): 1052–1069.

7. Richard L. Stroup and John C. Goodman, "Making the World Less Safe: The Unhealthy Trend in Health, Safety, and Environmental Regulation," National Center for Policy Analysis Policy Report no. 137, April 1989.

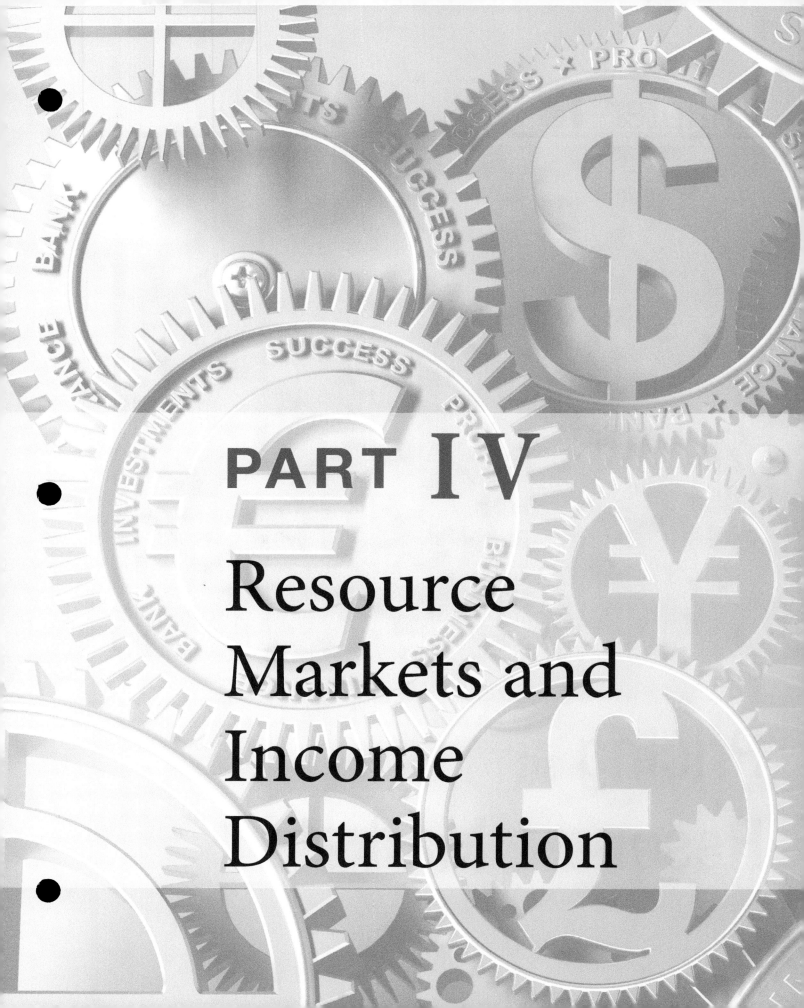

PART IV

Resource Markets and Income Distribution

Chapter 13

Pricing *in* Resource Markets

After reading this chapter, you will understand the following:

1. The demand for productive inputs

2. The supply curve for labor

3. The equilibrium of a competitive labor market

4. The equilibrium of a labor market with only one or a few employers

5. Why wages are not the same for all labor markets and for all workers in a given labor market

6. The determination of interest rates in the loanable funds market

7. What determines land and resource rents

Before reading this chapter, make sure you know the meaning of the following concepts:

1. Substitutes and complements

2. Elasticity

3. Income and substitution effects

4. Marginal physical product and diminishing returns

5. Perfect competition and price takers

6. Theory of monopoly and price searchers

7. Economic rent

Markets for factors of production, or resource markets, are among those that most frequently make the news. We read that incomes of financial managers have soared while wages of production workers have stagnated. Why? We read that prices of natural gas have fallen to record lows compared to prices of oil. Why? We read that China is rapidly building its stock of capital, in the forms of factories, power lines, and high-speed rail networks. Why?

Up to this point we have mentioned markets for resources only in passing. In this chapter, they will move to the center of the stage. The first part of the chapter will outline a general theory of demand for inputs. The second part focuses on markets for labor. The final section applies the theory to markets for capital and natural resources.

13.1 Demand for Inputs

In many ways, resource markets are like the product markets we have already studied. The theories of supply and demand and the tools of marginal analysis apply to resource markets just as they do to product markets. However, resource markets differ from product markets in one major respect: the buyers are firms, and the sellers often are households.

Objectives and Constraints

As elsewhere in microeconomics, the first step in building a theory of demand for resources is to specify the objectives and constraints that firms face. We will assume, as we have in earlier chapters, that the objective is profit maximization. We will consider three types of constraints.

1. *Production technology*   Technology limits the ways in which firms can combine inputs to produce outputs. We can represent technological constraints as marginal physical product curves when there is only one input. When there is more than one variable input, we can represent them using the isoquant technique explained in the appendix to Chapter 8.

2. *Demand for the product*   Firms buy resources not for their own sake but to use them to produce goods and services for sale. We call the demand for any input a **derived demand** because it reflects demand for the product that the input produces.

3. *Resource cost*   The third constraint is the cost of obtaining that input. In perfectly competitive input markets, that cost is the market price of the input. The situation in less competitive input markets, which we will look at later in the chapter, is more complex.

Derived demand

Demand for an input that reflects the demand for the product the input produces

Marginal Physical Product

As we saw in Chapter 8, the *marginal physical product* of a resource is the increase in output that results from a one-unit increase in the input of that resource, holding all other inputs constant. For example, suppose using one additional worker-hour of labor to cultivate a turnip field yields an additional output of five turnips when no other inputs are changed. If so, the marginal physical product of labor is five turnips per hour.

The marginal physical product of a resource varies according to the amount used. As the quantity of a single input increases while the quantities of all others remain fixed, the marginal physical product of the variable input begins to decrease beyond some point—the *law of diminishing returns*.

Figure 13.1 shows total and marginal physical product curves for a firm that is subject to diminishing returns over the range from 0 to 20 units of an input. As the amount of a single input increases while other inputs are held constant, output increases—but at a diminishing rate. The first unit of the input yields a marginal physical product of twenty units of output; the second a marginal physical product of nineteen units of output; and so on. After the twentieth unit of input, marginal physical product drops to zero. Beyond that point, adding more of the variable input will not yield more output unless the amounts of fixed inputs are also increased. For example, if the variable input in our example is labor, adding more than twenty workers will not increase output unless the amount of machinery available to them also increases. Beyond twenty units of input, the marginal physical product of the variable input drops to zero and the total physical product curve becomes horizontal.

FIGURE 13.1   TOTAL AND MARGINAL PHYSICAL PRODUCT OF AN INPUT

(a)

Quantity of Input (1)	Total Physical Product (2)	Marginal Physical Product (3)
0	0	
		20
1	20	
		19
2	39	
		18
3	57	
		17
4	74	
		16
5	90	
		15
6	105	
		14
7	119	
		13
8	132	
		12
9	144	
		11
10	155	
		10
11	165	
		9
12	174	
		8
13	182	
		7
14	189	
		6
15	195	
		5
16	200	
		4
17	204	
		3
18	207	
		2
19	209	
		1
20	210	

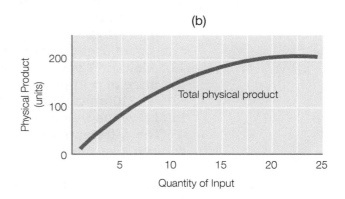

(b)

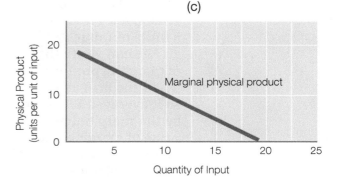

(c)

As the quantity of one resource input increases with the quantity of other inputs remaining unchanged, total physical product increases, but at a decreasing rate. As Parts (a) and (c) of this figure show, marginal physical product decreases as the quantity of the employed input increases. The decrease reflects the law of diminishing returns.

Marginal Revenue Product

**Marginal revenue
product**

The change in revenue that
results from the sale of the
output produced by one
additional unit of a resource

**Value of marginal
product**

Marginal physical product
multiplied by the product's
per-unit price

In deciding how much of a resource to use, a firm must consider not
only the physical quantity of output but also how much revenue it
will earn by selling the output. The change in revenue from selling the
output produced by one more unit of a resource is the **marginal revenue
product** of that resource. The relationship of marginal revenue product
to the demand for output depends on whether the firm in question is
a *price taker* or a *price searcher* in its output market.

A perfectly competitive firm is a price taker in its output market,
so its output price is constant regardless of the quantity sold. Marginal
revenue for such a firm equals the price of its output. For such a firm,
then, marginal revenue product is the same as the **value of marginal
product**, that is, marginal physical product times the output price.

If the firm is a price searcher in its output market, the price at which
it sells its output will vary as its output changes. That will be the case
in markets that are monopolies, oligopolies, or monopolistically competitive. As a price searcher, the firm must choose from among a menu
of price-quantity combinations given by its negatively sloped demand
curve. Because the price per unit decreases as output increases, marginal revenue per unit of output for a price searcher is always less than
price per unit. It follows, then, that the marginal revenue product for
such a firm is less than the value of marginal product.

Figure 13.2 shows marginal revenue product for a price searcher.
The figure uses the same total physical product schedule as in Figure
13.1. Column 3 presents the firm's product demand curve, showing that
the price of output drops from $1.40 per unit at 20 units of output to
$.45 at 210 units. Multiplying price by total physical product gives the
total revenue that corresponds to each quantity of input (column 4).

The differences between successive entries in the total revenue
column give the marginal revenue product data, shown in column 5.
For example, as input of the resource increases from 4 to 5 units, total
output increases from 74 to 90 units while the price falls from $1.13 to
$1.05 per unit. As column 4 shows, total revenue increases from $83.62
when the firm uses 4 units of the input to $94.50 when it uses 5 units.
That gives a marginal revenue product of $10.88 in the range from 4 to
5 units of input.

We can verify that marginal revenue product is less than the value
of marginal product (not shown in the figure). The product price is $1.13
when the firm uses 4 units of the input and $1.05 when it uses 5 units,
so it averages $1.09 over that range of output. Multiplying this average
by the marginal physical product of 16 (column 6 of the figure) gives a
value of marginal product of $17.44 at the midpoint of the output range
in question, compared with a marginal revenue product of $10.88.

As the price continues to fall, marginal revenue eventually becomes negative. Beyond that point, additional units of the input reduce
total revenue even though they increase total physical product. The
turning point comes at ten units of input. Beyond that level, marginal
revenue product is negative even though marginal physical product
remains positive.

FIGURE 13.2   MARGINAL REVENUE PRODUCT FOR A PRICE-SEARCHING FIRM

Quantity of Input (1)	Total Physical Product (2)	Price of Output (3)	Total Revenue (4)	Marginal Revenue Product (5)	Marginal Physical Product (6)	Marginal Revenue per Unit of Output (7)
0	0	—	0.00			
				$ 28.00	20	$ 1.40
1	20	$ 1.40	$ 28.00			
				22.90	19	1.21
2	39	1.31	50.90			
				18.36	18	1.02
3	57	1.22	69.26			
				14.36	17	.84
4	74	1.13	86.62			
				10.88	16	.68
5	90	1.05	94.50			
				7.88	15	.52
6	105	.98	102.38			
				5.32	14	.38
7	119	.91	107.70			
				3.18	13	.24
8	132	.84	110.88			
				1.44	12	.12
9	144	.78	112.32			
				.06	11	.01
10	155	.73	112.38			
				−1.00	10	−.10
11	165	.68	111.38			
				−1.76	9	−.20
12	174	.63	109.62			
				−2.24	8	−.28
13	182	.59	107.38			
				−2.48	7	−.35
14	189	.56	104.90			
				−2.52	6	−.42
15	195	.53	102.38			
				−2.38	5	−.47
16	200	.50	100.00			
				−2.08	4	−.52
17	204	.48	97.92			
				−1.66	3	−.55
18	207	.47	96.26			
				−1.16	2	−.58
19	209	.46	95.10			
				−.60	1	−.60
20	210	.45	94.50			

Note: Figures in columns 3, 4, 5, and 7 are rounded to the nearest cent.

This figure shows how marginal revenue product varies as the quantity of a resource input changes for a price searcher. As column 3 shows, price falls as output increases. Total revenue begins to decrease after 10 units of output (the point at which marginal revenue per unit of output becomes negative) even though marginal physical product remains positive. We can calculate marginal revenue product either as the difference between each entry in the total revenue column or as the product of marginal physical product and marginal revenue per unit of output.

At every level of input, the marginal revenue product of the input equals the marginal physical product times the marginal revenue per unit of output. This relationship is shown in columns 5 through 7 of Figure 13.2. Note that column 7 gives marginal revenue in dollars per unit of output, whereas column 5 gives marginal revenue product in dollars per unit of input.

Marginal Resource Cost

The third constraint that the firm must consider in determining how much of each resource to use is the cost of obtaining each additional unit of the resource, that is, its **marginal resource cost**.

We can begin by considering the case in which input markets are perfectly competitive, so that the firm is a price taker in those markets. That will be the case if the firm is only one of a large number of firms that are competing to buy a particular resource and if the amount of the resource it uses is only a small part of the total used by all firms. For a firm that buys as a price taker, the marginal resource cost equals the market price of the resource. For example, if the market wage rate for clerical workers is $7 an hour, the marginal resource cost for clerical workers' labor is $7 an hour for any firm that is a price taker in that market.

Profit Maximization

To maximize profits, a firm must use just enough of each input to equalize marginal revenue product and marginal resource cost. If marginal revenue product exceeds marginal resource cost, hiring one more unit of the input will add more to revenue than to cost and will increase profit. If marginal resource cost exceeds marginal revenue product, *reducing* the amount of that input by one unit will reduce cost by more than revenue and increase profit. Only when marginal revenue product and marginal resource cost are equal will it be impossible for any change in the amount of the input to increase profit. We can state this rule as the following equation

$$MRC = MRP$$

where MRC stands for marginal resource cost and MRP for marginal revenue product. The rule applies both to firms that are price takers in their output markets and to those that are price searchers in their output markets.

Figure 13.3 illustrates the profit maximization rule. Both the table and the corresponding graph assume that the firm is a price taker in the output market and that the market price of the output is $1 per unit. We also assume the firm is a price taker in the *resource market*, buying at $5 per unit. Note that up to the fifteenth unit of input, profit rises as the firm uses more of the input. The firm just breaks even on the purchase of the sixteenth unit of input. After that, profit decreases if more of the input is used. It is between the fifteenth and sixteenth units of input that marginal revenue product becomes exactly equal to marginal resource cost.

FIGURE 13.3   PROFIT MAXIMIZATION FOR A PRICE-TAKING FIRM

(a)

Quantity of Input (1)	Marginal Revenue Product (2)	Marginal Resource Cost (3)	Total Variable Cost (4)	Fixed Costs (5)	Total Revenue (6)	Total Profit (7)
1			$5	$100	$20	–$85
2	$19	$5	10	100	39	–71
3	18	5	15	100	57	–58
4	17	5	20	100	74	–46
5	16	5	25	100	90	–35
6	15	5	30	100	105	–25
7	14	5	35	100	119	–16
8	13	5	40	100	132	–8
9	12	5	45	100	144	–1
10	11	5	50	100	155	5
11	10	5	55	100	165	10
12	9	5	60	100	174	14
13	8	5	65	100	182	17
14	7	5	70	100	189	19
15	6	5	75	100	195	20
16	5	5	80	100	200	20
17	4	5	85	100	204	19
18	3	5	90	100	207	17
19	2	5	95	100	209	14
20	1	5	100	100	210	10

(b)

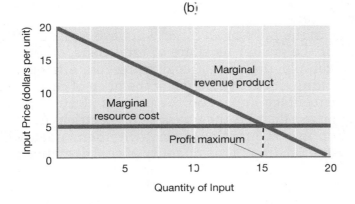

Maximizing profit requires that a firm buy just enough of each resource input to equalize marginal revenue product and marginal resource cost. Here we assume that the firm is a price taker in the market where it sells its output and that the product price is $1 per unit. The point of profit maximization occurs between 15 and 16 units of input.

Resource Demand Curves

Suppose that a firm is a price taker in an input market, whether it is a price taker in the output market or not. If so, its marginal revenue product curve for the input, like the one shown in Figure 13.3, is also its demand curve for the input. The reason is that the quantity of the input demanded by such a firm would be whatever quantity makes the input's price (and, hence, its marginal resource cost) equal to marginal revenue product.

We can extend the same principle to all firms employing a given resource in order to create a market demand curve. The resulting curve, like those of the individual firms, is a derived demand curve because demand for any input derives from the demand for the products the input produces, not directly from the usefulness of the input itself. The market demand for farmland is derived from the market demand for food, the market demand for bookstore clerks from the market demand for books, and so on.

Like the demand for outputs, the demand for inputs changes in response to changes in economic conditions. A change in the market price of any input will cause the quantity of the resource demanded to change; this we would represent by a movement along its demand curve. Changes in economic conditions other than a change in the input's price can cause a change in the demand for the input, which we would show as a *shift* in the demand curve.

The price elasticity of demand for a resource, as for any other good, is the ratio of the percentage change in the quantity demanded to a given percentage change in price, other things being equal. The degree of price elasticity of demand for a resource depends on several circumstances.

Because the demand for any input is derived from the demand for the product it produces, elasticity of demand for an input depends on the elasticity of demand for the product. Suppose, for example, that the demand for taxi services is elastic. If taxi fares are forced up because of an increase in drivers' wages, the quantity of taxi service demanded will fall sharply and there will be a correspondingly large effect on the quantity of drivers demanded.

A change in the price of an input will have a greater effect on the demand for it the greater its share of total costs, other things being equal. For example, the cost of coal represents a large share of the cost of generating electricity. Doubling the price of coal, therefore, will have a big percentage impact on the price of electricity and a correspondingly large effect on the quantity of electricity demanded. The resulting drop in the quantity of electricity demanded will, in turn, cause a substantial drop in the quantity of coal demanded.

Other things being equal, the demand for an input will be more elastic the easier it is to substitute other inputs for it. For example, clowns are an essential part of circus entertainment. If clowns' wages rise, a circus can substitute other inputs, such as trained animal acts, only to a limited degree without disappointing its customers. As a result, a doubling of clowns' wages would have only a small percentage effect on the quantity of clowns demanded. Elasticity of demand for given input also depends on the elasticity of supply of substitute inputs.

If taxi fares increase because drivers' wages go up, demand for taxi services will fall sharply, which will in turn affect the quantity of drivers demanded.

Changes in Demand for Resources

Three kinds of changes are capable of causing shifts in the demand curve for inputs of any productive resource.

A Change in Demand for Output   The principle of derived demand plays a key role in shifts in resource demand curves, as well as in movements along them, In particular, a change in demand for the product produced by an input (that is, a shift in the product demand curve) will cause a change in demand for the input. The source of changes in product demand can be either microeconomic or macroeconomic. A microeconomic example is the increase in demand for the labor of poultry workers because of a shift in consumer tastes from beef to chicken. A macroeconomic example is the rise and fall of the demand for labor as the economy experiences expansions and recessions over the course of the business cycle. Expansion brings tight labor markets and increased overtime work; recessions bring layoffs and unemployment.

A Change in the Price of Another Input   A second source of shifts in the demand curve for an input is a change in the price of some other input. The notions of *substitutes* and *complements* apply to inputs just as they do to consumer goods. For example, consider labor and farm machinery, both of which are inputs to production of corn. In Mexico, where labor is relatively cheap, relatively little machinery is used per bushel of corn produced. Farmers in the United States use more machinery, because labor is relatively expensive. We can see, then, that labor and machinery are substitutes in producing corn. On the other

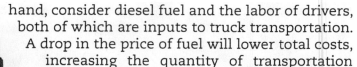

hand, consider diesel fuel and the labor of drivers, both of which are inputs to truck transportation. A drop in the price of fuel will lower total costs, increasing the quantity of transportation services demanded. As a result, the number of drivers hired will increase. We see, then, that labor and fuel are complements in the production of truck transportation.

Changes in Technology   Changes in technology are a third condition that affects the demand for inputs. Improvements in technology not only shift firms' cost curves but also their demand curves for inputs. Sometimes changes in technology will cause the demand for one input to rise while the demand for another falls. For example, the introduction of improved crop varieties in developing countries as part of the so-called green revolution has not only decreased the amount of land needed per unit harvested but also has increased the demand for chemical fertilizer. Sometimes, instead, a new technology reduces the quantities of *all* inputs demanded per unit of output. For example, e-mail dramatically shortened the time needed to produce and circulate a memo to colleagues working on a project within a firm. That reduced both the demand for clerical workers, messengers, and copying equipment.

Be aware, though, that reduced demand for inputs per unit of output does not mean a decrease in total demand for the input. The reason is that more efficient technology lowers prices and tends, over time, to increase the quantity of the product demanded. Often the increase will more than offset the reduced quantity of inputs per unit of output.

For example, look at the relationship between clerical workers and office equipment. In the eighteenth century, firms employed clerks to copy documents laboriously by hand. In the late nineteenth century, the typewriter replaced pen and ink. In the twentieth century, word processors and photocopiers replaced typewriters, until they in turn, gave way to e-mail and voice mail. Each technological innovation vastly reduced the number of clerical-worker hours needed to process a given volume of documents. At the same time, the quantity of document processing demanded grew dramatically, so that the entire clerical labor force is larger now than at any time in the past.

13.2 The Labor Market

Up to this point, we have discussed demand for inputs in general terms. When we turn to the supply side of resource markets, however, we cannot be so general. There are great differences in the conditions that affect supply for various factors of production. This section will focus on the supply of labor and the way demand and supply, together, determine wages. Later sections will take up markets for capital and natural resources.

The Labor Supply Curve

In Chapter 5, we looked at how the preferences and constraints that households face affect the choices they make as buyers of goods. Since the same households that buy goods also supply labor, we can use a similar approach here. We will begin with the labor supply decision for one worker and then turn to market labor supply curves.

Labor Supply for One Worker   All choices that people make as consumers involve trade-offs. The same is true with how they decide how much labor to supply. The key trade-off that shapes the labor supply decision is one between leisure and income. People value leisure for relaxation, recreation, and the time to do household chores. Time spent at leisure is time taken away from work, however, which means it is time diverted from earning income. In making the choice between work and leisure, consumers face two key *constraints*. First, there are only twenty-four hours each day. Second, market wage rates limit the amount of income earned per hour of work.

The hourly wage rate represents the opportunity cost of leisure, that is, the amount of income a worker must sacrifice in order to enjoy an added hour away from work. An increase in the wage rate affects the work-versus-leisure decision in two ways:

1. There is a *substitution effect* as the increased wage rate raises the opportunity cost of leisure. By itself, the substitution effect gives an incentive to work more in order to enjoy the higher standard of living that comes with increased income.

2. A higher wage rate also has an *income effect*. By itself, the income effect tends to reduce the number of hours worked. The reason for this is that leisure is a normal good—one people want more of as their incomes rise. Other things being equal, then, people (at least on average) seek shorter working hours and longer vacations as their incomes rise.

Figure 13.4 shows that the net effect of an increase in the wage rate depends on the relative strength of the substitution and income effects. At very low wages, the substitution effect tends to predominate. That means the quantity of labor supplied by any one worker at first increases as the wage rises. As it rises still more, though, the income effect grows stronger. Because most people treat leisure as a normal good, after they reach some income threshold (which varies from one person to another), they begin to "spend" part of any further wage increases by taking more time off from work. That pattern of behavior gives the labor supply curve for any one worker the backward-bending shape like the one in the figure. Over the positively sloped low-wage section, the substitution effect of wage changes is stronger; over the negatively sloped high-wage section, the income effect prevails.

FIGURE 13.4   THE LABOR SUPPLY CURVE FOR ONE WORKER

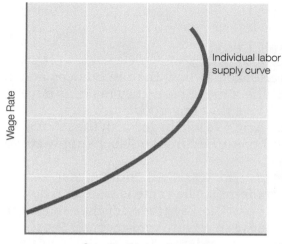

The substitution effect of a higher wage tends to increase the amount of work that a person is willing to do, because the extra income compensates for time taken away from leisure pursuits. At the same time, the income effect of a higher wage allows a person to take more time off from work and still enjoy a high standard of living. Taken together, the two effects tend to give the individual labor supply curve a backward-bending shape like this one.

Market Labor Supply Curves   Although the labor supply curves for any one worker may bend backward, the same need not be true of the market supply curve for any given type of labor. Consider, for example, the supply of electrical engineers in New York, of clerical workers in Chicago, or of farm laborers in Texas. Beyond some point, any one engineer, clerical worker, or laborer might respond to a wage increase by cutting back on the number of hours worked. For the market as a whole, however, that tendency would be more than offset by the entry of new workers from other occupations or areas. Other things being equal, if the wage rate for electrical engineers in New York rose, more engineering students would take up that specialty and more engineers would move to New York from Los Angeles. If the wage rate for clerical workers in Chicago rose, more people would switch to office work instead of, say, waiting tables. If the wage rate for farm laborers in Texas rose, people in that line of work would move to Texas from Arizona, Florida, and Mexico. As a result, for any given type of labor at any one time and place, the supply curve will usually have a positive slope throughout its range, even though the individual labor supply curves that underlie it may be backward bending.

The Equilibrium Wage in a Competitive Market

Once we have both supply and demand curves, determining the equilibrium wage rate for a competitive labor market is easy. Figure 13.5 shows hypothetical supply and demand curves for the market for clerical workers in Chicago. It assumes that many workers compete for jobs and a many employers compete for workers; thus everyone is a price taker on both sides of the market.

FIGURE 13.5   THE EQUILIBRIUM WAGE IN A COMPETITIVE LABOR MARKET

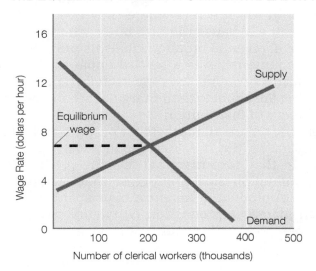

When both employers and workers are price takers in a labor market, the equilibrium wage occurs where the supply and demand curves intersect. Here the equilibrium wage rate is $7 an hour, and the equilibrium quantity of labor is 200,000 workers.

The equilibrium wage for this market is $7 an hour, with two hundred thousand workers employed. If the wage rate were lower, there would be a shortage of clerical workers. Some firms, unable to fill all their job openings, would offer premium wages to workers from other occupations or regions. Those offers would drive up the equilibrium wage. At any wage above $7 an hour, there would be a labor surplus. Some people seeking clerical jobs at the hoped-for high wage would not be able to find them. After a while, some job seekers would offer to work for less, pushing the wage rate down toward equilibrium. Others would give up and move into other occupations or regions, reducing the initial surplus.

In a labor market like this one where both employers and employees are price takers, the equilibrium wage rate equals the marginal revenue product of labor. In the special case in which all employers are price takers in the market where they sell their output as well as in the market where they purchase inputs, the equilibrium wage rate also equals the value of marginal product.

The Marginal Productivity Theory of Distribution

Marginal productivity theory of distribution

A theory of income distribution in which each input of production receives a payment equal to its marginal revenue product

Supply and demand determine how much each worker earns and how much labor firms will use in making each product. When employers are price takers in the markets where they buy inputs, their desire to maximize profit will cause them to hire each input up to the point where its marginal revenue product equals its price. In that case, each unit of each resource receives a reward equal to the contribution it makes to the firm's revenue. Economists call the idea that resources earn rewards that are equal to their marginal productivity the **marginal productivity theory of distribution**.

In an economy where all markets for outputs as well as inputs are perfectly competitive, the marginal productivity theory applies even more directly. In that case marginal revenue product equals output price times marginal physical product, so that each input receives its value of marginal product. If an extra hour spent pulling weeds in a cabbage patch increases production by twenty pounds and cabbage sells for $.50 per pound, the equilibrium wage rate must be $10 an hour—no more, no less.

The marginal productivity theory of distribution, as we have presented it, is a statement about how markets work. Some people find the principle attractive in another way, as well—as a matter of fairness. Under the marginal productivity theory, the reward of every worker is exactly equal to that worker's contribution to the productive process. If a worker or other resource owner contributes one more unit of input to the market, they will earn an income just equal to the resulting increase in the value of output. In that sense, the marginal productivity theory can be interpreted as a restatement, in the language of economic theory, of the old idea of "from each according to ability, to each according to work."

Monopsony

Not every input market meets the conditions for the marginal productivity theory of distribution. In particular, some firms are price searchers, not price takers, in their input markets. In labor markets, there may be only one or a few employers in a particular location or for a particular skill. Even when there are many employers, they may differ in terms of the characteristics other than wages. Some people might work for Acme because it is close to their neighborhood; some might prefer Zeus Company because the managers there are friendlier; and so on. In either case, when there are only a few employers or when employers differ in their attractiveness to workers, they cannot hire unlimited numbers of workers at a constant wage. If so, they will not be price takers and their labor supply curves will not be horizontal.

The extreme case, in which a single employer accounts for 100 percent of the demand in a resource market, is termed **monopsony**. This term, like monopoly, comes from Greek roots. *Monopsony* means "one buyer" just as *monopoly* means "one seller." In principle, we could also introduce the terms *oligopsony* (a few buyers) and *monopsonistic competition* (many buyers that are not alike). In practice, though, most economists use the term monopsony for all markets where buyers are price searchers.

Monopsony

A situation in which there is only a single buyer in a market; more generally, any situation in which a firm is a price searcher in a market in which it is a buyer

In a monopsony labor market, the wage is not a given. Instead, the employer faces a range of wage-quantity combinations that lie along a positively sloped labor supply curve. For example, compare the situation of a retail store in Los Angeles that wants to hire a few security guards with the situation of the U.S. government, which wants to hire soldiers for the army. The retail store is a price taker, or close to it, in the market for security guards. If the going wage for such guards is, say, $40,000 a year, it can call an agency or advertise online; and it will very likely get more applicants than it

The U.S. government is the only employer for soldiers; in contrast, there are many employers for private security guards.

needs to hire. In contrast, the U.S. government, as the employer of volunteer soldiers, is not a price taker. The number of soldiers the army can recruit depends, among other things, on the level of military pay. If the government wants to increase the number of soldiers it recruits, it can offer better pay, benefits, and enlistment bonuses.

The Marginal Resource Cost Curve

In order to find the point of equilibrium in a monopsonistic market, we need to change the way we treat marginal resource cost. Figure 13.6 shows we can do this for a firm that is a monopsonist in its local labor market—for example, a large insurance company that employs most of the clerical workers in a small town.

FIGURE 13.6 MARGINAL RESOURCE COST UNDER MONOPSONY

(a)

Quantity of Labor Supplied (Number of Workers) (1)	Wage Rate (Dollars per Hour) (2)	Total Resource Cost (Dollars per Hour) (3)	Marginal Resource Cost (Dollars per Hour) (4)
1	$ 3.02	$ 3.02	
			$ 3.06
2	3.04	6.08	
			3.10
3	3.06	9.18	
150	6.00	900.00	
			9.02
151	6.02	909.02	
			9.06
152	6.04	918.08	
200	7.00	1,400.00	
			11.02
201	7.02	1,411.02	
			11.06
203	7.04	1,422.08	

(b)

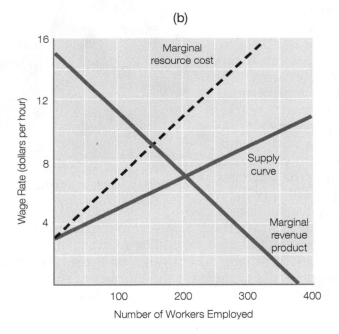

Under monopsony, marginal resource cost is greater than the price of the input. For example, suppose this employer wants to increase the quantity of labor it hires from 150 to 151 workers. To do so, it needs to raise the wage rate from $6 to $6.02 not just for the 151st employee but for all the previous 150 as well. Marginal resource cost in this range is $9.02 rather than $6.02 an hour. Profit is at a maximum where the marginal revenue product curve intersects the marginal resource cost curve (150 workers).

The labor supply curve in Figure 13.6 shows that each time employers raise the wage by two cents per hour, they attract one more worker to the market. For example, if the firm wants to hire 150 workers, it needs to pay $6.00 per hour. If it wants to hire 151, it has to raise the wage to $6.02 an hour. Normally, the increased wage will apply not just to the last worker hired but also to all workers. (We will consider the special case of wage discrimination, where an employer pays different wages to different workers for doing the same work in Chapter 16). If that is the case, moving from 150 to 151 workers raises total labor cost from $900 per hour to $909.02 per hour, which means a marginal resource cost of $9.02 per hour. Of that, $6.02 is the wage paid to the 151st worker, and $3 is the 2 cents per hour added to the pay of the 150 workers who were already on the job. The same principle applies to all points on the labor supply curve. Whatever the chosen starting point, the monopsonist's marginal resource cost is greater than the wage rate.

Figure 13.6 shows the relationship between labor supply and marginal resource cost both as a table, Part (a), and a graph, Part (b). Notice that the graph of the marginal resource cost curve lies above the supply curve at every point. When the supply curve is a straight line, as it is in this example, a simple rule of thumb makes it easy to draw the marginal resource cost curve: The horizontal distance from the vertical axis to the marginal resource cost curve is, at every wage rate, exactly half the distance from the vertical axis to the supply curve.

Monopsony Profit Maximization

Earlier we saw that for a competitive labor market, a firm maximizes profit at the quantity of labor for which marginal resource cost equals marginal revenue product. The same is true for a monopsonist. The only difference is that for an employer that is a price taker in the labor market, marginal resource cost equals the wage rate, while for a monopsonist the marginal resource cost is higher than the wage rate. In Figure 13.6, the monopsonist's marginal resource cost curve intersects that marginal revenue product curve at 150 units of labor. The supply curve shows that the wage rate must be $6 an hour to attract that number of workers.

Notice that for a monopsony, the equilibrium wage rate is lower than both the marginal resource cost and the marginal revenue product of labor. In our example, the equilibrium wage rate is $6 an hour (which is equal to the height of the labor supply curve), although the marginal revenue product is $9 an hour at the point at which the marginal revenue product and marginal resource cost curves intersect. Despite the gap between the wage rate and the marginal revenue product, adding to the amount of labor hired would not raise revenue enough to offset higher labor costs. The reason is that the cost of hiring another worker is not just the $6.02 an hour received by the 151st worker; instead, it is that sum plus the extra $.02 per hour that all 150 previously hired workers receive. The complete marginal resource cost for the 151st worker thus is $6.02 + $3.00, or $9.02 an hour, which is higher than that worker's marginal revenue product.

13.3 Why Wage Rates Differ

Pay differs widely, not just among occupations, but also for workers within a given labor market. This section turns to some extensions of marginal productivity theory that help explain why wage rates differ.

Non-Wage Job Characteristics

One reason wage rates differ is that pay alone is not the only thing that makes a job more or less attractive. Jobs also differ in terms of safety, prestige, comfort, and challenge. Other things being equal, workers are willing to supply their services at lower wages to employers that offer jobs with more attractive non-wage characteristics. Knowing that, many employers try to make the jobs they offer safe, attractive, and challenging. Employers who must attract workers to jobs that are inherently risky and uncomfortable often have to pay higher wages.

However, the need to pay more to attract workers to jobs with less desirable non-wage characteristics applies only when *other things are equal*. In practice, it turns out that many tedious, unpleasant, and even dangerous jobs pay low wages, while the high-salaried occupants of the executive suite work in air-conditioned comfort and eat lunches served on fine china. How can we explain this seeming paradox in terms of labor market theory?

Economists see nothing strange in the contrast between the heat and noise of the factory floor and the cool calm of the executive suite. They simply interpret the observed pattern as evidence that comfort on the job is a *normal good*. As people's incomes rise, they want more comfort. Employers must consider that fact when offering wages and working conditions to various employees.

Comfort on the job is a "normal good," so as people's incomes rise they want more comfort.

Suppose that a firm offered its warehouse workers a cut in pay from $7 an hour to $5 an hour ($2,000 a year) in return for replacing the vinyl tile in the warehouse coffee room with wool carpet and replacing the cheap posters on the wall with original artwork. Would it be surprising if they turned down the offer? Suppose the same firm offered its president a raise from $500,000 a year to $502,000 a year, in return for ripping out the carpet in the executive office and replacing its oil paintings with cheap posters? Would it be surprising if the president turned down the offer?

This principle applies on an international scale, as well. Major U.S. multinationals with plants in developing countries are often local leaders in terms of the wages and working conditions they offer. Their factories are often cleaner, better lit, and safer than those of their small, local competitors are. Yet, when critics compare the overseas plants of U.S. firms with factories in the United States, they often denounce them as "sweatshops." What is the truth? Are multinational corporations ruthlessly exploiting foreign workers? Or are those workers, who may be just making the first steps out of rural poverty, less willing to trade off hard cash wages for improvements in workplace amenities? There may be no simple answer to such questions.

Human Capital

Differences in the non-wage characteristics of jobs do not fully explain why wages differ. Ability also counts. If the supply of people with the abilities needed for the job of corporate president were as abundant as the supply of those with abilities needed for the job of warehouse worker, we would not expect such a big difference in pay to the two occupations.

Some people are born with special abilities, or at least with unusual potential. The enormous salaries of professional ballplayers, first-rate opera singers, and other superstars are a direct result of the scarcity of those abilities. The abilities people are born with are only part of the story, however. Training and education are at least as important as innate ability for most occupations, from lawyers and accountants to glassblowers and hairdressers.

Economists view the costs of training and education as a form of investment. Taking courses to become an accountant, in this view, is much like buying a dump truck in order to go into the gravel-hauling business. In both cases, someone makes an expenditure now to acquire something that will increase future earning power. The main difference is that the dump truck operator acquires capital in the form of a machine, whereas the accountant acquires **human capital**—capital in the form of learned abilities.

First rate opera singers and other superstars draw enormous salaries due to the scarcity of people with those abilities.

According to human-capital theory, the earnings of each occupation that requires special training must be high enough to make up for the opportunity cost of getting the training. For example, suppose you go to college to get a degree in accounting. Your opportunity costs include both out-of-pocket costs like tuition and books and also the income you could have earned if you spent those college years working at a job that did not require a college degree. Other things being equal, we expect occupations that require longer or more expensive training to pay more than those that require less. We would expect doctors to earn more than lawyers, lawyers to earn more than hairdressers, and so on—and that is in fact the case.[1]

Of course, the non-wage characteristics of jobs play a role in people's willingness to invest in various kinds of human capital. If some occupations are more exciting or prestigious than others, people will take them up even if the pay alone is not enough to justify the investment in training. For example, the training required to become a

Human capital

Capital in the form of abilities acquired through formal training or education or through on-the-job experience

ballet dancer may be as long and rigorous as that needed to become an orthodontist, but dancers, on the average, earn less than orthodontists do. The difference in pay presumably has something to do with the value the dancers place on the opportunity for artistic expression.

Formal education is not the only way to invest in human capital. On-the-job training is also important. In total, employers probably spend as much for on-the-job training as people spend on formal education at all levels. Both employers and employees benefit from on-the-job investment in human capital. Employers benefit from the ability to fine-tune the skills of their work forces to their investments in plant and equipment. At the same time, on the job training benefits workers not just through promotions and higher pay but also because it opens opportunities for more interesting and rewarding work.

Efficiency Wage Theory

Human-capital theory suggests that being able to do a job better will result in higher pay. Another theory suggests that the opposite may also be true—higher pay may lead to better on-the-job performance. Economists call this reverse linkage from higher pay to better performance **efficiency wage theory**.

Efficiency wage theory

The theory that higher wages can raise productivity by enough to increase profit

Efficiency wage theory helps us understand a puzzle that almost everyone has encountered at one time or another. Why do many firms pay a wage that is higher than needed to attract workers with minimum qualifications? Why is it that when you apply for an attractive job, it so often turns out that the employer has hundreds of applications on file and only a few openings? According to the simple supply-and-demand model, the profit-maximizing strategy for such a firm would be to lower the wage rate until the backlog of applicants falls to just the number needed to cover turnover. Yet that is often not what employers do.

There are several reasons why a higher wage may stimulate productivity. Better pay can improve morale, lower absenteeism, and decrease job turnover. Also, workers at high-wage firms will be less willing to risk losing their jobs because of poor performance, so they may work to the best of their abilities with less supervision.

The idea of paying extra to encourage quality work and cut turnover is far from new. In 1914, Henry Ford used efficiency wages when he cut turnover and increased productivity by raising his workers' pay to the unheard of level of $5 a day. *Applying Economic Ideas* 13.1 gives a modern example.

Taking all things together, we see that there are many reasons why wage rates differ. The principles of labor markets covered in this chapter will provide useful background for even broader questions that we will discuss in Chapters 15 and 16, which cover problems of labor market policy, discrimination, income distribution, and poverty.

Henry Ford used efficiency wages to reduce worker turnover and increase productivity.

Applying Economic Ideas 13.1

Costco versus Sam's Club in the Labor Market

Costco versus Sam's Club is one of the hottest rivalries in U.S. retail trade. Both companies follow the philosophy of "pile 'em high and sell 'em cheap." Both feature huge stores with rock bottom prices for a wide range of merchandise, much of it top-of-the-line brand names.

However, in the labor market, where they compete for workers, the two companies take different approaches. Costco pays its full-time U.S. employees about 50 percent more, on average, than Sam's Club, a division of Wal-Mart. New Costco employees receive a wage only slightly higher than that at Sam's Club, but they are able to work their way up the pay scale faster—and they stay longer, adding to the difference in average pay.

Benefits as well as wages differ at the two companies. According to the *Wall Street Journal*, 82 percent of Costco's employees have health insurance, compared with 44 percent for Wal-Mart. Costco pays 92 percent of insured workers' premiums, compared to 66 percent at Wal-Mart. Costco also contributes generously to its employees' 401(k) plans.

Costco also has a different attitude toward labor unions. Wal-Mart resists unionization vigorously. Costco does not actively encourage unionization, but it accepts workers' rights to unionize if they

Sam's Club warehouse

Costco Wholesale store

think doing so will improve their lot. About 20 percent of Costco's U.S. employees are unionized, many of them represented by the Teamsters.

The result of these differences in policy is a dramatic difference in employee loyalty. According to the *Financial Times*, Costco has an annual labor turnover of just 17 percent. Wal-Mart's is near the industry average of 44 percent.

"Paying good wages is not in opposition to good productivity," says Costco Chief Executive and President, Jim Sinegal, speaking to a reporter from *Business Week*. "If you hire good people, give them good jobs, and pay them good wages, generally something good is going to happen."

Sources: "James Sinegal, Costco: The Bargain Hunter," Business Week Sept. 23, 2002; "Costco's Dilemma: Is Treating Employees Well Unacceptable for a Public Corporation?" Wall Street Journal, March 26, 2004; "Pile High, Sell Cheap, and Pay Well," Financial Times, July 11, 2005; David Worrell, "Higher Salaries: Costco's Secret Weapon," AllBusiness.com, Dec. 6, 2011 (http://www.allbusiness.com/staffing-hr/16745820-1.html)

13.4 Capital and Interest

Capital, in the broadest sense, refers to all means of production that people make. Some capital takes discrete, tangible forms, such as tractors for a farm or excavators for a mining company. Improvements to land are another form of capital. For a farm, that might mean improved drainage; for a mining company, that might mean access roads. In addition, as we saw in the previous section, skills that an agronomist or mining engineer acquires through education or on the job are forms of human capital. In this section, we look at some features that all forms of capital share.

Capital and Roundabout Production

A trade-off between the present and the future is a fundamental feature of all forms of capital. Accumulating capital requires bearing opportunity costs now in order to reap a return later. Suppose, for example, that you want to catch fish from a lake. You might be able to catch a few fish by wading in and grabbing them with your bare hands. That way you would have some fish today, although not many. Instead, you could spend a day weaving string into a net and cutting a branch to use as a handle. You would go hungry today, but tomorrow you would be able to catch lots of fish, many more than with your bare hands. By taking time to make the net, you would be paying an opportunity cost in the form of forgone meals in order to eat more in the future.

The example of the fishing net shows why economists refer to production using capital as *roundabout* production. It is easy to find other examples. Making cars in an automated factory uses more capital than making them one by one using hand tools. Lots of labor and other resources go into building the factory—but once it is finished, a given number of workers can produce more cars at a lower cost. Digging a ditch to lead water to a field is a roundabout method of irrigation compared with carrying water to the field in buckets. Writing a specialized computer program to calculate a company's payroll is a roundabout method compared with working out the numbers each week with an all-purpose spreadsheet.

The Rate of Return on Capital

We can analyze the use of capital by using a variant on the marginal product technique we used for labor resources. Because we use the capital that we create today, and typically employ it over a long period in the future, we usually express its marginal product as a percentage, the **rate of return on capital**. For example, if we say that the rate of return on capital in a certain application is 10 percent per year, we mean that adding one dollar to the capital stock will increase output by about $.10 each year in the future. The law of diminishing returns causes the marginal physical product of capital to decrease as more

Rate of return on capital

The marginal product of capital expressed as an annual percentage rate capital is used, holding other inputs constant. As a result, the demand curve for capital, like the demand curves for other resources, has a negative slope.

Next we turn to the supply curve of capital, which we can explain in terms of the principle of diminishing marginal utility. To acquire more capital, we must forego more present goods. Reducing the quantity of goods available today raises their marginal utility. At the same time, acquiring more capital makes future goods more abundant, so their marginal utility falls. As a result, the marginal resource cost, or opportunity cost, of capital, which is the ratio of the marginal utility of present goods forgone to the marginal utility of future goods gained, increases as the quantity of capital invested increases. We can illustrate this principle with our fishing example. Spending more hours on net building means catching fewer fish today. As the quantity of fish available today falls, we become more reluctant to spend more time on the net today in return for a larger feast tomorrow. The rising marginal opportunity cost of capital gives a positively slope to the supply curve.

Time Preference

Other things being equal, people prefer goods now to goods in the future, a tendency that we call **time preference**. Time preference affects much of what we do throughout our lives. As young children, we "can't wait" to open our birthday presents; without time preference, we would attach no more utility to a new bicycle today than to a new bicycle next week. As, teenagers we "can't wait" to get a driver's license; as grandparents we "can't wait" for our first chance to hold a new grandchild.

Time preference does not mean it is never worth waiting, however, because "other things" are not always equal. Although we do not want to postpone something now to get something equally good later, we may be willing to put off something good now for something even better later. To return to our earlier fishing example, suppose you would be willing to forgo having ten fish today in order to have eleven fish tomorrow. In that case, your *rate of time preference* would be 10 percent per day.

If we express both time preference and the marginal productivity of capital in percentage terms, a simple relationship emerges: In an equilibrium state where the optimal quantity of capital is employed, the rate of return on capital and the rate of time preference will be equal.

Time preference

The tendency to prefer goods now to goods in the future, other things being equal

Interest and the Market for Loanable Funds

Up to now, we have worked in terms of physical units. The next step is to introduce money, both as a means of payment for goods and services and as a store of value that can be used to buy things later. Money makes possible another class of transactions involving time: borrowing and lending.

Borrowing and lending become attractive whenever two people's rates of time preferences differ. For example, suppose my rate of time preferences is higher than yours; that is, I place a higher value on enjoying things now. I will be willing to borrow from you at any interest rate that is lower than my rate of time preference. You will be willing to lend to me at any interest rate that is higher than your rate of time preference. Here are some other examples:

- Borrowing and lending may be motivated purely by impatience. For example, Bill is so eager to go skiing this year that he is willing to borrow the funds, with interest, from Jane. Jane, who is less impatient, thinks the interest she will earn is enough to make it worth putting off skiing until next year.

- People may borrow and lend to smooth out consumption over time. Al, who is just entering the job market, borrows to buy a car. Jose, who has already worked for several years, is saving for retirement. Jose will have even more money after he retires if he lends part of his savings to Al at a good rate of interest.

- One person sees better opportunities to use capital than another. Jill thinks that buying a greenhouse in order to start a cut-flower business will produce a rate of return of at least 20 percent. Mike thinks investing to expand his cookie store would yield a return of only 5 percent. That means it would be worthwhile for Mike to lend funds to Jill, rather than to invest in his own business, at any interest rate over 5 percent; and it would be worthwhile for Jill to borrow, rather than to forgo the business opportunity, at any interest rate less than 20 percent.

Loanable funds market

A general term for the set of institutions that facilitate borrowing and lending

Whatever the motives, we call the set of institutions that facilitate borrowing and lending the **loanable funds market**. Figure 13.7 shows that market. The negative slope of the demand curve indicates that, other things being equal, people will borrow more if the interest rate is lower. The positive slope of the supply curve indicates that they will lend more if the interest rate is higher. The intersection of the supply and demand curves determines the equilibrium interest rate. Behind those curves, in turn, stand the rate of return on capital and the rate of time preference, which will be equal at the margin when the loanable funds market is in equilibrium.

13.5 Markets for Natural Resources

We turn now from markets for capital to markets for natural resources. Natural resources come from the land, the sea, even the air, but economists traditionally focus on land. Not all land is alike. Features like location, climate, and mineral deposits make any given piece of land more suited to some activities than others. Some land is good for growing corn, some for building houses, some is rich with ores or energy, and still other land is best for wildlife habitat.

FIGURE 13.7   THE MARKET FOR LOANABLE FUNDS

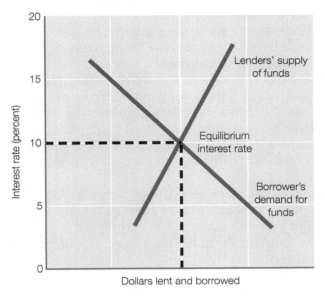

The demand curve for loanable funds shows that, other things being equal, people will borrow more as the interest rate falls. The supply curve for loanable funds shows that they will be more willing to make loans at higher rates of interest. The intersection of the two curves determines the equilibrium interest rate.

Pure Economic Rent

In an earlier chapter, we defined *economic rent* as any income that a factor of production receives in excess of its opportunity cost. The theory of rent goes back to the days of the classical economists two centuries ago, who saw the supply of land as fixed by nature. In economic terms, that means the supply of land is perfectly inelastic. They called the income earned by a factor of production whose supply is fixed a **pure economic rent**.

We can express the market price paid for land either in terms of an annual rental payment, or when the user buys land outright rather than renting it, a purchase price. There is a simple relationship between the value of a piece of land expressed as an annual rent and its selling price: The selling price of a piece of land is equal to the **capitalized value of its rent**, that is, the present value of all future rents the land is expected to earn.[2]

Differential Rent

The theory of pure economic rent deals with land as an abstraction. It implicitly assumes that all land is alike and that it is interchangeable in

Pure economic rent

The income earned by any resource whose supply is perfectly inelastic with respect to its price

Capitalized value of a rent

The present value of all future rents that a piece of land or other resource is expected to earn

Differential rent

The rents earned by
superior units of a resource
in a situation where units
of a resource differ in
productivity

all uses. In practice, land differs in terms of its fertility, its climate, and its location advantages. Land in Kansas has a comparative advantage in producing wheat, land in Cuba for producing sugar cane, and land in France's Rhone valley for growing wine grapes. For that reason, as economists since David Ricardo have recognized, not all land earns the same rent in a competitive market.

Consider Figure 13.8, which shows the marginal cost and average total cost of producing wheat on three different farms with different qualities of land. The costs include all outlays for labor, machinery, fertilizer, and other inputs except the land itself. At a market price of $5 per bushel, Farm A will produce 1,200 bushels per year, Farm B will produce 1,000 bushels per year, and Farm C will not find it worthwhile to grow wheat at all.

Given that market price and those outputs, Farm A receives total revenue of $5 per bushel and incurs average total costs of $3 per bushel. The $2 excess of revenue over cost is associated with the superior productivity of the land on Farm A. It is a special example of rent that we call **differential rent**.

At a market price of $5 a bushel for wheat, Farm B just breaks even on its total costs and earns no differential rent. What if the market price were to rise to $7 per bushel? In that case, Farm C would find it worthwhile to enter the market. Farm B would step up its output to 1,200 bushels per year and earn a differential rent equal to a little under $2 per bushel, and Farm A would increase its output to 1,400 bushels, causing its differential rent to rise to $3.50 per bushel.

Land is not the only factor of production that earns differential rents. Differential rent can arise in the case of any input that is not homogeneous. For example, earlier in the chapter, we noted that lawyers earn more on the average than truck drivers because of greater investment in human capital. Strictly speaking, that reasoning applies only to lawyers without special aptitudes. Some lawyers have not only the needed education but also a special ability to bewitch jurors and charm judges, allowing those lawyers to earn differential rents over and above the opportunity costs of acquiring their education.

Inframarginal Rents

Differential rents arise in markets where some units of a resource are more productive than others. Another kind of rent occurs in markets where units are equally productive but differ in terms of the willingness with which people supply them.

Consider Figure 13.9, which shows hypothetical supply and demand curves for the market for nurses. For the sake of discussion, assume that all nurses, once they have the needed training, are equally productive. However, not everyone is equally willing to be a nurse. In the figure, the first few people would be willing to enter the profession at a wage rate as low as $5 per hour. An increase to $7.50 per hour would attract five hundred thousand people to the profession, and further increases would draw in even more, as is shown by the supply curve. Given the demand curve, the equilibrium wage rate is $10 per hour, enough to attract 1 million people to the profession.

FIGURE 13.8   DIFFERENTIAL RENT

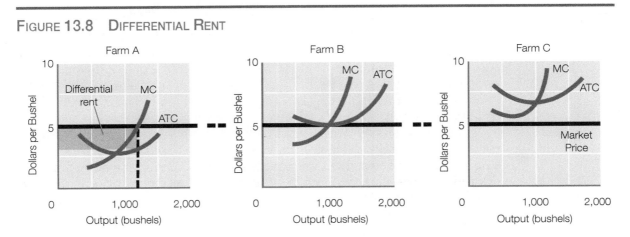

The theory of pure economic rent implicitly assumes that all land is alike. In practice, different pieces of land have different productivity. Those differences will affect rents. This figure shows marginal and average total cost curves for three wheat farms that differ only in terms of the quality of their land. Given a market price of $5 a bushel for wheat, Farm A earns a differential rent of $2 per bushel, equal to the difference between the cost of production on its highly productive land and the market rental on land. Farm B just breaks even at $5 per bushel and earns no economic rent, and Farm C does not produce at that price. If the price rose to $7, Farm C would enter the market, Farm B would begin to earn a differential rent, and Farm A would earn an even larger differential rent.

Why is it that some people are willing to enter the nursing profession at a lower wage than others? Like other economic choices, the answer depends in part on their objectives and constraints. Some people may be willing to enter the nursing profession at a low wage because they like the flexible hours and opportunities to serve others. People who don't like those aspects of nursing will do the job only for a higher wage. People also face different constraints, especially with regard to other job opportunities. The better their opportunities in other lines of work, the higher the wage they require to enter nursing.

Whether we view the matter in terms of objectives or constraints, or both together, the positive slope of the supply curve reflects the differing opportunity costs that people face. In a competitive labor market, all but the marginal worker—the one who is just attracted to the profession at the equilibrium wage—are paid more than their opportunity costs. Economists say they earn **inframarginal rents** equal to the difference between the equilibrium wage and the minimum they would accept rather than pursue other opportunities.

Inframarginal rents

The difference between the payment made to a unit of resource and the minimum needed to attract it to the use in question

FIGURE 13.9 INFRAMARGINAL RENT

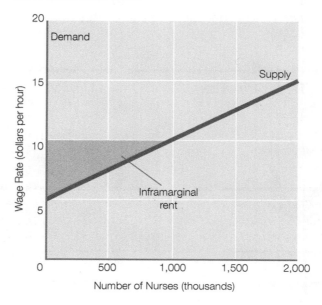

In some markets, units of a resource are equally productive but differ in terms of the willingness with which people supply them. This figure shows supply and demand curves for nurses. Some people would be willing to work as a nurse for as little as $5 per hour. As the supply curve shows, increasingly higher wage rates will draw more people into the market. At the equilibrium wage rate of $10 per hour, only the marginal nurse receives just the wage needed to work in this market. The others earn an inframarginal rent equal to the difference between the equilibrium wage rate and the minimum they would accept rather than pursue other alternatives.

Inframarginal rents help us understand why people are often so strongly attached to the job they currently hold that they see the loss of a job as a trauma comparable to a hurricane, a divorce, or a major illness. Why? For a person "on the margin," whose job pays just enough keep him or her in a given line of work rather than the next best, losing a job would be no big deal. The next-best job would be almost as good. But most workers in any given occupation are not at the margin. They hold jobs that pay significant inframarginal rents. If they have to change jobs, those rents, whether they take the form of a high wage or non-wage job satisfaction, will be lost.

Summary

1. **What determines the demand for productive inputs?** For a firm that is a price taker in its output market, the *marginal revenue product* of any input is equal to the input's *value of marginal product*—that is, marginal physical product times the product's price. For a firm that is a price searcher in the output market, it is equal to marginal physical product multiplied by the marginal revenue and thus is less than the value of marginal product. In both cases, the firm makes the maximum profit by buying each input up to the point where marginal revenue product equals *marginal resource cost*. The marginal revenue product curve is the resource demand curve for any firm that is a price taker in its input market. The demand for a resource is derived from the demand for the goods it is used to produce.

2. **What determines the supply curve for labor?** Labor supply curves depend on the trade-off that people make between leisure and income. The curve for an individual worker, and perhaps for the economy as a whole, may bend backward above a certain wage rate. However, the supply curve for a single labor market has a positive slope throughout its length.

3. **What are the characteristics of equilibrium in a competitive labor market?** In a labor market where employers are price takers, the equilibrium wage rate will be equal to the marginal revenue product of labor, a principle that economists call the *marginal productivity theory of distribution*. If employers are price takers in the output market, the equilibrium wage rate also will be equal to the value of the marginal product.

4. **What are the characteristics of labor market equilibrium with only one or a few employers?** A *monopsony* market is one in which firms are price searchers as buyers of inputs. The marginal resource cost curve for such a firm lies above the supply curve for labor. The equilibrium input is established at the intersection of the marginal resource cost curve and the marginal revenue product curve. In a monopsony, the equilibrium wage is below the marginal revenue product.

(Continues)

5. **Why are wages not the same for all labor markets and for all workers within a labor market?** Wages differ among markets and workers for several reasons. Differences in the non-wage characteristics of jobs or in the *human capital* possessed by individuals are sometimes the cause. According to *efficiency wage theory*, firms sometimes pay more than the minimum wage needed to attract workers because doing so results in higher productivity.

6. **What determines the interest rate in loanable funds markets?** The use of capital involves a trade-off between the present and the future. Reducing consumption now makes it possible to accumulate capital, which will increase output in the future. We call the marginal product of capital, expressed in percentage terms per unit of time, the *rate of return on capital*. In equilibrium, the rate of return on capital just offsets the *time preference*—the tendency to prefer goods now to goods in the future. People differ in terms of their time preference and the investment opportunities they perceive. Their differing preferences and perceptions give rise to borrowing and lending in the loanable funds market. The equilibrium rate of interest depends on the rate of return on capital and the rate of time preference.

7. **How do supply and demand determine rents for land and other resources?** *Pure economic rent* is the income earned by any factor of production whose supply is completely inelastic. The *capitalized value of a rent* determines the market price of land. Other factors, whose supply is perfectly inelastic, such as the special talents of athletes or performing artists, can also earn rents. Where various units of a factor differ in terms of productivity, the more productive units earn *differential rents*. Where they differ in terms of the willingness with which people supply them, units that people would willingly supply below the equilibrium price earn *inframarginal rents*.

Key Terms	**Page #**
Capitalized value of a rent	401
Derived demand	378
Differential rent	402
Efficiency wage theory	396
Human capital	395
Inframarginal rents	403
Loanable funds market	400
Marginal productivity theory of distribution	390
Marginal resource cost	382
Marginal revenue product	380
Monopsony	391
Pure economic rent	401
Rate of return on capital	398
Time preference	399
Value of marginal product	380

Problems and Topics for Discussion

1. **Outsourcing**   Firms sometimes "outsource" their labor needs by hiring workers in other countries where wages are lower. Suppose the opening of trade with some previously closed foreign economy creates new outsourcing opportunities for U.S. firms. How would the outsourcing affect the U.S. labor market? Illustrate your answer with a supply and demand diagram.

2. **Households as buyers in resource markets**   This chapter focuses on resource markets where the buyers are firms. When are households direct buyers of labor or other factors of production? What would lie behind the demand curve for labor hired by households?

3. **A case of backward-bending labor demand**   In his historical novel *Chesapeake*, James Michener describes the unsuccessful efforts of early European colonists to run their plantations using hired Native American labor. In one episode in the novel, Michener describes the frustration of a planter who finds that an offer of higher wages does not keep Native American workers from quitting their jobs in the fields after a few weeks of work. Instead, the workers seem to quit sooner when they receive more pay. Does what you have learned in this chapter shed any light on this situation? Discuss.

4. **Monopsony and monopoly**   Is a monopsonist always a monopolist, and vice versa? Try to imagine a firm that is a monopsonist in its factor market but a perfect competitor in its product market. Then try to visualize a firm that is a monopolist but not a monopsonist.

5. **The relationship between "how" and "for whom"**   Discuss the following statement: "It is a good idea to let resource markets determine how things are produced; but the matter of for whom things are produced should be handled according to need, not according to supply and demand." Is it possible to separate the "how" and "for whom" functions of resource markets?

6. **Trends in the pay of men and women**   The wage gap between men and women has narrowed somewhat in recent years and is likely to narrow further. Do you think the narrowing of the wage gap has anything to do with the facts that (a) women are more than proportionately represented in service occupations and (b) demand for services is growing faster than demand for goods? Discuss this, using the theory of derived demand.

7. **Wages and working conditions in the newly industrialized countries**   Evaluate the following statement: "We probably can't do much about the fact that workers in Bangladesh, Vietnam, and other newly industrialized countries are paid less than U.S. workers doing similar jobs. However, we should not tolerate the fact that they work under conditions that fall far short of U.S. standards for health, safety, comfort, and hours of work. We should either insist on better working conditions or stop importing goods made by workers who are exploited in that way." How would this proposal affect workers in the newly industrialized countries (a) if the threat to cut off trade worked and labor conditions in those countries were brought up to U.S. standards, and (b) if the threat failed and trade with the countries in question were cut off?

8. **Two ways to make bricks**   Consider two ways to make bricks. One is to form them by hand out of clay scooped from the ground and then bake them over an open fire. Using that method, you can make 100 bricks a month. Another way is to use a whole month's output of bricks to build a kiln for baking the bricks. When the kiln is complete, the hotter fire and lower fuel use make it possible to make 120 bricks per month with the same labor that previously made 100. Is the kiln an example of capital? Why or why not? If so, what is the rate of return on the investment in the kiln, stated as a percent per month? Under what rate of time preference would it be worth your while to build the kiln?

Case for Discussion:

Kansas Ponders Bill to Let Illegal Immigrants Take Unfilled Jobs

The U.S. national unemployment rate soared during the recession that began in late 2007, and it was slow to fall again. By early 2012, the national rate was still over 8 percent, down just a little from its peak of 10 percent. Some states—including Arizona, Alabama, and Georgia—tried to counter high unemployment by cracking down on illegal immigrants, whom many politicians and labor leaders saw as unfairly taking jobs from U.S. citizens and legal residents.

In Kansas, things were different. The unemployment rate in parts of western Kansas was as low as 4 percent. Economists say that a rate as low as 4 percent is effectively full employment; it reflects no more than normal turnover as workers change jobs. Many Kansas employers—especially those in agriculture, meat packing, landscaping, road construction, and hospitality industries—faced severe labor shortages. To overcome the shortages, a coalition of employers came up with a bright idea: Make it easier—and legal—for firms to hire illegal immigrants.

States have limited control over immigration policy, which by and large is a prerogative of the federal government. Kansas's legislators who crafted HB 2603 thought they saw a loophole, however. The federal government doesn't have the resources it would need to deport all illegal immigrants, so it prioritizes deportations of illegal immigrants with criminal records. Why not pass a state law that allows employers to hire illegals without criminal records, and at the same time, have the state apply to the federal government, on their behalf, for permission to work?

Not everyone was pleased with the idea. One of them was Kansas Secretary of State Kris Kobach. Kobach, a former law professor, helped draft Arizona's strict immigration control law. He called HB 2603 an "amnesty" and maintained that it had fatal legal flaws.

That left Kansas Governor Ken Brownback in a dilemma. As a Republican, he knew his party was pushing a hard line on immigration at the national level. On the other hand, many of those backing HB 2603, including the Kansas Chamber of Commerce and farm groups, were also stalwart Republicans. Meanwhile, as conflicting political, legal, and economic forces played themselves out, some jobs in Kansas remained unfilled, despite the high unemployment rate.

Sources: "Kansas Immigration Hardliner Fights Plan to Allow Undocumented Workers," Fox News, Feb. 1, 2012 (http://latino.foxnews.com/latino/politics/2012/02/01/kansas-business-leaders-want-state-to-allow-undocumented-to-work/); and Mariano Castillo, "Kansas bill seeks to pair undocumented immigrants, jobs," CNN, Feb. 2, 2012 (http://www.cnn.com/2012/02/02/us/kansas-immigrant-jobs-bill/index.html).

Questions

1. Draw a diagram illustrating the market for landscape workers in western Kansas, showing a labor shortage as described in the case.

2. If there is no new legislation, do you think the shortage will continue indefinitely? Or do you think employers will eventually increase wages by enough to fill the jobs? Discuss both possibilities in terms of the theory of labor supply and demand.

3. If the legislation does succeed, what will happen to the market for landscape workers? Would it be best to represent the effect of the law in terms of a shift in the demand curve, a shift in the supply curve, or a combination of the two?

4. Speaking from your own knowledge of the labor market rather than from theoretical considerations, why do you think unemployed people from other parts of the country are reluctant to fill landscaping and road building jobs in Kansas, despite a lack of work closer to home? In your own opinion, taking economic, legal, and political aspects of the question into consideration, do you favor or oppose the Kansas law?

Endnotes

1. Human-capital theory implies that workers with more education tend to earn more than workers with less education because the knowledge they acquire makes them more productive on the job. This theory has been challenged by some economists, who think that the primary function of education is to help employers screen job candidates for certain desirable traits, such as intelligence and self-discipline, that are not themselves acquired through education.

2. The method of discounting, introduced in the Appendix to Chapter 6, provides a fuller understanding of the relationship between the purchase price of a piece of land and its annual rental value.

Chapter 14

Insurance, Information, *and* Uncertainty

After reading this chapter, you will understand:

1. How insurance helps protect people from the risks of life

2. Information problems of the insurance business

3. Why speculators willingly accept risk

4. The socially useful purposes served by speculation

5. How auctions work

Before reading this chapter, make sure you know the meaning of the following concepts:

1. Diminishing marginal utility

2. Perfect competition

3. Economics of nonrenewable resources

4. Transaction costs

5. Opportunism

Information is among the most valuable of all scarce resources. Economists have long recognized its importance. More than half a century ago, Friedrich Hayek argued that efficient use of information is the central economic problem facing society (see *Who Said It? Who Did It?* 14.1). Hayek concluded that we can trace the success of markets as an economic institution to the effectiveness of market prices as a way of creating and transmitting information.

Who Said It? Who Did It? **14.1**

Friedrich von Hayek on Markets and Information

Friedrich von Hayek, a recipient of the Nobel Memorial Prize in Economic Sciences, was a pioneer in monetary theory and made fundamental contributions to many other branches of economics. Born and educated in Vienna, he was a key contributor to the *Austrian school of economics*. With such books as *The Road to Serfdom* and *The Constitution of Liberty*, he also gained a reputation as a political philosopher.

A distinguishing feature of the Austrian school is its focus on the process through which markets adjust to change. In Hayek's view, the key to understanding how they do so lies in their role of markets as creators and transmitters of information. In 1945, he presented his views in a classic article, "The Use of Knowledge in Society."

Suppose, wrote Hayek, that a major new use arises for some resource, say tin. It may be in manufacturing, electronics, medicine—it does not matter. The exact nature of the new use does not matter, either. All the users of tin really need to know is that the opportunity cost of using tin has gone up—that is, some of the tin they used previously can now be used more profitably elsewhere—and, as a consequence, they must economize on tin. Most of them do not need to know what the new use is. If only some of them know the nature of the new use and switch resources over to it, they will create a gap between the quantities supplied and demanded at the originally prevailing price. People who are aware of the resulting gap will fill it with new supplies, and the effect will spread rapidly. It will influence the uses not only of tin but also of its substitutes and of substitutes for the substitutes. It will affect the supply of all things made of tin, the supply of all things made of its substitutes, and so on. All of this will happen even though most of those involved remain unaware of the exact cause of the original disturbance.

How will people be notified of the change in the tin market? Not, in Hayek's view, through television, newspapers, or government directives, but through the market price of tin. It is a rise in the price of tin that will notify each user of the new, more urgent use.

Prices are an efficient means of communicating this information because they allow users to concentrate on the details of their own particular needs for tin, without having to know about all uses of tin. Prices give just enough information about opportunity costs to guide decisions in the right direction. As Hayek puts it, "The whole acts as one market, not because any of its members survey the whole field, but because their limited individual fields of vision sufficiently overlap so that through many intermediaries the relevant information is communicated to all."

In recent years there has been a resurgence of interest in the economics of information. A common theme in the literature of this topic is the need to understand that markets are more than curves crossing on a graph. They are the nerve fibers along which messages pass from one part of the economic organism to another, thereby allowing the whole to adapt to a constantly changing environment. Hayek's 1945 article remains a seminal contribution to the economics of information.

Source: Friedrich von Hayek on Markets and Information adapted from F. A. von Hayek, "The Use of Knowledge in Society," *American Economic Review* (September 1945): 519–530. Reprinted by permission of the *American Economic Review*.

In previous chapters, we have often encountered the notion of transaction costs, which include the costs of acquiring and exchanging information. Sometimes potential buyers and sellers opportunistically hide what they know as they maneuver to gain an advantage. Doing so increases transaction costs. The less information people have, the more risk and uncertainty they face. This chapter addresses a number of problems that have information and uncertainty as their common element. The first section of the chapter focuses on the insurance industry. The second section discusses speculation and its role in financial markets. The final section deals with auctions as a pricing strategy to deal with situations in which normal supply and demand mechanisms fail to supply all the information that buyers and sellers need for efficient resource allocation.

14.1 Insurance and Risk Pooling

We can never have full information about what the future will bring. Will there be enough rain for the corn crop? How good a job offer will I get if I major in economics instead of accounting? Whenever people do not know what will happen in the future, we say that they face risk.[1]

Attitudes Toward Risk

People's attitudes toward risk vary. Suppose, for example, that I owe you a dollar; and instead of simply paying, I offer you double-or-nothing on the flip of a coin. Heads, I pay you $2; tails, I pay you nothing. What I offer you is a fair gamble because the **expected value** of the outcome is the same as the $1 I owe you to begin with. (Expected value is the sum of the values of each outcome times the probability of that outcome. See *Applying Economic Ideas 14.1*.)

Expected value

For a set of possible outcomes, the sum of the probability of each outcome multiplied by the value of that outcome

Applying Economic Ideas **14.1**

Expected Value

The expected value of a set of possible outcomes is equal to the sum of the probability of each outcome multiplied by the value of each outcome. This concept has numerous applications in economics, statistics, games, and elsewhere.

Suppose, for example, that you hold one of fifty tickets in a lottery. The winner of the lottery will receive a prize worth $100. The expected value of a ticket is calculated as follows:

Probability of winning: .02
Value of winning outcome: $100
Probability of not winning: .98
Value of nonwinning outcome: 0
Expected value: (.02 × $100) + (.98 × 0) = $2.00

Sometimes some of the outcomes in the set under consideration have negative values. For example, suppose that you have a bright idea for a new Christmas toy. You will have to invest $100,000 to bring the toy to market. If it is successful you will recover the $100,000 you have invested and earn a profit of $500,000 besides. If the toy is a flop, you will lose your entire investment. Your experience in the toy business tells you that your idea has about one chance in five of succeeding. You calculate the expected value of your investment as follows:

Probability of failure: .8
Loss in case of failure: $100,000
Probability of success: .2
Profit in case of success: $500,000
Expected value of project:

    (.8 x –$100,000) + (.2 x $500,000)

    = –$80,000 + $100,000

    = +20,000

Conclusion: Although bringing out the new toy is a risky venture, it does have a positive expected value.

Winning numbers on a lottery ticket

Risk aversion

A preference for a certain outcome with a given value over a set of risky outcomes with the same expected value

Will you take the offer of double-or-nothing? If you prefer a risk-free outcome with a certain value rather than a set of risky outcomes with the same expected value, you are said to display **risk aversion**. A risk-averse person would turn down the double-or-nothing offer.

If you prefer the risky outcome with the same expected value as the risk-free outcome, you are said to display positive **risk preference**. A person with risk preference would accept the double-or-nothing offer. If you are indifferent between risky and risk-free outcomes with the same expected value, you are said to display **risk neutrality**.

There is a good reason, grounded in the theory of utility and consumer behavior, to expect most people to be risk averse most of the time. Imagine, as we did in Chapter 5, that we can measure utility in units called "utils." If you were able to measure the utility, not of just one good, but of your total wealth, in utils, you could draw a graph like the one in Figure 14.1. It shows that starting from zero, adding $1,000 to your total wealth would give you 200 utils. Another $1,000 would add 100 more utils, a third $1,000 would add 40 more, and a fourth $1,000 would add just 20 more.

Risk preference

A preference for a set of risky outcomes with a given expected value over a certain outcome with the same expected value

Risk neutrality

Indifference between a certain outcome with a given value and a set of risky outcomes with the same expected value

---

FIGURE 14.1   RISK AVERSION, UTILITY, AND WEALTH

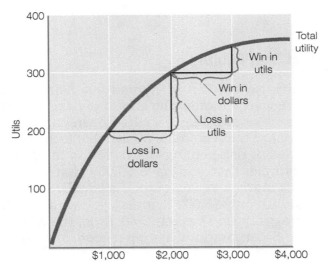

The total utility curve shown here is drawn on the assumption that utility can be measured in units called "utils." As you acquire more wealth, your total utility increases, but each added $1,000 adds less to total utility than the previous $1,000—an example of the principle of diminishing marginal utility. Suppose that you initially have a total wealth of $2,000, equivalent to 300 utils. A decrease in wealth of $1,000 would decrease your utility by 100 utils, but an increase in wealth of $1,000 would increase your utility by just 40 utils. That being the case, you would not find it attractive to wager $1,000 on the flip of a coin. The wager would have an expected value of –30 stated in utils, even though it would be a fair wager (zero expected value) in terms of dollars. This reasoning suggests that a person who is subject to diminishing marginal utility of wealth will tend to be risk averse.

The fact that each dollar added to your wealth increases your utility by less than the previous dollar reflects the principle of *diminishing marginal utility*. On the total utility graph in Figure 14.1, the marginal utility of wealth is equal to the slope of the total utility curve. As wealth increases, the slope of the total utility curve decreases, indicating that each added dollar of wealth adds a diminishing increment of utility.

To see the link between risk aversion and diminishing marginal utility, suppose you start with a total wealth of $2,000, and I offer to bet you $1,000 on the flip of a coin. Heads, I pay you $1,000; tails, you pay me $1,000. If you win, your total wealth will rise to $3,000. If you lose, you will be down to $1,000. In terms of money, it is a fair bet. Your expected value is zero, because the probability of a $1,000 gain is equal to that of a $1,000 loss; however, in terms of utility, the bet does not look so attractive. If you lose, your utility will drop by 100 utils, from 300 to 200. If you win, it will rise by just 40 utils, from 300 to 340. The expected value in utils of flipping the coin is $(-100 \times 0.5) + (40 \times 0.5) = -30$. Your *expected utility* drops by 30 utils if you accept the coin toss. You, therefore, decide to keep your $2,000 rather than flip the coin. Diminishing marginal utility makes you risk averse.[2]

The Principle of Risk Pooling

Risk pooling

A technique in which the risk of loss is shared among many people so that the impact of a loss on any one of them is small

Risk is part of life. No amount of human ingenuity can eliminate it. However, there are ways to soften the effects of risk. One way to do so is to share risks among several people so that the impact of an undesirable outcome on any one of them is small. We call that technique **risk pooling**.

Many examples of risk pooling can be found in financial markets. Suppose, for example, that you have $5,000 that you would like to invest in the stock market. Because stock is usually sold in units of one hundred shares, with only $5,000 to invest, you would probably end up putting all your eggs in one basket. Over time, the average return on stocks of major U.S. corporations has been good, but any company can run into trouble. If you were unlucky, a drop in the price of your chosen stock could wipe out a big chunk of your $5,000.

Risk pooling offers a solution to this problem for small investors. Suppose that you put your $5,000 together with similar amounts that one thousand other people want to invest. This would give you a pool of $5 million, which you could then invest in the stock of dozens or hundreds of different companies. You and your fellow investors would share equally in the profits and losses earned on stocks in the pool. Your pool would be called a *mutual fund*.

Now and then one of the companies represented in the pool of stocks would have a run of bad luck, but the unusual good fortune of another company would be likely to offset it. Your investment in the mutual fund would provide a degree of protection against changes in the fortunes of individual companies. Of course, a problem such as a recession or severe inflation in the economy as a whole could affect all companies at once and could still cause a loss for the fund. Pooling cannot eliminate all risk, but it can help.

Application of Risk Pooling to Insurance

BVT *Lab*

Flashcards are available
for this chapter at
www.BVTLab.com.

Financial risks are not the only ones that people face. There are many risks in everyday life as well, such as being in an automobile accident, being a victim of robbery, or becoming ill. People can protect themselves against the consequences of these risks through risk pooling in the form of *insurance*.

Suppose, for example, that you live in a house valued at $100,000. There is one chance in a thousand that your house will burn down in any given year. The expected dollar value of your loss from a fire is $100 per year. However, your expected loss in utility from a fire is much greater than the marginal utility of $100 cash because, although a fire is not likely, if one happened it would push you far down along the steep portion of your utility curve. What should you do?

One solution is to join with a group of your neighbors to form a mutual insurance fund. Suppose there are one thousand members in the group. Each time a member's house burned down, that person would receive $100,000 in compensation from the fund, and the members would kick in $100 each to cover the expense. On the average, you would have to pay just one claim for loss each year. If no houses burned down, you would pay nothing; if two burned down, you would pay $200; and so on. By adding more members—tens of thousands or even millions—the risk of variation in your annual contribution would become very small, so that an annual contribution very close to $100 would be a virtual certainty.

By forming the mutual insurance society, you and your neighbors convert a small risk of a catastrophic loss into a highly certain small loss. Risk pooling through insurance does not change the expected value of loss in dollar terms, but for risk-averse people it produces a big benefit in terms of expected utility. That is the fundamental principle underlying all forms of insurance.

Asymmetrical Information, Opportunism, and Transaction Costs of Insurance

In the real world, policyholders must pay premiums that exceed the expected value of claims because their premiums have to cover the costs of organizing and operating the insurance companies, as well as the cost of claims. Costs other than claims can account for as much as a quarter of each premium dollar for property insurers, somewhat less for life insurers. Such costs include the clerical costs of keeping the books and mailing out bills. In addition, they include some special transaction costs that arise because not everyone has access to the same information. To use the term favored by economists, insurance companies face a situation of **information asymmetry**.

Whenever information asymmetry exists, people who have information that others lack may behave opportunistically. Opportunistic behavior is an essential part of many games. Bluffing in poker is one example. Players always know more about their own hands than they

Information asymmetry

A situation in which some parties to a transaction have relevant information that other parties do not have

A pool hall hustler disguises his "true speed" by purposely playing poorly.

Adverse selection

The tendency of people facing the greatest risk of loss to be most likely to seek insurance

know about those of their opponents. By bluffing, they can project a misleading impression of their own hands, perhaps allowing them to win even when their cards are not good. Pool hall hustlers are examples in which asymmetric information becomes the basis for gamesmanship. In order to set up opponents for a big win, hustlers at first disguise their "true speed" by purposely playing poorly. Only when they have enticed their opponent to make a big bet do they suddenly reveal how well they can really play.

Adverse Selection   **Adverse selection** is the tendency of people who face the greatest risk of loss to be most likely to seek insurance. The people closest to a river are most likely to buy flood insurance; those who live in bad neighborhoods are most likely to buy burglary insurance; and so on.

Without measures to control adverse selection, insurance can become unavailable to many people. Suppose, for example, that there are two neighborhoods in a city, one of which is closer to a river than the other. Residents in the Riverside neighborhood face an expected loss from flood of $10,000 per year. Those in the Highlands neighborhood face an expected loss of just $1,000 per year.

If equal numbers of people from each neighborhood sign up for flood insurance, the average expected loss will be $5,500 per year. A premium set at that level (plus an allowance for clerical costs and other overhead costs) would just allow the company to break even over time. However, residents of Highlands would quickly recognize that it is not worth their while to sign up. Seeing that the premium far outweighs the expected loss, they would start dropping out. As they did so, the average expected loss of those remaining in the insurance plan would rise, as would the premium required for the company to break even. Eventually all the Highlanders would drop out, the premium would rise to $10,000 per year, and only the Riversiders would purchase insurance.

To generalize, if adverse selection is not controlled, insurance will be available only at rates corresponding to the worst risk category. People with low, but not zero, risk would like to buy insurance; however, they cannot practically do so because premiums are too high relative to the probability of loss they face. To control this tendency, firms employ *underwriters* whose job is to select and classify applicants into risk groups so that the company can calculate an appropriate premium for each group.

In the flood insurance example, the underwriter's job would be easy. Underwriters would put residents of Highlands in a low-risk class with a premium of $1,000 per year (plus an allowance for overhead costs), and residents of Riverside would go into a high-risk class with a premium of a little over $10,000. Yet, it is not always so easy to classify applicants into risk groups because only the insured may know some of the relevant information. If underwriters cannot tell who is high risk and who is low risk, they may have to raise premiums for everyone.

Adverse selection and the problems of asymmetric information are of central importance to health insurance, and to the ongoing debate over health insurance policy, as discussed in *Economics in the News* 14.1.

Economics in the News **14.1**

Adverse Selection and the Affordable Care Act

As of 2010, some 50 million Americans, or about 16 percent of the U.S. population, did not have health insurance. Adverse selection and the efforts of insurance companies to protect themselves from its economic consequences were among the main reasons for the low coverage.

One group of uninsured consisted of people with chronic, pre-existing health conditions like diabetes. Because people with chronic conditions have high health care costs, insurance companies find it unprofitable to insure them. They either charge very high premiums or exclude the chronically ill from coverage altogether. Another large group of uninsured are young, healthy people who think that their health risks are less than the averages on which insurance companies base their premiums. When young, healthy people drop out of the market for individual insurance, claims and premiums rise for those who do buy coverage. Squeezed from one side by the young and healthy and from the other side by the chronically ill, the number of people with access to reasonably priced individual policies has steadily decreased.

In the past, a majority of Americans have escaped the troubles of the market for individual health care coverage with the help of their employers. Insurers are willing to offer group policies to employers at reasonable premiums because employee groups spread the risk among large numbers of people, some of whom have higher than average and some lower than average risks. However, premiums for employers have risen, too. As a result, fewer companies are offering coverage. By 2010, just over half of the population had health care coverage through their place of work, down from a peak of two-thirds.

In an attempt to provide health care coverage to the growing numbers of uninsured, Congress passed the Patient Protection and Affordable Care Act (PPACA) in 2010. If fully implemented, PPACA would make it illegal for health insurance companies to exclude people from coverage because of pre-existing conditions, to drop coverage if they became ill, to exclude certain types of preventative care, or to put lifetime caps on coverage.

Congress passed the Patient Protection and Affordable Care Act in 2010.

However, the PPACA could not simply ignore the problem of adverse selection. By themselves, requirements to offer broad coverage to everyone, regardless of prior health condition, would raise insurers' costs and make it necessary for them to increase premiums. That, in turn, would increase the incentive for the young and healthy to forego coverage altogether. The result would be a vicious cycle in which coverage could become guaranteed, but unaffordable.

(Continues)

To overcome the problem of adverse selection, PPACA included a provision that people who chose not to buy insurance would have to pay an annual fee, initially set at $750, whether they bought coverage or not. The fee was intended either to induce people to buy insurance or, if not, to provide a source of funds to help run the system. The compulsory fee, however, proved highly controversial. A number of interested parties have challenged the fee in court. Eventually the Supreme Court will have to resolve the issue. Many observers think that if the court outlaws the compulsory fee, the problem of adverse selection will lead to the economic collapse of PPACA as a whole—and the country will be back to square one on the issue of universal health insurance.

Moral hazard

The tendency of people to expose themselves to risk if they know insurance will cover their losses

Moral Hazard   The term **moral hazard** refers to the tendency of people to expose themselves to risk if they know insurance will cover their losses. Sometimes a simple lack of care is involved. For example, a driver whose car is insured against theft might be less careful about locking it when it is parked. In other cases there is actual dishonesty, as, for example, if a landlord sets fire to a building to collect the insurance.[3]

Insurance companies take whatever measures they can to control moral hazard. Sometimes they insist on certain precautions as a condition for insurance. Thus, a hotel might be required to install a sprinkler system to qualify for fire insurance. To protect against fraud, insurance companies hire specialists to investigate the circumstances of suspicious claims. Finally, insurance companies try to prevent people from over-insuring. Selling someone $10,000 of theft insurance on a car that is worth only $5,000 is an invitation to a real or faked theft.

Efforts to control moral hazard, like efforts to control adverse selection, are never completely successful. Again, information asymmetry is a reason. The insurer simply cannot observe many kinds of opportunistic behavior. As a result, moral hazard makes insurance premiums higher than they would otherwise be, and the careless and dishonest benefit at the expense of the careful and upright.

14.2 Speculation and Its Role in the Economy

Speculation

Buying something at a low price in the hope of selling it later at a higher price

Our discussion of insurance focused on the desire to avoid risk, but there are other occasions when people voluntarily take on risk. **Speculation**—the activity of buying something at a low price in the hope of selling it later at a higher price—is one example. Speculators are present in many markets, including those for stocks, bonds, farm goods, precious metals, foreign currency, and real estate, to name just a few.

Speculation and Risk

Speculation is inherently risky. Suppose I buy stock in Exxon Mobil at $80 a share in the hope that rising world oil prices will boost the firm's profits, allowing me to sell the stock for $100 a share next year. Instead, the discovery of huge new oil reserves in Brazil sends world oil prices tumbling, and Exxon Mobil stock falls to $60. *C'est la vie*; it is all in a day's work for a speculator.

Why would I want to take such a risk? One explanation might be that unlike the majority of people, who are risk adverse, I have positive risk preference. But economists like to avoid explaining behavior in terms of preferences alone when other explanations are available. In this case, there is such an explanation. Even though I am risk averse and would not speculate on Exxon Mobil stock if I thought there was an equal chance that its price would rise or fall, I might do it if I thought there was a greater chance of an increase than of a decrease. For example, suppose that I think there were a 75 percent chance of an increase to $100 a share and just a 25 percent chance of a fall to $60 a share. In that case the expected value of the stock a year from now would be $50 ([.75 × $100] + [.25 × $60] = $90). If I bought the stock now at $80, my expected gain would be $10 a share. That expected gain could well be enough to overcome my aversion to risk.

This account of speculation raises another question. If the expected value of the stock next year were $90, why would anyone sell it for $80 today? There are two possible answers. One is that other people are even more risk averse than I am. The 25 percent chance of a loss so terrifies them that they will pass up the expected $10-per-share gain. The other answer is information asymmetry: Other people have not yet discovered the information I have that leads me to think world oil prices are significantly more likely to rise than to fall.

In practice, both factors may be at work. A smaller-than-normal degree of risk aversion probably explains why some people become professional speculators. Yet, their success as speculators depends on being the first to learn new information, whether through organized research or simply by keeping their ears to the ground.

Futures Contracts and Options

In the preceding example, speculation took the form of buying Exxon Mobil stock today and holding it for resale a year from now. Two other methods of speculation involve *futures contracts* and *options*.

A **futures contract** is an agreement to exchange something at a specified future date at a price that the parties agree on now. Suppose that I find another trader who expects the *spot price* for Exxon Mobil stock a year from now to be $80, the same as today's spot price. (The **spot price** is the price at which sellers offer a good for immediate sale.) I could enter into a futures contract with that trader under which I would agree today to buy ten thousand shares of Exxon Mobil stock a year from now at $80. If the spot price rises to $100 by then (as I think

BVT *Lab*

Improve your test scores. Practice quizzes are available at www.BVTLab.com.

Futures contract

An agreement to exchange something at a specified date in the future at a price that the parties agree on now

Spot price

The price at which sellers offer a good for immediate sale

there is a 75 percent probability that it will), I will make a killing because I can immediately resell the shares for $20 more than I paid for them under the terms of the futures contract. Of course, there is a risk (which I put at 25 percent) that the spot price will fall to $60. In that case, I am still bound by the futures contract to purchase the stock at $80 a share, $20 over its spot price at that time.

Win or lose, from my point of view as a speculator, the futures contract has an advantage over buying the stock at today's spot price and holding it for a year. The advantage is that I do not have to tie up my own funds by actually holding the stock. All the buying and selling is done a year from now on the date specified by the contract.

Options are a variation on the idea of agreeing now on the terms of a transaction that the parties will complete later. If I enter into an options contract to buy Exxon Mobil stock from you at $80 a share a year from now, you have the obligation to sell the stock to me at that price if I still want it; but if I change my mind, I have the right not to exercise the option. If the spot price goes up to $100, I make the purchase and profit from it. If the spot price falls below $80, I say, "Thanks but no thanks." Of course, you would not enter into such a "heads I win, tails I break even" deal unless there were some compensation to you. The compensation is in the form of an up-front fee (called a premium) of, say, $2 a share for accepting the options contract. If I exercise the options contract at a loss to you, the $2 fee helps you offset the loss. If I do not exercise the option, the $2 is a profit for you.

The kind of option just described, which gives me the right to buy from you at an agreed price, is called a *call option*. Another kind of option gives me the right, but not the obligation, to *sell* stock to you at some time in the future at a price we agree on now. Such a contract is called a *put option*. Call options and put options are commonly used not just for shares of stock, but also for bonds and commodities like wheat or oil.

Option

A contract under which one party obtains the right (but not the obligation) to buy or sell something from another party at a specified date in the future at a price on which they agree now

The Social Usefulness of Speculation

In terms of popularity and social respect, speculators rank about as high as poolroom hustlers. Still, speculators perform a number of socially useful functions.

Hedging   Although speculation itself involves the calculated acceptance of risks, speculators also make it possible for other traders to avoid risk. That is done through **hedging**, an operation that uses futures or options markets to offset one risk with another.

Suppose, for example, that you are a baker. You enter into a contract to sell 10 million loaves of bread to the Army at $.50 a loaf over the course of the next year. Your bid is based on the current price of flour, which, in turn, depends on the price of wheat. The price of wheat is currently $6 per bushel and people expect it to stay at that level over the next year, but no one is sure of that. If the price of wheat unexpectedly goes up, flour

Through hedging, the risk of gain or loss on wheat prices can be shifted to a speculator.

will become more expensive. That could wipe out your profit on the bread contract. What can you do to avoid the risk?

One way is to buy wheat futures at $6 a bushel. If the spot price of wheat rises, you will make a profit on your wheat futures contract that will offset the impact of a higher flour price on your bread profits. If the spot price of wheat falls, you will make a loss on the wheat futures contract, but cheaper flour will allow you to make a greater profit than you expected on the bread contract. Through hedging you have shifted the risk of gain or loss on wheat prices to a speculator. You can tend to your own specialty, which is baking bread.

Hedging
An operation in which futures markets or options markets are used to offset one risk with another

Transmission of Information   A second socially useful function of speculation is transmission to the public of information about expected future market conditions. That might seem paradoxical at first. Speculators clearly have an incentive to acquire information. They dig into the details of a business, hire research staffs, construct computer models, and so on. Our earlier example showed that speculators' profits depend on knowing information that other people do not know, however. Why would they share the results of their research with others?

The answer is that they cannot help doing so. Consider the example of oil prices and the prices of oil-company stocks. If my research indicates that the price of oil is likely to rise, I can profit by buying oil-company stock today (or trading in futures contracts or options, which amounts to the same thing). As soon as my fellow speculators and I start buying the stock, however, we bid up its market price. Other people look at the movement of the stock's price and say to themselves, "Somebody must think oil prices are going to rise. In fact, they must be sure enough of it to put their money on their information." The secret is out.

Speculation and Conservation   A final, socially useful function of speculation is to promote conservation by smoothing out trends in the use of scarce resources over time. Suppose that something—say natural gas—will become increasingly scarce in the future as reserves decrease. Optimal use of the resource over time requires that conservation efforts begin now; but the lower the current spot price, the less incentive there will be to conserve gas.

Enter the speculator. Anticipating future shortages, speculators buy up gas wells and cap them, hoping to sell later when the price is higher. By doing so they reduce the flow of gas to the market today, thereby driving up the current price. The rising price gives the needed incentive to spur conservation.

Of course, speculators also make mistakes. When they do so, they may destabilize prices and send false signals of scarcity to others. Whether or not that causes significant

Speculation can be used to promote conservation by smoothing out trends in the use of scarce resources.

problems depends, in part, on whether the speculators who make mistakes suffer losses as a result. If the speculators who make mistakes bear the losses, a process of market selection will tend to favor those who are most skilled at their job of discovering new information and putting it to use.

Unfortunately, sometimes people are able to speculate with other people's money. They then share the winnings from correct guesses while shifting the losses to others. For example, everyone has heard stories of "rogue traders" at securities firms who earn bonuses for a while by making lucky guesses on the direction of stock or commodity prices, but eventually lose millions or even billions of dollars of shareholders' money when they run out of luck. If shareholders and executives do not implement proper controls and appropriate bonus policies, they may encourage forms of speculation that destabilize, rather than stabilize markets.

14.3 The Economics of Auctions

In most of the markets we have discussed so far, sellers inform buyers in advance of the prices they will charge.[4] Buyers are offered the opportunity to buy as much or as little of the good as they want at that price, or not to buy at all.

For some goods, though, it is not feasible to announce prices in advance. Instead, the price is established at the actual moment when the transaction takes place. Markets for unique items that come on the market only rarely, such as works of art, are one example. Markets for perishable goods like cut flowers, where inventories cannot be stored, are another. Prices change from moment to moment in such markets to keep quantities supplied and demanded closely in balance. Markets for goods like racehorses or tobacco, which vary greatly in quality from one unit to the next, are still another example.

How do buyers and sellers get the information and incentives they need to use resources efficiently when a price is not established until a transaction actually takes place? How can the market ensure that scarce resources will move to their most highly valued uses? One answer is to use an auction. This section examines the economics of auctions with special emphasis on the way they handle information.

Types of Auctions

Reservation price

The maximum price that a buyer is willing to pay for a good or the minimum price at which a seller is willing to offer it

An auction always begins from a situation of asymmetric information. Suppose I want to sell a painting. I know my **reservation price** (the minimum I would accept to part with the painting), but I do not know the reservation prices of potential buyers (the maximum that they are willing to pay). Information is asymmetric on the buyers' side, too. Buyers know their own reservation prices, but they do not know that of the seller or those of other buyers. Needless to say, both buyers and sellers in an auction expect others to behave opportunistically. Each side seeks to gain an advantage while revealing as little as possible about its own reservation price.

The preceding paragraph describes an auction that is organized and conducted by the seller, who accepts bids from buyers. We can call these *sellers' auctions*. In other cases, a buyer, who solicits bids from a number of potential sellers, organizes the auction. We can call these *buyers' auctions*. For example, I might seek bids from a number of construction contractors to build a house. In such a case I know my reservation price (the maximum I am willing to pay), but not the reservation price (the minimum acceptable bid) of potential contractors. Also, the contractors do not know the minimum acceptable bids of other contractors.

Three types of auctions are common. The sellers' versions are described here, but buyers' versions of each also exist.

1. In an **English auction**, the bidding starts low and competing buyers successively call out higher bids until only one buyer is left. The object then goes to the high bidder.

2. In a **Dutch auction**, the bidding starts high, and the auctioneer calls out successively lower bids until one buyer indicates the price is acceptable and buys the item.

3. In a **sealed-bid auction**, all buyers submit bids simultaneously, and the object goes to the highest bidder.

English auctions are probably the most familiar type. They are frequently used for artwork, livestock, and charity fundraisers. Sealed-bid auctions are common in the buyer's version, in which competing contractors submit bids to build houses, pave roads, develop weapons systems, and so on. The United States Treasury also sells some kinds of securities through sealed-bid auctions. Formal Dutch auctions are not as common, although they are used in the Netherlands to sell fresh flowers. An informal version of the Dutch auction is often used to sell houses, used cars, and other items. The item is first advertised at a price that reflects the seller's most optimistic hopes. If there is no response, the seller gradually lowers the price until a buyer comes forward.

The Revenue-Equivalence Theorem

Which type of auction works best? Which will yield the highest price to the seller when there are many buyers? Which will elicit the lowest bid for the buyer when there are many sellers? The surprising answer is that under certain broad conditions, the three types of auctions can produce very nearly the same results on average. Economists call that proposition the **revenue-equivalence theorem**.

We can understand the essence of the revenue-equivalence theorem by means of an example. Suppose that I am selling a 2008

English auction

An auction in which bidding starts low and proceeds until the good is sold to the highest bidder

Dutch auction

An auction that begins with a high bid, which is lowered until a buyer is found

Sealed-bid auction

An auction in which all buyers submit bids at the same time, and the item is sold to the highest bidder

Revenue-equivalence theorem

The proposition that under certain general circumstances English, Dutch, and sealed-bid auctions will produce approximately the same winning bid

Honda Civic at a wholesale auction, to a group of experienced used-car dealers who plan to offer the car for resale. After estimating the resale value, each buyer mentally sets a reservation price for the car—one at which the resale transaction would just break even. Because the buyers are uncertain exactly how much they can get for the car, the reservation prices for a given car will differ from one buyer to another.

To begin with the simplest case, suppose that I use an English auction. The bidding starts at $1,000 and quickly moves to a point at which only two bidders, Janet and George, are left. Janet bids $2,400, and George answers with $2,450. Finally Janet bids $2,500 and George does not respond. Sold, to Janet, for $2,500. What have I learned? I have learned that George's reservation price was a little less than $2,500, while Janet's reservation price is at least $2,500. To generalize, an English auction will result in a sale at a price a little higher than the *second-highest* reservation price among the competing buyers.

Now consider the Dutch auction. I start the auction at $5,000, expecting no immediate takers, and there are none. At $3,000 I hit Janet's reservation price. Will Janet immediately jump in? No, because at $3,000 she would be buying the car for exactly the amount she thinks she will get when she resells it. There would be no profit, so Janet puts on a poker face and keeps quiet. Behind the poker face, she is putting all her experience to work to estimate the reservation price of the *second-highest* bidder. She guesses, correctly, that George values the car at just under $2,500. When the bid drops close to that level, Janet raises her hand and buys the car. Sometimes Janet will guess wrong, and George or someone else will get the car before she has a chance to bid. However, all the buyers are professionals. Their guesses will tend to be correct on the average. As a result, the average selling price at a Dutch auction will again be close to the reservation price of the second-highest bidder.

Finally, suppose that the auction is conducted by means of sealed bids. Janet's reasoning will be almost the same as in the Dutch auction. She certainly will not bid her reservation price of $3,000—that would guarantee that she would not make a profit. Her profit-maximizing strategy in a sealed-bid auction such as this one is to submit a bid close to her estimate of the reservation price of the second-highest bidder. With that strategy, she stands a good chance of getting the car for $2,500.

Under certain general conditions, then, the winning bid will be about the same for all three types of auction: close to the second-highest reservation price among the bidders. There are exceptions, however. Sometimes special characteristics of the product or the information available to buyers or sellers will make one type of auction work better than another. Presumably, buyers and sellers in various markets develop a feel for such things over time, so that when a particular type of auction would make a difference, that type is chosen.

All in all, auctions are a reasonably efficient solution to the problem of pricing unique goods under conditions of asymmetric information and opportunism. In sellers' auctions, goods tend to end up in the hands of those who value them most; in buyers' auctions, the winners tend to be those who can supply the goods at the lowest cost. Both buyers' and sellers' auctions maintain adequate incentives to call forth a supply of the goods and services that are in demand.

The Winner's Curse

Despite a generally favorable assessment of auctions, economists have identified a potential market failure that they call the **winner's curse**. The term refers to an alleged tendency for the winners of auctions to pay more than the item is worth or, in the case of buyers' auctions, to bid less than the cost of supplying the item.

The winner's curse is especially likely to be a problem with so-called *common-value* auctions. In such auctions, the item up for sale has the same actual value to all buyers, but the buyers do not know the exact value when they submit bids. A popular classroom demonstration asks students to bid on a jar of coins. They base their bids on guessing how many coins are in the jar. Bidding for oil drilling rights on government land is a real-world example. Competing bidders cannot know how much oil there is on a given tract until they drill; they must base their bids on estimates derived from indirect geological information.

Suppose that in a common-value auction each bidder's estimate is based on a method that, on average, accurately reflects the actual value of the item. For example, bids on a jar containing $10 worth of coins might range from $5 to $15, centered on the true average value of $10. Under these conditions the winner of the auction will be the bidder who has the bad luck to most overestimate the value of the coins. Someone will end up paying $15, or close to it, for $10 in coins, or $15 million for drilling rights worth $10 million, or whatever. In a buyers' auction, the curse would take the form of a winning bid to supply an item that failed to cover the supplier's costs—for example, a bid of $250,000 to pave a stretch of road that cannot be completed for less than $300,000.

Various writers have claimed to observe the winner's curse at work. Oil companies appear sometimes to overpay for the value of off-shore drilling rights. Publishers appear to overpay for the rights to best sellers. Nevertheless, many economists doubt that the curse is widespread. They reason that people would not participate in auctions year after year knowing that the auctions were cursed. Instead, they think that bidders learn how to protect themselves by submitting bids that are lower than their reservation prices—lower, that is, than their actual estimates of the value of the item.[5]

Winner's curse

The tendency for winners of an auction to pay more for a good or service than it is worth (or to offer to sell at a price below the cost of providing the good or service)

Summary

1. **How does insurance help protect people from the risks of life?** Most people are risk averse, meaning that they would prefer a certain outcome with a given value over a set of risky outcomes with the same expected value. Risk-averse individuals can protect themselves through risk pooling, a technique that shares losses among the members of a large group so that each faces the certainty of a small loss rather than a small risk of a large loss. Mutual funds and insurance are examples of risk pooling.

2. **What information problems does the insurance business face?** The insurance business faces two problems arising from *asymmetrical information*. The first, *adverse selection*, refers to the tendency of individuals facing the greatest risk to be most likely to seek insurance. The second problem, *moral hazard*, refers to behavior that increases the risk of loss, yet is undertaken in the knowledge that losses will be covered by insurance. Adverse selection and moral hazard, and efforts to control them, raise the transaction costs of providing insurance.

3. **Why do speculators willingly accept risk?** *Speculation*, the activity of buying at a low price in the hope of reselling at a higher price, is inherently risky. Risk-averse people will find speculation attractive only if they think they possess better information about future market conditions than other market participants do. Speculation can take the form of buying something in the *spot market*, holding it, and reselling in the spot market at a later date. Alternatively, speculators can use *futures contracts* or *options* to profit from expected changes in prices of goods that they do not currently own.

4. **What are the socially useful purposes of speculation?** Speculators make it possible for others to avoid risk by *hedging*—an operation that uses futures markets or options to offset one risk with another. A second socially useful function is the transmission of information about future economic developments via price changes that take place when speculators trade in spot, futures, or options markets. A third socially useful function of speculation is to promote conservation by smoothing out trends in the use of scarce resources over time.

5. **How do auctions work?** Auctions are a method of trading in markets in which prices are subject to variation with every transaction. Auctions are possible with one seller and many buyers, one buyer and many sellers, or sometimes many of each. In the *English auction,* bidding starts low and proceeds until one high bidder remains. A *Dutch auction* begins with a high bid, which the seller lowers until a buyer accepts it. In a *sealed-bid auction*, all buyers submit bids at the same time. The *revenue-equivalence theorem* states that under certain general conditions the expected winning bid is the same for all three types of auctions, although special circumstances may make one type work better than others for some purposes. An auction is said to be subject to a *winner's curse* if the winning bidder typically pays more than the item is worth (or bids less than the cost of supplying it, in a buyer's auction).

Key Terms

Problems and Topics for Discussion

1. **Hustlers and students**   Do you think it ever pays you to "hustle" your professor by seeming to be a poorer student than you are? For example, do you think it might be a good strategy sometimes to perform poorly on some small, early quizzes in a course, and then surprise your professor with a brilliant performance on the final exam? Compare this example of the exploitation of asymmetric information with the case of the pool hustler.

2. **Expected value**   Suppose that you are offered a chance to invest $5,000 in the production of a Broadway play. There is one chance in ten that the play will be a success. If it is a success, your share of the profit will be $50,000. If the play is a flop, you will get nothing back on your investment. What is the expected value of the investment? Under what conditions, if any, would you be willing to make the investment?

3. **Nuclear war insurance**   Home insurance policies often exclude coverage for damage caused by nuclear war. Why does the principle of risk pooling not work in the case of nuclear war? Can you think of any similar examples?

4. **Speculation**   The Black Knight has laid siege to Fairie Towne. As soon as he hears the news, Trader Sharp runs to the market in Fairie Towne and begins to buy all the wheat, corn, and potatoes he can get his hands on. Other citizens complain to the sheriff that Sharp is driving up the price of foodstuffs. The sheriff arrests Sharp and issues a decree that no merchant is allowed to raise the price of wheat, corn, or potatoes above the price that prevailed on the day before the siege.

   Which person's actions contribute more to helping Fairie Towne survive the siege as long as possible—Sharp's or the sheriff's? Discuss.

5. **Silent auctions**   St. John's Church decides to hold a "silent auction" to raise funds for new choir robes. Parishioners contribute quilts, jars of jam, and other items to be auctioned. The goods are put on display, with a box beside each item. People put slips of paper into the boxes with their names and the amounts they bid for various items. At the end of the evening, the winning bids are read off and the winning bidders pay for the items. All the proceeds go to the choir fund. In several cases, the winning bidder turns out to be the person who donated the item in the first place. Some people think this is cheating. Next time, they say, there should be a rule that people should not be allowed to bid on their own contributions. Other people think that no such rule is needed, but that people were stupid to buy their own items. If they were going to do that, why not simply contribute cash to the choir fund? What do you think?

6. **The winner's curse**   Fill some jars of different shapes and sizes with coins and auction them off by the sealed-bid method in your economics class. Do the results show evidence of a winner's curse? Discuss the results.

Case for Discussion:

The Market for Lemons

In 1970, George A. Akerlof caused a minor sensation in the economics profession with an article entitled "The Market for Lemons." The subject of the article was the market for used cars—more specifically, the market for bad used cars, or "lemons." The article drew attention to a potential source of market failure that had previously received little attention. This article, and related work, was later to win Akerlof the 2001 Nobel Prize in economics.

In simple terms, Akerlof's argument was as follows. Suppose that there are two kinds of used 2005 Honda Civics. The owners of some have maintained them lovingly and driven them carefully. They would not part with them for less than $8,000, and potential buyers would be willing to pay up to $10,000 for them. The other 2005 Civics have been hot-rodded around, have never had their oil changed, and cannot be counted on for reliable service. They are lemons. Owners would be happy to unload them for anything over $4,000; and buyers, if they knew what they were getting, would not pay more than $5,000.

If there were separate markets for good cars and lemons, there would be no problem; but, says Akerlof, there is a catch: Sellers know whether a car is a lemon, but buyers have no way to tell. Sellers of lemons will opportunistically misrepresent the quality of the cars, and buyers cannot observe their true quality.

Asymmetrical information strikes again. Not knowing which cars are which, buyers have to take their chances. If equal numbers of good cars and lemons were for sale, buyers would have a 50-50 chance of getting one or the other. The maximum they would pay for a Civic of unknown quality would be $7,500, the average of the value to them of the two types of cars. However, owners of good cars would not sell them for $7,500. They would rather go on driving them. That would leave only lemons on the market. Buyers would pay up to $5,000 for a lemon, a price at which owners would willingly sell. In the end, lemons would drive good cars out of the market altogether, even though potential buyers value the good cars more than sellers do. That would be a clear case of market failure.

As economists discussed the issue, it became clear that the lemons problem was not a completely new form of market failure but, rather, the old problem of adverse selection in a new guise. The tendency of lemons to drive good cars out of the market is much the same as the tendency of bad risks to drive good risks out of the insurance market. The difference is that the insurance example involves adverse selection among buyers, whereas the lemons problem involves adverse selection among sellers. In both cases, though, the root of the problem is asymmetrical information.

Source: George A. Akerlof, "The Market for Lemons: Qualitative Uncertainty and the Market Mechanism," *Quarterly Journal of Economics* (August 1970): 488–500. Copyright 1970 The MIT Press. Reprinted by permission.

Questions

1. Suppose you want to buy a good used car, and you are aware of the lemons problem. Given the numbers in the example, how much would you be willing to spend in order to break through the barrier of asymmetrical information, say, by paying an expert mechanic to make a detailed inspection of a car you want to buy?

2. Suppose you want to sell a good used car, but you know the lemons problem might make it hard for you to get a good price. What do you think you could do to convince a potential buyer that you were really offering a good car?

3. Individuals do not sell all used cars. Dealers who stay in business for a long time and want to build an honest reputation in order to get consumer referrals and repeat business put many up for sale. Do you think such an honest dealer with a good reputation would be better off to specialize in low quality or high quality used cars? Why?

Endnotes

1. Sometimes a distinction is made between uncertainty, meaning lack of information about the probabilities of future events, and risk, meaning a situation in which people do not know exactly what will happen but do know the mathematical probability of various possible outcomes. In this introductory discussion, however, we use the terms risk and uncertainty interchangeably.

2. If diminishing marginal utility implies risk aversion, why do people ever gamble? Economists have puzzled over this question for years. One hypothesis is that some people experience increasing marginal utility over some ranges of their utility function. (Imagine a utility graph that has several humps in it, like a playground slide.) A second hypothesis is that people overestimate the likelihood of winning. (That is what the poolroom hustler counts on.) A third hypothesis is that people get pleasure out of the act of gambling itself. (That seems to fit people who play poker for small stakes but would be bored playing for matches.) Take your pick.

3. Some insurance experts distinguish between moral hazard, meaning dishonest behavior on the part of the insured, and morale hazard, meaning merely careless behavior. Economists usually combine both types of behavior under the heading of moral hazard.

4. This section draws on an excellent review of the literature on auctions by R. Preston McAfee and John McMillan, "Auctions and Bidding," *Journal of Economic Literature* (June 1987): 699–738. For a shorter summary, see Paul Milgrom, "Auctions and Bidding: A Primer," *Journal of Economic Perspectives* (Summer 1989): 3–22.

5. For a good discussion of the winner's curse, see Richard H. Thaler, "The Winner's Curse," *Journal of Economic Perspectives* (Winter 1988): 191–202.

Chapter 15

Labor Markets, Discrimination, *and* Public Policy

After reading this chapter, you will understand the following:

1. Whether unions are economic maximizers

2. What unions do in addition to bargaining over wages and benefits

3. How discrimination and anti-discrimination policies affect wages and employment

4. The economics of equal pay for men and women

Before reading this chapter, make sure you know the meaning of the following concepts:

1. Monopsony

2. Human capital

3. Efficiency wage theory

4. Inframarginal rent

5. Transaction costs

6. Opportunism

7. Asymmetric information

8. Median voter model

9. Self-regarding and other-regarding preferences

Our discussion of labor markets in Chapter 13 focused on technical matters but gave little attention to labor market institutions. This chapter looks beyond supply and demand to examine how laws, organizations, customs, and attitudes shape the workings of the labor market in the real world. The first section looks at the role of labor unions, the second section takes up discrimination, and the final section looks at equal or unequal pay for men and women.

15.1 Labor Unions

Labor unions have been a part of the economy for more than two hundred years. *Applying Economic Ideas* 15.1 gives a brief history of the labor movement in the United States. Just what role have unions played in the past, and what do they do today? There seems to be no simple answer to this question. Unions do many things, and not all unions do the same things.

Applying Economic Ideas **15.1**

Labor Unions in the United States: A Brief History

The first labor unions appeared in the United States in the late eighteenth century. They were craft unions, that is, organizations of skilled workers practicing the same trade. None of them grew large or lasted long.

The first mass union—the Noble and Holy Order of the Knights of Labor—did not emerge until after the Civil War. It reached a peak membership of seven hundred thousand in 1886. Unlike the earliest unions, the Knights of Labor offered membership to anyone who worked for a living, not just skilled workers, but also miners, unskilled laborers, and even farmers. Its economic impact was limited, though, and it faded away almost as quickly as it had emerged.

Unions were created to improve wages and working conditions.

Meanwhile, craft unionism took on a new, more vigorous form under the leadership of Samuel Gompers, who founded the American Federation of Labor in 1881. Gompers had a narrowly economic view of unions. He saw them as tools to strengthen the bargaining power of skilled workers who, if they stood together, would be difficult for employers to replace. The AFL viewed organization of unskilled workers as a waste of time.

Although courts had recognized unions as legal as early as 1842, they continued to have their difficulties in court. In the early part of the twentieth century, courts applied the **Sherman Antitrust Act** to restrict union activities on the grounds that they were conspiracies in restraint of trade. Membership decreased during the 1920s.

The Great Depression of the 1930s brought high unemployment and a new swing of public sympathy toward unions, which many people saw as the best hope for hard-pressed workers. Unions won an important political victory with the passage of the **Norris-La Guardia Act of 1932**, which gave workers the right to strike and picket. The **Wagner Act**, which formally recognized the right of collective bargaining, followed in 1935.

Protected by the **Wagner Act**, the first large-scale industrial unions emerged in the 1930s. These, unlike craft unions, brought together skilled and unskilled workers in industries like steel and automobiles. By the end of the 1930s, 30 percent of nonagricultural workers were unionized; and in 1945, union membership hit an all-time peak at just over a third of the labor force.

After the war, the pendulum began to swing back again. The **Taft Hartley Act of 1947** added a list of unfair union labor practices to balance the **Wagner Act's** list of unfair employer practices. Spurred by corruption scandals, the **Landrum Griffin Act of 1959** put the government in the business of policing the internal affairs of unions. Attempts to organize workers in the South and West fell short of their goals. Unions gained in some service sectors and among government workers, but they continued to lose ground among industrial workers. By 2011, just 11.8 percent of U.S. workers belonged to unions, and just 6.9 percent in the private sector.

Unions, Wages, and Jobs

How do unions work? One way to approach that question is in terms of objectives, constraints, and rational choices, the same tools we used to look at firms and households. This approach emphasizes the economic power that union members achieve by presenting a united front. We begin with the case of a union that is formed in a competitive market and now seeks higher wages through the threat of a strike.

Figure 15.1 shows an initially competitive labor market in which the equilibrium wage rate is $8 an hour. Total employment at that wage is 300,000 worker-hours per year (point E_1). Now, suppose that the newly organized workers tell employers that they want $10 an hour or else they will go on strike. The graph shows the effect of the strike threat as a change in the shape of the supply curve. At first, the supply curve had the usual positive slope. After the strike threat, employers face a supply curve with a kink. The horizontal left-hand branch of the curve shows that if employers do not pay at least $10 an hour, no one will want to work. Workers will supply up to 400,000 hours if the wage is exactly $10 an hour. To hire more labor than that, the employers would have to raise the wage above what the union demands.

FIGURE 15.1   EFFECT OF UNIONIZATION IN A COMPETITIVE LABOR MARKET

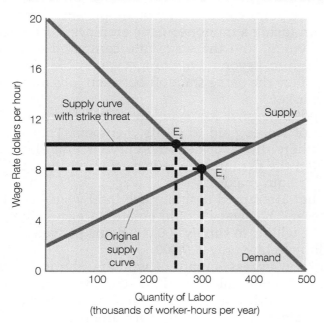

A union formed in a competitive labor market can use a strike threat to bargain for higher wages. Here, it threatens to strike unless the wage rises from its competitive level of $8 an hour ($E_1$) to $10 an hour. The supply curve for labor becomes horizontal at $10 an hour up to 400,000 worker-hours per year. The market reaches a new equilibrium at E_2, where the new supply curve intersects the demand curve. The wage is higher than before, but the quantity of labor employed is smaller.

If the employers accept the union's demand, they will react by shifting to a new equilibrium at point E_2, where the demand curve intersects the horizontal part of the new supply curve. There they will hire 250,000 worker-hours per year at $10 an hour.

In this example, the union can win a higher wage rate, but only at the expense of jobs for its members. How far up the demand curve should a union try to move in attempting to serve its members' interests? A recent estimate is that union workers in the United States earn about 14 percent more than their non-union counterparts. That does not seem like a big differential; but even so, union membership has fallen below 12 percent of the labor force, a record low. Does this tradeoff between wages and jobs represent some kind of rational maximizing behavior? The answer is not at all obvious.

At one extreme, suppose that a union tried to maximize the number of jobs open to its members. In Figure 15.1, that would require a wage of $8 an hour, as shown by the intersection of the supply and demand curves. At that wage, firms would use 300,000 worker-hours per year.

At any higher wage, employers would use less labor. At any lower wage, not enough workers would apply for work to fill the available jobs. The catch is that $8 an hour is the same as that in a competitive market without a union. An employment-maximizing union might represent workers politically or might provide social benefits, but it would not affect the wage rate.

The situation would be different if the employer were a monopsonist[1]. Up to the point where the labor supply and demand curves intersect, a union facing a monopsonistic employer could achieve gains in both employment and the wage rate compared with the monopsonistic equilibrium. Beyond that point (a wage of $8 per hour in Figure 15.1), it would face the same tradeoff between jobs and wages as in a competitive market.

Another possible goal for a union would be to bargain for the greatest total of wages paid to all its members. That would happen at the point where the labor demand curve is unit elastic, that is, its midpoint, when the demand curve is a straight line. In Figure 15.1, a wage of $10 per hour maximizes total wages.

A union that attempted to maximize total wages would face a dilemma, however. That wage would create an excess supply of labor. Workers will be willing to supply 400,000 hours per year, but employers would be willing to hire only 250,000.

Faced with an excess supply of workers, the union would have several choices. It could allow workers to compete for jobs on a first-come, first-served basis and not worry about who can get a job. Instead, it could try to divide the available work among all the workers who want jobs, limiting them to a certain number of hours per year. Still another approach would be for the union to act as a gatekeeper, making the final decision on which job applicants get to work and which do not get a job. Whatever approach it took to managing the excess supply of workers, the union would have to prevent nonunion workers from undercutting it by offering to work for less than the union wage.

Unions as Political Entities

Models of unions as rational maximizers face a key difficulty: Union members have no common interest that unites them in the way that profits unite a firm's owners.

To see why, consider a firm that is trying to decide whether a price increase would boost its profit. If the price increase raises revenue more than cost, the firm's owners will all benefit from the higher profit. If the owners, or their representatives on a board of directors, are able to vote, they will unanimously approve the increase in profit.

The situation of a union bargaining for a wage increase is fundamentally different. If the labor demand curve is inelastic at the current wage, raising it will increase total wages received by workers, but not all union members will necessarily share in the gain. Instead, as the employer moves up and to the left along the labor demand curve, some workers are likely to lose their jobs while those who remain on the job will reap all the gains. Theoretically, the union could share the gains with everyone by keeping all workers on the payroll and reducing hours per worker; however, that is not the usual practice.

If some workers gain and others lose their jobs when the wage goes up, it follows that each worker's "maximizing" wage is different from that of every other worker. Whether a given worker will favor a wage increase will depend on whether he or she fears a layoff. If, as is often the case, layoffs are made in reverse order of seniority, senior workers will favor relatively higher wages.

The Median Worker Model   Economists have borrowed concepts from public choice theory to analyze union behavior when the interests of members diverge. Bruce E. Kaufman has suggested using a variant of the median voter model. If union leadership is responsive to the wishes of a majority of members, he says, the target wage rate will correspond to the interests of the **median worker** —the one in the middle of the seniority scale. The idea is that the median worker plus all more-senior workers form a majority-voting bloc within the union. When workers vote on a contract that will increase wages at the expense of some job losses, the bloc of more-senior workers can, in principle, override the interests of less-senior workers, who are most threatened by layoffs.[2]

However, as Kaufman and others who take this approach recognize, the median worker model has some curious implications. Taken at face value, it suggests that 50 percent of the union plus one member would force through a wage increase that would get the rest of the membership laid off. The next year, half of those left would force through another such wage increase; and so on, until only one worker remained on the payroll. The fact that this does not happen suggests that the median worker model by itself does not give a full explanation of union behavior.

Other Factors   In practice, other factors offset the tendency for unions to shrink to the vanishing point, as would happen in the pure form of the median worker model. One is that union members are motivated, in part, by other-regarding as well as self-regarding preferences. Union members have a sense of solidarity that is best satisfied when all members of the group they care about have steady work at fair wages. Sometimes strong economic pressures can undermine that solidarity. For example, in recent years, the United Auto Workers union and several others have reluctantly accepted wage contracts that pay newly hired workers less for doing the same work, an arrangement that goes against union traditions. Despite such exceptions, a model of union behavior that ignores other-regarding preferences, like feelings of worker solidarity, cannot be complete.

In addition, theories should recognize that the self-regarding interests of leaders, as well as those of rank-and-file members, influence union behavior. Union leaders may want to keep membership large to enhance their own power, income, and prestige. They may also feel pressure from community leaders, such as city council members and newspaper editors, to behave in a "responsible" manner. If so, union leaders will balance the interests of their members against those of local government officials, members of the business community who do not want labor-management conflict to threaten the survival of an employer.

Whatever the specifics, no simple model like the profit-maximizing model of the firm can do justice to collective bargaining. Rather, we can best view unions, like we do democratic governments, as instruments for reconciling diverse interests.

What Else Unions Do

To focus entirely on unions' effects on wages would be misleading. Unions do many other things besides bargain over wages. That has been true from the earliest days when the Knights of Labor campaigned for worker education and self-improvement to the present, when unions provide social activities, help members with personal and family problems, and give members a voice in politics. Some of the things unions do reach beyond the scope of economics; but even on the economic level, unions affect more than wages.

The Union Voice in the Workplace   Most important, unions give workers a voice in running the workplace. They bargain with employers over health and safety conditions. They help settle workers' grievances over job assignments and conflicts with supervisors. They bargain over issues of fairness, such as the role of seniority in layoffs and recalls. In many plants, unions and management also cooperate to implement productivity-enhancing ideas from the shop floor.

The role of unions within the firm reflects the more general role of firms in the market economy. Firms exist because they reduce the cost of organizing complex transactions, especially those in which the parties must make a long-term commitment of specialized resources. Through their internal governing structures, firms facilitate coordination, control tendencies toward opportunistic behavior, and adapt to changes in the business environment. Unions contribute to the accomplishment of these tasks. Consider the following points in particular:

1. Workers often make commitments of specialized resources, such as acquiring firm-specific job skills or moving to a location where few alternative jobs are available. Those commitments bind the firm and the workers to each other and make separations more costly for both sides. Unions can potentially reduce the transaction costs of managing such long-term relationships.

2. Both workers and managers face temptations to behave opportunistically. Supervisors and line managers help prevent shirking by workers. For balance, workers need union shop stewards and grievance procedures to prevent arbitrary actions by supervisors. By providing a framework for resolving such problems, unions boost worker morale and cut turnover.

3. Circumstances may change unexpectedly for better or worse. If a firm prospers, workers will want to claim a share of the rewards. If it falters, workers may have to share hardships to ensure the firm's survival. New technologies may sharply change working conditions and require new skills. Collective bargaining often provides a way of making the necessary adjustments to change.

Firms Without Unions   It is fair to ask, if unions are so helpful in facilitating coordination and cutting transaction costs, why has union membership been falling for nearly half a century? There are at least three answers.

First, some researchers think that U.S. unions have simply priced themselves out of the market. During the 1950s and 1960s, unions gained wage differentials some 20–25 percent above labor market rates for nonunion workers. Economists David Blanchflower and Richard Freeman conclude that such differentials were "probably economically justified when the United States was the clear world economic leader." Today, however, in a more competitive world economy, they have become "a major liability to the development of unionism in the country." They note that differentials over market rates earned by workers in other countries are significantly smaller, which may explain the fact that union membership has not declined elsewhere as it has in the United States[3].

Second, although unions are sometimes partners with management in improving quality and raising productivity, there is a darker side to unions' voices in company affairs. There have been episodes in history when unions fought new technologies that they feared would eliminate jobs. Unions have sometimes tried to prevent women, members of minority groups, and immigrants from gaining access to jobs that traditionally went to white males. They have sometimes stirred up worker hostility to make themselves seem more needed. There have even been cases when unions battled competition from nonunion workers with threats and violence. Such episodes have not enhanced the reputation of unions among the public.

Third, managers have gradually learned that they can achieve productive labor relations without unions. In the nineteenth and early twentieth centuries, bosses often treated workers as robots. Management attitudes of that period created a fertile climate for the growth of unions. Today, top nonunion firms often go out of their way to give workers a voice in company affairs. *Applying Economic Ideas 15.2* contrasts management practices then and now. The fact that some top nonunion firms are willing to pay high wages to a highly productive work force is consistent with efficiency wage theory as discussed in an earlier chapter.

15.2 Minorities and Women in the Labor Force

As we have seen, workers join unions, not just in the hope of higher wages, but also in the pursuit of social goals. However, neither unions nor market forces have eliminated perceived inequalities and injustices.

One persistent focus of concern has been the gap in earnings between men and women. According to data from the Bureau of Labor

Neither unions nor market forces have eliminated the gap in earnings between men and women.

Applying Economic Ideas 15.2

Labor-Management Relations

Bob Stinson knew what labor-management relations were like in the automobile industry before the advent of unions.

"I started working at Fisher Body in 1917 and retired in 1962, with 45 and 8/10 years service," he told an interviewer. "Until 1933, no unions, no rules: You were at the mercy of your foreman.

"I left the plants so many nights hostile. If I were a fella big and strong, I think I'd a picked a fight with the first fella I met on the corner. It was lousy. Degraded. You might call yourself a man if you was on the street; but as soon as you went through the door and punched your card, you was nothing more or less than a robot. Do this; go there; do that. You'd do it."

Today the "do this, go there, do that" style of management is out at top U.S. nonunion companies. In 1981, Fred K. Foulkes made a study of management practices at several top U.S. firms. He concluded that such firms see the main advantage of operating in a nonunion environment as higher productivity, not lower wages. The higher productivity comes partly from lower employee turnover and less absenteeism, partly from greater worker loyalty, and partly from wider acceptance of new technology.

Managers of nonunion companies tend to give their workers a voice in company affairs.

Since the time of Foulkes' study, the U.S. economy has become much more globalized. One striking development has been the growing number of plants owned by international automakers such as Toyota, Honda, Mercedes, and BMW. Those plants are rarely unionized, but they pay well and treat their workers well. Their competition, in turn, has influenced both unions and management at U.S. automakers to improve their labor relations.

Sources: The Stinson quotes are from an interview in Studs Terkel, *Hard Times: An Oral History of the Great Depression* (New York: Pantheon Books, 1970), 129. The material on management practices today is based on Fred K. Foulkes, "How Top Nonunion Companies manage Employees," *Harvard Business Review* (September–October 1981): 90–96.

Statistics, as of 2010, median real weekly earnings of women were about 82 percent of those for men. However, as Figure 15.2 indicates, the gender gap in the United States has narrowed substantially in recent years and has nearly disappeared for younger women.

FIGURE **15.2**

RATIO OF WOMEN'S TO MEN'S PAY IN THE UNITED STATES, 1979–2010

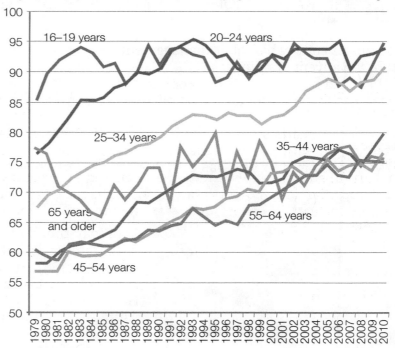

Women's earnings as percent of men's, median usual weekly earnings of full-time wage and salary workers, in current dollars, by age, 1979–2010 annual averages

As this chart shows, women earn less than men, on average, in all age groups. However, the gap has decreased over time and has nearly disappeared for younger workers.

Source: Bureau of Labor Statistics, *The Editor's Desk,* July 22, 2011 (http://www.bls.gov/opub/ted/200/ted_20110722.htm)

Men's and women's wages also differ significantly by ethnic group. Bureau of Labor Statistics data show that as of 2010, Asian men had the highest earnings, White men earned 82 percent as much as Asian men, Black men 68 percent as much, and Hispanic men 60 percent as much. At the same time, Asian women earned 83 percent as much as Asian men; White women 81 percent as much as White men; Black women 94 percent as much as black men, and Hispanic women 91 percent as much as Hispanic men.[4]

In part, the wage gaps are the result of different human-capital endowments of men, women, and minorities. Important factors include years of formal education, years of job experience, amount of on-the-job training, and time spent out of the labor force after completion of schooling. Some of those differences may reflect discrimination that takes place outside the labor market, and some may reflect cultural differences or differences in preferences. Such indexes of human capital appear to account for about half of the wage gap.

(The exact numbers vary from one group to another and from one study to another.) The remaining half is more difficult to attribute to human capital or other easily observable economic factors. We now turn to the unexplained part of the wage gap, which may be a result of discrimination in labor markets, and with policies designed to correct the effects of discrimination.

An Economic Model of Discrimination

Employers practice **labor market discrimination** against a group of workers if they are unwilling to hire members of that group at the same wage rate that they pay to equally productive members of a more favored group.

Figure 15.3 applies labor market theory to the effects of discrimination. Part (a) shows supply and demand curves for workers in the favored group. The demand curve, as usual, is the based on marginal revenue product. Part (b) shows supply and demand curves for workers in the disfavored group. In that market, the demand curve lies to the

Labor market discrimination

A situation in which employers are unwilling to hire members of a disfavored group at the same wage rate that they pay to equally productive members of a more favored group

FIGURE 15.3   EFFECTS OF DISCRIMINATION ON WAGE RATES AND HOURS WORKED

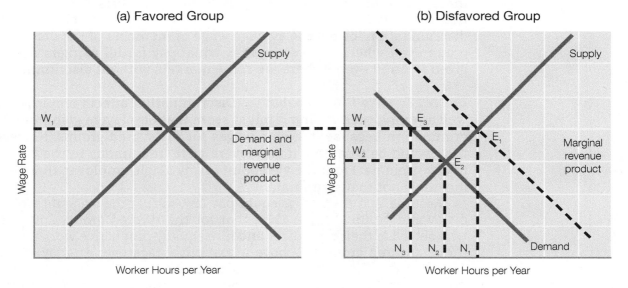

This figure shows the effect of discrimination in a labor market that contains a group of workers who are favored by employers and a group of workers who are disfavored. We assume the two groups are equal in terms of productivity, but the demand curve for the disfavored group lies to the left of the corresponding marginal revenue product curve. If there are no equal-pay laws, the disfavored group's pay will fall to W_2, below the level of W_1 received by members of the favored group. If the law requires equal pay, both groups will receive wage W_1, but fewer members of the disfavored group find work. Many members of the disfavored group who would be willing to work in this occupation at wage W_1 will move into other, less attractive sectors of the job market or into unemployment. With or without the equal-pay law, then, discrimination is harmful to the disfavored group.

left of the marginal revenue product curve because employers will hire members of the disfavored group only if they are more productive than members of the favored group are—or if they are equally productive but will work for less.

Equilibrium Under Discrimination   Two types of equilibrium are possible under discrimination. First, assume there are no legal limits on discrimination. In this case, the wage rate for the disfavored group will fall to W_2 compared with a rate of W_1 for the favored group. Workers from the two groups will then work side-by-side, doing the same job, but will receive different pay. All members of the disfavored group who want to work at wage W_2 will be able to find jobs in this market. In the second case, assume the law prohibits paying different wages to members of different groups for doing the same work. In that case, employers must pay wage W_1 to members of both the favored and the disfavored groups. As a result, they will employ only N_3 worker-hours per year from the disfavored group. The effect of the equal-pay law on members of the disfavored group is mixed. On the one hand, members of that group who remain employed earn more than they would without the law. On the other hand, fewer workers from the disfavored group get jobs at wage W_1. Those who do not get jobs in this market either remain unemployed or move to some other sector of the labor market, possibly one in which employers do not discriminate. However, whether employers in those markets discriminate or not, wages will fall because of greater labor supply. In the end, then, discrimination lowers the average wage of members of the disfavored group even when the law requires equal pay for all workers doing a given job, and even if there are some markets without discrimination.

Competition and Discrimination   Discrimination affects employers as well as employees. At first it might seem that employers gain from discrimination because it lowers wages for disfavored groups. However, that would be true only if employers were unanimous in their intent to discriminate. From the viewpoint of any single employer, there is an incentive not to discriminate.

Assume that there is no equal-pay law, so that the wage rate for the disfavored group is lower than that for the favored group. Employers who set aside their prejudices and hire equally productive workers from the disfavored group will have a cost advantage over employers who discriminate. That advantage would allow them to undercut competitors' prices, either driving them out of the market or forcing them to change their hiring practices. In the long run, then, competition would tend to erode both the practice of discrimination and the pay gap.

All in all, the situation of discrimination in the labor market is somewhat like that of a cartel. Discriminating employers or cartel members can gain as long as they are united; at the same time, however, each has an incentive to cheat on the system. Just as the profit motive tempts cartel members to violate price and output agreements, so too it tempts employers to abandon established patterns of discrimination.

Applying Economic Ideas 15.3 illustrates the effects of competition with the case of discrimination in the South during the Jim Crow era. In that case, competition and the profit motive threatened to undermine discrimination to such an extent that states found it necessary to pass laws that supported discrimination by employers.

Applying Economic Ideas 15.3

Discrimination and the Law in the Jim Crow South

In the southern United States in the Jim Crow era (the 1890s through the early 1950s), there was no lack of discrimination against black workers. Especially in the early part of the period, white plantation owners dominated the economy and employed large numbers of blacks. As a group, they had an interest in holding down the wages of black farmworkers, both to boost their own profits and to maintain the dominant position of the white race in social and political life.

Headquarters for workers favoring approval of Kansas City's Public Accommodation ordinance in an election April 7, 1964

There was one problem, however. The greed of many white employers overcame racial solidarity. Despite warnings in newspapers that "white men must stick together," the employers competed for black labor. Black workers often left their jobs for higher-paying ones, especially at harvest time, when labor was in short supply. In addition, labor recruiters from the North would appear in the South to entice black workers to come to work in the North's growing industries at wages that, while low by today's standards, were nonetheless better than those southern planters offered.

To protect the traditional system of exploitation against erosion by market forces, most southern states passed special labor laws in the period between 1890 and 1910. Following are some examples:

- Enticement laws made it a crime for white employers to "entice" a worker who had a contract with another employer. The aim was to prevent competition for workers that might bid up wages.

- Contract enforcement laws made it a crime for a black worker to break a labor contract with a white employer in order to seek work elsewhere. The standard contract period was one year. The aim was to prevent competition at harvest time when the demand for labor was strongest.

(Continues)

- Vagrancy laws made it a crime for any person who was able to work to "wander or stroll in idleness." The aim was to keep black workers in the labor force and to prevent them from spending time between jobs shopping around for the best wage offer.

- Emigrant-agent laws curbed the activities of labor recruiters from other states or even other counties. For example, a law passed by the city of Montgomery, Alabama, imposed a $100 fine or six months in jail on anyone who printed, published, wrote, delivered, posted, or distributed any advertisement that tried to persuade people to leave the city to seek work elsewhere.

- The convict lease system allowed prisons to lease black prisoners to private employers, including those convicted of violating contract or vagrancy laws. Being on the chain gang was worse than being a slave. Since the lease was short term, the employer, unlike a slave owner, did not even have an interest in preserving the worker's health.

In a study of the Jim Crow labor laws, economist Jennifer Roback finds that they were effective in keeping wages down and limiting migration. She concludes that without the laws competition would, over time, have undermined racial exploitation of workers.

Source: Jennifer Roback, "Exploitation in the Jim Crow South: The Market or the Law?" *Regulation* (September–December 1984): 37–44. A longer version of the article appears in the *University of Chicago Law Review* (Fall 1984).

Some Qualifications Although competition is a force that tends to break down labor market discrimination, there is no guarantee that it will eliminate discrimination altogether. For example, suppose employers are monopsonists in their local labor markets. An employer that faces a positively sloped supply curve in the labor market is in a position similar to that of a seller that faces a negatively sloped demand curve in the product market. It is profitable for a seller to practice price discrimination, if the market consists of two or more segments with different price elasticities of demand. The seller then charges a higher price in the market where elasticity of demand is lower.

Similarly, in labor markets, a monopsonistic employer can discriminate if it can identify groups according to their elasticity of supply. The profit-maximizing strategy would then be to pay a lower wage to the groups with the least elastic supply. Those would tend to be the groups that have the least attractive alternative employment opportunities, often including women and minorities.

In still other cases, competition may fail to eliminate discrimination because it originates with customers or fellow employees rather than with the employer. If customers do not want service from members of a minority group, they will take their business to employers who do not hire such workers. The discriminating employers may then be at a competitive advantage overall even if they have to pay higher wages, as theory suggests they will.

In other cases, workers from dominant groups may not want to work with minority-group members. An employer who wants to hire a mixed labor force may then have to pay higher wages than one who hires only members of the dominant group. That could give the discriminating employer an advantage over the nondiscriminating employer, despite the tendencies discussed earlier.

Finally, in some cases employers may not be responsive at all to market forces. Government agencies are an example. It is no accident that some of the early targets of the drive for equal pay for women were city and state governments. Also, some economists have argued that managers of large corporations do not always share their shareholders' interest in maximum profits. If the white male managers of such a corporation like to hire only other white males, even when more highly qualified women or minority candidates are available, they may be able to get away with doing so, at least for a time, even if the firm's profits suffer.

Discrimination and Asymmetrical Information

The preceding discussion assumes that someone *wants* to discriminate—that employers, fellow workers, or customers prefer not to deal on an equal basis with members of another group. It is possible, though, that discrimination can occur even when all parties would prefer not to discriminate. That can happen when employers wrongly think that an individual member of a certain group shares characteristics that may be statistically valid for the group as a whole but are not true of that individual—a phenomenon sometimes termed *statistical discrimination*.

One example concerns the tendency of women, on average, to spend more time out of the labor force than men do. No one disputes that the number of years a person spends in the labor force has a positive effect on productivity and wages. Suppose that I am looking for entry-level workers to train for career positions, and that I am convinced that women and men who spend equal years with my firm will turn out to be equally productive in their jobs. I have just interviewed two young, unmarried candidates who are alike in all respects except that one is a woman. Which do I hire?

If I am a rational profit maximizer, and if I intend to offer the same wage to both candidates, I hire the man. I have no way of knowing how many years each candidate will remain in the job, but the statistical probability is that the man will stay longer. Suppose, though, that you are the woman who does not get the job. *You know* that you are career bound, and that you, unlike many women, will not drop out of the labor force to raise children. *You know* that you will be just as productive as the male candidate will. You feel discriminated against, and you are right to feel that way.

The problem here is one of asymmetric information: I do not know as much about your future employment plans as you do, and I have no way of finding out. Can I ask? No. First, it is illegal. Even to ask about your family intentions can violate antidiscrimination regulations. Moreover, it would be pointless to ask. You might currently intend to stay with the job but later change your mind. Even if you intend to drop out of the labor force the minute you got married, there is no reason for you to tell the truth. Asymmetric information and opportunism compound each other. In this case, they prevent me, the employer, from learning what I would like to know about you, the employee, in order to make a decision that is in all ways fair and efficient.

Now, the story just told contains some implicit assumptions that make it a worst-case scenario. In many cases, there are other sources of information available to an employer who is not lazy or prejudiced. For example, if a job requires math skills, it would be ridiculous for an employer to exclude women on the basis of a belief that "women are not good at math." The generalization is not valid to begin with, and in any event an employer could find out a candidate's math skills by testing or looking at college transcripts.

Also, the story assumes that employers cannot structure contracts in a way that protects them against employees who leave their jobs before the employer reaps the full benefits of their on-the-job training. Seniority-based salary scales, bonus systems, and deferred compensation in the form of pensions and other devices can protect the employer against excessive turnover among employees of either gender.

Empirical studies suggest that the problem of asymmetric information does not always prevent employers from rewarding women and men equally when they are equal in terms of labor force attachment. One study showed, for example, that men who never marry and women who never marry have comparable labor force histories, whereas married women spend fewer than half as many years in the labor force as never-married women. Within the category of never-marrieds, the study found that women earn 99 percent as much as men, even though married women earned substantially less than married men did. Another study focusing on college professors showed that never-married women actually did better in terms of salary and promotions than never-married men[5].

Such studies suggest that labor markets—like markets for other goods and services—find ways of at least partially overcoming the problem of asymmetric information. Still it is likely that at least some cases of perceived labor market discrimination are due to information asymmetry.

Federal Antidiscrimination Policies

Since the 1960s, the federal government has instituted a number of policies to combat discrimination in the labor market. The first of these was the Equal Pay Act of 1963. As explained earlier, however, mandating equal pay is not enough to fully protect disfavored groups against the effects of discrimination. In the face of employer discrimination, an equal-pay law alone may only reduce the number of workers hired from the disfavored group.

The Civil Rights Act of 1964 made a more direct attack on employment discrimination. Title VII of that act outlaws discrimination of any kind based on race, color, religion, sex, or national origin. The law applies to firms with fifteen or more employees and to labor unions.

In the years since, there has been much debate and litigation about what constitutes discrimination. The current interpretation is that any practice is suspect if it has a "disparate impact" on various groups. A practice with a disparate impact can be justified only if an employer proves that it is relevant to job performance. For example, the government might challenge a minimum height for employees on the ground that it has a disparate effect on women. An employer might be able to justify the requirement by proving, say, that only a person taller than the minimum height could safely operate a certain piece of equipment.

A third important federal policy is Executive Order 11246, which President Lyndon Johnson signed in 1965. That order sets antidiscrimination standards for all companies doing business with the federal government, so it covers most major firms. A key feature of the order is that major federal contractors must file *affirmative-action programs*. Under an affirmative-action program, a firm pledges to do more than simply not discriminate: it conducts a statistical analysis of its work force and takes concrete steps, through recruitment, training programs, and the like, to hire women and members of minority groups for jobs where few of them have found employment. Federal law explicitly forbids the establishment of numerical quotas for hiring on the ground that they constitute discrimination against white males. However, some people still criticize affirmative-action measures as de facto quotas.

A number of empirical studies have tried to determine the effectiveness of federal antidiscrimination policy. They have focused on reductions in wage gaps among various groups before and after passage of the key civil rights acts. Such studies have found federal policy to have a modest, but measurable, favorable impact on the earnings of minority men. They appear to have had a strong effect in helping to close the wage gap between black and white women. Their effects on the earnings of white women have been negligible, however. In some cases, affirmative action has caused displacement of white women by minority-group members of both genders.[6]

Occupational Segregation and Gender Inequality

In many respects, theory and policy issues having to do with discrimination by race and gender are similar, but there are some notable differences. One of the differences concerns segregation by occupation. Occupational segregation by gender is much stronger than segregation by race. For example, there are black and white truck drivers and black and white home health care workers; but the truck drivers, whatever their race, are mostly men, while the home health workers are mostly women.

Figure 15.4, taken from a recent study by the Government Accounting Office, gives some examples of occupational segregation. The graph focuses on workers with low educational attainment, for which occupational segregation and wage disparities are more pronounced. The study makes clear that there are two different sources of inequality between low-educated men and women. First, low-educated women earn about 15 percent less than men even when they work in the same occupation. Second, low-educated women are more likely to be numerous in lower-paid occupations like personal care than in higher-paid occupations like construction.

FIGURE 15.4

REPRESENTATION OF LESS-EDUCATED WOMEN AND MEN BY OCCUPATION

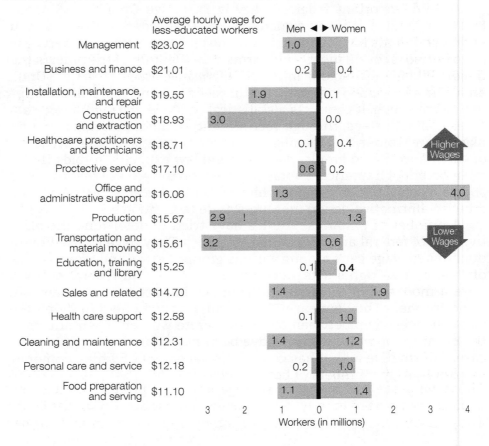

A recent study from the Government Accounting Office found that occupational and wage disparities between men and women were greater for low-educated than high-educated workers. This chart shows that part of the reason is the fact that low-educated women tend to be overrepresented, relative to men, in lower wage occupations like personal care than in higher-paid occupations like construction. However, even when low-educated women and men work in the same occupation, the women earn about 15 percent less, on average.

Source: GAO, "Gender Pay Differences," GAO-12-10, October 2011, p. 15. (http://www.gao.gov/assets/590/585721.pdf)

Origins of Occupational Segregation   The source of occupational segregation by gender is one of the most controversial topics in labor market economics. There are two very different views on this matter.

According to one view, occupational segregation reflects choices made by women, choices that have both cultural and economic origins. Cultural factors might lead women into nurturing occupations such as teaching and personal care and men into more physical occupations such as construction or mining. As cultural images change, occupational choices change, too. For example, the idea of women as doctors and lawyers seemed strange to many people a generation ago, but today very close to half of medical and law students are women.

According to the opposite view, occupational segregation reflects choices made by men. In this model, men choose first. They decide which occupations they would like, leaving the rest for women. Economist Barbara Bergman conjectures that the earmarking of jobs by sex has its origin in social systems that decree that women are and should be inferior in status to men. The result is that men feel uncomfortable when working side by side with women as equals, and even more so when working under the supervision of women. To avoid this discomfort, men confine women to a limited set of job categories.[7]

Just a generation ago the idea of women as doctors and lawyers seemed strange to many people.

In both views, supply and demand determine wages within each occupation. The disagreement is over why the supply of women in certain occupations is as great as it is despite low pay. In the one view, women choose those occupations voluntarily because they have attractive nonwage characteristics. In the other view, men leave women no other place to go.

The Comparable-Worth Remedy   The different views on the origins of occupational segregation by gender have different policy implications. Those who see occupational segregation as a product of women's choices see no need for any remedy beyond those already on the books. Those measures prohibit paying different wages to men and women doing the same work and, through affirmative action, grant women access to nontraditional occupations. Those who see occupational segregation as male dominance of labor markets want more, however. They want equal pay for women now, without waiting for massive cultural and occupational shifts to occur.

One suggested way to do this is to institute equal pay for work of *comparable worth*. Under that approach, employers would use statistical job evaluation techniques to measure the worth of work in different occupations, such as those of personal care worker and truck driver. Each job would earn points for traits like physical demand, initiative, and responsibility. The results would give a formula for pay recommendations.

BVT *Lab*

Visit www.BVTLab.com to explore the student resources available for this chapter.

Skeptics see the concept of equal pay for comparable work not only as unnecessary but also as actively harmful, for several reasons.

First, they say, job evaluations fail to account for supply and demand. Suppose that petroleum engineers and lawyers receive equal job evaluation points and were assigned equal pay. Later, there is a boom in the oil industry, increasing the demand for engineers but having little effect on the demand for lawyers. If firms could not bid up wages to attract the extra engineers they need, positions would go unfilled. Similarly, during a downturn in the industry, petroleum engineers would experience layoffs because their employers would not be able to offer them the option of continued employment at reduced pay.

Second, job evaluation techniques are inherently subjective. Different point scales and different evaluators produce different relative values for the same pair of jobs. For these reasons, private firms that already use such scales as part of their human resources management use them only as one factor among many in setting wages.

Finally, the critics point out that raising wages in traditionally female-dominated jobs would cause firms to cut back on employment in those occupations. Hospitals would use more automated monitoring equipment in order to economize on personal care. Insurance companies would substitute computers for clerical workers. The reduced employment opportunities would offset the wage gains for women in the affected occupations.

Advocates of comparable worth acknowledge that job evaluation techniques are imperfect. They agree that assigning every wage decision in the country to a computer would be a bad idea, and they deny that this is their intention. Rather, they claim that intelligently applied, job evaluations and other comparable-worth policies can contribute to a more just and productive labor market.

Summary

1. **Are unions economic maximizers**? In a competitive labor market, any increase in the wage won by unions tends to reduce employment. Some models of unionization emphasize maximization of employment or the wage bill. Other models view unions as political structures, applying concepts like the *median worker model* that come from public choice theory.

2. **What do unions do in addition to bargaining wages and benefits?** Besides affecting wages, unions give workers a voice in the workplace. In that sense, we can see unions as part of the way firms coordinate complex transactions under conditions of long-term commitment of specialized resources, opportunism, and change. Managers of top nonunion firms recognize that productivity rises when workers have a voice in company affairs.

3. **How do discrimination and anti-discrimination policies affect wages and employment of various groups?** A firm practices *labor market discrimination* against a group of workers if it is unwilling to hire members of that group at the same wage rate as equally productive members of a more favored group. Discrimination by employers will reduce the wages of members of the disfavored group if there are no legal restrictions, and it will reduce employment of members of the disfavored group even if the law requires equal pay for equal work. Competition tends to erode discrimination by employers but not discrimination by customers or fellow workers. Where there is asymmetric information about worker characteristics, discrimination is possible even though employers would prefer not to discriminate, other things being equal.

4. **What are the economics of equal or unequal pay for men and women?** The degree of occupational segregation is much greater by gender than by race, and occupations that have traditionally had a majority of women pay less than those that have traditionally had more men. To correct this situation, some have proposed that workers performing jobs of comparable worth receive equal pay.

Key Terms   Page

Problems and Topics for Discussion

1. **Unions and monopsony**   Turn to Figure 13.6, in the preceding chapter, which shows supply, demand, and marginal resource cost curves for a monopsonist. The equilibrium wage under monopsony is $6 per hour. Suppose now that the workers threaten to go on strike unless they receive at least $8 per hour, and the employer accepts this demand. What happens to the supply curve of labor, given the union's wage demand? What happens to the marginal resource cost curve? Compared with the initial equilibrium, what happens to the wage rate? To the number of workers? Is there a limit to how high this union can raise wages without sacrificing the jobs of members? If so, what is the limit?

2. **Unionization on campus**   Are the non-teaching staff of your university members of a union? The teaching faculty? Are any efforts under way to unionize either of these groups? Interview one member of the non-teaching staff and one member of the faculty to learn their attitudes toward unionization.

3. **Labor unions and cartels**   Review the section on cartels in Chapter 11. In what ways do unions resemble cartels? How do they differ from cartels? Do you think that public policy should treat unions and producer cartels differently? Discuss.

4. **Labor unions in the news**   Search the Internet for news about labor unions and collective bargaining. Have recent rounds of bargaining centered on issues of wages and benefits or on such matters as job security and productivity? Give examples.

5. **Discrimination at Hertz**   In 1981 two women who had worked as automobile rental agents at Hertz Corporation filed a suit saying that they had encountered discrimination when they had applied repeatedly for jobs as station manager, but male candidates got the jobs. Although most rental agents were women, few had ever received promotions to the position of station manager. Hertz's manager in the city where the women worked had told them that a woman should not have the job of station manager because she couldn't go away for training and because, in the manager's view, "a woman's place is in the kitchen." The judge in the case decided in favor of the women. Do you think that the judge's decision was a proper one? Would it have been better to wait for competition to eliminate the discrimination, or do you think there was no real discrimination? Discuss.

Case for Discussion

Wal-Mart Case Shows Difficulties of Fighting Discrimination Through Class Actions

In June 2011, the United States Supreme Court, in a 5 to 4 decision, threw out a class action lawsuit against Wal-Mart on behalf of a group of women employees who claimed they had been victims of employment discrimination. At least 1.5 million current and former Wal-Mart employees had an interest in the outcome of that suit.

The lawsuit alleged that women were discriminated against both in pay and promotion. According to the plaintiffs, in 2007, at the time of the original lawsuit, women managers at Wal-Mart earned $89,280 on average while men made $105,682. Women hourly workers earned $17,459 compared with $18,609 for male hourly workers. In addition, women held only 34 to 40 percent of managerial jobs at Wal-Mart.

The Supreme Court decision did not rule directly on the issue of whether or not the plaintiffs had suffered discrimination. The key issue, instead, was whether they had sufficient common grounds for their complaints to meet the legal standards for a class action suit. In claiming that they did not, lawyers for Wal-Mart pointed out that the company had an explicit policy at the national level that prohibited discrimination.

Lawyers for the plaintiffs replied that despite the company-wide policy Wal-Mart gave substantial discretion to local managers in making actual hiring and promotion decisions. They submitted testimony by William T. Bielby, a sociologist specializing in social framework analysis. Bielby testified that he had collected "scientific evidence about gender bias, stereotypes, and the structure and dynamics of gender inequality in organizations." On the basis of that evidence, he concluded that Wal-Mart's culture might foster pay and other disparities by allowing subjective decisions by local managers. Such practices, he argued, allowed stereotypes to sway personnel choices, making "decisions about compensation and promotion vulnerable to gender bias."

Writing for the court majority, Justice Antonin Scalia contended that was not enough to justify bringing a class action suit. He viewed any possible discrimination against women employees to be the result of disparate decisions by local managers, not company-wide policy. The suit lacked the "glue" needed to hold the reasons for all the individual decisions together.

Sources: Based in part on Christopher Caldwell, "Licensed to Curb a Retail Leviathan," *The Financial Times,* February 11, 2007; Steven Greenhouse, "Court Approves Class-Action Suit Against Wal-Mart," *The New York Times,* February 7, 2007; Adam Liptak, "Justices Rule for Wal-Mart in Class-Action Bias Case," *The New York Times,* June 20, 2011.

Questions

1. In an early phase of the Wal-Mart litigation, Court of Appeals Judge Andrew J. Kleinfeld wrote that it was unrealistic to conclude that illegal discrimination was the sole cause of Wal-Mart's female employees failing to advance to better jobs. What other factors might play a role? Which of these factors, in your view, represent "choices made by men," and which would be "choices made by women?"

2. Data presented by the plaintiffs suggest that Wal-Mart was able to attract qualified female managers at wages less than those it paid to equally qualified males for comparable jobs. If so, could Wal-Mart further increase its profits by replacing some of its higher-priced male managers with equally competent, but less expensive, women? Why do you think Wal-Mart had not done so? Do you think economic or non-economic motivations lie behind the under-representation of women in managerial jobs?

3. National data, across all occupations, showed that at the time the lawsuit was brought women in the United States earned about 81 percent as much as men. At Wal-Mart, according to data submitted by plaintiffs in this lawsuit, women managers earned about 85 percent as much as men and women hourly workers about 94 percent as much as men. Those numbers suggest that Wal-Mart, although not perfect, was doing better than the average for all U.S. businesses in providing equal compensation for its female and male employees. Do you think that should have had a bearing on the way the case is decided? Discuss.

Endnotes

1. See Chapter 14 for an explanation of monopsony in labor markets.

2. Bruce E. Kaufman, *The Economics of Labor Markets and Labor Relations* (Hinsdale, IL: Dryden Press, 1986), 461–463.

3. David Blanchflower and Richard Freeman, "Going Different Ways: Unionism in the United States and Other Advanced OECD Countries," NBER Working Paper No. 3342, 1992

4. Bureau of Labor Statistics, Highlights of Women's Earnings in 2010, Report 1031, July 2011, http://www.bls.gov/cps/cpswcm2010.pdf.

5. These and other studies are discussed in Walter Williams, *Explaining the Economic Gender Gap* (Dallas: National Center for Policy Analysis, 1983).

6. For a brief summary of the empirical literature, see Kaufman, *Economics of Labor Markets,* 392–393.

7. See Barbara Bergman, "Does the Marker for Women's Labor Need Fixing?" *Journal of Economic Perspectives* (Winter 1989): 43–60.

Chapter 16

Income Distribution
and Poverty

After reading this chapter, you will understand the following:

1. How to measure the equality of income distribution

2. How the distribution of income has changed over time

3. How to measure poverty and how it differs from inequality

4. How policies for alleviating poverty affect the labor market

5. How the government uses transfer payments to alleviate poverty

Before reading this chapter, make sure you know the meaning of the following concepts:

1. Income and substitution effects

2. Human capital

3. Public choice theory

4. Economics of discrimination

This chapter takes up the issues of income distribution and poverty. In part, these issues are an extension of the theory of resource markets. As we saw in Chapter 13, workers and owners of capital and natural resources earn incomes from the factors of production they supply. Entrepreneurs earn profits or experience losses by finding and taking advantage of new opportunities. Yet economic theory offers only a partial explanation of income distribution. At best, it can tell us the outcome of market forces, other things being equal; but in the real world, "other things" are definitely not equal.

Culture, politics, geography and a host of other considerations affect the point from which people start when they enter the marketplace. People are born with different skills and talents. They grow up in different countries and different regions or school districts within a country. Some inherit large amounts of capital and natural resources; some do not. As they go through life, people encounter different attitudes and prejudices of others. The decisions they make about their educations, the places they choose to live, who they marry, and business risks they take—all cause their incomes to vary still more. As a result, some earn little or nothing, while others earn millions of dollars a year.

In addition to market forces, public policies also influence income distribution. Transfer payments such as disability payments and Temporary Assistance for Needy Families (TANF) raise the incomes of poor families, while tax systems in most countries also affect income distribution by taxing the poor comparatively less than the wealthy.

This chapter will take a comprehensive look at the determinants of inequality and poverty, and at the public policies to alleviate them.

Figure 16.1
Before and After-Tax Lorenz Curves for the U.S. Economy, 2007

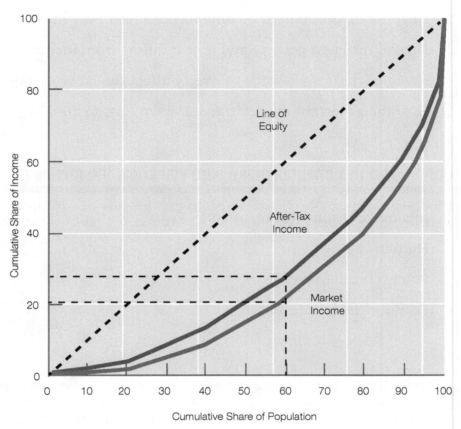

This figure uses a Lorenz curve to show the degree of inequality in the United States, both before tax (market income) and after tax. The horizontal axis represents the percentage of the population and the vertical axis the percentage of all income earned by those at or below each population percentile. In an economy with equal income distribution, the poorest 20 percent of the population would earn 20 percent of all income; the poorest 40 percent would earn 40 percent of all income, and so on. In that case, the Lorenz curve would be a straight line from one corner of the box to the other. This diagram shows that the 60 percent of the U.S. population earned just 21 percent of market income and 27 percent of after-tax income. As a result, the Lorenz curves sag toward the lower right-hand corner of the box. The degree of inequality can be measured by the Gini coefficient—the ratio of the shaded area between the Lorenz curve and the line of perfect equality to the area of the whole triangle beneath the line of equality.

Source: Congressional Budget Office, Trends in the Distribution of Household Income between 1979 and 2007, October 2011, Box 2.

16.1 Income Distribution: Measurement and Trends

Measuring Income Distribution

Figure 16.1 provides a good place to begin a discussion of how inequality is measured. The diagram shows a **Lorenz curve**—a visual picture of income distribution. It is drawn as a square with the horizontal axis representing a percentage of the population and the vertical axis a percentage of income earned by those at or below each population percentile. Reading this particular Lorenz curve, we see that as of 2007, the 60 percent of the population with the lowest incomes earned 21 percent of pre-tax income (market income) and 27 percent of after-tax income. If income distribution were completely equal, the Lorenz curve would follow the straight line of perfect equality. The more unequal the distribution, the more the Lorenz curve sags below the line of equality. In a society where one person earned all the income and no one else had anything at all, the Lorenz curve would coincide with the axes.

The fact that the Lorenz curve moves farther from the line of equality as inequality increases provides a simple way to reduce the concept of inequality to a single number. The **Gini coefficient**, devised in 1912 by the Italian statistician Corrado Gini, is the ratio between the shaded area lying between the Lorenz curve and the line of equality to the whole triangle lying beneath the line of equality. If income is distributed perfectly equally, the Gini coefficient is zero. If one person has all the income, the Gini coefficient is 1. The **Gini index** is the Gini coefficient multiplied by 100. For example, in Figure 16.1, the Gini index for after tax income is 48.9.

Figure 16.2, which gives data on income distribution in selected countries, shows that inequality varies greatly around the world. Latin America and Africa stand out as regions of the greatest inequality. The high-income countries of Europe, along with Canada and Australia, are more equal. The median Gini index for in-country income distribution in the full set of 140 countries from which this sample came is 39. That leaves the United States, at 45, a little less equal than the global median. A separate World Bank study of global inequality estimates that the Gini Index for the whole world, throwing together everyone from the poorest people in poor countries to the wealthiest people in the richest countries, is about 66—more unequal than the in-country distribution for all but the very least equal individual countries.

Income distribution in many individual countries— including the United States, China, South Africa, and Russia—has become less equal in recent decades. At the same time, though, global income distribution has become more equal. The explanation of this seeming paradox is that many very large, poor countries—such as China, India, and Brazil—have had greater increases in per capita income than the world's wealthiest countries. Because poor Chinese workers have become a lot less poor while wealthy Swiss bankers have become only moderately richer, the whole world income distribution has become more compressed.

Lorenz curve

A graph that represents the degree of income inequality in an economy

Gini coefficient

A measure of inequality of income equal to zero under conditions of perfect equality and to one under perfect inequality

Gini index

The Gini coefficient expressed as a percentage

FIGURE 16.2
GINI COEFFICIENTS OF INCOME INEQUALITY FOR SELECTED COUNTRIES

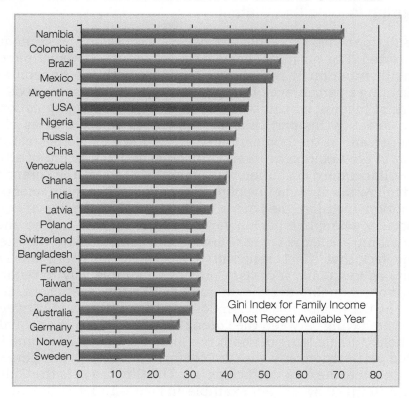

The Gini index is a measure of inequality that has a value of 0 under conditions of perfect equality and 100 under perfect inequality. The United States, at 45, is a little less equal than the median of 39 for the full set of 140 countries from which this sample came. The cross-country Gini Index for the whole world, throwing together the poorest people in poor countries and the wealthiest people in the richest countries, is about 66—more unequal than the in-country distribution for all but the least equal individual countries.

Source: CIA World Factbook

U.S. Income Distribution Trends and Their Causes

Income distribution differs not only from country to country but also over time within any country. Figure 16.3 provides two views of the way income distribution changed in the United States from 1979 to 2007. (For better comparison, the years at both ends of the comparison period came at the conclusion of an economic expansion, just before the onset of a recession.)

FIGURE 16.3
INCOME DISTRIBUTION TRENDS IN THE UNITED STATES, 1979–2007

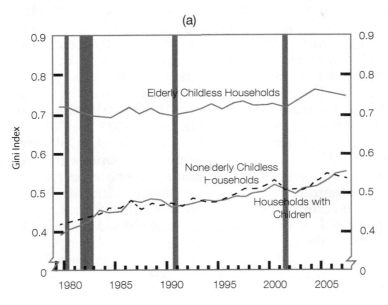

(a)

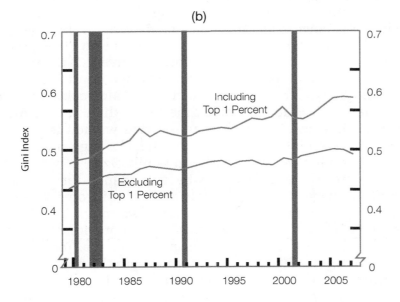

(b)

This figure gives two views of increasing inequality in the United States. Part (a) shows that elderly, childless households experienced only a small increase in inequality, while income distribution among younger households with children became much less equal. Part (b) shows that much of the increase in inequality over the period is attributable to the rapidly increasing incomes of the top 1 percent of the population. The absolute income of that group tripled over the period, and their share of all income doubled.

Source: Congressional Budget Office, Trends in the Distribution of Household Income between 1979 and 2007, October 2011, Figures 8 and 9.

Part (a) shows that inequality increased at different rates for various groups. The distribution of income for elderly, childless households became only slightly less unequal over the period. The greatest increase in inequality was for younger households with children. The difference reflects the fact that younger households depended more on market income, which became less equally distributed. Elderly households depended more on savings and Social Security benefits, for which the distribution changed less rapidly.

Part (b) shows that much of the overall increase in inequality over the period was attributable to the top 1 percent of the income distribution, for whom income tripled between 1979 and 2007. There are several possible explanations for the rapid increase in incomes of the very wealthiest members of the population. One is that incomes of superstars like athletes and musicians have risen as new technology has allowed them to reach larger audiences. Another focuses on the very high pay of top corporate executives. Still another explanation focuses on the growing share of all income earned by top professionals in the fields of law and finance. Whatever the reason, the share of all market income earned by the top 1 percent of households grew from 9.6 percent in 1979 to 18.6 percent in 2007.

The Effect of Demographic Changes   The distribution of income by individuals is somewhat less unequal than the distribution by households since the lowest-income households are, on average, smaller than those at the top of the income distribution. The poorest 20 percent of households include only about 15 percent of the population, whereas the richest 20 percent include nearly a quarter of the population. Demographic changes appear to be of increasing importance. For example, in 2006, for the first time fewer than half of American women were married. The rate of unmarried women is greater and increasing more rapidly for low-income than for high-income households, which reinforces the disparity in family size.

Furthermore, there appears to be a tendency for an increased number of marriages among partners of similar income levels. At the risk of using an overly stylized illustration, we might imagine that in the past, male doctors married wives who did not enter the labor force while male laborers married female grocery clerks. Today, the male doctors are marrying female lawyers while both the male laborers and female grocery clerks are marrying later, if at all. Such changing patterns of marriage would have the effect of increasing income inequality among households even if the degree of income equality among all male and female individuals were to remain unchanged.

Changes in Relative Wages of Skilled and Unskilled Workers   Some of the most dramatic changes in income inequality occurred within the category of wage and salary income, which makes up the largest source of income for the population as a whole. During the 1980s, there was a sharp increase in the earnings of college-educated workers relative to those with a high-school education or less. That change continued, although at a slower rate, during the 1990s. Because college-educated workers already earned more than the less educated to begin with, that change added to overall inequality. Economists have offered several explanations for the trend:

- *Skill-biased technological change* One explanation for the increased return to education is skill-biased technological change. Computerization of manufacturing has increased the demand for college-educated workers more rapidly than that group increased as a percentage of the labor force.

- *Immigration and trade* Another explanation for the relative increase in pay of more educated workers lies in immigration and trade. If immigrants, including illegal immigrants, were less skilled than the average U.S.-born labor force, the relative supply of low-skill workers would have increased at the same time the relative demand for low-skill workers was falling. In many cases, instead of importing workers, U.S.-based firms have moved low-skill production processes abroad, with much the same effect on relative demand and supply for low-skilled workers.

- *Decline of unionization* Some observers think that the decline of labor unions in the United States, a process that began earlier but continued during the 1980s and after, may also have contributed to inequality. In the past, unionized manufacturing jobs were among the best-paying alternatives for workers with a high-school education or less. Now such jobs are fewer, and less educated workers more often take low-paid service jobs.

- *Growth of the financial sector* Still another reason for growth of inequality is the growth of the financial sector. The financial sector not only hires more highly educated workers than do nonfinancial sectors, it pays more to workers at equal educational levels. Overall, between 1979 and 2007, pay in the financial sector rose from about average for the economy to 180 percent of the average.

Progressive tax

A tax that takes a larger share of higher incomes, making the distribution of income more equal after the tax than before

Regressive tax

A tax that takes a larger share of lower incomes, making the distribution of income less equal after the tax than before

The above explanations are not mutually exclusive. It is likely that each has played some role in the trend toward greater inequality of income in the United States over the past quarter century.

Taxes and Income Distribution Figure 16.1 showed that the distribution of income is more equal after taxes and transfer payments than before. We say that a tax is **progressive** if the distribution of after-tax income is more equal than that of before-tax income and **regressive** if the opposite is true. Personal income taxes are an example of a progressive tax, while sales taxes and payroll taxes are regressive.

The distribution of after-tax income in the United States is more equal than the distribution of before-tax income

FIGURE 16.4   INDEXES OF PROGRESSIVITY OF FEDERAL TAXES

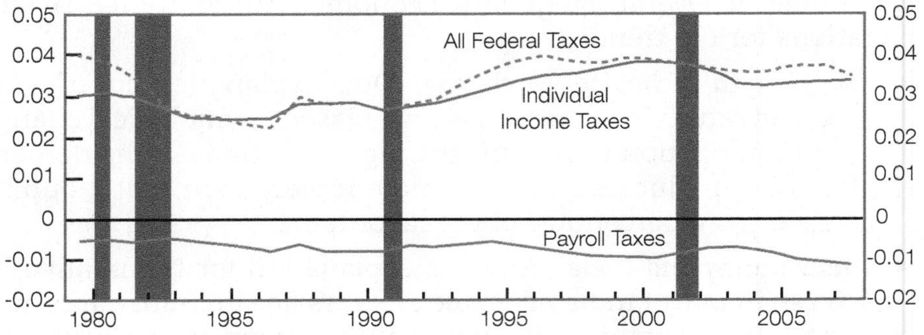

This figure shows the progressivity of federal taxes as measured by an index that shows their effects on income distribution. A positive value for the index shows a progressive tax that makes after-tax distribution more equal; a negative value shows a regressive tax that makes after-tax distribution less equal. The income tax is progressive; the payroll tax is regressive. On the whole, the federal tax system has become slightly less progressive over the past three decades.

Source: Congressional Budget Office, Trends in the Distribution of Household Income between 1979 and 2007, October 2011, Figure 19.

Figure 16.4 shows indexes of the distributional effects of federal taxes, based on the degree to which they equalize the distribution of income. A positive value indicates a progressive tax; a negative value indicates a regressive one.

The federal income tax is an example of a progressive tax because the tax rate rises for larger incomes. Economists call the amount of tax paid on the last dollar of income the marginal tax rate. The top marginal tax rate, as of 2012, was 35 percent. The most recent change was a decrease from 39.6 percent, which took place in two steps from 2001 to 2003. Over the whole period, the top marginal tax rate has varied from as high as 70 percent in 1979 to as low as 28 percent in the late 1980s. On balance, the progressivity of the federal income tax was about the same in 2007 as it had been in 1979.

The federal payroll tax, in contrast, is regressive. At present, the payroll tax consists of a Social Security tax of 6.2 percent levied on employees and another 6.2 percent levied on employers, plus a 1.45 percent tax on employees and employers for Medicare, for a total tax rate of 15.6 percent. (In 2011-2012, Congress temporarily lowered the employee Social Security rate to 4.2 percent.) The tax is regressive for two reasons. First, it falls only on income from labor (wages, salaries, and self-employment income), which makes up a larger share of total income for lower-income households. Second, there is a cap, currently set at $106,800, beyond which labor income is not subject to tax.

As Figure 16.4 shows, the payroll tax is not only regressive but also has become more so over time. Moreover, now it accounts for a larger share of total federal taxes than in the past. In the 1950s, only about 10 percent of all federal tax revenue came from the payroll tax. By 1979 that had risen to about 30 percent, and by 2007 it had reached 40 percent. The growing importance of the payroll tax is one of the main reasons that the federal tax system as a whole has become somewhat less progressive over time.

It is worth noting that although the tax system has become slightly less progressive, the share of total income taxes paid by wealthy taxpayers has increased. For example, from 1979 to 2007, the share of federal taxes paid by the top 10 percent increased from 41 percent to 55 percent, and the share paid by the top 1 percent of taxpayers increased from 15 percent to 28 percent. Meanwhile, the share of all federal taxpayers paid by the lowest 60 percent of earners decreased from 23 percent to 14 percent.

The explanation for the seeming paradox is that the share of total income received by high earners has increased even faster than their taxes. For example, while the share of all taxes paid by the top 1 percent roughly doubled, their share of total income increased by 275 percent.

Poverty and Antipoverty Policy

Poverty and inequality are related concepts, but the relationship is not a simple one. Inequality is a statistical concept, whereas poverty is sociological. Poverty means a lack of means to provide for the basic goods and services that people in a given society see as usual and necessary. As discussed in *Applying Economic Ideas* 16.1, there are countries in the world where almost everyone is poor and others where almost no one is poor, even though income is nowhere distributed equally.

Applying Economic Ideas **16.1**

Poverty in the United States and Around the Globe

Without denying that poverty is a problem in the United States, to keep things in perspective we need to recognize that even low-income families in the United States are incomparably richer than the poor in many regions of the world.

In 2008, the World Bank published a new set of estimates that used an income of $1.25 per day as a measure of extreme poverty. Some 1.4 billion people, or more than a quarter of the world population, fell below that level.

The figure of 1.4 billion poor people was an improvement from the count of 1.9 billion extremely poor people in 1981, but the improvement has been uneven. While economic growth and globalization has lifted hundreds of millions of people out of poverty in China and India, more than half of the population of Sub-Saharan Africa continues to experience extreme poverty. In the poorest countries, like Ethiopia, four out of five people fall below this threshold. By comparison, an income of $1.25 per day, or $1,825 per year for a family of four, was just 8 percent of the U.S. government's official poverty threshold for 2008. In the United States, almost no one qualifies as extremely poor by the World Bank's standards.

More than a quarter of the world population falls below the level of extreme poverty or income below $1.25 a day.

It is hard to understand just what it means to live on less than $1.25 a day. Hunger is perhaps a more intuitive concept. The World Hunger Education Service estimates that some 925 million people, almost 14 percent of the world's population, do not have enough food. Of these, 239 million live in Sub-Saharan Africa, and just 19 million in developed countries.

On the other hand, not all the news is bad, even for the bottom billion. A recent book by Charles Kenny, *Getting Better,* explains that certain key non-income measures of the quality of life have been improving, even in countries where per capita GDP has stagnated. For example, in 1950, life expectancy in the poorest 20 percent of countries was only about half that in the richest 20 percent. Today, people in the poorest countries live two-thirds as long as those in the richest countries. The improvement has come about, in part, because some of the most basic inputs to good health—including clean water, sanitation, vaccines, and antibiotics—have become cheaper even in the poorest countries.

Kenny notes that there has also been progress in education. From 1950 to 2000, the share of the world's population who could read and write increased from about half to four-fifths. Women's literacy rates increased even faster over the period, rising from a global average of less than two-thirds that of men to around four-fifths that of men by the end of the twentieth century.

Sources: World Bank, Poverty Data: A Supplement to 2008 World Development Indicators (http://sitere-sources.worldbank.org/DATASTATISTICS/Resources/WDI08supplement1216.pdf); World Hunger Education Service, "2012 World Hunger and Poverty Facts and Statistics," (http://www.worldhunger.org/articles/Learn/world%20hunger%20facts%202002.htm); and Charles Kenny, *Getting Better,* Basic Books, 2011.

Measuring Poverty in the United States

Official Poverty Data   The U.S. government first developed an official definition of poverty in the 1960s. Molly Orshansky of the Social Security Administration, who took an approach that was as much commonsense as scientific, did the original work. She began with the idea that people had to eat. The Department of Agriculture published estimates of the cost of an economy food plan that would provide a balanced diet at the lowest possible cost given market prices. Of course, an income equal to the cost of the economy food plan would not be enough to keep a family out of poverty because it would leave nothing for other basic needs like clothing and shelter. To take those needs into account, Orshansky set the poverty threshold—the dividing line between the poor and the nonpoor—at three times the cost of the economy food plan, a multiplier derived from data that showed that low-income families spent about a third of their income on food. In 1964, the poverty threshold for a family of four was set at $3,104. By 2011, that had grown to $22,350.

Figure 16.5 shows how officially-measured poverty has changed in the United States since 1960. Part (a) shows that a strong economy and a set of policy initiatives known as the "War on Poverty" brought officially-measured poverty down sharply during the 1970s. Since that time, the poverty rate has changed little, rising and falling with the business cycle.

Part (b) of Figure 16.5 shows that within the flat trend of total poverty, the distribution of poverty among population groups has changed greatly. Historically, the elderly had the highest poverty rates. Increased Social Security benefits, wider use of private retirement savings, and increased housing wealth has changed that; the elderly now have the lowest poverty rates. Poverty rates are now highest for children, although even for that group the rate is down from the 1960s. A disturbing feature of the chart is the upward trend of poverty among the working-age population, which reached an all-time high in 2010.

A New View of Poverty   The Census Bureau's own staff and independent analysts have long known that the official poverty measure is deeply flawed. One problem is that it counts only the cash income of poor families and fails to take into account the value of in-kind government benefits like SNAP (formerly food stamps) and housing benefits. A second problem is that its multiplier of three, applied to the economy food plan, fails to take into account the changing costs of budget elements other than food. Other problems include inadequate attention to regional differences in living costs and an inadequate view of family structure.

FIGURE **16.5** POVERTY TRENDS, 1960–2010

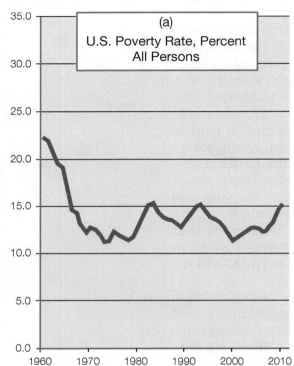

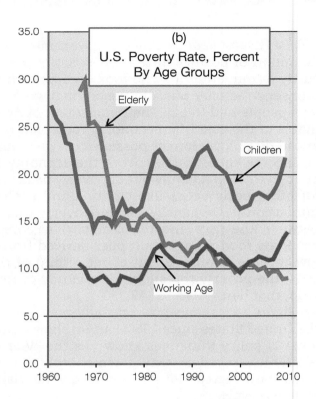

According to the official definition, 15.1 percent of the U.S. population was poor as of 2010. The percentage has varied within a narrow range since the 1970s. Meanwhile, poverty has become less prevalent among the elderly population and more common for people of working age. The poverty rate for children is the highest of the major groups.

Source: U.S. Bureau of the Census

In 2011, in an attempt to deal with these criticisms, the Census Bureau published what it called a Supplemental Poverty Measure (SPM), which does not replace the official measure but does try to address some of its shortcomings. The SPM begins from a minimum budget that includes, not just food, but food, clothing, shelter, and utilities (FCSU). The FCSU budget is then multiplied by 1.2 to allow for other items. It is also adjusted for family size and regional differences in housing costs. The SPM then compares the poverty budget to a measure of resources that adjusts the old cash income concept in three ways. First, it adds the value of in-kind benefits that are available to meet FCSU needs. Second, it adjusts for taxes and cash transfer payments. Third, it subtracts other necessary expenses, the largest of which are work-related childcare and out-of-pocket medical expenses.

The resulting poverty thresholds are only a little higher than under the official measure: $24,391 vs. $22,113 for a family of four in rental accommodations. To put it in perspective, we can break the numbers down to see the kind of lifestyle such an income allows. Imagine a family of two adults and two children with a total income of $30,000 after taxes, including the cash value of SNAP and other in-kind benefits. Suppose they are healthy and manage to keep their out-of-pocket medical costs down to $400 a month, perhaps using an employer-subsidized high-deductible insurance plan. Suppose they can juggle work schedules to avoid all-day childcare costs, allowing them to hold work-related expenses to $809 per year. That would leave them right at the poverty line. Almost all of their cash income would go to meet food, clothing, shelter, and utility needs. They would have just $391 a month for phone bills, gasoline, appliance repairs, and maybe Internet service, if they wanted to give their kids a chance to be part of the modern world.

Overall, the SPM does not change the poverty rate very much. The SPM estimates the poverty rate for the entire population at 16 percent in 2010, compared with 15.2 for the official measure. The surprises come in how that poverty impacts specific population groups.

In particular, the SPM records just 18.2 percent of children as poor, down from 22.5 percent by the official measure. The working age poverty rate rises from 13.7 percent to 15.2 percent, and the rate for the elderly from 9 percent to 15.9 percent. To put it a different way, the SPM tells us that 60 percent of all poor people are of working age, which means more than twice as many working-age as children.

The SPM makes an even bigger difference for the income status of the working-age population if we look at near-poverty, that is, incomes from 1 to 2 times the poverty threshold. Under the official measure, 16.3 percent of the working-age population fell in that income bracket. Under the SPM, the figure rises to 29 percent. That means almost 45 percent of the U.S. working age population are living on incomes less than double the poverty level.

Another stereotype to suffer erosion concerns poverty and family structure. According to the SPM, 37.3 percent of poor people, the largest group, are members of two-parent households, up from just 30.5 percent under the official measure. Households headed by women, which contain the greatest number of people under the official measure, come in second, with 36.6 percent of the poor. There are many more poor individuals (mostly children) in households headed by one female parent than in those with a single male parent, but the gap narrows significantly. Yes, having two parents still offers some protection against poverty, but not as much as the official data implies.

According to the SPM, minorities are still at greater risk of poverty than whites are, but once again the stereotypes do not hold as sharply as under the official poverty measure. The poverty rate for whites rises from 13.1 percent to 14.3 percent. That for blacks falls from 27.5 percent to 25.5 percent while the poverty rate for Hispanics just edges out that for blacks under the new measure, rising from 26.7 percent to 28.2 percent. Although Asians continue to suffer far less poverty than other minorities, their poverty rate shows the greatest increase under the new measure, rising from 12.1 to 16.8 percent.

The bottom line is that the new view of poverty does not completely dispel the old stereotypes, but it significantly undermines them. In every dimension, the picture is less of two Americas and more of one America. Yes, the white, home owning, working age population is still more prosperous than the population of minority children and working-age single mothers in rental housing; but the differences between the groups, by every metric, are narrower than we thought.

16.2 Fighting Poverty through the Labor Market

At one time, responsibility to support low-income individuals rested with families, local communities, and private charities. In some countries, that remains true to this day. In the United States and other high-income countries, however, national governments have instituted major policies to fight poverty. In many European countries in the mid-twentieth century, governments led by Labor or Social Democratic parties instituted comprehensive "welfare state" policies. In the United States, the 1930s saw the advent of Social Security to combat poverty among the elderly. President Lyndon Johnson declared a "War on Poverty" in 1964, which resulted in a reduction of poverty to its present rate of 12 to 15 percent, down from rates higher than 20 percent in the 1950s. In the 1990s, a major legislative effort, led by President Bill Clinton and receiving broad bipartisan backing in Congress, resulted in extensive reform of antipoverty policy. This section briefly summarizes the main types of policies used to fight poverty in high-income countries.

Without a doubt, work is the most effective of all antipoverty programs, at least in high-income countries. In the United States, the poverty rate for families with at least one full-time worker is about a fifth of that for families with no workers. Not surprisingly, then, governments have tried to combat poverty by improving wages and job prospects of people who might otherwise fall into poverty.

A broad range of public policies improves people's work prospects. Take education, for example. In the United States, the poverty rate for people without a high-school diploma is nearly double the national average, while the poverty rate for college graduates is less than a quarter of the average. Public health policies also combat poverty since poor health is something that cuts many people from the labor market. Important though such policies are, this section will focus on a narrower group of labor market policies that aim to ensure that those who do work will not fall into poverty.

Minimum wage laws are one such labor market policy. Although those who work are less likely to be poor than those who do not, it remains true that even in the United States, one of the world's highest income countries, almost 6 percent of people in families with a full-time worker have incomes below the poverty threshold. In 1938, Congress passed the first federal minimum wage law, which required employers to pay $.25 per hour. Since then it has raised the federal minimum wage several times. In 2007, Congress enacted a schedule of increases raising the minimum wage to its current level of $7.25 per hour. That is enough to raise a single full-time worker above the poverty threshold.

However, even at the increased minimum wage, it would require two minimum-wage workers to keep a family of four out of poverty—and even that might not be enough if work-related expenses are included, as they are in the Supplementary Poverty Measure discussed above. Several states and a few cities mandate a wage above the federal rate. As of 2012, Washington State had the highest minimum wage, $9.04.

To some extent, unintended consequences of minimum wage laws may undermine their effectiveness in reducing poverty. They make some low-skilled workers better off; but at the same time they reduce the quantity of low-wage workers demanded, as restaurants shift to shorter hours, automated gates replace parking lot attendants, and so on. The strength of the unintended effects is not clear. During periods like the early 2000s, when the minimum wage was low in comparison to average wages, the effects appear to have been small.

An additional disadvantage of a minimum wage as an antipoverty policy is that not all low-wage workers are poor. In the United States, something like half of all workers with minimum wage jobs come from households in the top half of the income distribution. They include students working part time and living with their families, low-paid spouses in households where both husband and wife work, and so on. At the same time, a minimum wage does little or nothing to help the many poor families in which no one holds a full-time job. Rather than relying on wages, those families support themselves with income from pensions, disability payments, welfare, and other nonwage sources.

Unemployment Compensation

Unemployment compensation is another labor market policy that helps combat poverty. Like minimum wages, however, unemployment compensation can have unintended consequences. One of those is to lengthen the time workers spend searching for a new job before they accept an offer. Up to a point, a longer period of job search is not all bad. It takes time and careful search to match workers to the jobs for which they are best suited. If people had to take the first job that came along, the labor market might operate less efficiently.

Countries differ in the way they balance the various effects of unemployment compensation. The United States and some other English-speaking countries emphasize a time limit on unemployment payments. They offer payments high enough to keep the unemployed out of poverty without replacing the full income of their previous jobs. Also, they often require beneficiaries to take part in training and job-search programs and to accept jobs that pay less than those previously lost.

Many countries of continental Europe are more generous in terms of time limits, compensation levels, and retraining requirements. Economist Stephen Nickell made a intercountry comparison of countries with different unemployment compensation policies. He found that countries with higher benefits offered for longer periods tend to have both higher unemployment rates and more long-term unemployment as a share of total unemployment. Spurred in part by such concerns, Germany and some other European countries have reformed unemployment policies to moderate their unintended consequences.

Still other labor market policies can have direct or indirect effects on poverty. Policies to combat discrimination against women and minorities are examples. Policies that facilitate formation of labor unions are another. Policies that aim to increase job security by making it harder to dismiss workers, or to replace full-time with part-time workers, are yet another. All of these run the risk that while helping some workers, they may make it more difficult for others to find jobs.

Helping the Poor with Cash and In-kind Transfers

When most people think of antipoverty program, they are less likely to think of labor market policies than of programs that give the poor cash or in-kind transfers. Beginning in 1935, the U.S. government undertook a *cash transfer* program called Aid to Families with Dependent Children (AFDC). In 1997, Temporary Assistance for Needy Families (TANF) replaced AFDC. The best-known in-kind transfer program is the Supplemental Nutrition Assistance Program (SNAP). Many people still refer to the program as "food stamps," even though the old paper food coupons have been phased out. This section examines the intended and unintended consequences of such programs and the reforms to them in the 1990s.

The new debit card is replacing paper food stamps. Food stamps are one of the best known in-kind transfer programs.

Incentive Effects of Transfer Programs Transfer programs, like policies centered on the job market, have the intended consequence of raising the incomes of people who would otherwise be poor. Both types of programs also have unintended consequences. For transfer programs, the unintended consequences that have attracted the most attention are changes in work incentives. Figure 16.6 demonstrates the incentive effects of income transfer programs.

Suppose that the poverty threshold P for a certain family is determined to be $20,000, and suppose that the family's earned income is Y. We call the difference between P and Y the *poverty gap* for the family. One way to ensure that the family will not be poor would be to give them a cash grant equal to the poverty gap. For example, a family with no earned income would get a grant of $20,000; one with $6,000 of earned income would get $14,000; and families with earned income over $20,000 would get no grant.

Under such a program, the total disposable income for various families would follow the line PQRS. The program would succeed in its intended effect of keeping the family out of poverty. Unfortunately, it would have a strong negative impact on work incentives. The family would get no financial benefit whatsoever from earnings up to $20,000.

FIGURE 16.6   WORK INCENTIVES AND TRANSFER PROGRAMS

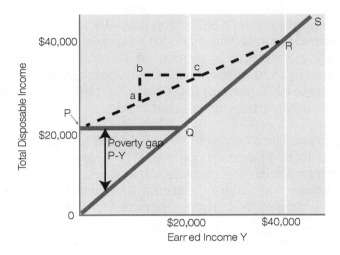

In this figure, the poverty threshold is P ($20,000) and earned income is Y. The poverty gap is the difference between P and Y. If a family is paid exactly what is needed to fill the poverty gap, its total disposable income follows the path PQRS as earned income increases. In that case, work incentives are zero up to point Q. If the program is modified to include a benefit reduction rate of 50 percent (the ratio ab/bc), total disposable income follows the path PRS. Work incentives are increased, but now some payments go to families whose earned income is already above the poverty threshold.

Taking into account the effort of holding a job, not to mention job-related expenses like transportation, clothing, and childcare, many families might prefer not to work even if a job paying $20,000, or even a little more, were available.

Alternatively, it would be possible to tie payments to earned income. A family with no income would still receive $20,000, but the amount would fall only by part of a dollar for each dollar of earned income. Economists refer to the amount by which benefits of a transfer program decrease for each added dollar of earned income as the **benefit reduction rate**. In Figure 16.6, the benefit reduction rate is the ratio of line ab to line bc.

If the benefit reduction rate were 50 percent, the family's total disposable income would follow the path PRS in Figure 16.6. That would provide a much stronger work incentive than a program that cut benefits off sharply when a family reached the poverty threshold. However, reducing the benefit reduction rate means that some families now receive transfers even though their earned income is greater than the poverty threshold. For example, a family with $24,000 earned income, previously ineligible for assistance, would receive a grant of $8,000 under a program with a basic benefit equal to $20,000 and a benefit reduction rate of 50 percent. Whether such a program would cost less overall depends on how people respond to work incentives and how many families there are, to begin with, at various income levels.

Benefit reduction rate

The amount by which benefits of a transfer program decrease for each added dollar of earned income

Net marginal tax rate

The sum of the benefit reduction rate and the rate of income tax

Negative income tax

An antipoverty program under which low-income people receive grants from the government and high-income people pay taxes, subject to a net marginal tax rate of less than 100 percent for everyone

The situation gets even more complex if earned income is subject to an income or payroll tax. If so, the amount by which total disposable income increases for each dollar of earned income depends on both the tax rate and the benefit reduction rate. We call the sum of the two the **net marginal tax rate**. Suppose, for example, that we tax all earned income, starting at zero, at 20 percent. If we combine that tax with the 50 percent benefit reduction rate for the transfer program, we get a net marginal tax rate of 70 percent for income up to $20,000 and a net marginal tax rate of 20 percent above that level.

Reform: The Earned Income Tax Credit   In 1962, University of Chicago economist Milton Friedman proposed integrating all antipoverty transfer programs with the income tax system. He called the scheme a **negative income tax**. Low-income families would receive payments from the government and higher income families would make payments to it, with the net marginal tax rate held low enough for everyone to provide adequate work incentive.

Friedman made his proposal at a time when most welfare programs had very high net marginal tax rates, sometimes more than 100 percent. Such high rates occurred because the benefit reduction rates and tax rates of various programs are additive. For example, if a family received an AFDC grant with a benefit reduction rate of 67 percent, a food-stamp grant with a benefit reduction rate of 50 percent, and paid Social Security payroll taxes of 14 percent, its net marginal tax rate would be 131 percent. For each $100 earned, the family would end up $31 poorer in terms of total disposable income.

Friedman's ideas helped focus the attention of economists and policy makers on the inefficiencies, not to say the injustices, of existing antipoverty programs. More and more, people came to perceive AFDC, food stamps, and similar programs as "paying people to be poor." In response to these criticisms, governments at both the federal and state levels undertook many experiments in welfare reform during the 1970s and 1980s. Some of them were small-scale experiments with negative income taxes that aimed to measure the response of poor families to changes in benefit reduction rates. Others changed details of the implementation of antipoverty programs. Many of them showed promising results. In the 1990s, they culminated in major reforms of the welfare system at the national level. Remarkably, they took place with wide bipartisan support at a time when different political parties controlled the White House and Congress.

One of the most important reforms, enacted in 1993, was the expansion of a previously small federal program known as the Earned Income Tax Credit (EITC). Under the EITC, families with low earned incomes receive a federal tax credit for each dollar earned. The EITC operates on top of other existing federal taxes. For very low incomes, the EITC exceeds taxes due on earned income, so taxpayers receive a check from the government. For higher incomes, the EITC may be less than taxes due, but it still reduces tax owed. The net marginal tax rate is the sum of the EITC rate and applicable rate of other income and payroll taxes.

The EITC is a variant on the negative income tax concept, but one that contains even more potent work incentives for the lowest-income workers than did Friedman's original proposal. Up to the maximum EITC threshold, payments actually rise rather than fall when earned income increases. The benefit reduction rate up to the maximum benefit limit is not just low but negative.

In its study of Supplemental Poverty Measures, the Census Bureau staff found that EITC was the single most effective antipoverty program. Without EITC, the SPM measure of the poverty rate, which had an estimated value of 16 percent for 2010, would have risen to 18 percent.

TANF and Related Reforms   In 1996, three years after expanding the EITC, Congress passed another major set of reforms under the clumsy title Personal Responsibility and Work Opportunity Reconciliation Act (PRWORA). The PRWORA reforms are difficult to summarize because, although they establish certain federal guidelines, individual states are responsible for implementing them. In practice, state programs vary greatly. Without examining all the variants, the main features of PRWORA were as follows:

- Temporary Assistance for Needy Families (TANF) replaced Aid to Families with Dependent Children (AFDC), which had been the main welfare program up to that time.

- Training programs and work incentives underwent expansion. Participation was mandatory for most families, and incentives like additional childcare grants became available to working parents.

- Beyond a set time limit, new regulations required TANF recipients to make a transition to self-sufficient employment.

The response to PRWORA was dramatic. In the late 1990s, welfare roles, measured as the number of families receiving AFDC or TANF, decreased sharply; and labor force participation rates increased, especially for single women with children. The reforms did not bring a permanent reduction in the overall poverty rate for the United States. However, for single women with children, the poverty rate declined significantly, from over 35 percent in 1992 to under 25 percent by 2000.

A large amount of research has attempted to explain just why welfare roles fell and labor force participation increased in the late 1990s. All of it seems to agree that, in combination, the EITC and PRWORA reforms made a helpful contribution to these trends. However, it remains difficult to determine exactly which parts of the reforms worked and how well. One reason is that the reforms took place against the background of a booming labor market that would have reduced welfare roles and increased employment even if there had been no reforms. Another reason is that many reforms came into effect at once. However, it is important to emphasize, as the data reported in Figure 16.5 showed, that however well reformed welfare systems performed in times of prosperity, they did not prevent sharp increases in poverty rates during the recession that began in 2007.

BVT *Lab*

Visit www.BVTLab.com to explore the student resources available for this chapter.

Summary

1. **How do economists measure income inequality?** The most widely used measure of inequality is the Gini coefficient or Gini index. The Gini coefficient is 0 under conditions of perfect equality and 1 under conditions of perfect inequality. The Gini index converts this to a percentage by multiplying by 100. The United States has a Gini index of about 45 for personal income before tax, somewhat less equal than the median for countries of the world.

2. **How has the distribution of income changed over time?** The income distribution in the United States reached its historically most equal point in the 1960s and 1970s. Since that time inequality has steadily increased. For example, between 1979 and 2007, the share of income that the top 1 percent of households received increased from about 9 percent to about 18 percent. Several factors can explain increasing inequality—including skill-biased technological change, downward pressure of wages of low-skill workers from trade and immigration, and a tax system that is less progressive than in the past.

3. **How does poverty differ from inequality, and what methods are available to measure it?** Poverty implies a lack of ability to meet basic needs. The U.S. Census Bureau sets an official poverty threshold equal to three times the cost of buying a minimum adequate diet for a family. Since the 1970s, the percentage of households in poverty in the United States has varied from about 12 to 15 percent, with no strong trend one way or the other. On a global scale, the World Bank sets a poverty threshold of $1.25 per day, or $1,825 per year for a family of four. That is much lower than the U.S. poverty threshold, which was $22,113 in 2010.

4. **How do policies for alleviating poverty affect the labor market?** One way to raise people out of poverty is to improve their prospects in the job market. Indirectly, policies supporting education and public health contribute to this goal. Direct efforts to improve earnings and job security include minimum wages, unemployment compensation, and measures to discourage layoffs, part-time work, and overtime. All of these policies may improve the income of the employed but also have the possible unintended consequence of raising the unemployment rate.

5. **How does the government use transfer payments to alleviate poverty?** Transfer programs aim to eliminate poverty by making up the gap between the poverty threshold and earned income. Their most troublesome unintended effect is the risk of discouraging work effort. Work incentives are stronger when benefit reduction rates and net marginal tax rates are low. Reforms in the 1990s, including widening the EITC and replacing AFDC with TANF, have helped to limit poverty rates.

Key Terms	Page #
Benefit reduction rate	479
Gini coefficient	465
Gini index	465
Lorenz curve	465
Negative income tax	480
Net marginal tax rate	480
Progressive tax	469
Regressive tax	469

Problems and Topics for Discussion

1. **Poverty versus inequality**   "It is a mistake to think of poverty in terms of absolute needs. The best way to measure poverty would simply be to consider the bottom fifth of the income distribution in each country to be 'poor' and the rest to be 'nonpoor.'" Do you agree, disagree, or agree in part with the preceding statement? Is the approach applicable to very rich countries? To very poor countries?

2. **Updating poverty rates**   The U.S. Census Bureau publishes official poverty data each year, and issues many special studies in between their annual publications. Visit their web site (http://www.census.gov/hhes/www/poverty/index.html) and update as many of the charts and data in this chapter as you can.

3. **Occupy Wall Street**   In 2011, a movement called Occupy Wall Street undertook protests against the shift of income from the lower 99 percent of the population toward the wealthiest 1 percent. Test your Internet search skills by learning more about that movement and its demands. Has the movement faded away, or has it continued?

4. **International wage competition**   One reason given for increasing inequality in the United States is downward pressure, from international competition, on the earnings of low-skill workers. Review Chapter 7 on international trade. Does standard international trade theory offer any support for the idea that trade could put downward pressure on wages of low-skill U.S. workers? Explain.

5. **Cash versus in-kind transfers**   What are the relative merits of cash and in-kind transfers? Review Chapter 5, paying particular attention to the concepts of marginal utility and consumer equilibrium. Suppose that Program A gives a family a $1,000 cash benefit and Program B gives it $1,000 worth of goods in kind, but in proportions that are not chosen by the family itself. Which program would be likely to give the family greater utility?

6. **Transfer payments and the nonpoor**   Discussions of "waste" in poverty programs often focus on the fact that some benefits go to families whose incomes are above the poverty line. After reading this chapter, do you agree that it is wasteful to pay benefits to some nonpoor families? Would you favor a program that cut off all benefits as soon as a family reaches the poverty threshold? In what ways might such a program itself be wasteful? Discuss.

7. **Fight Poverty—Get a Job**   A popular bumper sticker reads "Fight Poverty—Get a Job!" The slogan presumably means to do more than call attention to the fact that those who work are less likely to be poor. Rather, its purpose seems to be to evoke a set of subjective judgments related to "deserving" versus "undeserving" poor, willingness to work versus opportunity as reasons for not working, and so on. What is your position on these issues? Discuss.

Case for Discussion

San Francisco's Living Wage

San Francisco has the highest minimum wage in the country. After being raised to $10.24 per hour for 2012, it reached a level nearly $3 higher than the federal minimum wage.

Some people are more enthusiastic about the high minimum wage than others are. The Los Angeles Times reported that the increased minimum wage will help Ace Wiseman, 27, a recent graduate of San Francisco State University who cleans tables for minimum wage in a Sunset District pizzeria, buy a few more groceries, and maybe start paying off student loans. At the same time, Daniel Scherotter, executive chef and owner of Palio D'Asti, an Italian restaurant in the downtown financial district, said the higher minimum wage had caused him to cut his kitchen staff and shift pastry production outside the city. "It's hurting the people it's trying to help," he told a reporter.

High as it seems, the minimum wage is not high enough for members of San Francisco's Living Wage Coalition. The Coalition defines a living wage as what a person must earn if he or she works full time and must support a family at a level that meets basic needs recognized by the community. Needs considered include food, housing, medical expenses, transportation, and others. According to the coalition's "living wage calculator," a single person in San Francisco would have to earn $12.65 per hour to meet the standards, while a single wage earner supporting a spouse and two children would have to earn $32.70 per hour, more than three times the city's minimum wage.

More than one hundred cities around the United States have adopted living wage ordinances; in practice, they apply to only small numbers of workers, typically employees and contractors of city governments. The unavoidable subjectivity of the living wage concept is one major reason more governments do not use it to set minimum rates of pay. A thorough review of the subject by Richard Anker for the International Labor Organization acknowledges that there is no generally accepted methodology for calculating a numerical value for the minimum wage. Issues in dispute include what needs should be covered, whether all adults in a family should be expected to work, and how to account for differences in family size and locational differences in the cost of living.

Sources: Mark Lishifer, "San Francisco Minimum Wage is Set to Become the Highest in the U.S.," Los Angeles Times, Dec. 27, 2011 (http://articles.latimes.com/2011/dec/27/business/la-fi-minimum-wage-20111227); San Francisco Living Wage Coalition (http://www.livingwage-sf.org/); Richard Anker, "Estimating a Living Wage: A Methodological View," International Labor Organization, Conditions of Work and Employment Series No. 29, 2011 (http://www.ilo.org/wcmsp5/groups/public/---ed_protect/---protrav/---travail/documents/publication/wcms_162117.pdf)

Questions

1. What are the advantages and disadvantages of a higher minimum wage from the point of view of workers will low skills? From the point of view of those with higher skills, who will, in any event, earn more than the minimum?

2. If a city government implements the living wage concept as a basis for paying its employees, should it use the same minimum for all workers, or should workers with larger families receive more? What would be the pros and cons of each approach?

3. Compare two policy strategies for ensuring that no families fall below the poverty level. One is a transfer strategy, which leaves the determination of wage rates entirely up to labor supply and demand, and then uses a negative income tax or earned income tax credit to ensure that each family's total income is above the poverty line. The other is a living wage strategy, which sets a minimum wage at a level high enough to ensure that a family with two full-time workers and two children earns enough, without transfer payments, to raise family income above the poverty level. What would be the advantages and disadvantages of each strategy?

Endnotes

1. Research by the World Bank's Branco Milanovic summarized in Robert Wade, "Winners and Losers," *The Economist* (April 26, 2001).

2. This section draws on an analysis of Census Bureau's supplemental poverty measure originally published on Ed Dolan's Econ Blog at Economonitor.com (http://www.economonitor.com/dolanecon/2011/11/08/understanding-the-new-view-of-poverty-1-the-erosion-of-stereotypes/), used by permission of the author.

3. The Census Bureau study can be found online at http://www.census.gov/prod/2011pubs/p60-241.pdf.

4. Stephen Nickell, "Unemployment and Labor Market Rigidities: Europe vs. North America," *Journal of Economic Perspectives* (Summer 1997): 55–74.

glossary

a

Absolute advantage
The ability of a country to produce a good at a lower cost, in terms of quantity of factor inputs

Access fee
The part of a two-part pricing strategy paid for the right to become a customer

Accounting profit
Total revenue minus explicit costs

Adverse selection
The tendency of people facing the greatest risk of loss to be most likely to seek insurance

Antitrust laws
A set of laws that regulate market structure and the competitive behavior of firms

b

Barrier to entry
Any circumstance that prevents a new firm in a market from competing on an equal footing with existing ones

Benefit reduction rate
The amount by which benefits of a transfer program decrease for each added dollar of earned income

Bounded rationality
The assumption that people intend to make choices that best serve their objectives, but have limited ability to acquire and process information

Budget line
A line showing the various combinations of goods and services that consumers can buy at given prices with a given budget

c

Capital
All means of production that are created by people—including tools, industrial equipment, and structures

Capitalized value of a rent
The present value of all future rents that a piece of land or other resource is expected to earn

Cartel
A group of producers that jointly maximize profits by fixing prices and limiting output

Change in demand
A change in the quantity of a good that the buyers are willing and able to purchase that is caused by a change in some condition other than the price of that good; a shift in the demand curve

Change in quantity demanded
A change in the quantity of a good that buyers are willing and able to purchase that results from a change in the good's price, other things being equal, shown by a movement from one point to another along a demand curve

Change in quantity supplied
A change in the quantity of a good that suppliers are willing and able to sell that results from a change in some condition other than the good's price, shown by a shift in the supply curve

Change in supply
A change in the quantity of a good that suppliers are willing and able to sell that results from a change in the good's price, other things being equal, shown by a movement along a supply curve

Closed monopoly
A monopoly that enjoys the protection of legal restrictions on competition

Coase theorem
The proposition that private agreements will efficiently resolve problems of externalities, regardless of the initial assignment of property rights, provided that there are no transaction costs

Comparative advantage
The ability to produce a good or service at a relatively lower opportunity cost than someone else

Complementary goods
A pair of goods for which an increase in the price of one causes a decrease in demand for the other

Conditional forecast
A prediction of future economic events in the form "If A, then B, other things being equal"

Conglomerate mergers
Mergers of firms in unrelated markets

Constant returns to scale
A situation in which there are neither economies nor diseconomies of scale

Consumer equilibrium
A state of affairs in which a consumer cannot increase the total utility gained from a given budget by spending less on one good and more on another

Consumer surplus
The difference between the maximum that a consumer would be willing to pay for a unit of a good and the amount that he or she actually pays

Contestable market
A market in which barriers to entry and exit are low

Cross-elasticity of demand
The ratio of the percentage change in the quantity of a good demanded to a given percentage change in the price of some other good, other things being equal

d

Deadweight loss
A loss of consumer or producer surplus that is not offset by a gain to someone else

Demand
The willingness and ability of buyers to purchase goods

Demand curve
A graphical representation of the relationship between the price of a good and the quantity of that good that buyers demand

Derived demand
Demand for an input that reflects the demand for the product the input produces

Differential rent
The rents earned by superior units of a resource in a situation where units of a resource differ in productivity

Direct relationship
A relationship between two variables in which an increase in the value of one variable is associated with an increase in the value of the other

Diseconomies of scale
A situation in which long-run average cost increases as output increases

Dutch auction
An auction that begins with a high bid, which is lowered until a buyer is found

Dynamic efficiency
The ability of an economy to increase consumer satisfaction through innovation and technological change

e

Econometrics
The statistical analysis of empirical economic data

Economics
The social science that seeks to understand the choices people make in using scarce resources to meet their wants

Economic efficiency
A state of affairs in which it is impossible to make any change that satisfies one person's wants more fully without causing some other person's wants to be satisfied less fully

Economic rent
Any payment to a factor of production in excess of its opportunity cost

Economies of scale
A situation in which long-run average cost decreases as output increases

Efficiency in distribution
A situation in which it is not possible, by redistributing existing supplies of goods, to satisfy one person's wants more fully without causing some other person's wants to be satisfied less fully

Efficiency in production
A situation in which it is not possible, given available knowledge and productive resources, to produce more of one good without forgoing the opportunity to produce some of another good

Efficiency wage theory
The theory that higher wages can raise productivity by enough to increase profit

Elastic demand
A situation in which quantity demanded changes by a larger percentage than price, so that total revenue increases as price decreases

Elasticity
A measure of the response of one variable to a change in another, stated as a ratio of the percentage change in one variable to the associated percentage change in another

Empirical
Based on experience or observation

English auction
An auction in which bidding starts low and proceeds until the good is sold to the highest bidder

Entrepreneurship
The process of looking for new possibilities— making use of new ways of doing things, being alert to new opportunities, and overcoming old limits

Equilibrium
A condition in which buyers' and sellers' plans exactly mesh in the marketplace, so that the quantity supplied exactly equals the quantity demanded at a given price

Excess burden of the tax
The part of the economic burden of a tax that takes the form of consumer and producer surplus that is lost because the tax reduces the equilibrium quantity sold

Excess quantity demanded (shortage)
A condition in which the quantity of a good demanded at a given price exceeds the quantity supplied

Excess quantity supplied (surplus)
A condition in which the quantity of a good supplied at a given price exceeds the quantity demanded

Expansion path
A line on an isoquant diagram showing the least-cost production points for various levels of output

Expected value
For a set of possible outcomes, the sum of the probability of each outcome multiplied by the value of that outcome

Explicit costs
Opportunity costs that take the form of explicit payments to suppliers of factors of production and intermediate goods

Externalities
The effects of producing or consuming a good whose impact on third parties other than buyers and sellers of the good is not reflected in the good's price

f

Factors of production
The basic inputs of labor, capital, and natural resources used in producing all goods and services

Fixed costs
The explicit and implicit opportunity costs associated with providing fixed inputs

Fixed inputs
Inputs that cannot be increased or decreased in a short time in order to increase or decrease output

Full rationality
The assumption that people make full use of all available information in calculating how best to meet their objectives

Futures contract
An agreement to exchange something at a specified date in the future at a price that the parties agree on now

g

Giffen good
An inferior good accounting for a large share of a consumer's budget that has a positively sloped demand curve because the income effect of a price change outweighs the substitution effect

Gini coefficient
A measure of inequality of income equal to zero under conditions of perfect equality and to one under perfect inequality

Gini index
The Gini coefficient expressed as a percentage

Government failure
A situation in which a government policy causes inefficient use of resources

h

Heckscher-Ohlin theorem
The proposition that countries tend to export goods that make intensive use of the factors of production that the country possesses in relative abundance

Hedging
An operation in which futures markets or options markets are used to offset one risk with another

Hierarchy
A way of achieving coordination in which individual actions are guided by instructions from a central authority

Horizontal mergers
Mergers of firms that compete in the same market

Human capital
Capital in the form of abilities acquired through formal training or education or through on-the-job experience

i

Implicit costs
Opportunity costs of using resources that firm's owners (or the firm itself as a legal entity) contribute without receiving explicit payment

Import quotas
A limit on the quantity of a good that imported over a given period

Income effect
The part of the change in quantity demanded of a good whose price has fallen that is the result of the increase in real income resulting from the price change

Income elasticity of demand
The ratio of the percentage change in the quantity of a good demanded to a given percentage change in consumer incomes, other things being equal

Indifference curve
A graphical representation of an indifference set

Indifference map
A selection of indifference curves for a single consumer and pair of goods

Indifference set
A set of consumption choices, each of which yields the same utility so that no member of the set is preferred to any other

Inelastic demand
A situation in which quantity demanded changes by a smaller percentage than price, so that total revenue decreases as price decreases

Inferior goods
A good for which an increase in consumer incomes results in a decrease in demand

Information asymmetry
A situation in which some parties to a transaction have relevant information that other parties do not have

Inframarginal rents
The difference between the payment made to a unit of resource and the minimum needed to attract it to the use in question

Inventory
A stock of a good awaiting sale or use

Inverse relationship
A relationship between two variables in which an increase in the value of one variable is associated with a decrease in the value of the other

Investment
The act of increasing the economy's stock of capital, that is, its supply of means of production made by people

Isoquantity line (isoquant)
A line showing the various combinations of inputs that are sufficient to produce a given quantity of output

l

Labor
The contributions to production made by people working with their minds and their hands

Labor market discrimination
A situation in which employers are unwilling to hire members of a disfavored group at the same wage rate that they pay to equally productive members of a more favored group

Law of demand
The principle that an inverse relationship exists between the price of a good and the quantity of that good that buyers demand, other things being equal

Law of diminishing returns
The principle that as one variable input increases while all others remain fixed, the firm will eventually reach a point beyond which the marginal physical product of the variable input will begin to decrease

Limit pricing
A strategy in which the dominant firm in a market charges less than the short-run profit maximizing price in order to limit the likelihood of entry

Loanable funds market
A general term for the set of institutions that facilitate borrowing and lending

Logrolling
The practice of trading votes among members of a legislative body

Long run
A time horizon that is long enough to permit changes in both fixed and variable inputs

Lorenz curve
A graph that represents the degree of income inequality in an economy

m

Macroeconomics
The branch of economics that studies large-scale economic phenomena, particularly inflation, unemployment, and economic growth

Marginal-average rule
The rule that marginal cost must equal average cost when average cost is at its minimum

Marginal cost
The increase in cost required to increase the output of some good or service by one unit

Marginal cost of abatement
The cost of reducing waste discharged into the environment by one unit

Marginal external cost
The total additional cost to all affected parties of an added unit of pollution

Marginal physical product
The amount by which output, expressed in physical units, increases as a result of adding one unit of a variable input, other things being equal

Marginal productivity theory of distribution
A theory of income distribution in which each input of production receives a payment equal to its marginal revenue product

Marginal rate of substitution
The rate at which a consumer can substitute one good for another with no gain or loss in satisfaction

Marginal resource cost
The amount by which a firm's total resource cost increases when the firm uses an additional unit of a given resource

Marginal revenue
The amount by which total revenue changes when output changes by one unit

Marginal revenue product
The change in revenue that results from the sale of the output produced by one additional unit of a resource

Marginal utility
The amount of added utility gained from a one-unit increase in consumption of a good, other things being equal

Market
Any arrangement people have for trading with one another

Market failure
A situation in which a market fails to coordinate choices in a way that achieves efficient use of resources

Market performance
The degree to which markets work efficiently in providing arrangements for mutually beneficial trade

Market structure
The key traits of a market, including the number and size of firms, the extent to which the products of various firms are different or similar, ease of entry and exit, and availability of information

Median voter model
A model showing that there is a tendency for decisions in a democracy to reflect the interests of voters whose preferences lie near the middle of the scale

Microeconomics
The branch of economics that studies the choices of individual units—including households, business firms, and government agencies

Minimum efficient scale
The output level at which economies of scale cease

Model
A synonym for theory; in economics, often applied to theories that take the form of graphs or equations

Monopoly
A situation in which there is only a single seller of a good or service

Monopolistic competition
A market structure in which there are many small firms, a differentiated product, and easy entry and exit

Monopsony
A situation in which there is only a single buyer in a market; more generally, any situation in which a firm is a price searcher in a market in which it is a buyer

Moral hazard
The tendency of people to expose themselves to risk if they know insurance will cover their losses

n

Nash equilibrium
An equilibrium solution to a game in which each player's strategy is optimal given the other players' choice of strategy

Natural monopoly
An industry where long-run average cost is at a minimum when only one firm serves the market

Natural resources
Anything that people can use as a productive input in its natural state, such as farmland, building sites, forests, and mineral deposits

Negative income tax
An antipoverty program under which low-income people receive grants from the government and high-income people pay taxes, subject to a net marginal tax rate of less than 100 percent for everyone

Negative slope
A slope having a value less than zero

Net marginal tax rate
The sum of the benefit reduction rate and the rate of income tax

Normal goods
A good for which an increase in consumer income results in an increase in demand

Normal profit (normal return on capital)
The implicit opportunity cost of capital contributed by the firm's owners (equity capital)

o

Ockham's razor
The principle that simpler theories are to be preferred to more complex ones when both are consistent with given observations

Oligopolistic interdependence
The need to pay close attention to the actions of rival firms in an oligopolistic market when making price or production decision

Oligopoly

A market structure in which there are only a few firms, at least some of which are large in relation to the size of the market

Open monopoly

A monopoly where one firm temporarily becomes the sole supplier of a product but has no special protection from competition

Opportunity cost

The cost of a good or service measured in terms of the forgone opportunity to pursue the best possible alternative activity with the same time or resources

Option

A contract under which one party obtains the right (but not the obligation) to buy or sell something from another party at a specified date in the future at a price on which they agree now

Other-regarding preferences

A set of objectives that includes not only the material welfare of the decision maker but also the material welfare of others and their attitudes

p

Perfect competition

A market structure in which there are a large number of small firms, a homogeneous product, freedom of entry and exit, and equal access to information

Perfectly elastic demand

A situation in which the demand curve is a horizontal line

Perfectly inelastic demand

A situation in which the demand curve is a vertical line

Political rent seeking (rent seeking)

The process of seeking and defending economic rents through the political process

Positive slope

A slope having a value greater than zero

Present value

The value today of a sum payable in the future (In mathematical terms, the present value of a sum V_p, payable t years in the future, discounted at r percent interest, would grow to the value V_t in t years; the present value formula is $V_p = V_t/(1 + r)^t$.)

Price fixing

Attempt by two or more firms to cooperate in setting prices

Price taker

A firm that sells its output at prices determined by forces beyond its control

Price discrimination

The practice of charging different prices for various units of a single product when the price differences are not justified by differences in cost

Price elasticity of demand

The ratio of the percentage change in the quantity of a good demanded to a given percentage change in its price, other things being equal

Price elasticity of supply

The ratio of the percentage change in the quantity of a good supplied to a given percentage change in its price, other things being equal

Price leadership

A situation in which price increases for all or most of the other firms in the market match decreases by a dominant firm in an oligopoly, known as the price leader

Price searcher

A firm that faces a negatively sloped demand curve for its product

Principle of diminishing marginal utility

The principle that the greater the consumption of some good, the smaller the increase in utility from a one-unit increase in consumption of that good

Producer surplus

The difference between what producers receive for a unit of a good and the minimum they would be willing to accept

Production possibility frontier

A graph that shows possible combinations of goods that an economy can produce given available technology and factors of production

Progressive tax

A tax that takes a larger share of higher incomes, making the distribution of income more equal after the tax than before

Property rights
Legal rules that establish what things people may use or control, and the conditions under which they may exercise control

Protectionism
Any policy that shields domestic industries from import competition

Public choice theory
The branch of economics that studies how people use the institutions of government in pursuit of their own interests

Public goods
Goods that (1) cannot be provided for one person without also being provided for others and (2) when provided for one person can be provided for others at zero additional cost

Pure economic profit
The sum that remains when we subtract both explicit and implicit costs from total revenue

Pure economic rent
The income earned by any resource whose supply is perfectly inelastic with respect to its price

r

Rate of return
A firm's accounting profit expressed as a percentage of its net worth

Rate of return on capital
The marginal product of capital expressed as an annual percentage rate

Rationality
Acting purposefully to achieve an objective, given constraints on the opportunities that are available

Regressive tax
A tax that takes a larger share of lower incomes, making the distribution of income less equal after the tax than before

Reservation price
The maximum price that a buyer is willing to pay for a good or the minimum price at which a seller is willing to offer it

Revenue
Price multiplied by quantity sold

Revenue-equivalence theorem
The proposition that under certain general circumstances English, Dutch, and sealed-bid auctions will produce approximately the same winning bid

Risk aversion
A preference for a certain outcome with a given value over a set of risky outcomes with the same expected value

Risk neutrality
Indifference between a certain outcome with a given value and a set of risky outcomes with the same expected value

Risk pooling
A technique in which the risk of loss is shared among many people so that the impact of a loss on any one of them is small

Risk preference
A preference for a set of risky outcomes with a given expected value over a certain outcome with the same expected value

s

Scarcity
A situation in which there is not enough of a resource to meet all of everyone's wants

Sealed-bid auction
An auction in which all buyers submit bids at the same time, and the item is sold to the highest bidder

Self-regarding preferences
A set of objectives that depend only on the material welfare of the decision maker

Short run
A time horizon within which a firm can adjust output only by changing the amounts of variable inputs it uses while fixed inputs remain unchanged

Simple monopoly
A monopoly that offers its output at the same price to all customers and allows them to buy as much or as little as they want at that price

Slope
For a straight line, the ratio of the change in the y value to the change in the x value between any two points on the line

Speculation
Buying something at a low price in the hope of selling it later at a higher price

Spontaneous order
A way of achieving coordination in which individuals adjust their actions in response to cues from their immediate environment

Spot price
The price at which sellers offer a good for immediate sale

Static efficiency
The ability of an economy to get the greatest degree of consumer satisfaction from given amounts of resources and technology

Substitute goods
A pair of goods for which an increase in the price of one causes an increase in demand for the other

Substitution effect
The part of the increase in quantity demanded of a good whose price has fallen that is the result of substitution of that good for others that are now relatively more costly

Sunk costs
Once-and-for-all costs that a firm cannot recover once it incurs them

Supply
The willingness and ability of sellers to provide goods for sale in a market

Supply curve
A graphical representation of the relationship between the price of a good and the quantity of that good that sellers are willing to supply

t

Tangent
A straight line that touches a curve at a given point without intersecting it

Tariff
A tax on imported goods

Theory
A representation of the relationships among facts

Time preference
The tendency to prefer goods now to goods in the future, other things being equal

Total physical product
The total output of a firm, measured in physical units

Transaction costs
The costs, other than production costs, of carrying out a transaction

Transitivity
The principle that if A is preferred to B and B is preferred to C, A must be preferred to C

Two-part pricing
A pricing strategy in which people must pay for the right to be a buyer before choosing how much to buy at a given price

u

Unit elastic demand
A situation in which price and quantity demanded change by the same percentage so that total revenue remains unchanged as price changes

User charge
The per-unit price offered in a two-part pricing strategy to qualified customers who have paid the access fee

Utility
The pleasure, satisfaction, or need fulfillment that people obtain from the consumption of goods and services

v

Value of marginal product
Marginal physical product multiplied by the product's per-unit price

Variable costs
The explicit and implicit costs of providing variable inputs

Variable inputs
Inputs that can be varied within a short time in order to increase or decrease output

Vertical mergers
Mergers of firms with a supplier-purchaser relationship

W

Winner's curse
The tendency for winners of an auction to pay more for a good or service than it is worth (or to offer to sell at a price below the cost of providing the good or service)

photo credits

chapter 9

Shutterstock, 266; iStockphoto (top), 277; Wikimedia Commons (bottom), 277; Shutterstock, 286; Shutterstock, 295

chapter 10

Wikimedia Commons, 298; iStockphoto, 301; Shutterstock, 302; Shutterstock, 311; Wikimedia Commons, 312; Wikimedia Commons, 314; Gregor Kervina/Shutterstock, 316; iStockphoto, 321; Shutterstock, 326

chapter 11

Shutterstock, 328; Stuart Monk/Shutterstock, 333; iStockphoto, 336; Wikimedia Commons, 338; Shutterstock, 347

chapter 12

Shutterstock, 350; iStockphoto (top), 352; Shutterstock (bottom), 352; AP Wide World Photos, 354; iStockphoto (both), 355; Wikimedia Commons, 358; Shutterstock, 366; Shutterstock, 371

chapter 13

iStockphoto, 375; Vacclav/Shutterstock, 376; Shutterstock, 385; Shutterstock, 386; Wikimedia Commons, 391; Shutterstock, 394; iStockphoto, 395; Rob Wilson/Shutterstock, 396; iStockphoto (top), 397; AP Wide World Photos (left & right), 397; Shutterstock, 410;

chapter 14

iStockphoto, 412; Wikimedia Commons, 414; iStockphoto (both), 416; Shutterstock, 420; iStockphoto (top), 421; Wikimedia Commons (bottom), 421; Shutterstock, 424; Shutterstock, 425; Shutterstock, 434

chapter 15

David Burrows/Shutterstock, 436; iStockphoto (top), 438; Wikimedia Commons (bottom), 438; Shutterstock, 444; iStockphoto, 445; iStockphoto (top), 449 AP Wide World Photos (bottom), 449; Shutterstock, 455; Shutterstock, 460

chapter 16

iStockphoto, 462; iStockphoto, 469; iStockphoto, 472; Wikimedia Commons, 472; Wikimedia Commons, 478; Shutterstock, 486

index